The XML Handbook™
Third Edition

ISBN 0-13-055068-X

90000

9 780130 550682

The Charles F. Goldfarb Series on Open Information Management

"Open Information Management" (OIM) means managing information so that it is open to processing by any program, not just the program that created it. That extends even to application programs not conceived of at the time the information was created.

OIM is based on the principle of data independence: data should be stored in computers in non-proprietary, genuinely standardized representations. And that applies even when the data is the content of a document. Its representation should distinguish the innate information from the proprietary codes of document processing programs and the artifacts of particular presentation styles.

Business data bases—which rigorously separate the real data from the input forms and output reports—achieved data independence decades ago. But documents, unlike business data, have historically been created in the context of a particular output presentation style. So for document data, independence was largely unachievable until recently.

That is doubly unfortunate. It is unfortunate because documents are a far more significant repository of humanity's information. And documents can contain significantly richer information structures than data bases.

It is also unfortunate because the need for OIM of documents is greater now than ever. The demands of "repurposing" require that information be deliverable in multiple formats: paper-based, online, multimedia, hypermedia. And information must now be delivered through multiple channels: traditional bookstores and libraries, the World Wide Web, corporate intranets and extranets. In the latter modes, what starts as data base data may become a document for browsing, but then may need to be reused by the reader as data.

Fortunately, in the past ten years a technology has emerged that extends to documents the data base's capacity for data independence. And it does so without the data base's restrictions on structural freedom. That technology is the "Standard Generalized Markup Language" (SGML), an official International Standard (ISO 8879) that has been adopted by the world's largest producers of documents and by the World Wide Web.

With SGML, organizations in government, aerospace, airlines, automotive, electronics, computers, and publishing (to name a few) have freed their documents from hostage relationships to processing software. SGML coexists with graphics, multimedia and other data standards needed for OIM and acts as the framework that relates objects in the other formats to one another and to SGML documents.

The World Wide Web's HTML and XML are both based on SGML. HTML is a particular, though very general, application of SGML, like those for the above industries. There is a limited set of markup tags that can be used with HTML. XML, in contrast, is a simplified subset of SGML facilities that, like full SGML, can be used with any set of tags. You can literally create your own markup language with XML.

As the enabling standard for OIM of documents and structured data, the XML/SGML family of standards necessarily plays a leading role in this series. We provide tutorials on SGML, XML, and other key standards and the techniques for applying them. Our books vary in technical intensity from programming techniques for software developers to the business justification of OIM for enterprise executives. We share the practical experience of organizations and individuals who have applied the techniques of OIM in environments ranging from immense industrial publishing projects to websites of all sizes.

Our authors are expert practitioners in their subject matter, not writers hired to cover a "hot" topic. They bring insight and understanding that can only come from real-world experience. Moreover, they practice what they preach about standardization. Their books share a common standards-based vocabulary. In this way, knowledge gained from one book in the series is directly applicable when reading another, or the standards themselves. This is just one of the ways in which we strive for the utmost technical accuracy and consistency with the OIM standards.

And we also strive for a sense of excitement and fun. After all, the challenge of OIM—preserving information from the ravages of technology while exploiting its benefits—is one of the great intellectual adventures of our age. I'm sure you'll find this series to be a knowledgable and reliable guide on that adventure.

About the Series Editor

Dr. Charles F. Goldfarb is the father of markup languages, a term that he coined in 1970. He invented the SGML language in 1974 and later led the team that developed it into the International Standard on which both HTML and XML are based. He serves as editor of the Standard (ISO 8879) and as a strategic consultant to developers of SGML and XML applications and products. He is based in Saratoga, CA. You can find him on the Web at www.xmltimes.com.

About the Series Logo

The rebus is an ancient literary tradition, dating from 16th century Picardy, and is especially appropriate to a series involving fine distinctions between things and the words that describe them. For the logo, Andrew Goldfarb incorporated a rebus of the series name within a stylized SGML/XML comment declaration.

The Charles F. Goldfarb Series on Open Information Management

XML Titles

Goldfarb, Pepper, and Ensign

SGML Buyer's Guide:™ Choosing the Right XML and SGML Products and Services

Megginson
- Structuring XML Documents

McGrath
- XML by Example: Building E-commerce Applications

Leventhal, Lewis, and Fuchs
- Designing XML Internet Applications

Jelliffe
- The XML and SGML Cookbook: Recipes for Structured Information

DuCharme
- XML: The Annotated Specification

Floyd
- Building Web Sites with XML

Morgenthal and la Forge
- Enterprise Application Integration with XML and Java

McGrath
- XML Processing with Python

Goldfarb and Prescod
- The XML Handbook™ Third Edition

General Titles

Ensign

$GML: The Billion Dollar Secret

Martin
- TOP SECRET Intranet: How U.S. Intelligence Built Intelink—The World's Largest, Most Secure Network

The XML Handbook™

Third Edition

- Charles F. Goldfarb
- Paul Prescod

PH PTR
Prentice Hall PTR, Upper Saddle River, NJ 07458
www.phptr.com

Editorial/Production Supervision: *Faye Gemmellaro*
Acquisitions Editor: *Mark L. Taub*
Editorial Assistant: *Sarah Hand*
Marketing Manager: *Kate Hargett*
Manufacturing Manager: *Alexis R. Heydt*
Cover Design: *Anthony Gemmellaro*
Cover Design Direction: *Jerry Votta*
Series Design: *Gail Cocker-Bogusz*

Prentice Hall books are widely used by corporations and government agencies for training, marketing, and resale.

The publisher offers discounts on this book when ordered in bulk quantities. For more information, contact: Corporate Sales Department, Phone: 800-382-3419; Fax: 201-236-7141; E-mail: corpsales@prenhall.com; or write: Prentice Hall PTR, Corp. Sales Dept., One Lake Street, Upper Saddle River, NJ 07458.

Printed in the United States of America

10 9 8 7 6 5 4 3 2 1

ISBN 0-13-055068-X

Prentice-Hall International (UK) Limited, *London*
Prentice-Hall of Australia Pty. Limited, *Sydney*
Prentice-Hall Canada Inc., *Toronto*
Prentice-Hall Hispanoamericana, S.A., *Mexico*
Prentice-Hall of India Private Limited, *New Delhi*
Prentice-Hall of Japan, Inc., *Tokyo*
Pearson Education Asia Pte. Ltd.
Editora Prentice-Hall do Brasil, Ltda., *Rio de Janeiro*

This book, and the CD-ROM included with it, contain software and descriptive materials provided by (or adapted from materials made publicly available by) product developers, vendors, and service providers. Said software and materials have not been reviewed, edited, or tested, and neither the Authors, Contributors, Series Editor, Publisher, Sponsors, or other parties connected with this book are responsible for their accuracy or reliability. Readers are warned that they use said software and materials at their own risk, and are urged to test the software and confirm the validity of the information prior to use.

To Linda – With love, awe, and gratitude.

Charles F. Goldfarb

For Lilia – Your support makes it possible and your love makes it worthwhile.

Paul Prescod

Overview

Part 1   The Who, What, and Why of XML   2

Chapter 1   **Why XML?**   **4**

Chapter 2   **Just enough XML**   **28**

Chapter 3   **The XML usage spectrum**   **54**

Chapter 4   **Better browsing through XML**   **66**

Chapter 5   **Taking care of e-business**   **82**

Chapter 6   **XML Jargon Demystifier™**   **92**

Part 2   Middle-tier Servers   106

Chapter 7   **Personalized frequent-flyer website**   **108**

Chapter 8   **Building an online auction website**   **120**

Chapter 9 **Anatomy of an information server** **138**

Chapter 10 **Wells Fargo & Company** **150**

Chapter 11 **Bidirectional information flow** **158**

Part 3 E-commerce 170

Chapter 12 **From EDI to IEC: The new Web commerce** **172**

Chapter 13 **XML and EDI: Working together** **194**

Chapter 14 **Collaboration in an e-commerce supply web** **208**

Chapter 15 **Lead tracking by Web and email** **218**

Chapter 16 **An information pipeline for petrochemicals** **228**

Part 4 Portals 236

Chapter 17 **Enterprise Information Portals (EIP)** **238**

Chapter 18 **Portal servers for e-business** **252**

Chapter 19 **RxML: Your prescription for healthcare** **264**

Part 5 Syndication 274

Chapter 20 **XMLNews: A syndication document type** **276**

Chapter 21 **Wavo Corporation** **288**

Chapter 22 **Information and Content Exchange (ICE)** **300**

Part 6   Publishing   316

Chapter 23 **Frank Russell Company**   **318**

Chapter 24 **PC World Online**   **340**

Chapter 25 **MTU-DaimlerChrysler Aerospace**   **356**

Part 7   Content Management   364

Chapter 26 **Tweddle Litho Company**   **366**

Chapter 27 **Efficient content management**   **376**

Chapter 28 **Document storage and retrieval**   **390**

Chapter 29 **Enterprise data management**   **406**

Part 8   Content Acquisition   422

Chapter 30 **Developing reusable content**   **424**

Chapter 31 **Converting renditions to abstractions** **438**

Chapter 32 **Planning for document conversion** **450**

Chapter 33 **XML mass-conversion facility**   **470**

Chapter 34 **Integrating legacy data**   **482**

Part 9   Schemas   496

Chapter 35 **Building a schema for a product catalog** **498**

Chapter 36 **Schema management at Major Bank**   **512**

Chapter 37 **Building your e-commerce vocabulary**   **524**

Chapter 38 **Repositories and vocabularies 534**

Part 10 Stylesheets   552

Chapter 39 **The role of stylesheets**   **554**

Chapter 40 **A stylesheet-driven tutorial generator**   **562**

Chapter 41 **Designing website stylesheets 578**

Part 11 Navigation   590

Chapter 42 **Extended linking**   **592**

Chapter 43 **Topic maps: Knowledge navigation aids**   **606**

Chapter 44 **Application integration using topic maps**   **624**

Part 12 Infrastructure   636

Chapter 45 **Java technology for XML development**   **638**

Chapter 46 **Building a rich-media digital asset manager**   **648**

Chapter 47 **New directions for XML applications**   **662**

Part 13 XML Tutorials   674

Chapter 48 **XML basics**   **676**

Chapter 49 **Creating a document type definition**   **702**

Chapter 50 **Entities: Breaking up is easy to do**   **736**

Chapter 51 **Advanced features of XML**   **760**

Chapter 52 **Reading the XML specification**   **776**

Part 14   Related Tutorials   786

Chapter 53 **Namespaces**   **788**

Chapter 54 **XML Path Language (XPath)**   **800**

Chapter 55 **Extensible Stylesheet Language (XSL)**   **828**

Chapter 56 **XML Pointer Language (XPointer)**   **860**

Chapter 57 **XML Linking Language (XLink)**   **874**

Chapter 58 **Datatypes**   **894**

Chapter 59 **XML Schema (XSDL)**   **908**

Part 15   Resources   926

Chapter 60 **Free resources on the CD-ROM**   **928**

Chapter 61 **Other \XML-related books**   **964**

Index   **970**

Contents

Preface xlviii

Foreword lviii

Prolog lxii

Part 1 The Who, What, and Why of XML 2

Chapter 1 Why XML? **4**
Introductory Discussion

1.1 | Text formatters and SGML 7

1.1.1 *Formatting markup* 7

1.1.2 *Generalized markup* 9

1.1.3 *Common data representation* 10

1.1.4 *Customized document types* 10

1.1.5 *Rule-based markup* 15

1.2 | XML markup 17

1.2.1 *Documents and databases* 18

1.3 | Road to XML 19

1.3.1	*HTML and the Web*	*20*
1.3.2	*HTML gets extended – unofficially!*	*21*
1.3.3	*The World Wide Web reacts*	*22*
1.4 |	**EDI, EAI and other TLAs**	**23**
1.4.1	*Electronic Data Interchange (EDI)*	*24*
1.4.2	*Enterprise Application Integration (EAI)*	*25*
1.5 |	**Conclusion**	**26**

Chapter 2 Just enough XML 28
Introductory Discussion

2.1 |	**The goal**	**30**
2.2 |	**Elements: The logical structure**	**31**
2.3 |	**Unicode: The character set**	**33**
2.4 |	**Entities: The physical structure**	**34**
2.5 |	**Markup**	**36**
2.6 |	**Document types**	**37**
2.6.1	*Defining document types*	*38*
2.6.2	*HTML: A cautionary tale*	*39*
2.6.3	*Declaring a DTD*	*40*
2.7 |	**Well-formedness and validity**	**42**
2.8 |	**Hyperlinking**	**43**
2.9 |	**Stylesheets**	**45**
2.10 |	**Programming interfaces and models**	**46**
2.10.1	*Parsing*	*46*
2.10.2	*APIs*	*47*
2.11 |	**XML and Protocols**	**48**
2.11.1	*The protocol stack*	*49*
2.11.2	*Writing the Web*	*49*
2.11.3	*Remote procedure call*	*50*
2.11.4	*Object protocols*	*51*
2.12 |	**Conclusion**	**53**

Chapter 3   **The XML usage spectrum**   **54**

Introductory Discussion

3.1 | Is XML for documents or for data?   55

3.2 | A wide spectrum of application opportunities   56

   3.2.1 *Presentation-oriented publishing*   58

   3.2.2 *Message-oriented middleware*   60

3.3 | Opposites are attracted   61

3.4 | MOM and POP – They're so great together!   63

3.5 | Conclusion   65

Chapter 4   **Better browsing through XML**   **66**

Introductory Discussion

4.1 | Beyond HTML   67

   4.1.1 *An HTML table*   68

   4.1.2 *An XML table*   68

   4.1.3 *Extensible HTML (XHTML)*   71

   4.1.4 *Specialized document types*   71

4.2 | Database publishing   72

4.3 | Multimedia   73

4.4 | Metadata   74

   4.4.1 *Platform for Internet Content Selection*   74

   4.4.2 *Resource Description Framework*   75

   4.4.3 *Topic maps*   76

4.5 | Content syndication   77

4.6 | Science on the Web   77

4.7 | Portals and personalization   78

4.8 | Alternative delivery platforms   79

   4.8.1 *XML goes wireless*   80

   4.8.2 *Downloading the library*   80

4.9 | Conclusion   81

Chapter 5   Taking care of e-business   **82**
Introductory Discussion

5.1 | Commerce frameworks   84

  5.1.1 *CommerceNet eCo framework*   84

  5.1.2 *Trading Partner Agreement Markup Language*   85

  5.1.3 *ebXML*   85

  5.1.4 *BizTalk Framework*   86

5.2 | Going Vertical   87

  5.2.1 *RosettaNet*   87

  5.2.2 *Open Financial Exchange (OFX)*   88

  5.2.3 *Health Level Seven (HL7)*   89

5.3 | Repository stories   90

5.4 | Conclusion   91

Chapter 6   XML Jargon Demystifier™   **92**
Introductory Discussion

6.1 | Structured vs. unstructured   94

6.2 | Tag vs. element   95

6.3 | Document type, DTD, and markup declarations   96

6.4 | Document, XML document, and instance   97

6.5 | Schema and schema definition   98

6.6 | What's the meta?   98

  6.6.1 *Metadata*   98

  6.6.2 *Metalanguage*   99

6.7 | Notations and characters   99

6.8 | Coding, encoding, and markup   100

6.9 | Documents and data   100

  6.9.1 *It's all data!*   100

  6.9.2 *Comparing documents to data*   101

6.10 | And in conclusion   102

Part 2   Middle-tier Servers   106

Chapter 7   **Personalized frequent-flyer website 108**
Introductory Discussion

7.1 | Client/server frequent-flyer sites   109
7.2 | What's wrong with this Web model?   110
7.3 | A better model for doing business on the Web   111
7.4 | An XML-enabled frequent-flyer website   113
7.5 | Understanding the Softland Air scenario   116
7.6 | Towards the Brave New Web   118

Chapter 8   **Building an online auction website   120**
Application Discussion

8.1 | Getting data from the middle tier   122
8.1.1 | *Defining the XML document structure*   124
8.1.2 | *Using ASP files to generate XML documents*   124
8.1.3 | *Generating XML from multiple databases*   127
8.1.4 | *Generating XML from both databases and XML data sources*   130
8.2 | Building the user interface   130
8.2.1 | *Using procedural scripts*   132
8.2.2 | *Using descriptive data binding*   133
8.3 | Updating the data source from the client   134
8.4 | Conclusion   135

Chapter 9   **Anatomy of an information server   138**
Tool Discussion

9.1 | E-business applications   139
9.1.1 | *Web catalogs*   140
9.1.2 | *Knowledge management*   140
9.1.3 | *Supply chain integration*   141
9.1.4 | *Enterprise application integration (EAI)*   141
9.2 | Requirements for an information server   142

9.3 | How eXcelon works   143

   9.3.1 eXcelon Data Server   143

   9.3.2 eXcelon Xconnects   144

   9.3.3 eXcelon Toolbox   145

Chapter 10 **Wells Fargo & Company**   **150**
Case Study

10.1 | Website requirements   151

10.2 | The challenge: Leverage all the information   152

10.3 | The new intranet system   154

10.4 | How the system works   155

10.5 | Conclusion   156

Chapter 11 **Bidirectional information flow**   **158**
Application Discussion

11.1 | infoShark plays its CARD!   160

11.2 | Application scenario: Metro Police   160

   11.2.1 *Diverse user population*   160

   11.2.2 *Marketing crime data*   164

11.3 | Other features of CARD   165

   11.3.1 *Rich metadata*   165

   11.3.2 *Inter-schema sharing*   166

   11.3.3 *CARD automation*   168

Part 3   E-commerce   170

Chapter 12 **From EDI to IEC: The new Web commerce**   **172**
Introductory Discussion

12.1 | What is EDI?   173

   12.1.1 *Extranets can't hack it*   174

   12.1.2 *XML can!*   175

   12.1.3 *Integrated e-commerce*   175

12.2 | The value of EDI   176

12.3 | Traditional EDI: Built on outdated principles 179

12.3.1 *The history of EDI* 179

12.3.2 *EDI technology basics* 179

12.3.3 *The problems of traditional EDI* 181

12.4 | Leveraging XML and the Internet 185

12.4.1 *XML* 187

12.4.2 *The Internet* 188

12.4.3 *Internet technologies* 189

12.4.4 *XML data storage* 190

12.4.5 *Data filtering* 191

12.5 | Conclusion 192

Chapter 13 XML and EDI: Working together 194

Introductory Discussion

13.1 | What is integrated e-commerce? 196

13.1.1 *Web storefronts* 196

13.1.2 *E-commerce portals* 197

13.1.3 *Integrated e-commerce* 198

13.2 | Traditional EDI and XML compared 200

13.2.1 *Message formats* 201

13.2.2 *The different flavors of XML and EDI* 201

13.3 | An XML-EDI trading system 203

13.3.1 *XML to EDI* 204

13.3.2 *EDI to XML* 204

13.4 | The future of e-commerce 206

Chapter 14 Collaboration in an e–commerce supply web 208

Application Discussion

14.1 | It's all about collaboration! 209

14.1.1 *Loosely-coupled collaboration* 210

14.1.2 *Tightly-coupled collaboration* 210

14.2 | Modes of e-commerce 211

14.3 | An e-commerce scenario   211

14.3.1   *Part One: Originate purchase order*   212

14.3.2   *Part Two: Update order status*   214

Chapter 15   Lead tracking by Web and email   218

Case Study

15.1 | The challenge   220

15.2 | The solution   220

15.2.1   *One: Create and send XML email*   221

15.2.2   *Two: Receive and verify XML email*   223

15.2.3   *Three: Process XML email and update database*   225

**Chapter 16   An information pipeline for
                 petrochemicals   228**

Case Study

16.1 | The petrochemical marketplace   229

16.1.1   *Upstream flow*   229

16.1.2   *Downstream flow*   230

16.1.3   *The bottleneck!*   230

16.2 | Integrating with XML   231

16.2.1   *Coexistence with EDI*   231

16.2.2   *Significant information flows*   232

16.3 | Achieving a free-flowing information pipeline   233

16.3.1   *Internal information flows*   233

16.3.2   *External information flows*   233

16.3.3   *Mergers and acquisitions*   234

16.3.4   *XML integration aids*   234

16.4 | Conclusion   234

Part 4   Portals   236

Chapter 17 **Enterprise Information Portals (EIP)**   **238**
Introductory Discussion

17.1 | Information is the global economy   239

17.2 | Enterprise Information challenges   242

17.2.1 *Managed data*   *242*

17.2.2 *Unmanaged data*   *243*

17.3 | Enterprise information portals   245

17.3.1 *The role of XML*   *245*

17.3.2 *The golden rule of content*   *246*

17.3.3 *EIP empowers the enterprise*   *246*

17.4 | A framework for portals   247

17.4.1 *Strategy*   *248*

17.4.2 *Design & architecture*   *249*

17.4.3 *Software*   *249*

17.5 | Summary   251

Chapter 18 **Portal servers for e-business**   **252**
Tool Discussion

18.1 | Portal server requirements   253

18.1.1 *Performance*   *253*

18.1.2 *Content distribution*   *254*

18.1.3 *Business process integration*   *254*

18.2 | Architecture of an e-business portal server   255

18.2.1 *XML application server*   *256*

18.2.2 *Content delivery services*   *259*

18.2.3 *Business integration services*   *261*

18.3 | Other portal server facilities   262

18.3.1 *Integration agents*   *262*

18.3.2 *Administration and configuration*   *263*

**Chapter 19   RxML: Your prescription for
             healthcare   264**
Case Study

19.1 | Doing as well as can be expected – Not!   267
19.2 | The prescription: a health portal system   267
19.3 | Connectivity counts   269
19.4 | Aggregation adds value   270
19.5 | Personalization assures usability   272
19.6 | Linking up the supply chain   273
19.7 | Conclusion   273

Part 5   Syndication   274

**Chapter 20   XMLNews: A syndication
             document type   276**
Application Discussion

20.1 | Structure of a news story   278
20.2 | Structure of an XMLNews-Story document   279
20.3 | Rich inline markup   283
20.4 | Media objects   287

Chapter 21   Wavo Corporation   288
Case Study

21.1 | The challenge   289
21.2 | Wavo's MediaXpress service   292
21.2.1 *Transport layer*   293
21.2.2 *Content layer*   294
21.2.3 *Business layer*   296
21.3 | Summary   298

**Chapter 22   Information and Content
             Exchange (ICE)   300**
Application Discussion

22.1 | Beyond the newswire   301
22.1.1 *Value networks*   302

22.1.2   *Intermediaries as market makers*   *302*

22.2 | Syndication requirements   303

22.3 | ICE: A cool and solid solution!   304

22.3.1   *ICE capabilities*   *304*

22.3.2   *An ICE implementation*   *305*

22.4 | An ICE scenario   308

22.4.1   *Syndicator and subscriber set up a business agreement*   *309*

22.4.2   *Syndicator and subscriber set up a subscription*   *309*

22.4.3   *Subscriber receives content*   *312*

Part 6   Publishing   3|6

Chapter 23 Frank Russell Company   **318**
Case Study

23.1 | Background   319

23.2 | Project strategy considerations   320

23.2.1   *Proceeding from a theoretical abstraction to practical*
         applications   *321*

23.2.2   *Phasing deliverables with measurable return*
         on investment   *321*

23.2.3   *Continuing research in parallel with focused*
         development projects   *321*

23.2.4   *Alignment with overall corporate strategies*   *322*

23.2.5   *Executive sponsorship*   *322*

23.3 | Identifying the needs   323

23.3.1   *Business requirements*   *323*

23.3.2   *Technical requirements*   *324*

23.4 | Create an abstract architecture   325

23.5 | Implement applications   327

23.5.1   *Real-world design issues*   *328*

23.5.2   *Phased implementation plan*   *330*

23.6 | Conclusion   338

Chapter 24 PC World Online   **340**
Case Study

24.1 | The challenge   341

24.1.1 *Complex conversion requirements*   342

24.1.2 *Time-consuming HTML markup*   344

24.1.3 *Richly-structured information sources*   344

24.2 | Templates and databases were not enough   345

24.3 | XML provides a solution   346

24.3.1 *Content creation and storage*   346

24.3.2 *Data delivery*   348

24.3.3 *Improved workflow*   349

24.4 | Results and benefits   350

24.4.1 *Publish to and from multiple formats*   350

24.4.2 *Reuse*   351

24.4.3 *Tailored information for site visitors*   351

24.4.4 *Reduced cost and time to market*   353

24.4.5 *Improved quality*   354

24.4.6 *Future-proofing with a standard*   354

24.4.7 *Job satisfaction*   354

24.5 | Summary   355

Chapter 25 MTU–DaimlerChrysler Aerospace   **356**
Case Study

25.1 | The challenge   357

25.2 | The solution   358

25.2.1 *Selecting content to be customized*   360

25.2.2 *Content editing*   360

25.2.3 *Integration and republishing*   361

25.3 | The result   361

Part 7   Content Management   364

Chapter 26   Tweddle Litho Company   366
Case Study

26.1 | Auto manufacturing is large-scale publishing   368

26.2 | Global markets, global information   369

26.3 | Needed: An XML component management system   370

26.4 | Improving the translation process   372

26.5 | One Source, multiple delivery formats   374

26.5.1 *Printed delivery*   374

26.5.2 *Online delivery*   374

26.6 | Conclusion   375

Chapter 27   Efficient content management   376
Tool Discussion

27.1 | How today's process works   378

27.1.1 *Original creation workflow*   378

27.1.2 *Revisions and updates*   379

27.2 | How to make the process efficient   380

27.2.1 *Dealing with file conversions*   380

27.2.2 *Preventing duplicate content proliferation*   384

27.2.3 *Personalized delivery*   385

27.3 | Conclusion   388

Chapter 28   Document storage and retrieval   390
Tool Discussion

28.1 | Storage strategies   391

28.1.1 *Selection criteria*   392

28.1.2 *An integral storage example*   393

28.2 | Indexing and retrieval   394

28.2.1 *XML Path Language (XPath)*   394

28.2.2 *A simple XML query language*   400

28.3 | Conclusion   404

Chapter 29 Enterprise data management   406
Tool Discussion

29.1 | Applications and XML   408

29.1.1 *Data sharing and communication*   408

29.1.2 *Customized presentation of data*   409

29.2 | Requirements for enterprise data management   409

29.2.1 *Data storage and management*   409

29.2.2 *Data views and interchange*   411

29.2.3 *Query facilities*   412

29.2.4 *Integration with existing systems*   412

29.3 | XML database operations   412

29.3.1 *Reading XML from a database*   413

29.3.2 *Writing XML into a database*   417

29.3.3 *Indexing and searching*   418

29.4 | Internet file system   418

29.5 | An e-commerce example   419

29.6 | Conclusion   421

Part 8   Content Acquisition   422

Chapter 30 Developing reusable content   424
Application Discussion

30.1 | The content developer's dilemma   425

30.1.1 *What do solution developers want from XML?*   426

30.1.2 *What do content creators need from XML?*   426

30.1.3 *Creation and deployment requirements may not
         conform*   427

30.2 | Content development strategy   427

30.2.1 *Beyond the basic*   428

30.3 | Editing XML abstractions   429

30.3.1 *Guided editing*   430

30.3.2 *Editing non-valid documents*   430

30.4 | Linking and navigation   432

30.4.1 *Abstract links*   432

30.4.2 *Extensible and portable links*   434

30.4.3 *Extensible tools*   435

**Chapter 31 Converting renditions to
abstractions**   **438**
Application Discussion

31.1 | Concepts of document conversion   439

31.1.1 *Starting with abstractions*   440

31.1.2 *Starting with renditions*   440

31.1.3 *Two key concepts*   441

31.1.4 *Style and structure*   441

31.2 | The conversion process   442

31.2.1 *Choosing a DTD and root element*   442

31.2.2 *Creating tagging rules*   442

31.2.3 *Tagging content*   446

Chapter 32 Planning for document conversion   **450**
Application Discussion

32.1 | The Data Conversion Laboratory methodology   452

32.2 | Phase 1: Concept and planning   454

32.2.1 *Project concept*   454

32.2.2 *Materials evaluation*   455

32.2.3 *Rough-cut pricing estimate*   457

32.2.4 *Project feasibility analysis*   458

32.3 | Phase 2: Proof-of-concept   458

32.3.1 *Project initiation*   459

32.3.2 *Sample set definition*   459

32.3.3 *Inventory materials*   460

32.3.4 *Data conversion guidelines*   460

32.3.5 *Data conversion specification*   461

32.3.6 *Software and pilot conversion*   461

32.3.7 *Pricing*   462

32.3.8 *Go/no-go decision*   462

32.3.9 *Planning for future phases*   463

32.4 | Phase 3: Analysis, design and engineering 463

32.4.1 *Production process planning*   464

32.4.2 *Production quality planning*   465

32.4.3 *Production ramp-up*   466

32.5 | Phase 4: Production   466

32.6 | Conclusion   467

Chapter 33   XML mass-conversion facility   470
Tool Discussion

33.1 | The challenge   471

33.1.1 *Why XML is different*   472

33.1.2 *Tagging consistency*   472

33.1.3 *Diversity of project types*   472

33.1.4 *Text accuracy*   473

33.2 | The solution   473

33.2.1 *Applicable lessons from the past*   473

33.2.2 *Technology-driven workflow*   474

33.3 | Conclusion   481

Chapter 34   Integrating legacy data   482
Application Discussion

34.1 | What is legacy data?   483

34.1.1 *Unlocking legacy data*   484

34.1.2 *The benefit of Y2K*   484

34.2 | E-commerce with legacy data   485

34.2.1 *Y2K-compliant date exchange*   486

34.2.2 *International invoicing*   488

34.2.3 *Automated bid response*   489

34.3 | Legacy data flow   490

34.3.1 *Usage scenarios*   491

34.3.2   *XML-based legacy data flow*   492

34.3.3   *XML communication server*   494

34.3.4   *Data repositories*   494

34.4 | Legacy data challenges   495

  Part 9   Schemas   496

  Chapter 35 **Building a schema for a product catalog**   **498**

Friendly Tutorial

35.1 | Online catalog requirements   499

35.2 | Design considerations   500

35.3 | Datatypes   502

35.4 | The design   502

35.4.1   *The catalog*   503

35.4.2   *Manufacturer*   504

35.4.3   *Product*   504

35.4.4   *Promotion*   506

35.4.5   *The big picture*   506

35.5 | Schema definition notations   507

35.5.1   *XML 1.0 DTD declarations*   508

35.5.2   *W3C XML Schema Definition Language (XSDL)*   509

35.5.3   *Microsoft XML-Data*   509

35.6 | A sample document   509

35.7 | Conclusion   509

  Chapter 36 **Schema management at Major Bank**   **512**

Case Study

36.1 | The situation   513

36.1.1   *Inconsistent, incompatible efforts*   514

36.1.2   *Lack of understanding of existing schemas*   514

36.1.3   *Dramatic variations in vocabulary and style*   515

36.1.4 *Versions, versions everywhere*   *515*

36.2 | Schema management as a solution   516

36.2.1 *Schema categorization and documentation*   *517*

36.2.2 *Schema relationships*   *517*

36.2.3 *Version control*   *518*

36.2.4 *Schema standardization*   *518*

36.3 | The plan of attack   518

36.3.1 *Create standards and guidelines*   *519*

36.3.2 *Define a corporate e-commerce vocabulary*   *520*

36.3.3 *Create reusable building blocks*   *521*

36.3.4 *Populate the schema repository*   *522*

36.3.5 *Organize for future growth*   *522*

36.4 | Conclusion   522

Chapter 37 Building your e-commerce vocabulary   **524**

Tool Discussion

37.1 | Why do you need an e-commerce vocabulary?   525

37.2 | Where do schemas come from?   526

37.2.1 *Building a new schema*   *526*

37.2.2 *Borrowing an existing schema*   *527*

37.3 | Capturing existing business semantics   527

37.3.1 *Relational databases*   *528*

37.3.2 *Electronic Data Interchange (EDI)*   *528*

37.3.3 *Program data structures*   *529*

37.3.4 *Logical models*   *531*

37.3.5 *Repositories*   *531*

37.3.6 *Customized sources*   *531*

37.4 | Reuse for e-commerce   531

37.4.1 *Editing and refining*   *532*

37.4.2 *Schema generation*   *532*

37.4.3 *Managing the vocabulary*   *532*

Chapter 38 Repositories and vocabularies   534
Resource Description

38.1 | Repositories   535

  38.1.1 *xml.org*   536

  38.1.2 *BizTalk repository*   536

  38.1.3 *Unofficial registries*   537

38.2 | Public vocabularies   538

  38.2.1 *Business systems*   538

  38.2.2 *Content creation, maintenance, and distribution*   542

  38.2.3 *Math and science*   545

  38.2.4 *Software development*   547

  38.2.5 *Vertical industry*   548

Part 10   Stylesheets   552

Chapter 39 The role of stylesheets   554
Tool Discussion

39.1 | The need for intelligent publications   556

39.2 | Creating a stylesheet   556

  39.2.1 *Associating processing with document components*   558

  39.2.2 *Specifying processing*   559

39.3 | Delivering the results   560

**Chapter 40 A stylesheet-driven tutorial
generator   562**
Case Study

40.1 | Touring a tutorial   563

40.2 | The tutorial XML document   566

40.3 | Generating the tutorial   567

  40.3.1 *Main menu panel*   568

  40.3.2 *Information panels*   569

  40.3.3 *Section indexes*   570

  40.3.4 *XSL-FO file*   571

40.3.5   *JPEG files*   *571*

40.3.6   *ZIP file*   *574*

40.3.7   *PDF file*   *575*

40.4 | Conclusion   *575*

Chapter 41 Designing website stylesheets   **578**
Application Discussion

41.1 | Server delivery strategy   580

41.1.1   *Accessing all the data*   *580*

41.1.2   *Serving the data efficiently*   *581*

41.2 | Designing document types for navigation   583

41.2.1   *Cross-referencing*   *583*

41.2.2   *Traversing to referenced nodes*   *585*

41.2.3   *Defining an ID attribute*   *585*

41.3 | Filtering with XSL   587

41.4 | Rendering XML documents as speech   588

41.5 | Conclusion   589

Part 11   Navigation   590

Chapter 42 Extended linking   **592**
Application Discussion

42.1 | The shop notes application   593

42.1.1   *What is extended linking?*   *594*

42.1.2   *Displaying extended links*   *595*

42.1.3   *Notes survive to new versions of manuals*   *596*

42.1.4   *Vendors can use the notes*   *597*

42.2 | Other applications of extended linking   597

42.2.1   *Public resource communities of interest*   *598*

42.2.2   *Guidance documents*   *599*

42.2.3   *Computer-augmented memory*   *600*

42.2.4   *Intellectual property management*   *601*

42.3 | Strong link typing   601

42.3.1	*Hiding the installation log*	*602*
42.3.2	*Why do we need strong link typing?*	*602*
42.3.3	*Anchor role identification*	*603*
42.4 |	Conclusion	603

Chapter 43 **Topic maps: Knowledge navigation aids** **606**

Friendly Tutorial

43.1 |	Topic maps in a nutshell	608
43.1.1	*Topic and topic type*	*609*
43.1.2	*Topic occurrence and occurrence role*	*610*
43.1.3	*Indexes and glossaries*	*610*
43.1.4	*Topic association and association type*	*612*
43.1.5	*Thesauri and semantic networks*	*614*
43.1.6	*Scope*	*615*
43.1.7	*Public subject*	*616*
43.1.8	*Facets*	*616*
43.2 |	Applications of topic maps	616
43.2.1	*Reference work publishing*	*616*
43.2.2	*Technical documentation*	*618*
43.3 |	Tool support for topic maps	619
43.3.1	*Topic map design*	*619*
43.3.2	*Creation and maintenance*	*620*
43.3.3	*Exchange of topic maps*	*621*
43.3.4	*Navigating a map*	*621*
43.3.5	*As we think ...*	*622*
43.4 |	Conclusion	623

Chapter 44 **Application integration using topic maps** **624**

Application Discussion

44.1 |	Distributed objects	625
44.1.1	*Navigating the object ocean*	*626*

44.1.2 *Mapping control flow*   626

44.1.3 *Workflow*   627

44.2 | Architecture for application integration   628

44.2.1 *Context manager*   628

44.2.2 *Semantic manager*   629

44.2.3 *Service manager*   630

44.3 | A simple workflow example   630

44.4 | A compound workflow example   632

44.5 | Conclusion   634

Part 12   Infrastructure   636

Chapter 45 **Java technology for XML development**   **638**

Tool Discussion

45.1 | SAX and DOM implementations   640

45.1.1 *The SAX API*   640

45.1.2 *The DOM API*   643

45.2 | XML middleware services   644

45.2.1 *Business 1*   645

45.2.2 *Business 2*   646

Chapter 46 **Building a rich-media digital asset manager**   **648**

Application Discussion

46.1 | Architecture of a rich-media digital asset manager   649

46.2 | Object-oriented messaging   651

46.2.1 *Neutral serialization*   652

46.2.2 *Cost-effectiveness*   654

46.3 | Scripting with XML   655

46.3.1 *An* AssetProcessor *class*   656

46.3.2 *Batching assets for processing*   657

46.4 | Element structure and storage structure   658

46.5 | XML-based rich-media distribution   659

Chapter 47 **New directions for XML applications** **662**

Application Discussion

47.1 | Performance analysis   664

47.1.1 *Remote data collection*   *664*

47.1.2 *A clean solution ... with SOAP!*   *664*

47.2 | Coming soon to a television near you ...   666

47.2.1 *Distribution system design*   *667*

47.2.2 *Adding a subscriber*   *667*

47.3 | Performance enhancement   669

47.3.1 *Load balancing and routing*   *669*

47.3.2 *XML content matching*   *671*

47.3.3 *Other* XML Director *capabilities*   *673*

Part 13 XML Tutorials   674

Chapter 48 **XML basics** **676**

Friendly Tutorial

48.1 | Syntactic details   678

48.1.1 *Case-sensitivity*   *678*

48.1.2 *Markup and data*   *679*

48.1.3 *White space*   *680*

48.1.4 *Names and name tokens*   *680*

48.1.5 *Literal strings*   *681*

48.1.6 *Grammars*   *683*

48.2 | Prolog vs. instance   684

48.3 | The logical structure   684

48.4 | Elements   686

48.5 | Attributes   689

48.6 | The prolog   691

48.6.1 *XML declaration*   *692*

48.6.2 *Document type declaration*   *694*

48.7 | Markup miscellany   695

48.7.1 *Predefined entities*   695

48.7.2 *CDATA sections*   697

48.7.3 *Comments*   699

48.8 | Summary   701

**Chapter 49 Creating a document type
definition**   **702**

Friendly Tutorial

49.1 | Document type declaration   704

49.2 | Internal and external subset   707

49.3 | Element type declarations   710

49.4 | Element type content specification   711

49.4.1 *Empty content*   711

49.4.2 *ANY content*   712

49.4.3 *Mixed content*   712

49.5 | Content models   714

49.5.1 *Mixed content models*   718

49.6 | Attributes   719

49.6.1 *Attribute-list declarations*   720

49.6.2 *Attribute defaults*   722

49.6.3 *Attribute types*   724

49.7 | Notation Declarations   732

Chapter 50 Entities: Breaking up is easy to do   **736**

Tad Tougher Tutorial

50.1 | Overview   737

50.2 | Entity details   741

50.3 | Classifications of entities   742

50.4 | Internal general entities   744

50.5 | External parsed general entities   745

50.5.1 *External parsed entity support is optional*   746

50.6 | Unparsed entities   747

50.7 | Internal and external parameter entities   748

50.8 | Markup may not span entity boundaries   751

  50.8.1 *Legal parameter entity reference*   754

50.9 | External identifiers   755

  50.9.1 *System identifiers*   756

  50.9.2 *Public identifiers*   757

50.10 | Conclusion   758

  Chapter 51   Advanced features of XML   760
  Friendly Tutorial

51.1 | Conditional sections   761

51.2 | Character references   763

51.3 | Processing instructions   765

51.4 | Special attributes and newlines   770

51.5 | Standalone document declaration   771

51.6 | Is that all there is?   774

  Chapter 52   Reading the XML specification   776
  Tad Tougher Tutorial

52.1 | A look at XML's grammar   778

52.2 | Constant strings   779

52.3 | Names   781

52.4 | Occurrence indicators   782

52.5 | Combining rules   784

52.6 | Conclusion   785

  Part 14   Related Tutorials   786

  Chapter 53   Namespaces   788
  Friendly Tutorial

53.1 | Problem statement   790

53.2 | The namespaces solution   791

53.2.1   *Namespace prefixes*   *792*

53.2.2   *Scoping*   *793*

53.2.3   *Attribute names*   *795*

53.3 | Namespaces and DTDs   796

53.4 | Are namespaces a good thing?   799

Chapter 54   XML Path Language (XPath)   **800**
Tad Tougher Tutorial

54.1 | XPath applications   802

54.1.1   *User scenarios*   *802*

54.1.2   *Specifications built on XPath*   *803*

54.2 | The XPath data model   804

54.2.1   *Sources of the model*   *805*

54.2.2   *Tree addressing*   *806*

54.2.3   *Node tree construction*   *807*

54.2.4   *Node types*   *809*

54.3 | Location paths   811

54.3.1   *Basic concepts*   *811*

54.3.2   *Anatomy of a step*   *815*

54.3.3   *Our story so far*   *820*

54.3.4   *Predicates*   *822*

54.4 | ID function   826

54.5 | Conclusion   827

**Chapter 55   Extensible Stylesheet Language
(XSL)**   **828**
Friendly Tutorial

55.1 | Transformation vs. rendition   830

55.2 | Formatting objects   832

55.3 | In the meantime   833

55.4 | XSL stylesheets   834

55.5 | Rules, patterns and templates   835

55.6 | Creating a stylesheet   836

  55.6.1   *Document-level template rule*   *836*

  55.6.2   *Literal result elements*   *838*

  55.6.3   *Extracting data*   *838*

  55.6.4   *The* `apply templates` *instruction*   *839*

  55.6.5   *Handling optional elements*   *840*

  55.6.6   *Reordering the output*   *841*

  55.6.7   *Sharing a template rule*   *842*

  55.6.8   *Data content*   *842*

  55.6.9   *Handling inline elements*   *843*

  55.6.10   *Final touches*   *844*

55.7 | Top-level instructions   846

  55.7.1   *Stylesheet combination*   *846*

  55.7.2   *Keys*   *847*

  55.7.3   *Whitespace handling*   *850*

  55.7.4   *Output descriptions*   *851*

  55.7.5   *Numeric formats*   *852*

  55.7.6   *Attribute sets*   *852*

  55.7.7   *Namespace alias*   *852*

55.8 | Variables and parameters   853

55.9 | XSL formatting objects   854

55.10 | Referencing XSL stylesheets   857

55.11 | Conclusion   858

Chapter 56   **XML Pointer Language (XPointer)**   **860**

  Friendly Tutorial

56.1 | XPointers: The reason why   861

56.2 | Uniform Resource Identifiers   862

56.3 | URI references   863

56.4 | ID references with XPointers   864

56.5 | XPointer abbreviations   865

56.6 | Extensions to XPath		867
56.6.1	*Ranges*	868
56.6.2	*Point functions*	870
56.6.3	*Other extension functions*	870
56.6.4	*Multiple XPointer parts*	871
56.7 | The role of XPointers		872
56.8 | Conclusion		872

Chapter 57   XML Linking Language (XLink) **874**
Friendly Tutorial

57.1 | Basic concepts		876
57.2 | Simple links		878
57.2.1	*Link roles*	880
57.2.2	*Is this for real?*	881
57.2.3	*Link behaviors*	883
57.3 | Extended links		887
57.3.1	*Locator elements*	887
57.3.2	*Arcs*	889
57.4 | Linkbases		890
57.5 | Conclusion		892

Chapter 58   Datatypes **894**
Friendly Tutorial

58.1 | Datatype requirements		896
58.2 | XML Schema Datatypes		897
58.2.1	*Built-in datatypes*	898
58.2.2	*User-derived datatypes*	903
58.3 | Using datatypes		904
58.3.1	*XML Schema definition language (XSDL)*	904
58.3.2	*XML DTDs*	905
58.4 | Conclusion		906

Chapter 59   XML Schema (XSDL)   **908**
Tad Tougher Tutorial

59.1 | DTDs and schemas   910
59.1.1 *Next generation schemas*   911
59.1.2 *XSDL syntax*   912
59.2 | A simple sample schema   912
59.2.1 *Baseline DTD*   912
59.2.2 *Declaring an element type*   913
59.2.3 *Declaring attributes*   917
59.2.4 *Declaring schema conformance*   917
59.3 | Additional capabilities   918
59.3.1 *Locally-scoped element types*   918
59.3.2 *Element types versus types*   919
59.3.3 *Schema inclusion*   922
59.3.4 *Other capabilities*   923

Part 15   Resources   926

Chapter 60   Free resources on the CD-ROM   **928**
Resource Description

60.1 | Software featured on the covers   929
60.1.1 *XMLSolutions Corporation free software*   930
60.1.2 *IBM alphaWorks XML software suite*   930
60.1.3 *Adobe FrameMaker+SGML XML/SGML
             editor/formatter*   931
60.1.4 *eXcelon Stylus XSL stylesheet manager*   931
60.1.5 *Extensibility XML Authority schema editor* 931
60.1.6 *infoShark ViewShark XML relational data viewer* 932
60.1.7 *Arbortext Adept Editor LE*   932
60.1.8 *Enigma INSIGHT XML publishing software*   932
60.2 | IBM alphaWorks   933
60.2.1 *The alphaWorks idea*   933

60.2.2 *XML at alphaWorks*   934

60.3 | An eXtravagance of free XML software   938

60.3.1 *Parsers and engines*   939

60.3.2 *Editing and composition*   951

60.3.3 *Control information development*   953

60.3.4 *Conversion*   954

60.3.5 *Electronic delivery*   956

60.3.6 *Document Storage and Management*   957

60.4 | The XML SPECtacular   958

60.4.1 *W3C base standards*   958

60.4.2 *W3C XML applications*   961

60.4.3 *Other specifications*   962

Chapter 61   Other XML-related books   **964**

Resource Description

61.1 | Program development with XML   966

61.2 | Websites and Internet   967

61.3 | DTDs and schemas   967

61.4 | XML reference   968

61.5 | An awesomely unique XML/SGML application   968

61.6 | Learning the foundations of XML   969

Index   **970**

Preface

XML is taking over the world!

I saw the proof a few days ago in the newsletter for a major mutual fund. A profile of one of the fund's top holdings praised the company's great prospects because of its leadership in XML technology – *and the article didn't even explain what XML is!*

If a financial analyst thinks that XML is common knowledge, can world domination be far behind?

I'm delighted at the analyst's enthusiasm, but I don't think the knowledge is all that common yet – which is why Paul and I wrote this book. We know – and we want to share with you – the reasons why XML is taking over the world. We want you to understand how it is enabling all sorts of wonderful services for Web users and amazing new opportunities for website developers and businesses.

HTML – the HyperText Markup Language – made the Web the world's library. XML – the Extensible Markup Language – is its sibling, and it is making the Web the world's commercial and financial hub.

In the process, the Web is becoming much more than a static library. Increasingly, users are accessing the Web for "Web pages" that aren't actually on the shelves. Instead, the pages are generated dynamically from information available to the Web server. That information can come from databases on the Web server, from the site owner's enterprise databases, or even from other websites.

And that dynamic information needn't be served up raw. It can be analyzed, extracted, sorted, styled, and customized to create a personalized Web experience for the end-user. For this kind of power and flexibility, XML is the markup language of choice.

You can see why by comparing XML and HTML. Both are based on SGML – the International Standard for structured information – but look at the difference:

In HTML:

```
<p>P200 Laptop
<br>Friendly Computer Shop
<br>$1438
```

In XML:

```
<product>
<model>P200 Laptop</model>
<dealer>Friendly Computer Shop</dealer>
<price>$1438</price>
</product>
```

Both of these may appear the same in your browser, but the XML data is *smart* data. HTML tells how the data should *look*, but XML tells you what it *means*.

With XML, your browser knows there is a product, and it knows the model, dealer, and price. From a group of these it can show you the cheapest product or closest dealer without going back to the server.

Unlike HTML, with XML you create your own tags, so they describe exactly what you need to know. Because of that, your client-side applications can access data sources anywhere on the Web, in any format. New "middle-tier" servers sit between the data sources and the client, translating everything into your own task-specific XML.

But XML data isn't just smart data, it's also a smart document. That means when you display the information, the model name can be a different font from the dealer name, and the lowest price can be highlighted in green. Unlike HTML, where text is just text to be rendered in a uniform way, with XML text is smart, so it can control the rendition.

And you don't have to decide whether your information is data or documents; in XML, it is always both at once. You can do data processing or document processing or both at the same time.

With that kind of flexibility, it's no wonder that we're starting to see a Brave New Web of smart, structured information. Your broker sends your account data to Quicken using XML. Your "push" technology channel definitions are in XML. Everything from math to multimedia, chemistry to CommerceNet, is using XML or is preparing to start.

You should be too!

Welcome to the Brave New XML Web.

What about SGML?

This book is about XML. You won't find feature comparisons to SGML, or footnotes with nerdy observations like "the XML empty-element tag does not contradict the rule that every element has a start-tag and an end-tag because, in SGML terms, it is actually a start-tag followed immediately by a null end-tag".[1]

Nevertheless, for readers who use SGML, it is worth addressing the question of how XML and SGML relate. There has been a lot of speculation about this.

Some claim that XML will replace SGML because there will be so much free and low-cost software. Others assert that XML users, like HTML users before them, will discover that they need more of SGML and will eventually migrate to the full standard.

Both assertions are nonsense ... XML and SGML don't even compete.

XML is a simplified subset of SGML. The subsetting was optimized for the Web environment, which implies data-processing-oriented (rather than publishing-oriented), short life-span (in fact, usually dynamically-generated) information. The vast majority of XML documents will be created by computer programs and processed by other programs, then destroyed. Humans will never see them.

Eliot Kimber, who was a member of both the XML and SGML standards committees, says:

> There are certain use domains for which XML is simply not sufficient and where you need the additional features of SGML.

---

1. Well, yes, I did just make that nerdy observation, but it wasn't a footnote, was it?

These applications tend to be very large scale and of long term; e.g., aircraft maintenance information, government regulations, power plant documentation, etc.

Any one of them might involve a larger volume of information than the entire use of XML on the Web. A single model of commercial aircraft, for example, requires some four million unique pages of documentation that must be revised and republished quarterly. Multiply that by the number of models produced by companies like Airbus and Boeing and you get a feel for the scale involved.

I agree with Eliot. I invented SGML, I'm proud of it, and I'm awed that such a staggering volume of the world's mission-critical information is represented in it.

I'm thrilled that it has been such an enabler of the Web that the Society for Technical Communication awarded joint Honorary Fellowships to the Web's inventor, Tim Berners-Lee, and myself in recognition of the synergy.

But I'm also proud of XML. I'm proud of my friend Jon Bosak who made it happen, and I'm excited that the World Wide Web is becoming XML-based.

If you are new to XML, don't worry about any of this. All you need to know is that the XML subset of SGML has been in use for a decade or more, so you can trust it.

SGML still keeps the airplanes flying, the nuclear plants operating safely, and the defense departments in a state of readiness. You should look into it if you produce documents on the scale of an Airbus or Boeing. For the rest of us, there's XML.

About our sponsors

With all the buzz surrounding a hot technology like XML, it can be tough for a newcomer to distinguish the solid projects and realistic applications from the fluff and the fantasies. It is tough for authors as well, to keep track of all that is happening in the brief time we can steal from our day jobs.

The solution to both problems was to seek support and expert help from our friends in the industry. We know the leading companies in the XML arena and knew they had experience with both proven and leading-edge applications and products.

In the usual way of doing things, had we years to write this book, we would have interviewed each company to learn about its products and/or application experiences, written the chapters, asked the companies to review them, etc., and gone on to the next company. To save time and improve accuracy, we engaged in parallel processing. I spoke with the sponsors, agreed on subject matter for their chapters, and asked them to write the first draft.

All sponsored chapters are identified with the name of the sponsor, and sometimes with the names of the experts who prepared the original text. I used their materials as though they were my own interview notes – editing, rewriting, deleting, and augmenting as necessary to achieve my objective for the chapter in the context of the book, with consistent terminology and an objective factual style. I'd like to take this opportunity to thank these experts publicly for being so generous with their time and knowledge.

The sponsorship program was directed by Linda Burman, the president of L. A. Burman Associates, a consulting company that provides marketing and business development services to the XML and SGML industries.

We are grateful to our sponsors just as we are grateful to you, our readers. Both of you together make it possible for *The XML Handbook* to exist. In the interests of everyone, we make our own editorial decisions and we don't recommend or endorse any product or service offerings over any others.

Our twenty-seven sponsors are:

- Adobe Systems Incorporated, `http://www.adobe.com`
- Arbortext, `http://www.arbortext.com`
- Artesia Technologies, `http://www.artesiatech.com`
- DataChannel, Inc., `http://www.datachannel.com`
- Data Conversion Laboratory, `http://www.dclab.com`
- Documentum, `http://www.documentum.com`
- Enigma, Inc., `http://www.enigma.com`
- Excelon Corporation, `http://www.exceloncorp.com`
- Extensibility, Inc., `http://www.extensibility.com`
- Frank Russell Company, `http://www.russell.com`
- IBM Corporation, `http://www.ibm.com/xml`
- InfoShark, Inc., `http://www.infoshark.com`
- Infoteria Corporation, `http://www.infoteria.com`
- Innodata Corporation, `http://www.innodata.com`
- Intel Corporation, `http://www.intel.com/eBusiness`
- IPNet Solutions, `http://www.ipnet-solutions.com`

- IXIASOFT, `http://www.ixiasoft.com`
- Kinecta Corporation, `http://www.kinecta.com`
- Microsoft, `http://msdn.microsoft.com/xml`
- Oracle Corporation, `http://www.oracle.com/xml`
- Quark, Inc., `http://www.quark.com`
- Sequoia Software Corp., `http://www.sequoiasoftware.com`
- Sun Microsystems, `http://java.sun.com/xml`
- Wavo Corporation, `http://www.wavo.com`
- XCare.net, `http://www.xcare.net`
- XMLSolutions Corporation, `http://www.xmls.com`
- XyEnterprise, `http://www.xyenterprise.com`

How to use this book

The XML Handbook has fifteen parts, consisting of 61 chapters, that we intend for you to read in order.

Well, if authors didn't have dreams they wouldn't be authors.

In reality, we know that you, our readers, have diverse professional and technical backgrounds and won't all take the same route through a book this large and wide-ranging. Here are some hints for planning your trip.

In addition to the Table of Contents, you can get the best feel for the subject matter by reading the introductions to each part. They are less than a page and usually epitomize the subject area of the part in addition to introducing the chapters within it.

Part One contains introductory tutorials and establishes the terminology used in the remainder of the book. Please read it first.

Parts Two through Twelve cover different application domains. The chapters are application discussions, case studies, and tool category discussions, plus some introductory discussions and tutorials. You can read them with only the preceding parts (especially Part One) as background, although technical readers may want to complete the remaining tutorials first.[1]

---

1. The chapters in these parts are illustrated by their sponsors' experiences and products. The organization into parts only classifies the subject matter of the chapters; there is no attempt to classify the products. A tool used to illustrate the middle-tier servers part, for example, might be an appropriate choice for a portal or a publishing system.

Those can be found in Parts Thirteen and Fourteen. We strove to keep them friendly and understandable for readers without a background in subjects not covered in this book. Chapters whose subject matter thwarted that goal are labeled as being a tad tougher so you will know what to expect, but not to discourage you from reading them.

Part Fifteen is a guide to the CD-ROM and to other XML-related books in this series.

Acknowledgments

The principal acknowledgment in a book of this nature has to be to the people who created the subject matter. In this case, I take special pleasure in the fact that all of them are friends and colleagues of long standing in the SGML community.

Tim Bray and C. Michael Sperberg-McQueen were the original editors of the XML specification, later joined by Jean Paoli. Dan Connolly put the project on the W3C "todo list", got it started, and shepherded it through the approval process.

But all of them agree that, if a single person is to be thanked for XML, it is Jon Bosak. Jon not only sparked the original ideas and recruited the team, but organized and chairs the W3C XML Working Group.

As Tim put it: "Without Jon, XML wouldn't have happened. He was the prime mover."

Regarding the content of the book, Paul and I would like to thank Jean Paoli, Jon Bosak, G. Ken Holman, Bob DuCharme, Eliot Kimber, Andy Goldfarb, Lars Marius Garshol, and Steve Newcomb for contributing great material; Bryan Bell, inventor of MIDI and document system architect extraordinaire, for his advice and support; Steve Pepper and Bob DuCharme for talent-spotting; and John Bedunah for his insights into XSL.

We also thank Lilia Prescod, Thea Prescod, and Linda Goldfarb for serving as our useability test laboratory. That means they read lots of chapters and complained until we made them clear enough.

Prentice Hall PTR uses Adobe FrameMaker and other Adobe graphic arts and publishing software to produce the books in my series. We thank the late Lani Hajagos of Adobe for providing Paul and me with copies and, more importantly, for her encouraging support and suggestions when I first proposed this book. Her untimely passing was deeply felt by the markup language community, who greatly valued her friendship and counsel.

We also thank David Turner of Microsoft for providing copies of its drawing tools.

Paul and I designed, and Paul implemented, an SGML-based production system for the book. It uses James Clark's Jade DSSSL processor, FrameMaker+SGML, and some ingenious FrameMaker plug-ins designed and implemented by Doug Yagaloff of Caxton, Inc. We thank Doug, and also Randy Kelley, for their wizard-level FrameMaker consulting advice.

But a great production system is nothing without a great production manager. We thank Camille Trentacoste for being ours. Her rare combination of technical skill and artistic sensibility[1] was perfect for bridging the gap between the technology-obsessed authors and the Prentice-Hall production team. Her 1000 kilowatt personality and wicked sense of humor didn't hurt one bit either!

Andy Goldfarb served as artist-on-demand, art director, and document converter extraordinaire. We also thank Peter Snell for exercising his formidable logistic and diplomatic skills to develop our two CD-ROMs from the contributions of several hundred people.

This was my fourth project in which Linda Burman served as industry relations consultant. I thank her – again – for her sage counsel and always cheerful encouragement.

My personal thanks, also, to Mark Taub, our Editor-in-Chief at Prentice Hall PTR, for his help, encouragement, and management of the project.

I'd also like to acknowledge a major debt to two people who have supported and encouraged my work for the last six years – since the very day in 1994 that I retired from IBM to become an independent consultant. Yasufumi Toyoshima and Charles Brauer, of Fujitsu Network Communications, epitomize vision and leadership in technical management. They saw the potential for a Web-friendly, grammatically simple SGML subset long before myself or anyone else I know.

As the senior author, I gave myself this preface to write. I'm senior because Paul's folks were conceiving him about the same time that I was conceiving SGML. In return, Paul got to write the history chapter, because for him it really is history.

This gives me the opportunity to thank Paul publicly for the tremendous reservoir of talent, energy, and good humor that he brought to the project. The book benefitted not just from his XML knowledge and fine writing skills, but from his expertise in SGML, Jade, and FrameMaker that enabled

---

1. Meaning she can deal with Windows and Unix even though she prefers to work on a Mac!

us to automate the production of the book (with the previously acknowl-
edged help from our friends).

Thanks, Paul.

Charles F. Goldfarb
Saratoga, CA
September 4, 2000

Foreword

XML everywhere
By Jean Paoli
Product Unit Manager, XML Technologies
Microsoft Corporation
Co-editor of the XML Recommendation

When HTML came onto the scene it sparked a publishing phenomenon. Ordinary people everywhere began to publish documents on the Web. Presentation on the Web became a topic of conversation not just within the computer industry, but within coffeehouses. Overnight, it seemed as though everyone had a Web page.

I see the same phenomenon happening today with XML. Where data was once a mysterious binary blob, it has now become something ordinary people can read and author because it's text. With XML, ordinary people have the ability to craft their own data, the ability to shape and control data. The significance of this shift is difficult to overstate, for not only does it mean that more people can access data, but that there will undoubtedly be more data to access. We are on the verge of a data explosion. One ignited by XML.

By infusing the Web with data, XML makes the Web a better place for people to interact, to do business. XML allows us to do more precise searches, deliver software components, describe such things as collections of

Web pages and electronic commerce transactions, and much more. XML is changing not only the way we think about data, but the way we think about the Web.

And by doing so, it's changing the way we think about the traditional desktop application. I have already witnessed the impact of XML on all types of applications from word processors and spreadsheets to database managers and email. More and more, such applications are reaching out to the Web, tapping into the power of the Web, and it is XML that is enabling them to do so. Gone are the days of the isolated, incompatible application. Here are the days of universal access and shared data.

I joined Microsoft in the summer of 1996 with great faith in the Standard Generalized Markup Language (SGML) and a dream that its potential might one day be realized. As soon as I arrived at Microsoft, Jon Bosak of Sun Microsystems and I began discussing the possibility of creating an XML standard. Jon shared my enthusiasm for a markup language such as XML, understanding what it could mean to Web communication.

My goal in designing an XML standard was to produce a very simple markup language with as few abstractions as possible. Microsoft's success is due in no small part to its ability to develop products with mass-market appeal. It is this mass-market appeal that I wanted to bring to XML. Together with Jon and other long-time friends from the SGML world, C.M. Sperberg-McQueen, James Clark, Tim Bray, Steve DeRose, Eve Maler, Eliot Kimber, Dave Hollander, Makoto Murata, and Peter Sharpe, I co-designed the XML specification at the World Wide Web Consortium (W3C). This specification, I believe, reflects my original goals.

It was truly an exciting time. For years, we had all been part of a maverick band of text markup enthusiasts, singing its praises every chance we had, and before us was an opportunity to bring XML into the mainstream, maybe even into the operating system. At last, we were getting our chance to tell the World of the thing we had been so crazy about for all this time.

By the fall of 1996, many groups inside Microsoft, including Office, the Site Server Electronic Commerce Edition, the Data Access Group, to cite a few, were searching for an open format to enable interoperability on the Web. It was then that I began working with the managers of Internet Explorer 4, with the passionate Adam Bosworth, with Andrew Layman, with Thomas Reardon, to define the Channel Definition Format (CDF). CDF, the first major application of XML on the Web, became an immediate and incredible success, and XML started catching on like wildfire across the Web.

I remember those weeks and months that followed as a time where it seemed that every day another new group within Microsoft began coding applications using XML. Developers, left and right, were turning on to XML. They frenetically began to develop applications using XML, because XML gave them what they wanted: an easy-to-parse syntax for representing data. This flurry of activity was so great that by October of 1997, almost a year after my arrival at Microsoft, Chairman Bill Gates announced XML as "a breakthrough technology." Since that time we've never looked back.

This book is an excellent starting point where you can learn and experiment with XML. As the inventor of SGML, Dr. Charles F. Goldfarb is one of the most respected authorities on structured information. Charles has had a very direct influence on XML, as XML is a true subset of SGML, and he clearly understands the impact that XML will have on the world of data-driven, Web-based applications.

Charles and I share a common vision, that the most valuable asset for the user or for a corporation, namely the data, can be openly represented in a simple, flexible, and human-readable form. That it can easily travel from server to server, from server to client, and from application to application, fostering universal communication with anyone, anywhere. This vision can now be realized through XML.

Enjoy the book!

Redmond, April 24, 1998
Jean Paoli
Product Unit Manager, XML Technologies
Microsoft Corporation
Co-editor of the XML Recommendation

Prolog

XML: Looking back and looking forward
By Jon Bosak
XML Architect, Sun Microsystems
Chair, W3C XML Coordination Group

The World Wide Web is a medium that gained acceptance where earlier attempts had failed by providing the right combination of simplicity and fault tolerance. Now it faces the job of reinventing itself as a scalable, industrial-strength infrastructure strong enough to carry both human communication and electronic commerce into the new century. The story of XML and its companion standards is the story of that reinvention.

XML arose from the recognition that key components of the original Web – HTML tagging, simple hypertext linking, and hardcoded presentation – would not scale up to meet future needs. Those of us involved in industrial-strength SGML-based electronic publishing before the Web came into existence had learned the hard way that nothing substantially less powerful than SGML would work over the long run.

We also realized that any solution not based on SGML – the only formal International Standard that addresses this problem – would likely employ a proprietary binary format that would require special proprietary tools. XML is the creation of a small group of SGML experts who were motivated in large part by a desire to ensure that the Web of the future would not be dominated by standards controlled by a single vendor or nation. Its adoption by the world's largest computer software and hardware companies marks a significant turning point in the struggle to keep data free.

XML is a tremendous victory for open standards. It is freely extensible, imposing no limits on the ability of users to define markup in any combination of the world's major natural languages; it is character-based and human-readable, which means that XML documents can be maintained using even the most primitive text processing tools; and it is relatively easy to implement, so users can look forward to an abundance of inexpensive commercial XML processing tools and an ever-growing number of free ones.

Most importantly, XML provides a standard framework for making agreements about communication. It allows people sharing a common data exchange problem to work out an open solution to that problem – without interference from third parties, without dependence on large software vendors, without bindings to specific tools, without language restrictions, and in a way that lets anyone with a similar problem use the same solution. While the task of defining such standards within each industry and user community still lies before us, the framework for doing so is now in place.

Nevertheless, we must not lose sight of the larger goal. True interoperability requires not just interoperable syntax, but interoperable semantics. This ultimate goal cannot be achieved with anything less than the standardization of meaning itself, at least in those areas in which we wish to achieve automatic interoperability.

The coming standardization of domain-specific element types and attributes will establish the semantically meaningful labeling of content in particular industries, but it cannot address the behavioral aspect. While interoperable behavior can always be specified using a platform-neutral programming language like Java, such a powerful tool is often disproportionate to simple tasks. Just as we cannot ask our airline pilots to be aircraft engineers, we cannot require every creator of meaning to also be a programmer.

In the areas of hypermedia linking and presentation of rendered data, we can and must establish standardized techniques for behavioral specification that are declarative enough to be usable by nonprogrammers and yet powerful enough to get the job done in industrial contexts of unlimited scale. In both areas we are being held back by early superficial successes with simple mechanisms that are easy to learn but place unacceptable limits on what can be done, just as the early success of HTML held back the adoption of extensible markup.

The parallels to be drawn among the recent histories of markup, linking, and presentation are striking.

- In all three cases, early visionaries went much farther than the majority of adopters were ready to follow.
- In all three cases, breakthroughs in public consciousness were made by relative newcomers whose major contribution was to radically simplify the early, more advanced techniques in a way that made them accessible to the first wave of implementors.
- In all three cases, the original work is now being reconsidered, as those who understand the essential coherence of the original, larger view labor patiently to reconstruct mechanisms adequate for the demands of the future.
- And in all three cases, the biggest roadblock to deployment of the more advanced solutions is the success of the limited ones that got the Web off the ground.

I have no doubt that we will eventually succeed in replacing today's anemic realization of hypertext with something closer to the ideal articulated by the visionaries of the 1960s and worked out in the research projects of the 1970s and 1980s. I also have no doubt that we will eventually achieve interoperability of formatting behavior in a way that preserves the delivery of textual semantics to Web clients while simultaneously enabling the level of typographic control associated with printed newspaper and magazine publishing. My certainty is based not on a logical analysis of the future but simply on the same from-the-trenches understanding of basic needs that motivated me to begin the XML project in the first place.

What is not clear is how long it will take for Web implementors to realize the limitations of their existing conceptions of hyperlinking and style specification in the way that the more advanced among them now understand the limitations of HTML markup. But whether it takes two years or ten, the next steps are as necessary as was the first step to XML.

The XML Handbook can help us take those steps.

Los Altos, August 1999
Jon Bosak
XML Architect, Sun Microsystems
Chair, W3C XML Coordination Group

The Who, What, and Why of XML

- ▌ Why XML?
- ▌ Just enough XML
- ▌ XML in the real world
- ▌ XML and your browser
- ▌ XML and e-business
- ▌ The XML Jargon Demystifier

Part One

This part is the essential introduction to everything else in the book, which is why we named it Part One! Please read it from beginning to end because each chapter builds on the preceding ones.

For example, Chapter 2's *Just enough XML* tutorial relies on insights and markup fundamentals presented in their historical and business contexts in Chapter 1. That knowledge lets Chapter 3 tackle the most fundamental issue for XML: the relationship between documents and data and what that means for applications and products.

By Chapter 4 we've covered enough to understand XML's impact on human communication through the Web, and then, in Chapter 5, how it enables computer-to-computer communication for e-business.

Finally, in Chapter 6 we can apply what we have learned to an examination of the most important terms related to XML – the ones that people misuse the most! You'll learn what they really mean, and how to decipher the intended meaning when others get them wrong.

Reading this part will prepare you for the application and tool discussions in Parts Two through Twelve. High-tech readers may want to complete the tutorials in Parts Thirteen and Fourteen first, but others can just dip into the tutorials on a need-to-know basis.

Why XML?

- What is XML, really?

- Origins in document processing

- Abstraction vs. rendition

- Documents and data

Chapter

1

The buzz around the Extensible Markup Language is revolutionary: there is talk about changing the way software is written, sold and used. All of the major software companies are enthusiastic about XML. New standards based upon it are released daily.

As you may have noticed, the XML book rack has grown from the *XML Handbook* and a couple of others to scores of books on every imaginable technical variation and combination. Where did this language come from and why is it so important?

The computer world's excitement can be summarized in two words: *information interchange*. XML is about making computer systems work together through the exchange of everything from simple numbers to elaborate data structures and human-readable texts.

For instance, to let Web browsers interwork with drawing tools like Corel Draw and Adobe Illustrator, the World Wide Web Consortium created an XML-based language called the Scalable Vector Graphics language (SVG).

Similarly – but in a totally different domain – a group of accounting software vendors defined an XML-based language called Open Financial Exchange (OFX).[1]

Analysis   XML is a framework for any project that involves moving information from place to place, even between different software products and platforms.

Once computers can interchange information, they can work together. This in turn allows people to work together more efficiently. It does not matter whether you are buying and selling, writing a manifesto or collecting data on the fertility rates of fruit flies – XML can be used for any kind of information interchange.

Many of the most influential companies in the software industry promote XML as the next step in the Web's evolution. How can they be so confident about something so new? More important: how can *you* be sure that your time invested in learning and using XML will be profitable?

We can all safely bet on XML because the central ideas in this new technology are in fact very old and have been proven effective across several decades and thousands of projects. The easiest way to understand these ideas is to go back to their source, the *Standard Generalized Markup Language* (SGML).

XML is, in fact, a streamlined subset of SGML, so SGML's track record is XML's as well. SGML has enabled information interchange within and between some of the world's largest companies for more than a decade. SGML was intended for document processing but as time goes by it has become increasingly clear that with extensible markup technologies like SGML and XML, data processing and document processing are the same thing! If you understand where it all comes from, you'll understand where it – and the Web – are going.

---

1. If you're going to work with XML, you'll need to get used to contrived acronyms with the letter "X" in them.

1.1 | Text formatters and SGML

XML comes from a rich history of text processing systems. *Text processing* is the sub-discipline of *computer science* dedicated to creating computer systems that can automate parts of the document creation and publishing process. Text processing software includes simple word processors, advanced news item databases, hypertext document presentation systems and other publishing tools.

The first wave of automated text processing was computer typesetting. Authors would type in a document and describe how they would like it to be formatted. The computer would print out a document with the described text and formatting.

We call the file format that contained the mix of the actual data of the document, plus the description of the desired format, a *rendition*. Some well-known rendition notations include *troff*, *Rich Text Format* (*RTF*), and *LaTeX*.

The system would convert the rendition into something physically perceivable to a human being – a *presentation*. The presentation medium was historically paper, but eventually electronic display.

Typesetting systems sped up the process of publishing documents and evolved into what we now know as desktop publishing. Newer programs like *Microsoft Word* and *Adobe PageMaker* still work with renditions, but they give authors a nicer interface to manipulate them. The user interface to the rendition (the file with formatting codes in it) is designed to look like the presentation (the finished paper product). We call this *What You See Is What You Get* (*WYSIWYG*) publishing. Since a rendition merely describes a presentation, it makes sense for the user interface to reflect the end-product.

1.1.1 *Formatting markup*

The form of typesetting notation that predates WYSIWYG (and is still in use today) is called *formatting markup*. Consider an analogy: you might submit a manuscript to a human typesetter for publication. Imagine it had no formatting, not even paragraphs or different fonts, but rather was a single continuous paragraph that was "marked up" with written instructions for how it should be formatted. You could write very precise instructions for layout: "Move this word over two inches. Bold it. Move the next word

beside it. Move the next word underneath it. Bold it. Start a new line here."
and so forth. It might look like Figure 1-1.

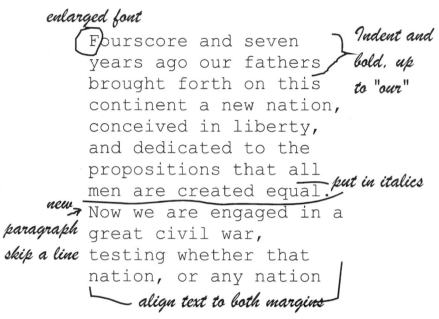

Figure 1-1   A manuscript "marked up" by hand

Formatting markup is very much the same. We "circle" text with instructions called *tags* or *codes* (depending on the particular formatting markup language). Here is an example of markup in one popular formatting markup language called LaTeX.

Example 1-1. A document with formatting markup

This is a marked up document. It contains words that are italicized because they are in a foreign language: \it{oo la la}, bold-faced because they are \bf{important}, small because they are \small{not important} and large, just because \large{we like large text!}

In this markup language, the curly braces describe the extent of the formatting. So the italics started with the "\it" command extend until the end of the word "la". Because the markup uses only ordinary characters on typical keyboards, it can be created using existing text editors instead of special word processors (those came later).

1.1.2 *Generalized markup*

This process is adequate if your only goal is to type documents into the computer, describe a rendition and then print them. Around the late sixties, people started wanting more from their documents. In particular, IBM asked a young researcher named Charles Goldfarb (the name may sound familiar) to build a system for storing, finding, managing, and publishing legal documents.

Goldfarb found that there were many systems within IBM that could not communicate with each other. They could not interchange information! Each of them used a different command language. They could not read each other's files, just as you may have had trouble loading *WordPerfect* files into *Word* and vice versa. The problem then, as now, was that they all had a different *representation* (sometimes also called a *file format*) for the information.

In the late sixties, Goldfarb and two other IBM researchers, Ed Mosher and Ray Lorie, set out to solve this problem. The team recognized (eventually) that the language would need to support three basic features:

Common data representation: markup
Various computer programs and systems would need to be able to read and write information in the same representation.

Markup should be extensible
There are an infinite variety of different types of information that must be exchanged. The markup language must be extensible enough to support them all.

Document types need rules
There must be a mechanism for formally describing the rules shared by documents of a common type.

1.1.3 *Common data representation*

The need for a common data representation is easy to understand. Tools cannot interchange information if they do not speak the same language. As an analogy, consider the popularity of Latin terms in describing chemical and legal concepts and categories. To a certain extent, chemists and lawyers have chosen Latin as a common language for their fields. It made sense in the text processing context that the common language should be some form of markup language, because markup was well understood and very compatible with existing text editors and operating systems. Markup is like a common language shared by many disciplines.

1.1.4 *Customized document types*

Second, the three realized that the common format should be *specific* to legal documents while at the same time being general enough to be used for things that are completely unrelated to the law. This seems like a paradox but it is not as impossible as it sounds!

This is a little more subtle to grasp, but vital to understanding XML. The team could have invented a simple language, perhaps similar to the representation of a standard word processor, but that representation would not have allowed the sophisticated processing that was required. Lawyers and scientists both use Latin, but they do not use the same terminology. Rather they use Latin words as building blocks to create domain specific vocabularies (e.g. "habeas corpus", "ferruginous"). These domain specific vocabularies are even more important when we are describing documents to computers. Markup is the lingua franca but it must be customized (extended!) for each community, consortium or problem domain.

Just as Latin can be used to describe anything under the sun, XML can be used for legal and scientific projects, for electronic business and also for poetry. XML is great for everything from long, complicated academic documents to the business transaction documents that allow commerce to flow around the planet: purchase orders, requests for quotation, bills of lading and so forth. Because XML is so expressive, the business transaction documents can be created and consumed by computers; increasingly, they can transact business with little or no human intervention.

1.1.4.1 Computers are dumb

Usually we take for granted that computers are not very good at working with text and documents. We would never, for instance, ask a computer to search our hard disk and return a document that was a "letter" document, that was to "Martha" and that was about "John Smith's will". Even though this example seems much simpler than something a lawyer or chemist would run into, the fundamental problems are the same.

Most people recognize that the computer is completely incapable of understanding the concepts of "letter", "Martha" or "a will". Instead we might tell it to search for those words, and hope that we had included them all in the document. But what would happen if the system that we wanted to search was massive? It might turn up hundreds of unrelated documents. It might return documents that contained strings like "Martha, will you please write me a letter and tell me how John is doing?"

The fundamental problem is that the computer does not in any way understand the text. The solution is to teach the computer as much about the document as possible. Of course the computer will not understand the text in any real sense, but it can pretend to, in the same way that it pretends to understand simple data or decimal numbers.[2] We can make this possible by reducing the complexity of the document to a few structural *elements* chosen from a common vocabulary.

The elements that we use are not chosen just for the computer but also because they have significance to people and our sociological systems. One important example of this is in electronic commerce vocabularies. If corporate policy or national law requires a certain form of document be produced in order to conduct a certain kind of business then XML allows that document type to be moved directly into a digital representation. The system can move from a manual process to a digital one without breaking any rules or laws.

1.1.4.2 Computers can be trained

Once we "teach" computers about documents, we can also program them to do things they would not have been able to otherwise. Using their new

---

2. We hope we haven't disillusioned anyone here. Computers may seem to know everything about math, but it is all a ruse. As far as they are concerned, they are only manipulating zeros and ones.

"understanding" they can help us to navigate through large documents, organize them, and automatically format the documents for publication in many different media, such as hypertext, print or tape.

In other words, we can get them to process text for us! The range of things we can get them to do with the documents is much wider than what we would get with WYSIWYG word processors or formatting markup. In the world of transaction documents, the computer typically rips the documents apart and can do a variety of things with the bits: store them in databases, perform financial computations or anything else necessary to a business process.

Let us go back to the analogy of the typesetter working with a document marked up with a pen on paper to see why this is so powerful.

Imagine if we called her back the next day and told her to "change the formatting of the second chapter". She would have a lot of trouble mentally translating the codes for presentation back into high level constructs like sections and paragraphs.

To her, a title would only look like a line of text with a circle around it and instructions to make it italicized and 18 point. Making changes would be painful because recognizing the different logical constructs would be difficult. She probably could eventually accomplish the task by applying her human intuition and by reading the actual text. But computers do not have intuition, and cannot understand the text. That means that they cannot reliably recognize logical structure based totally on formatting. For instance they cannot reliably distinguish an italicized, 18 point title from an italicized, 18 point warning paragraph.

Even if human beings were consistent in formatting different types of documents (which we are not) computers would still have trouble. Even in a single document, the same formatting can mean two different things: italics could represent any kind of emphasis, foreign words, mathematical notations, scholarly citations or other conventions.

Note that this all comes back to our theme of information interchange, but in a subtle way. The human being has information about a document that may not show up in any particular formatted print-out (rendition) of the document. The author knows which documents are letters and which are not. The author knows which words are foreign and which are emphasized for rhetorical effect. A markup language can serve as a vehicle for the human to transmit this information *to the computer*.

We'll see that in some applications we can use markup to let computers talk to computers also! In fact, we can build systems in which each participant does not know or care whether its conversation partner is mechanical or biological.

1.1.4.3   Abstractions and renditions

Computers are not as smart as we are. If we want the computer to consider a piece of text to be written in a foreign language (for instance for spell checking purposes) then we must label it explicitly `foreign-language` and not just put it in italics! We call "foreign language" the *abstraction* that we are trying to represent, and we call the italics a particular rendition of the abstraction.

Formatting information has other problems. It is specific to a particular use of the information. Search engines cannot do very interesting searching on italics because they do not know what they mean. In contrast, the search engine could do something very interesting with `citation` elements: it could return a list of what documents are cited by other documents.

Italics are a form of markup specific to a particular application: formatting or printing. In contrast, the citation element is markup that can be used by a variety of applications. That is why we call this form of structural markup *generalized markup*. Generalized markup is the alternative to either formatting markup or WYSIWYG (lampooned by XML users as What You See is *All* You Get). Generalized markup is about getting more.

Because of the ambiguity of formatting, XML users typically do not bother to capture the document's presentational features at all, though XML would allow it. We are not interested, for instance, in fonts, page breaks and bullets. This formatting information would merely clutter up our abstract document's representation. Although typographic conventions allow the computer to print out or display the document properly, we want our markup to do more than that. As you can imagine, removing all ambiguity is especially important in commerce applications where millions of dollars may hinge on the proper completion of a transaction.

1.1.4.4   Stylesheets

Of course we must still be able to generate high quality print and online renditions of the document. Your readers do not want to read XML text directly. Instead of directly inserting the formatting commands in the XML document, we usually tell the computer how to generate formatted renditions *from* the XML abstraction.

For example in a print presentation, we can make the content of TITLE elements bold and large, insert page breaks before the beginning of chapters, and turn emphasis, citations and foreign words into italics. These rules are specified in a file called a *stylesheet*. The stylesheet is where human designers can express their creativity and understanding of formatting conventions. The stylesheet allows the computer to automatically convert the document from the abstraction to a formatted rendition.

We could use two different stylesheets to generate online and print renditions of the document. In the online rendition, there would be no page breaks, but cross-references would be represented as clickable hypertext links. Generalized markup allows us to easily produce high-quality print and online renditions of the same document.

We can even use two different stylesheets in the same medium. For instance, the computer could format the same document into several different styles (e.g. "New York Times" style vs. "Wired Magazine") depending on the expressed preferences of a Web surfer, or even based on which Internet service provider they use.

We can also go beyond just print and online formatting and have our document be automatically rendered into braille or onto a text-to-speech machine. XML is highly endorsed by those who promote the *accessibility* of information to the visually impaired.

Generalized markup documents are also "future-proof". They will not have to be redone to take advantage of future technologies. Instead, new stylesheets can be created to render existing documents in new ways.

Future renditions of documents might include three-dimensional virtual reality worlds where books are rendered as buildings, chapters as rooms and the text as wallpaper! Once again, the most important point is that these many different renditions will be possible without revising the document. There are millions of SGML documents that predate the Web, but many of them are now published on it.

Typically, they were republished in the Web's Hypertext Markup Language (HTML) without changing a single character of the SGML source's markup or data, or editing a single character of the generated HTML. The same will be true of the relationship between XML and future representations.

The key is abstraction. SGML and XML can represent abstractions, and from abstractions you can easily create any number of renditions. This is a fact well-known to the world's database programmers, who constantly generate new renditions – reports and forms – from the same abstract data. In this sense, XML brings some of the rigor of the database world to the document world, where it has typically been lacking.

In the electronic commerce world, stylesheets can be used to make an information-dense computer-to-computer message into a visual rendition fit for human consumption. Perhaps your company policy is to require purchase orders beyond some limit to be considered by an executive. A stylesheet could turn an abstract, data-oriented XML document into a familiar rows-and-columns purchase order that can be printed, touched and stapled to a wall. If some executives are more comfortable working online, a different stylesheet could turn it into a transient computer window with the purchase order information at the top and two buttons: "Accept" and "Reject" at the bottom. The same information can have different renditions depending on your corporate policies and systems of the day.

1.1.5 *Rule-based markup*

Charles and his team (remember them?) had a third realization: if computer systems were to work with these documents reliably, the documents would have to follow certain rules. In retrospect we can see that this is important for interchanging information of all sorts, whether it is traditionally considered a document or not.

For instance a courtroom transcript might be required to have the name of the judge, defendant, both attorneys and (optionally) the names of members of the jury (if there is one). Since humans are prone to make mistakes, the computer would have to enforce the rules for us.

In other words the legal markup language should be specified in some formal way that would restrict elements appropriately. If the court stenographer tried to submit a transcript to the system without these elements being properly filled in, the system would check its *validity* and complain that it was *invalid*.

Once again, this concept is very common in the database world. Database people typically have several layers of checking to guarantee that improper data cannot appear in their databases. For instance *syntactic* checks guarantee that phone numbers are composed of digits and that people's names are not. *Semantic* checks ensure that business rules are followed (such as "purchase order numbers must be unique"). The database world calls the set of constraints on the database structure a *schema*.

Of course, court transcripts have a different structure from wills, which in turn have a different structure from memos. So you would need to rigorously define what it means for each type of document to be valid. In SGML terminology, each of these is a *document type* and the formal definition that describes each type is called a *document type definition* (DTD) or *schema definition*. We use the word *document type* (or *schema*) to refer both to a vocabulary and the constraints on the vocabulary's use.

Once you have a document type worked out, you can describe for the computer how to print or display documents that conform to it with a *stylesheet*. So you might say that the address line in memos would be bold, or that there should be two lines between speeches in a court transcript. These processes can work reliably because documents are constrained by the document type definition.

For instance, a letter cannot have a postscript ("P.S.") at the beginning of the document nor an address at the end. Because there is no convention for formatting such a letter, a stylesheet would typically not do a good job with it. In fact, it might crash, as some word processors do when they try to load corrupted documents. The document type definition protects us from this.[3]

The rigor of a formal document type is just as important when the creator of the document is a computer (e.g. a purchasing system) and the receiver is also a computer (e.g. a delivery system). If your company lives and dies by its supply of widgets, you cannot afford for a miscommunication to cause a purchase to fail. You need both parties to know in advance what they should provide as requests and what they should expect back as responses. You need seamless interchange. As they say in the space exploration business, "Failure is not an option."

---

3. Of course, computer programmers will always invent new excuses for crashing software.

1.2 | XML markup

Enough hype about generalized markup! You probably want to know what it looks like. To mark up a letter, we could identify the components of the letter like this:

Example 1-2. A simple memo

```
<memo>
<to>Martha Crealock</to>
<from>Joan Joplin</from>
<re>John Smith's will</re>
<p>John Smith wants to update his will. Another wife left him.</p>
</memo>
```

This text would be part of an XML document. The markup identifies components, called elements, of the document in ways that the computer can understand. The start-tag "<to>" marks the beginning of an element and the end-tag "</to>" marks the end of the element. Each element is an instance of an *element type*, such as to, from, re and p.

If you use an XML-aware word processor, you may never work with markup at the textual tag level, but you would still annotate sections of the document in this way (using the graphical interface that the tool provides).

Instead of each element type describing a formatting construct, each one instead describes the logical role of its elements – the *abstraction* it represents. The goal is for the abstraction to be descriptive enough and suitably chosen so that particular uses of the document (such as printing, searching and so forth) can be completely automated as computer processes acting on the elements.

For instance, we can search for a document that is "to" Martha, about ("re") John Smith's will. Of course the computer still does not understand the human interaction and concepts of sender and receiver, but it does know enough about the document to be able to tell me that in a "to" element of this particular document, the word "Martha" appears. If we expanded the letter a little to include addresses and so forth, we could also use an appropriate stylesheet to print it as a standard business letter.

1.2.1 *Documents and databases*

We can make our letter example even more precise and specific:

Example 1-3. Another letter

```
<memo>
<to>marthac@thelegaleagles.com</to>
<from>joanj@thelegaleagles.com</from>
<regarding>
<document-retrieval-request>will</document-retrieval-request>
<customer-name>John Smith</customer-name>
<customer-number>802-31348-5749</customer-number>
</regarding>
<comment>John Smith wants to update his will. Another wife left
him.</comment>
</memo>
```

XML does not require this level of detail, but it allows it. If you are familiar with databases, you might recognize that this looks database-ish in the sense that the customer number could be stored in a special index and you could easily search and sort this document based on customer numbers, document retrieval requests and so forth.

But you can only do this sort of thing if your letter processing system understands your company's concepts of customer-numbers and your documents consistently provide the information. In other words, you must define your own set of element types just as the IBM team did.

In fact, many people have noticed that XML documents resemble traditional relational and object database data in many ways. Once you have a language for rigorously representing documents, those documents can be treated more like other forms of data.

But the converse is also true. As we have described, XML documents have many features in common with databases. They can preserve the abstract data and prevent it from being mingled with rendition information.

Furthermore, you can actually use generalized markup to represent data that is not what we would traditionally think of as documents, but too complex to be directly handled in conventional databases. In this brave new world, DNA sequences are data, and so are molecular diagrams and virtual reality worlds. A document is just an interchangeable form of data! In other words, generalized markup allows us to blow the doors off the word "document" and integrate diverse types of data. This database-ization of documents and document-ization of data is one of the major drivers of the XML excitement. Prior to XML, the Web had no standard data interchange format for even moderately complex data.

Only a few people could see years ago that SGML might one day change the entire world of databases and electronic commerce. But XML's unique usefulness as a data interchange representation was a direct consequence of the IBM team's three fundamental concepts:

- Markup as a common data representation
- Extensibility through document types (vocabularies)
- Verification that documents follow rules (document types/schemas).

1.3 | Road to XML

In 1969, the IBM team developed a language that could implement their vision of markup that would allow the construction of sophisticated, robust systems that are not specific to a particular piece of application software or vendor. They called it the *Generalized Markup Language* (which, not coincidentally, has the same initials as the names Goldfarb, Mosher and Lorie).[4]

However, it wasn't until 1974 that Goldfarb proved the concept of a "validating parser", one that could read a document type definition and check the accuracy of markup, without going to the expense of actually processing a document. As he recalls it: "At that point SGML was born – although it still had a lot of growing up to do."

Between 1978 and 1986, Goldfarb acted as technical leader of a team of users, programmers and academics that developed his nascent invention into the robust International Standard (ISO 8879) they called the *Standard Generalized Markup Language.*

That team, with many of the same players still involved, is now JTC1/SC34, which continues to develop SGML and related standards. Two of the most important are *HyTime*, which standardizes the representation of hyperlinking features, and DSSSL, which standardizes the creation of stylesheets.[5]

---

4. In fact, Goldfarb coined the term "markup language" for the purpose.

The SGML standard took a long time to develop, but arguably it was still ahead of the market when it was created. Over those years, the basic concepts of GML were broadened to support a very wide range of applications. Although GML was always extensible and generalized, the SGML standard added many features and options, many intended for niche markets. But the niches had to be catered for: some of the niche users have document collections that rival the Web in size!

By the time it was standardized in 1986, SGML had become large, intricate and powerful. In addition to being an official International Standard, SGML is the de facto standard for the interchange of large, complex documents and has been used in domains as diverse as programming language design and airplane maintenance.

1.3.1 *HTML and the Web*

In 1989, a researcher named Tim Berners-Lee proposed that information could be shared within the CERN European Nuclear Research Facility using hyperlinked text documents. He was advised to use an SGML-ish syntax by a colleague named Anders Berglund, an early adopter of the new SGML standard. They started from a simple example document type in the SGML standard.[6] and developed a hypertext version called the *Hypertext Markup Language* (HTML).

Relative to the 20 year evolution of SGML, HTML was developed in a hurry, but it did the job well. Tim called his hypertext system the *World Wide Web* and today it is the most diverse, popular hypertext information system in existence. Its simplicity is widely believed to be an important part of its success. The simplicity of HTML and the other Web specifications allowed programmers around the world to quickly build systems and tools to work with the Web.

---

5. Knowing the full names probably won't help much, but just in case, HyTime is short for "Hypermedia/Time-based Structuring Language" and DSSSL (pronounced "dis-sal") is short for "Document Style Semantics and Specification Language". We warned you that it wouldn't help much.
6. That DTD was based on the very first published DTD, from a 1978 IBM manual written by Goldfarb, derived in turn from work that he and Mosher had done in the early 70's.

HTML inherited some important strengths from SGML. With a few exceptions, its element types were generalized and descriptive, not formatting constructs as in languages like TeX and Microsoft Word. This meant that HTML documents could be displayed on text screens, under graphical user interfaces, and even projected through speakers for the sight impaired.

HTML documents used SGML's simple angle bracket convention for markup. That meant that authors could create HTML documents in almost any text editor or word processor. The documents are also compatible with almost every computer system in existence.

On the other hand, HTML only uses a fixed set of element types. As we discussed before, no one document type can serve all purposes, so HTML only adopted the first of GML's revelations, that document representations must be standardized. It is not extensible and therefore cannot be tailored for particular document types, and it was not very rigorously defined until years after its invention. By the time HTML was given a formal DTD, there were already thousands of Web pages with erroneous HTML.[7]

1.3.2 *HTML gets extended – unofficially!*

As the Web grew in popularity many people started to chafe under HTML's fixed document type. Browser vendors saw an opportunity to gain market share by making incompatible extensions to HTML. Most of the extensions were formatting commands and thus damaged the Web's interoperability. The first golden rule – standardization – was in serious danger.

For instance Netscape's popular CENTER element cannot be "pronounced" in a text to speech converter. A BLINK element cannot be rendered on some computers. Still, this was a fairly understandable reaction to HTML's limitations.

One argument for implementing formatting constructs instead of abstractions is that there are a fixed number of formatting constructs in wide use, but an ever growing number of abstractions. Let's say that next year biologists invent a new formatting notation for discussing a particular type of DNA. They might use italics to represent one kind of DNA con-

---

7. Today there are tens of thousands with misleading or downright erroneous informational content, so perhaps bad HTML markup is not that big a problem in the overall scheme of things.

struct and bold to represent another. In other words, as new abstractions are invented, we usually use existing formatting features to represent them. We have been doing this for thousands of years, and prior to computerization, it was essentially the only way.

We human readers can read a textual description of the meanings of the features ("in this book, we will use Roman text to represent...") and we can differentiate them from others using our reasoning and understanding of the text. But this system leaves computers more or less out of the loop.

For instance superscripts can be used for trademarks, footnotes and various mathematical constructs. Italics can be used for references to book titles, for emphasis and to represent foreign languages. Without generalized markup to differentiate, computers cannot do anything useful with that information. It would be impossible for them to translate foreign languages, convert emphasis to a louder voice for text to speech conversion, or do calculations on the mathematical formulae. Over time, the Web became more and more optimized for a single delivery platform: whichever Web browser had the most market share on a particular day. Handhelds, braille printers and other alternative devices became marginalized.[8]

1.3.3 *The World Wide Web reacts*

As the interoperability and diversity of the Web became more and more endangered by proprietary formatting markup, the World Wide Web Consortium (headed by the same Tim Berners-Lee) decided to act. They attacked the problem in three ways. First, they decided to adopt the GML convention for attaching formatting to documents, the stylesheet.

They invented a simple HTML-oriented stylesheet language called *Cascading Style Sheets* (CSS) that allowed people to attach formatting to HTML documents without filling the HTML itself with proprietary, rendition-oriented markup.

Second, they invented a simple mechanism for adding abstractions to HTML. We will not look at that mechanism here, because XML makes it obsolete. It allowed new abstractions to be invented but provided no mechanism for constraining their occurrence. In other words it addressed two of GML's revelations: it brought HTML back to being a single standard,

---

8. Although, thanks to XML, that is starting to change, as we shall see.

more or less equally supported by the major vendors, and it allowed people to define arbitrary extensions (with many limitations).

But they knew that their stool would not stand long on two of its three legs. The (weakly) extensible HTML and CSS are only stopgaps. For the Web to move to a new level, it had to incorporate the third of GML's important ideas, that document types should be formally defined so that documents can be checked for validity against them.

Therefore, the World Wide Web Consortium decided to develop a subset of SGML that would retain SGML's major virtues but also embrace the Web ethic of minimalist simplicity. They decided to give the new language the catchy name *Extensible Markup Language* (XML). They also decided to make related standards for advanced hyperlinking and stylesheets.

The first, called the *Extensible Linking Language* (XLink), is inspired by HyTime, the ISO standard for linking SGML documents, and by the Text Encoding Initiative, the academic community's guidelines for applying SGML to scholarly applications.

The second, called the *Extensible Style Language* is a combination of ideas from the Web's Cascading Style Sheets and ISO's DSSSL standard.[9]

XML was specifically designed to enhance reliable interchange on the Web. At about the same time, the Internet became popular as a place to do business: to buy and sell things. People saw that in the future, computers would do the buying and selling completely independently of human beings. They would also need a robust, sophisticated information interchange language. In other words, electronic business needed XML.

1.4 | EDI, EAI and other TLAs

By 1998, many understood that XML was not just a tool for Web servers sending information to Web browsers. Many people who had previously considered their problem domains to be separate came to see them as really variations on the same things.

---

9. This description necessarily presented as linear, straightforward, and obvious a process that was actually messy and at times confusing. It is fair to say that there were many people outside the World Wide Web Consortium who had a better grasp on the need for XML than many within it, and that various member corporations "caught on" to the importance of XML at different rates.

Each of these domains is known by a *Three Letter Acronym (TLA)*. When you combine these with the various XML-world specs and standards the result is a terminological alphabet soup. Pick up your spoon, we'll help you through!

1.4.1   *Electronic Data Interchange (EDI)*

One of the first groups to sense the coming convergence between documents and data was the Electronic Data Interchange (EDI) community. EDI is the technology that large companies typically use to buy, sell and interchange information with each other.

Most people agree that XML is easier to work with and more extensible. Where EDI only scratched the surface of the business world, XML-based e-commerce should penetrate down even to small companies. The thing that differentiates this sort of e-commerce from the kind you can find on any old website is that it is *integrated*.

With integrated e-commerce (IEC), your system is integrated directly or indirectly with your partner's system so that transactions can be verified and logged automatically in your internal systems. In contrast, buying a book (even this book!) from Amazon's website is not integrated e-commerce because there is no way that the purchase could be automatically entered into your local accounting system or sent to your boss for approval. Amazon, of course, uses a great deal of IEC when buying from *its* suppliers.

The venture capital world has chosen to embrace the somewhat confusing term "business to business e-commerce"(B2B) for this application. We consider the term confusing because one business could buy products from another business through a Web storefront and it would not typically be termed B2B, even though it was "business to business" and "e-commerce". What the pundits (fund-its?) really mean is *integrated* e-commerce.

So if buying from Amazon isn't IEC, what would be? Imagine if you bought a thousand widgets and your computer system automatically generated and delivered a purchase order and then updated your inventory while the receiving system automatically entered the order into its order system. Whew! That's a lot of automation! The opportunity to automate things is the fundamental strength of the integrated e-commerce paradigm.

The integrated solution allows a new class of *Business Process Automation (BPA)* software. BPA software allows businesses to describe their business process workflows in terms of the steps necessary to complete the process.

Where human oversight is necessary, BPA software routes the information to the right person and solicits approval or input. BPA extends the concept of workflow by allowing processes to go beyond the boundaries of an organization. Of course this depends on standards – and most of these standards will be based upon XML.

There will also be a role for intermediaries that help businesses find each other and conduct transactions. Depending on their features, you can think of them as brokers or exchanges. Fortunes will be made and lost in this new application domain.

1.4.2 *Enterprise Application Integration (EAI)*

The fourth TLA that we will tackle is Enterprise Application Integration (EAI). We have described how XML helps businesses to communicate with each other. It is just as good at helping the parts of a business to communicate. This area of XML use is termed Enterprise Application Integration (or just Application Integration).

EAI is important because it is necessary before integrated e-commerce can really begin to save money. The accounting system must be integrated with inventory. Inventory must be integrated with delivery systems. Deliveries must be integrated with billing, which is a part of accounting and so forth. "The thigh bone's connected to the leg bone, the leg bone's connected to the ankle bone..." XML is today's choice for the cartilage between the bones in your organizational skeleton.

XML can be directly generated by many large-scale enterprise accounting, Enterprise Resource Planning (ERP), Customer Relationship Management (CRM), Supply Chain Management (SCM) and related packages. Even systems that do not natively "speak" XML can be made to do so through third-party or in-house extensions. When the vocabularies do not exactly match up (in other words, before there is a widely adopted standard vocabulary for a particular task) we can *transform* XML from one vocabulary into another.

In a sense, EAI and integrated e-commerce are two sides of the same coin. EAI is a kind of integration within your corporate boundaries in order to present better information to employees and systems. Integrated e-commerce is a form of integration that spans corporate boundaries in order to improve the flow of information and products among partners.

1.5 | Conclusion

EAI, EDI, B2B, IEC, ERP: XML touches every acronym.

XML is likely to be the basis for most structured information interchange in the future. If you buy a car on the Web, your browser will signal your decision with an XML document in one vocabulary. The auto dealer will replenish its stock of cars from the car company through another XML document using another vocabulary. The auto manufacturer will buy parts from its suppliers by sending out an automated request for quotes in XML in an e-business auction vocabulary and suppliers will respond in XML. In other words, whenever two computers need to communicate with each other, there is a role for XML.

In many ways, none of this is new. Ancients used documents to communicate around their kingdoms and across centuries. Cavemen used documents (also known as wall paintings) to communicate their hopes and fears. XML allows computers to get into the conversation.

Analysis   Now we've seen the origins of XML, and some of its key ideas. Unlike lots of other "next great things" of the high-tech world, XML has solid roots and a proven track record. You can have confidence in XML because the particular subset of SGML that is XML has been in use for a dozen years.

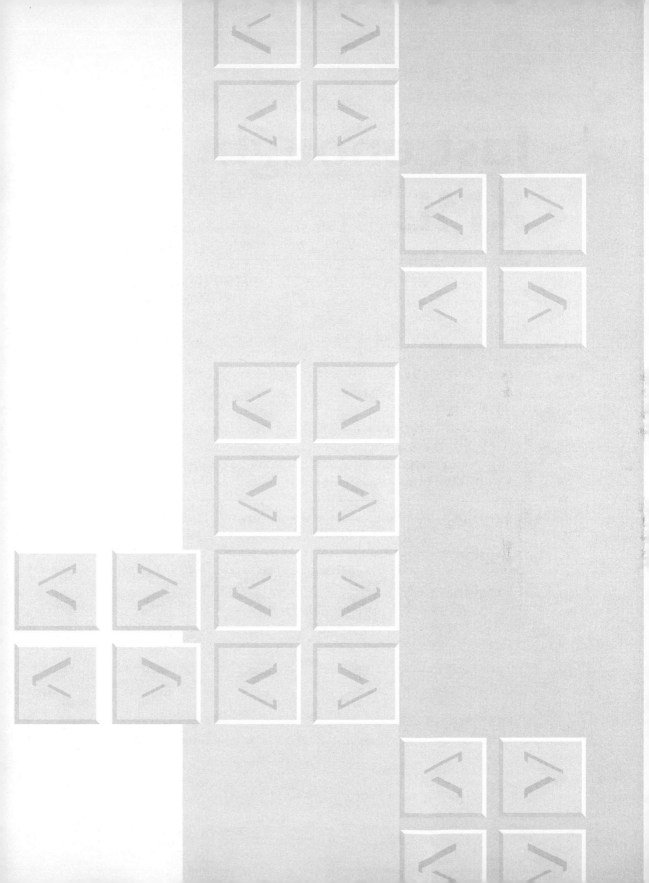

Just enough XML

- Elements
- Character set
- Entities
- Markup
- Document types

Chapter

2

In this chapter we will explore the fundamental concepts of XML documents and XML systems. If XML were a great work of literature then this chapter would be the Cliff notes. The chapter will introduce the ideas that define the language but will avoid the nitty-gritty details (the syntax) behind the constructs. As a result, some concepts may remain slightly fuzzy because you will not be able to work with them "hands on". Our tutorial chapters will provide that opportunity.

This early presentation of these ideas will allow you to see XML's "big picture". We will do this by walking through the design process for an XML-like language. Hopefully by the end of the process, you will understand each of the design decisions and XML's overall architecture.

Our objective is to equip you with "just enough" XML to appreciate the application scenarios and tool descriptions in the following parts of the book, but being over-achievers we may go a little too far. Feel free to leave at any time to read about XML in the real world.

2.1 | The goal

First we should summarize what we are trying to achieve. In short, "What is XML used for?" XML is for the *digital representation* of documents. You probably have an intuitive feel for what a document is. We will work from your intuition.

Documents can be large and small. Both a multi-volume encyclopedia and a memo can be thought of as documents. A particular volume of the encyclopedia can also be called a document. XML allows you to think of the encyclopedia whichever way will allow you to get your job done most efficiently. You'll notice that XML will give you these sorts of options in many places. XML also allows us to think of an email message as a document. XML can even represent the message from a police department's server to a police officer's handheld computer that reports that you have unpaid parking tickets.[1]

When we say that we want to *digitally represent* documents we mean that we want to put them in some kind of computer-readable notation so that a computer can help us store, process, search, transmit, display and print them. In order for a computer to do useful things with a document, we are going to have to tell it about the structure of the document. This is our simple goal: to represent the documents in a way that the computer can "understand", insofar as computers can understand anything.

XML saves money by allowing programmers to reuse a piece of code called an XML *processor* or *parser*. The former term is used in the XML spec, but the latter is more often used in discussions. The processor parses the markup and passes the data to whatever application the programmer is writing. There are parsers available for almost every language on every platform and most of them are available freely on the Web!

XML documents can include pictures, movies and other multimedia, but we will not actually represent the multimedia components as XML. If you think of representation as a translation process, similar to language translation, then the multimedia components are the parts that we will leave in their "native language" because they have no simple translation into the "target language" (XML). We will just include them in their native formats as you might include a French or Latin phrase in an English text without explicit translation. Most pictures on the Web are files in formats called

---

1. Sorry about that.

GIF or JPEG and most movies are in a format called MPEG. An XML document would just refer to those files in their native GIF, JPEG or MPEG formats. If you were transcribing an existing print document into XML, you would most likely represent the character-text parts as XML and the graphical parts in these other formats.

2.2 | Elements: The logical structure

Before we can describe exactly how we are going to represent documents, we must have a model in our heads of how a document is structured. Most documents (for example books and magazines) can be broken down into components (chapters and articles). These can also be broken down into components (titles, paragraphs, figures and so forth). It turns out that every document can be viewed this way, though some fit the model more naturally than others.

In XML, these components are called *elements*. Each element represents a logical component of a document. Elements can contain other elements and can also contain the words and sentences that you would usually think of as the text of the document. XML calls this text the document's *character data*. This hierarchical view of XML documents is demonstrated in Figure 2-1.

Markup professionals call this the *tree structure* of the document. The element that contains all of the others (e.g. book, report or memo) is known as the *root element*. This name captures the fact that it is the only element that does not "hang" off of some other element. The root element is also referred to as the *document element* because it holds the entire logical document within it. The terms *root element* and *document element* are interchangeable.

The elements that are contained in the root are called its *subelements*. They may contain subelements themselves. If they do, we will call them *branches*. If they do not, we will call them *leaves*.

Thus, the chapter and article elements are branches (because they have subelements), but the paragraph and title elements are leaves (because they only contain character data).[2]

---

2. This arboreal metaphor is firmly rooted in computer science. However, markup experts have recently extended it with the term "grove". This term recognizes that a single document may best be viewed as multiple trees.

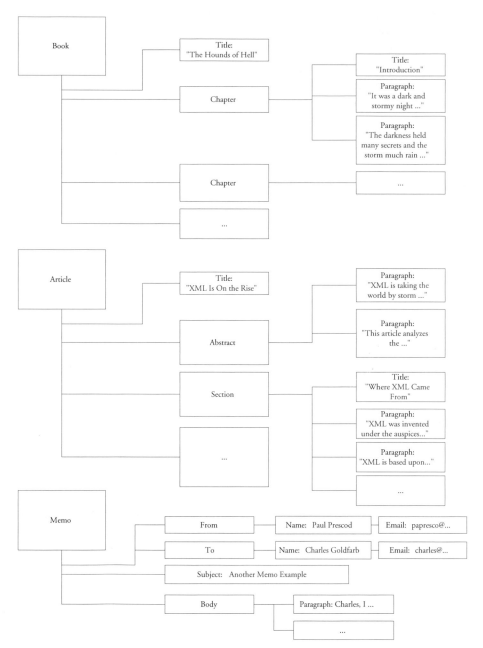

Figure 2-1   Hierarchical views of documents

Elements can also have extra information attached to them called *attributes*. Attributes describe properties of elements. For instance a CIA-record element might have a security attribute that gives the security rating for that element. A CIA database might only release certain records to certain people depending on their security rating. It will not always be clear which aspects of a document should be represented with elements and which should be represented with attributes, but we will give some guidelines in Chapter 49, "Creating a document type definition", on page 702.

Real-world documents do not always fit this tree model perfectly. They often have non-hierarchical features such as cross-references or hypertext links from one section of the tree to another. XML can represent these structures too. In fact, XML goes beyond the powerful links provided by HTML. More on this in 2.8, "Hyperlinking", on page 43.

2.3 | Unicode: The character set

Texts are made up of characters. If we are going to represent texts, then we must represent the characters that comprise them. So we must decide how we are going to represent characters at the bits and bytes level. This is called the *character encoding*. We must also decide what characters we are going to allow in our documents. This is the *character set*. A particularly restrictive character set might allow only upper-case characters. A very large character set might allow Eastern ideographs and Arabic characters.

If you are a native English speaker you may only need the fifty-two upper- and lower-case characters, some punctuation and a few accented characters. The pervasive *7 bit ASCII character set* caters to this market. It has just enough characters (128) for all of the letters, symbols, some accented characters and some other oddments. ASCII is both a character set *and* a character encoding. It defines what set of characters are available and how they are to be encoded in terms of bits and bytes.

XML's character set is *Unicode*, a sort of ASCII on steroids. Unicode includes thousands of useful characters from languages around the world.[3] However the first 128 characters of Unicode are compatible with ASCII

---

3. It also includes some not-so-useful characters – there is an entire section dedicated to "dingbats" and there is a proposal to include "Klingon", the artificial language from Star Trek™.

and there is a character encoding of Unicode, *UTF-8* that is compatible with 7 bit ASCII. This means that at the bits and bytes level, the first 128 characters of UTF-8 Unicode and 7 bit ASCII are the same. As if by magic, every ASCII document is automatically a Unicode document. This feature of Unicode allows authors to use standard plain-text editors to create XML immediately.

2.4 | Entities: The physical structure

An XML document is defined as a series of characters. An XML processor (or parser) starts at the beginning and works to the end. XML provides a mechanism for allowing text to be organized non-linearly and potentially in multiple pieces. The processor reorganizes it into the linear structure.

The "piece-of-text" construct is called an *entity*. An entity could be as small as a single character or as large as all the characters of a book.

Entities have *names*. Somewhere in your document, you insert an *entity reference* to make use of an entity. The processor replaces the entity reference with the entity itself, which is called the *replacement text*. It works somewhat like a word processor macro.

For instance an entity named "sigma", might contain the name of a Greek character. You would use a reference to the entity whenever you wanted to insert the sigma character. An entity could also be called "introduction-chapter" and be a chapter in a book. You would refer to the entity at the point where you wanted the chapter to appear.

One of the ideas that excited Ted Nelson, the man who coined the word *hypertext*, was the idea that text could be reused in many different contexts automatically. An update in one place would propagate across all uses of the text. For instance you could define your company name as an entity and update all occurrences of it automatically.

The feature of XML that allows documents to be broken into many physical files is called the *external entity*. External entities are often referred to merely as entities, but the meaning is usually clear from context. An XML document can be broken up into many files on a hard disk or objects in a database and each of them is called an entity in XML terminology. Entities could even be spread across the Internet. Whereas XML elements describe the document's logical structure, entities keep track of the location of the chunks of bytes that make up an XML document. We call this the *physical structure* of the document.

Note   The unit of XML text that we will typically talk about is the entity. You may be accustomed to thinking about files, but entities do not have to be stored as files.

For instance, entities could be stored in databases or generated on the fly by a computer program. Some file formats (e.g. a *zip* file) even allow multiple entities to reside in the same file at once. The term that covers all of these possibilities is entity, *not* file. Still, on most Web sites each entity will reside in a single file so in those cases external entities and files will functionally be the same. This setup is simple and efficient, but will not be sufficient for very large sites.

External entities help to break up large files to make them editable, searchable, downloadable and otherwise usable on the ordinary computer systems that real people use. Entities allow authors to break their documents into workable chunks that can fit into memory for editing, can be downloaded across a slow modem and so forth.

Without entities, authors would have to break their documents unnaturally into smaller documents with only weak links between them (as is commonly done with HTML). This complicates document management and maintenance. If you have ever tried to print out one of these HTML documents broken into a hundred HTML files then you know the problem. Entities allow documents to be broken up into chunks without forgetting that they actually represent a single coherent document that can be printed, edited and searched as a unit when that makes sense.

Non-XML objects are referenced in much the same way and are called *unparsed entities*. We think of them as "data entities" because there is no XML markup in them that will be noticed by the XML processor. Data entities include graphics, movies, audio, raw text, PDF and anything else you can think of that is not XML (including HTML and other forms of SGML).[4] Each data entity has an associated *notation* that is simply a statement declaring whether the entity is a GIF, JPEG, MPEG, PDF and so forth.

Entities are described in all of their glorious (occasionally gory) detail in Chapter 50, "Entities: Breaking up is easy to do", on page 736.

2.5 | Markup

We have discussed XML's conceptual model, the tree of elements, its strategy for encoding characters, Unicode, and its mechanism for managing the size and complexity of documents, entities. We have not yet discussed how to represent the logical structure of the document and link together all of the physical entities.

Although there are XML word processors, one of the design goals of XML was that it should be possible to create XML documents in standard text editors. Some people are not comfortable with word processors and even those who are may depend on text editors to "debug" their document if the word processor makes a mistake, or allows the user to make a mistake. The only way to allow authors convenient access to both the structure and data of the document in standard text editors is to put the two right beside each other, "cheek to cheek".

As we discussed in the introduction, the stuff that represents the logical structure and connects the entities is called markup. An XML document is made up exclusively of markup and character data. Both are in Unicode. Collectively they are termed *XML text*.

This last point is important! Unless the context unambiguously refers to data, as in "textual data", when we say "XML text", we mean the markup and the data.

 *Caution*   The term XML text refers to the combination of character data and markup, not character data alone. Character data + markup = text.

---

4. Actually, a data entity could even contain XML, but it wouldn't be treated as part of the main XML document.

Markup is differentiated from character data by special characters called *delimiters*. Informally, text between a less-than (<) and a greater-than (>) character or between an ampersand (&) and a semicolon (;) character is markup. Those four characters are the most common delimiters. This rule will become more concrete in later chapters. In the meantime, Example 2-1 is an example of a small document to give you a taste of XML markup.

Example 2-1. A small XML document

```
<?xml version="1.0"?>
<!DOCTYPE Q-AND-A SYSTEM "http://www.q.and.a.com/faq.dtd">
<Q-AND-A>
<QUESTION>I'm having trouble loading a WurdWriter 2.0 file into
WurdPurformertWriter 7.0. Any suggestions?</QUESTION>
<ANSWER>Why don't you use XML?</ANSWER>
<QUESTION>What's XML?</QUESTION>
<ANSWER>It's a long story, but there is a book I can
recommend...</ANSWER>
</Q-AND-A>
```

The markup between the less-than and greater-than is called a *tag*.

You may be familiar with other languages that use similar syntax. These include HTML and other SGML-based languages.

2.6 | Document types

The concept of a document type is fairly intuitive. You are well aware that novels, bills of lading and telephone books are quite different, and you are probably comfortable recognizing documents that conform to one of these categories. No matter what its title or binding, you would call a book that listed names and phone numbers a phone book. So, a document type is defined by its elements. If two documents have radically different elements or allow elements to be combined in very different ways then they probably do not conform to the same document type.

2.6.1 *Defining document types*

This notion of a document type can be formalized in XML. A *document type definition (DTD)* or *schema definition* consists of a series of definitions for element types, attributes, entities and notations.

The DTD declaration syntax is the original mechanism for doing this. DTDs are built into XML. Schemas are a newer, more sophisticated (and also more complicated) arrival to the party. Schemas and document types share concepts, so at a high level the terms can be used interchangeably. Of course when we get down to the details, schema definitions and DTDs look quite different, even though the underlying concepts are similar.

The DTD or schema definition declares which element types, etc., are legal within the document and in what places they are legal. A document can claim to conform to a particular DTD in its *document type declaration*.[5] There is also a mechanism for referring to a schema through a specialized attribute.

Other terms for document type include "message format" or "message layout." We don't use them because we believe that there is an important distinction between the term "document" and "message". A book is a document. The information that the book conveys is its message. In other words, the message is the informational content of the document. According to this definition, a message cannot really have a layout or format.

DTDs and schemas are powerful tools for organizational standardization in much the same way that forms, templates and style-guides are. A very rigid DTD that only allows one element type in a particular place is like a form: "Just fill in the blanks!". A more flexible DTD is like a style-guide in that it can, for instance, require every `list` to have two or more `items`, every `report` to have an `abstract` and could restrict `footnotes` from appearing within `footnotes`.

DTDs are critical for organizational standardization, but they are just as important for allowing robust processing of documents by software. For example, a letter document with a `chapter` in the middle of it would be most unexpected and unlikely to be very useful. Letter printing software would not reliably be able to print such a document because it is not well defined what a chapter in a letter looks like. Even worse is a situation where

---

5. The document type declaration is usually abbreviated "DOCTYPE", because the obvious abbreviation would be the same as that for document type definition!

a document is missing an element expected by the software that processes it. If your mail program used XML as its storage format, you might expect it to be able to search all of the incoming email addresses for a particular person's address. Let us presume that each message stores this address in a `from` element. What do we do about letters without `from` elements when we are searching them? Programmers could write special code to "work around" the problem, but these kinds of workarounds make code difficult to write.

2.6.2 *HTML: A cautionary tale*

HTML serves as a useful cautionary tale. It actually has a fairly rigorous structure, defined in SGML, and available from the World Wide Web Consortium. But everybody tends to treat the rules as if they actually came from the World Wrestling Federation – they ignore them.

The programmers that maintain HTML browsers spend a huge amount of time incorporating support for all of the incorrect ways people combine the HTML elements in their documents. Although HTML has an SGML DTD, very few people use it, and the browser vendors have unofficially sanctioned the practice of ignoring it. Workarounds are expensive, time consuming, boring and frustrating, but the worst problem is that there is no good definition of what these illegal constructs mean. Some incorrect constructs will actually make HTML browsers crash, but others will merely make them display confusing or random results.

In HTML, the `title` element is used to display the document's name at the top of the browser window (on the title bar). But what should a browser do if there are two titles? Use the first? Use the last? Use both? Pick one at random? Since the HTML standard does not allow this construct it certainly does not specify a behavior. Believe it or not, an early version of Netscape's browser showed each title sequentially over time, creating a primitive sort of text animation. That behavior disappeared quickly when Netscape programmers realized that authors were actually creating invalid HTML specifically to get this effect! Since authors cannot depend on nonsensical documents to work across browsers, or even across browser versions, there must be a formal definition of a valid, reasonable document of a particular type. In XML, the DTD provides a formal definition of the element types, attributes and entities allowed in a document of a specified type.

There is also a more subtle, related issue. If you do not stop and think carefully about the structure of your documents, you may accidently slip back into specifying them in terms of their formatting rather than their abstract structure. We are accustomed to thinking of documents in terms of their rendition. That is because, prior to GML, there was no practical way to create a document without creating a rendition. The process of creating a DTD gives us an opportunity to rethink our documents in terms of their structure, as abstractions.

2.6.3 *Declaring a DTD*

Example 2-2 shows examples of some of the declarations that are used to express a DTD. Example 2-3 shows the equivalent DTD as a schema definition.

Example 2-2. Markup declarations

```
<!ELEMENT Q-AND-A (QUESTION,ANSWER)+>
<!-- This allows: question, answer, question, answer ... -->
<!ELEMENT QUESTION (#PCDATA)>
<!-- Questions are just made up of textual data -->
<!ELEMENT ANSWER (#PCDATA)>
<!-- Answers are just made up of textual data -->
```

Caution   A DTD is a concept; markup declarations are the means of expressing it. The distinction is important because other means of expressing DTDs are being proposed. However, most people, even ourselves, don't make the distinction in normal parlance. We just talk about the declarations as though they are the DTD that they describe, unless doing so would be ambiguous.

Example 2-3. Schema definition

```
<schema xmlns:qa='http://www.q.and.a.com/'
        targetNamespace='http://www.q.and.a.com/'>
 <element name="Q-AND-A">
 <complexType>
  <sequence minOccurs="1" maxOccurs="unbounded">
   <element ref="qa:QUESTION"/>
   <element ref="qa:ANSWER"/>
  </sequence>
 </complexType>
 </element>
<!-- This allows: question, answer, question, answer ... -->
 <element name="QUESTION" type="string"/>
<!-- Questions are just made up of textual data -->
 <element name="ANSWER" type="string"/>
<!-- Answers are just made up of textual data -->
</schema>
```

Some XML documents do not have a schema definition or document type declaration. That does not mean that they do not conform to a document type. It merely means that they do not claim to conform to some formally defined document type definition.

If the document is to be useful as an XML document, it must still have some structure, expressed through elements, attributes and so forth. When you create a stylesheet for a document you will depend on it having certain elements, on the element type names having certain meanings, and on the elements appearing in certain places. However it manifests itself, that set of things that you depend on is the document type.

You can formalize that structure in a DTD. In addition to or instead of a formal computer-readable DTD, you can also write out a prose description. You might consider the many HTML books in existence to be prose definitions of HTML. Finally, you can just keep the document type in your head and maintain conformance through careful discipline. If you can achieve this for large, complex documents, your powers of concentration are astounding! Which is our way of saying: we do not advise it. We will discuss DTDs more in Chapter 49, "Creating a document type definition", on page 702 and schemas in Chapter 59, "XML Schema (XSDL)", on page 908.

2.7 | Well-formedness and validity

Every language has rules about what is or is not valid in the language. In human languages that takes many forms: words have a particular correct pronunciation (or range of pronunciations) and they can be combined in certain ways to make valid sentences (grammar). Similarly XML has two different notions of "correct". The first is merely that the markup is intelligible: the XML equivalent of "getting the pronunciation right". A document with intelligible markup is called a *well-formed* document. One important goal of XML was that these basic rules should be simple so that they could be strictly adhered to.

The experience of the HTML market provided a cautionary tale that guided the development of XML. Much of the HTML on the Web does *not* conform to even the simplest rules in the HTML specifications. This makes automated processing of HTML quite difficult.

Because Web browsers will display ill-formed documents, authors continue to create them. In designing XML, we decided that XML processors should actually be prohibited from trying to recover from a *well-formedness* error in an XML document. This was a controversial decision because there were many who felt that it was inappropriate to restrict XML implementors from deciding the best error recovery policy for their application.

The XML equivalent of "using the right words in the right place" is called *validity* and is related to the notion of document types. A document is *valid* if it declares conformance to a DTD in a document type declaration and actually conforms to the DTD.

Documents that do not have a document type declaration are not really *invalid* – they do not violate their DTD – but they are not valid either, because they cannot be validated against a DTD.

If HTML documents with multiple titles were changed over to use XML syntax, they would be *well-formed* and invalid because they would not conform to the DTD (known as XHTML). If we remove the document type declaration, so that they no longer claim to conform to the XHTML DTD, then they would become merely well-formed but neither valid nor invalid.

> *Caution*   For most of us, the word "invalid" means something that breaks the rules. It is an easy jump from there to concluding that an XML document that does not conform to a DTD is free to break any rules at all. So for clarity, we may sometimes say "type-valid" and "non-type-valid", rather than "valid" and "invalid".

You should think carefully before you decide to make a document that is well-formed but not valid. If the document is one-of-a-kind and is small, then making it well-formed is probably sufficient. But if it is to be part of any kind of information system (even a small one) or if it is a large document, then you should write a DTD or schema for it and validate whenever you revise it. When you decide to build or extend your information system, the fact that the document is guaranteed to be consistent will make your programming or stylesheet writing many times easier and your results much more reliable.

2.8 | Hyperlinking

If you have used the Web, then you probably do not need to be convinced of the importance of hyperlinking. One thing you might not know, however, is that the Web's notions of hyperlink are fairly tame compared to what is available in the best academic and commercial hypertext systems. XML alone does not correct this, but it has an associated standard called *XLink* that goes a long way towards making the Web a more advanced hypertext environment.

The first deficiency of today's Web links is that there are no standardized mechanisms for making links that are external to the documents that they are linking from. Let's imagine, for example that you stumble upon a Web page for your favorite music group. You read it, enjoy it and move on. Imagine next week you stumble upon a Web page with all of the lyrics for all of their songs (with appropriate copyrights, of course!). You think: there should be a link between these two pages. Someone visiting one might want to know about the other and vice versa.

What you want to do is make an *external link*. You want to make a link on your computer that appears on both of the other computers. But of course you do not have the ability to edit those two documents. XLink will allow this external linking. It provides a representation for external links, but it does not provide the technology to automatically publish those links to the world. That would take some kind of *link database* that would track all of the links from people around the world. Needless to say this is a big job and though there are prototypes, there is no standardized system yet.

You may wonder how all of these links will be displayed, how readers will select link sheets and annotations, how browsers will talk to databases and so forth. The simple answer is: "nobody knows yet."[6]

Before the first Web browser was developed there was no way to know that we would develop a convention of using colored, underlined text to represent links (and even today some browsers use other conventions). There was also no way to know that browsers would typically have "back" buttons and "history lists". These are just conventions that arose and browser features that became popular.

This same process will now occur with external links. Some user interface (perhaps a menu) will be provided to apply external link sheets, and there will probably be some mechanism for searching for link sheets related to a document on the Web. Eventually these will stabilize into standards that will be ubiquitous and transparent (we hope!). In the meantime, things are confused, but that is the price for living on the cutting edge. XLink moves us a notch further ahead by providing a notation for representing the links.

Another interesting feature of XML extended links is that they can point to more than one resource. For instance instead of making a link from a word to its definition, you might choose to link to definitions in several different dictionaries. The browser might represent this as a popup menu, a tiny window with the choices listed, or might even open one window for each. The same disclaimer applies: the XML Link specification does not tell browsers exactly what they must do. Each is free to try to make the most intuitive, powerful user interface for links. XML brings many interesting hypertext ideas from university research labs and high-tech companies "to

---

6. But we've got some ideas. See Chapter 42, "Extended linking", on page 592.

the masses." We still have to work out exactly how that will look and who will use them for what. We live in interesting times!

2.9 | Stylesheets

To a certain extent, the concerns described above are endemic to generalized markup. Because it describes structure, and not formatting, it allows variations in display and processing that can sometimes disturb people.

However, as the Web has evolved, people have become less and less tolerant of having browser vendors control the "look and feel" of their documents. An important part of all communication, but especially modern business communication, is the idea of style. Stylesheets allow us to attach our own visual style to documents without destroying the virtue of generalized markup. Because the style is described in a separate entity, the stylesheet, software that is not interested in style can ignore it.

For instance most search engines would not care if your corporate color is blue or green, so they will just ignore those declarations in the stylesheet. Similarly, software that reads documents aloud to the sight-impaired would ignore font sizes and colors and concentrate on the abstractions – paragraphs, sections, titles and so forth.

The Web has a very simple stylesheet language called *Cascading Style Sheets* (CSS), which arose out of the early battles between formatting and generalized markup in HTML. Like any other specification, CSS is a product of its environment, and so is not powerful enough to describe the formatting of documents types that are radically different in structure from HTML.

Because CSS is not sufficient, the World Wide Web Consortium has developed a complementary alternative called the *Extensible Stylesheet Language* (XSL). XSL has many features from CSS, but also borrows some major ideas from ISO's DSSSL stylesheet language. XSL is extensible, just as XML is, so that it will be appropriate for all document types and not just for HTML.

2.10 | Programming interfaces and models

This subject may seem intimidating if you are not a programmer – possibly even if you are! But we are just going to take a high-level view of a few constructs that will be helpful in understanding the chapters that follow. We'll cover the XML geek-speak Top Term List: Parsing, APIs, DOM, and SAX.

2.10.1 *Parsing*

Great as XML is for representing data, eventually that data has to be processed, which requires the use of one or more programs. One of the nice things about writing XML applications is that there is an abundance of reusable component and utility software available to help.

All great programmers try to reduce their work! If every programmer reinvented the wheel when it came to basic processing of XML, no programmer would ever get around to building applications that *use* XML. Instead of implementing basic XML processing over and over again, programmers tend to download or buy packages that implement various types of XML services.

The most basic reusable service is parsing. Parsing is about ripping apart the textual representation of a document and turning it into a set of conceptual objects.

For example, a processor looking at the document in Example 2-1 would recognize the characters <QUESTION> to be a start-tag, and would know that they signaled the start of a QUESTION element. The tag is part of the representation; the element is the conceptual object.

If the processor were also validating the document according to the DTD in Example 2-2, it would make sure that an ANSWER element followed the QUESTION element.

As a human being, you do parsing subconsciously. Because you've learned about elements and attributes, when you look at XML text you can think about the document in those conceptual terms.

But without an XML *processor*, a computer program can only see the characters. It's sort of the opposite of not seeing the forest for the trees. Without some form of parsing, an XML application cannot see the tree because of all of the characters!

2.10.2 *APIs*

There are many good XML parsers out there for use with many different programming languages. There are so many that it is hard to choose. A software developer would hate to pick one and be wedded to it forever. The programmer might want to change some day to a faster or cheaper one, or from a non-validating processor to a validating one.

Switching processors ("parsers") is easy if the two "look" the same to the programmer. You can plug in different brands and types of light bulbs into the same socket because of the standardization of the socket. The equivalent concept in software components is the standardization of *Application Processing Interfaces (APIs)*.

2.10.2.1   The DOM

The World Wide Web Consortium has standardized an API for working with XML. It is called the *Document Object Model* and it is available in Version 5 Web browsers. If you write code for Microsoft's *DOM* implementation, it should be relatively easy to make that code also work on Netscape's DOM.

But the DOM is not only for use in browsers. It can also be used on the server side. You can use the DOM to read, write and transmit XML on your Web server. DOM-based programs can talk to some XML content management systems. The DOM is very popular for general XML processing. It has been implemented, for example, for use with Python and Perl scripts and with the C++ and Java™ programming languages, among others. In fact, Microsoft's DOM implementation is a built-in part of Windows 2000 itself.

2.10.2.2   SAX

The DOM is popular and useful but it is not the be-all and end-all of XML parsing APIs. It is a little bit like putting a plane on automatic pilot. You point your DOM-building processor at an XML document and it returns you an object tree based on the structure of the document.

But if the document is five hundred megabytes of text and resides on the "other side" of the Internet, your program will just wait. And wait. And wait. When you finally get the data it will fill your computer's memory and some of its disk space. If you are having a bad day it might fill up everything and then crash the computer.

In a situation like this, you would rather just get tiny bits of the data as they come in. An *event-based parser* allows this mode of operation. Event-based parsers let your application work on the bit of the data that the parser finds at each "event" in the document.

For example, each XML start-tag corresponds to a "start element" event. Each end-tag corresponds to an "end element" event. Characters and other constructs have their own events. The event-based XML parser tells the application what it sees in the document as if through a peep-hole. It does not try to describe the larger picture to the application. This sort of event-driven mode is more efficient even for small documents, but it is not as convenient as a tree-based parser.[7]

The most popular event-based API is the *Simple API for XML*. SAX was developed by XML processor users and developers in an open discussion group called *XML-DEV.* Despite the name, SAX is not actually any simpler than the DOM. It is much more efficient and low-level, however. The price for efficiency is convenience. The processor only provides you with a peep-hole view, so if your application needs more than that, you'll need to write your own code to understand the "big picture" of the parsed document.

These two APIs are pervasive in the XML processing world. There are many other services that we could envision for XML handling: link management, searching and so forth. It is likely that these will be built either on top of or as extensions to these two popular APIs.

2.11 | XML and Protocols

Computers are like humans in that they cannot communicate with each other except by dint of a shared language. Just like humans, they cannot communicate if both parties speak at the same time so there must be some concept of back and forth, send and receive, talk and listen. The specification of how this happens is termed a protocol.

---

7. If you concluded from this description that a DOM processor in effect uses an event-based parser as it constructs the DOM, you are right.

Once again we are visiting the domain of programmers, but we'll try to keep the conversation at a level that will be meaningful to others – a diplomatic protocol discussion, so to speak!

2.11.1 *The protocol stack*

You seldom just use one protocol. Protocols build on each other. At the lowest level, your computer's network interface card speaks the Ethernet protocol and your modem uses protocols with cryptic names like V.32, V.42, V.32bis, and V.42bis. This level of protocol just lets the bits go back and forth.

Above this physical level of communication, you typically want to talk to the Internet. The TCP/IP protocol allows this. It lets "packets" of bits go to specific addresses on the Internet.

Next you are likely to want to do email, surf the Web or something like that. Email uses the POP and SMTP protocols. The Web uses the HTTP protocol. These protocols let you have a "conversation" about specific subjects; they define what is in the packets.

If you want two computers to have a new sort of conversation, you need to invent a new protocol. For instance to get computers to talk about network management, the Internet Engineering Task Force invented the Simple Network Management Protocol.

XML documents are usually transmitted by the HTTP protocol. In turn, many protocols have been built on top of XML. We'll look at three of them: WebDAV, XML-RPC, and SOAP. We'll even explain what the acronyms mean!

2.11.2 *Writing the Web*

The early Web allowed little more interactivity than following links. Later, it became possible to build real, interactive Web applications. This is a quantum leap but it still does not go as far as Tim Berners-Lee had hoped. He wanted Web *publishing* to be so easy that anyone could do it with any software package whenever they felt like it. We are not there yet.

The problem is that the protocol used to communicate between Web clients and servers (HTTP) is only really designed to get information. The early Web designers never got around to finishing the half of the specification that would standardize writing back to the Web. A variety of half-solutions have arisen. Some people use the older File Transfer Protocol (FTP). Some use product-specific protocols like Microsoft's "Frontpage Extensions". Neither of these is a true, standardized Web protocol.

Another half-solution is to allow publishing through a small "text entry box" on a Web page. Some bulletin-board websites use this technique. If you have ever edited more than a few lines in this environment, you will know how inconvenient it is – like mowing the lawn with hand-clippers.

Finally we have a real Web protocol for writing to Web sites. It is called *WebDAV* because it allows *Web-based Distributed Authoring and Versioning*.

WebDAV uses XML extensively to represent complex, structured values that can be associated with documents for searching and management. WebDAV is already supported by the Microsoft Office 2000 line of software products and the Apache Web server. That means it has already passed a significant milestone: most people buying new computers will have WebDAV-enabled content creation capability and most people deploying new Web servers will have free access to a WebDAV implementation. Even so, it takes time for these technologies to become ubiquitous and popular. Nevertheless, WebDAV promises to correct a long-acknowledged limitation of the World Wide Web.

2.11.3   *Remote procedure call*

A procedure is a basic unit of program behavior. In many languages, computer programs are made by stringing together calls from one procedure to another. A *Remote Procedure Call (RPC)* protocol extends this paradigm to calls between computers.

You can do remote procedure calls in XML using a specification called XML-RPC. Example 2-4 is the XML portion of an XML-RPC message that invokes a procedure called `calculateTax`. The `methodCall` element invokes the procedure. The `methodName` element names the procedure to be called. The `param` elements provide the information that the calculation requires.

Example 2-5 shows the response to the remote procedure call in Example 2-4. The Alaskan sales tax is $1.87.

The primary virtue of XML-RPC is that the programmer does not need to think about this stuff at all. In many programming languages, they will

Example 2-4. XML-RPC method call

```
<?xml version="1.0"?>
<methodCall>
  <methodName>calculateTax</methodName>
  <params>
    <param><value><i4>Alaska</i4></value></param>
    <param><value><i4>41</i4></value></param>
  </params>
</methodCall>
```

Example 2-5. XML-RPC method response

```
<?xml version="1.0"?>
<methodResponse>
  <params>
    <param><double>1.87</double></param>
  </params>
</methodResponse>
```

just call a procedure, using traditional procedure call syntax and all of the remote procedure stuff happens automatically.

Some programmers consider this approach heresy and would rather control the details of the transmission themselves. Neither side is right or wrong. Suffice to say that the right approach depends on a variety of factors including how fast and secure your network is and how much time you have available to solve a problem!

2.11.4   *Object protocols*

The dominant mode of thinking about software problems is in terms of "objects." An object in a computer is just like an object in the real world. Each object has properties and behaviors. You can send messages to objects to ask them to do something. You can also update the properties.

2.11.4.1   What is an object?

Everything from a bank account to an entire bank can be represented as an object. You could add money to the bank account by sending it a message, or you could negotiate to open a new account with the bank object. Though religious wars still rage on, most programmers feel that working with objects is a little easier and somewhat more sophisticated than working only with procedures.

Most modern programming languages provide some way of building objects. Many operating systems provide ways of communicating between objects written in various languages. On Windows™ systems, there is the Component Object Model (COM). On Unix™, Linux and other systems, it is often CORBA.

These object communication specifications have never caught on for communicating between machines. Developers have shown a clear preference for text-based inter-machine communication mechanisms. Binary communication mechanisms are essentially made up of strings of numbers and are not easy to understand without special tools.

Inter-object communication mechanisms – known as inter-object protocols – can work well with XML. Since XML can represent any information, the inter-object protocols can be expressed as XML elements instead of in terms of raw integers. This means that the messages can be inspected with standard textual tools and processed with any programming language, even simplistic or primitive ones.

2.11.4.2   Simple Object Access Protocol (SOAP)

The most popular specification in this category is *Simple Object Access Protocol (SOAP)*. SOAP is a derivative of XML-RPC with a little more support for object-oriented features. SOAP is still far from being as sophisticated as the binary inter-object protocols, but it is also far less complicated.

But SOAP is interesting for more reasons than having some support for object-oriented communication. SOAP is intrinsically designed to be a protocol for building protocols – just as XML is a markup language for inventing new markup languages! SOAP-based protocols are extensible, just as XML vocabularies are extensible, and SOAP's proponents are working on schema languages for SOAP interactions just as there are schema definition languages for XML. In other words, SOAP extends XML's virtues into back-and-forth communication protocols.

SOAP does not have any formal standards status yet but it is promoted by Microsoft and has been implemented for many programming languages on several platforms. It is even becoming popular in the Linux world, which tends to be suspicious of Microsoft-sponsored technologies. Something like SOAP is certainly going to be standardized at the W3C in the next couple of years. Whether it is very like SOAP, or like SOAP only in concept remains to be seen.

SOAP also goes beyond XML-RPC in that it can be used in *asynchronous* systems. If you go to an ice cream store to ask for some ice cream, you expect to leave with ice cream. On the other hand, if you go into a government office and ask for a passport you expect to make your request now but get your passport in the mail later. That's an asynchronous situation. A protocol is asynchronous if the person making the request does not wait around for a response but rather expects it to arrive some time later. SOAP has specific support for these kinds of situations.

2.12 | Conclusion

There are a lot of new ideas here to absorb, but we'll be repeating and re-emphasizing them as we move along. At this point, though, we're ready to look at the spectrum of XML usage in the real world.

The XML usage spectrum

Introductory Discussion

- Real-world concepts

- Documents vs. data

- Message-oriented middleware (MOM)

- Presentation-oriented publishing (POP)

ike the Jets and the Sharks, the factions never mixed.[1]
On the one hand there were the document-heads armed with word processors and formatters. On the other, the data-heads from the relational database world. It's time for a truce – no, an alliance. XML finally makes clear an internal truth: documents and data are the same thing. To be precise, documents are the interchangeable form of data!

3.1 | Is XML for documents or for data?

What is a document?
The dictionary says:

"Something written, inscribed, engraved, etc., which provides evidence or information or serves as a record".

---

1. Depending on your cultural proclivities, these are either athletic teams or the rival gangs in West Side Story.

Documents come in all shapes and sizes and media, as you can see in Figure 3-1. Here are some you may have encountered:

- Long documents: books, manuals, product specifications
- Broadsides: catalog sheets, posters, notices
- Forms: registration, application, etc.
- Letters: email, memos
- Records: "Acme Co., Part# 732, reverse widget, $32.50, 5323 in stock"
- Messages: "job complete", "update accepted"

An e-commerce transaction, such as a purchase, might involve several of these. A buyer could start by sending several documents to a vendor:

- Covering note: a letter
- Purchase order: a form
- Attached product specification: a long document

The vendor might respond with several more documents:

- Formal acknowledgment: a message
- Thank you note: a letter
- Invoice: a form

The beauty of XML is that the same software can process all of this diversity. Whatever you can do with one kind of document you can do with all the others. The only time you need additional tools is when you want to do different kinds of things – not when you want to work with different kinds of documents.

And there are lots of things that you can do.

3.2 | A wide spectrum of application opportunities

Sorry about that, we've been reading too many marketing brochures. But it's true, nevertheless.

Figure 3-1 Documents come in all shapes and sizes.

At one end of the spectrum we have the grand old man of generalized markup, *POP* – Presentation-Oriented Publishing. You can see him in Figure 3-2.

At the other end of the spectrum is that darling of the data processors, *MOM* – Message-Oriented Middleware. She smiles radiantly from Figure 3-3.

Let's take a closer look at both of them.

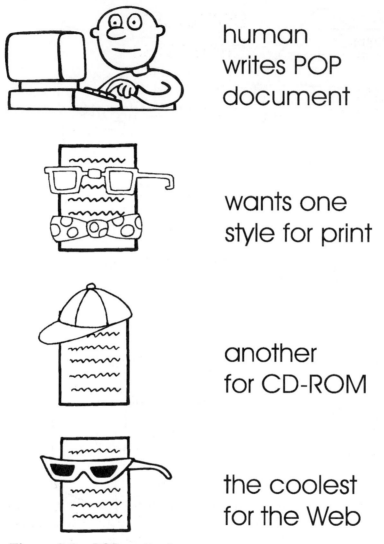

Figure 3-2   POP application.

3.2.1 *Presentation-oriented publishing*

POP was the original killer app for SGML, XML's parent, because it saves so much money for enterprises with Web-sized document collections.

POP documents are chiefly written by humans for other humans to read.

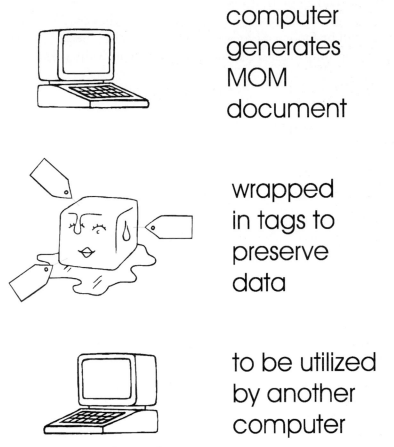

computer
generates
MOM
document

wrapped
in tags to
preserve
data

to be utilized
by another
computer

Figure 3-3   MOM application.

Instead of creating formatted renditions, as in word processors or desktop publishing programs, XML POP users create unformatted abstractions. That means the document file captures what is *in* the document, but not how it is supposed to look.

To get the desired look, the POP user creates a stylesheet, a set of commands that tell a program how to format (and/or otherwise process) the document. The power of XML in this regard is that you don't need to choose just one look – you can have a separate stylesheet for every purpose.[2] At a minimum, you might want one for print, one for CD-ROM, and another for a website.

POP documents tend to be (but needn't be) long-lived, large, and with complex structures. When delivered in electronic media, they may be interactive. How they will be rendered is of great importance, but, because XML is used, the rendition information can be – and is – kept distinct from the abstract data.

3.2.2 *Message-oriented middleware*

MOM is the killer app – actually, a technology that drives lots of killer apps – for XML on the Web.

Middleware, as you might suspect from the name, is software that comes between two other programs. It acts like your interpreter/guide might if you were to visit someplace where you couldn't speak the language and had no idea of the local customs. It talks in the native tongue, using the native customs, and translates the native replies – the messages – into your language.

MOM documents are chiefly generated by programs for other programs to read.

Instead of writing specialized programs (clients) to access particular databases or other data sources (servers), XML MOM users break the old two-tier client/server model. They introduce a third tier, the "middle tier", that acts as a data integrator. The middle-tier server does all the talking to the data sources and sends their messages to the client as XML documents.

That means the client can read data from anywhere, but only has to understand data that is in XML documents. The XML markup provides the metadata (i.e. information about the data) that was in the original data source schema, like the database table name and field names (also called "cell" or "column" names).

The MOM user typically doesn't care much about rendition. He *does* care, though, about extracting the original data accurately and making some use of the metadata. His client software, instead of having a specialized module for each data source, has a single "XML parser" module. The parser is the program that separates the markup from the data, just as it does in POP applications.

---

2. We know that all office suites offer some degree of stylesheet support today, but XML (well, GML) did it first, and still is the only way to do it cleanly.

And just like POP applications, there can be a stylesheet, a set of commands that tell a program how to process the document. It may not look much like a POP stylesheet – it might look more like a script or program – but it performs the same function. And, as with POP stylesheets, there can be different MOM stylesheets for different document types, or to do different things with message documents of a single document type.

There is an extra benefit to XML three-tier MOM applications in a networked environment. For many applications, the middle-tier server can collect all of the relevant data at once and send it in a single document to the client. Further querying, sorting, and other processing can then take place solely on the client system. That not only cuts down Web traffic and overhead, but it vastly improves the end-user's perceived performance and his satisfaction with the experience.

MOM documents tend to be (but needn't be) short-lived, non-interactive, small, and with simple structures.

3.3 | Opposites are attracted

To XML, that is!

How is it that XML can be optimal for two such apparently extreme opposites as MOM and POP? The answer is, the two are not really different where it counts.

In both cases, we start with abstract information. For POP, it comes from a human author's head. For MOM, it comes from a database. But either way, the abstract data is marked up with tags and becomes a document.

Here is a terminally cute mnemonic for this very important relationship:

Data + Markup = DocuMent

Aren't you sorry you read it? Now you'll never forget it.

But XML "DocuMents" are special. An application can do three kinds of processing with one:

- *Parse it*, in order to extract the original data. This can be done without information loss because XML represents both metadata and data, and it lets you keep the abstractions distinct from rendition information.

- *Render it*, so it can be presented in a physical medium that a human can perceive. It can be rendered in many different ways, for delivery in multiple media such as screen displays, print, Braille, spoken word, and so on.
- *Hack it*, meaning "process it as plain text without parsing". Hacking might involve cutting and pasting into other XML documents, or scanning the markup to get some information from it without doing a real parse.

The real revelation here is that data and documents aren't opposites. Far from it – they are actually two states of the same information.

The real difference between the two is that when data is in a database, the metadata about its structure and meaning (the schema) is stored according to the proprietary architecture of the database. When the data becomes a document, the metadata is stored as markup.

A mixture of markup and data must be governed by the rules of some *notation*. XML and SGML are notations, as are RTF and Word file format. The rules of the notation determine how a parser will interpret the document text to separate the data from the markup.

Notations are not just for complete documents. There are also *data object notations*, such as GIF, TIFF, and EPS, that are used to represent such things as graphics, video (e.g., MPEG), and audio (e.g., AVI). Document notations usually allow their documents to contain data objects, such as pictures, that are in the objects' own data object notations.

Data object notations are usually (not always) in *binary*; that is, they are built-up from low-level ones and zeros. Document notations, however, are frequently *character-based*. XML is character-based, which is why it can be hacked.

In fact, a design objective of XML was to support the "desperate Perl hacker"[3] – someone who needs to write a program in a hurry, using a scripting language like Perl, and who doesn't use a real XML parser. Instead, his program scans the XML document as though it were plain text. The program might search for markup strings, but can also search for data.

---

3. As used here, and by most knowledgeable computer people, "hacker" has none of the "cracker" stigma given the term in the popular press. The only security compromised by a desperate Perl hacker is his job security, for leaving things to the last minute!

Since databases and documents are really the same, and MOM and POP applications both use XML documents, there are lots of opportunities for synergy.

Figure 3-4　Dynamic servers: The MOM and POP store.

3.4 | MOM and POP – They're so great together!

Classically, MOM and POP were radically different kinds of applications, each doing things its own way with different technologies and mental models. But POP applications frequently need to include database data in their document content – think of an automotive maintenance manual that has to get the accurate part numbers from a database.

Similarly, MOM applications need to include human-written components. When the dealer asks for price and availability of the automotive parts you need, the display might include a description as well.

With the advent of generalized markup, the barriers to doing MOM-like things in POP applications began to disappear. Some of the POP-like applications you'll read about later in the book appear to have invented the middle tier on their own. And now, with the advent of XML, MOM applications can easily incorporate POP functionality as well.

What is now emerging is a new generation of composite systems, dynamically serving both persistent POP information and dynamic MOM data. They use databases to store information components so they can be controlled, managed, and assembled into end-products in the same way as components of automobiles, aircraft, or other complex devices. Think of them as the MOM and POP store (Figure 3-4).[4]

In fact, we'd go so far as to say there is no longer a difference in kind between the two, only a difference in degree. There really is "an endless spectrum of application opportunities". It is a multi-dimensional spectrum where applications need not be implemented differently just because they process different document types. The real differentiators are other document characteristics, like persistence, size, interactivity, structural complexity, percentage of human-written content, and the importance of eventual presentation to humans.[5]

At the extremes, some applications may call for specialized (or optimized) techniques, but the broad central universe of applications can all be implemented similarly. Much of the knowledge that POP application developers have acquired over the years is now applicable to MOM applications, and vice versa. Keep that in mind as you read the application descriptions and case studies.

That cross-fertilization is true of products and their underlying technologies as well. All of the product descriptions in this book should be of interest, whether you think of your applications as chiefly being MOM or being POP. It is the differences in functionality and design that should cause you to choose one product over another, not their marketing thrust or apparent orientation. We've included detailed usage examples for leading tools in each category so you can look beyond the labels.

---

4. Generations ago the Mom and Pop store (grocery, convenience, etc.) was the achievement of the entrepreneurial couple who'd lifted themselves out of the working class. Today they'd have an Internet start-up and be striving for a successful IPO!

5. The relationship between documents and data is explored further in 6.9, "Documents and data", on page 100.

3.5 | Conclusion

We've covered the key concepts of XML itself and the spectrum of its uses. The next few chapters will zoom in on applications at both ends of the spectrum.

Better browsing through XML

Introductory Discussion

- Beyond HTML
- Database publishing
- Multimedia
- Metadata
- Content syndication
- Science on the Web

Chapter

4

The XML effort is new ground in many senses. The Web has never before had access to the new features that XML offers. It will take a while for the Web culture to understand the strengths (and weaknesses) of the new language and learn how to properly deploy it. Still, XML is already becoming a building block for the next generation of Web applications and specifications.

4.1 | Beyond HTML

XML was originally conceived as a big brother to HTML. As its name implies, XML can be used to extend HTML or even define whole new languages completely unlike HTML.

For instance, a company might want to offer technical manuals on the Web. Many manuals have a formatting for tables (e.g. a table listing a software product's supported languages) and repeat the formatting on several tables in the manual (perhaps once per program in a package). The formatting of these tables can be very intricate.

The rows, for example may be broken into categories with borders between them. The title of each column and row might be in a particular font and color. The width of the columns might be very precisely described. The final row ("the bottom line") might be colored. HTML could provide the formatting markup that the layout would require, but it would require a lot of duplication. In fact, it would be such a hassle that most companies would choose to use a graphic or an *Adobe Portable Document Format* (PDF) file instead.

4.1.1 *An HTML table*

To demonstrate how XML can help, we will use a sample table from the specification for HTML tables, shown in Table 4-1. We will simplify the table somewhat, but the XML solution will still be shorter (in characters) and easier to read than the HTML source in Example 4-1.

If there are many of these tables the cumulative effort of doing this manual work can add up to a large burden, especially since it must be maintained as products change. Even with an HTML authoring tool, you will probably have to do the layout manually, over and over again. As if this internal expense was not disturbing enough, every person who reads the annual report over the Web must download the same formatting information row after row, column after column, table after table, year after year. Right thinking Web page authors will understand that this situation is not good. The repetition leads to longer download times, congested servers, dissatisfied customers and perhaps irate managers.

4.1.2 *An XML table*

The XML solution would be to invent a simple extension to HTML that is customized to the needs of the manual. It would have table elements that would only require data that varies from table to table. None of the redundant formatting information would be included. We would then use a sophisticated stylesheet to add that information back in. The beauty of the stylesheet solution is that the formatting information is expressed only in one place. Surfers only have to download that once. Also, if your company decides to change the style of the tables, all of them can be changed at once

Table 4-1   Code-page support in Microsoft Windows

Code Page ID	Name	Windows NT 3.1	Windows NT 3.51	Windows 95
1200	Unicode (BMP of ISO 10646)	X	X	
1250	Windows 3.1 Eastern European	X	X	X
1251	Windows 3.1 Cyrillic	X	X	X
1252	Windows 3.1 US (ANSI)	X	X	X
1253	Windows 3.1 Greek	X	X	X
1254	Windows 3.1 Turkish	X	X	X
1255	Hebrew			X
1256	Arabic			X
1257	Arabic			X
1361	Korean (Johab)			X

Example 4-1. HTML markup for Table 4-1

```
<TABLE>
<CAPTION>CODE-PAGE SUPPORT IN MICROSOFT WINDOWS</CAPTION>
<COLGROUP align="center">
<COLGROUP align="left">
<COLGROUP align="center" span="2">
<COLGROUP align="center" span="3">
<THEAD valign="top"><TR><TH>Code-Page<br>ID<TH>Name
<TH>Windows<br>NT 3.1<TH>Windows<br>NT 3.51<TH>Windows<br>95
<TBODY>
<TR><TD>1200<TD>Unicode (BMP of ISO/IEC-10646)<TD>X<TD>X<TD>
<TR><TD>1250<TD>Windows 3.1 Eastern European<TD>X<TD>X<TD>X
<TR><TD>1251<TD>Windows 3.1 Cyrillic<TD>X<TD>X<TD>X
<TR><TD>1252<TD>Windows 3.1 US (ANSI)<TD>X<TD>X<TD>X
<TR><TD>1253<TD>Windows 3.1 Greek<TD>X<TD>X<TD>X
<TR><TD>1254<TD>Windows 3.1 Turkish<TD>X<TD>X<TD>X
<TR><TD>1255<TD>Hebrew<TD><TD><TD>X
<TR><TD>1256<TD>Arabic<TD><TD><TD>X
<TR><TD>1257<TD>Baltic<TD><TD><TD>X
<TR><TD>1361<TD>Korean (Johab)<TD><TD><TD>X</TABLE>
```

merely by changing the stylesheet. Example 4-2 shows what that might look like.

Example 4-2. XML version of Table 4-1

```
<CODE-PAGE-TABLE>
<CP NUM="1200" NAME="Unicode (BMP of ISO/IEC-10646)"
   PLATFORMS="NT3.1 NT3.51"/>
<CP NUM="1250" NAME="Windows 3.1 Eastern European"
   PLATFORMS="NT3.1 NT3.51 WIN95"/>
<CP NUM="1251" NAME="Windows 3.1 Cyrillic"
   PLATFORMS="NT3.1 NT3.51 WIN95"/>
<CP NUM="1252" NAME="Windows 3.1 US (ANSI)"
   PLATFORMS="NT3.1 NT3.51 WIN95"/>
<CP NUM="1253" NAME="Windows 3.1 Greek"
   PLATFORMS="NT3.1 NT3.51 WIN95"/>
<CP NUM="1254" NAME="Windows 3.1 Turkish"
   PLATFORMS="NT3.1 NT3.51 WIN95"/>
<CP NUM="1255" NAME="Hebrew"
   PLATFORMS="WIN95"/>
<CP NUM="1256" NAME="Arabic"
   PLATFORMS="WIN95"/>
<CP NUM="1257" NAME="Baltic"
   PLATFORMS="WIN95"/>
<CP NUM="1261" NAME="Korean (Johab)"
   PLATFORMS="NT3.1 NT3.51 WIN95"/>
</CODE-PAGE-TABLE>
```

The difference between this XML version and the HTML version is not as dramatic as in some examples, but the XML version is clearer, has fewer lines and characters and is easier to maintain. More important, the stylesheet can choose to format this in many different ways as time goes by and tastes change. All the XML version represents is the actual information about Windows code pages, not the tabular format of a particular presentation of it. The markup is also clearer (to someone interested in code pages!) because the element type names (CODE-PAGE-TABLE, CP) and attribute names (NAME, PLATFORMS, NUM) relate directly to the world of code pages and not to the world of HTML tables. A table is just one way to display this data today! We may choose another way tomorrow.

One thing to note is that the extra download of a stylesheet does take time. It makes the most sense to move formatting into a stylesheet when that formatting will be used on many pages or in many parts of the same page. The goal is to amortize the cost of the download over a body of text.

A similar caveat applies to the time it takes to make the stylesheet and design the table elements. Doing so for a single table would probably not be cost effective. Our example above basically shifts the complexity from the document to the stylesheet, on the presumption that there will probably be many documents (or at least many tables) for every stylesheet. In general, XML is about short-term investment in long-term productivity.

4.1.3 *Extensible HTML (XHTML)*

What if you are not interested in the extra investment that XML usually requires? You can get some of its benefits "on the cheap" with XHTML. *XHTML* is a version of HTML that uses XML syntax. The element types are all identical to those in ordinary HTML, so you do not have to learn new ones.

XHTML's major benefit is the availability of XML parsers. HTML's definition has always been very loose. Major browsers do not offer a way to validate documents and often accept non-conforming HTML-like text as if it were really HTML. XHTML disallows this practice. XHTML documents must always be well-formed and valid. At least one browser can already validate XHTML documents and report errors. Because of this "cleanliness", XHTML is much easier to work with than old-fashioned HTML. Future versions of XHTML will be extensible so that you can add a few of your own element types to the standard XHTML mix.

4.1.4 *Specialized document types*

The real savings come when you move to a full-fledged industry- or company-specific XML document type. Once you have made that investment you can sometimes realize more radical productivity gains than you first intended. That's because your documents, like your database, now holds abstract data – not rendered, as in HTML.

Imagine that you use XML tables to publish the financial information in your company's annual report. Your accountants may be able to use their software's report writing feature to directly transfer accounting information into the XML table. This can save one more opportunity for typos between the accountants' printout and the Web author's keyboard. There might also be opportunities for automation at the other end of the spectrum. Other software might transform the XML table directly into a format required for submission to some government agency.

4.2 | Database publishing

The last example hints at the way XML can interact with systems that are not typically associated with documentation. As documents become abstractions, they can become integrated with the other abstract data in an organization. Some of the same techniques can be used to create them (such as report writing software or custom graphical user interfaces) and some of the same software will be able to read them (such as spreadsheets and database software). One already popular application of XML is the publishing of databases to the Web.

Consider for instance a product database, used by the internal ordering system of a toy manufacturer. The manufacturer might want the database to be available on the Web so that potential clients would know what was available and at what price. Rather than having someone in the Web design department mark up the data again, they could build a connection between their Web server and their database using the features typically built into Web servers that allow those sorts of data pipes.

The designers could then make the product list beautiful using a stylesheet. Pictures of the toys could be supplied by the database. In essence, the Web site would be merely a view on the data in the database. As toys get added and removed from the database, they will appear and disappear from the view on the Website. This mechanism also gives the Website maintainer the freedom to update the "look and feel" of the Website without dealing with the database or the plumbing that connects it to the Web server! Publishing information from a database to the Web is pretty well understood these days, but XML allows standardization, rigor and a separation of the tasks of programmers and Web designers.

XML is already becoming an important tool for interchange of database information. Databases have typically interchanged information using simple file formats like one-record per line with semi-colons between the fields. This is not sufficient for the new object-oriented information being stored and generated by databases. Objects must have internal structure and links between them.

XML can represent objects by using elements and attributes to provide a common representation for transferring database records between databases. You can imagine that one database might produce an XML document representing all of the toys the manufacturer produces. That document could be directly loaded into another database either within the company or at a customer's site. This is a very interesting way of thinking about documents, because in many cases human beings will never see them. They are documents produced by and for computer software.

One is shown in Example 4-3.

Example 4-3. A products database in XML

```
<TOYS>
<ITEM>
<TITLE>GI John</TITLE>
<MANUFACTURER>War Toys Inc.</MANUFACTURER>
<PRICE>50.95</PRICE>
<IN-STOCK>3000</IN-STOCK>
</ITEM>
<ITEM>
<TITLE>Leggo!</TITLE>
<MANUFACTURER>Grips R US</MANUFACTURER>
<PRICE>64.95</PRICE>
<IN-STOCK>2000</IN-STOCK>
</ITEM>
<ITEM>
<TITLE>Hell On Wheels</TITLE>
<MANUFACTURER>Li'l Road Warriors</MANUFACTURER>
<PRICE>150.95</PRICE>
<IN-STOCK>3200</IN-STOCK>
</ITEM>
</TOYS>
```

4.3 | Multimedia

XML can be a central component in a rich multimedia system. Consider the *Scalable Vector Graphics (SVG)* specification. This World Wide Web Consortium specification allows vector graphics to be represented entirely in XML, as shown in Example 4-4.

Vector graphics are described in terms of lines and shapes instead of individual points. This makes them relatively efficient (compared to bitmaps) and much easier to work with. Once the Web adopts this standard vector

Example 4-4. Diagram represented in SVG

```
<?xml version="1.0" standalone="no"?>
<!DOCTYPE svg PUBLIC "-//W3C//DTD SVG August 1999//EN"
  "http://www.w3.org/Graphics/SVG/SVG-19990812.dtd">
<svg width="4in" height="3in">
<desc>Two groups, each of two rectangles</desc>
<g style="fillcolor:red">
  <rect x="100" y="100" width="100" height="100" />
  <rect x="300" y="100" width="100" height="100" />
</g>
<g style="fillcolor:blue">
  <rect x="100" y="300" width="100" height="100" />
  <rect x="300" y="300" width="100" height="100" />
</g>
</svg>
```

graphics notation, it will be easy to move these graphics between software products like *Adobe Illustrator*™ and *CorelDraw*™. SVG support is not yet built into browsers but is available through plug-ins.

The *Synchronized Multimedia Integration Language (SMIL)* is an XML document type for describing multimedia presentations. SMIL allows sequencing of audio, video, text and graphic components. SMIL is used in the *RealPlayer G2*™ product.

4.4 | Metadata

There is a special type of data that interests owners and users of large information collections. It is called *metadata*: information about information. Metadata is starting to become crucial to Web searching and navigation.

4.4.1 *Platform for Internet Content Selection*

The first standardized metadata specification for the Web was developed before XML and is called the *Platform for Internet Content Selection (PICS)*. PICS allows the filtering of inappropriate material from computer screens based on external descriptions of content.

The "violent content" label on a video tape is a perfect example of metadata. The data provided, "violent content" describes the contents of the tape – it is data about data. PICS is an electronic version of that label.

Parts of the PICS family of standards are based upon XML. It took almost two years to get PICS into the XML world. This is because on the way to developing PICS the W3C created an intermediate layer called *Resource Description Framework (RDF)*.

4.4.2 *Resource Description Framework*

RDF is not a document type: it is a convention for designing XML documents so that they can more easily be interpreted as metadata.[1] According to the W3C definition, metadata is data about data intended to make computer filtering, sorting and other processing easier.

RDF's central concept is the "property". An RDF document can associate many properties with documents on the Web. Some of those properties can be from the PICS vocabulary but there are many other RDF vocabularies that are unrelated to content filtering, such as those used in Example 4-5.

Example 4-5. Describing the owner of a document in RDF

```
<RDF:assertions href="http://www.bar.com/some.doc">
  <bib:author>
  <RDF:resource>
      <bib:name>John Smith</bib:name>
  <bib:email>john@smith.com</bib:email>
  <bib:phone>+1 (555) 123-4567</bib:phone>
    </RDF:resource>
  </bib:author>
</RDF:assertions>
```

In one sense, this sounds very complicated: PICS is based on RDF which is based on XML. But on the other hand, it will not be so complicated in practice. PICS will have a set of element types that you must learn to apply according to the XML syntax described in this book. RDF, the middle layer,

---

1. At least that is what it looks like from an XML user's point of view. A metadata user would say that RDF is a model for metadata and XML is a particular way of representing that model. Six of one...

will only be visible to the wizards who invent new ways of cataloging, describing and organizing information – the librarians of the future.[2]

4.4.3 *Topic maps*

A related development comes from the *International Organization for Standardization (ISO)*. *Topic maps* are a specific type of metadata designed to allow the construction of logical "maps" of information. Topic maps are designed to help us navigate through the massive amounts of information on the Web. You can think of topic maps as a very sophisticated indexing mechanism for online information. We think of them as the GPS for the Web![3]

Topic maps' sophistication comes in the idea of *scoping*. With scoping, you can label a particular characteristic (roughly, an index entry) as only being applicable within a certain context.

For example, if you label characteristics as being applicable only in a particular language, a query for information on a topic would only return occurrences in your native tongue. If you labeled characteristics as being either "biological" or "psychological", then a search for the word "evolution" would return only biological topics or only psychological ones, depending on your query.

Tip   There is a friendly tutorial on topic maps in Chapter 43, "Topic maps: Knowledge navigation aids", on page 606.

---

2. Luckily, the librarians of the present are very much involved in these standardization efforts.
3. The exact relationship between RDF and topic maps is somewhat unclear to everybody concerned. Formally, they are unrelated but it seems like there is some opportunity for cooperation in the future. The experts are looking into this as we speak!

4.5 | Content syndication

Content syndication is about using metadata to move documents, such as news articles, from place to place. It is a problem domain that is tailor-made for XML because when you put XML and the Internet together you have a powerful information distribution infrastructure.

The alphabet soup of competing and cooperating standards is too long to cover in depth, but we can name a few:

- *ICE* is the *Information Content and Exchange* specification from the vendor consortium of the same name. It is described in Chapter 22, "Information and Content Exchange (ICE)", on page 300.
- *XMLNews* from Wavo and David Megginson has its roots in the newspaper business. It is discussed in Chapter 21, "Wavo Corporation", on page 288.
- *RSS*, the *RDF Site Specification* is a lightweight standard from Netscape that has been embraced by the Open Source and Linux communities.

4.6 | Science on the Web

Although the Web was originally invented in a physics laboratory for communication among physicists, it never developed into a great system for communicating mathematical formulae. Markup for mathematics is more complex than it seems at first to non-mathematicians.

The World Wide Web Consortium has created an XML-based language called *MathML*. Although the major browsers do not support MathML directly, you can get MathML support through Java applets, browser plug-ins and specialized browsers.

A rendition of a mathematical formula is shown in Figure 4-1. Its MathML markup is illustrated in Example 4-6.

The *Chemical Markup Language* (CML) is an XML-based language for describing the management of molecular information on computer networks. Using a Java viewer that is under development, users can view and manipulate molecules in 2 and 3 dimensions.

$$x^2 + 4x + 4 = 0$$

Figure 4-1   Rendition of a mathematical formula

Example 4-6. MathML markup for the formula in Figure 4-1

```
<mrow>
  <mrow>
    <msup>
      <mi>x</mi>
      <mn>2</mn>
    </msup>
    <mo>+</mo>
    <mrow>
      <mn>4</mn>
      <mo>&invisibletimes;</mo>
      <mi>x</mi>
    </mrow>
    <mo>+</mo>
    <mn>4</mn>
  </mrow>
  <mo>=</mo>
  <mn>0</mn>
</mrow>
```

Bioinformatic Sequence Markup Language is a standard for representing DNA, RNA and protein sequence information. One day your doctor may download your DNA into XML and then upload it into a petri dish to make a mini-you. We hope you'll be well-formed!

4.7 | Portals and personalization

At the beginning of the Internet revolution, knowledge workers were like kids in a candy store. The information they needed became easily available. Now the stomach-ache is setting in. The information that they need is buried in gigabytes of information they do not need.

A portal is a website designed to help users find their way through information. The first portals only helped people to find other websites. Then public portals started to add interactive features such as stock quotes and weather reports. Later, they started to allow users to build customized "home pages" including their favorite stock quotes, local weather reports and other information specific to them. This is termed *personalization*. In addition to public portals like Yahoo™, there are also many portals used within large companies. These are termed *Enterprise Information Portals*(EIPs) or *digital dashboards*. We discuss EIPs in detail in Part [no number], "Portals".

XML serves as a fundamental building block for personalized portals. XML can be used to bring various information resources into one common structure. From there, XML tools such as parsers, search engines and transformation engines can slice and dice the information into bite-sized pieces applicable to the user. The vocabulary details of the information returned by various enterprise systems may vary, but they can be *transformed* into a common vocabulary using any programming language or the XSLT transformation language.

In a sense, an Enterprise Information Portal serves as a friendly user interface to the unified system that results from Enterprise Application Integration (see 1.4, "EDI, EAI and other TLAs", on page 23). EAI systems use XML because it is good for integrating various data sources. The EIP adds another feature of XML: XML documents can easily be formatted for presentation to a human being using stylesheets.

We'll say it again: XML brings the worlds of document and data processing together.

4.8 | Alternative delivery platforms

One of the original benefits of generalized markup was its ability to make information available to new delivery devices. When the Web was young, some of the first serious content providers were established SGML users. Information that predated the Web by years could be easily served as HTML through an automated conversion. Now the web as-we-know-it is the legacy platform (not paper) and new devices such as electronic books and hand-held computers are the up and coming, new, new thing.

4.8.1 *XML goes wireless*

As you may have heard, desktop Web browsers are already passè. The next wave is wireless. And your new surfboard is the *Wireless Application Protocol (WAP)*. WAP is the term for the collection of standards that are driving the move to Internet access over handheld computers, mobile telephones, wrist watches and other go-anywhere technologies. Web browsing is not the only interesting application, either. Many people argue that hand-held instant messaging will be even more popular and important.

Not all of the WAP family of standards are based on XML. The main XML-specifications are *WBXML* and *WML/HDML*.

WBXML, is, as you might have guessed, a schema for television shows on the Warner Brothers Network. Okay, not really. WBXML is WAP Binary XML. The philosophy behind WBXML is that small machines typically have very slow connectivity to the Internet. WBXML documents are compressed XML files that can be more efficiently sent back and forth over tiny little Internet pipelines. WML and HDML are markup languages for small devices. HDML is being phased out in favor of WML.

WAP allows the Web to be presented on cell phones in real time. There is a separate language called SyncML for synchronizing data between small platforms (such as mobile phones or palm pilots) and desktop computers. SyncML would allow you to program your desktop calendar software to inform your cell phone about your meeting times. SyncML will also be very popular for moving contact information (electronic business cards) to, from and between handheld devices.

4.8.2 *Downloading the library*

Surfing your stock quotes is great while you are on the run, but what about when you want to curl up by the fire with a novella? Futurists have promised us electronic books for almost as long as they have promised us flying cars. Business interests are starting to believe that electronic books are now feasible and worth research and investment. We should all have one any day now. No word yet on the flying cars.

The Open eBook Forum creates and maintains standards relating to electronic books. The forum is made up of hardware and software companies, electronic book publishers and related organizations. A common standard for electronic books will allow those books to work on media as diverse as laptop computers, text-to-speech readers and palm computers.

The Open eBook specification is fairly simple in that it combines existing specifications into a single unified whole. The basic syntax for eBooks is XML. The "core" vocabulary is a variant of XHTML but the language is designed to be extensible to any XML vocabulary. Books are rendered using the Cascading Style Sheet (CSS) language. Metadata is represented using a vocabulary known as Dublin Core.

The Open eBook spec is not so much an invention as a standardized combination of specifications defined elsewhere. It is likely to drive the adoption of XML down into portable reading devices.

4.9 | Conclusion

XML is set to revolutionize the Web and all forms of information delivery. This will allow more sophisticated means of communication between computers and people and among people.

In the next chapter we'll talk about applications that dispense with people. Computers talk to one another to automatically accomplish tasks that have traditionally been labor-intensive and error prone.

Taking care of e-business

- Electronic business

- ebXML and BizTalk

- Electronic marketplaces

On the one end of the XML spectrum are the POP applications designed primarily for human consumption. XHTML, WAP and other similar specifications will increase the availability and sophistication of online information in these sorts of applications. On the other end of the spectrum there are MOM applications wherein computers talk to each other with minimal human intervention.

There is no requirement that MOM applications involve e-commerce, but as a notorious criminal said when asked why he robbed banks: "That's where the money is." It's also where most of the current research and energy are directed. Many people are working extremely hard to completely integrate commerce between organizations.

We discussed generic machine-to-machine protocols such as SOAP and XML-RPC in Chapter 2, "Just enough XML", on page 28. Now we'll look at the applications they support in the rapidly growing area of integrated e-commerce. There are many different standards under development in this area. They sometimes overlap, compete and maybe even contradict each other. That's merely a consequence of the fact that we are in the early days of XML-based e-business.

The dream of automated supply chain management is unmediated computer-to-computer, business-to-business integrated e-commerce. When you buy a television set, you are really buying a bundle of parts that one company bought from other companies to assemble for you. Those parts are made up of raw materials that were bought from somewhere else. Some company sold the service of removing the waste materials from these processes. Every company in this *supply chain* also had to buy desks, paper clips, and overhead projectors.

In the future the vast majority of these products will be bought over the Internet. A large subset will be bought automatically, without human intervention, through XML-based systems. When the warehouse runs low on staples, a computer will recognize this situation through the inventory and order more. Before a plant runs short of steel, it will order some from whichever supplier promises the best price that day.

5.1 | Commerce frameworks

The word framework is deliberately vague. It is an environment in which to frame other work: not something directly usable by itself. XML itself can be considered a framework!

You cannot simply download a framework and begin to work. Rather you use it as guidance in designing the particular details of your document types and software. If many document types adhere to the same framework then some portion of your implementation code can be reused between document types.

The electronic business frameworks we are about to discuss are based upon XML. They consist of a mix of vocabularies, best practice recommendations and markup conventions.

5.1.1 *CommerceNet eCo framework*

Conducting business among known trading partners is all very well and good, but first you must find appropriate partners. This can be a difficult task all by itself. Once you have found them, you must configure your software to be able to speak with theirs. The eCo Interoperability Framework provides a single common protocol through which e-commerce systems can describe themselves, their services and their interoperability requirements.

The eCo Interoperability Framework has two parts. The *eCo Architecture* defines the way businesses describe themselves and their integrated e-commerce services. They may also list the markets or trading communities to which they belong. The *eCo Semantic Recommendations* codify best practices for developing XML-based integrated e-commerce document types. The recommendations also include a "starter set" of example business documents, such as purchase orders and invoices.

5.1.2 *Trading Partner Agreement Markup Language*

Once you have found a trading partner, but before you start trading, you may need some form of formal agreement on the terms of your partnership. IBM has developed a language called the Trading Partner Agreement Markup Language (tpaML) for electronic contracts. IBM has submitted tpaML to the Organization for the Advancement of Structured Information Standards (OASIS) for standardization.

According to the announcement:

> The foundation of tpaML is the Trading Partner Agreement (TPA), which defines how trading partners will interact at the transport, document exchange and business protocol layers. A TPA contains the general contract terms and conditions, participant roles (buyers, sellers), communication and security protocols and business processes, (valid actions, sequencing rules, etc.).

In other words, TPA documents formalize the agreement required before two businesses can begin trading.

5.1.3 *ebXML*

Getting all of the world's computers to talk to and negotiate with each other will not be easy. There are many reasons that the problems are tricky and XML does not remove them all. Consider the variety of international human languages. Even within a country, there are huge variances in terminology and process between and within industries. Someone needs to standardize terminology, message structures and product and business codes.

The United Nations and OASIS have set up a joint project to tackle this problem. It is known as *ebXML*. According to the OASIS website:

> ebXML (www.ebXML.org) is an International Initiative established by UN/CEFACT and OASIS in late 1999 with a mandate to undertake an 18-month program of work to research and identify the technical basis upon which the global implementation of XML (Extensible Markup Language) can be standardized. The goal of ebXML is to facilitate open trade between organizations regardless of size by enabling XML to be used in a consistent manner to exchange electronic business data.

Because ebXML has the formal support of the United Nations, it is likely to become a very important standard internationally. The first ebXML deliverable was a specification for transport, routing and packaging (known collectively as TRP). In addition to being associated with the government of governments, the ebXML group have set themselves some aggressive deadlines, so this project is worth watching closely.

5.1.4 *BizTalk Framework*

BizTalk™ is a series of technologies from Microsoft. There is the BizTalk Framework (an electronic business framework), the BizTalk server (which is Microsoft's implementation of the framework) and the BizTalk repository.

The BizTalk Framework is a set of guidelines for XML best practices. The framework describes how to publish schemas in XML and how to use XML messages to integrate software programs together in order to build new solutions.

The framework includes a vocabulary for wrapping XML documents in an "envelope" that manages message routing, workflow and security. BizTalk has no pre-defined e-business document types such as Purchase Order or Request For Quotation. Those would be the contents of the envelope and would likely be defined by ebXML or an industry consortium.

The BizTalk envelope is a little more descriptive than the sort of envelopes we use in the paper world. It describes the sender and receiver of the message, how it should be delivered, whether a return receipt is required, what sort of processing deadlines are in force and other, similar *quality of service (QoS)* details.

5.2 | Going Vertical

In addition to generalized, common frameworks, there are dozens of organizations adopting XML to particular industries. These are termed *vertical* applications or *verticals*. It is not possible to discuss them all here[1] Instead, we will focus on a few examples. These verticals seem to be achieving real success and can serve as models for other, similar activities.

5.2.1 *RosettaNet*

RosettaNet is an non-profit consortium that develops and deploys standard electronic business interfaces. RosettaNet exists to combat the problem of "supply chain misalignments" in the information technology industry. The supply chain is the path from raw materials to finished products. In the information technology business, this would include everything from silicon to chips to parts to software.

A supply-chain misalignment is an inefficiency caused by poor information flow between organizations in a supply chain. As a child you may have played the game "telephone" where information was relayed from person to person, getting more and more garbled as it traveled. A supply chain has the same problems. These problems are particularly severe in the computer hardware industry because things change so rapidly and margins are very thin. A small company that makes too many or too few computer chips may not have an opportunity to correct its mistake.

RosettaNet is the name of the organization and also of the electronic business framework developed by the consortium. Partners use RosettaNet specifications to "align" their internal business processes and create inter-company information flows. The RosettaNet framework describes dictionaries of common definitions for computer and business terminology. RosettaNet also defines many standardized business processes known as Partner Interface Processes (PIPs).

In June, 1999, RosettaNet released a 3,600-word "dictionary" of IT products. The group has also created dozens of XML-based PIPs. These guidelines amount to dialogs between computers conducted entirely in XML. The PIPs enables manufacturers, distributors, resellers, customers

---

1. There's a helpful catalog, including website links, in Chapter 38, "Repositories and vocabularies", on page 534.

and other supply chain members to execute those processes in a standard fashion. Existing PIPs cover basic supply chain functions such as distributing new product information, transferring shopping carts, managing purchase orders and querying technical information. Others are under development.

Examples of PIPs include "Request Quote", "Query Price and Availability" and "Change Basic Product Information". These standards form a common integrated e-commerce language. They align processes between supply chain partners on a global basis, rather than using individually or bilaterally developed methods.

Judged by technical specification output, RosettaNet is advancing quickly. Corporations in the Information Technology (IT) industry have also released a flurry of press releases pledging support for the RosettaNet processes. Members of the RosettaNet Board of Directors are typically vice-presidents or directors of large companies in the IT industry.

RosettaNet has a well-defined methodology which has led quickly to formal specifications. The specifications are still very new and have not been widely adopted in industry. We will keep our eyes on them!

5.2.2 *Open Financial Exchange (OFX)*

The Open Financial Exchange is the name of a technical specification created by Intuit, CheckFree and Microsoft. OFX allows financial institutions (banks, brokerages and billers) to communicate with one another and their clients about account transactions.

OFX is one of the most mature uses of generic markup in the consumer software world, having originated as an SGML application. It is supported on the client side by accounting packages such as *Microsoft Money* and Intuit's *Quicken*, and on the server side by numerous financial institutions.

OFX supports four major kinds of services: banking, bill presentment, bill payment and investment.

5.2.2.1 Banking

Using the OFX Banking services, your client software (e.g. *Quicken, Microsoft Money* or *Peachtree*) could communicate directly with your bank. That means that your banking transactions can appear in your accounting software automatically. Bad news: covering up the trail left by transfers into the "poker money" account is about to get tricky.

Information can flow the other way also. Using an OFX-based accounting program, you could transfer money from account to account instead of through a separate website (or, heaven forbid, a branch office). Now your spouse can transfer the money back into the "university fund" account without leaving the house!

Customers can even schedule transfers in advance so that the disputed money is sent to the university account (or the university!) as soon as the paycheck clears. All of these features apply both to regular accounts and to credit card accounts. Spending money has never been so easy!

5.2.2.2   Bill presentment and payment

OFX-based bill payment is exactly as boring as it sounds. Accounting software can direct the bank to automatically pay your bills for you when they arrive. You can specify which bills should be payed automatically and which should be done manually. Bill presentment allows billers (typically utility companies) to actually deliver the bill for a product you consumed to your accounting software.

5.2.2.3   Investment

Although OFX does not currently allow customers to buy and sell investments through their accounting software, it does allow you to download information about your holdings and transactions for presentation in the accounting package.

5.2.3 *Health Level Seven (HL7)*

Health Level Seven is the dominant industry consortium for health care. HL7 has been around since 1987 and is moving now to embrace XML. Although HL7's XML support is still in its infancy, we include it here in order to demonstrate that XML is being deployed for extremely mission-critical applications.

The most widely used HL7 specification is the Application Protocol for Electronic Data Exchange in Healthcare Environments. This is a messaging standard that enables various health care applications to exchange data within and between organizations.

Version Three of the HL7 specifications will use XML extensively. According to them: "HL7 has developed the Patient Record Architecture (PRA), an XML-based clinical document architecture that provides an exchange model for documents of varying levels of complexity. Using the PRA, Version 3 will enable systems to create XML documents that incorporate HL7 message content, to generate messages from document content, and exchange and process messages and documents between disparate systems."

HL7 reminds us that XML is used in life and death applications. It was specifically designed for systems that cannot be permitted to fail. Those of us that develop XML specifications and tools must take this responsibility seriously and keep reliability as a major focus.

5.3 | Repository stories

As you can see, there are hundreds of schemas, DTDs, frameworks and other specifications swirling around XML like leaves in a storm. This is as it should be. XML is a building block. There can never be one or ten or one hundred "definitive" XML document types. Actually, there are going to be new ones invented all of the time, as new situations arise.

As we come to understand the human genome, we will need genome markup languages. When we send robotic probes to other planets, NASA may well deliver the results of experiments to the Web in various appropriate markup languages. Believe it or not, there is already a Spacecraft Markup Language![2]

Fortunately, organizations have begun to establish repository sites on the Web to catalog vocabularies and schemas in process. We discuss them in Chapter 38, "Repositories and vocabularies", on page 534.

---

2. It might be presumptuous to predict that XML would be the basis for communication at Federation Headquarters. The aliens may already have their own Galactic Markup Language.

5.4 | Conclusion

The first wave of the Internet revolution made access to information easier than it had ever been before. The second wave made commerce between individuals and businesses easier. Now the third wave will eliminate vast amounts of paperwork and inefficiency in processes that are conducted between businesses. XML is a key enabler of this more integrated business world. It serves as the foundation for industry-neutral frameworks and industry-specific vertical markets.

XML Jargon Demystifier™

Introductory Discussion

▮ Structured vs. unstructured

▮ Tag vs. element

▮ Document type, DTD, and markup declarations

▮ Schema and schema definitions

▮ Notations and characters

▮ Documents and data

6

One of the problems in learning a new technology like XML is getting used to the jargon. A good book will hold you by the hand, introduce terms gradually, and use them precisely and consistently.

Out in the real word, though, people use imprecise terminology that often makes it hard to understand things, let alone compare products. And, unlike authors,[1] they sometimes just plain get things wrong.

For example, you may see statements like "XML documents are either well-formed or valid." As you've learned from this book, that simply isn't true. *All* XML documents are well-formed; some of them are also valid.[2]

In this book, we've taken pains to edit the application and tool chapters to use consistent and accurate terminology. However, for product literature and other documents you read, the mileage may vary. So we've prepared a handy guide to the important XML jargon, both right and wrong. Think of it as a MOM application for XML knowledge.

---

1. We should be so lucky!
2. So does that mean a merely well-formed document is "invalid"? No, for the reasons described in 2.7, "Well-formedness and validity", on page 42. Hey, we didn't promise to justify XML jargon, just to explain it.

6.1 | Structured vs. unstructured

Structured is arguably the most commonly used word to characterize the essence of markup languages. It is also the most ambiguous and most often misused word.

There are four common meanings:

structured = abstract

XML documents are frequently referred to as structured while other text, such as renditions in notations like RTF, is called *unstructured*. Separating "structure from style" is considered the hallmark of a markup language. But in fact, renditions can have a rich structure, composed of elements like pages, columns, and blocks. The real distinction being made is between "abstract" and "rendered".

structured = managed

This is the meaning that folks with a database background usually have in mind. Structured information is managed as a common resource and is accessible to the entire enterprise. Unfortunately, there are also departmental and individual databases and their content isn't "structured" in quite the same sense.

structured = transactional

This is another way of thinking about database data. Structured data is captured from business transactions, comes in easily identified granules, and has metadata that identifies its semantics. In contrast, *freeform data* is normally buried in reports, with no metadata, and therefore must be "parsed" (by reading it!) to determine what it is and what it means.

structured = possessing structure

This is the dictionary meaning, and the one used in this book. There is usually the (sometimes unwarranted) implication that the structure is fine-grained (rich, detailed), making components accessible at efficient levels of granularity. A structure can be very simple – a single really big component – but nothing is unstructured. All structure is well-defined and "predictable" (in the sense of consistent), it just may not be very granular.

These distinctions aren't academic. It is very important to know which "structured" a vendor means.

What if your publishing system has bottlenecks because you are maintaining four rendered versions of your documents in different representations? It isn't much of a solution to "structure" them in a database so that modifying one version warns you to modify the others.

You'll want to have a single "structured" – that is, abstract – version from which the others can be generated. And if you find that your document has scores of pages unrelieved by sub-headings, you may want to "structure" it more finely so that both readers and editors can deal with it in smaller chunks.

Keep these different meanings in mind when you read about "structured" and "unstructured". In this book, we try to confine our use of the word to its dictionary meaning, occasionally (when it is clear from the context) with the implication of "fine-grained".

6.2 | Tag vs. element

Tags aren't the same thing as elements. Tags describe elements.

In Figure 6-1 the package, metaphorically speaking, is an element. The contents of the package is the content of an element. The tag describes the element. It contains three names:

- The *element-type name* (`Wristwatch`), which says what type of element it is.
- A *unique identifier*, or ID (`9842-3729`), which says which particular element it is.
- The name of an attribute that describes some other property of the element: `Manufacturer="Hy TimePiece Company"`.

When people talk about a *tag name*:

1. They are referring to the element-type name.
2. They are making an error, because tags aren't named.

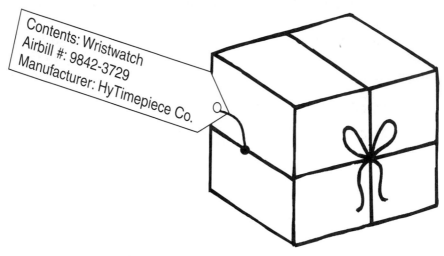

Contents: Wristwatch
Airbill #: 9842-3729
Manufacturer: HyTimepiece Co.

Figure 6-1   What's in a tag?

6.3 | Document type, DTD, and markup declarations

A *document type* is a class of similar documents, like telephone books, technical manuals, or (when they are marked up as XML) inventory records.

A *document type definition* (*DTD*) is the set of rules for using XML to represent documents of a particular type. These rules might exist only in your mind as you create a document, or they may be written out.

Markup declarations, such as those in Example 6-1, are XML's way of writing out DTDs.

Example 6-1. Markup declarations in the file `greeting.dtd`.

```
<!ELEMENT greeting (salutation, addressee) >
<!ELEMENT salutation (#PCDATA) >
<!ELEMENT addressee  (#PCDATA) >
```

It is easy to mix up these three constructs: a document type, XML's markup rules for documents of that type (the DTD), and the expression of those rules (the markup declarations). It is necessary to keep the constructs separate if you are dealing with two or more of them at the same time, as when discussing alternative ways to express a DTD. But most of the time, even in this book, "DTD" will suffice for referring to any of the three.

6.4 | Document, XML document, and instance

The term *document* has two distinct meanings in XML.

Consider a really short XML document that might be rendered as:

Hello World

In one sense, the *conceptual document* that you see in your mind's eye when you read the rendition is the *real document*. Communicating that conception is the reason for using XML in the first place.

In a formal, syntactic sense, though, the complete text (markup + data, remember) of Example 6-2, is the *XML document*. Perhaps surprisingly, that includes the markup declarations for its DTD in Example 6-1. The XML document, in other words, is a character string that *represents* the real document.

In this example, much of that string consists of the markup declarations, which express the greeting DTD. Only the last four lines describe the real document, which is an instance of a greeting. Those lines are called the *document instance*.

Example 6-2. A greeting document.

```
<?xml version="1.0"?>
<!DOCTYPE greeting SYSTEM "file://greeting.dtd">
<greeting>
<salutation>Hello</salutation>
<addressee>World</addressee>
</greeting>
```

6.5 | Schema and schema definition

The programming and database worlds have introduced some new terminology to XML.

We now speak of a document type as a kind of *schema*, a conception of the common characteristics of some class of things. Similarly, a DTD is a *schema definition*, a representation of a schema.

A notation for schema definitions is called a *schema definition language*. Markup declarations serve that purpose for DTDs, while XML instances do the job for schema definitions. And as with DTDs, the word "schema" can serve for all these purposes when there is no ambiguity.

6.6 | What's the meta?

Nothing. What did you think was the meta?[3]

There are two "meta" words that come up regularly when computer types talk about XML: metadata and metalanguage.

6.6.1 *Metadata*

Metadata is data about data. The date, publisher's name, and author's name of a book are metadata about the book, while the data of the book is its content. The DTD and markup tags of an XML document are also metadata. If you choose to represent the author's name as an element, then it is both data and metadata.

If you get the idea that the line between data and metadata is a fluid one, you are right. And as long as your document representation and system let you access and process metadata as though it were data, it doesn't much matter where you draw that line.

Be careful when talking to database experts, though. In their discipline "metadata" typically refers only to the schema.

---

3. Sorry about that!

6.6.2 *Metalanguage*

You may hear some DTDs referred to as languages, rather than document types. HTML is a prominent example. There's nothing special about them, it is just another way of looking at the way a markup language works.

Remember that an XML document is a character string that represents the conceptual document. The rules for creating a valid string are like the rules of a language: There is a *vocabulary* of element type and attribute names, and a *grammar* that determines where the names can be used.

These language rules come from the DTD, which in turn follows the rules of XML. A language, such as XML, which you can use to define other languages (such as DTDs), is called a *metalanguage*. XML document types are sometimes called *XML-based languages*.

6.7 | Notations and characters

Normally, the characters in a document are interpreted one at a time. They are given the meaning assigned by the document character set, which for XML documents is Unicode. So the character a is interpreted as the letter "a" and the character < is interpreted as the mathematical symbol "less-than".

A character-based *notation* is a set of rules for interpreting a *sequence* of characters at once, and giving the sequence a meaning that is different from the character-set meaning of the individual characters. The HTML notation, for example, interprets <a name=b> as the start-tag of an "a" element.

Computer languages (including markup languages and languages defined by markup languages), document and data formats like RTF and JPEG, and the string representations of datatypes, are all examples of notations.

The distinction between various kinds of notations can be rather esoteric. The important thing is that characters don't have their usual meaning. You need a *parser* to figure out what that meaning is. But XML is simple enough that, after reading Part Thirteen of this book, you should be able to parse XML documents yourself.

6.8 | Coding, encoding, and markup

People refer to computer programs as *code*, and to the act of programming as *coding*.

There is also the word *encoding*, which refers to the way that characters are represented as ones and zeros in computer storage. XML has a declaration for specifying an encoding.

You'll often see (in places other than this book) phrases like "XML-encoded data", "coded in HTML", or "XML coding".

But using XML isn't coding. Not in the sense of programming, and not in the sense of character encoding. What those phrases mean are "XML document", "marked-up in HTML", and "XML markup".[4]

6.9 | Documents and data

We presented the easy illustrated guide to the documents and data relationship in Chapter 3, "The XML usage spectrum", on page 54, but it's worth summarizing the high points here.

6.9.1 *It's all data!*

In an XML document, the text that isn't markup is data. You can edit it directly with an XML editor or plain text editor. With a stylesheet and a rendering system you can cause it to be displayed in various ways.

In a database, you can't touch the data directly. You can enter and revise it only through forms controlled by the database program. However, rendition is similar to XML documents, except that the stylesheet is usually called something like "report template".

The important thing is that, in both cases, the data can be kept in the abstract, untainted by the style information for rendering it. This is very different from word processing documents, of course, which normally keep their data in rendered form.

---

4. Although dynamic HTML pages contain so much scripting that the phrase "HTML coding" is sometimes warranted.

6.9.2   *Comparing documents to data*

Since documents contain data, what are people doing when they compare or contrast documents and data?

They are being human. Which is to say, they are using a simplified expression for the complex and subtle relationship shown in Table 6-1. They are comparing the typical kind of data that is found in XML and word processing (WP) documents with business process (BP) transactional data, which usually resides in databases.

Table 6-1   (typical data in) **Documents and** (business process) **Data**

	XML data	BP data	WP data
Presentability	Abstraction	Abstraction	Rendition
Source	Written	Captured	Written
Structure	Hierarchy+ links	Fields	Paragraphs
Purpose	Presentation	Processing	Presentation
Representation	Document	Database	Document

Note that the characteristics in the table are typical, not fixed. For example, as we've shown many times in this book, XML data can be a rendition and WP data can be an abstraction. In addition, XML data could:

- Be captured from a data entry form or a program (rather than written);
- Consist of simple fields like those in a relational table (rather than a deeply nested hierarchy with links among the nodes); and
- Be intended for processing (rather than presentation).

In casual use, the term "document" connotes the data characteristics shown in Table 6-1 for "XML data" or "WP data", whichever is being referred to.

When "data" is contrasted with "document", it means the "BP data" column of the table. However, in other contexts, it could refer to "XML data" or all data.

We are more specific whenever a different meaning is intended in this chapter (and elsewhere in the book).

 *Caution*   The true relationship between documents and data isn't as widely understood as it ought to be, even among experts. That is in part because the two domains existed independently for so long. This fact can complicate communication.

6.10 | And in conclusion

The matrix in Figure 6-2 ties together a number of the concepts we've been discussing.

The top row contains two conceptual documents, as they might appear in your mind's eye. Actually, they are two states of the same document, the one we saw in Example 2-1.[5]

The left column shows the document in its abstract state, while the right column shows it rendered.

The bottom row shows the computer representations of the abstraction and the rendition. The abstraction uses the XML notation while the rendition uses HTML. The horizontal arrow indicates that the rendition was generated from the abstraction.

The diagram illustrates some important points:

■ Abstraction and rendition are two *presentability* states that a document can be in. Renditions are ready to be presented; abstractions aren't.

■ Renditions can be generated from abstractions automatically.

---

5. But for clarity only the second pair of QUESTION and ANSWER elements is shown here.

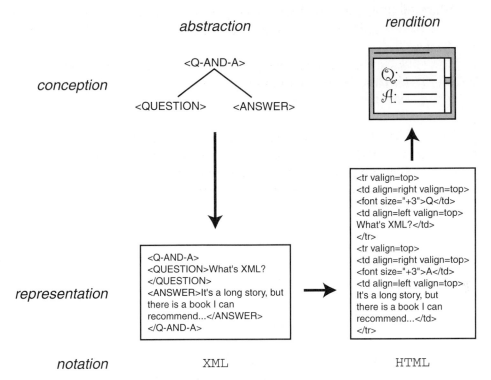

Figure 6-2   A rendition can be generated from an abstraction

- Markup languages can represent both abstractions and renditions; "structuring in XML" is no guarantee that you'll get an abstraction.
- The *computer representation* of a document incorporates two concepts: presentability and notation. In other words, the representation of a document is either an abstraction or a

rendition, and is either in an XML-based language or some other notation.

Hint   The road ahead diverges at this point. If your main interest is in what XML can do for you, rather than what makes it tick, proceed with the application and tool discussions in Part Two, "Middle-tier Servers", through Part Twelve, "Infrastructure". On the other hand, if you took clocks apart as a child, you may want to read Part Thirteen, "XML Tutorials", and Part Fourteen, "Related Tutorials", before continuing.

Middle-tier Servers

- Three-tier Web applications
- Content aggregation
- XML information servers
- Bidirectional information flow

Part Two

The advent of the personal computer (PC) popularized a two-tier networking model called *client/server*. Servers are typically large computers that control proprietary databases and act as *data sources*. They "serve" that data to end-users whose software, running on PCs (the "clients"), requests it.

Both client and server have to understand the proprietary representation in which the data is interchanged. And if a client needs data from several data sources, it has to deal with multiple servers and be able to understand the proprietary data formats of all of them.

XML is changing all that because it is a universal data representation. XML facilitates a three-tier model, in which a single *middle-tier* server can be an intermediary that aggregates data from multiple sources and presents all of it at once to the client.

In this part, we'll first look at a three-tier Web application from the end-user's perspective, then take a closer look at how a middle-tier server works. We'll analyze the architecture of an information server, see how servers are used in the investment industry, and examine bidirectional information flow.

Personalized frequent-flyer website

Introductory Discussion

▊ Three-tier XML Web application

▊ What makes websites "hot"

▊ Client/server Web model has changed

▊ Website personalization

Contributing experts: Dianne Kennedy of XMLXperts Ltd., http://www.xmlxperts.com, and Bruce Sharpe of SoftQuad Inc., http://www.sq.com

7

If the original frequent-flyer website model had been the ultimate in doing business on the Web, then business on the Web would never have taken off. This chapter explains how the middle tier gives a lift to those high-flying e-businesses.

I f you surf the Web as well as travel by air, you have probably stopped by your favorite airline frequent-flyer website. Let's consider how that experience would have been in the early days of the Web.

It might have been fun to find the site and to see all the last minute bargains offered for frequent flyers. Perhaps those specials were initially enough to motivate you to return to the site, if only to dream of taking a vacation in the middle of your biggest project!

7.1 | Client/server frequent-flyer sites

Beyond viewing the posted specials, perhaps you interacted with the site in a limited way, by entering your frequent flyer number to see your current point balance. But during heavy traffic hours on the Web, such interactions can take quite a long time.

And once you know how many points you've accumulated, what about the whole series of new questions it stimulates for which the website can't provide an answer. At that point, you must resort to calling the toll-free number to learn more about your award options and eventually book a flight.

Bottom line: once the novelty wears off, this Web experience, like countless others, is less than satisfying.

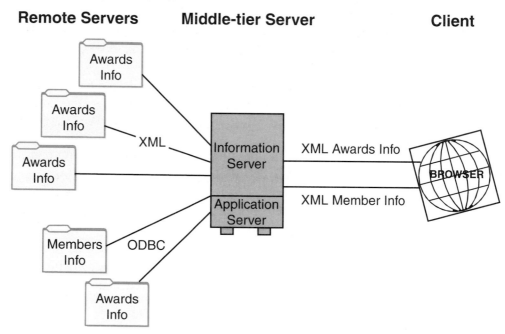

Figure 7-1   Three-tier XML processing architecture.

7.2 | What's wrong with this Web model?

The original Web model that we've described here is a "client/server" model. In this model, any personalized interaction takes place on the Web server you have contacted. As a result, there is little of it.

Instead, the Web pages you saw were static brochures rendered in HTML to provide eye-appealing display. In fact, some of the websites that were rated the "hottest" in that early market were those that provided multi-media sizzle – heavy on graphics, streaming media, animation, and sound. Personalized content, while an increasingly important consideration, had not yet become the primary distinguishing characteristic of a "hot" website. But as the Web continued its shift from simply providing entertainment value to facilitating business transactions, it became clear that personalization was the way to win customers.

In an airline frequent-flyer website, there is a great deal of HTML information that the customer can view. If this information and its associated links changes daily, the website becomes more interesting and is more likely to generate return visits. Likewise, interactivity generates more site traffic.

But in the two-tier client/server model, interactivity requires lengthy periods where the customer must be "connected" to remote servers. Queries from the customer go to the server, and resulting responses are shipped back to the customer for viewing in HTML. Unfortunately, a Web server can handle only a limited number of connections at one time.

Every time a new piece of information is requested, a transaction between the client's Web browser and remote Web servers is required. Sooner or later the number of transactions slows the server and the customer experiences lengthy time-outs when queries are processed and data is transferred back to the browser.

7.3 | A better model for doing business on the Web

Today, XML has enabled a new breed of Web server software, one that allows the Web developer to add a new "middle-tier" server to the Web model. This new three-tier Web architecture is illustrated in Figure 7-1.

Remember, in the old Web model, the customer using a browser such as *Internet Explorer* or *Netscape Navigator* on the client interacted directly with data sources on remote servers. The client maintained its connection throughout the interactive session. Each query was sent a response in HTML which could be directly viewed by the client browser. Maintaining the connection between the client and server was critical.

In the new three-tier Web model, the information that fits the profile of the customer is retrieved at once from remote databases by software on the middle tier, either as XML documents or through an ODBC or similar database connection. From that point, continued interaction with the remote databases is no longer required. The connection to the remote servers can be, and is, terminated.[1]

Once all information that fits the customer profile has been assembled by software on the middle tier, it is sent in XML to the client. Now the requirement for further interaction between the client and the middle-tier server is eliminated as well.

Figure 7-2   "Welcome to *Softland Air*"

Rich XML data, directly usable by client applications and scripting languages like *JavaScript*, has been delivered to the client. The connection

---

1. Incidentally, the term "three-tier" is a relative one. Any of the remote servers could itself be the client of a three-tier application, so if you are actually counting tiers between the end user and the farthest data source, the number could be much higher than three. Nevertheless, the architectural model remains three-tiered.

between the client and middle-tier server can now be terminated. At this point, all computing becomes client-based, resulting in a much more efficient use of the Web and a much more satisfying customer experience.

To understand the new three-tier Web model better, one must understand the role XML plays as an enabling technology. One must also understand how efficient delivery of structured abstract data to the client makes all the difference.

7.4 | An XML-enabled frequent-flyer website

Initially, differences between the *Softland Air* XML-enabled frequent-flyer website shown in Figure 7-2 and existing sites may not be apparent. Both provide a pleasing HTML-rendered site brochure. Both enable you to select the services you wish to use. But here the similarities end. New business functions, not possible with non-XML sites, quickly become apparent.

Figure 7-3   "Members, sign in here"

From the initial *Softland Air* screen you can select the "frequent flyer" option, which causes the page in Figure 7-3 to be displayed. The frequent-flyer page asks you to enter your membership identification number.

Once you have entered your membership number, a personalized, interactive Web experience begins. The next screen that is displayed (Figure 7-4) not only returns your number of frequent flyer points, but shows you destinations for which you have already qualified for awards. This screen will vary from member to member, based upon the points a member has in the frequent-flyer database and other personal information the database holds, such as city of origin.

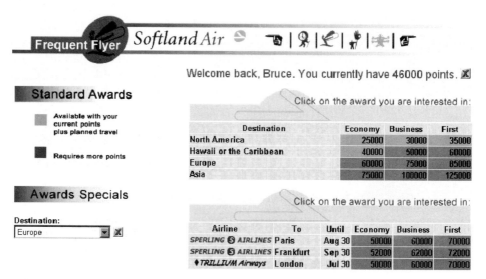

Figure 7-4 Personalized frequent-flyer information

In addition to showing you the awards you have already earned, the *Softland Air* website enables you to select destinations of interest. You can see that you have 46,000 points and are qualified to go anywhere in North America in economy through first class. You can also go to Hawaii or the Caribbean by economy class. You do not qualify to go to Europe, but you can see that you nearly have enough points for a European trip.

Suppose you are interested in going to Europe. To learn more about options to get there, you would select a destination on the "Awards Specials" part of the screen. This destination information is added to your profile, along with your city of origin and the number of points you currently have. It will be used to personalize the ongoing transactions.

Once you have selected a destination, the Web page in Figure 7-5 shows you awards, both on *Softland Air* and on partner airlines, that fit the destination you have selected. From this screen you can see what destinations in Europe most nearly fit with the number of award points you hold. As you do not currently qualify for a trip to Europe, you can use the "Planned Trips" portion of the screen to determine what trips you can take by this summer in order to qualify for the award you want.

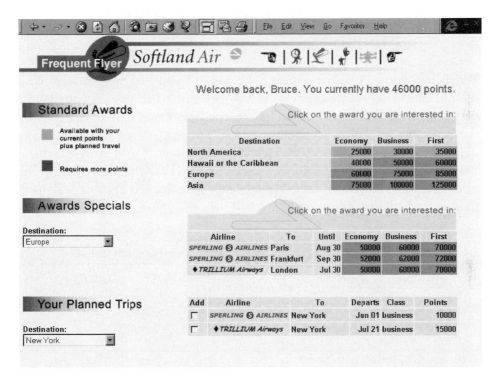

Figure 7-5   Trip planning

Using the screen in Figure 7-5, you can plan trips and even book tickets. In this way you can put enough miles in the bank to be able to earn the award to Europe.

Notice how the entire transaction is personalized for the client interacting with the website. It is also important to note that aside from logging on to enter your membership number and select the frequent-flyer transaction, all other transactions occurred on the PC in your home or office. Because the middle-tier server can aggregate data from remote sources, package it as XML documents, and send it to the client, a continuous connection to the servers is not required.

This model is one that leading business sites on the Web have striven for and can now achieve. And XML, working with an information server in the middle tier, is the reason.

7.5 | Understanding the *Softland Air* scenario

When you connect to the *Softland Air* website you first sign in with your membership ID. Your membership number is used to extract your name, the number of award points you have earned, and your city of origin from the "member information" database. This information is sent from remote databases to the middle-tier server, which combines it into an XML document (see Example 7-1). Once the data is in XML, the member name, city of origin, and number of award points can be addressed and used by middle-tier and client applications.

Example 7-1. XML document generated from member information database

```
<CUSTOMER
  MEMBERID="1AB345"
  FIRST="Bruce"
  LAST="Sharpe"
  POINTS="46000"
  CITY="Vancouver"/>
```

At this point, the middle-tier software knows who signed on. It can request all relevant awards information from both its own awards database and the remote databases maintained by its partner airlines. Example 7-2 shows the XML data for award specials items from remote awards databases. Note that because this data is in XML, we can easily see the number of points required for each award, the partner airline name, the city of origin, the destination, and the dates the special runs. Again, this information is available for use by both middle-tier and client-side processing based on member queries.

Example 7-2. XML document generated from award specials database

```
<special_item
  economy="50000"
  business ="60000"
  first  ="70000"
  partner_name="Sperling Airlines"
  from_city="Vancouver"
  to_city="Paris"
  start  ="02/Apr/1998"
  end   ="Aug 30"/>
<special_item
  economy="52000"
  business ="62000"
  first  ="72000"
  partner_name="Sperling Airlines"
  from_city="Vancouver"
  to_city="Frankfurt"
  start  ="02/Apr/1998"
  end   ="Sep 30"/>
<special_item
  economy="50000"
  business="60000"
  first="70000"
  partner_name-"Trillium Airways"
  from_city="Vancouver"
  to_city="London"
  start="01/Apr/1998"
  end="Jul 30"/>
```

The middle-tier server can also request all planned flight point earnings from all remote flight information databases, as shown in Example 7-3. We can easily see the number of points that would be earned from each flight, the partner airline name, the city of origin, the destination, and the date of flight and class of service. This information is available for use by middle-tier and client-side processing.

The information that is sent to the middle tier is compact, personalized, and precise. It differs from HTML because it contains the actual abstract data, not the look of the screen. Middle-tier software acts to assemble and deliver the right information at the right time, minimizing Web traffic and providing a higher degree of user interaction and satisfaction.

Example 7-3. XML document with flight point earnings

```
<flight
   points="10000"
   partner_name = "Sperling Airlines"
   from_city = "Vancouver"
   to_city = "New York"
   depart="Jun 01"
   flightclass="business"/>
<flight
   points="15000"
   partner_name = "Trillium Airways"
   from_city = "Vancouver"
   to_city = "New York"
   depart="Jul 21"
   flightclass="business"/>
```

7.6 | Towards the Brave New Web

The World Wide Web continues to evolve rapidly. Today the hottest web-sites are still those that provide multimedia sizzle. But as the shift continues from simply providing entertainment value to facilitating business transactions, dynamic personalized content is increasingly becoming hot.

Products like those described in this book allow the website developer to add a new middle-tier server to the Web model. It is this middle tier that enables business transactions in a way that was simply not possible before XML.

The *Softland Air* scenario shows how a middle-tier server, using XML as a structured information interchange representation, enables personalized data aggregation and organization from multiple remote databases, and interactive delivery to client browsers based upon end-user requirements.

Building an online auction website

Application Discussion

▌ Three-tier Web application

▌ Dynamic generation of XML documents

▌ Extracting data from XML documents

▌ Creating a user interface

▌ Demo on CD-ROM

Sponsor: Microsoft Corporation, http://msdn.microsoft.com/xml

Contributing expert: Charles Heinemann

Chapter

8

An online auction is the epitome of a complex real-time interactive application – not to mention being the hottest business-to-consumer (B2C) business model on the Web! This chapter describes a realistic *Auction Demo* that shows how simply the core functions of an auction can be implemented as an XML three-tier Web application.

T he Auction Demo is a three-tier Web application that simulates an online auction using technologies that have been available since Internet Explorer 4.0 (IE 4.0). It allows you to view the items available for auction, place bids on those items, and monitor the bids placed by fellow bidders.

Like other three-tier Web applications, the *Auction Demo* has data sources on the back end, a user interface on the client, and a Web server in the middle. We'll see how it was developed, using just three permanent Web pages:

userInterface.htm

This page uses *Dynamic HTML* (DHTML) to allow the Web browser to present the auction information to the user. It contains scripts that collect or update data on the middle tier by requesting *Active Server Pages* (ASP).

auction.asp

This page is an ASP file. When userInterface.htm requests this page, the scripts in it are executed on the server. The scripts generate auction.xml, an XML document that contains the latest auction data, which is delivered to the client.

makebid.asp

This page is requested by userInterface.htm when the user wants to make a bid. It is executed on the middle tier, causing the data source to be updated with the new bid information.

The user interface (UI) for the *Auction Demo* is shown in Figure 8-1. It is the rendition of the userInterface.htm *Dynamic HTML* page, which is downloaded to the client when the user clicks on a link to the auction.

That page has scripts within it that handle all the client-side activity. That includes requesting data from the middle tier in order to display the most current values of the items and bids. We'll see later how the UI page does its thing, but first let's look at how the middle tier collects and transmits the data. It does so by packaging the data as XML documents.

8.1 | Getting data from the middle tier

The role of the middle tier in a Web application is to gather information from data sources and deliver it in a consistent manner to clients. In the *Auction Demo* we start with a single data source, an ODBC-compliant database. (Later we'll see how multiple data sources of different kinds can be accessed.)

The "Auction" database used for the *Auction Demo* is a relational database with two tables, an "Item" table and a "Bids" table. The "Item" table contains data about each of the items up for auction. It is shown in Figure 8-2.

For the sake of clarity, we'll just cover the "Item" table in this chapter (the "Bids" are handled similarly). You can see the full demo in the Microsoft folder on the CD-ROM. We want to deliver the data in that table in the form of an XML document, so the client's user interface page won't have to know anything about the actual data source.

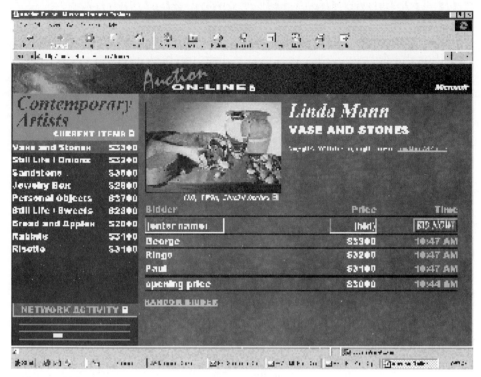

Figure 8-1   The *Auction Demo* user interface.

Title	Artist	Dimensions	Materials	Year
Vase and Stones	Linda Mann	20x30 inches	Oil	1996
Still Life / Onions	Linda Mann	20x30 inches	Oil	1997
Sandstone	Linda Mann	20x30 inches	Oil	1995
Jewelry Box	Linda Mann	20x30 inches	Oil	1994
Personal Objects	Linda Mann	20x30 inches	Oil	1995
Still Life / Sweets	Linda Mann	20x30 inches	Oil	1994
Bread and Apples	Linda Mann	20x30 inches	Oil	1995
Rabbits	Linda Mann	20x30 inches	Oil	1996
Risotto	Linda Mann	20x30 inches	Oil	1995

Figure 8-2   The *Auction Demo* item table.

8.1.1 *Defining the XML document structure*

The key to creating useful XML documents is the proper structuring of the data. For the *Auction Demo*, that means deciding how a record in the "Item" table will be represented as an ITEM element in XML. There is a straightforward mapping, shown in the data-less element in Example 8-1.

Example 8-1. Template for an ITEM element.

```
<ITEM>
  <TITLE></TITLE>
  <ARTIST></ARTIST>
  <DIMENSIONS></DIMENSIONS>
  <MATERIALS></MATERIALS>
  <YEAR></YEAR>
</ITEM>
```

For each field in the "Item" table, there is a corresponding subelement of the ITEM element.

To generate XML documents with these ITEM elements, the *Auction Demo* uses ASP files.

8.1.2 *Using ASP files to generate XML documents*

XML can be generated on the middle tier using *Active Server Pages*. ASP offers an environment in which Web authors can create documents dynamically by intermixing markup languages with in-line scripts. The scripts can be written in a variety of scripting languages, including *JScript* and *VBScript*, and can invoke server-side components to access databases, execute applications, and process information.

When a browser requests an ASP file, it is first processed by the server, which delivers a generated Web page containing standard markup.

In an ASP file, commands and scripts are delimited by "<%" and "%>". Everything not so delimited is markup or data that will appear in the generated page. For example, consider the trivial ASP file in Example 8-2.

Example 8-2. Sample ASP file.

```
<%@ LANGUAGE = VBScript%>
<%DIM Total = 2%>
<AMOUNT><%=Total%></AMOUNT>
```

The file, after establishing that the scripting language is *VBScript*, creates the variable "Total" with the value "2". The following line generates an XML "AMOUNT" element whose content is generated by executing the small script, which in this case retrieves the value of "Total".

When the browser requests this file, it will actually receive the XML document that is generated from the file, as shown in Example 8-3.

Example 8-3. XML document generated by sample ASP file.

```
<AMOUNT>2</AMOUNT>
```

Note that the ASP syntax (<%...%>) does not cause an XML parsing error. That is because the ASP file is not itself an XML document. The ASP file is processed on the server and only the generated XML document is returned to the client.

In the case of the *Auction Demo*, the file auction.asp is used to access the "Auction" database and generate XML containing the data within the "Item" and "Bids" tables. The ability to generate XML on the middle tier makes it possible to provide the Web application with content that can be manipulated on the client and refreshed without having to refresh the entire user interface.

In Example 8-4, auction.asp begins like the ASP file in Example 8-2, by declaring the scripting language. The next two lines are the XML declaration and the start-tag of the root element (AUCTIONBLOCK) of the XML document to be generated, which we will call "auction.xml".

Example 8-4. Start of auction.asp.

```
<%@ LANGUAGE = VBScript %>
<?xml version="1.0"?>
<AUCTIONBLOCK>
```

Next, a connection to the "Auction" database is established and that connection is opened:

Example 8-5. Connecting to the database.

```
<%
Set Conn = Server.CreateObject("ADODB.Connection")
Conn.Open "Auction","Auction","Auction"
%>
```

A "record set" variable (ItemRS) is now established to contain each record of the "Item" table as it is accessed, and a "Do While" loop is begun to perform the access.

Example 8-6. Preparing to access the "Item" records.

```
<%
Set ItemRS = Conn.Execute("select * from item")
Do While Not ItemRS.EOF
%>
```

Next, the template in Example 8-1 is used to create the XML ITEM element that will be generated. Just as in Example 8-2, a small script is inserted as the content of each subelement of ITEM within auction.asp. In this case, the script extracts the corresponding field's data from the record set.

Example 8-7. Markup and scripts to generate an **ITEM** element.

```
<ITEM>
  <TITLE><%=ItemRS("Title")%></TITLE>
  <ARTIST><%=ItemRS("Artist")%></ARTIST>
  <DIMENSIONS><%=ItemRS("Dimensions")%></DIMENSIONS>
  <MATERIALS><%=ItemRS("Materials")%></MATERIALS>
  <YEAR><%=ItemRS("Year")%></YEAR>
</ITEM>
```

After an ITEM element is generated, the script moves to the next record in the record set. The loop is then repeated. Once all of the records have been run through, the root element is ended.

Example 8-8. Repeating the loop and ending the document.

```
<%
ItemRS.MoveNext
Loop
%>
</AUCTIONBLOCK>
```

The complete auction.asp file is in Example 8-9.

Example 8-10 is an abridged version of the XML document (auction.xml) generated by the auction.asp file in Example 8-9.

8.1.3 *Generating XML from multiple databases*

One powerful reason to generate XML documents on the middle tier is that they can contain data that is sourced from multiple independent databases. The technique is similar to what we've already seen. The only difference is that multiple database connections are made instead of one.

The ASP file in Example 8-11 does just this, generating a single XML document with data from the databases "Gallery1" and "Gallery2".

Example 8-9. The complete auction.asp file.

```
<%@ LANGUAGE = VBScript %>
<?xml version="1.0"?>
<AUCTIONBLOCK>
<%
Set Conn = Server.CreateObject("ADODB.Connection")
Conn.Open "Auction","Auction","Auction"
Set ItemRS = Conn.Execute("select * from item")
Do While Not ItemRS.EOF
%>
  <ITEM>
    <TITLE><%=ItemRS("Title")%></TITLE>
    <ARTIST><%=ItemRS("Artist")%></ARTIST>
    <DIMENSIONS><%=ItemRS("Dimensions")%></DIMENSIONS>
    <MATERIALS><%=ItemRS("Materials")%></MATERIALS>
    <YEAR><%=ItemRS("Year")%></YEAR>
  </ITEM>
<%
ItemRS.MoveNext
Loop
%>
</AUCTIONBLOCK>
```

Example 8-10. Abridged auction.xml document generated by auction.asp.

```
<?xml version="1.0"?>
<AUCTIONBLOCK>
  <ITEM>
    <TITLE>Vase and Stones</TITLE>
    <ARTIST>Linda Mann</ARTIST>
    <DIMENSIONS>20 X 30 inches</DIMENSIONS>
    <MATERIALS>Oil</MATERIALS>
    <YEAR>1996</YEAR>
  </ITEM>
  <ITEM>
  . . .
  </ITEM>
  . . .
</AUCTIONBLOCK>
```

The XML generated by the ASP file in Example 8-11 looks structurally just like Example 8-10, an AUCTIONBLOCK element with multiple ITEM children. However, the data content originates from two different data sources.

Also notice that, for the DIMENSIONS, MATERIALS, and YEAR elements, the source fields in the "Gallery2" database are actually labeled dif-

Example 8-11. Generating one XML document from two databases.

```
<%@ LANGUAGE = VBScript %>
<?xml version="1.0"?>
<AUCTIONBLOCK>
<%
'The connection to the Gallery1 data source is made
Set Conn = Server.CreateObject("ADODB.Connection")
Conn.Open "Gallery1","Gallery1","Gallery1"
Set ItemRS = Conn.Execute("select * from item")
Do While Not ItemRS.EOF
%>
  <ITEM>
    <TITLE><%=ItemRS("Title")%></TITLE>
    <ARTIST><%=ItemRS("Artist")%></ARTIST>
    <DIMENSIONS><%=ItemRS("Dimensions")%></DIMENSIONS>
    <MATERIALS><%=ItemRS("Materials")%></MATERIALS>
    <YEAR><%=ItemRS("Year")%></YEAR>
  </ITEM>
  <%
  ItemRS.MoveNext
  Loop
  %>
<%
'The connection to the Gallery2 data source is made
Set Conn = Server.CreateObject("ADODB.Connection")
Conn.Open "Gallery2","Gallery2","Gallery2"
Set ItemRS = Conn.Execute("select * from item")
Do While Not ItemRS.EOF
%>
  <ITEM>
    <TITLE><%=ItemRS("Title")%></TITLE>
    <ARTIST><%=ItemRS("Artist")%></ARTIST>
    <DIMENSIONS><%=ItemRS("Size")%></DIMENSIONS>
    <MATERIALS><%=ItemRS("Medium")%></MATERIALS>
    <YEAR><%=ItemRS("Date")%></YEAR>
  </ITEM>
  <%
  ItemRS.MoveNext
  Loop
  %>
</AUCTIONBLOCK>
```

ferently from the corresponding fields in "Gallery1." One benefit of consolidating the data on the middle tier is that the semantics can be identified consistently, and therefore made more easily accessible.

8.1.4 *Generating XML from both databases and XML data sources*

The middle tier can source data of different kinds, not just databases. In Example 8-12, the ASP file, as in previous examples, first accesses data from "Gallery 1", an ODBC compliant database. However, it then adds data from "Gallery 3", a source of XML documents.

The Gallery3 XML document is processed by the *MSXML* parser (details below), which allows access to the document's data content. Note that there is no way – and no need – to tell whether Gallery3 is a persistent document, or was generated by another middle-tier application.

Also, look at the YEAR element. Just as with the Gallery2 database in the previous example, the original semantic label – in this case the DATE generic identifier – is changed on the middle tier to ensure consistency.

8.2 | Building the user interface

The user interface is critical to the success of any application. It must allow the user to interact with the application in an efficient and straightforward manner. The user interface for the *Auction Demo* was built using DHTML.

DHTML is a set of features introduced in *Internet Explorer 4.0* for creating interactive and visually interesting Web pages. It is based on existing HTML standards and is designed to work well with applications, *ActiveX* controls, and other embedded objects.

With DHTML a developer can create a robust and efficient UI without additional support from applications or embedded controls, or even return trips to the server. A *Dynamic HTML* page is self-contained, using styles and scripts to process user input and directly manipulate the HTML markup and other text within the page.

Let's see how userInterface.htm creates the *Auction Demo* interface by using scripts and the *IE 4.0 Document Object Model*. Two basic techniques are employed: procedural scripts and descriptive binding.

Example 8-12. Generating one XML document from a database and another XML document.

```
<%@ LANGUAGE = VBScript %>
<?xml version="1.0"?>
<AUCTIONBLOCK>
<%
Set Conn = Server.CreateObject("ADODB.Connection")
Conn.Open "Gallery1","Gallery1","Gallery1"
Set ItemRS = Conn.Execute("select * from item")
Do While Not ItemRS.EOF
%>
  <ITEM>
    <TITLE><%=ItemRS("Title")%></TITLE>
    <ARTIST><%=ItemRS("Artist")%></ARTIST>
    <DIMENSIONS><%=ItemRS("Dimensions")%></DIMENSIONS>
    <MATERIALS><%=ItemRS("Materials")%></MATERIALS>
    <YEAR><%=ItemRS("Year")%></YEAR>
  </ITEM>
  <%
  ItemRS.MoveNext
  Loop
  %>
<%
'Here the connection to the Gallery3 data is made
Set XML = Server.CreateObject("msxml")
XML.URL = "http://datasource3/Gallery3.xml"
Set Items = XML.root.children
For I = 0 to Items.length - 1
%>
  <ITEM>
    <TITLE><%=Items.item(I).children.item("TITLE").text%>
    </TITLE>
    <ARTIST><%=Items.item(I).children.item("ARTIST").text%>
    </ARTIST>
    <DIMENSIONS><%=Items.item(I).children.item("DIMENSIONS").text%>
    </DIMENSIONS>
    <MATERIALS><%=Items.item(I).children.item("MATERIALS").text%>
    </MATERIALS>
    <YEAR><%=Items.item(I).children.item("DATE").text%>
    </YEAR>
  </ITEM>
<%Next%>
</AUCTIONBLOCK>
```

8.2.1 *Using procedural scripts*

Internet Explorer 4.0 includes the *MSXML* parser, which exposes the parsed XML document as a *document object model*.[1] Once exposed, scripts can access the data content of the XML elements and dynamically insert the data into the user interface.

The userInterface.htm code in Example 8-13 applies *MSXML* to auction.xml, the XML document generated by auction.asp. That creates an *ActiveX* object representing the parsed document.

Example 8-13. Creating the auction document object.

```
var auction = new ActiveXObject("msxml");
auction.URL = "http://Webserver/auction.asp";
```

In Example 8-14, the script next retrieves the root element. It then navigates the tree until it locates the TITLE element within the first ITEM element of auction.xml. The innerText property is used to insert the data content of TITLE into the user interface as the value of the "item_title" attribute, which appears on a DIV element.

Example 8-14. Extracting data from the auction document object.

```
var root = auction.root;
var item0 = root.children.item("ITEM",0);
var title = item0.children.item("TITLE").text;
document.all("item_title").innerText = title;
<DIV ID="item_title"></DIV>
```

One of the benefits of using procedural scripts to display XML documents is that you can manipulate the data content of an XML element before you display it. For example, if you wanted to display the dimensions of each painting using the metric system, rather than feet and inches, your

---

1. The Auction Demo was developed before the W3C completed development of the common document object model (DOM) for XML and HTML. However, the IE 4.0 Document Object Model attempted to maintain compliance with the W3C draft as it evolved and IE5 supports the W3C DOM. The final spec for the DOM is on the CD-ROM.

script could simply convert the content of the DIMENSIONS element from inches to centimeters.

8.2.2 *Using descriptive data binding*

The *IE 4.0 XML Data Source Object* (XML DSO) is a declarative alternative to the procedural scripts described in the last section. The XML DSO is an applet (see Example 8-15) that enables the data of XML elements to be bound as the content of HTML elements.

Example 8-15. The *IE 4.0 XML Data Source Object* applet.

```
<APPLET ID=auction CODE=com.ms.xml.dso.XMLDSO.class MAYSCRIPT
     WIDTH=0 HEIGHT=0>
  <PARAM NAME="url" VALUE="auction.asp">
</APPLET>
```

In Example 8-15, the "url" parameter points the XML DSO to auction.asp, which causes auction.xml to be generated on the middle tier. A persistent XML source could also have been used.

In Example 8-16, data binding is used to populate the part of the user interface that shows the painting and the caption beneath it.

Example 8-16. Data binding with the XML DSO.

```
<TD>
  <DIV STYLE=
  "margin-left:16px;margin-top:16px;margin-right:16px">
    <DIV ID=pict></DIV>
    <DIV CLASS="details">
      <SPAN DATASRC=#auction DATAFLD=MATERIALS></SPAN>,
      <SPAN DATASRC=#auction DATAFLD=YEAR></SPAN>,
      <SPAN DATASRC=#auction DATAFLD=DIMENSIONS></SPAN>
    </DIV>
  </DIV>
</TD>
```

With the XML DSO applet embedded in the Web page, no scripting is required to bind the data content of XML elements to HTML elements. Instead, the name of the document object (ID of the APPLET in Example

8-15) is specified as the value of the DATASRC attribute, and the generic identifier of the XML element is specified for the DATAFLD attribute.

One advantage of displaying XML with the XML DSO is that the XML document is processed asynchronously to the rendering of the page. Therefore, if the inventory of paintings were very large, the initial elements of the XML document could be displayed even before the last elements were processed.

8.3 | Updating the data source from the client

We have seen how userInterface.htm on the client obtained data to display to the user by invoking auction.asp on the middle tier. It can also enable the user to make his own bid by invoking another middle tier page, makebid.asp.

In the *Auction Demo*, the user bids by overwriting the price and bidder name in the first row of the bid table. A bid therefore consists of the "title" of the item currently displayed, the "price" of the new bid, and the name of the new "bidder".

These data items must be passed as parameters to makebid.asp, which executes a script to process them and update the database. The script returns to the client a "return message" XML document: a single element containing information about the status of the processing.

The script in userInterface.htm (see Example 8-17) begins by assigning the title of the current item up for auction to the "title" variable, the value of the "price" text box to the "price" variable, and the value of the "bidder" text box to the "bidder" variable.

It then creates the return message document object, which will state whether makebid.asp successfully updated the database. The three variables are passed as parameters to the ASP file when it is invoked.

Example 8-17. Sending a new bid to makebid.asp.

```
var title = current_item.children.item("TITLE").text;
var price = price.value;
var bidder = bidder.value;
var returnMsg = new ActiveXObject("msxml");
returnMsg.URL = "http://auction/makebid.asp?title=" +
  title + "&price=" + price + "&bidder=" + bidder;
```

In Example 8-18, makebid.asp (called by userInterface.htm in Example 8-17) assigns the values of the parameters "title", "price", and "bidder" to variables with the same names.

The "BidRS" record set object is then created and a connection to the "Auction" database is made. Note that the connection is made for both reading and writing. The "Bids" table is then opened and the new information is added to the record set, after which the connection is closed. The process is much the same as it was for auction.asp, except that the database is written to instead of just being read.

Finally, makebid.asp generates the return message document with the status of the update.

8.4 | Conclusion

The entire *Auction Demo* was built using the methods described above. You can get a head start on building a similar Web application by modifying these scripts to suit your particular requirements.

XML enables Web applications by providing dynamic, accessible content that can be navigated and manipulated on the client. In addition, it enables the updating of content without having to refresh the entire user interface. This ability saves time by reducing round trips to the server for information that already exists on the client.

With XML, users can manage data over the Internet just as they presently do on their local machines. As a result, the Web is made a more interactive and interoperable medium. As the information superhighway has

Example 8-18. The makebid.asp file updates the database.

```
<%@ LANGUAGE = VBScript %>
<%
  title = Request.QueryString("title")
  price = Request.QueryString("price")
  bidder = Request.QueryString("bidder")

  Set BidRS = Server.CreateObject("ADODB.RecordSet")
  connect = "data source=Auction;user id=sa;password=;"
  BidRS.CursorType = 2
  BidRS.LockType = 3  ' read/write
  BidRS.Open "Bids", connect

  BidRS.AddNew
  BidRS("item") = title
  BidRS("price") = price
  BidRS("bidder") = bidder
  BidRS.Update
  BidRS.Close
%>
<STATUS>OK</STATUS>
```

transformed itself into the data superhighway, Web applications similar to the *Auction Demo* are allowing far better utilization of the vast resources made available by the Web.

Analysis   The Auction Demo clearly illustrates the architecture of a three-tier application. It uses the middle tier as a transient data aggregator and normalizer. In the next chapter we take a closer look at the requirements and architecture of a middle-tier information server.

Anatomy of an information server

Tool Discussion

∎ Middle-tier information server

∎ E-business applications

∎ Graphical development tools

Sponsor: eXcelon Corporation, http://www.exceloncorp.com

Contributing experts: eXcelon Corporation staff

A major role for middle-tier servers is enabling electronic business applications. Whether they serve as portal systems, application integrators, or publishing systems, they are all information servers. And in e-business, you *are* your information, so your server had better be capable of making all of it available – regardless of the data format!

E lectronic business, whether business-to-consumer (B2C) or business-to-business (B2B), is more than just replacing manual tasks with electronic automation. B2B in particular requires that you leverage information. Not just managed, finely-structured, abstract information in corporate databases, but all information. That includes information located in office documents, flat files, and Web pages, whether generated by employees, customers, partners or prospects.

An XML-based information server can provide the means of capturing and maintaining this information, as well as serving it to e-business applications. In effect, the server becomes an infrastructure platform upon which the application is built.

9.1 | E-business applications

Let's look at four categories of e-business application that will help us understand the requirements for information servers.

9.1.1 *Web catalogs*

The typical Web product catalog contains large numbers of products, each with different characteristics that appeal to customers. For example, a monitor and a printer are both pieces of computer equipment, but they have vastly different marketing characteristics.

For the monitor, you need to communicate screen size and pixel resolution. For the printer, you need to communicate speed, footprint and dots-per-inch resolution. Static Web page catalog technology, however is limited to a set of identical characteristics for every product: name, SKU, price, etc.

You'd like to go beyond those limitations and communicate the product-specific characteristics. Furthermore, you'd like to include targeted marketing materials with each product, such as product reviews, specifications, and comparison tables. Perhaps you'd even like to include the comments of other customers.

9.1.2 *Knowledge management*

As we make the transition from the industrial age to the information age, there is an increasing realization that the most valuable asset of an enterprise is the knowledge of its employees. Knowledge management applications attempt to gather, maintain, and disseminate that knowledge.

The value of any knowledge management system correlates directly to the percentage of total knowledge assets that the system can leverage. The managed enterprise database is typically only a small portion of that knowledge. Most of it is in the documents created by individuals using office productivity tools. It can reside anywhere in the enterprise.

Effective delivery of knowledge is also important. A good system must be customizable to the point where different users can get different views of the same document, according to their needs and roles in the enterprise. And because knowledge generation is continuous, data capture must be as well. The system should allow users to append information to documents and contribute content to the system dynamically, while also enabling new audiences to be added without disrupting the rest of the system.

9.1.3 *Supply chain integration*

A *supply chain*, as the name implies, is a relationship in which one partner supplies things to another. An aircraft manufacturer, for example, is supplied with electronic equipment and other parts from various vendors and subcontractors, and then in turn supplies the aircraft to an airline. Records must be kept of all of this activity, including documents with legal significance, such as purchase orders and invoices.

Traditional business-to-business technology for this purpose, such as electronic data interchange (EDI), is gradually being supplemented or supplanted by Web-based versions, which are much more flexible. We will discuss these issues at greater length in Part [no number], "E-commerce".

An information server should allow you to modify the content, products, customers, etc. of your supply chain applications without requiring any changes to the application code itself. These modifications should be possible dynamically, without disrupting the operation of your application.

9.1.4 *Enterprise application integration (EAI)*

In an ideal world, all of the business applications of an enterprise – purchasing, invoicing, general ledger, inventory, etc. – would be designed to work together and share data. Indeed, many companies have deployed Enterprise Resource Planning (ERP) systems to accomplish this very objective.

But despite the enormous popularity of ERP software, most enterprises are very far from that ideal state. In fact, the separate departmental systems of most companies are no better able to communicate with one another than are the systems of independent participants in a supply chain. And just as supply chain integration has become a killer app for the public Web, enterprise application integration is becoming the killer app for intranets.

An EAI system requires a *data hub*, which provides a single point of access and unified view of all enterprise data that you can query, update, delete, etc. An information server can fulfill this role.

9.2 | Requirements for an information server

From this brief survey of some key e-business application categories, we can identify several requirements for an information server. A common thread is flexibility with respect to data handling, something that use of XML facilitates.

access to all kinds of data

Corporate data can be found in a variety of sources, including relational databases, flat files, the Web, email, and prepackaged applications. Because of the flexibility of XML, any information on a hard drive or any shred of information that is thought up can be turned into well-formed XML. An information server should present and support a single view of all information as being well-formed XML documents, thereby making all data usable as e-business information.

extensibility

E-business applications require the ability to add new attributes to a data model in an ad hoc fashion, akin to scribbling an isolated fact in the margins of an incident report. XML allows you to extend individual elements by adding subelements and attributes independently without breaking existing query and retrieval operations. A server should exploit the extensibility of XML by enabling you to build extended applications without impacting database administration.

development tools

Server software should include a suite of tools to facilitate application development and the adoption of XML. The technology is evolving rapidly, so well-designed tools that can guide you through adopting and successfully employing new technology tend to be a necessity, not a luxury.

persistence and granularity

The server should store and manage XML documents either as well-formed XML document strings (whether or not valid), or in a pre-parsed form from which the original strings can be restored. The document should be accessible at any level of granularity needed by an application.

9.3 | How *eXcelon* works

The *eXcelon eBusiness Information Server*, from eXcelon Corporation, is an example of an information server that addresses these e-business requirements (among others). It has three components: *eXcelon Data Server*, *Xconnects*, and *eXcelon Toolbox*. The data server is the core run-time component that supports the applications, while *Xconnects* are modules that provide back-end connectivity to data sources. The *Toolbox* is a suite of tools to speed application development.

9.3.1 *eXcelon Data Server*

The *eXcelon Data Server* includes a complete XML database that manages and stores information. At run time, it supports the applications either by delivering information to them directly through Web server extensions, or via an application server through component object model (COM) or *Java* interfaces.

It also supports XML-based queries using XQL, XPath, and XSLT, which give highly-granular access to XML data. Query performance can be enhanced with XML indexes, which are content-based and therefore do not compromise concurrency.

The heart of the *Data Server* is the data engine, which stores XML documents as hierarchically-linked objects. It stores files that use other document and data representations – such as images, audio, and HTML files – as binary large objects (BLOBs). The data engine supports basic create, read, update, and delete functionality, which you can enhance with *Java* or COM server extensions.

The *eXcelon Data Server* can be the actual managed repository for non-relational data and/or a front-end that manages access to existing sources of data. It can also work in parallel with relational databases.

The server also creates and maintains caches for each Web server and application server to provide high performance, in-memory database support. It keeps these caches up-to-date and transactionally consistent even when scaling across a large application server farm.

eXcelon supports the extensibility of XML by enabling you to extend an XML data record without disrupting any applications that are connected to the *Data Server.* If you extend the knowledge base, either through *Studio* or by simply editing an XML document, the server will store and manage that new attribute without requiring a schema evolution and without breaking any current requests.

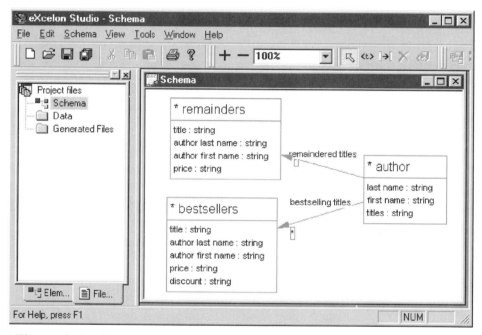

Figure 9-1   A schema being defined in *eXcelon Studio*

9.3.2 *eXcelon Xconnects*

Xconnects are modules that convert data into XML and load it into *eXcelon*. The modules can be designed to incorporate any method of translation as well as two-way synchronization, and can be built to custom requirements with an array of third-party tools and APIs.

9.3.3 *eXcelon Toolbox*

eXcelon Toolbox is an integrated tool set for building and managing XML e-business applications. It includes three tools, which are described in this section.

9.3.3.1   *eXcelon Studio*

eXcelon Studio, shown in Figure 9-1, allows you to define XML document types for your application graphically. You can describe document and element types with their attributes and connect them with one-to-one or one-to-many relationships.

The tool automatically generates *eXcelon Server* extensions in both *Java* and COM to manipulate your XML data using the W3C Document Object Model (DOM). It also generates HTML forms for data entry.

Studio is using XML Document Content Description (DCD) as its schema representation until one is approved by the W3C. It can read an existing XML document, reverse engineer the schema, and allow you to extend it. This facility makes it easier to incorporate new information.

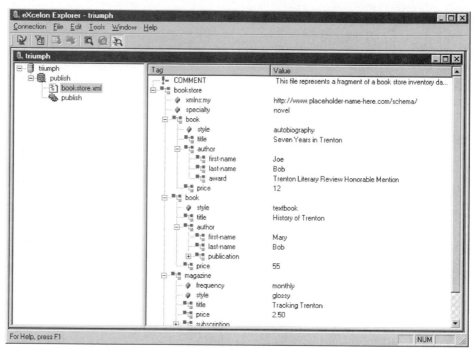

Figure 9-2   A book store inventory in *eXcelon Explorer*

9.3.3.2   *eXcelon Explorer*

The *eXcelon Explorer*, shown in Figure 9-2, is a graphical user interface (GUI) for organizing and browsing your XML data. It has a familiar file system metaphor: you can create folders and move both XML and non-XML files with a simple drag and drop.

Explorer includes a *Query Wizard*, shown in Figure 9-3, to build queries visually. It supports ad hoc querying by dynamically generating a list of the attributes provided by the applicable schema. If you take advantage of XML's extensibility and add an attribute to even a single element, *eXcelon* updates the document type schema and the *Query Wizard* dynamically adapts to the change.

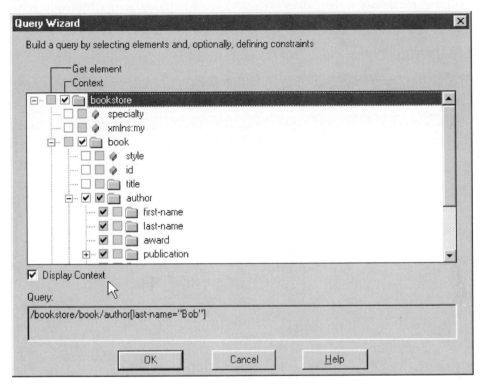

Figure 9-3   Using *Query Wizard* to search for books by Bob

9.3.3.3   *eXcelon Manager*

The *eXcelon Manager*, shown in Figure 9-4, provides a central point for all administration. You can create XML document stores, define users and

assign their access rights, distribute and load-balance across multiple servers, and create additional caches for increased concurrency.

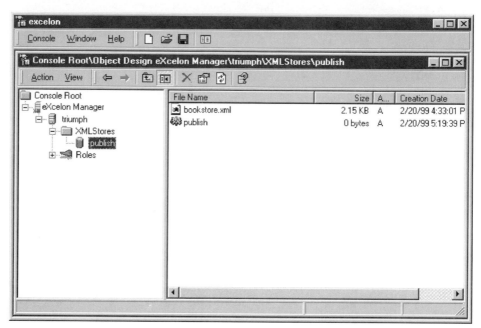

Figure 9-4   eXcelon Manager administration tool

Tip   *There is a free trial of eXcelon software on the CD-ROM
that accompanies this book.*

Wells Fargo & Company

- Intranet deployment
- XSL stylesheets
- Portal information server

Sponsor: eXcelon Corporation, http://www.exceloncorp.com

Contributing experts: eXcelon Corporation staff

Chapter

10

The Web may be the world's library, but as it grows it becomes increasingly difficult to keep the shelves organized. Instead of stocking them with static HTML pages, why not generate the pages as needed, from your ever-changing content? This chapter shows how one company did it.

Retirement plans are big business! Wells Fargo & Company's Institutional Trust Group (ITG) is one of the world's largest, with more than $260 billion in assets under administration and more than 650,000 people participating in its IRAs and other retirement plans. The ITG is consistently top-ranked for customer satisfaction among all U.S. institutional retirement organizations.

10.1 | Website requirements

In order to make its services more competitive, Wells Fargo realized that there was an enormous amount of useful information in the company that needed to be used more effectively. But there was no system in place that could deliver this information to employees. If the company could devise such a system, it would go a long way toward ensuring that the ITG would continue to maintain its leading position.

Specifically, the company needed a system that could do the following:

- Access and use any piece of information in the company, whether located in a database, on someone's desktop, or on a Web server...anywhere.
- Enable customization of the information so that specific content is delivered to specific users, right down to the level where different users get different paragraphs within personalized versions of the same document.
- Capture knowledge by allowing users to append information to documents and contribute ad hoc content to the system dynamically.
- Provide highly targeted searching capabilities so people can get the exact information they need, when they need it.
- Enable new audiences and information to be added dynamically, without disrupting the rest of the system.

Wells Fargo met these requirements by implementing an XML-based knowledge management system based on the *eXcelon eBusiness Information Server* from eXcelon Corporation (see Chapter 9, "Anatomy of an information server", on page 138).

10.2 | The challenge: Leverage all the information

Wells Fargo's new knowledge management system is replacing the company's old intranet, which was based on static HTML pages and was too rigid to accommodate the company's requirements.

There was an enormous amount of valuable information, such as newsletters, memos, requests for proposals, etc., scattered throughout the organization. It was not being leveraged because there was no practical way to deliver this information, which was increasing by dozens of documents every week. It was virtually impossible to publish and manage it using static HTML pages.

XML was chosen as the solution to the problem because it could be used to represent any kind of information – both managed (i.e., information kept in a formal database) and unmanaged (everything else). Furthermore, because information constantly changes, XML's extensibility would enable

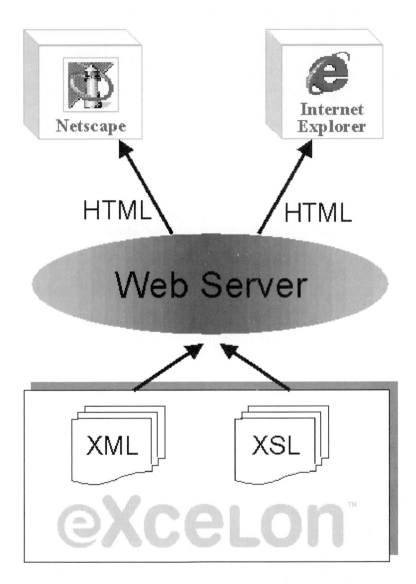

Figure 10-1   Information flow in the Wells Fargo intranet

the bank to constantly update and extend its knowledge base without disrupting the system.

10.3 | The new intranet system

The new system, which is shown in Figure 10-1, was deployed in just two months using the development tools in the *eXcelon Toolbox*. It currently supports three distinct audiences: general Wells Fargo employees, general employees who are frequent visitors, and ITG employees.

The system meets all of the requirements, and then some. capabilities, including:

Universal information access

Because *eXcelon* is not restricted to a single data representation, virtually every piece of information in the organization can be used in the knowledge management system. These range from *Word* documents and email messages to finely-structured and managed relational database information.

Highly targeted content delivery

The bank added "audience type" attributes to its content, which enables the system to deliver specific content to specific users.

Enhanced sales support

The company is now able to implement a "service selector" feature. It enables salespeople to enter profile information for prospective customers (number of employees, etc.) and to receive a customized package of the product and service marketing materials that are most appropriate.

Continually evolving content

Wells Fargo can exploit XML's extensibility to continuously evolve and improve the content on the site. For example, the sales force now has access to the multitudes of newsletters and management memos generated each week. And individuals can append information to the content, thereby enabling them to share their knowledge with the rest of the sales force. This will get easier in the future when a new extension is deployed that will enable employees to publish *Microsoft Office* content directly into *eXcelon*, in XML.

Example 10-1. Service description document

```xml
<?xml version="1.0"?>
<?xml:stylesheet type="text/xsl" href="Service.xsl"?>

<ITGServiceTypes>
<Service>
<Name>Small Business 401K</Name>
<Description>Small Business 401(k) is a cost-effective
retirement plan program that offers small businesses many of
the features normally available only in larger plans.
Features include daily valuation, a toll-free number and
employee communication services.</Description>
<PlanType>401k</PlanType>
<Link>http://cartalk.cars.com/columns/cc/latest.html</Link>
</Service>

<Service>
<Name>OMNI Bundled Regional Services</Name>
<Description>ITG ranks in the top 20 providers of plan
administration, recordkeeping and investment
services.</Description>
<PlanType>OMNI</PlanType>
<Link>http://www.microsoft.com/msdn</Link>
</Service>

<Service>
<Name>OMNI Bundled National Services</Name>
<Description>ITG ranks in the top 20 providers of plan
administration, recordkeeping and investment
services.</Description>
<PlanType>OMNI</PlanType>
<Link>http://www.netscape.com</Link>
</Service>

</ITGServiceTypes>
```

10.4 | How the system works

The system uses XML and XSL so that both the content and the Web layout can be changed independently. This strategy allows new services and information to be added without the assistance of a webmaster.

The data flow is shown in Figure 10-1. The client completes a search form that requests an *Active Server Page* from the Web server, which interprets the page and issues a data request to *eXcelon*. The latter returns an

XML document and an XSL stylesheet to the Web server, which processes them and generates HTML pages that are delivered to the client.

The abbreviated illustration of such an XML document in Example 10-1 shows how Wells Fargo describes its services. Note the element called PlanType, which assigns each service to a category.

The XSL stylesheet with which the Web server creates the HTML rendition of the document is shown in Example 10-2. It uses the PlanType element to select and display only services that are associated with OMNI plans.

Example 10-2. Stylesheet to display only OMNI plans

```
<?xml version="1.0"?>
<xsl:stylesheet xmlns:xsl="http://www.w3.org/TR/WD-xsl"
                xmlns="http://www.w3.org/TR/REC-html40">
   <xsl:template match="/">
      <xsl:for-each select="//Service[PlanType='401k']">
         <xsl:apply-templates/>
            <a>
               <xsl:attribute name="href">
                  <xsl:value-of select="Link"/>
               </xsl:attribute>
               <xsl:value-of select="Name"/>
            </a>
            <p></p>
            <xsl:value-of select="PlanType"/>
            <blockquote>
               <font size="-1">
                  <xsl:value-of select="Description"/>
               </font>
            </blockquote>
      </xsl:for-each>
   </xsl:template>
</xsl:stylesheet>
```

10.5 | Conclusion

Wells Fargo's *eXcelon*-based knowledge management system is enabling its employees to be better informed and better prepared to do their jobs. They can respond more quickly to customer inquiries and deliver better sales offerings to prospective customers. Furthermore, the company no longer incurs the expense of maintaining and revising static HTML pages.

Bidirectional information flow

Application Discussion

▌ CARD: Commerce Accelerated Relational Data

▌ Interface to back-end relational data sources

▌ Supports update as well as access

Sponsor: Infoshark, Inc., http://www.infoshark.com
Contributing experts: Barbara Bouldin and Jay Eberly

Chapter

11

Perhaps the most challenging part of implementing a three-tier Web application is the need for an interface between the information server and each and every back-end data source. It is particularly daunting when the data flow is bidirectional; that is, when the client can modify the data source. This chapter describes a strong CARD to have in your hand for those projects.

The essence of the three-tier Web architecture, as we have seen, is that information can be delivered to the client in a convenient and consistent form, regardless of how and where it is stored. In sophisticated interactive applications, the reverse is also true. That is, the end user, by using his friendly local interface, can cause changes to be made in the back-end data source.

But what seems a friendly and convenient act to the enterprise's customer or supplier is often viewed as a horror by the database administrator (DBA): unmanaged strangers modifying his carefully managed database!

Even within an enterprise, where there is much greater control and supervision, no one really updates a database directly. Instead, the requested changes are captured in "transaction files". The actual transactions take place only under controlled conditions, in which the integrity of the database can be maintained. Because the files are a complete record of the updates, the transactions can be "rolled back" to a previous point of integrity if an error should occur.

What if something similar could be done for Web-based transactions?

11.1 | infoShark plays its CARD!

Enter the *Commerce Accelerated Relational Data* (CARD) schema, a schema developed by infoShark for representing relational data and its metadata in XML. The main goal of CARD is to provide a common language, complete with basic business rules, for a bidirectional XML-based information flow.[1]

Documents conforming to CARD can represent the necessary information to re-create relational databases and populate them with their data. This information includes such things as primary and foreign key relationships, indices, constraints, and native datatypes. CARD documents can be used by a business to provide a subset of a production database to its business partners.

Furthermore, the CARD schema provides for pricing individual pieces of data contained in a CARD document instance. As the 21st century fulfills its promise as the "Age of Information", that pricing metadata should prove an appropriate recognition – and practical enabler – of information's new role as an electronically tradable commodity.

11.2 | Application scenario: Metro Police

To get an idea of what CARD can do, let's look at a potential application in a law enforcement information system.

11.2.1 *Diverse user population*

A large metropolitan law enforcement agency – call it "Metro Police" – built a *Crime Data Bank* using Oracle databases. Several classes of user need to access and update this information: crime analysts, detectives, patrolmen in mobile units, pawnbrokers, and other law enforcement agencies. (See Figure 11-1).

---

1. CARD conforms to the current draft of the W3C schema definition language. It is freely available at schema repositories such as `http://www.xml.org` and `http://www.biztalk.org`, and from infoShark.

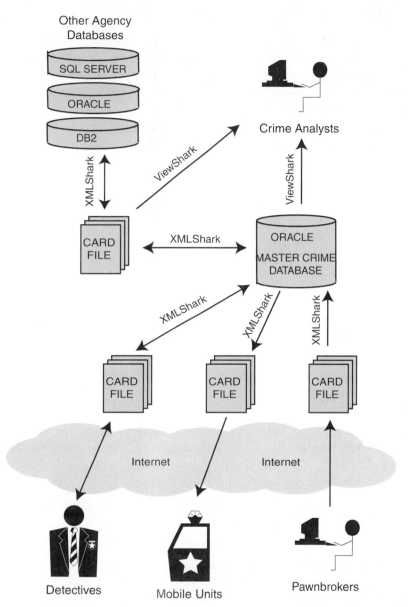

Figure 11-1 *Crime Data Bank* access

11.2.1.1   Crime analysts

Crime analysts need the ability to navigate and analyze the information in all the databases. They require free access to any data that is not considered private, such as the identity of minors.

However, the database administrator does not want the analysts working directly with production databases. That could create a serious performance degradation during a time that critical and urgent information might be needed by officers for prevention of a crime.

Instead, XML CARD files could be generated and those files could be queried instead of the actual databases. This arrangement would limit database traffic to production data, while allowing the analysts to peruse the information at will. Moreover, the XML could easily be transformed into a convenient form for analysis, such as a spreadsheet.

11.2.1.2   Detectives

Detectives are constantly acquiring new information that they want updated in the databases. The same performance, security, and privacy concerns need to considered for them as for the analysts. Like the analysts, it would also be useful for the detectives to work on a CARD file that could in turn be used to update the database.

In order for a detective's updates to be most effective, they must be applied quickly, which in essence means the update must be done from remote locations. Furthermore, the remote access will most probably be accomplished via a PDA. This situation dictates a minimal datastream size.

CARD supports this requirement by allowing a document to contain updated data only, when the original data and metadata are unchanged, as shown in Example 11-1.

Example 11-1. CARD document with altered data only

```
<alterData>
  <data dbStructureName="Crime Data Bank"
       dbSchemaName="investigation"
       tableName="crime">
  ...
  </data>
</alterData>
```

11.2.1.3   Patrolmen

Like detectives, patrolmen also have a need to access information on demand with their PDAs. In fact, it would be advantageous if critical information could be transmitted to them at the crime scene by others. XML CARD files could be used in conjunction with voice technology to achieve this goal.

11.2.1.4   Pawnbrokers

More than 90% of all items that appear in a pawn shop have been stolen. There is, therefore, a legal requirement that copies of all pawn receipts be forwarded to the relevant law enforcement authority. Every week the Metro Police receives thousands upon thousands of receipts with no efficient mechanism for updating the *Crime Data Bank*. And as pawnbrokers are manifestly not part of the official law enforcement community, this class of user introduces additional security exposure.

Once again, CARD can afford an effective and secure way for updating the database with this information. The pawnshop owners and managers could create CARD files via the Internet which could then be used to update the *Crime Data Bank*, as shown in Figure 11-2.

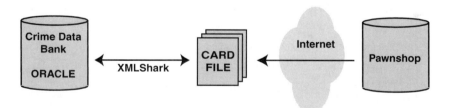

Figure 11-2   Internet database update using a CARD file

As all user updating occurs in the CARD file, the DBA can continue to enforce tight control over who changes or even accesses what data, where, and when. This control is accomplished through standard and pre-established permissions, privileges, and authorization to utilize the *Crime Data Bank*.

11.2.1.5   Law enforcement agencies

In addition to utilizing its own information, Metro Police also shares information with other law enforcement agencies, such as the U.S. Bureau of Alcohol, Tobacco, and Firearms (ATF) and the U.S. Federal Bureau of Investigation (FBI). This information flow is shown in Figure 11-3.

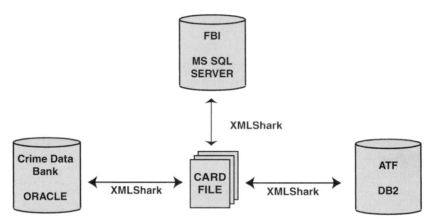

Figure 11-3   Inter-agency data sharing

The shared databases need not be homogeneous. The FBI database might be in *SQL Server*, for example, while the ATF database is in *DB2*. CARD supports the relational database model generically, rather than in the context of a specific database management system (DBMS), so it is capable of representing the information of both agencies.

11.2.2 *Marketing crime data*

Metro Police plans to recoup development costs for the *Crime Data Bank* application by selling the information to other law enforcement agencies. In Example 11-2, note the `currencyValue`, `currencyCode`, and `description` attributes of the `card` element. They allow the information within the document to be described and a price specified for it.

Example 11-2. Data for sale

```
<card name="crime data" distributor="Metro Police"
     currencyValue="499" currencyCode="USD"
     description="Metro area crime reports: 2000-2001">
  <dbStructures>
    ...
  </dbStructures>
  <existingData>
    <rows dbStructureName="Crime Data Bank"
        dbSchemaName="investigation"
        tableName="crime">
    ...
    </rows>
  </existingData>
</card>
```

11.3 | Other features of CARD

CARD has many features besides those described in the Metro Police scenario. Here are a few of the highlights.

11.3.1 *Rich metadata*

The CARD schema provides for the representation of existing data, its metadata, and alterations to the data. Any or all of these can be interchanged in a single document, or each can be in a dedicated document. We saw an example of alterations in Example 11-1 and of existing data in Example 11-2.

The business rules under which an enterprise operates are frequently expressed as constraints on values in the enterprise database. Such constraints are an example of the metadata that can be represented in CARD documents. For example, an *Oracle8i* database might enforce a rule that a manager's base salary must be a minimum of $75,000 per year but cannot exceed $100,000. A CARD representation is shown in Example 11-3.

Similarly, in *MicroSoft SQL Server*, the relationship between the products a customer has ordered and the product's inventory level is contained in the foreign keys (Example 11-4).

By including metadata along with the data, the information supports bidirectional processing, as shown in Example 11-5. If just the data itself

Example 11-3. Managerial salary constraint in *Oracle8i*

```
<checkConstraints>
  <checkConstraint name="cc_oo1" enabled="yes">
    <checkConstraintValue language="PLSQL">
      <![CDATA[salary >= 75000 and salary <= 100000]]>
    </checkConstraintValue>
    <columnLink columnLinkName="column.sales.employee.salary"/>
  </checkConstraint>
</checkConstraints>
```

Example 11-4. Relationship in *Microsoft SQL Server*

```
<foreignKey name="fk_001"
            keyLinkName="key.sales.product.pk_001"
            enabled="yes"
            cascadeDelete="no">
  <columnLink columnLinkName="column.sales.customer.prod_id"/>
</foreignKey>
```

had been present, without the metadata that describes its context, it would not be possible to add, delete or change the data.

11.3.2 *Inter-schema sharing*

It is common for different databases or schemas to use different names for semantically identical information. For example, one database might refer to its employee identifier column as emp while another uses emp_id.

CARD provides the ability to represent the identical nature of these columns by establishing a shared common name for them, as shown in Example 11-6.

The same technique can be used for relating identical information across industry schemas. It is not hard to imagine that a company might need to represent the same data according to the HL7 schema created by the health care industry and the SWIFT schema created by the financial industry (see Figure 11-4).

Example 11-5. Metadata supporting bidirectional processing

```
<alterData>
  <data dbStructureName="DotCommerce Data"
        dbSchemaName="sales"
        tableName="employee">
    <insertData>
      <columnValue columnName="emp_id" isNull="no">
        <![CDATA[1.234]]>
      </columnValue>
    </insertData>
    <deleteData>
      <columnValue columnName="emp_id" isNull="no">
        <![CDATA[5.678]]>
      </columnValue>
    </deleteData>
    <updateData>
      <columnValue columnName="emp_id" isNull="no">
        <![CDATA[5.678]]>
      </columnValue>
      <previousData>
        <columnValue columnName="emp_id" isNull="no">
          <![CDATA[1.234]]>
        </columnValue>
      </previousData>
    </updateData>
  </data>
</alterData>
```

Example 11-6. Shared common names

```
<columns>
  <column name="emp" linkName="column.sales.employee.emp"
          nativeType="number" precision="3" scale="5"
          length="5" defaultValue="1.234" nullable="no"
          commonName="EMPLOYEE-IDENTIFIER"/>
</columns>
...
<columns>
  <column name="emp_id" linkName="column.sales.employee.emp_id"
          nativeType="number" precision="3" scale="5"
          length="5" defaultValue="1.234" nullable="no"
          commonName="EMPLOYEE-IDENTIFIER"/>
</columns>
```

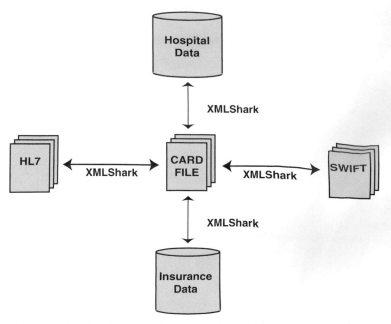

Figure 11-4   Sharing identical information among industries with different schemas

11.3.3   *CARD automation*

infoShark has developed a suite of tools for automatically generating and parsing CARD documents, viewing CARD documents, subsetting and combining data, and transforming to other formats, such as *Excel*.

   Tip   You can try out CARD for yourself using the copy of ViewShark, infoShark's CARD viewer, on the CD-ROM that accompanies this book.

E-commerce

- **❚** Electronic Data Interchange (EDI)
- **❚** Business-to-business (B2B)
- **❚** Supply chain integration
- **❚** Trading exchanges
- **❚** Integrated E-commerce (IEC)

Part Three

E-commerce is all about the elimination of manual procedures among trading partners. The eventual goal is to have each partner's system exchange information directly with all the others.

The most visible manifestations of e-commerce are *Web storefronts* — websites where an online catalog replaces a paper catalog and mailed-in order forms. These sites enter transactions directly into the vendor's system, but the purchaser must do everything manually.

Historically, though, business supply chain automation, in the form of Electronic Data Interchange (EDI), has been the major driver of e-commerce. EDI is vital to those companies rich enough to have implemented it, but for smaller trading partners it is unattainable.

In the following chapters, we'll see why traditional EDI has reached its limit and how XML and the Web can help it realize its full potential. The key to the value of EDI is its *integration* into the business systems of all trading partners, something that the storefront does not accomplish. With XML-based EDI, a truly integrated e-commerce is now possible, for partners of all sizes.

From EDI to IEC: The new Web commerce

Introductory Discussion

▌ Electronic Data Interchange (EDI)

▌ Integrated e-commerce (IEC)

▌ Leveraging XML and the Internet for EDI

▌ Supply chains and supply webs

Contributing expert: Mike Hogan of POET Software Corporation, http://www.poet.com.

12

XML and the Internet are dramatically altering the Electronic Data Interchange (EDI) landscape. By driving down costs and complexity, they are creating a revolutionary form of business-to-business integrated e-commerce (IEC) that complements EDI and vastly extends its reach. IEC is becoming a truly ubiquitous technology that is reshaping business as we know it. This chapter introduces EDI and explains its evolution to IEC.

O ver the past several decades, corporations have invested trillions of dollars in automating their internal processes. While this investment has yielded significant improvements in efficiency, that efficiency is only beginning to be extended to external processes.

In effect, companies have created islands of automation that are isolated from their vendors and customers – their trading partners. The interaction among companies and their trading partners remains slow and inefficient because it is still based on manual processes.

12.1 | What is EDI?

Electronic Data Interchange (EDI) has been heralded as the solution to this problem. *EDI* is defined as the exchange of data between heterogeneous systems to support transactions.

EDI is not simply the exportation of data from one system to another, but actual interaction between systems. For example, Company B is a supplier to Company A. Instead of sending purchase orders, bills and checks in hard copy form, the two might connect their systems to exchange this same data electronically.

In the process they could benefit in many other ways, including faster turnaround on orders, better inventory control, reduced financial float, complete real-time information about orders and inventory for improved decision-making, reduced costs for manual data input, and more. Companies that have implemented EDI rave about the various benefits.

In fact, these benefits can be expanded to a chain of suppliers. For example, Company C might be a supplier to Company B above. If companies B and C implement EDI, then Company A gains the additional benefits of superior integration with their entire *supply chain* of suppliers.

12.1.1 *Extranets can't hack it*

There is a significant gap between the business benefits described above and the actual implementation of EDI. This is because the actual implementation of "traditional EDI" is fundamentally flawed. It is difficult and costly to implement and, even worse, it requires a unique solution for each pair of trading partners. This situation is analogous to requiring a unique telephone line to be wired to each person to whom you wish to speak.

Many people falsely proclaimed the Internet as the solution to this problem. By implementing EDI over a single network, our problems would be solved. This "solution" was so exciting it was even given its own name, the extranet. Unfortunately, a network with a common protocol is still only a partial solution.

This is because the systems implemented in each company are based on different platforms, applications, data formats (notations), protocols, schemas, business rules, and more. Simply "connecting" these systems over the Internet does not, by itself, solve the problem. To use the phone system analogy again, this is analogous to wiring each business into the global phone network, only to realize that each company's phone system is unique, and incompatible with every other phone system.

And given the trillions of dollars companies have invested in automation, they are not simply going to replace these systems with new "compatible" solutions, assuming such things existed.

12.1.2 *XML can!*

The eXtensible Markup Language (XML) provides a solution for EDI over the Internet. XML is a universal notation (data format) that allows computers to store and transfer data that can be understood by any other computer system. XML maintains the content and structure, but separates the business rules from the data. As a result, each trading partner can apply its own business rules. This flexibility is critical to creating a complete solution for EDI.

There are additional technologies that are also part of the complete solution. Security, for example, is critical to EDI. Transactional integrity, connection stability, authentication and other services are also critical to implementing a complete solution. These requirements are addressed by technologies that are layered on top of the Internet. We refer to them generically as *Internet-based services*.

The final piece of the EDI solution is data storage. XML introduces a unique set of requirements for hierarchical naming and structure. It also requires rich relationships and complex linking. XML's use in EDI adds further requirements for metadata and versioning. These requirements levy heavy demands on database technology.

12.1.3 *Integrated e-commerce*

By combining XML, the Internet, Internet-based services and database connectivity, we have a complete solution for universal *integrated e-commerce (IEC)*. IEC, which complements and extends EDI, is changing our entire business landscape. EDI is metamorphosing from a handful of unique interconnections, defined by the supply chain, into a "supply web". The supply web is an intelligent common fabric of commerce over the Internet. Trading communities and exchanges are examples of supply webs.

According to Metcalfe's Law – formulated by Robert Metcalfe, the inventor of *Ethernet* – the value of a network is roughly proportional to the square of the number of users. Imagine what this means when your EDI "network" expands from a one-to-one proposition, to a true network that encompasses practically every company in the world. Suddenly, the trillions of dollars companies have invested in internal automation increase in value by several factors. By the same token, this information can also be extended to customers, adding significant value to the vendor-customer relationship, thereby enhancing customer loyalty.

This is a pivotal time in the history of technology. With the emergence of XML, all of the pieces are available to create a universal mechanism for EDI. The Internet provides the transport. XML provides the flexible, extensible, structured message format. Various Internet-based services provide solutions for security, transactional integrity, authentication, connection stability, network fail-over and more.

Add to this sophisticated data storage and you have all of the pieces necessary to unite corporate islands of automation into a single coherent fabric of electronic commerce. IEC has already achieved dramatic improvements in efficiency, cost-savings, superior access to real-time data for analysis and decision-making, superior inventory management, and more.

Integrated e-commerce will have a profound impact on business-to-business (B2B) and business-to-consumer (B2C) relationships. The many problems with current implementations of EDI have relegated it to large enterprises and selected industries. However, the combination of the Internet, Internet-based technologies, and XML is opening up EDI – as enhanced by IEC – not only to small-to-medium enterprises (*SMEs*), but also to individuals (Example 12-1).

IEC will experience growth and market penetration that will rival the email market. It has already begun to blossom on the Web and become an everyday part of our lives. It will eventually usher in a new era in computing. The Internet will complete its metamorphosis from a transport for Web pages into a ubiquitous and seamless foundation for every imaginable transaction. In the future, IEC will touch every aspect of computing.

We will be examining these propositions in detail, and the technology that makes them possible.

12.2 | The value of EDI

While traditional EDI is very costly and difficult to implement, the potential benefits are very significant. Companies that have implemented EDI rave about benefits like improved efficiency, vendor management, cost savings, superior access to information for decision making, tighter inventory control, customer responsiveness, and it is a competitive advantage that can be marketed to attract new customers.

Example 12-1. The value of data interchange.

Mike opens his company expense report, and in the microsecond it takes to launch, he reminisces about the old days when he had to fill out these things himself. Now the computer does it for him. Mike recently took a trip to Utah to close a major deal. In the process he purchased a plane ticket, a rental car and various meals. In the old days, he used to enter all of these charges manually into an expense program...not any more.

Mike uses a corporate American Express card for these purchases. When he opens the expense report, it automatically connects to American Express and presents a list of new charges. Mike selects the charges that are appropriate for this expense report.

American Express sends this data to Mike's computer, which automatically formats the data into his expense report. Mike then clicks the send button and the expense report is sent to his manager to approve. Then the company's bank instantly wires the money to Mike's bank account.

Behind the scenes, all these companies are establishing connections, as needed, to share information in a secure and reliable manner using XML and the Internet. But Mike doesn't concern himself with what goes on behind the scenes; he's off to close another big deal in Washington.

EDI was initially implemented to improve efficiency by enabling companies to eliminate costly and slow manual methodologies, like the processing of purchase orders and bills. It was thought that by allowing the computers of two or more companies to share this information, they could achieve dramatic improvements in efficiency.

However, the largest savings are derived from a complete shift to EDI that allows companies to completely eliminate their hard copy processes. The traditional 80/20 rule applies in reverse to EDI, meaning that it is the last 20% of your trading partners to convert to EDI who account for 80% of the potential savings.

This is because even with 80% of your trading partners using EDI, you must still maintain the same manual processes for the remaining 20% who don't. While most companies have not been able to completely convert from hard copy processes to EDI, the 20% savings companies have realized have still been very significant. With integrated e-commerce enabling companies to completely eliminate their manual processes, the savings will improve dramatically.

With EDI, companies are also able to manage their supply chains much more efficiently. Through EDI, companies have been able to reduce the average time from issuance of an order to receipt of goods from several weeks, to a matter of days. By improving inventory control, companies are able to minimize their investment in costly inventory, while still being able to address spikes in business. For industries where inventory costs are a significant part of their business, like manufacturing, this represents a significant cost savings.

EDI also reduces the financial float by eliminating the typical order generation, delivery and processing, by 5-7 days. By combining EDI with Electronic Funds Transfer (EFT) companies can also reduce the financial float by 8-10+ days. Based on the amount of money involved, this can represent a significant savings.

EDI also provides companies with superior real-time information upon which to base decisions. Everyone recalls stories of companies who simply didn't have the data to realize how bad things were, until it was too late. With EDI, companies have access to complete data in real-time. The ability to collect, manipulate and measure information about your relationships with vendors and customers can be critical to your company's success.

Customer responsiveness is becoming increasingly important. Many companies have leveraged technology to dramatically improve customer responsiveness. A good example of this is Federal Express, who pioneered the concept of a website where customers can track the status of their packages.

The site is possible only because of FedEx's end-to-end dedication to EDI. By capturing information about the package status at each step in the process, and making this information accessible to customers, they have made themselves leaders in customer support. This is critical to building and growing businesses, especially in the Internet age.

Some companies who have implemented EDI with one customer, have gone on to market this capability to other potential customers, as a unique selling point. This has enabled them to grow their business. As IEC becomes more ubiquitous, the tide could even shift to the point where companies will not accept vendors who are not IEC-capable. That is because of the dramatic savings that vendors can achieve by a complete conversion to EDI.

12.3 | Traditional EDI: Built on outdated principles

EDI is a process for exchanging data in electronic format between heterogeneous applications and/or platforms in a manner that can be processed without manual intervention.

12.3.1 *The history of EDI*

EDI dates back to the 1970s, when it was introduced by the Transportation Data Coordinating Committee (TDCC). The TDCC created transaction sets for vendors to follow in order to enable electronic processing of purchase orders and bills.

At the time, the technology landscape was very different from what it is today. Lacking ubiquitous powerful CPUs, a common transport, and a file format that allows for flexibility, they defined strict transaction sets. These transaction sets addressed the needs for data content, structure and the process for handling the data. In other words, the business rules were embedded into the transaction set.

The incorporation of business rules into the definition of the transaction set causes many problems, because:

1. Business rules vary from company to company;
2. Business rules for one size company may be completely inappropriate for companies of another size;
3. Business rules are subject to change over time according to changes in market dynamics.

In short, the use of fixed and rigid transaction sets, while necessary at the time, have limited the value of EDI, and therefore stunted its growth.

12.3.2 *EDI technology basics*

Traditional EDI transaction sets are defined by standards bodies such as the United Nations Standard Messages Directory for Electronic Data Interchange for Administration, Commerce and Transport (*EDIFACT*), and the

American National Standards Institute's (ANSI) Accredited Standards Committee X12 sub-group.

Transaction sets define the fields, the order of these fields, and the length of the fields. Along with these transaction sets are business rules, which in the lexicon of the EDI folks are referred to as "implementation guidelines".

To actually implement EDI, the trading partners would follow these steps:

1. Trading partners enter into an agreement, called a trading arrangement.
2. They select a Value Added Network (VAN).
3. The trading partners typically either contract for, or build themselves, custom software that maps between the two data set formats used by these trading partners.
4. Each time a new trading partner is added, new software would have to be written to translate the sender's data set for the recipient. In other words, you start from scratch with each new trading partner.

Transaction sets are typically transmitted over expensive proprietary networks, which generally base charges on a mixture of fixed fees and message lengths. These fees can become quite substantial, but they are typically overshadowed by the cost to build and maintain the translation software. The VANs provide value-added services such as:

1. Data validation (compliance) and conversion
2. Logging for audit trails
3. Customer support
4. A secure and stable network
5. Accountability
6. Transaction roll-back to support uncommitted transactions

It is important to note that EDI is not simply the exportation of data from one system to another, but a bidirectional mechanism for interaction between systems. Because these disparate systems typically employ different file formats (data notations), schemas, data exchange protocols, etc., the process of exchanging data is very difficult.

12.3.3 *The problems of traditional EDI*

Traditional EDI suffers from many problems that have limited its growth. One of the most significant problems is the fact that it is based on the transfer of fixed transaction sets. This rigidity makes it extremely difficult to deal with the normal evolution necessary for companies to introduce new products and services, or evolve or replace their computer systems.

In addition, these transaction sets include strict processes for handling the data. These processes are not universally acceptable to companies in various industries and of various sizes. This problem is compounded by a standardization process that is too slow to accommodate the accelerating pace of business today.

In addition, the high fixed costs of implementation have been too much to justify for SMEs. In short, there are a host of problems which, despite the benefits of EDI, have prevented its universal adoption.

12.3.3.1 Fixed transaction sets

EDI is currently built on transaction sets that are fixed in nature. For example, a contact field might include the individual's name, title, company, company address and phone number. However, the company does not have the flexibility to add or subtract fields.

Why is this important?

Companies cannot be frozen in time by a fixed transaction set. This prevents them from evolving by adding new services or products, changing their computer systems and improving business processes. This inflexibility inherent in the current custom solutions required to map data between each trading partner pair is untenable, despite the significant benefits of EDI (Example 12-2).

12.3.3.2 Slow standards evolution

EDI standards are defined by standards bodies that are structurally ill-equipped to keep up with the rapid pace of change in the various business environments they impact, as illustrated by Example 12-2.

These standards accommodate many companies with very different needs. They also encompass not just the ontology, but the associated busi-

Example 12-2. Problems of traditional EDI: Healthcare

The transaction sets created for the healthcare system were defined for the traditional indemnity model, where the insurance company pays the doctor on a per visit basis. However, the movement toward managed care was not foreseen in this transaction set. Since managed care pays the doctor a set fee per patient, but does not reimburse on a per visit basis, the standard transaction set simply doesn't work.

The typical doctor sees a mixture of patients, some having managed care insurance and others with indemnity insurance. In order to accommodate this scenario, the doctor is forced to create a false "per visit" fee for managed care patients. This false fee, which is required in order to "complete" the transaction set, creates havoc with the doctor's other billing systems, which EDI was supposed to help.

Rigid transaction sets that enforce process as well as content are simply not flexible enough to address the ever-changing business environment.

---

ness processes. As a result, it is very slow and difficult, if not impossible, to develop one-size-fits-all solutions.

The current process for defining standards for transaction sets can take years. This simply will not work in today's business environment, which is characterized by accelerated change and increased competition. However, in an effort to jump-start the creation of industry ontologies in the form of DTDs for XML, the work of the traditional EDI standards bodies could be enormously valuable.

Historically, technology standards that are defined and managed in a top-down fashion, like EDI standards, have been replaced by bottom-up standards that allow for independent and distributed development. In other words, technologies like XML, that support greater flexibility and diversity, while providing compatibility between implementations, typically replace inflexible managed solutions like fixed transaction sets.

12.3.3.3   Non-standard standards

Despite the perception of standardization, there remains some flexibility in the interpretation of traditional EDI standards. The simple fact of the matter is that companies have unique needs, and these needs must be translated into the information they share with their trading partners.

In practical terms, the customer is at a significant economic advantage in defining these "standards", vis-a-vis the supplier. As a result, suppliers are forced to implement one-off solutions for each trading partner. In many of the industries where EDI is more prevalent, the suppliers also tend to be the smaller of the two partners, which makes the financial proposition even worse (see 12.3.3.4, "High fixed costs", on page 183).

Because of the various informational needs of companies, it is impractical to expect that EDI standards can be a one-size-fits-all proposition. The variables of company size, focus, industry, systems, etc. will continue to create needs that are unique to each company. As evidence, consider the amounts companies spend on custom development and customization of packaged applications.

12.3.3.4   High fixed costs

While large companies tout the financial and operational benefits of EDI, these same benefits have eluded the SMEs. That is because of the high fixed costs of implementation, which must be balanced against savings that are variable.

Depending on the level of automation, implementing EDI for a large enterprise is not substantially more expensive than it is for SMEs. In fact, it can be more expensive for the SMEs. Larger companies can often implement a single EDI standard, while the SMEs must accommodate the various standards of their larger partners. This can be very expensive.

Yet, ironically, the benefits are variable. So, if savings are 2% of processing costs, this might not be a substantial number for the manufacturer of car seat springs, but it can be a huge number for GM, Ford or Chrysler. SMEs simply do not have the scale to compensate for the high fixed costs of traditional EDI.

Because of this some of the SMEs that claim to implement EDI are actually printing a hard copy of the data feeds and re-typing them in their systems. The reason they implemented this faux-EDI is to meet customer requirements, because they simply do not have the transactional scale to justify the investment in traditional EDI. Something had to be done to bring down those costs (Example 12-3).

Example 12-3. Problems of traditional EDI: Retail

One large retailer requires its vendors to implement EDI in order to qualify as a vendor. However, like all traditional EDI implementations, the data set is unique to the retailer.

For small companies, implementing this system can be quite an investment. Retail is a very fast-paced industry, because it is forced to cater to ever-changing customer demands. As a result, some suppliers to this retailer have implemented this costly technology, only to later lose their contract with the retailer. In fact, because of the significant investment in technology these companies were forced to make, they have sued the retailer.

If this technology were universally applicable, the vendor's investment in a single customer would be eliminated, as would the retailer's legal liability.

12.3.3.5   Fixed business rules

Business rules are encapsulated in the definition of the transaction sets as implementation guidelines. However, business rules are not something that can be legislated, nor can they be rigid.

Business rules that are applicable for a large enterprise, may be completely inappropriate for an SME. To make matters worse, business rules for a medium-sized enterprise may be wholly inappropriate for a small enterprise.

These business rules will also vary between industries. Even companies of the same size that are in the same industry will implement different business rules. What's more, business rules change over time. The earlier healthcare example demonstrates this point.

Traditional EDI focuses too much on process as an integral part of the transaction set. This is a fatal flaw. New technologies, like XML, support the separation of process, or business rules, from the content and structure of the data. Achieving this separation is critical to widespread adoption of EDI.

The linkage between transaction sets and business rules creates additional problems. The real-life implementation of EDI typically requires custom solutions for each trading partner pair. This creates havoc when trying to implement or modify global business rules.

For example, if your company changed business policy to begin accepting purchase orders, which you had refused to accommodate in the past, you would have to manually change the individual software for each trading partner. You could not make these changes on a global basis using traditional EDI.

This problem also impacts your ability to upgrade or replace your internal systems, since they are uniquely woven into the EDI software in place. In essence, you can become locked into systems that may become obsolete by the time you actually implement the total solution.

12.3.3.6   Limited penetration

EDI penetration has been very limited, when compared to the penetration rates of other automation technologies. Yet the majority of the value of EDI is derived by complete elimination of the hard-copy processes EDI is meant to replace.

As mentioned above, EDI benefits do not follow the 80/20 rule, because converting the first 80% of your vendors to EDI results in only 20% of the potential cost savings. The remaining 80% of the costs remain, since the company is forced to maintain all of the old manual process in tandem with the electronic processes. The most significant savings come only from completely replacing all manual processes with EDI.

The real value of any network is in its adoption by users. Remember Metcalfe's Law: The value of any network is roughly proportional to the number of users squared.

But EDI, in its current state, is *not* a single interlinked network. On the contrary it is a series of one-to-one chains of data flow. As a result, it is vulnerable to alternative "networked" solutions like those enabled by XML, the Internet, Internet-based services, and database connectivity.

12.4 | Leveraging XML and the Internet

Now that we've established the tremendous benefits of EDI, and the structural problems of traditional EDI, the obvious question is: "How can we fix the problems?"

Fortunately, new technologies are coming together to completely reshape the EDI landscape. Today, EDI is currently implemented in a 1-to-1 manner between trading partners. These partnerships can then be extended through tiers to create a supply chain.

This is all changing!

The new paradigm is the *supply web*. The supply web is based on utilization of XML, the Internet, Internet-based services and database connectivity to create a network, or "web", of trading partners.

Implementation and operational costs are plummeting, trading partners are able to implement one-size-fits-all solutions, and adoption is skyrocketing. And the benefits will not be limited to the trading partners, they will be driven down to end-users as well. EDI will become as commonplace as email.

In short, EDI will dramatically alter the business computing landscape, moving the world forward from our current islands of automation toward a single fabric of commerce tying together businesses and end-users.

Traditional EDI is based on the technologies that existed in the 1970s. Now it is time to build a new EDI architecture on current technologies like XML, the Internet, Internet-based services and database connectivity.

- XML provides the ability to separate the data and structure from the processes.
- The Internet provides the ubiquitous connectivity upon which a Web of interconnected trading partners can flourish.
- Internet technologies provide a layer of security, authentication, transactional support and more, to support the needs of EDI.
- Database connectivity means that XML data, and the business rules that interact with that data, can be communicated among disparate systems by means of middle-tier data filters and aggregators.

Together, these technologies are removing the barriers that prevented widespread adoption of EDI. By leveraging these technologies, EDI functionality is becoming more flexible, more powerful, and less expensive – and integrated e-commerce will ultimately become ubiquitous.

12.4.1 *XML*

XML is closely related to HyperText Markup Language (HTML), the original document representation of the World Wide Web, as both are based on SGML. While HTML enables the creation of Web pages that can be viewed on any browser, XML adds tags to data so that it can be processed by any application. These tags describe, in a standardized syntax, what the data is, so that the applications can understand its meaning and how to process it (Example 12-4).

For example, in HTML a product name and a price might be somewhere in the text. But the computer only knows that there is a collection of characters and numbers. It cannot discern that this data represents a product name and price. As a result, little can be done with the data.

With XML, however, the product name is tagged (e.g. `product_name`), as is the product price (e.g. `product_price`). More importantly, there is an association between the product price and the product name.

This information results in significant additional value. For example, a user can now search for the best price on a specific product.

Example 12-4. XML insulates applications from diversity: Customer record

The following example demonstrates one of the values of XML. Below are three different types of message documents from three different companies (A,B and C). Each describes its respective company's customer data:

Company A:
```
<Person name="Mike Hogan" phone="6502864640"
        email="mph@poet.com" />
```
Company B:
```
<Person name="Mike Hogan" street address="999 Baker Way"
        city="San Mateo" zip="94404" phone="6502864640"/>
```
Company C:
```
<Person name="Mike Hogan" phone="6502864640"/>
```

The XML parser parses, or disassembles, the messages to show the "person" element, which has associated attributes ("name", "phone", etc.). These attributes, as you can see, differ in content and organization.

However, if your application was written to extract a person's name and phone number, it could work equally well with each of these document types without modification. In fact, if these companies evolve their data to include additional information, your application continues to function without modification. This flexibility is one of the benefits of XML.

XML documents must be "well-formed", which means that most document-type information – grammar and hierarchy – can be embedded in the tags that "mark up" the individual document. There can also be an associated *document type definition* (DTD), containing additional meta-information that describes the data.

In either case, XML is self-describing. As a result, applications can be very flexible in their ability to receive, parse and process very diverse sets of information. This enables companies to write a single application that will work with diverse sets of customers. In fact, such a system is even capable of processing information from new trading partners in an ad hoc fashion. This capability completely changes the dynamics of EDI.

Using XML, companies can separate the business rules from the content and structure of the data. By focusing on exchanging data content and structure, the trading partners are free to implement their own business rules, which can be quite distinct from one another. Yet, using templates, companies can work with legacy EDI, non-XML datatypes as well (as we will see in Chapter 13, "XML and EDI: Working together", on page 194).

12.4.2 *The Internet*

Many companies heralded the cost savings and ubiquity of the Internet as the death knell for VANs. However, this future has not come to pass...yet.

The boldest of these claims was based on the notion that the extranet would redefine the new computing paradigm. What these pundits failed to realize was that the Internet alone does not address the needs of the EDI community.

The EDI community is generally limited to the largest enterprises. EDI is mission critical, and requires a dependable network. It also requires a level of security that couldn't be found on the Internet. To put it simply, the savings were not sufficient to justify the switch.

Furthermore, connectivity is only a small part of the problem, the largest issue is the exchange of data in a universal fashion.

All these issues have now been addressed.

- Technology is now available to provide dial-up services to support the Internet in addressing up-time and throughput for mission critical information.
- Security has improved dramatically.

- The use of XML has broadened the EDI customer base to include SMEs and individuals. This new group of customers is much more price-sensitive, so they are inclined to seek an Internet-based solution.
- The ability to exchange data in a more democratic and ad hoc manner is causing an explosion in the average number of EDI connections.

The average number of traditional EDI trading partners, for those companies who utilize EDI at all, is *two*. Building EDI solutions based on XML, and operating this over the Internet, which offers a low-cost ubiquitous transport, is dramatically expanding the value of EDI, according to Metcalfe's Law.

12.4.3 *Internet technologies*

Internet technologies have improved, and continue to improve dramatically, now providing a critical mass of technologies that is capable of replacing the services of VANs. Consider the following list of VAN services, each followed by the Internet-based alternatives that offer greater functionality and flexibility:

Data validation and conversion
XML DTDs, XML validation, templates, and structure-based data feed interpretation.

Intermediary-based logging for audit trails
XML-savvy repositories employed by all trading partners enables rich logging for audit trails. Combining these with electronic signatures ensures system and company identification.

Consulting, customer service and customer support
This function could be handled by VANs capable of making the transition to Internet technologies, or by the other legions of consultants.

Security and accountability

Public key cryptography, certificate authorities, digital signatures can assure secure transactions.

Connection reliability, stability

New technologies in bandwidth allocation, general improvement in the stability of the Internet and alternative fail-over solutions like dial-up continue to move the Internet toward supporting critical real-time data flow. (Remember, it was originally designed to withstand nuclear attack!)

Trading partner negotiation

Directories (X.500, LDAP, NDS, Active Directory), certificate authorities, digital signatures, email, Internet versions of the Better Business Bureau, etc., can support this function.

Transactional support (roll-back, etc.)

The improvements in remote messaging systems and transaction processing monitors provide a layer of transaction support that is capable of adding transactional integrity even on unstable networks.

12.4.4 *XML data storage*

In other technological transitions, data storage has been a moot point, since the data could be mapped more-or-less directly into relational tables or file systems. More recently, object-oriented database management systems became available for this purpose.

XML data, however, is composed of self-describing information elements that are richly linked, and that utilize a hierarchical structure and naming mechanism. These qualities enable new data-access capabilities based on the tree structure, such as context-sensitive queries, navigation, and traversal.

"Native" XML-based support for these new capabilities can be provided by a value-added content management layer above the DBMS, and by native-format "document-centric" databases.

12.4.5 *Data filtering*

The source of the vast majority of EDI-related information is currently in mainframes and relational databases. This data will be marked-up on the fly with XML tags. XML data will also come from data sources such as:

- XML content management systems
- Various Internet resources
- EDI-XML documents, both full documents like purchase orders and short inter-process messages
- Result sets from applications, also in XML

These diverse sources must be communicated with by a middle-tier "data filter" that can speak to each source in a manner that the source will recognize. The data must then be filtered in source-dependent ways, based on one's confidence in the data, application of consistent business logic, resolution of the various element-type name ontologies, response mechanisms, security, caching for performance, etc. Only then can the application address the data in a consistent manner and receive consistent responses from the middle tier, as shown in Figure 12-1.

The middle tier could maintain valuable meta-information that would add structure and context to the data stream. Such information could include:

- Routing for the query, response, etc.
- Source of the information (to indicate credibility, etc.)
- Time stamps
- Data, DTD, and tag normalization
- Context and navigation aids

Further details on XML content management and the use of storage systems in the management of XML data can be found in Part [no number], "Content Management".

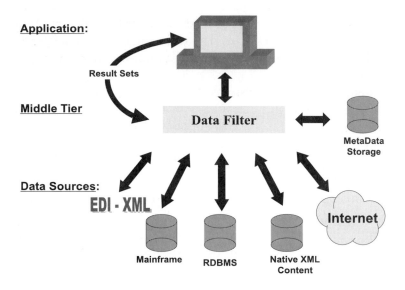

Figure 12-1   Data filter in an XML-based EDI system

12.5 | Conclusion

After decades of investment in corporate data centers, we have created islands of automation inside companies. Their isolation from trading partners limits the value companies can recognize from these systems.

EDI offers the ability to change all of this. EDI offers benefits like:

- improved efficiency
- supply chain management
- real-time data and metrics
- better planning
- superior execution
- control systems
- resource management
- cost savings
- superior access to information for decision making
- customer responsiveness

However, traditional EDI is very difficult and expensive to implement. Because of problems like rigid transaction sets that embed business rules, slow standards development, high fixed costs, and limited market penetration, EDI has not achieved broad adoption. Fortunately, XML-based technology is now available to address these problems and, in the process, reshape the use of EDI.

XML, the Internet, Internet-based services and database connectivity are combining to complement EDI and enhance commerce, in the form of integrated e-commerce. Instead of forcing companies to adapt their systems and business processes to the EDI data, this data can now adapt dynamically to the companies' existing systems.

Where traditional EDI was isolated to certain industries and to the largest enterprises, integrated e-commerce will become as ubiquitous as email. Trading communities have evolved from EDI's one-to-one supply chain to IEC's richly interconnected web of trading partners forming the supply web.

This supply web is resulting in dramatic improvements in efficiency. Companies are slashing costs, while improving access to critical information. This information will be pushed all the way to the end-user, providing superior customer support as well.

XML and EDI: Working together

Introductory Discussion

▌ Approaches to e-commerce

▌ Traditional-EDI and XML e-commerce compared

▌ Leverage existing EDI with XML

Sponsor: XMLSolutions Corporation, http://www.xmls.com

Contributing experts: Jeffrey Ricker and Drew Munro

Chapter

13

Large companies have invested millions in their existing successful EDI systems. XML can enhance that investment by extending them to a Webful of EDI-less trading partners. This chapter explains how traditional EDI and XML can work together.

In a few short years, the Internet has changed the fundamental rules for conducting business.

Now consider EDI: Large companies have been using it with their major trading partners for nearly 20 years. But, as we have seen, traditional EDI commerce has proven itself to be too complicated and expensive for most small and many midsize companies. As a result, EDI has never been adopted widely enough to cause any such fundamental change.

Now, however, there is an e-commerce that all companies can afford. The Internet and XML have lowered the barriers to e-commerce, in both cost and complexity. But they are not replacing EDI, they are extending it to bring e-commerce to small and midsize companies. XML complements EDI and, in so doing, finally turns the vision of EDI into the reality of integrated e-commerce.

13.1 | What is integrated e-commerce?

In traditional commerce, each customer and vendor may be automated internally, but they are individually isolated. They traverse the gulf between their systems by manual processes such as mail, email, fax, meetings and phone calls. This *manual gulf* between "islands of automation" is illustrated in Figure 13-1.

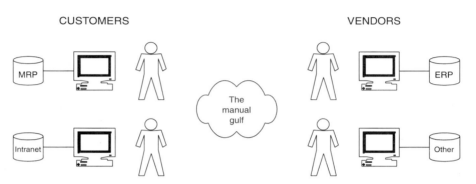

Figure 13-1   A manual gulf separates trading partners in traditional commerce

The objective of *integrated e-commerce (IEC)* is to bridge that manual gulf; that is, to eliminate manual trade processes by allowing the internal applications of different companies to exchange information directly.

Not all e-commerce is integrated e-commerce, but a lot of it is. At present, there are three major approaches, which vary in the extent to which they fully realize this goal.

13.1.1 *Web storefronts*

Web storefronts provide a Web interface to a vendor's catalog of products or services, as illustrated in Figure 13-2. Customers can place orders directly into a vendor's internal system through a Web storefront. Famous examples include Amazon.com and Dell Computer.

Web storefronts have proven immensely popular with customers, and they clearly can achieve economic and other objectives for vendors. How-

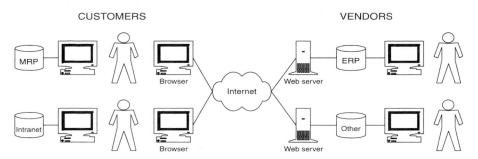

Figure 13-2   Web storefronts automate only one side of trading

ever, in terms of achieving the full potential of integrated e-commerce, they are unilateral.

Nothing is automated on the customer's side. He must go to each website separately and manually search through the catalogs. He must also enter orders manually through a Web form and simultaneously update his internal ERP system or intranet application.

For a large manufacturer with 40,000 suppliers, Web storefronts are not much of an improvement over printed catalogs and telephones.

13.1.2 *E-commerce portals*

Some companies have proposed *e-commerce portals* to automate both vendors and customers. With e-commerce portals, customers go to only one website – the portal website – to view vendor catalogs and place orders. Vendors go to the same portal to view and respond to orders (see Figure 13-3).

E-commerce portals bridge the manual gap better than Web storefronts, and can offer the convenience and quick ramp-up of an outsourced solution. However, there are tradeoffs to be considered in this approach:

- Both vendors and customers must update their ERP systems from the portal. Can this task be automated?
- A company's e-commerce data resides outside that company on the portal website. Is the security risk acceptable?
- E-commerce portals may charge a subscription fee and may also charge for every transaction. In essence, they are charging

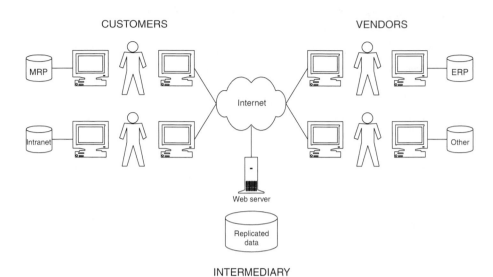

CUSTOMERS   VENDORS

Internet

Web server

Replicated
data

INTERMEDIARY

Figure 13-3   E-commerce portals rely on an intermediary

companies to access their own information. Would another approach be more cost-effective?

Caution   *E-commerce portals should not be confused with the popular types of information portal that are discussed in Part [no number], "Portals"; they are a type of application service provider (ASP) (see Chapter 14, "Collaboration in an e-commerce supply web", on page 208).*

13.1.3 *Integrated e-commerce*

EDI was the first attempt at integrated e-commerce. Although its users reap great benefits from it, there are only about 300,000 of them worldwide. The reasons for this were explored in Chapter 12, "From EDI to IEC: The new Web commerce", on page 172.

The basic premise of EDI, however, is right on track. EDI eliminates manual processes by allowing the internal applications of different companies to exchange information directly.

Today, thanks to XML, companies such as XMLSolutions Corporation can offer business-to-business e-commerce systems that accomplish the original goal of allowing the internal applications of trading partners to share information directly, as illustrated in Figure 13-4.

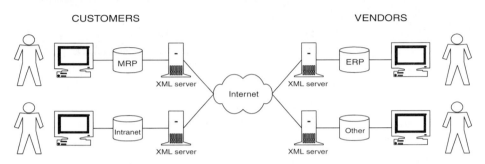

Figure 13-4 XML-based integrated e-commerce bridges the manual gulf

Intranets are ubiquitous today. Most, if not all, ERP systems have Web-based interfaces, which makes them intranets. Midsize and small companies that do not have ERP systems also have intranets. With XML-based EDI, any company can view its trading partners through its own corporate intranet, rather than through its hundreds of suppliers' individual websites or a third-party website.

The financial services industry has been a leader in bringing the benefits of integrated e-commerce to individuals. Its offerings reflect the approaches to e-commerce we have discussed here. When you go to your broker's website to execute trades and examine your statement, you are using a Web storefront. But when your broker sends the information to *Quicken* and you execute trades from your ledger, that's integrated e-commerce.[1]

---

1. We use the term "integrated e-commerce" in preference to "business-to-business (B2B)" e-commerce because not all B2B e-commerce is integrated into internal applications. Also, as seen in this example, integrated e-commerce isn't limited to businesses.

13.2 | Traditional EDI and XML compared

The stark differences between traditional EDI e-commerce and XML e-commerce stem from the basic characteristics of the two technologies, as compared in Table 13-1.

The creators of EDI were very concerned about size of their messages. Bandwidth for EDI networks is very expensive even today. EDI messages are therefore very compressed and use codes to represent complex values. For the same reason, all the metadata is stripped from the messages, which makes them very hard to read and debug.

The complexity of EDI makes EDI programmers hard to train and expensive to keep, which in turn makes EDI applications expensive to buy and maintain. Complexity drives cost.

Table 13-1   EDI and XML e-commerce solutions compared

Traditional EDI	XML e-commerce
Optimized for compressed messages	Optimized for easy programming
Requires dedicated EDI server costing $10,000 to $100,000	Requires Web server costing $0 to $5000
Uses value-added network (VAN) charging $1 to $20 per message or more	Uses your existing Internet connection
EDI message format takes months to master	XML message format learned in hours
Requires costly program development	Requires only scripts and stylesheets

13.2.1 *Message formats*

Example 13-1 and Example 13-2 provide a comparison between traditional EDI and XML. To demonstrate the difference to yourself, try to find the purchase order number in each document.

Example 13-1. Sample EDI purchase order

```
ISA*00*      *00*  *08*61112500TST      *01*DEMO WU000003
*970911*1039*U00302000009561*0*P?
GS*PO*6111250011*WU000003 *970911*1039*9784*X*003020
ST*850*397822
BEG*00*RE*194743**970911
REF*AH*M109
REF*DP*641
REF*IA*000100685
DTM*010*970918
N1*BY*92*1287
N1*ST*92*87447
N1*ZZ*992*1287
PO1*1*1*EA*13.33**CB*80211*IZ*364*UP*718379271641
PO1*1*2*EA*13.33**CB*80211*IZ*382*UP*718379271573
PO1*1*3*EA*13.33**CB*80213*IZ*320*UP*718379271497
PO1*1*4*EA*13.33**CB*80215*IZ*360*UP*718379271848
PO1*1*5*EA*13.33**CB*80215*IZ*364*UP*718379271005
CTT*25
SE*36*397822
GE*1*9784
IEA*1*000009561
```

13.2.2 *The different flavors of XML and EDI*

EDI comes in two distinct flavors, X12 and EDIFACT. X12 is the American standard that evolved over the years from the most basic attempts at exchange in the 1960s to full-blown billion-dollar networks. EDIFACT is the international standard, endorsed by the United Nations and designed from the ground up beginning in 1985. Both flavors have several version releases of their message formats. Compatibility between versions is not always straightforward.

XML e-commerce is currently even more diversified, with proposed standards that use XML only and others that are XML-EDI hybrids. Some of the most important are listed here.

Example 13-2. Sample XML purchase order

```
<?xml version="1.0" ?>
<?xml:stylesheet?>
<purchase-order>
<header>
   <po-number>1234</po-number>
   <date>1999-02-08</date><time>14:05</time>
   </header>
<billing>
   <company>XMLSolutions</company>
   <address>
      <street>601 Pennsylvania Ave. NW</street>
      <street>Suite 900</street>
      <city>Washington</city>
      <st>DC</st><postcode>20004</postcode>
      </address>
   </billing>
<order items="1" >
   <item>
      <reference>097251</reference>
      <description>Widgets</description>
      <quantity>4</quantity>
      <unit-price>11.99</unit-price>
      <price>47.96</price>
      </item>
   <tax type="sales" >
      <tax-unit>VA</tax-unit>
      <calculation>0.045</calculation>
      <amount>2.16</amount>
      </tax>
   ...
```

- CommerceNet, a business consortium, is developing eCo.
- RosettaNet, another consortium, is working on XML standards for product catalogs.
- CommerceOne has created the common business library (CBL), in part funded by a government grant from the US National Institute for Standards and Technology (NIST).
- OASIS and UN/CEFACT are building industry consensus for a technical framework called *ebXML* that will enable consistent use of XML for the exchange of business data.
- Ariba has rallied several companies around commerce XML (cXML), a proposed standard for catalogs and purchase orders.
- Microsoft has loosely grouped many of these technologies under what it calls *BizTalk*.

- The XML-EDI Group has proposed a naming convention for representing EDI messages in XML. Essentially, they have built-on and preserved the hard-won consensus for the X12 taxonomy by using X12 names in XML tags.
- Still other groups, such as the Open Buying Initiative (OBI), are proposing standards for simply moving EDI X12 messages over HTTP.

13.3 | An XML-EDI trading system

Traditional EDI works. You can rely on it. There is no greater accolade for a technology. Large companies have spent millions on their EDI systems, which are mission-critical and unlikely to be abandoned. The objective now should be to leverage this sound base and extend it to more trading partners.

Simply sending EDI X12 or EDIFACT messages over HTTP – the Web transport protocol – won't do the job. Although EDI's transport system is primitive, it is not EDI's governing limitation.

The expense of EDI is rooted in its complexity, and its complexity is based in its compressed, cryptic message formats. XML can overcome this complexity by storing the metadata within the text of the message. And XML also happens to be designed for HTTP.

Traditional EDI users can extend their electronic trading base by installing XML-EDI translators on their Web servers, as shown in Figure 13-5. The translation must go both ways: XML to EDI for messages starting from the small company and EDI to XML for messages starting from the large company traditional EDI user.

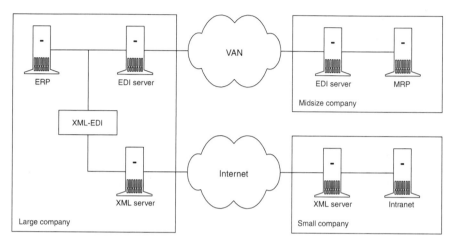

Figure 13-5   An XML-EDI trading system

13.3.1   *XML to EDI*

XML-EDI translators are already available, many relying on proprietary technology and unique scripting languages. Others, including XMLSolutions' *XEDI Translator* use XSL to specify the transformation, as shown in Figure 13-6.

Although XSL is most commonly used to transform XML into HTML for presentation, it is perfectly well-suited to transform XML into any representation, including EDI. And as it is an open standard, it is likely to benefit from the availability of free and open-source implementations and a large body of skilled developers.

13.3.2   *EDI to XML*

XSL cannot be used directly for the inverse conversion, as it can only transform from XML. The problem is well-known from the long experience in SGML and XML systems of having to convert word processing documents to generalized markup. The solution is also well-known: an intermediate

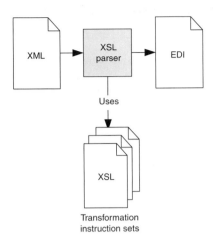

Figure 13-6   XSL is well-suited for transforming XML into EDI

trivial translation from the foreign notation to the markup language. A translation, in other words, that changes only the representation of the document, not the meaning. Then XSL can be applied to accomplish more powerful transforms.

This technique is illustrated in Figure 13-7, which shows an EDI parser as the intermediate translator. The EDI parser has an application programming interface (API) very similar to the XSL parser (and the XML parser for that matter). The EDI parser makes an XML message out of the EDI message by replacing EDI codes with their full names and making XML elements out of the EDI segments and elements. This process follows the XML-EDI Group's concept of preserving the X12 taxonomy when translating to XML.

Once the EDI message is a well-formed XML document, XSL can transform it into various XML-EDI message standards, such as cXML, Rosetta-Net or BizTalk.

Because there are many kinds of XML and many kinds of EDI, an XML-EDI translator is not a one-to-one system but rather a many-to-many system. Such a translator can therefore also serve as an XML to XML translator and an EDI to EDI translator.

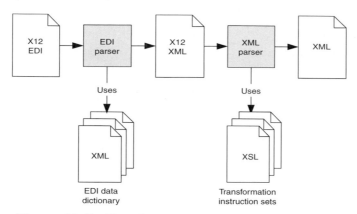

Figure 13-7   Transforming EDI to XML requires an intermediate step

13.4 | The future of e-commerce

The objective of integrated e-commerce is to eliminate manual processes by allowing the internal applications of different companies to exchange information directly. Stated more generically, *integrated e-commerce* is systems integration that crosses the boundary of the enterprise.

That definition encompasses more than just the automation of supply chain paperwork. It envisions a future framework that also automates business processes and workflow between trading partners, and that accommodates those few trading partners that might never automate as well.

XML and EDI working together is the first step toward that future.

Tip   A free copy of the ExeterXML Server from the XMLSolutions e-commerce suite is available on the CD-ROM.

Collaboration in an e-commerce supply web

Application Discussion

- Collaborative intensity and intimacy
- Multiple delivery protocols
- Purchasing scenario
- E-commerce portal ASP

Sponsor: IPNet Solutions, http://www.ipnet-solutions.com

Contributing expert: Jamie N. Graham

Chapter

14

The efficiency of an e-commerce supply web depends on the collaboration among the trading partners: How much they are willing to share, and how intimately they can share it. In this chapter we look at an e-commerce scenario in detail to see how collaboration works.

I n Chapter 13, "XML and EDI: Working together", on page 194, we saw a number of approaches to e-commerce: Web storefronts, e-commerce portals, and integrated e-commerce. Let's take a closer look at what these approaches really involve.

14.1 | It's all about collaboration!

Parties to an e-commerce transaction are *collaborators*, both in a business sense and in terms of how their computer systems relate to one another. The extent of collaboration can vary in both domains.

In the business context, the variation is in the *intensity* of the relationship. Do the parties merely expose and exchange information by electronic means, or do they collaborate even further by using their computers to automate the negotiation of transactions and relationships?

In the system implementation context, collaboration varies in the *intimacy* of the implementation. There are two kinds: loosely-coupled and tightly-coupled. Both are illustrated in Figure 14-1.

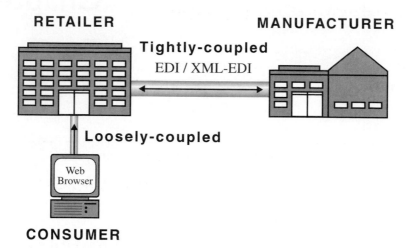

Figure 14-1   Loosely-coupled and tightly-coupled e-commerce

14.1.1 *Loosely-coupled collaboration*

The Web storefront is an example of loosely-coupled collaboration. It is based on browser-to-server information sharing.

Using XSL stylesheets, transactional information can be presented by Web browsers in familiar renditions, such as purchase orders and invoices. The same model applies to non-traditional presentation devices, such as personal digital assistants (PDAs) and cell phones.

The hallmark of a loosely-coupled collaboration is that at least one trading partner uses an interface that is not supplied by its own computer system.

14.1.2 *Tightly-coupled collaboration*

Integrated e-commerce and EDI are examples of tightly-coupled collaboration. It is based on server-to-server or server-to-PC information sharing. Using XML, trading partners can expose, exchange and negotiate dynamically in real-time based on predefined business rules.

The hallmark of a tightly-coupled collaboration is that each trading partner uses an interface supplied by his own system.

14.2 | Modes of e-commerce

We can now take a closer look at the three e-commerce approaches we have been discussing and analyze them in terms of their intensity and intimacy of collaboration. The results are shown in Table 14-1.

Table 14-1   Collaboration in e-commerce: intensity vs. intimacy

	Loosely-coupled	**Tightly-coupled**
Low intensity	Manual process	[Rare]
Medium intensity	Web storefront	E-commerce portal
High intensity	[Rare]	Integrated e-commerce

Note that, in principle at least, the intensity and the intimacy of a collaboration are independent of one another. Regardless of the intensity of the relationship, the implementation could be either loosely- or tightly-coupled. However, as the table indicates, just as in social relationships it is rare to find intimacy that does not correlate with intensity!

Table 14-1 also reveals why comparing our three approaches to e-commerce can be an apples-to-oranges exercise. The e-commerce portal differs from the Web storefront in the *intimacy* of the collaboration, while it differs from integrated e-commerce in the *intensity*.

Keep these considerations in mind as we examine a typical transaction.

14.3 | An e-commerce scenario

The scenario is a purchasing transaction. There are two parts: A retailer issues a purchase order to a manufacturer who later updates the status of the order. However, instead of a simple two-party supply chain, there is actually a three-party supply web, since the retailer uses a logistics company to track its orders.

The scenario is based on an actual system implemented by IPNet using components of its *eBizness Suite*. In order to minimize the implementation impact for the trading partners, a loosely-coupled solution was designed. The transactions were managed by an independent system that acted as an e-commerce portal ASP.

Let's look at the two transactions in detail, considering the roles of the Retailer, Logistics Co., E-commerce Portal ASP, and Manufacturer. They communicate by a variety of Internet protocols, including email, File Transfer Protocol (FTP), and the HyperText Transfer Protocol (HTTP) used by Web browsers.

14.3.1 *Part One: Originate purchase order*

In this part, Retailer sends a purchase order (P.O.) to Manufacturer, who acknowledges it. The information flow is illustrated in Figure 14-2.

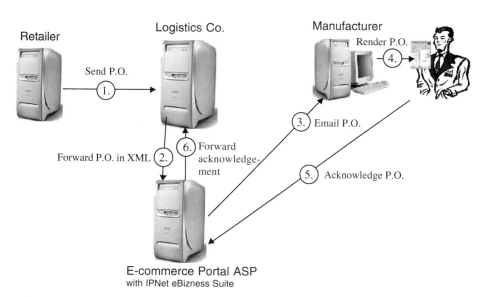

Figure 14-2   Originating a purchase order

1. Retailer sends a P.O. to Logistics Co. Their systems are tightly-coupled and the data format is proprietary.

2. Logistics Co. converts the P.O. to XML-EDI and sends the XML document, via FTP, to E-commerce Portal ASP. The first line item of the P.O. is shown in Example 14-1.

3. All of the functions of E-commerce Portal ASP are implemented by IPNet *eBizness Suite*. The software here links the XML-EDI P.O. to a stylesheet and sends it by email to Manufacturer.

4. Manufacturer's browser renders the P.O. in accordance with the stylesheet. The rendered P.O. is shown in Figure 14-3.

5. Manufacturer acknowledges the P.O. by clicking on a button in the browser rendition. The acknowledgment is transmitted back to E-commerce Portal ASP by HTTP.

6. The *eBizness Suite* software at E-commerce Portal ASP notifies Logistics Co. of the acknowledgment by email. As nothing is out of the ordinary, there is no need for Retailer to be notified.

Example 14-1. 1st line item of P.O. record in XML

```
<order-record-dtl Action="X">
<ItemID>0CF10</ItemID>
<ItemSubgroup Curve="N">
  <ItemSubgroupCode>BO</ItemSubgroupCode>
  <ItemSubgroupValue>00</ItemSubgroupValue>
</ItemSubgroup>
<ItemSubgroup Curve="Y">
  <ItemSubgroupCode>IZ</ItemSubgroupCode>
  <ItemSubgroupValue>000</ItemSubgroupValue>
</ItemSubgroup>
<Factory><FactoryCode>06009</FactoryCode></Factory>
<PlannedShipMode>
  <PlannedShipModeCode>J</PlannedShipModeCode>
</PlannedShipMode>
<OrderedQty1>100</OrderedQty1>
<OrderedUM1>EA</OrderedUM1>
<UnitPrice>7</UnitPrice>
<Currency><CurrencyCode>USD</CurrencyCode></Currency>
<TotalPrice>700</TotalPrice>
<Currency><CurrencyCode>USD</CurrencyCode></Currency>
</order-record-dtl>
```

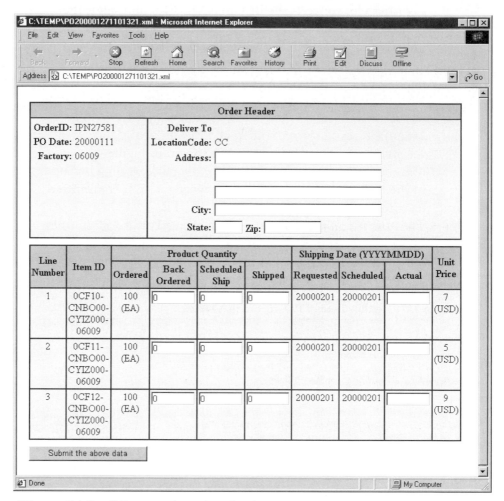

Figure 14-3 P.O. record rendered in browser

14.3.2 *Part Two: Update order status*

In this part, Manufacturer updates the P.O. status and notifies Retailer. The information flow is illustrated in Figure 14-4.

1. Manufacturer's browser renders a P.O. Status Notification in accordance with a stylesheet supplied by E-Commerce Portal ASP. The rendered form is shown in Figure 14-5.

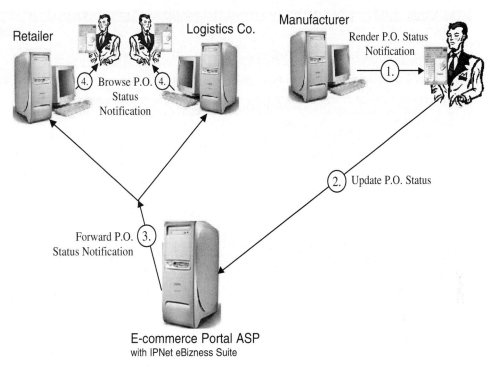

Figure 14-4   Updating P.O. status

2.   Manufacturer completes the form in the browser – quantity, shipping details, etc. – which sends it in XML-EDI to E-commerce Portal ASP via HTTP. The first line item of the P.O. Status Notification is shown in Example 14-2.

3.   The *eBizness Suite* software at E-commerce Portal ASP sends copies of the P.O. Status Notification to Retailer and Logistics Co. by email.

4.   Personnel at Retailer and Logistics Co. can view the rendered form in their browsers, as shown in Figure 14-5.

5.   (Not shown in diagram.) If the necessary tightly-coupled connections exist, E-commerce Portal ASP could automatically update the ERP systems of Retailer and/or Manufacturer via EDI or XML-EDI to reflect the change in P.O. status.

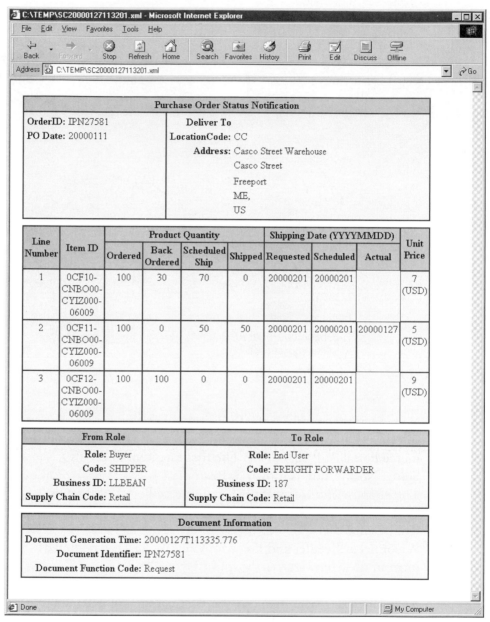

Figure 14-5   P.O. status notification rendered in browser

Example 14-2. P.O. status notification in XML

```
<ProductLineItem>
<shipDate><DateStamp/></shipDate>
<ProductQuantity>100</ProductQuantity>
<backOrderedQuantity>
  <ProductQuantity>30</ProductQuantity>
</backOrderedQuantity>
<scheduledShipQuantity>
  <ProductQuantity>70</ProductQuantity>
</scheduledShipQuantity>
<shippedQuantity>
  <ProductQuantity>0</ProductQuantity>
</shippedQuantity>
<LineNumber>1</LineNumber>
<productUnit><ProductPackageDescription><ProductDescription>
  <GlobalProductIdentifier>0CF10-CNBO00-CYIZ000-06009
  </GlobalProductIdentifier>
</ProductDescription></ProductPackageDescription></productUnit>
<countryOfOrigin>
  <GlobalCountryCode>US</GlobalCountryCode>
</countryOfOrigin>
<requestedShipDate>
  <DateStamp>20000201</DateStamp>
</requestedShipDate>
<unitPrice><FinancialAmount>
  <GlobalCurrencyCode>USD</GlobalCurrencyCode>
  <MonetaryAmount>7</MonetaryAmount>
</FinancialAmount></unitPrice>
<scheduledShipDate>
  <DateStamp>20000201</DateStamp>
</scheduledShipDate>
</ProductLineItem>
```

Lead tracking by Web and email

▌ Data collection with Web forms

▌ Integration of outsourced website with internal system

▌ Email for XML data transport

Sponsor: Infoteria Corporation, http://www.infoteria.com

Contributing experts: Todd Headrick

If your sales leads come from your outsourced website, and your sales tracking is done on your internal system, how do you integrate the two? XML, as we have seen, solves the data representation aspects of the problem. But how will the XML documents be transported from the outsourced system to yours? For one company there was an easy answer: You get mail!

S ince the dawn of computerized data processing, forms with pre-defined fields have been used for capturing information. Table 15-1 shows some of the more common forms used on intranets and Internet Web servers.

Table 15-1 Examples of internal and external forms

Internal Forms	External Forms
HR employee info change	Event registration
401K enrollment form	Trial software download
User survey	Customer support request
Office move request	Request for price quotation
Office supplies request	Purchase order

15.1 | The challenge

For Subject Software Company, the trial software download form is an important source of sales leads. Like many companies, Subject Software manages its own internal system for sales force automation, customer support, order entry, and other business-unit applications, as well as enterprise email. However, its website is operated by its Internet Service Provider (ISP) and is not connected to its internal system.

As a result, the sales leads from the trial software downloads had to be imported manually from the outsourced website. This was done on a weekly basis, using a *comma-separated values (CSV)* text file. Subject Software needed to integrate its website with its internal system, as shown in Figure 15-1.

The company was able to accomplish this goal using Infoteria Corporation's *XML Solution Components*. The new design is a message-oriented middleware solution. It uses XML documents and the Internet email infrastructure to move the sales lead information quickly from the website to the internal sales systems. Lead processing is now automatic, and occurs almost immediately after a person downloads trial software from the outsourced website.

Let's take a closer look at the new system.

15.2 | The solution

The architecture of the new system is illustrated in Figure 15-2. An XML document contains information collected at the outsourced website. It is transmitted to the internal *Notes/Domino* sales-tracking system using the Internet email infrastructure as the transport.

The process consists of three parts:

1. Create and send XML email
2. Receive and verify XML email
3. Process XML email and update database

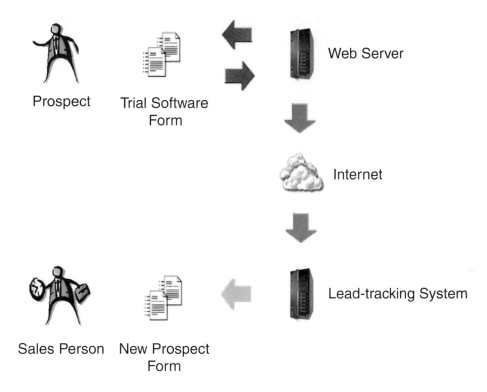

Internet Service Provider

Prospect   Trial Software
             Form

Web Server

Internet

Sales Person   New Prospect
               Form

Lead-tracking System

In-house System

Figure 15-1   Integrating sales leads generated at an outsourced website

15.2.1 *One: Create and send XML email*

When a user fills out a form to download a trial version of software from the outsourced website, a RegisterUser.CGI script is invoked. That script calls the Send_XML_Lead subroutine, an excerpt from which is shown in Example 15-1.

Send_XML_Lead creates a download XML document, like that shown in Example 15-2. It incorporates the document in an email message and calls the SendMail component of the Web server operating system to send the message to the lead-tracking inbox on the internal system's mail server.

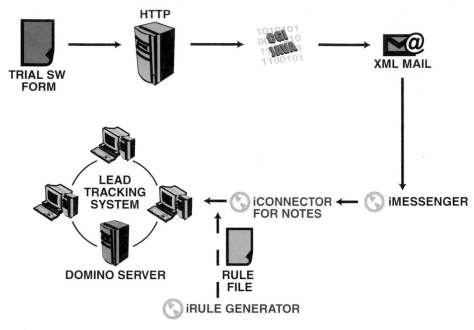

Figure 15-2   Lead-tracking system architecture

Example 15-1. Excerpt from Send_XML_Lead subroutine

```
sub send_xml_lead {
  if ($FORM{'email'} ne '') {
  open (LEAD, ">$leadtemp") || die "Can't open $leadtemp!\n";
  print LEAD "To: SalesLeads\@infoteria.com\n";
  print LEAD "From: Infoteria <website@infoteria.com>\n";
  print LEAD "Reply-To: website\@infoteria.com\n";
  print LEAD "Content-Transfer-Encoding: 7bit\n";
  print LEAD "Content-Type: text/plain\n";
  print LEAD "Subject: $fullname ($product $edition) \n\n";
  print LEAD "<\?xml version=\"1.0\" encoding=\"UTF-8\"?>\n";
  print LEAD "<Download>\n";
  print LEAD "<Person>\n";
  print LEAD "  <FirstName>$FORM{'fname'}</FirstName>\n";
  print LEAD "</Person> \n";
  ...
  print LEAD "</Download>\n";
  close (LEAD);
  system("$convprog -SJ $leadtemp|$mailprog -t");
  }
}
```

Example 15-2. XML document created by CGI Script in Example 15-1

```
<?xml version="1.0" encoding="UTF-8"?>
<Download>
<Person>
  <FirstName>Robert</FirstName>
  <LastName>Blacken</LastName>
  <FullName>Robert Blacken</FullName>
  <MailAddress>rblacken@infoteria.com</MailAddress>
  <JobTitle>CIO</JobTitle>
</Person>
<Company>
  <CompanyName>Infoteria</CompanyName>
  <OfficeAddress>900 Cummings Center</OfficeAddress>
  <OfficeCity>Beverly</OfficeCity>
  <OfficeState>Massachusetts</OfficeState>
  <OfficeZip>01915</OfficeZip>
  <OfficeCountry>United States</OfficeCountry>
  <OfficePhone>978-922-4029</OfficePhone>
</Company>
<Other>
  <Comment>Evaluating software for new app</Comment>
  <Categories>Download - iPEX for Solaris</Categories>
</Other>
</Download>
```

15.2.2 *Two: Receive and verify XML email*

The second part of the process is handled inside the company's firewall, on its internal system. The download XML documents containing the sales leads are stored in a mail queue on the company's Lotus *Domino* mail server.

Infoteria's *iMESSENGER*™ product pulls the email into a working directory, using the IMAP4 protocol. It verifies the sender's email address and the document type of the XML documents (in this case, Download). This information determines the subsequent processing, as we'll see shortly.

iMESSENGER is message-oriented middleware whose behavior is configurable by the configuration tool shown in Figure 15-3. That figure illustrates some of the settings that were used for this application. The program was set to run at one minute intervals and to use D:\SalesLead\XML as the working directory.

The configuration tool supports multiple categories of XML email in one or more email queues. It does so by allowing different behaviors to be

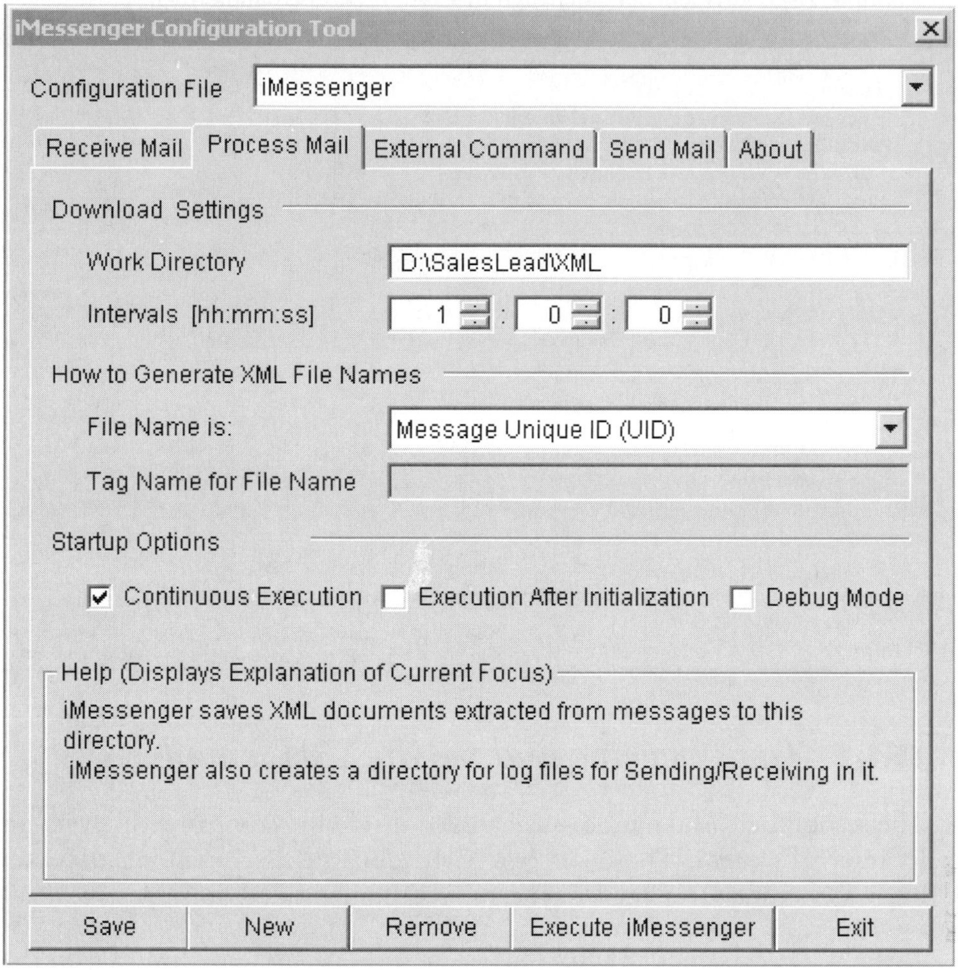

Figure 15-3　*iMESSENGER* Configuration Tool

specified for different XML document types and/or sender's email addresses.

15.2.3 *Three: Process XML email and update database*

After verification, the XML document is processed according to the business rules defined for the particular sender and document type. The rules can cause *iMESSENGER* to invoke DOS batch (.BAT) files or executable programs (.EXE). They also cause the internal system database to be updated with data extracted from the XML document.

Because Subject Software's internal system uses Lotus *Notes*, they were able to use Infoteria's *iCONNECTOR for Notes*™ to update the lead-tracking database. That tool includes *iRuleGenerator*™, a graphical interface for defining the rules for extracting data from XML elements and updating the corresponding database fields. The defined rules are represented in XML.

Example 15-3 shows a subset of the XML *rule* document used in this application. It maps the element types of a download document onto the fields of the Personform in the *Domino* lead-tracking system.

Example 15-3. Excerpt from `rule` document

```xml
<?xml version="1.0" encoding="UTF-8"?>
<rule:rule
  xmlns:rule=
    "http://www.xmlns.org/system/jp/co/infoteria/rule/"
  xmlns:notes=
    "http://www.xmlns.org/system/jp/co/infoteria/tdf/notes/"
  default-space="strip"
  indent-result="yes">
<rule:template
  match="/database/table[@name=&quot;Person&quot;]/record">
  <Download>
  <Person>
    <FirstName>
      <rule:apply-templates
        select="field[@name=&quot;FirstName&quot;]"
        mode="_Download_Person_FirstName_.text."/>
    </FirstName>
    <LastName>
      <rule:apply-templates
        select="field[@name=&quot;LastName&quot;]"
        mode="_Download_Person_LastName_.text."/>
    </LastName>
    ...
  </Person>
  ...
  </Download>
</rule:template>
</rule:rule>
```

Although Subject Software's system uses Lotus *Notes* and *Domino*, the principles apply to any email system and to any database management system.

 Tip   A trial version of *iMESSENGER* is available on the CD-ROM that accompanies this book.

An information pipeline for petrochemicals

Case Study

- Petrochemical industry marketplace

- Integration with XML

- Enabling free information flows

Sponsor: XMLSolutions Corporation, http://www.xmls.com

Contributing experts: Kathleen House and John Evdemon

Chapter

16

When does a supply chain become a supply noose? When a company is so dependent on its suppliers that market analysts won't evaluate it solely on its individual performance. That's the case in the petrochemical industry, where a slip from one primary vendor can create a logistical nightmare of missed and delayed communications for 50 other companies. What better reason to grease the skids for rapid adoption of integrated e-commerce!

The petrochemical industry is a subsidiary of the oil and gas industry. As such, as well as in its own right, it is a huge and highly diverse horizontal market.

But is also a complex vertical market!

16.1 | The petrochemical marketplace

Depending on the selling and buying position for a particular product range, business units within a large petrochemical company, like Shell or Exxon, compete against their corporate siblings. The product flows upstream and downstream from the refineries often cross the traditional boundaries of competition.

16.1.1 *Upstream flow*

The upstream flow begins with OPEC and its control over the pricing of the crude oil flowing out of the ground. In the upstream flow we see the global purchase, transportation, and warehousing of the crude oil that eventually flows into the refineries.

The top-tier petrochemical companies and their oil and gas parents exert their own control over the industry by creating highly intertwined combinations of joint ventures, strategic partnerships, business unit ownerships, and non-disclosed horizontal agreements. Horizontal domination then occurs as petrochemical firms secure their production by entering into agreements with oil and gas supplier companies. To compete effectively, most large petrochemical companies own and control companies along the complete vertical industry chain – upstream as well as downstream.

16.1.2   *Downstream flow*

Once the crude has been refined, the downstream process occurs. It involves an amazing diversity of activities, including:

- Buying and/or retrieving refined oil products
- Transportation and warehousing
- Purchasing non-oil products
- Producing and selling half-finished products
- Manufacturing consumer products
- Ensuring quality and process control
- Pipelining
- Administration
- Product enhancement
- Product development

16.1.3   *The bottleneck!*

The critical bottleneck in this market is the information exchange among internal partners, outside vendors, distributors, and ancillary services. Data from one distributor's lab analysis of crude oil, for example, may enter the system in the form of a spreadsheet compiled by a customized (and usually non-standard) program. Yet the receiving ERP system might need the data in its own format to populate its back-end database.

Maintaining communications for a pair of such sending and receiving systems currently requires highly-experienced (not to mention highly-paid) computer programmers on each end. This labor-intensive process impacts negatively on companies' return on investment (ROI).

The petrochemical industry urgently needs a cost-effective means of utilizing these highly-segmented downstream information flows and connecting them to existing EDI, ERP, and legacy systems. It must be possible to pass data in a timely, efficient and standard manner, to and from varied sources, without reinvesting in another transactional, ERP-related system.

16.2 | Integrating with XML

After making an initial investment in their business software systems of choice, companies want to maximize their investment and use the technology long enough to realize positive ROI. Particularly on the downstream end of the petrochemical Industry, most companies do not make such a capital outlay lightly. To them, software has not been perceived as part of the core business model.

16.2.1 *Coexistence with EDI*

XML can be used to empower existing software without reinvesting in a new application. Integrating the petrochemical industry with XML means linking existing legacy applications, not reengineering the wheel. Supply chain logistics surrounding the flow of petrochemical products can be used to evaluate the ease of transferring data between companies.

For example, in the trading of chemical related products and services, such as logistics and packaging, the Internet delivers cost savings in materials alone of approximately 10-20%. The only way to offer these cost savings to small suppliers is to offer them via e-commerce capabilities, but *without* a full EDI implementation.

The benefit to the larger companies of doing so is that they gain the ability to expand their existing market share and reach markets more quickly. The key to survival in this industry is maintaining well-established networks for distribution and supplies.

Figure 16-1 illustrates the co-existence of EDI and XML-based systems within a supply web. The utilization of an already existing system leverages the investment in that system and does not throw away the years of effort involved in creating the EDI-system mappings to back-end legacy data.

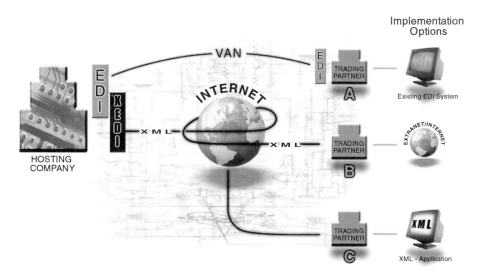

Figure 16-1   EDI and XML-based systems within a supply web

16.2.2 *Significant information flows*

The petrochemical industry business processes with the most significant information flows are:

- Exchange of information regarding the selling and buying of crude oil
- Transportation, pipelining, and warehousing: internally and among business partners
- Quality and process control
- Quoting and selling of half-finished products and consumer products
- Customer support

It is logical to extract this information from existing EDI systems and simply extend the reach of that information over the Internet to smaller companies. In other words, to create an integrated e-commerce environment in which traditional EDI and XML-EDI coexist and complement one another.

16.3 | Achieving a free-flowing information pipeline

By examining the downstream business processes more closely, it becomes clear that XML can enable the internal and external flows of information to avoid critical blockages.

16.3.1 *Internal information flows*

A typical example involves a large petrochemical company with activities in various joint ventures, and in manufacturing of high quality finished products. This firm also needs to acquire half-finished products from other large firms to produce other finished goods, outside of its core product line.

The interconnectivity within this company must encompass thousands of internal businesses and their individual data processing systems. There are multiple plants in multiple countries, each with vendors supplying supplying systems tailored for those countries and their languages.

XML can enable communication among these diverse systems. Moreover, because of its use of Unicode, it can support multiple natural languages.

16.3.2 *External information flows*

Many companies force the constraints of industry standards organizations upon their suppliers. These companies can only assure on-time deliveries when information is readily available to all partners in their supply web – all the time!

For example, a supplier of jet fuel to the world's major airports cannot afford to have a late delivery. There would be a domino effect that could cause plane delays, resulting in major expenses to the airlines and other industries – not just petrochemicals.

A company's supply chain may be secure, but how reliable is the information feeding that chain? The key to survival is maintaining well-established networks for distribution and supplies – and for distributing accurate contemporaneous information to all trading partners. XML makes it easy for legacy systems to communicate both internally and externally.

16.3.3 *Mergers and acquisitions*

A merger of multiple companies does not necessarily equate to smooth, fast integration, nor realistic savings. In fact, most merged companies experience a period where the inability to share transactional data seamlessly (because of the technical complexity) causes breakdownd in what were once the most streamlined of business processes.

Consider two Fortune 500 petrochemical companies with ten to fifteen core legacy applications each. Both utilize EDI, e-commerce, and Web-based procurement processes. Imagine them trying to merge their data, hoping to leverage their core competencies to new levels.

Streamlining this process by conventional programming techniques is as likely as getting oil to flow back up the pipeline. XML gives companies the ability to utilize their existing applications to communicate with all vendors and business partners, without forcing costly implementations on those who cannot afford the capital investment.

16.3.4 *XML integration aids*

To communicate accurately with business partners while using XML, systems must maintain links between industry standards and company-specific standards. Tools for schema management, such as XMLSolutions' *Schema Central*, can be helpful in this regard. They are discussed in Chapter 36, "Schema management at Major Bank", on page 512.

16.4 | Conclusion

Ancillary businesses surrounding the petrochemical industry are expected to grow to 25% of its in the next 2 years. To accommodate this growth, the industry needs integrated e-commerce. Those petrochemical companies that adopt it can become well-oiled internal information exchanges. The others will likely become the fossils of the future.

Portals

- Doorways to information
- Enterprise Information Portals (EIP)
- Digital dashboards

Part Four

A portal is a doorway, and in the language of the World Wide Web, a "portal site" is one that users visit first. It acts, literally, as the user's doorway to all of the resources of the Web.

Now organizations are constructing their own portals – not all-encompassing sites for the masses, like traditional Web portals, but *Enterprise Information Portals* (EIP). An EIP is a doorway to a focused set of resources, intended for a specific audience, like the employees, customers, and suppliers of a business. Most importantly, an EIP can serve as a single coherent view of information aggregated from disparate sources by e-commerce systems and integration servers.

In this part, we'll explore the reasons for EIPs and the systems needed to build them. We'll look at an EIP in detail: an imaginary but possible portal that you'll wish your doctor had.

Enterprise Information Portals (EIP)

Introductory Discussion

- Global information economy

- Enterprise information challenges

- Framework for EIP development

Sponsor: DataChannel, Inc., http://www.datachannel.com

Contributing experts: DataChannel, Inc. staff

> The industrial age is dead. Long live the information age! But the information revolution will be as devastating to the unprepared enterprise as the industrial revolution was to cottage industry. This chapter will help you prepare.

We are witnessing an economic transformation that is unparalleled in history. The stabilization and acceptance of the Internet is resulting in its becoming the primary platform for conducting business. Information is at the core of this rapidly emerging transformation as it is presented, shared, and exchanged to transact business everywhere.

Essentially, information is used to support every business decision made within an enterprise. This shift towards a global information economy via the Internet has created a new playing field in the electronic business marketplace. Electronic business is becoming a major defining element of an enterprise's market capitalization.

17.1 | Information is the global economy

Corporations around the globe, large and small, recognize this transformation and the potential power of their information. Over the past five years millions of dollars have been spent to develop ways to better capture and efficiently use existing data. These include:

back office systems
> Enterprise Resource Planning (ERP), financials, human resources, engineering, process automation/workflow, project management, etc.

front office systems
> Sales force automation, customer relationship management, help desk, marketing automation, etc.

personal productivity systems
> Word processor, spreadsheet, presentation, contact manager, Personal Information Manager, etc.

Front office and back office systems capture and create a tremendous amount of managed information. However, with personal productivity tools readily available, company employees, partners, and customers have all created a wealth of unmanaged information as well – some 80% of a typical company's information base! (See Figure 17-1.)

The global information economy discovery is upon us and with it, two distinct realizations:

- The first realization is the fact that this tremendous IT investment in back office, front office, and personal productivity systems has paid off. As a result of investing in the available technology, companies can now create and capture information from every transaction, inquiry, resource, supplier, partner, and customer.
- The second realization as it relates to the first, however, is even more revealing. There are significant barriers to accessing information by the people who need it to make critical business decisions. If not addressed appropriately, these barriers will prevent anyone from intelligently managing the information to its fullest potential, thereby potentially stunting the growth of this economic transformation that has recently emerged.

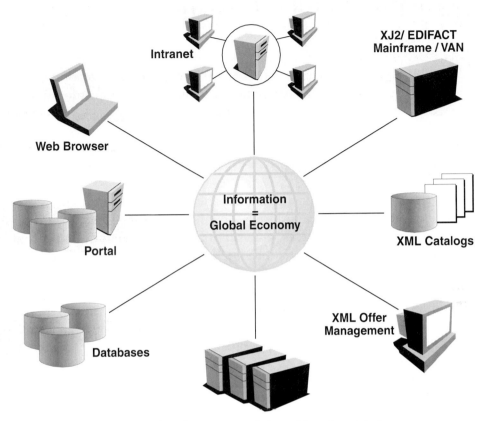

Figure 17-1   Managed and unmanaged data drive the global economy.

Today, this global information economy is one without geographic, industry, or computing boundaries. Intranets, extranets, and the Internet all become arteries of the seamless information highway without specified origins or destinations. The catch is, however, that any enterprise wishing to participate successfully in the new economy must transform itself to enable common access and integration to *all* information from *all* roads.

That it means it must learn how to deal effectively with the many challenges that now exist to the effective utilization of enterprise information.

17.2 | Enterprise Information challenges

There are several challenges and roadblocks preventing information access and the systems interoperability required to unleash critical information. They exist for both managed and unmanaged data.

17.2.1 Managed data

Managed data is information that is built and maintained by the enterprise. It consists of controlled repositories of information like business documents, policies and procedures, enterprise applications, and customer and product databases. While managed data has connotations of being more useful than unmanaged data, it presents its own unique challenges to those wishing to access and use it efficiently.

17.2.1.1 Legacy systems

While computing systems tout openness and standards, the fact remains that a significant amount of business information resides in legacy systems, which effectively means proprietary systems. These can be anything from a mainframe or enterprise application, to one of the many customized solutions built by a company's Information Technology (IT) or Management Information Systems (MIS) department.

Even a newly-implemented solution creates a legacy problem if it is not entirely compatible with existing technology. The more such legacy systems are incorporated within the IT infrastructure, the more difficult it becomes to integrate disparate data as needed.

And integrating the data is the primary issue only if the user is lucky enough to find it in the first place! Often, the primary challenge is just being able to *access* the data.

17.2.1.2 Disconnected data sources

Although each managed-data system can demonstrate effectiveness to some degree, they constitute "islands of automation" that are disconnected from each other. Routine reports and access to each individual data source are common and expected. However, creating a report that integrates information from more than one system, and doing it routinely, requires customized development.

It also requires ongoing maintenance, as the various technologies change and upgrade. IT organizations typically spend between 25% and 40% of their budget on application integration and system compatibility.

17.2.1.3   Restricted application development

Even the most heterogeneous system environment requires some degree of integration. It is provided by IT departments, who respond to customization requests and ad-hoc queries from users. IT groups also build proprietary applications to meet the specific needs of their business that cannot be met with generic manufactured software.

To remain competitive, corporations must be able to develop solutions for their exact business model. A company cannot rely on its systems to give it a competitive advantage unless the systems are updated just as quickly as the market changes. Employing incompatible systems in the same environment handicaps IT's ability to respond.

17.2.1.4   Proprietary access

Each of these heterogeneous data sources has its own registry of authorized users and administrators. The administrative burden to manage the limitless permutations of users and systems can be overwhelming.

It is not uncommon to find several machines on the same manager's desktop to help manage users and systems. In a typical back-office scenario, one might find a terminal for accessing account history, a workstation to manage the ERP system, and a PC with Internet access and/or reporting tools.

17.2.2 *Unmanaged data*

While managed data is captured by enterprise applications, it is the day-to-day work that creates the vast majority of information throughout an organization. Most of this work is done using personal productivity tools and is "managed" in an impromptu, even chaotic way.

Moreover, users of these tools frequently take managed data and "unmanage" it by manipulating information from multiple managed sources into a single document or report. These new information resources are stored and shared in numerous ways. File systems, document management systems, email, hard copy, fax, and messaging middleware all contribute to exponential growth of unmanaged data communications and exchange.

17.2.2.1   Ad-hoc productivity tools

Desktop productivity tools have become standard issue in corporations around the world. They free users to manage their own environments and allow them to create documents and files on demand.

However, this freedom comes with a price. Typically, there is no organized way to share, exchange, or validate these outputs. Sometimes a report may be created in a spreadsheet, the next time in a word processor, or even specially programmed and faxed in a hard-copy version.

17.2.2.2   Chaotic access and exchange

Access to personally-created information is haphazard. Such disjointed access mechanisms cause uneven distribution and, as a result, misunderstandings. Groupware solutions have addressed this problem with only limited success. While they create a collaborative platform for creating and exchanging data, managing access for persons outside the group is still a challenge. Furthermore, information must be kept in the application's proprietary representation, limiting those who can access the data.

17.2.2.3   Restricted publication rights

Once information has been compiled and processed, it can be published to a community of users. Today's intranets provide the useful function of allowing end-users to store critical, unmanaged information and make it available to a community of users. However, the administrative burden of maintaining these systems can become cost-prohibitive.

A bottleneck occurs when users who want to publish to the corporate intranet are required to do so through administrators who control the access rights. There are further difficulties when they want to publish to only a subset of the corporate community and there is no way to manage access rights on a per-user basis.

17.3 | Enterprise information portals

Tying together diverse and proprietary systems presents significant challenges. Breaking down the barriers erected by disparate applications, intranets, extranets, and the Internet is the final step in creating an enterprise ready for the global information economy. The result is the Enterprise Information Portal (EIP).

A *portal* – a system to manage access to information – is nothing more than a door to the information of the enterprise. If the information is not readily accessible or organized, the door opens to a wall. An information portal is, therefore, only as good as the information it can access.

Legacy systems, enterprise applications, database systems, and other applications may provide portals to the information they store. The failure comes, however, when those systems must communicate with each other, or the information in them must contribute to a greater application.

For an EIP to succeed, it must be properly designed to access all the information. A single standard of computing is the elusive Holy Grail of IT professionals, yet, it is now within grasp. In the same way that enterprises around the globe have accepted the Internet Protocol (IP) as the standard for *transmitting* data, they now have the opportunity to adopt a global standard for *representing* the data that is transmitted – XML.

17.3.1 *The role of XML*

XML is not only the Web standard for exchanging data, it is also becoming the standard for business transactions in legacy systems environments. When an enterprise wants to move data across dissimilar systems, transforms are required. As we have seen, XML makes it possible to create such transforms quickly.

The power and beauty of generalized markup languages is that they maintain the separation of the rendition seen at the user interface from the structured abstract data, allowing the seamless integration of data from diverse sources. Customer information, purchase orders, research results, bill payments, medical records, catalog data and other information can be converted to XML on the middle tier of a three-tier enterprise architecture, allowing abstract data to be exchanged online as easily as HTML pages display rendered data today.

17.3.2 *The golden rule of content*

A single rule can save countless hours of work and vast expense. This rule, put simply: *Content must be abstract and kept separate from rendition.*

By following this rule, after some preparation, users, developers, and IT professionals will be able to create *dynamic applications*. In these applications, the rendition of the information may differ each time a query is made, or may change depending on the profile of the user.

But because the rendition is independent of the content, the interface need not depend upon the access rules or the structure of the data being presented. Content sources maintain their integrity while dynamically becoming integrated with data from other sources, as illustrated in Figure 17-2. This is possible only because there are no ties to the presentation that might otherwise encumber the processing of the data content.

The rule can also eliminate integration overhead when maintaining data. Typically, when an update routine from a single transaction affects data in more than one system, heavy integration is required.

However, when the golden rule of content is observed, multiple data sources can be updated dynamically without requiring a user to have explicit rights to each of them. That's because user access rights are associated with specific reports and other presentations, which are no longer connected with the abstract content.

17.3.3 *EIP empowers the enterprise*

Abstract data content makes the EIP possible, which empowers the enterprise in new ways:

DYNAMIC Documents | Applications

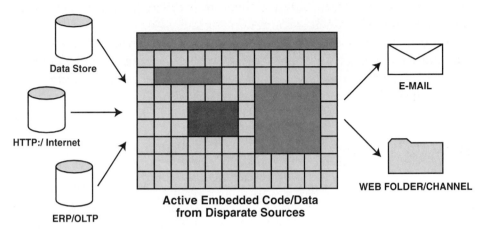

Figure 17-2   Integrating reusable elements from disparate sources

- Business managers can now engage their customers using data from formerly isolated distinct systems, and consolidate the information for delivery to the customer's browser.
- The information infrastructure can be extended beyond the boundaries of a corporation and include an extended community of customers, partners, and suppliers.
- New offers can be configured literally in a moment's notice and back office support systems can readily respond to the new requirements.

The latter prospect is especially critical for commodity-type businesses that rely on services and fast response to maintain a competitive edge. Financial institutions and telecommunications companies in particular must adapt their offerings quickly because of the tremendous competitive threat that exists in their markets.

17.4 | A framework for portals

To transform an enterprise's computing environment into an EIP capable of capitalizing on the information economy requires a well-architected strategy and a framework in which the necessary software and services can be applied. DataChannel's approach, which is based on the consulting and training experience of its ISOGEN division, is called *XMLFramework*.™ It is pictured in Figure 17-3.

The critical horizontal layers ("Training" and "Professional Services") are required to support each of the other solution offerings to one degree or another, depending on the customer's unique business and IT infrastructure requirements.

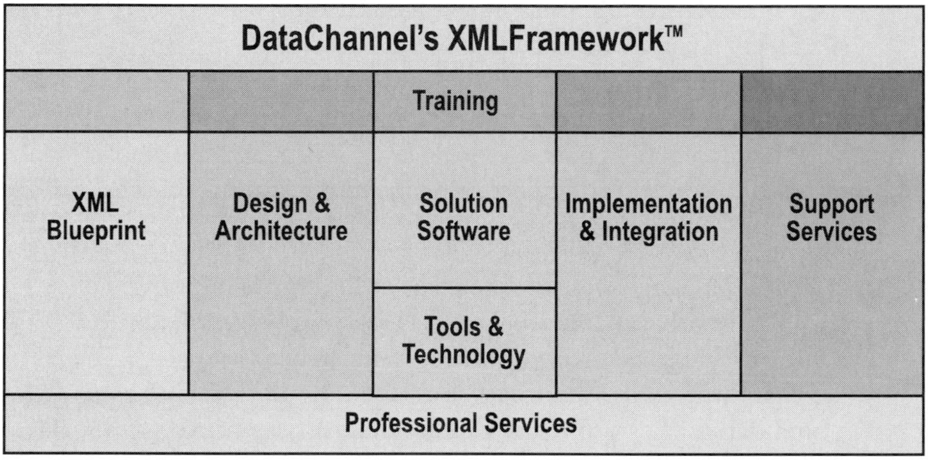

Figure 17-3   The DataChannel *XMLFramework*

17.4.1 *Strategy*

A cornerstone of the solution is a comprehensive, customized strategy, which DataChannel calls the *XMLBluePrint*.™ Designed by both business management and IT professionals, the blueprint identifies and describes the roadblocks to realizing the enterprise's strategic imperatives, and how XML can be applied to address strategic and technological challenges.

17.4.2 *Design & architecture*

IT design and architecture are then developed that support the *XMLBlue-Print*. XML metadata markup and integration design criteria are defined for the customer's entire cross-platform environment.

17.4.3 *Software*

There is a multitude of software offerings for EIP development, much of it described in this book and/or available on its CD-ROM. They tend to fall into two broad categories:

Focused software
> This is software designed for a specific function, such as editors, parsers, publishing systems, etc.

Platforms
> These are systems of various kinds that provide a platform into which focused software can be plugged and integrated (Figure 17-4). There are lots of platform systems in this book, targeted for specific application domains, such as middle-tier servers, commerce integrators, portal systems, and content management systems.

For example, DataChannel offers *RIO*, shown in Figure 17-5, as an XML-enabled platform for publishing, managing, and retrieving information. Its functions include end-user Web publishing, personalized information delivery with notification, multi-tier administration, and an extensible security architecture.

DataChannel also offers focused software that plugs into *RIO*, such as the following programs:

WEBView Extensions
> This offering allows seamless viewing of over 200 document file formats through a standard Web browser without installing additional applications.

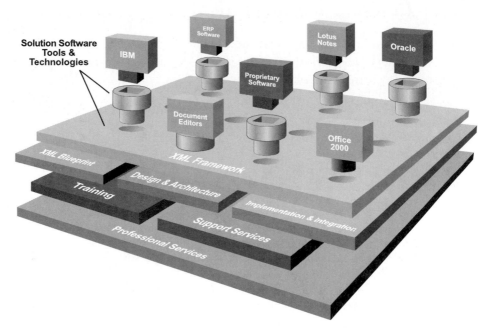

Figure 17-4 Platforms support and integrate other software.

XJParser

This is a validating parser for the *Java* platform that enables server-side and client-side parsing. It is based on Microsoft's XML parser technology. DTD/schema, XML-data subset, and namespaces capabilities allow application developers to integrate XML support into existing or new products through the W3C DOM interface.

XSL Processor

This is a server-based XSL engine that provides XML-to-XML or XML-to-HTML transformations. It includes support for pattern matching as well as Microsoft's proposed query language specification.

XML Generator

This product can automatically transform character data from tab- or comma-delimited files into XML documents. By means of

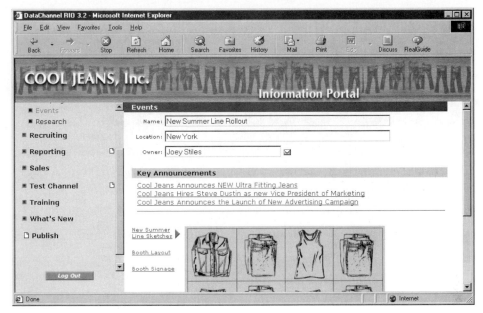

Figure 17-5   *DataChannel RIO* client interface

a template, the *XML Generator* can automatically map your data fields to XML elements.

17.5 | Summary

A company must mobilize its resources to compete effectively in today's global information economy. With IT infrastructure encompassing such a large percentage of those resources, there is a compelling case for an organization to transform its enterprise architecture to adapt to its changing business requirements, overcome computing boundaries, and truly leverage its information, both managed and unmanaged. XML technology and a systematic approach like that embodied in DataChannel's *XMLFramework* can accomplish that goal.

Portal servers for e-business

Tool Discussion

■ Portal server requirements

■ Architecture of an e-business portal server

■ Other portal server facilities

Sponsor: Sequoia Software Corp., http://www.sequoiasoftware.com
Contributing expert: Bryan Caporlette

In today's e-business environment, an enterprise information portal is literally a "digital dashboard" that allows employees, suppliers, and customers to interact with an enterprise. The EIP accepts and delivers information, ranging from formal publications to dynamic business process data, anywhere the Internet can reach – with or without wires! The resulting requirements for portal servers are quite demanding, as this chapter reveals.

o meet the needs of today's interactive e-business portals, a portal server must do many things. It combines the functions of an application server, workflow manager, content manager, end-to-end publishing system, and database – either as a single product or a set of interconnected ones. But however they are implemented, the requirements are the same.

18.1 | Portal server requirements

The requirements for interactive e-business portals can be divided into three categories: performance, content distribution, and business process integration.

18.1.1 *Performance*

Performance, for a portal server, means reliability, availability, and scalability. An application server is required that can provide sophisticated load distribution and communication capabilities that allow an enterprise to scale its portal in multiple directions. It must be possible for administrators to add hardware to stress points as they expand the reach of the portal to new users and data sources.

18.1.2　*Content distribution*

It is no longer feasible to require that a portal user have access to a powerful PC and a large monitor. The reach of the EIP has extended to network PCs, thin clients, and mobile devices – including phones and personal digital assistants (PDA).

Content sources are also expanding. They now include ERP and MRP systems, legacy business applications, Internet sites, syndicated information sources, and information services integrated within the portal. To cope with the increasing variety of content, the server must offer a quickly extensible environment for adding new content sources.

A further requirement for content distribution is personalization. Users must be able to filter the content to satisfy personal profiles, and at the same time be able to specify a rendition style that best suits their personal needs and the capabilities of the delivery device.

18.1.3　*Business process integration*

The portal server must allow an enterprise to define complex business flows in a modular and flexible way. These modules can be thought of as *integration agents* because their individual small actions can have the combined effect of implementing a large and complex process.

For example, Figure 18-1 shows the workflow for an expense report that is submitted to the portal as an XML document. The first integration agent validates the report against the company expense report schema. The next agent interrogates the amount and, depending on the dollar value, either sends the report directly to the accounting department for processing, or else routes it to the manager's inbox for review and approval.

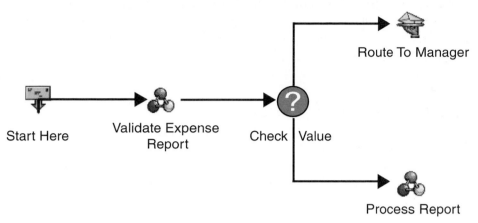

Figure 18-1   Expense report flow

18.2 | Architecture of an e-business portal server

To understand the workings of portal servers and discuss their requirements, it is helpful to have an architectural model in mind as a frame of reference. Figure 18-2 depicts the architecture of an XML-based portal server
at a level where the components relate directly to the requirements categories we have been discussing.

There are three major components, and XML plays a significant role in
each of them:

- The XML Application Server (XAS) addresses performance
  issues by providing the necessary reliability and scaling. All
  data is packaged in XML "envelopes", thereby creating a
  messaging architecture that is easily connected to other
  systems, both internal and external.
- *Content Delivery Services* (CDS) brokers end-user requests for
  information and generates the appropriate response. Because
  the XML representation separates the abstract data from any
  specific presentation format, the data can easily be reformatted
  for multiple delivery devices.

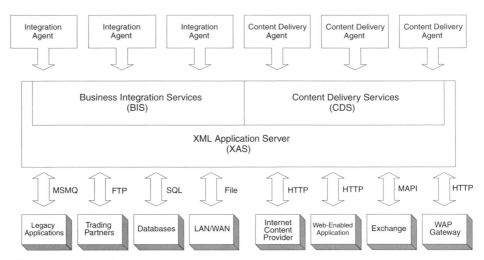

Figure 18-2 Portal server architecture

- ■ *Business Integration Services* (BIS) automates work processes within the portal. A sophisticated rules engine can interrogate the XML envelopes in order to make routing decisions.

We will examine each of these components in detail in the following sections. Bear in mind that we are discussing an architecture, not a specific implementation. Although we use a single integrated product to illustrate the functionality, it would also be possible to satisfy the requirements by using several intercommunicating dedicated products.

18.2.1   *XML application server*

The XML application server provides load balancing and a messaging architecture.

18.2.1.1   Portal clusters

The load balancer distributes work among sets of portal servers known as *portal clusters*. Each cluster has a *cluster server*, which stores information about the portal cluster's configuration. That information is stored persistently in a relational database, which provides backup and replication capabilities.

The cluster environment provides fail-over capabilities that ensure that the portal is always available. When a message is sent to a load-balanced server, the XAS awaits a response from it. If that machine does not respond in a timely manner, the application server may re-submit the request to the next available portal server, or enter a failure event into the auditing system. The administrator can set a threshold for failures, which will determine the number of negative responses a given machine can have prior to becoming deactivated within the cluster.

18.2.1.2 Messaging architecture

XML messages are the interface between the portal server and external systems. All communications with the XAS, whether business objects (e.g. documents) or remote procedure calls (e.g. search requests), are encapsulated in XML envelopes.

18.2.1.2.1 Messaging protocols

The application server abstracts the notion of envelopes through the definition of *message types*. Message types provide the routing and metadata information necessary to transmit data between an application and the portal by means of a *message protocol*. There are several industry initiatives for message protocols, including Microsoft's *BizTalk*, *ICE* (discussed in Chapter 22, "Information and Content Exchange (ICE)", on page 300, and *RosettaNet*). The XAS, because it abstracts the message types, is not limited to a single protocol.

There are two directions a message might take, depending on the message type. Presentation requests coming from a browser or Wireless Access Protocol (WAP) gateway are routed to the *Content Delivery Services* component. Business objects, such as documents and business interactions, are routed to the *Business Integration Services* component.

18.2.1.2.2 Receivers and senders

Receivers and senders are modules that provide access to the portal. They are shown at the bottom of Figure 18-2.

Receivers listen for new messages coming into the portal. Senders transmit messages to external applications. The modular design allows the XAS to provide support for any data communications protocols, including HTTP, MSMQ, SMTP, COM, FTP, and directory polling.

This flexible support for data communications protocols allows the portal server to interoperate with enterprise application integration (EAI) tools. The portal server is thereby able to leverage corporate experience and expenditures on existing EAI applications.

18.2.1.3   Load balancing

As messages flow into the portal, a message processor communicates with the load balancer to distribute the processing across the known load-balanced servers within the cluster.

Once a load-balanced server is selected, XAS instantiates a new transaction to process the message. Depending on the success or failure of the transaction, XAS will log one or more events into the auditing component. The auditing component provides system monitoring and health status for all portal services.

18.2.1.4   Rules engine

The XAS dispatcher routes messages to the appropriate services, such as integration agents. It has a sophisticated rules engine that interrogates the Document Object Model (DOM) of the XML envelope.

Rules are test conditions that are evaluated to determine the route a message will take through the portal. The rules include XML Path Language (XPath) expressions that address values in the DOM.

For example, the rule in Example 18-1 might be used at the Check value decision point in Figure 18-1 to route the expense report. It compares the value attribute of the total element of an expense-report document to "500.00".

Example 18-1. Rule containing an XPath expression

```
%/expense_report/total/@value% > 500.00
```

18.2.2   *Content delivery services*

The *Content Delivery Services* component controls the delivery of data to an end user. It allows for personalization of the rendered information, the portal desktop, and individual content sources.

18.2.2.1   Rendition

CDS exploits the fact that XML allows abstract information content to be separate from formatting style, so data can be rendered in the needed form on delivery.

This separation enables the portal to service requests coming in from Web servers or Wireless Access Protocol gateway servers. CDS dynamically associates an XSL stylesheet with each XML document, based on the type of device on which it will be presented (e.g. Web browser, cellular phone, personal digital assistant). It then generates HTML or Wireless Markup Language (WML), as appropriate.

The rendering engine is controlled by rules that establish a one-to-many relationship of XSLT stylesheets to XML schemas. When a user requests a document, the rendering engine uses the rules to select a stylesheet, apply that stylesheet to the XML document, and deliver the result. The rules that select the stylesheet can be based on the user's name and/or role within the portal (explained later), as well as the type of requesting device.

In fact, rendition rules can also specify selection criteria based on the content of the document. For example, a rule might test for the payment method of an order, represented by the content of the `payment.method` element. The rules could apply different style sheets to the document depending on whether the payment method is Visa, Mastercard, or American Express.

18.2.2.2   Personalization

The essence of a portal is the personalized aggregation and delivery of information from multiple sources. The delivery point is the desktop, which is populated with information by means of *content delivery agents (CDA)*.

18.2.2.3   Personalized desktop

Figure 18-3 shows an example of a portal desktop, as generated by Sequoia's *XML Portal Server (XPS)*™. The tabs at the upper left allow different pages to be selected.

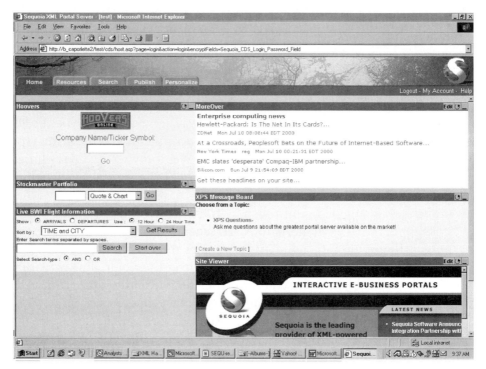

Figure 18-3   Desktop in Sequoia's *XML Portal Server*

The portal desktop is controlled by a template, which specifies the content and layout. Customization of the template occurs at two levels: roles and individual personalization.

18.2.2.3.3   Roles

The types of pages and CDAs available to a user are controlled by assigning each user to one or more "roles". A role corresponds conceptually to a mode of use of the portal, such as engineer, manager, administrator, etc.

In system terms, a role is a collection of pages, CDAs, and a default theme (i.e. a color scheme and background). As users log into the portal, their roles are used to generate the original desktop.

18.2.2.3.4   Individual personalization

The rightmost tab in Figure 18-3 allows the desktop to be personalized. With it the user can change the layout of any page. Content source windows can be moved around, added, and hidden. In addition, the user can select from a set of pre-configured themes that control the color and background images of the desktop.

18.2.2.4   Content delivery agents (CDA)

The portal administrator can associate content delivery agents with pages. A CDA is a program or script that creates a window for communicating with a data source. These include:

- Internet content providers (e.g. *Hoovers, CNBC*, etc.).
- Application programs (e.g. *Exchange, Lotus Notes*).
- Internal integration agents (see 18.3.1, "Integration agents", on page 262).

A CDA can provide a personalization option to elicit property settings for the data source, such as news categories, mail servers, or stock symbols. The CDA tailors the content delivered based on the user's current preferences.

18.2.3   *Business integration services*

The *Business Integration Services* component enables the administrator to automate business processes within the portal. The dispatcher controls the path through which a message flows.

Message paths could be simple, routing a message to an index server or content repository. However, they could also follow complex alternative routes among integration agents and decision points that must be resolved by use of the rules engine.

In BIS, unlike XAS, the rules can test not just the XML envelope, but the contained business object itself. If the object is an XML document, its content can be tested to determine the path.

A flow design tool enables the portal administrator to define routes graphically, using icons for integration agents and decision points, as in Figure 18-1. Icons for subflows allow the reuse of common business processes.

18.3 | Other portal server facilities

Sequoia's *XML Portal Server (XPS)* implements the architecture we have been discussing in a single integrated product. In addition to providing the three core architectural components, it comes packaged with a set of integration agents and an administration tool.

18.3.1 *Integration agents*

Integration agents can provide the following functions:

taxonomy

This agent provides a mechanism for organizing relevant information into a hierarchical view.

content management

The content management agent provides persisten local storage of information, including configuration management features.

smart summary

This agent provides summary views of data aggregated within the portal.

transformation

The transformation agent uses XSLT to map data from one XML schemas to another.

data entry

This agent maps HTML form designs to XML schemas in order to generate XML documents from the completed forms.

Indexing

The indexing agent creates both XML-based contextual indices and full-text indices of information flowing through the portal.

scripting

The scripting agent provides a mechanism for extending the functionality of the portal through scripts written in a variety of languages.

18.3.2 *Administration and configuration*

The sheer number of components and configuration options available within a portal server can be daunting even to contemplate, let alone to deal with in a production environment. The interface provided by a server implementation is therefore as important a consideration as the functionality.

Product vendors are aware of this fact. Sequoia's *XML Portal Server*, for example, includes a *Portal Management Console* that provides a single point of administration and configuration for the entire portal environment.

RxML: Your prescription for healthcare

Case Study

▋ Health portal system

▋ Dynamic patient summary

▋ Information aggregation

▋ Supply chain automation

Sponsor: Sequoia Software Corp., http://www.sequoiasoftware.com

Contributing expert: Bryan Caporlette

Chapter

19

When it comes to electronic information processing, the U.S. medical system is "terminally" ill, so to speak. Systems rarely share data, even in the same medical organization, and there is little chance that your doctor can usefully access all your records for a diagnosis. This chapter prescribes a cure.

I magine you're feeling under the weather, so you make an office visit to your primary care physician.

Dr. Caps enters the examination room with a portable device instead of a clipboard. From that device he can access a patient summary record that contains your complete medical history, follow-up visits, current medications, and your favorite pharmacy. This information has been pooled together from various sources in the ABC Medical Center to create a single integrated logical view.

After an initial evaluation, Dr. Caps orders a throat culture to check for streptococcus bacteria. A laboratory order request, in the form of an XML document, is transmitted to the microbiology department. A culture is obtained by the nurse and sent to the lab. The culture results will be sent directly to the doctor's electronic in-basket, where he can evaluate them to determine the appropriate course of action.

Until determination of the culture result, he prescribes Keflex for coverage. He chooses Keflex, rather than amoxicillin, because the patient summary indicates that in a previous "encounter" (office visit, etc.) you reported an adverse reaction to amoxicillin.

The prescription is sent electronically to your local MRC pharmacy, where it will be awaiting your arrival as you head home for some much needed rest. Following your departure, the billing department will automatically generate an XML invoice that is electronically submitted to Blue Triangle, your healthcare provider.

That all-important patient summary is made possible for Dr. Caps through a collection of electronically stored medical information, aggregated and distributed through a *health portal system*, as shown in Figure 19-1. It enables you, as a patient, to receive the best service, and clinicians to make the most informed decisions regarding your care.

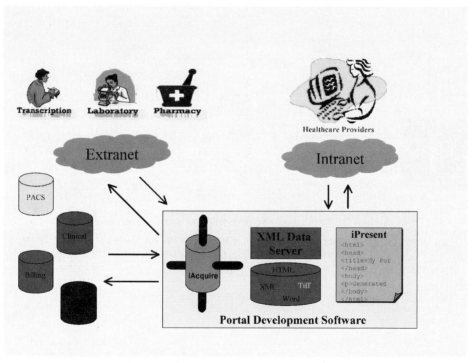

Figure 19-1   Health portal system

19.1 | Doing as well as can be expected – Not!

As you have probably noticed, real-world experiences with the healthcare industry do not resemble the integrated environment we've portrayed. Let's say you were born in upstate New York, went to school in Ohio, and now live in Silicon Valley. More likely than not, you have had to receive medical attention at each of these locations.

Most of us have been asked repeatedly to fill out the same forms, with our demographic and medical histories. The onus has been on us to remember our doctors' names, dates of injury and illness, arcane names for medications we are taking, and allergies that have been discovered over a lifetime. This information has been stored multiple times, in multiple systems, in multiple geographic locations.

Unless you have been fortunate enough to have the same doctor your whole life, your physicians probably haven't had all the information necessary to render the best diagnosis. Stories of duplicate laboratory tests, negative reactions to unknown medical allergies, and misdiagnosis due to missing or incorrect information abound within the industry.

There are many reasons the care we receive falls short of our expectations. Organizations have to deal with a copious amount of information. However, providing access to this information to the correct person at the correct time is often impossible.

The typical healthcare organization information system deploys between 30 and 70 applications. These applications are spread across multiple functional departments, hardware platforms, and geographical locations, which impedes effective use of their information. Other barriers include security considerations and the cost of software licenses.

19.2 | The prescription: a health portal system

Fortunately, there is a cure for this condition. Health portal systems like the one used by Dr. Caps in our example can exist. They are just examples of Enterprise Information Portals, which organizations can build using products like Sequoia's *XML Portal Server*.

A *health portal system* provides a single point of access for all your medical information. Clinicians log into the portal, after which they have sophisticated search and navigation capabilities to access a comprehensive library of information.

These capabilities enable the clinician to locate your patient summary record quickly. The patient summary is an aggregate view of your complete medical history, made up of information components extracted from the numerous systems deployed by the health enterprise. Figure 19-2 depicts what Dr. Caps saw in our example.

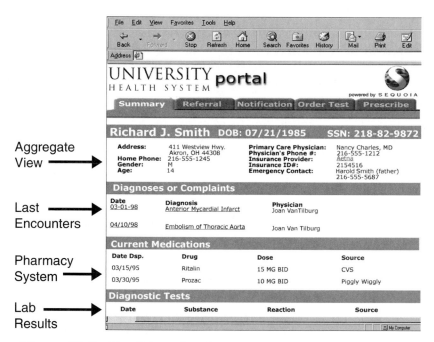

Aggregate View →

Last Encounters →

Pharmacy System →

Lab Results →

Figure 19-2   Rendition of patient summary

In addition to those internal systems, the portal provides access to medical libraries and external systems, such as laboratory results and pharmaceutical ordering systems. Its all done by the portal system's acquisition component and its connectors.

19.3 | Connectivity counts

The portal software in Figure 19-1 is Sequoia's *XML Portal Server*; its acquisition component is labeled *iAcquire* and it uses senders and receivers to communicate with connectors that tap into various disparate systems. The connectors communicate with software applications, extract data from them, and package that data in XML messages that are passed on to the XML data server.

The connectors are a flexible bunch. One might be communicating directly with a radiology system, capturing the images and routing them into the portal. Another connector could be listening through a TCP/IP port for health industry standard (HL7) messages being transmitted from the "admit, discharge, transfer" application.

Yet another connector might poll an FTP directory that has been set up for our transcription service company to submit operative reports and other transcribed documents. As the documents are sent into the directory, the connector grabs them and converts the information into XML.

This functionality doesn't just happen. The portal administrator must train the system to perform the transformations by defining connectors. Systems typically provide a graphical user interface (GUI) that enables easy mapping of source data elements into their target XML document. Some, like Sequoia's *XML Portal Server*, provide other features that make the administrator's life easier, such as DTDs that allow automatic import of standard HL7 messages. Once defined, the connectors are deployed across the enterprise to begin collecting the data needed by Dr. Caps.

But these connectors are not just one-way data pumps. The administrator can also enable connectors to dynamically query data stored in an electronic medical records (EMR) application. When Dr. Caps needs to find out if you have had streptococcus recently, the data server can formulate a search request. This request is serviced in real-time by the connector, communicating to the EMR application through an ODBC interface. Perhaps he will recommend a vitamin C supplement to your diet.

Figure 19-3 illustrates the acquisition component of Sequoia's *XML Portal Server* and its connectors, which are labeled *Accessor* in the diagram.

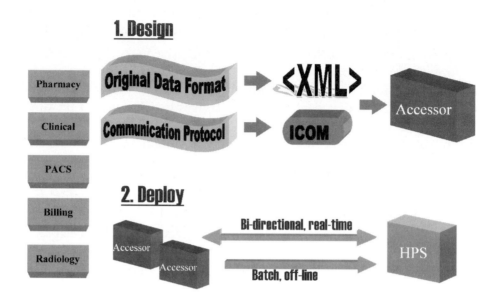

Figure 19-3   Sequoia's *XML Portal Server* and its *Accessor* connectors

19.4 | Aggregation adds value

As information flows into the portal's XML data server, it must be organized in a way that facilitates easy, intuitive access by Dr. Caps.

Information overload could become a problem, if information is not properly presented to the physician. The obvious first step is to provide a categorization facility to help organize the data into folders. XML provides the ability to define element types such as patient name, encounter date, and attending physician that can be used to place documents into a particular folder.

However, the unique capability of a true enterprise information portal is that it can aggregate data from disparate sources to create a comprehensive view of your overall health. This is where XML really plays a significant role.

Imagine trying to assimilate information from a proprietary ASCII format, the results of an SQL query, and an operative report in some word processor format. But, if the connectors are doing their transformation job properly and sending only XML into the portal, a new breed of aggregate XML objects can be built dynamically from these sources.

The aggregate XML object in this case is a patient summary. The template that causes it to be created is shown in Figure 19-4. The template is an XML document with no data. The empty elements act as queries that retrieve the data of the same element types in other documents – the "data sources".

Actual patient summaries are constructed by filling in copies of the template with data extracted dynamically from the data sources as they enter the system. The patient summary becomes the universal access point for all information, with hyperlinks into the original data source documents supplementing the summary where appropriate.

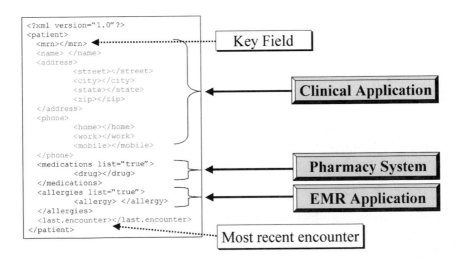

Figure 19-4   Template for patient summary

19.5 | Personalization assures usability

Not everyone needs to see, or should see, all the information flowing into the system. The portal can deliver personalized renditions of the XML information to the clinicians by using XSL stylesheets. These provide very granular personalization, applying transformation rules at the element level.

The portal applies XSL on the server-side, where it can employ a powerful rules engine to associate multiple stylesheets with the same document. Users can define profiles that choose their preferred stylesheet.

Personalization doesn't only apply to the presentation. Access and document routing can be controlled through XML documents so that physicians can automatically be sent a "today's appointments" report listing the day's schedule.

The portal can also limit access to patient records to their own doctors. For example, the access rule in Example 19-1 ensures that only Dr. Caps has access to the lab report in Example 19-2, where he is identified as the attending physician. The %doctor_name% variable accesses the user's login identity.

Example 19-1. Access rule for lab reports

```
Access Rule: Grant Read where
    Lab.report\attending.physician$eq$%doctor_name%
```

Example 19-2. Lab report

```
<lab.report>
<patient>
<name>John Smith</name>
<mrn>ID939393</mrn>
</patient>
<attending.physician>Dr. Caps</attending.physician>
<result>
<test>
<name>Throat culture</name>
</test>
</result>
</lab.report>
```

19.6 | Linking up the supply chain

Healthcare enterprises struggle constantly with managing all their external suppliers. The typical organization must deal on a daily basis with laboratories, physicians, transcription services houses, and most importantly, the benefit providers (Blue Triangle in your case).

The portal's ability to automate the relationship with provider organizations is one of the key benefits to the healthcare facility. The billing department will extract XML information from the portal to create an electronic billing invoice, passing it through an XML-enabled transaction server for transmittal over a secure extranet connection to Blue Triangle. Blue Triangle, in processing the invoice, verifies your benefits eligibility with Healtheon prior to transmitting a payment voucher back to ABC Medical Center.

Internet banking services will also impact the payment system. Soon you might be able to authorize electronic payment of your co-pay amount directly from your checking account.

19.7 | Conclusion

XML-powered health portals with dynamic patient summaries transform the healthcare experience. Patients receive better, faster healthcare service while clinicians gain greater access to information that enables them to make the best decisions.

Healthcare organizations also realize significant benefits. Their service reputation improves even while they cut costs because doctors don't order the same tests multiple times. In addition, automated billing lowers costs further while improving cash flow.

Hint   *You can learn more about building enterprise information portals with Sequoia's XML Portal Server in Chapter 18, "Portal servers for e-business", on page 252.*

Syndication

- Information feed syndication
- XMLNews
- Information and Content Exchange (ICE)

Part Five

Syndication – the delivery of content to multiple subscribers simultaneously – is as old as the newspaper business. In some sense, syndication is the original supply chain. However, unlike EDI, syndicators deliver the actual merchandise electronically, not just the transaction data.

In today's Web, syndication has become important to businesses in general, not just the media industry. Enterprises now subscribe to such "syndicated information" as supplier catalogs and technical data.

In this part we'll first examine a document type for news syndication. Then we'll look at the operations of a major syndication service – the Web equivalent of the newswire – that brings real-time information feeds to portals.

Finally, we'll look at an emerging industry standard for ordering and delivering syndicated information.

XMLNews:
A syndication document type

Application Discussion

∎ News syndication initiative

∎ *XMLNews-Story* document type

∎ Instances with varying degrees of markup

Sponsor: Wavo Corporation, http://www.wavo.com/

Contributing experts: Bonnie Robinson and David Megginson

Chapter

20

Portals feed on *feeds* – continuous information streams like the newswire, which has carried syndicated articles from services like Reuters and the Associated Press since the dawn of the telegraph. Now the news feed is being updated for the Internet, thanks to XML.

The XMLNews initiative promotes the use of XML in the news syndication industry, building on existing specifications and providing new ones where needed. To date, two specifications have been published: XMLNews-Meta and XMLNews-Story.

XMLNews-Meta

This XML application defines metadata records for news objects. It conforms to the Resource Description Framework (RDF), developed by the World Wide Web Consortium for the exchange of metadata.

XMLNews-Meta is not limited to traditional, character-based wire stories. Because it holds the metadata in a separate document, you can use it for any kind of news information, including textual news stories, photos, audio or video clips, or even virtual 3-D worlds and interactive scripts.

XMLNews-Meta is described in Chapter 21, "Wavo Corporation", on page 288.

XMLNews-Story

This specification defines the representation of news stories in XML. It is a streamlined but fully-compatible subset of the larger News Industry Text Format (NITF) standard, developed by the International Press Telecommunications Council (IPTC; http://www.iptc.org/iptc/) and the Newspaper Association of America (NAA; http://www.naa.org/).

NITF itself is designed to replace ANPA 1312, a modem format currently used by most major wire services.

This chapter illustrates *XMLNews-Story* (and NITF) by showing how to create and then enhance a simple news story.

20.1 | Structure of a news story

Although there is a lot of variety in presentation, most news stories share a basic logical structure. Figure 20-1 shows the parts of a basic news story.

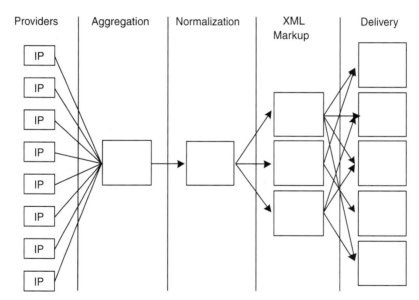

Figure 20-1   Structure of a news story

headline

    The headline "Kansas gets $5.7 Million Relief" is the main title of the story. The purpose of a headline is both to grab a reader's attention and to provide some information about what will appear in the story. As a result, the headline is usually presented in such a way that it stands out from the rest of the story.

subheadline

In addition to the headline, this story contains a subheadline "Money will help dislocated workers," which provides additional information about the contents of the story. The subheadline is usually rendered so that it is less prominent than the headline, but more prominent than the rest of the news story. In certain rare cases, a story might have more than one subheadline.

byline

The byline credits the author of the story. It is called the "byline" because, in English, it often begins with the word "by". Many news stories do not have bylines, and for those that do, the byline might contain a person's name, several people's names, an organization's name, or just a generic word like "staff", as is the case with this story.

dateline

Some news stories contain a dateline, like "Wichita, Kansas, May 6, 1999." If the dateline is present, it contains the location (or locations) from which the story was filed, and sometimes, the date as well.

body

The body (or "copy") contains the actual news story itself. A simple news story consists only of character text divided into a series of paragraphs. More complicated news stories contain other types of information, such as photographs, figures, and tables.

20.2 | Structure of an XMLNews-Story document

The XML element types used in an *XMLNews-Story* document (and in a full NITF document) reflect this basic story structure. Figure 20-2 shows the top-level element structure, which borrows heavily from HTML. The root element type, `nitf`, contains two subelements, `head` and `body`.

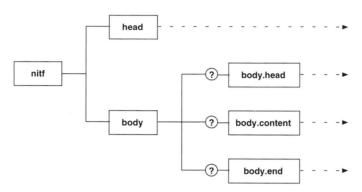

Figure 20-2   *XMLNews-Story* top-level structure

As in HTML, the `head` element contains non-printing information about the document, such as the title for cataloging purposes (which may or may not be the same as the headline).

Unlike HTML, though, the *XMLNews-Story* `body` element is further subdivided into three parts:

`body.head`
> This element contains the headline, subheadlines, byline, and dateline, together with other (optional) information.

`body.content`
> This element contains the actual story body.

`body.end`
> This element contains the (aptly-named for XML) `tagline`, a small copyright or distribution notice that often appears at the end of a printed story.

To actually create a story, you need to insert the root `nitf` element; it is also a good idea to include the XML declaration, stating the version of

XML used (currently, "1.0") and, optionally, the character encoding, as seen in Example 20-1:

Example 20-1. XML declaration and `nitf` root element

```
<?xml version="1.0" encoding="UTF-8"?>
<nitf>
</nitf>
```

If you wish to create a valid XML document, you must also include a document type declaration with the system identifier for the *XMLNews-Story*, as shown in Example 20-2.

Example 20-2. Adding the document type declaration

```
<?xml version="1.0"?>
<!DOCTYPE nitf SYSTEM
  "http://www.xmlnews.org/dtds/xmlnews-story.dtd">
<nitf>
</nitf>
```

An XML-aware editing tool can insert all of this for you automatically (see Figure 20-3).

You must include a `head` element followed by a `body` element. The `head` element contains a `title` element with the title of the news story, as shown in Example 20-3. This is the title for cataloging purposes; it may be the same as the headline, but does not have to be.

Example 20-3. head, `title`, and `body` elements

```
<head>
<title>Gore announces Emergency Relief</title>
</head>
<body>
</body>
```

The body of the story is divided into three parts. The `body.head` element contains the headline, subheadline, byline, and dateline, together with the name of the distributor, as shown in Example 20-4.

Example 20-4. The body.head element

```
<body.head>
  <hedline>
    <hl1>Kansas gets $5.7 Million Relief</hl1>
    <hl2>Money will help dislocated workers</hl2>
  </hedline>
  <byline>
    <bytag>Staff</bytag>
  </byline>
    <distributor>ACME Newswire</distributor>
  <dateline>
    <location>Wichita, Kansas</location>
    <story.date>May 6, 1999</story.date>
  </dateline>
</body.head>
```

The body.content element contains the main body of the story, divided into paragraphs, as shown in Example 20-5.

Example 20-5. The body.content element

```
<body.content>
<p>Vice President Al Gore announced today that Kansas will
receive $5,731,224 in emergency funds to help workers who
lost their jobs as a result of the tornadoes that struck the
state this week.</p>
<p>Nearly $2 million of the funds will be awarded
immediately to provide temporary jobs to help with the clean
up and restoration efforts of the affected communities.
Early estimates indicate that at least that at least 30
businesses were damaged or destroyed as a result of
Tuesday's tornadoes, including the total destruction of
Norland Plastics in Haysville, KS, the town's primary
employer with a full-time payroll of 234 workers.</p>
<p><q>I know that these tornadoes have taken quite a toll on
the people of Kansas,</q> Gore said. <q>I want them to know
that the Federal government is available to help them start
rebuilding their neighborhoods and their lives.</q></p>
</body.content>
```

The body.end element contains a tagline with a copyright notice for the fictional provider ACME Newswire, as shown in Example 20-6.

Example 20-6. The body.end element

```
<body.end>
<tagline><copyrite>Copyright (c) 1999 by ACME Newswire. All rights
reserved.</copyrite>
</tagline>
</body.end>
```

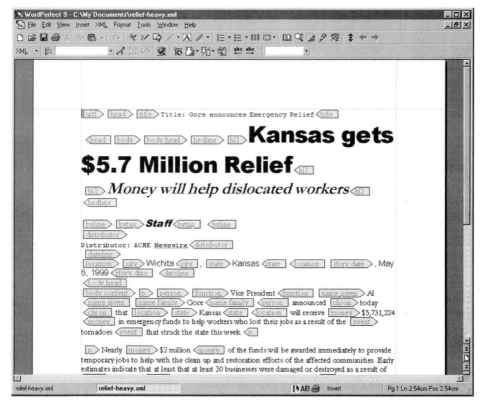

Figure 20-3   Creating an *XMLNews-Story* document in an XML-aware
word processor.

20.3 | Rich inline markup

In addition to basic, high-level structural markup, the *XMLNews-Story* document type also supports rich inline markup, which can improve the quality of news feeds.

The existing ANPA 1312 standard allows newswire stories to contain some presentational inline codes, to mark font shifts within a paragraph for example. NITF and *XMLNews-Story* replace these codes with XML elements specifying not how a word or phrase should look, but what it actually means.

There are seventeen inline elements allowed (but not required) in the body of a news story:

chron
A phrase that refers to a specific date and time (such as "today", or "last February"). It optionally includes a normalized date and time in ISO 8601 format.

copyrite
A copyright statement.

event
A word or phrase referring to an event, such as a holiday, a natural disaster, an election, or an awards ceremony.

function
A word or phrase referring to a person's function, such as "President," "well-known reporter," "astronaut," or "right-wing lobbyist."

location
A word or phrase referring to a geographical location, such as a country, city, town, region, neighborhood, or building.

money
A word or phrase referring to a monetary item. It optionally includes the currency in ISO 4217 format.

num
A word or phrase referring to a quantity, including fractions.

object.title
A word or phrase referring to the title of an object such as a book, movie, television show, or song.

org

> A word or phrase referring to an organization such as a government, a non-profit organization, a university, or a publicly-traded company.

person

> A word or phrase referring to a person.

virtloc

> A word or phrase referring to a virtual location such as a URL or an e-mail address.

a

> A word or phrase that is the source of a hyperlink (from HTML).

br

> A line break (from HTML).

em

> An emphasized word or phrase (from HTML).

lang

> A word or phrase in a different language or dialect from the main story. It may optionally include the ISO 629 language code, with or without an ISO 3166 country code as a qualifier.

pronounce

> A word or phrase that may be difficult to pronounce. It includes a phonetic spelling or other guide to pronunciation.

q

> A direct quotation. (It is not necessary to add quotation marks when you use this element).

None of the additional markup is required. However, including it can make the news story much more valuable, because consumers can perform more intelligent indexing, filtering, cataloging, and searching. For example, an online news service could generate an index of every person mentioned in the day's news, and a user could search for "Buffalo" the city without finding matches for "buffalo" the animal.

Example 20-7 is the first paragraph of the body of the original story:

Example 20-7. The first paragraph of the body of the original story

```
<p>Vice President Al Gore announced today that Kansas will
receive $5,731,224 in emergency funds to help workers who
lost their jobs as a result of the tornadoes that struck the
state this week.</p>
```

For many uses, simply delimiting the paragraph is sufficient; however, a news distributor could add value to a news story by introducing some basic inline markup, as shown in Example 20-8:

Example 20-8. Introducing some basic inline markup

```
<p><person>Vice President Al Gore</person> announced today
that <location>Kansas</location> will receive
<money>$5,731,224</money> in emergency funds to help workers
who lost their jobs as a result of the
<event>tornadoes</event> that struck the state this week.</p>
```

Now, a news filtering system can tell that this story discusses the event "tornadoes" rather than, say, the airplane, and the person "Gore" rather than a street or town with the same name.

An archivist might choose to add even more markup to the same paragraph to allow highly-sophisticated searching and analysis, as shown in Example 20-9:

Example 20-9. An archivist's additional markup

```
<p><person><function>Vice President</function>
<name.given>Al</name.given>
<name.family>Gore</name.family></person> announced <chron
norm="19990506">today</chron> that
<location><state>Kansas</state></location> will receive
<money unit="USD">$5,731,224</money> in emergency funds to
help workers who lost their jobs as a result of the
<event>tornadoes</event> that struck the state this
week.</p>
```

With this rich inline markup, it would be possible for a British publication to perform automatic currency conversion from U.S. dollars to pounds sterling; for a search engine to distinguish the word "Kansas" as a state name from the word "Kansas" as part of a city name; or for an filtering program to find stories about people with "Gore" as a last name but not a first name.

Initially, at least, most news providers and distributors will likely not adopt markup as rich and complex as that in the last example, but the markup is available when needed.

20.4 | Media objects

Even traditional printed news stories often contain non-textual items such as photographs or illustrations, and a news story from a new media provider might also contain live content like audio or video clips. NITF and *XML-News-Story* provide support for photographs, images, and audio and video clips.

 Tip   You can find more about XMLNews on the CD-ROM. Check the Wavo folder in the Sponsor Showcase.

Wavo Corporation

Case Study

■ *MediaXpress* Internet syndication service

■ From delivery service to value-added aggregator

■ Automatic markup

■ *XMLNews-Meta* document type

Sponsor: Wavo Corporation, http://www.wavo.com/

Contributing experts: Deren Hansen and Charles deTranaltes

Chapter

21

The "wire" in newswire used to refer to telegraph wires. Nowadays it's virtually virtual, as news increasingly moves by other means, including the Internet. Learn how one company went from being a wire substitute to a value-added data aggregator with the help of XML.

For more than 15 years, Wavo Corporation has been in the business of moving media, particularly news. Every day it distributes thousands of stories from major newswire providers like the Associated Press, Dow Jones, and Reuters.

In the fall of 1998, the company launched a strategic initiative to integrate the technologies from its various divisions into an industry-standard system for aggregating, normalizing, and delivering commercial news services via the Internet. From the beginning, it was clear that XML would be the glue that bound these technologies together into a system whose whole was greater than the sum of its parts.

21.1 | The challenge

Wavo's business initially revolved around delivering a provider's data to customers in the provider's own format. To that end, the company developed a system to broadcast streaming, real-time data via satellite or FM transmitter. As shown at "A" in Figure 21-1, broadcasts are made to a proprietary receiver (IDR) that, in turn, feeds client computer systems.

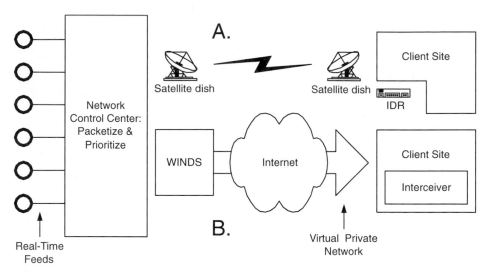

Figure 21-1   Wavo's streaming, real-time data delivery systems.

With the advent of the Internet, the company expanded its palette of delivery mechanisms by creating the Wavo Internet News Delivery Service (WINDS). The WINDS system creates a virtual private network to deliver real-time, streaming information across the Internet. It is shown at "B" in Figure 21-1

Once the distribution infrastructure was in place, the company discovered there was a market for news aggregation services. Commercial news consumers, such as major corporations, wanted one source from which they could receive news feeds from a number of providers.

Those providers deliver their data using proprietary (sometimes idiosyncratic) formats. And where they do use one of the several pre-XML standards for news, Wavo found, they follow the standard rigorously – except when they don't!

Shielding downstream data consumers from the idiosyncrasies of the various raw feeds turned out to be a real opportunity. Syntactic normalization, or having a single representation for all delivered data, was the obvious first step. It is shown in Figure 21-2.

Some information providers send metadata to classify their stories by categories, such as industry, location, and subject. As one might expect, each provider that generates metadata has its own taxonomy and data representation. Wavo realized that semantic normalization, or classifying stories

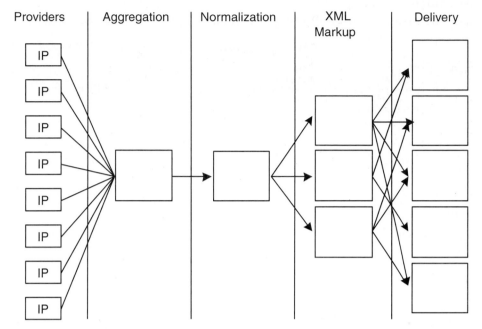

Figure 21-2   Data flow through Wavo's MediaCentral.

according to a common metadata scheme regardless of the source of the story, would add tremendous value to what up till then had been simply a delivery business.

In reviewing this mix of problems and capabilities, Wavo formulated this list of required characteristics of its new system:

consolidated

News from multiple providers is available from a single supplier.

blended

Data is delivered on a single channel; packets are commingled to allow news delivery from multiple sources in a timely fashion.

standardized

A single industry-standard data representation is used for all news sources.

structured
> The structure of the abstract content is preserved in the data representation.

faithful
> The provider's original representation is either preserved or can be reconstructed.

consistent
> The terminology used in the markup means the same thing for all sources.

richly-marked
> The context of proper nouns, such as company names, locations, product names, etc. is identified by markup in the running text.

classified
> Stories are classified for easier retrieval.

21.2 | Wavo's *MediaXpress* service

Wavo's strategic initiative was named *MediaXpress* and was put into production in 1999. It resulted in the three-layer system shown in Figure 21-3.

Layer 1
> High-volume transport services for real-time data.

Layer 2
> Content acquisition and normalization at the network head-end and an application framework for the client site.

Layer 3
> Business and administration layer.

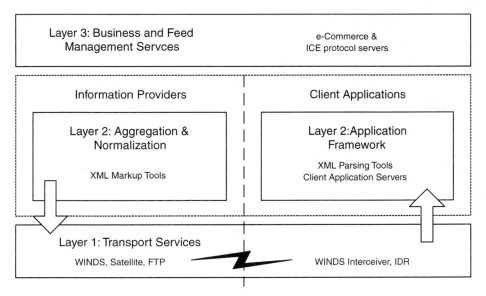

Figure 21-3   The *MediaXpress* system

21.2.1 *Transport layer*

Transport services are available in a variety of configurations, ranging from premium services like satellite broadcast and WINDS to ancillary mechanisms such as FTP and HTTP. The feed distribution system enforces usage, re-distribution, and syndication policies.

The system can provide real-time data delivery without sacrificing the benefits of rich markup. Real-time data is processed at the network head-end and immediately broadcast via WINDS or the satellite network. Receivers running at the customer site automatically produce a minimally marked XML version of the story.

At the same time, that same data stream is also processed at the head-end to create richly marked versions of the real-time stories, complete with metadata and inline tagging. The new versions of the real-time stories are then sent to replace the minimally marked versions of the story delivered earlier.

21.2.2 *Content layer*

The information feeds are translated from their original format into richly marked-up XML documents. There are two kinds of automatic markup applied: normalized associated metadata, and contextual inline markup of significant elements.

On the client side, in addition to transport layer components like WINDS receivers, the service includes a set of applications, demonstration systems, and sample code.

21.2.2.1   Metadata normalization

Some information providers supply metadata with their stories. Such metadata sets typically include fields for geographic region, industry, company name, company code (usually its ticker symbol), and so on. Each information provider has its own set of metadata symbols and usage policies. For example, one provider may only report the geographic region with which a story is concerned, while another might indicate all the countries mentioned in the story.

All provider metadata is preserved, but *MediaXpress* also provides normalized metadata as follows:

- Company names are extracted from the stories and associated with their standard ticker and other symbols.
- Geographic regions are extracted and associated with standard aggregate geographic codes.
- All other proper names are extracted and associated as metadata.
- Detailed industry and event categories are assigned after content analysis.

21.2.2.2   Contextual inline markup

MediaXpress marks up proper nouns (i.e., persons, places, and things) in the body of a story so that one can distinguish between persons and organizations. For example, a sentence such as:

Example 21-1. One word in several contexts.

```
Professor Rice, of Rice University, is an authority on rice.
```

after automatic markup would become:

Example 21-2. Tags identify contexts of words.

```
<person>Professor Rice</person>, of <org>Rice University</org>, is
an authority on rice.
```

21.2.2.3   Markup languages

MediaXpress uses *XMLNews-Meta* and *XMLNews-Story* as its XML document types.

*XMLNews-Story*which is described in Chapter 20, "XMLNews: A syndication document type", on page 276, is a subset of the News Industry Text Format (NITF), an XML document type under development by the International Press Telecommunications Council (IPTC) and the Newspaper Association of America (NAA). It is used for the news stories themselves.

However, the value-added metadata and other elements needed by the system to transmit and process a story are included in a second XML document. You can think of it as a work order and envelope for the story itself. This companion metadata document conforms to the *XMLNews-Meta* document type, which is an application of RDF. An example is shown in Example 21-3.

The relationship between *XMLNews-Meta* and *XMLNews-Story* is shown in Figure 21-4. Decoupling the two provides a great deal of flexibility.

For example, *XMLNews-Story* is limited to associating a single story with its media elements, such as images, audio, and video. *XMLNews-Meta*, however, can associate multiple stories with one another, such as a main article and several sidebars. It can also deliver other document types, such as database records of stock quotes.

Example 21-3. XMLNews-Meta document

```
<?xml version="1.0"?>
<rdf:RDF xmlns:rdf="http://www.w3.org/1999/02/22-rdf-syntax-ns#"
 xmlns:xn="http://www.xmlnews.org/namespaces/meta#">
   <rdf:Resource
    about="199903300001K00002DK000031000009.xml">
      <xn:resourceID>199903300001K00002DK000031000009
        </xn:resourceID>
      <xn:format>text/xml</xn:format>
      <xn:providerName>Dow Jones &amp; Company, Inc.
        </xn:providerName>
      <xn:providerCode>73</xn:providerCode>
      <xn:serviceName>Today's Business Sections via DowVision
        </xn:serviceName>
      <xn:serviceCode>97</xn:serviceCode>
      <xn:receivedTime>1999-03-30T00:01-05:00
        </xn:receivedTime>
      <xn:publicationTime>1999-03-30T00:01-05:00
        </xn:publicationTime>
      <xn:title>When the stock market plunged in October 1987
        </xn:title>
      <xn:subjectCode>DOW:N/LCL</xn:subjectCode>
      <xn:locationCode>DOW:R/US</xn:locationCode>
      <xn:copyright>Copyright 1999</xn:copyright>
   </rdf:Resource>
</rdf:RDF>
```

XMLNews-Meta is also extensible. By employing XML namespaces, users can add their own metadata and document associations.

21.2.3 *Business layer*

MediaXpress has an e-commerce system that allows customers to acquire software, pay for continuing service, and purchase content from participating publishers without human intervention.

The Information and Content Exchange (ICE) protocol is employed to handle information subscriptions, user counts, usage logs, delivery schedules, updates, event logs, trouble reports, redistribution, re-syndication, and so on. The ICE protocol supports automatic negotiation of delivery schedules and requests to resend content. (For more on ICE, see Chapter 22, "Information and Content Exchange (ICE)", on page 300.)

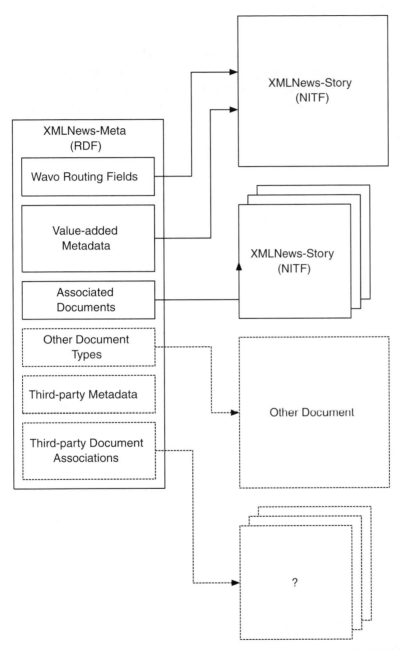

Figure 21-4   Relationship between *XMLNews-Meta* and *XMLNews-Story*

21.3 | Summary

Wavo's *MediaXpress* service is an ambitious undertaking whose success depends on XML. XML is the organizing principle that brings a number of formerly separate technologies together into a cohesive system. All data, regardless of its provider, enjoys the benefit of standardized XML markup, consistent metadata associations, and rich contextual inline markup.

Information and Content Exchange (ICE)

Application Discussion

- The new role of syndication
- Syndication requirements
- An ICE scenario

Sponsor: Kinecta Corporation, http://www.kinecta.com

Contributing expert: Lucien Rhodes

Syndication isn't just for the media industry any more. The growth of value networks and Web portals is making it a vital tool for integrated e-commerce, as trading partners face the need to keep one another updated with current information. Negotiating syndication subscriptions used to be a time-consuming and expensive process, but now there's a cool way to do it!

oday's media industry is dominated by giant content providers – syndicators – that deliver everything from news articles to television programs to a legion of newspapers, networks, and TV stations – subscribers – for publication or broadcast. Syndication – the delivery of content to multiple subscribers simultaneously – began in the earliest days of the newspaper business. It was automated by the telegraph, with reporters and local newspapers transmitting articles to big city newspapers.

In fact, the newspaper business is perhaps the oldest example of an automated supply chain. Unlike the EDI supply chain, however, which delivers only data about commercial transactions, the newswire delivers the actual goods – the news articles.

22.1 | Beyond the newswire

We've seen how the traditional newswire functions are managed when the "wire" is the Internet, with the help of XML. But the Internet also offers the possibility of automating the business side of syndicated content delivery.

And the Internet has also expanded the market for syndication. As integrated e-commerce becomes pervasive, ordinary businesses need to syndicate content and subscribe to content syndicated by others. Two trends in particular are creating this demand: the growth of value networks, and the increasing number of intermediaries serving as market makers.

22.1.1 *Value networks*

A *value network* is a group of businesses that cooperate to create and deliver products and services. Content syndication can be a valuable tool for coordinating and managing the activities of such a network.

For example, consider a high-tech manufacturer. The manufacturer may design new products but outsource the actual manufacturing. The manufacturer needs to manage the set of manufacturing documents its outsourcing partners are using, such as work instructions, assembly procedures, and engineering drawings.

As new manufacturing documents are distributed, effective dates and expiration dates need to be assigned to them. The manufacturer also needs to be assured that all documents are successfully delivered. It also needs notification of any problems as they arise, so they can be resolved promptly.

The manufacturer also needs to supply marketing collateral to its distributors. Marketing documents could include a mix of descriptive text, graphics, and business data, with each document having its own effective date and expiration date. The documents might also need to incorporate each distributor's unique branding.

While manufacturing and marketing documents are certainly not editorial news content, this B2B syndication process shares many of the characteristics of news syndication.

22.1.2 *Intermediaries as market makers*

In the case of value networks, syndication supports the efficient coordination of business partners who have already developed a close working relationship. In other, more fragmented markets, syndication can play a role in helping potential buyers and vendors to find one another in the first place.

In such markets, intermediaries have a key role to play. They aggregate many vendors' marketing collateral, product specifications, data sheets, catalogs, and the like at a single website, so buyers can more easily find what they want. Syndication is used to keep the website current.

In addition, the site can offer subscriptions for buyers who are interested in a specific product. New content is syndicated to the buyer as soon as it becomes available.

22.2 | Syndication requirements

Just as with traditional EDI, sharing online information among a network of partners can be expensive, as adding a new partner requires time-consuming, customized, manual processes. The syndicator must negotiate special requirements with each new subscriber, such as delivery times and frequency, notification, reporting, and monitoring. For example:

Flexible delivery
To operate properly and scale across a wide range of relationships, content syndication must support several delivery techniques. Some subscribers can accept delivery of content at any time, others only at specified times – for instance, off-peak hours. Some subscribers may request specific data at agreed-upon times; others will be set up to receive "pushed" data asynchronously.

Delivery guarantees
Some content items, such as press releases, are embargoed until a certain date and should not be accessible until that date. Also, most content has a shelf life and should be subject to expiration.

Time value
Some content has a time value for delivery. For example, subscribers to a financial service that delivers stock quotes every ten minutes need a guarantee that the quotes will either arrive on time, or that the subscribers will be advised of failure.

22.3 | ICE: A cool and solid solution!

These requirements and other needs of Web-based content syndication are addressed by the Information and Content Exchange (ICE). ICE is an XML-based protocol that defines the business rules and processes needed for reliable content syndication among Web servers. It was developed by a consortium of more than 80 software developers, technology suppliers, content owners, and publishers.

22.3.1 *ICE capabilities*

The ICE protocol defines a model for the ongoing management of syndication relationships, including the roles and responsibilities of syndicators and subscribers. Here are some key capabilities:

- Syndicators can describe business rules, such as usage constraints and intellectual property rights.
- Syndicators can create and manage catalogs of subscription offers. These can be accessed by type of content and by content source.
- ICE uses XML to represent the messages that syndicators and subscribers exchange. The ICE message structure keeps the content payload completely independent of the protocol itself, so virtually any data can be exchanged – from text to streaming video. ICE accommodates data conforming to industry specifications such as RosettaNet and Publishing Requirements for Industry Standard Metadata (PRISM).
- Subscribers can specify a variety of "push" or "pull" delivery modes, as well as delivery times and frequency.
- Subscribers can specify content update parameters, such as incremental or full updates.
- ICE allows content to be obtained from, and delivered to, a wide variety of content repository types. These include databases, content management systems, file directories, Web servers, PDAs, and Internet appliances.
- ICE can work with any reliable transport protocol. The standard HTTP POST "request/response" transport model,

for example, allows fully symmetric ICE implementations in which both syndicators and subscribers can initiate requests.

22.3.2 *An ICE implementation*

Figure 22-1 shows the architecture of an ICE implementation, Kinecta's *Java*-based *Interact* system.

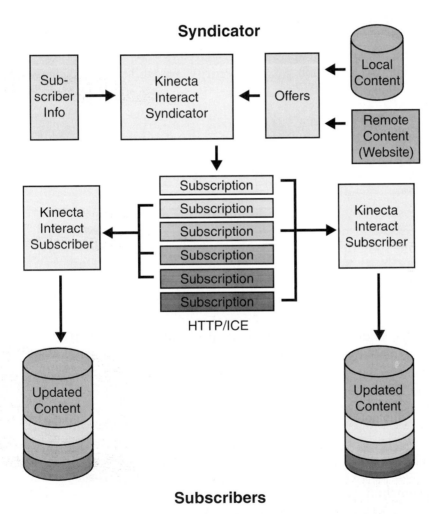

Figure 22-1   Architecture of the *Kinecta Interact* ICE platform

In this particular ICE platform, there are two separate software components named – logically enough – the *Syndicator* and the *Subscriber*.

22.3.2.1   Syndicator functions

The *Syndicator* application lets syndicators manage the packaging and syndication of content, including such essential tasks as:

Creating subscription offers
Syndicators can identify content types and content sources, such as local directories and databases or remote locations, and package the content as subscription offers. They can also define management information, such as security, availability, and shelf life.

Defining subscribers
Syndicators can identify subscribers and the addresses of the receiving computers. They can also provide passwords and other administrative information.

Turning subscription offers into subscriptions
The *Syndicator* can match subscribers to the offers they want. It can define subscription pairs one at a time, or in groups.

Distribute subscription offers to recipients
The *Syndicator* maintains records of offers, subscribers, and subscriptions in its database, and uses these records to control the availability and distribution of offers using the ICE and HTTP protocols. User-configurable logging tracks management and transmission events at the appropriate level of detail, and can automatically report anomalies and problems.

22.3.2.2   Subscriber functions

The *Subscriber* software provides tools and processes to manage content downloads, including:

Defining subscriptions

Subscribers can choose specific subscriptions from a catalog of subscription offers put up by the syndicator.

Defining download rules

Subscribers can specify which subscriptions will be polled for and accepted, how often polling will be done, and where the received content will be stored.

Transforming received content

Subscribers can customize and transform downloaded content. For example, a company might insert its own branding and ads in the content before posting it on its website.

Monitoring content

Subscribers can control event logging and notification priorities.

22.3.2.3   User interface

GUIs are not required by the ICE protocol and ICE transactions can be completed without them, but the appeal of a user-friendly interface is obvious. In *Kinecta Interact*, for example, all ICE operations of the *Syndicator* and the *Subscriber* are carried out through an interface that is partially illustrated in Figure 22-2. The interface code automatically generates ICE XML message documents from the data provided by the user.

22.3.2.4   ICE messages

An ICE message is a valid XML document whose document type is `ice-payload`; subordinate element types describe ICE operations and data. ICE payloads can contain any number of either requests or responses, but not a mixture of both. ICE payloads are exchanged as request/response pairs.

ICE does not restrict the type of content that is the subject of a transmission; the ICE message is effectively an envelope. The content can be incorporated as a subelement of the ICE message if doing so won't cause the document to be invalid XML. Alternatively, a URL to the actual content can be incorporated.

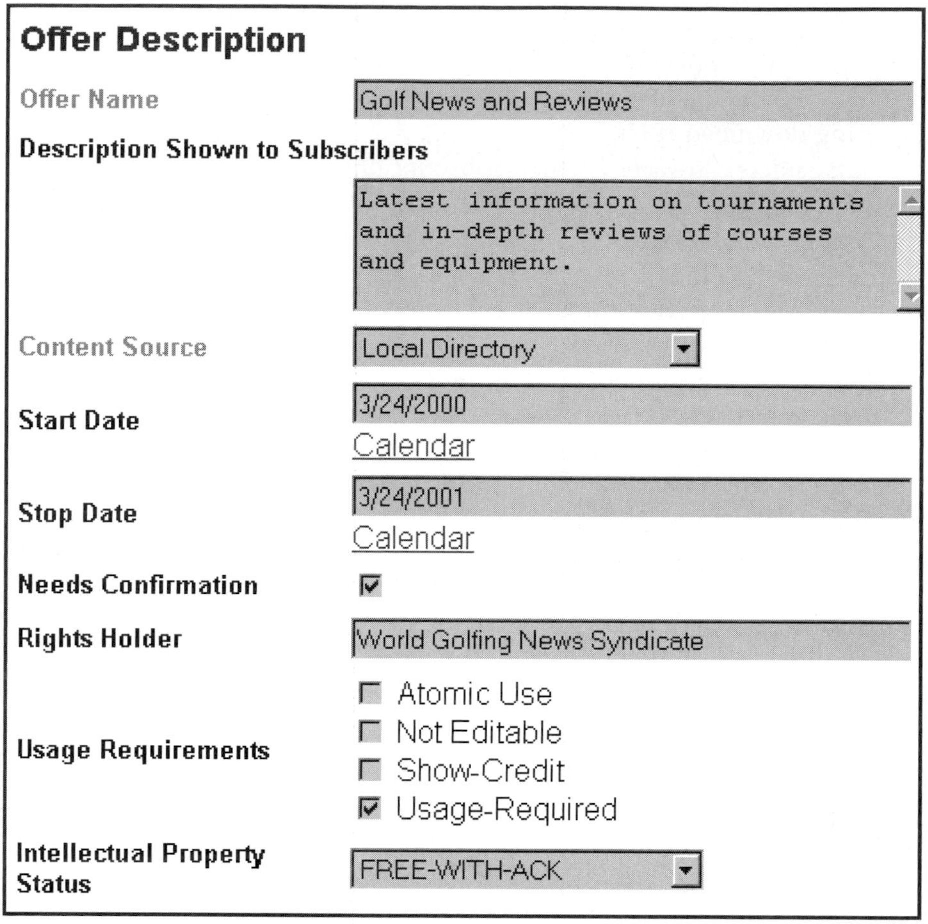

Offer Description

Offer Name	Golf News and Reviews

Description Shown to Subscribers

Latest information on tournaments
and in-depth reviews of courses
and equipment.

Content Source	Local Directory ▾
Start Date	3/24/2000
	<u>Calendar</u>
Stop Date	3/24/2001
	<u>Calendar</u>
Needs Confirmation	☑
Rights Holder	World Golfing News Syndicate
Usage Requirements	☐ Atomic Use
	☐ Not Editable
	☐ Show-Credit
	☑ Usage-Required
Intellectual Property Status	FREE-WITH-ACK ▾

Figure 22-2   A GUI interface for ICE transactions

22.4 | An ICE scenario

Let's look at a step-by-step example illustrating one of the most basic ICE exchanges between a syndicator and a subscriber. Here the syndicator, the Best Code Company, a software developer, sets up and delivers a subscription to Tech News, a trade journal for the high technology industry.

22.4.1 *Syndicator and subscriber set up a business agreement*

Syndication relationships begin with a business agreement. Best Code and Tech News agree on such terms as payment issues, usage rights, and subscription lifetime. The business agreement negotiation typically happens outside ICE and can involve person-to-person discussion, legal review, and contracts.

22.4.2 *Syndicator and subscriber set up a subscription*

Once the business agreement is in place, ICE comes into play as Best Code and Tech News start exchanging ICE messages to create a subscription. The exchange can involve negotiation about the mechanics of the subscription, such as when the content is delivered, what delivery guarantees are made, whether delivery is done by push or pull, and so forth.

22.4.2.1 Subscriber requests catalog of subscription offers

Example 22-1 shows an ICE message in which Tech News uses `ice-get-catalog` to request a subscription catalog from Best Code. Tech News identifies itself to Best Code using a Universal Unique Identifier (UUID), as defined by the Open Group.

22.4.2.2 Syndicator responds with catalog containing one offer

In Example 22-2, Best Code uses `ice-offer-type="subscription"` to tell Tech News that the catalog contains a single subscription offer for press releases. `ice-delivery-rule mode="pull"` tells Tech News that this particular subscription offer will be delivered by the "pull" delivery method.

Example 22-1. Request for a catalog of subscription offers

```
<?xml version="1.0"?>
<!DOCTYPE ice-payload SYSTEM "http://www.ice-ag.org/ICE.dtd">
<ice-payload ice.version="1.1"
             payload-id="74"
             timestamp="2000-09-22T04:37:00">
<ice-header>
  <ice-sender sender-id="37AB3FDO-D2CA-11d3-BBE9-723B75000000"
              name="tech news"
              role="subscriber"/>
  <ice-user-agent>Kinecta Subscriber 3.0</ice-user-agent>
</ice-header>
<ice-request request-id="74">
  <ice-get-catalog/>
</ice-request>
</ice-payload>
```

Example 22-2. Catalog containing one offer

```
<?xml version="1.0"?>
<!DOCTYPE ice-payload SYSTEM "http://www.ice-ag.org/ICE.dtd">
<ice-payload ice.version="1.1"
             payload-id="74"
             timestamp="2000-09-22T04:37:03">
<ice-header>
  <ice-sender sender-id="37AB3FD1-D2CA-11d3-BBE9-723B75000000"
              name="best code"
              role="syndicator"/>
  <ice-user-agent>Kinecta Syndicator 3.0</ice-user-agent>
</ice-header>
<ice-response response-id="74">
  <ice-code numeric="200" phrase="OK"/>
  <ice-catalog>
    <ice-contact description="Call her if something crashes."
                 name="Marcia Programmer, CEO, Code Co.">
Marcia Programmer mprog@bcode.com
(123) 456 7890
    </ice-contact>
    <ice-offer type="subscription"
               description="code co. press releases">
      <ice-delivery-policy>
        <ice-delivery-rule mode="pull"/>
      </ice-delivery-policy>
    </ice-offer>
  </ice-catalog>
</ice-response>
</ice-payload>
```

22.4.2.3 Subscriber sends a request to subscribe to the offer

Tech News thinks the press releases are exciting stuff and promptly asks to sign up for the subscription offer. It agrees to pull the content from Best Code's site and with `minfreq="P300S"` requests 5 minute intervals at most (Example 22-3.

Example 22-3. Request for a subscription

```
<?xml version="1.0"?>
<!DOCTYPE ice-payload SYSTEM "http://www.ice-ag.org/ICE.dtd">
<ice-payload ice.version="1.1"
             payload-id="75"
             timestamp="2000-09-22T04:40:00">
<ice-header>
  <ice-sender sender-id="37AB3FD0-D2CA-11d3-BBE9-723B75000000"
              name="tech news"
              role="subscriber/>
  <ice-user-agent>Kinecta Subscriber 3.0</ice-user-agent>
</ice-header>
<ice-request request-id="75">
  <ice-offer type="subscription"
             description=" code co. press releases">
    <ice-delivery-policy>
      <ice-delivery-rule mode="pull" minfreq="P300S"/>
    </ice-delivery-policy>
  </ice-offer>
</ice-request>
</ice-payload>
```

22.4.2.4 Syndicator accepts request and responds with subscription

Best Code indicates that a subscription has been established by enclosing the agreed-upon offer within an `ice-subscription` element. Best Code gives Tech News an ID number of "1" for the subscription and also confirms the delivery method and "pull" time (Example 22-4).

Example 22-4. Acceptance of subscription request

```
<?xml version="1.0"?>
<!DOCTYPE ice-payload SYSTEM "http://www.ice-ag.org/ICE.dtd">
<ice-payload ice.version="1.1"
             payload-id="75"
             timestamp="2000-09-22T04:40:03">
<ice-header>
  <ice-sender sender-id="37AB3FD1-D2CA-11d3-BBE9-723B75000000"
              name="best code"
              role="syndicator"/>
  <ice-user-agent>Kinecta Syndicator 3.0</ice-user-agent>
</ice-header>
<ice-response response-id="75">
  <ice-code numeric="200" phrase="OK"/>
  <ice-subscription subscription-id="1">
    <ice-offer type="subscription"
               description="best code press releases">
      <ice-delivery-policy>
        <ice-delivery-rule mode="pull" minfreq="P300S"/>
      </ice-delivery-policy>
    </ice-offer>
  </ice-subscription>
</ice-response>
</ice-payload>
```

22.4.3 *Subscriber receives content*

Once the subscription is set up, Tech News is ready to receive content. Tech News starts by asking for new content. Best Code responds with a message describing the changes to the content in the subscription. These changes can include new content and can also include requests to delete existing content. In this way, Best Code can control the precise content for that subscription on the Tech News site. Together with the actual content, the messages may also specify other subscription parameters such as effective date and expiration date.

22.4.3.1   Subscriber requests initial subscription content

Tech News uses `ice-get-package` to ask for subscription content. `current-state="ICE-INITIAL"` indicates that this is an initial request for this subscription, which alerts Best Code to download the full content (Example 22-5).

Example 22-5. Request for initial subscription content

```
<?xml version="1.0"?>
<!DOCTYPE ice-payload SYSTEM "http://www.ice-ag.org/ICE.dtd">
<ice-payload ice.version="1.0"
             payload-id="951723923006951723922044"
             timestamp="07:45:22,044">
<ice-header>
  <ice-sender sender-id="37AB3FD0-D2CA-11d3-BBE9-723B75000000"
              name="tech news"
              role="subscriber"/>
  <ice-user-agent>Kinecta Subscriber 3.0</ice-user-agent>
</ice-header>
<ice-request request-id="951723923012951723922044">
  <ice-get-package current-state="ICE-INITIAL"
                   subscription-id="1"/>
</ice-request>
</ice-payload>
```

22.4.3.2 Syndicator responds with full content of subscription

In Example 22-6, Best Code delivers the content of its subscription, consisting of an `ice-package` with two press releases. The first release is part of the message – the content of an `ice-item` element. The second release, however, is not actually in the message. Instead, its location is given in the `url` attribute of an `ice-item-ref` element.

The `ice-package` element also conveys other information. `editable="true"` gives Tech News permission to edit the content, while `new-state="2"` establishes the state of the subscription. The next time Tech

Example 22-6. Delivery of subscription content

```xml
<?xml version="1.0"?>
<!DOCTYPE ice-payload SYSTEM "http://www.ice-ag.org/ICE.dtd">
<ice-payload ice-version="1.1"
             payload-id="9534103105879951724229302"
             timestamp="07:50:29,743">
<ice-header>
  <ice-sender sender-id="37AB3FD1-D2CA-11d3-BBE9-723B75000000"
              name="best code"
              role="syndicator"/>
  <ice-user-agent>Kinecta Syndicator 3.0</ice-user-agent>
</ice-header>
<ice-response response-id="9534084755799951724229302">
  <ice-code numeric="200" phrase="OK"
            message-id="9517239230129951723922044" />
  <ice-package editable="true"
               new-state="2"
               old-state="ICE-INITIAL"
               package-id="9537749528891951724229302"
               subscription-id="1">
    <ice-item item-id="1" name="press release 1"
      subscription-element=
        "http://10.10.1.53:8891/1762994087/PressRelease1.DOC"
      content-filename="PressRelease1.DOC">
Press Release 1
Latest news: we've released our first press release!
    </ice-item>
    <ice-item-ref
      item-id="2-951719746000"
      name="press release 2"
      subscription-element=
        "http://10.10.1.53:8891/1762994087/PressRelease2.DOC"
      url="http://10.10.1.53:8891/1762994087/PressRelease2.DOC"
      content-filename="PressRelease2.DOC"/>
  </ice-package>
</ice-response>
</ice-payload>
```

News requests content, it will receive only content added or changed since this delivery, instead of receiving the entire content load all over again.

Tip   This example showed a basic ICE transaction. The protocol is capable of far more complex negotiations, as you can learn by visiting `http://www.icestandard.org/`.

Publishing

- Online and offline from single source
- Extranet delivery of high-quality printing
- Customizing supplier's documentation

Part Six

Publish or perish!

For decades that has been the mandate for academics seeking an assured career path. Today it is the mandate for enterprises of all kinds that are hostage to documentation requirements. If the manuals, reports, and marketing materials aren't ready, it is the products and business opportunities that will perish – not the career of some assistant professor.

And publishing today doesn't necessarily mean just a uniform static message on the corpses of dead trees: It means websites, CD-ROMs, multimedia, wireless, personalized delivery, and – yes – paper as well.

In this part we'll see how several companies have used XML to meet the demands of this new publishing environment, on and off the Web, in industries as diverse as financial management and computer magazine publishing. We'll also look at a problem of the information supply chain: How can you customize your supplier's documents safely and seamlessly?

Frank Russell Company

- Extranet XML financial publishing
- Business and technical requirements identification
- Structure-driven style

Sponsor: Frank Russell Company, http://www.russell.com

Contributing experts: Bryan Bell and Randy Kelley

This chapter is the chronicle of an extraordinary project: demanding requirements, ambitious goals, leading-edge technology, business school management techniques, and – did we mention "mission-critical"? – a trillion dollars riding on the outcome. And XML figures in it as well.

As a leading investment management and asset consulting firm, Frank Russell Company improves the financial security of people throughout the world. Russell provides investment solutions for institutions and individuals, guiding the investment of more than $1 trillion for clients in more than 25 countries.

23.1 | Background

During the eighties, Russell pioneered the use of color presentations and "high touch" relationship management with its group of clients. Recently, Russell has experienced explosive growth in the investment management division, marketing private mutual fund products to the institutional marketplace, and retail funds through a group of selected distribution partners.

Immediately you can visualize the tension between high quality/high touch and explosive growth. There needed to be a strategy to address the increasing production volume demands without sacrificing quality or profit margins. This led to a requirement for automation.

Russell traditionally viewed its printed client books as products. This project was the first to begin to stress that the importance of the book is really Russell's content, and that the book itself is merely a rendition.

Russell had been using the "print, then distribute" metaphor for decades. But as the newer digital technologies and communication processes were taking hold, and the World Wide Web's popularity became undeniable, the Russell Advanced Technology Lab began an effort to evangelize, design, produce and deliver a new metaphor: "distribute, then print".

Along with this shift in metaphors come real quality control issues, especially revolving around color printing. Not only were the traditional problems of re-purposing content for different media (i.e. for paper, CD-ROM, electronic, FAX, and email) an issue, but also an entirely new set of work-flow and editing issues was recognized with respect to the re-use of component objects from within the created documents.

Also, the trend to customizing the content product – moving from generic content to a specialized product for an individual information consumer, a "market of one" – was extremely interesting to Russell.

This chapter chronicles both the team's journey and the Russell solution that is currently in production.

23.2 | Project strategy considerations

Russell has steadily been increasing its own awareness that it truly is a large publishing concern, producing millions of pages of color and black and white output for its clients every year. And as a major financial intellectual property publisher, it is also realizing that printing and electronic delivery systems play a very strategic role in its continued growth and success.

There were five principle strategic considerations for the conduct of the project:

- Proceeding from a theoretical abstraction to practical applications.
- Phasing deliverables with measurable return on investment.
- Continuing research in parallel with focused development projects.
- Alignment with overall corporate strategies.
- Executive sponsorship.

23.2.1 *Proceeding from a theoretical abstraction to practical applications*

The project team, though capable of grasping both the short- and long-term objectives for the enterprise, required a methodology to manage scope creep. It chose to divide the tasks into two clear groups:

- the theoretical research and related effort towards general solutions; and
- day-to-day development.

The team was always able to have discussions from the abstract down to the practical by mapping them onto the architecture and life cycle models. When new technologies or vendor products came onto the radar, it was able to discuss them in the context of both the theory and practical project impact using a systematic method.

23.2.2 *Phasing deliverables with measurable return on investment*

This concept may sound similar to the concept of milestones, but is really quite different. This method assumes that there is *no* other project beyond the goals of this one.

It also assumes that this project must justify its own return on investment and bear management review based on its own merits.

Another key element is the openness of each phase's architecture, so that later phases can be bolted on seamlessly with very little trauma to users or developers.

23.2.3 *Continuing research in parallel with focused development projects*

Scope creep is an ever-present danger in technology. Change is a constant. Managing new inputs from press, rumors, research, and outside influence is a constant pressure on fixed milestones and deliverables.

The project team chose discretion as the better part of valor by separating the tasks of research and development into two distinct activities. The development tasks have clearly documented milestones, schedules, and budgets, with methodology in place to monitor their success weekly.

The research tasks are managed more loosely, with overall topics of interest. They use annual funding, rather than project-based funding, and measure deliverables by the published output from the team.

The team believes that this separation keeps developers on the hook for cleaner deliverables and return on investment, while still allowing a response to the crucial happenings that are a day-to-day part of the technology world.

23.2.4 Alignment with overall corporate strategies

Any technology project can be fraught with risk. Any technology project can solve a specific technical application and add value if properly executed. Russell's experience was that the real grand slam winner projects are the ones that support the overall mission, culture, vision, and business objectives of an enterprise.

In theory every part of an enterprise is supposed to be working on things that contribute to the goals of the entire enterprise. Straying too far from this principle increases risk and confuses observers, whereas following this principle makes a project's justification much easier to defend and publicize.

23.2.5 Executive sponsorship

For several reasons, this is the most powerful thing you can do to enhance a project's chance for success:

- Executives are generally seasoned professionals who have earned a place of authority by knowing how to exploit strengths and manage around weaknesses.
- Executives are generally the best funded portion of an enterprise.

- Executives generally have a clear understanding of the long-term objectives of the enterprise.
- Executives generally have a feeling for the short-term pressures on operations.

These executive qualities enhance a group's ability to make sure their work is done with the support and point-of-view of the senior management and shareholders.

23.3 | Identifying the needs

Russell began to realize the extremely high importance of publishing to the company when it found out the cost. A study determined that almost 1/3 of every expense dollar worldwide was attributable to documents and their production, printing and distribution.

23.3.1 *Business requirements*

The question then became: "How to distribute financial services publications better to a geographically diverse audience, while maintaining premium typographical quality, data integrity, security and compliance?"

Compliance
Russell operates in a heavily regulated environment. There is a legal requirement to reproduce documents related to a customer from many years in the past.

Premium typographic quality
Russell customers typically evaluate large amounts of financial information in a limited time. Russell adds tremendous value for their customers by simplifying and clarifying these numbers through the use of text, graphics, charts, and color.

Data integrity
It is extremely important that the document received by a customer is identical to the one that was sent to it.

Security

Because of the confidential nature of financial information, it is imperative that only the appropriate people can view these files.

23.3.2 *Technical requirements*

There were significant technical requirements to be met in addition to the business requirements.

Scalability

At Russell, a *Quarterly Investment Review* (QIR) runs from 20-125 pages, averaging around 50 pages. There are hundreds of clients who each get a customized QIR each quarter. Multiple writing, editing, assembly, and compliance steps are required throughout the process.

Low licensing impact for reader software

The problem with end-user licensing of software is that it penalizes a business for the success of a document.

Ease of use

To us, the lab team, ease of use is the single most important factor in the true success of a product.

Cross-platform

Russell cannot control the platforms that its customers use. It has to provide its information in an easily accessible form on virtually every platform available.

Multilingual capability

Russell has offices in London, New York, Winston-Salem, Paris, Hong Kong, Toronto, Tokyo, Sydney, and Auckland. Russell has clients in 25 countries.

23.4 | Create an abstract architecture

Russell's Advanced Technology Lab team set off to learn about the state of the art in publishing systems, SGML, PDF, and document delivery systems.

Russell had been a pioneer of Postscript assembly and color graphics in the financial services industry. Now the Lab team desired to modernize Russell's publication capabilities to support lower than page granularity and the "distribute then print" metaphor. The team felt that this type of system could meet Russell's business objectives.

The team, working with consultants, created a "Request For Information and Statement of Direction" for a system to purchase (Figure 23-1).

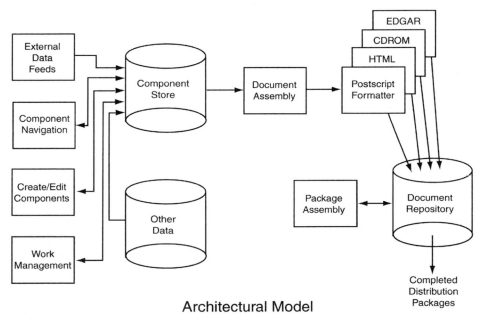

Architectural Model

Figure 23-1 Architectural model of desired system.

The team also performed research on document life cycles and included the life cycle requirements shown in Figure 23-2.

Russell searched the SGML community for a publishing solution to meet its requirements and found no single commercial product in the marketplace. It then asked the big question: "Why isn't there one already"? The

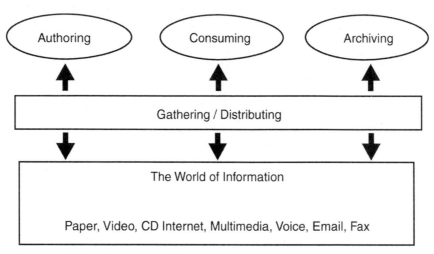

Figure 23-2   Document life cycle requirements.

team felt that there were many companies and institutions with document problems similar to, if not more complex than, Russell's.

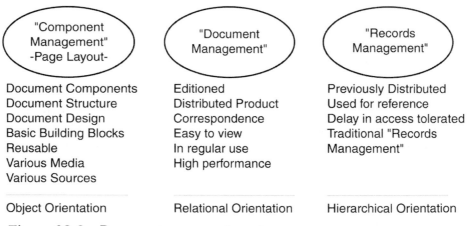

Figure 23-3   Document system orientations.

So the team spent several more months analyzing vendor capabilities and mapping them onto the life cycle graphic until it finally found what it felt was a possible reason. Namely, that the creating, consuming, and archiving stages of a document's life require different system capabilities and orientations: component management, document management, and records management, respectively (Figure 23-3).

Armed with this insight, the team developed the knowledge management model shown in Figure 23-4.

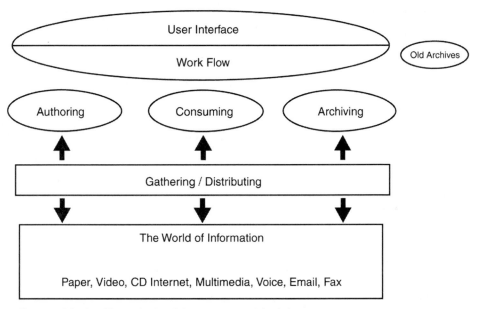

Figure 23-4   Knowledge Management Model

Russell's management and the Lab team then decided to build and integrate a solution out of *commercially available off-the-shelf* (*COTS*) products. The team decided to break the deliverables into different phases that would be integrated upon completion.

23.5 | Implement applications

The team's initial choice for an application was the *Quarterly Investment Review*. The QIR is representative of many of Russell's publications because it consists of a combination of generic, proprietary, customer-specific, and reusable components.

23.5.1 *Real-world design issues*

In order to apply the theoretical architecture to specific application designs for the QIR publications, the team had to come to grips with real-world issues of internetworking and document representation (file format) standards, to name a few.

23.5.1.1   Internetworking

The WWW family of technologies was chosen for its popularity. Its open-standard nature met the team's basic technical requirements for global electronic delivery, easy access, cheap per-seat licensing costs, cross-platform availability, and security.

The extranet model best served Russell's clients in this application. That is, WWW technologies connected, via public and/or private networks, to a restricted website.

23.5.1.2   Document representation

The Russell team is very firmly attached to the notion that document representation is the key to an organization's success with knowledge management. In the *SGML Buyers Guide* (1998), the authors clearly express this point: *"Don't let the software you buy determine the representation. Let the representation you need determine the software you buy"*.

In Russell's case, they needed to choose document representations for all three stages of the document life cycle.

During the creation stage, documents are most useful in an abstract unrendered representation, in which the data can easily be reused and reprocessed. During the consumption and archiving stages, however, the document must be in a rendered form so that it can be presented and displayed quickly and consistently.

23.5.1.2.1   Abstract document representation

At the time the work began, SGML was the only document representation that preserved the abstract data and had the "industrial strength" for Russell's requirements. So Russell used it.

XML, as a streamlined subset of SGML, is by definition, not as feature-rich. However, like its parent it preserves the abstraction, and it seems to be more than adequate for Russell's purposes. XML's capabilities, along with its new-found popularity, promise to bring great momentum to the entire document industry.

23.5.1.2.2 Rendered document representation

Portable Document Format (PDF) was chosen for the rendered document representation. The archiving requirement, that it must be readable for a minimum of ten years time, was the dominant deciding criterion.

Large document collections have been faced with this need for some time; for example, those of the Library of Congress and Department of Defense in the U.S. At Russell and many other enterprises, the final format-ted image of a document must be retrievable to meet business needs for compliance and reference. Russell's strong desire to use electronic documents to meet its goals was dependent upon a satisfactory decision in this single topic.

Russell first considered using SGML to meet its archiving requirements. It has successfully been used for simple partial renditions (e.g., HTML), but fully rendered final-form and graphics are outside its design objectives. Although it is undeniably the best representation for long-term preservation of text, that is not what Russell meant by archiving. To be compliant, from Russell's archive it must be possible to retrieve exactly what the client printed originally.

Russell made the choice to use PDF because it met the rendered image requirement for both text and graphics, was widely used across many plat-forms, had a publicly specified format, and supported a large set of the world's languages. It was also attracted to PDF's usability for email distri-bution and on-screen display.

PDF supports full text search, linking, and page by page loading. It has a development kit available, a compressed file size, interactive forms, cheap seats, and also prints extremely well.

23.5.2 *Phased implementation plan*

The work involved some parallel processing, with secondary teams doing research and advanced studies on upcoming phases. The implementation teams, however, focused on the deliverables.

One team was assigned to create archiving requirements for the corporation. Another team worked on object databases and SGML abstractions.

A third team worked on graphical design. Its goal was to constrain the number of presentation layouts in order to optimize for batch processing. Finally, a fourth team had the task of tracking and understanding key standards like SGML, XML, Hytime, and various related W3C activities.

23.5.2.1   Phase I: Records management business study

The technical work on this phase was deferred. The main candidate for an archiving product was in the middle of an acquisition, which created an unacceptable business risk.

However, Russell did conduct a two-year study on document archiving requirements for its Investment Management Business. Once the business case for records management was made, Russell hired a full-time professional archivist to champion the deployment of the technology.

23.5.2.2   Phase II: Document management of PDF files

Russell's corporate Information Technology department had previously deployed a document management system. The project team used it in the interests of corporate harmony, and worked with its vendor's R&D department on the beta version of an application to make documents available over the Web.

This product allows you to build a query on a Web-based form (Figure 23-5), which can be tailored to meet application requirements.

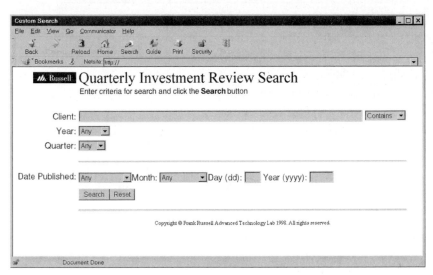

Figure 23-5   Document management search screen.

The query results are delivered as an HTML frame (Figure 23-6), the form of which can also be customized. Russell's users found that it made the interface to the product's library services, particularly document check-out, much more appealing than it had been.

23.5.2.3   Phase III: Document assembly and formatting

The objective of this phase was to create structured documents in SGML that could be auto-assembled, and to implement auto-check-in to the document management system.

As the assembly and formatting phase of the project began, the team focused on the issues of: How much structure is needed?, What are the quality levels required for the publication in its final form? What should the user interface experience be like for editing sections, book assembly and releasing books to the document management system?

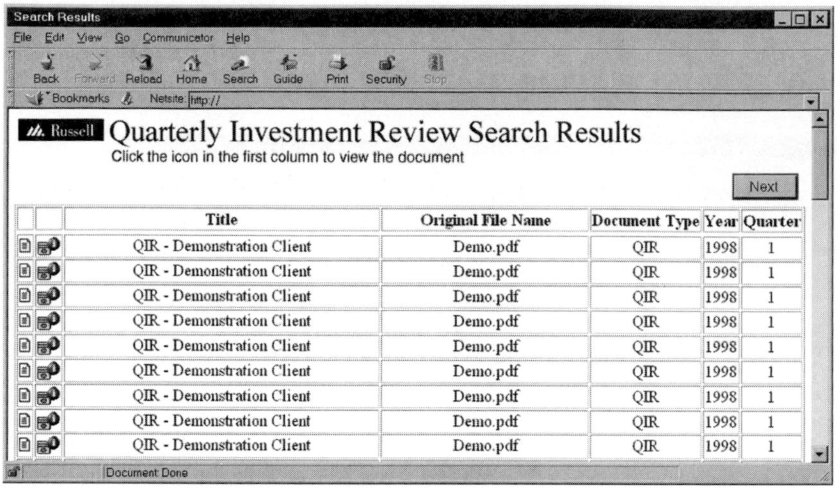

Figure 23-6   Document management search results.

Russell decided to purchase a product that supported integrated structured editing, layout, and typographic control.

The users for this phase are a small group of document editors who compile and author the QIR documents for clients at Russell. Their typical quarterly work cycle involves revising the previous quarter's document files, graphics, and tables, and launching a new composite book for each client. New document pages are created approximately 10% of the time.

The users are trained in popular word processors, spreadsheet, and graphics packages, but have no experience in SGML. They are accustomed to setting the indents, font style, size of a page, and common typography settings. They are often under the spotlight to make a production deadline in hours and therefore must be able to make edits quickly with minimal amount of new steps. They are only interested in software that makes their life easier.

The team quickly found that the system must make the SGML transparent to the user, that the layout must be WYSIWYG, and that the application should assist in the creation of a consistent layout throughout the book.

23.5.2.3.3   How structure was used

The approach taken was to replace the use of paragraph style codes with meaningful SGML element-type names. The document was then formatted in real time, based on the element types, thereby giving the users their customary WYSIWYG effect.

A welcome side-effect was that the list of element-type choices was much smaller than the full list of paragraph styles typically presented by a WYSIWYG editor, because of the context enforced by the DTD. In addition, the product has a guided creation feature, which automatically inserts required elements. It allowed us to lay out a typical page easily, and still allowed deviations by making choices permitted by the DTD.

One area of improvement to the overall professionalism of the book was in the consistency of format and layout. In the old system, each page was laid out individually and it often deviated slightly as editing continued over several quarters of revisions.

The new system, however, used a series of matched templates created by a professional typographer, and it used structure to drive the formatting of the text. The resultant books were consistent, and compliant with corporate guidelines. This achievement was a significant win since "document police" (people trying to enforce style quality control issues from a corporate perspective) are not often welcome.

23.5.2.3.4   Document editing

With all of these facilities available, the team found that it needed to simplify the application menus. Doing so would limit access to designer pallets and provide users with a simpler interface to this complex and powerful tool.

Simplifying was done by using the application's custom user interface feature. It required no programming, although some developer expertise is required.

Training the users on the new system consisted of five sessions of one day in length, including hands on lab sessions. The editing tool took 50% of the training time, with the remaining time being spread on a general introduction, graphics, book building, and lab sessions. The users quickly grasped the system's capabilities and found it to be a huge improvement over the previous system.

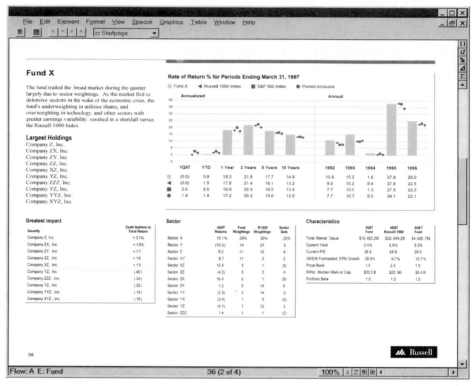

Figure 23-7   Fund page example in editing system.

23.5.2.3.5   *How much structure is needed?*

Once Russell made the decision to use a structured representation of its publications, the challenge became to decide how much structure was appropriate and for what reasons. The team approached this from two viewpoints: long-term and short-term.

The long-term objectives of using structure were to add value to the intellectual property and aid with reuse, navigation, automation and archiving.

The short-term goals were to enforce consistency in the typography, assure better quality control, and facilitate the aggregation of disparate content sources into single publications with a high degree of automation. Other short-term goals were to facilitate document assembly with automation, and to improve the user's experience.

23.5.2.3.6   Final-form quality requirements

Russell's output quality requirements are extremely high (Figure 23-7). When it looked at the commercially available database-driven publishing systems and dynamic Web page assemblers, none were capable of presenting publications as well as Russell's legacy systems. Also, although the Web publishing systems were great for producing pages from the current state of the database, they were not capable of satisfying Russell's compliance requirements.

23.5.2.3.7   Book assembly

The team wanted to make the user experience during book building as straightforward as possible by presenting only immediately relevant information. It built a simple windowing scheme, based on a customer database, that presented the bookbuilding experience on two screens (Figure 23-8 and Figure 23-9).

Along with the customer name and the component bill of materials list selections, the book building interface also gathers the metadata required for check-in to the document management system and stores it for later use. This may seem trivial, but it completely removes the user pain from the document management check-in process.

23.5.2.3.8   Releasing books to the document management system

Final preparation of a book for review and release is invoked by a single custom menu item, `Publish`, on the *File* menu. The `Publish` command creates a PostScript file of the book, which is then distilled into a PDF file (Figure 23-10). During this process, the PDF file is updated with the document management system check-in metadata that was gathered during the book building.

The `Publish` command eliminates a large number of print and configuration item choices for the user and controls the way PDF files are created. This plug-in also automatically generates bookmark hyperlinks for the PDF table of contents from the SGML structural element hierarchy.

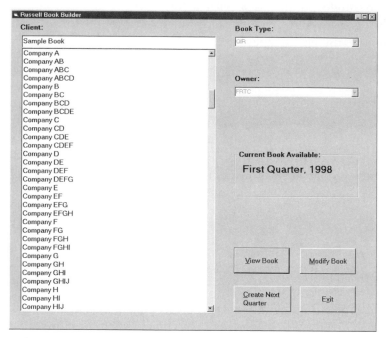

Figure 23-8   Russell BookBuilder (1 of 2)

23.5.2.4   Phase IV: XML and the future

In 1995 Russell began a pure research project into the notion of "Knowledge Management Systems". These are automated systems that would be the next logical extension for publishing, collaborative creation, and electronic delivery.

Russell believes that XML systems are the beginning of an entirely new age of documents. In the same way that ASCII allowed people to interchange bits in the past, adoption of XML as the data representation will allow people to exchange "bits with meaning" in the future.

That was the original promise of SGML, but Russell feels the SGML community, for whatever reasons, fell short on realizing that promise to its fullest commercial degree. Russell's view is that XML is SGML done right for the masses, which still leaves SGML there for those for whom XML falls short.

Russell believes the marriage of XML, databases, WWW, EDI, and publishing technologies is going to be the cornerstone of extremely significant

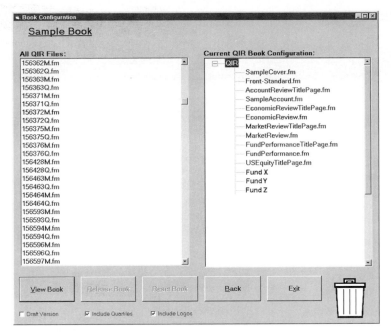

Figure 23-9 Russell BookBuilder (2 of 2)

developments over the next decade. Areas most likely to be affected will include content aggregation, simplified database connectivity, document distribution, and electronic commerce.

Russell also feels there is great danger in "almost open" or "almost standard" representations and technologies. The power and future of information technologies is determined by the degree of vendor and platform independence that they offer for the long term.

For the long term – not one version or two versions, but years and decades later. At Russell, they never lose sight of that goal. It is the company's information, stored in an open representation, that Russell expects to bring it true value in the future.

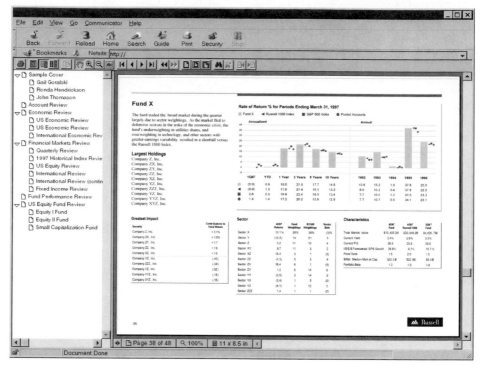

Figure 23-10   Fund page example in PDF book.

23.6 | Conclusion

In the past internetworking of systems was complex. Now, with the World Wide Web and TCP/IP, internetworking is routine and affordable. The next frontier is content interoperability.

Interoperability has always been a challenge. The people at Russell Advanced Technology Labs believe that XML is the interchange/interface language of the future, and that it will do for content interoperability what the WWW and TCP/IP did for internetworking.

Russell says: "We built an SGML application three years ago because it was the right thing to do. We have now converted it to XML because it is the right thing to do. The SGML to XML conversion took one developer three days."

While others discuss the potential values of XML, Russell is already enjoying the benefits of a production extranet XML publishing system.

PC World Online

Case Study

▌ Major commercial website

▌ Dynamic content delivery

▌ Print and online

Sponsor: Arbortext, http://www.arbortext.com

Contributing expert: Susan Örge

Chapter

24

It is hard enough to keep a website on any subject current and interesting. But when you are the world's largest computer monthly, keeping up with your subject matter is an immense challenge. Learn how *PC World Online* does it from this chapter.

T he website PC World Online is the electronic version of PC World magazine, one of the world's foremost sources of computer information and the largest monthly computer publication. It maintains over 8,000 pages and draws nine million page views per month (Figure 24-1). In addition to deriving diverse and often complex content from its print counterpart, the PC World Online group originates online news and features, a shareware library, and more. PC World Online also repackages content for several third party licensees.

The site serves its readership well by offering timely, useful information that encourages repeat visits. As more competition enters the arena every day, sites such as *PC World Online* must continually strive to sustain their competitive edge.

24.1 | The challenge

Because of a changing landscape of increasingly sophisticated audience expectations, Matt Turner, Director of Applications Development, and Rebecca Freed, Managing Editor, faced a challenging task in 1998. How

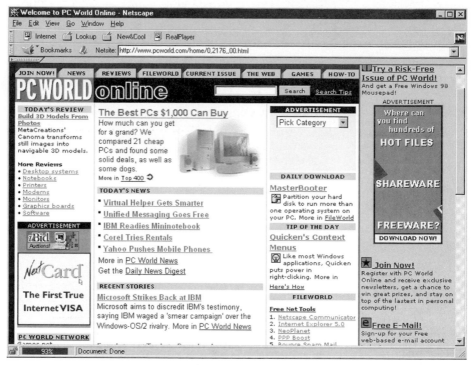

Figure 24-1   *PC World Online* home page

could *PC World Online* pull information from multiple sources, in many different formats, and serve it dynamically on the web, while keeping up with the breakneck speed of the publishing business?

On top of all of this, how could the online publication transform the thousands of pages of then static information into a more useful, dynamic site? After investigating a number of different solutions including standard template/database HTML Web publishing tools, Turner felt that XML was the only technology that rose to this challenge. Today, XML is the basis for all of *PC World Online*'s diverse content delivery needs.

24.1.1 *Complex conversion requirements*

PC World Online's editorial management process is painstakingly complex. The edit team is a central point where a variety of content types come from many different unstructured sources and formats, which the team must then deliver in other formats.

Before it implemented an XML-based publishing system, *PC World Online* had been using a home-grown production process that required four to five people to manually convert each month's *PC World* print articles into HTML (Figure 24-2). Among other problems, this process caused an unacceptable drain on resources while not allowing the group to create, store or access metadata about the content. As a result, the team was kept from building personalized content views or reusing content in different areas of the site.

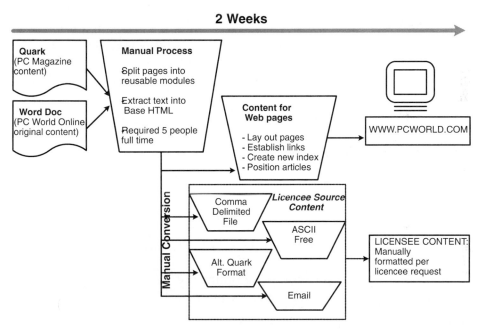

Figure 24-2   Converting articles before XML

Here are some examples of articles in the different source formats:

- **From the magazine**: A feature article from the magazine that is nine pages long, has sidebars, five charts, four screen shots and four art images. The print magazine delivers all of its content to *PC World Online* as a *Quark* document. The edit team must then convert that content to HTML and several other licensee-specific formats while maintaining consistency in style and content between the print version and the Web version.

- **From the online editors**: An online feature article of the same length and complexity, but on a different topic. This article may also have unique structures and layout for the online medium.
- **From the online editors**: A four-paragraph online news story.

These articles must be delivered dynamically in the following formats:

- **To the Web**: *PC World Online* produces HTML formats for at least five different website sections, as well as special formats such as an HTML "Print from Browser" version.
- **Via email**: These are text versions sent to readers who subscribe to information on specific topics of interest.
- **To licensees**: Licensee content in several formats including delimited ASCII and *Quark*.
- **To future formats**: *PC World Online* intends to deliver content using technologies, such as DHTML and XML, that are supported by newer browsers.

24.1.2   *Time-consuming HTML markup*

Even for articles originally written for online use, the editors' copy flow and review process was painstaking, as shown in Figure 24-3.

24.1.3   *Richly-structured information sources*

The *PC World Online* group wanted a system that could store these documents with their complexity intact so they could easily publish high-quality information electronically. For example, the print version uses spot art, color and placement cues, which conveys a strong sense of structure to the reader. Matt Turner was convinced that he could preserve this structure so

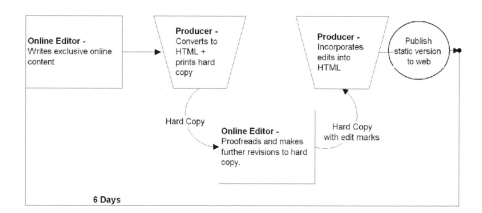

Figure 24-3   Workflow for original online content before XML

that the Web versions could display the same information-rich layouts as the print counterpart.

24.2 | Templates and databases were not enough

PC World Online was already producing some of its simpler information using a template and database Web publishing system, a traditional method of website production. Turner suspected that he could implement a more sophisticated version of this system for all of *PC World Online*'s content.

A typical template and database system for Web publishing combines a database that stores information content along with templates that specify where the content will go when it is rendered. When a site is published, the system automatically flows the information from a database through the template to generate a series of HTML pages. This type of tool has allowed many sites to automate the delivery of Web content.

Turner, however, found that his more complex information required transformation of the content, something that a template and database system could not accomplish. For example Turner found it impossible to use this kind of software to generate from the HTML markup the special marks that his licensees required.

Additionally, since a template and database system typically stores an entire body of an article in one "field," the editors lacked the fine granularity they needed to control the formatting of the more elaborately-structured article elements. Instead, the editors had a propensity to insert "rogue" tags arbitrarily to achieve specific formatting results. It was therefore impossible for Turner to base any automated procedure on the article content markup, and therefore impossible to control the format automatically at the time of publication. This situation also hindered *PC World Online* from producing the many diverse delivery formats that were required.

24.3 | XML provides a solution

In reviewing document management approaches, Turner learned about XML and chose it as the means of managing *PC World Online*'s complex content. Instead of forcing content into the rigid tabular structure of a relational database, XML can describe any document in terms of its natural structure as a hierarchy, or "tree", with links among the leaves and branches. This model allowed *PC World Online* to preserve the full richness of an article's structure.

24.3.1 *Content creation and storage*

Within three days, the team, working with a consultant, created a DTD for the website's content. The DTD defines element types, such as headlines and paragraph, that are common to most articles, It also defines more specialized element types, such as tips and product reviews, that are particular to a specific kind of article. These relationships are illustrated in Figure 24-4.

Within days, and with almost no training, editors were using this DTD in conjunction with Arbortext products to create their first issue in XML. Figure 24-5 shows an article and its XML markup as it appears when edited using Arbortext software.

Figure 24-6 shows the same article when rendered on the *PC World Online* site.

Soon after, the group began transforming all of its content to XML. The new system significantly reduced the time spent preparing the documents

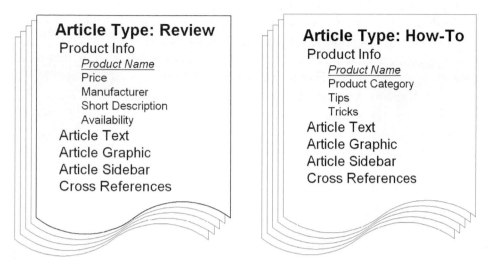

Figure 24-4 Articles can contain reusable elements.

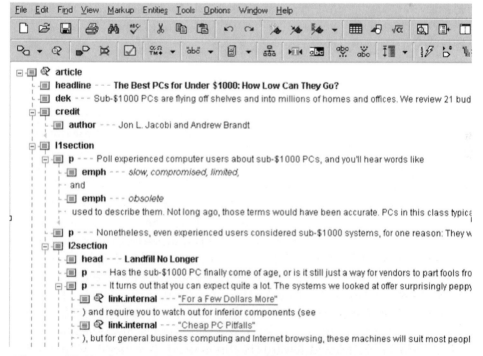

Figure 24-5 An article being edited with Arbortext software

Figure 24-6   The article in Figure 24-5 on the *PC World Online* site

for the Web and licensee formats. *Quark* desktop publishing documents were first converted to an equivalent XML document type, then processed with Arbortext software to refine the XML to conform to the *PC World Online* DTD.

This conversion process not only preserves the richness of the original article, but often allows the team to enrich it even further. For example many stories now include links to the URLs of companies whose products are reviewed, plus charts and product images that are tailored for the Web.

24.3.2 *Data delivery*

Once the articles are in XML, content delivery becomes a much easier, more effective task. That is because an XML-aware database system stores the actual XML document intact. This differs from the template and database system, which can only store lightly-tagged HTML data in simple "fields." One advantage of true XML storage is that data retrieval is much more powerful. Because of the hierarchical structure of XML data, it is just as easy to retrieve complete articles as it is to retrieve a single headline.

But there are additional rewards beyond powerful retrieval. While data is extracted, it is transformed to HTML or other representations by processing it according to an XSL stylesheet. Since *PC World Online* must transform the XML documents into a myriad of output formats, this ability to do it automatically makes for a tremendous time-savings over the previous method of conversion and cleanup of articles. Additionally, it gives the added power of transforming the actual data content depending on the output.

24.3.3 *Improved workflow*

The new XML system has changed the way *PC World Online* produces its website. Today, every page is generated from the data store of XML documents. The group now uses the workflow illustrated in Figure 24-7, a significant change from the original workflow in Figure 24-2.

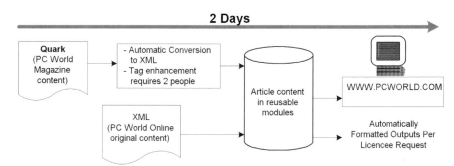

Figure 24-7 XML-based workflow

Once *PC World Online* editors sign off on the valid XML documents they have created, these documents are checked into a relational database and article-level attributes are decomposed into index fields. Although the database is similar to that in a traditional template and database system, there are significant differences. Whereas the traditional systems store lightly-tagged HTML, here a valid, richly-tagged XML document is stored.

When a request is made to view an article, the appropriate XSL stylesheet is invoked and the record containing the article is retrieved from the database. The XSL stylesheet then governs the processing and translation of the XML data to the selected format, such as HTML, and combines the returned fields for presentation. This workflow is the same for all uses of the content, including the Web pages and the licensee format.

The new workflow has been particularly effective for original online content. Contrast the flow in Figure 24-8 with that in Figure 24-3.

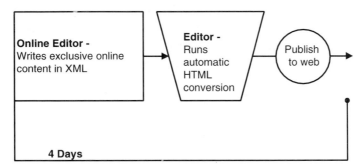

Figure 24-8   Workflow for original online content with XML

24.4 | Results and benefits

PC World Online's new XML system has satisfied the original requirements and yielded a number of significant benefits.

24.4.1 *Publish to and from multiple formats*

XML has enabled automatic conversion of documents from other formats, greatly reducing the time spent doing manual conversions. Converting content into the forms required by licensees had been as time-consuming as producing the articles in the first place. Now the same system that produces the articles can automatically produce the licensee content in whatever format is needed.

As a bonus, *PC World Online* is able to offer a variety of renditions just for the Web. These include a simplified printable Web page format and modified renditions for affiliated websites. All of these are simply alternative results from the automatic processing of XML.

PC World Online is always seeking ways to raise the visibility of its brand. That often means disseminating excerpts from its trove of content through affiliate sites that can reach audiences that its primary website would not reach. XML has made this a much easier process.

24.4.2 *Reuse*

Reuse from a central data store avoids the integrity problems of duplicated data. If information is derived from an original article, there is only one source version to create and maintain and therefore no need to manage and synchronize multiple versions of the same information. One example of reuse is the website's "product finder" (shown in Figure 24-9), with which site visitors can choose a product category and view a list of products and their review ratings. The product finder is automatically compiled from existing product review articles, so there is no need to create and maintain multiple versions of the information.

24.4.3 *Tailored information for site visitors*

Because *PC World Online* articles are marked up with information-rich tags, tailored subsets of the content can be presented to users. This is a radical departure from the usual method of search and retrieval, where a list of documents is returned when a keyword is searched.

As shown in Figure 24-10, with XML, an individual reader can request and receive only specific elements of the articles of interest. For example, a site visitor may ask for modems, their ratings, and their prices, and get only the parts of articles that contain this information.

Readers can also choose from different assemblies of the same content; for example, it is now easy for *PC World Online* to add a "product tips and tricks" section to its site, showing only the `tips` and `tricks` elements of `How-To` articles. This is a new presentation of the content that is separate from the articles themselves.

And at last, with the help of XSL stylesheets, the group can automatically transform complicated articles (some have a dozen or more highly specialized sections) so they can be displayed differently in different sections of the website.

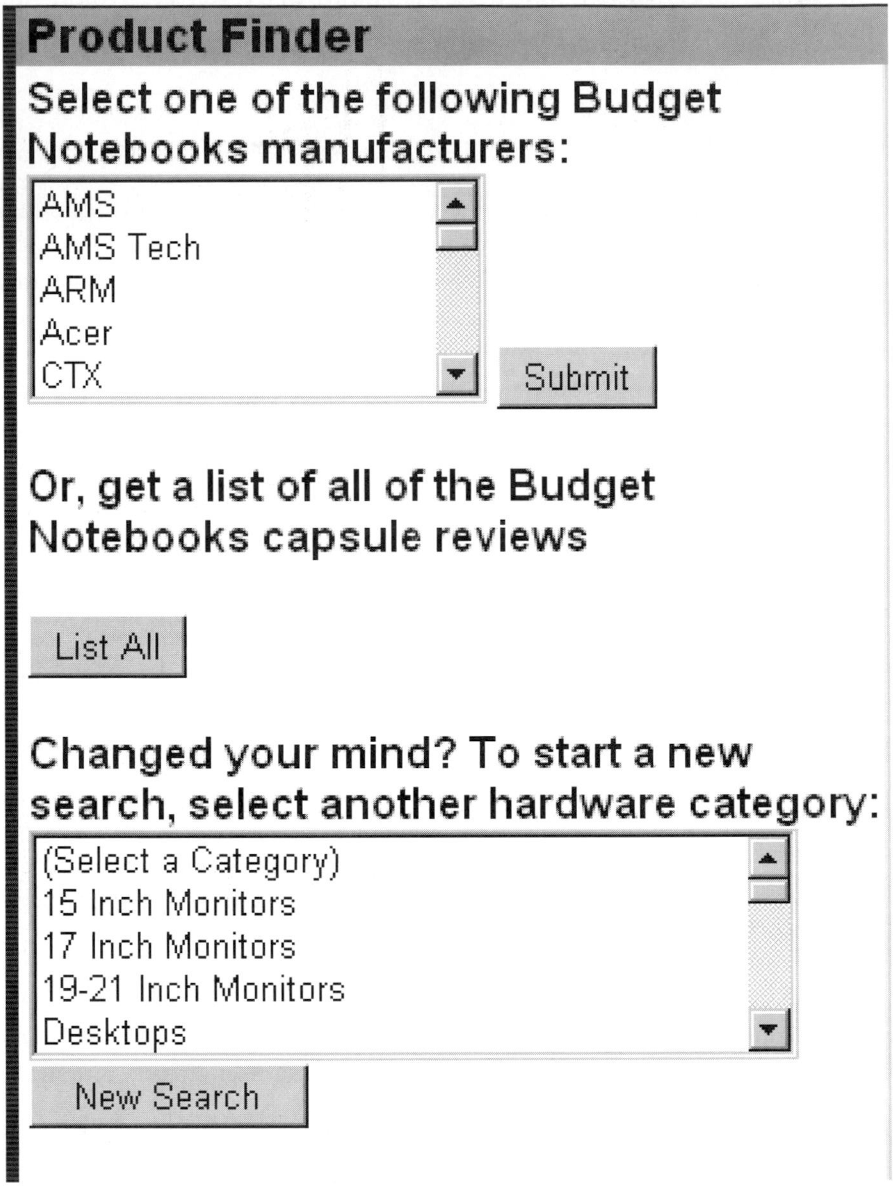

Product Finder

Select one of the following Budget Notebooks manufacturers:

AMS
AMS Tech
ARM
Acer
CTX

[Submit]

Or, get a list of all of the Budget Notebooks capsule reviews

[List All]

Changed your mind? To start a new search, select another hardware category:

(Select a Category)
15 Inch Monitors
17 Inch Monitors
19-21 Inch Monitors
Desktops

[New Search]

Figure 24-9   Product finder

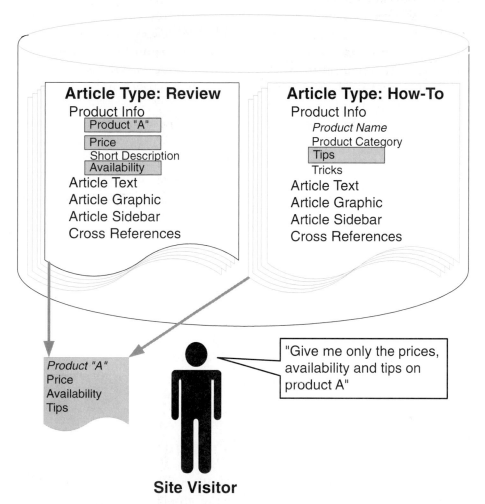

Figure 24-10   Querying for specific data elements

24.4.4 *Reduced cost and time to market*

By simplifying the process of creating, locating, and delivering information, the *PC World Online* team has increased productivity while reducing costs. Rebecca Freed, Managing Editor, reported that their XML system has cut the time to go from print to Web from two days to two hours. They have reinvested this time in creating higher-quality articles.

Additionally, editors now enter copy directly into the XML system, while server-side programs write out the actual HTML pages. Once the article is created, it is ready to go to the Web with little or no manual tagging or reformatting required on the part of the site producers. This is a huge savings in time that used to be spent updating index pages and pouring text into templates by hand.

Editors also handle the entire correction process, saving time and minimizing additional rounds of corrections. Granting this direct access to editors has streamlined production 100 percent.

Using Arbortext's structured editing environment, editors can access the articles and change the markup, while maintaining conformity to the document structure outlined in the DTD.

24.4.5 *Improved quality*

The editors and production staff are constantly seeking ways to enrich the ways in which their content can be accessed, navigated, presented and used. XML has been the key to fulfilling this goal.

Moreover, the easy-to-use, XML-based, automated system allows editors – who understand the content – to do their own markup, resulting in better quality control.

24.4.6 *Future-proofing with a standard*

The new XML system has allowed quick adaptability to new delivery formats as they evolve. For example, with some simple stylesheet adjustments, the system could produce content in forms that future browsers will accept. These might include XML versions for client-side XSL processing, or renditions for users of hand-held PDA devices such as the *Palm Pilot*.

24.4.7 *Job satisfaction*

Formerly, site producers spent time formatting and reworking what the editors had already written. Now they can use that time to add new capabilities to the site, while editors can exercise a greater degree of control over the final presentation of the articles.

24.5 | Summary

PC World Online must create original Web content as well as flow content from its print-based publication into electronic formats. With XML and Arbortext products, the company was able to overhaul production, allowing editors to edit and produce their own content to improve production efficiency.

Additionally, the new system laid the groundwork for a complete XML data store, which will enhance the reusability of data and become the backbone of *PC World Online* for years to come. Results to date include faster content delivery, editor efficiency, design consistency, flexibility, improved reuse of information, customized content, and elimination of Web production bottlenecks.

Turner and Freed predict that the advantages that *PC World Online* has reaped from XML will cause it to be adopted by *PC World Magazine* as well.

MTU-DaimlerChrysler Aerospace

Case Study

- Aerospace industry "green pages"
- Customizing supplier documentation
- Information supply chain

Sponsor: Enigma, Inc., http://www.enigma.com

Contributing experts: Enigma, Inc. staff

> How do you introduce your own changes to
> someone else's documents and see a seamless result?
> The fine-grained structuring of XML made it possible
> for DaimlerChrysler, as you'll see in this chapter.

The relationship between equipment manufacturers and the independent and customer organizations that service their equipment is highly dependent on the transfer of knowledge for maintenance operations. In most cases, unique knowledge is maintained by both the manufacturer and the servicer. To fully utilize this knowledge, manufacturers must be able to deliver intelligent publications, and servicers must be able to customize these publications.

25.1 | The challenge

The MTU-Maintenance division of DaimlerChrysler Aerospace is a maintenance and repair organization for aircraft engines. It performs maintenance on engines produced by the leading engine manufacturers and receives maintenance manuals and parts catalogs from each of them.

As with all airlines and maintenance facilities, DaimlerChrysler has tasks, procedures and parts information that are specific to its operations. These modifications are commonly referred to as "Customer Originated Changes", or COCs.

Historically, COCs have been maintained as paper documents, that are 'slip-sheeted' into the manufacturer's larger paper publications. These added pages were printed on green paper so they would stand out from the original publication, and are still known in the industry today as "green pages".

As the manufacturers began to deliver "intelligent" SGML- and XML-based publications, the green page paper COCs still needed to be referenced. Thus, the full benefit of digital data could not be realized.

An intelligent electronic publication is characterized by tables of contents, hyperlinking, topic specific searching and navigation. DaimlerChrysler sought a way to integrate its own modifications, while maintaining all the intelligence and usability features available in the manufacturer publications.

25.2 | The solution

Using Enigma's *Xtend* software, DaimlerChrysler implemented a complete digital maintenance publication process. Its workflow is shown in Figure 25-1.

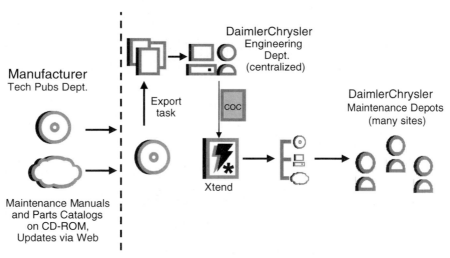

Figure 25-1   Xtend workflow

The system allows authorized DaimlerChrysler employees to update the publications that are used by all the staff mechanics. The process for adding COCs to these publications is as follows:

1. First, the authorized employee selects a task to be customized, using the original publication.
2. Next, the original content is modified with an editor, with templates used to automate the capture of XML metadata.
3. The modified content is dynamically integrated into the original publication and made available to all employees.

Let's look at each step more closely.

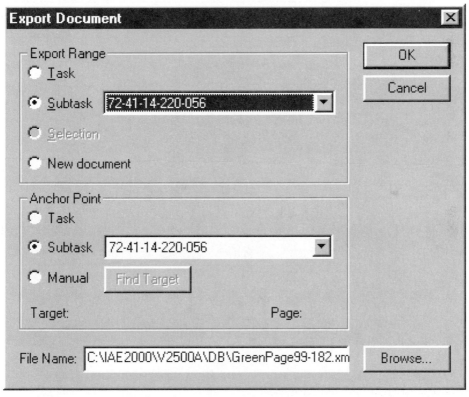

Figure 25-2   Subtask selection for customization

25.2.1   *Selecting content to be customized*

The authorized user can select any task or subtask to export for customization, as shown in Figure 25-2. The customized COC will be anchored to the original for referencing purposes.

Once the desired subtask is selected, the dialog box shown in Figure 25-3 is presented, enabling the capture of XML metadata. This information is maintained for document management purposes and is also automatically placed within the document content.

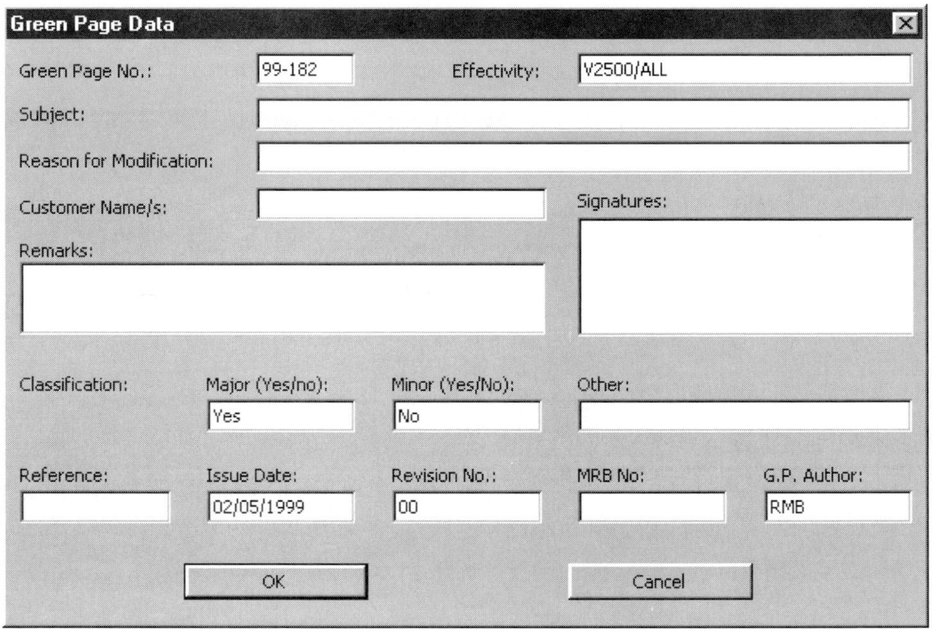

Figure 25-3   Metadata capture

25.2.2   *Content editing*

In Example 25-1 we see an excerpt from the source document that contains the text of the exported subtask.

The author can modify or add any content to this text. However, some elements, such as the `grphcref` graphic reference, are significant in order to reintegrate the COCs into the original publication. To assure that such

Example 25-1. Source document structure

```
<task chapnbr="72-41-14" func="200">
  <title>Examine the HP Compressor Rotating Air Seal</title>
  <subtask chapnbr="72-41-14" func="220" seq="056">
    <title>Maintenance Equipment Specification</title>
    <list1>
      <l1item>
        <para>Identify proper engine bay utilization as follows:
        </para></l1item>
      <l1item>
        <para>Remove access cover as shown in
          <grphcref refid="GR94030">Figure 901</grphcref>
        </para></l1item>
    </list1>
  </subtask>
```

information is not accidentally modified in the editing phase, it is marked as non-editable.

In addition to adding and modifying textual data, the author can add new hyperlinks and graphics.

25.2.3 *Integration and republishing*

After creating the COCs, the content is updated for distribution via the network to all maintenance users. Since the original publication typically is very large (100's of megabytes), it is critical that the update process be able to work with just the new and modified content.

25.3 | The result

As a result of the customization process, technicians at DaimlerChrysler have access to the entire knowledge-base of maintenance information - both from the original manufacturer as well as accumulated knowledge from within their organization.

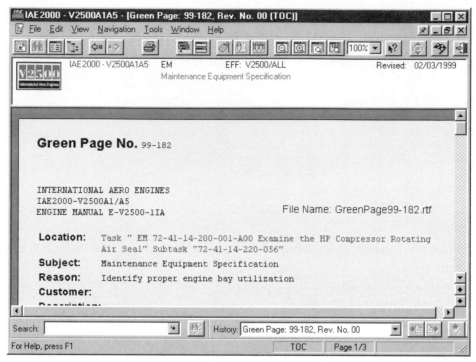

Figure 25-4   Customized information for the maintenance technician

Because all the content is available within a single publication (as shown in Figure 25-4), the technician no longer needs to correlate manually between multiple information sources.

Tip   *Other aspects of the Enigma publishing solution are described in Chapter 39, "The role of stylesheets", on page 554.*

Content Management

- Efficient content management
- Component management
- Document storage and retrieval
- Enterprise data management

Part Seven

Content is king!

Whether it's a website, your car's owner's manual, or a newspaper, the style may get your attention but the content is why you are there and why you will (or won't) return.

And the demand for new content – and new ways of packaging and delivering it – is growing by leaps and bounds. This calls for increased efficiency in the creation, processing, and delivery of content.

As a result, enterprises are increasingly realizing that content is a valuable corporate asset, one that needs to be managed with the same care as other valuable property.

In this part we'll look at the systems that have been developed for content management. We'll set the stage with a classic application, then look at content management systems that employ varying strategies: component management and integral document storage.

Finally we'll examine the role of the enterprise database system in content management.

Tweddle Litho Company

- Automotive manuals in 30 languages

- XML content management

- Natural language translation

Sponsor: XyEnterprise, http://www.xyenterprise.com

Contributing experts: Jon Parsons and Judy Cox

For the perfect introduction to content management and its benefits, you need look no further than the glove box of your car – and the manuals in the language of whichever of 60 countries you bought it in. This chapter will show you how that miracle of logistics is accomplished.

When you lease or buy an automobile, you become dependent on documentation.

You know that the glove box will contain an owner's manual, a maintenance schedule, a warranty maintenance book, and a book that describes your radio and/or CD player. You expect them to completely and accurately describe the car you are in. What's more, when you take the car in for service, you rely on the service technician having the information needed for the model and year of your car in a language he or she can read – no matter where in the world you are.

Ensuring that the information is there and available when needed is a big task, a task made achievable by XML and a content management system. Let's look at how that task is accomplished at Tweddle Litho Company, producer of more than half of the world's automotive owner and glove box documentation.

26.1 | Auto manufacturing is large-scale publishing

For a successful worldwide launch of a new car, the manufacturer needs a full range of publications. The owner's guide, audio guide, and warranty material must be present in each vehicle. A service manual must be available to the service providers in every country.

These documents must be translated into as many as 30 different languages. Each document must be modified to conform to the national regulations for each country that imports the car. Cars shipped to Mexico, for example, must include jumper cables, and the documentation must reference this.

Producing those documents for a single new vehicle launch is a huge undertaking. Producing them for all of a manufacturer's models is a monumental one.

And one that compounds over time, because each model changes to a greater or lesser degree each year. And for each of the models, in each of the years, in each of the languages, the information must be available in print, on the Web, and on CD-ROM. Figure 26-1 illustrates the complexity.

Many auto manufacturers choose to outsource these projects to a full-service technical publishing house such as Tweddle Litho Company of Clinton Township, Michigan.

Founded in 1954 as a small printing company, Tweddle Litho pioneered computerized photocomposition and typesetting. As technologies changed, the company seized the opportunity to move further upstream from publishing to encompass the entire data management cycle, including writing, translation, and other related services.

Today, with customers such as Ford Motor Company, General Motors, Chrysler, Nissan, and Volvo, Tweddle Litho produces approximately 55 percent of all the automotive owner's literature worldwide.

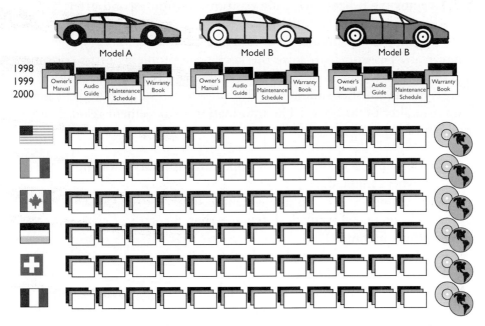

Figure 26-1 Managing information for multiple models and model years in many languages and three delivery formats is a complex task.

26.2 | Global markets, global information

As Tweddle's business grew, so did the requirements for internationalizing the information it managed for its customers. It soon became acquainted with the difficulties of the translation process:

- Passing information to translation houses, communicating about "what was really meant", and answering questions about context
- Tracking the status and progress of the translations underway – and what had been returned
- Retranslating what had already been translated – and hadn't changed – when only a small portion of a document was modified

Managing the process manually was time consuming and prone to error. It also required a large editorial staff.

In 1997 Tweddle undertook to find and apply a technology that would strategically position it to solve the large-scale problems of its customers. Tweddle knew it had to be prepared to support a vehicle release in 30 languages in 60 countries simultaneously. It needed to support 40 vehicle lines with a total of 6000 books. The information management team defined a number of objectives:

- Designing a friendlier more appealing visual style for the owner's manuals
- Creating a global, culturally neutral style
- Meeting local regulations (engineering, regulatory/safety, environmental)
- Reducing time to produce the information
- Reducing overall cost
- Increasing usability of the information
- Anticipating future uses of the information
- Managing artwork

Not everything on their list could be addressed by software, but the issues of time, cost, and reuse of the information could. They concluded that proper management of their information assets required generalized markup and a component-based information management system that could handle it.

26.3 | Needed: An XML component management system

By delimiting and labeling each of the individual elements of a document, XML enables both people and software to manipulate information as units useful for the purpose at hand. No longer is it necessary to deal with a whole document or even a complete chapter when only a small piece – perhaps only one or two paragraphs, a table, or step or two in a procedure – changes.

These units of information are called *components*. Figure 26-2 shows how XML identifies them.

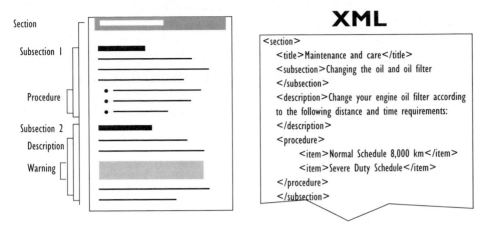

Figure 26-2   XML supports the use of document components

By managing these units separately and combining them into larger chunks of information – sections or chapters or books – only when needed, Tweddle could give only those units that changed to the translators. That level of precision enormously reduces redundant work.

In addition to providing the focus they needed for translation, a component management approach also let them reuse information in multiple documents. They could write a piece once, use it in several different places, and when changes occurred, update the component only once and have the changes replicated in each place it was used.

Even more, a component-based management system allowed them to build different views of the data. For example, a technical writer may be focusing on air conditioning or braking systems for a given auto model. The writer can look into the database and find all the procedures for that kind of system. Another writer, creating a view for a different model, might find that it included many of the same procedures because the systems were similar in both autos.

Tweddle developed its solution using *Parlance Document Manager*. The architecture for component storage is shown in Figure 26-3.

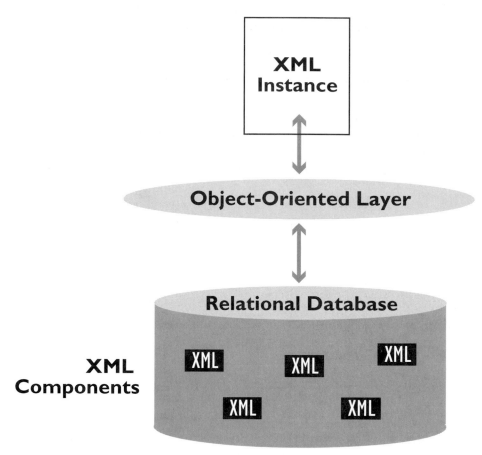

Figure 26-3   Content storage with *Parlance Document Manager*

26.4 | Improving the translation process

Component management allowed translation to be focused on revised components only, a concept illustrated in Figure 26-4.

The translation workflow at Tweddle is based upon the use of in-country translators; that is, native speakers of a language living in the country for which the information is destined. In this workflow, there is a significant exchange of information at "arm's length" between Tweddle and the translators. A key aim in managing the translation process is to preserve context so that the translator has sufficient information to make sound decisions about which word to choose in rendering one language into another.

When changes are made to a previously translated document, *Parlance* creates a translation package for the translator that includes a proof version that shows how the component looked in the last printed book, the previous XML source file for the component, the revised XML source file, and a list of differences. The package provides the context the translator needs.

The system creates the translation package automatically, triggered by the changes made when the revised component is returned to the repository. It is checked out for translation and the translation package is delivered electronically to the translator. Once the translation is complete, the revised translation component is checked back into the database and its status is automatically noted by the workflow manager.

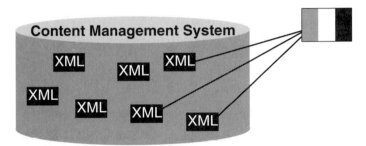

Figure 26-4 Only revised components are sent to the translator.

A further advantage of component management is the ability to coordinate parallel work on the same document. "One of our European car manufacturers does some of its own writing using the system," said Tom Dupont, Vice President of Sales at Tweddle Litho. "It writes some parts in German while we continue to write other parts in English. We have the ability to do original source writing in two different languages and still maintain the common use of data."

26.5 | One Source, multiple delivery formats

A key advantage of using XML is that markup reflects the structure of an element, totally apart from how it is to be rendered. This separation of abstract content from rendered format allows delivery of the information in multiple formats from a single source.

26.5.1 *Printed delivery*

When all revisions and translations are complete, *Parlance* assembles a complete version of the book from its components. This XML instance is then sent to XPP, which automatically composes and paginates the XML instance into finished documents.

"In the past, it took up to six months to deliver a translated book," said Dupont. "We are now getting the same results in 3 weeks and we are even able to support the release of a foreign language document prior to release of the domestic English version."

Tweddle has been setting up remote printing facilities around the world in response to a growing need for on-demand printing. "One of our European customers routinely has us prepare its service literature in 22 languages and then prepare deliverables in both print and CD-ROM formats," said Dupont. "Instead of shipping a large quantity of bulky books, we send the files electronically to be printed in Belgium for European distribution, in Singapore for Asian distribution, and so on."

26.5.2 *Online delivery*

Owner's literature will probably stay a paper-based product for quite some time because inside a car, at present, there are few practical alternatives for viewing it electronically. However, a few of the auto manufacturers have already eliminated paper deliverables completely for documents other than the owner's manuals.

"Another big trend is the move away from paper toward electronic files for customer assistance representatives," said Dupont. "Rather than sorting through one hundred manuals, each 1,400 to 2,000 pages long, the customer service representative today expects to access a searchable database to quickly find the appropriate procedure for a specific problem."

26.6 | Conclusion

XML enables solutions to complex information management problems such as Tweddle's because:

- XML can enforce the strict separation of abstract content from rendered format.
- XML enables the management and manipulation of small units of data that can be reused and assembled into multiple documents.
- XML can represent the structure of the abstract content, which is the same regardless of the natural language of the text.

Together with a component management system that supports and uses these advantages, XML solves immediate business problems while preserving a flexible and open foundation for whatever changes technology may bring.

Efficient content management

Tool Discussion

- Efficient production and efficient consumption
- File conversion
- Component management
- Personalized delivery

Sponsor: Arbortext, http://www.arbortext.com

Contributing expert: PG Bartlett

Chapter 27

Moving at Web speed requires efficiency for
information publisher and information consumer
alike. XML-based content management systems can
help you achieve that goal. This chapter will show
you how.

O rganizations that publish large amounts of vital business information face several challenges in keeping that content fresh,
accurate and relevant. Whether that information includes internal documents such as engineering specifications, manufacturing instructions or human resource policies, or external documents such as
diagnostic manuals or product catalogs, the information is vital to the
smooth functioning of an organization.

The Web has dramatically and forever altered the expectations of those
who receive information - the information consumers. They have learned
that the Web has the power to deliver information that suits their individual needs for accessibility, content and form. They have learned that the
Web can deliver all the information they need - and only the information
they need - at the moment of need. And they want that information delivered in the form that's most useful to them: print or electronic, online or
offline.

In a word, both the producers and consumers of information today seek
efficiency. The producers need efficient creation, management and utilization of the information. The consumers want the delivery of the information to be efficient for them: personalized and targeted to their needs.

Tools, systems and processes designed for the relatively slow pace and inflexibility of a print-oriented world are not efficient in either respect. Unfortunately for most enterprises, that is all they have.

27.1 | How today's process works

Today's corporate publishing systems are typically based on print-oriented tools that were developed before the Web.

27.1.1 *Original creation workflow*

To meet the need for Web delivery of information, organizations usually try to bolt on additional tools and processes. The result? A workflow that resembles Figure 27-1 for the creation of their vital business information.

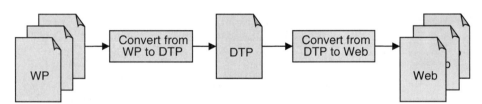

Figure 27-1 Original creation workflow

There are three steps:

1. Contributors, such as subject matter experts, capture their knowledge in word processor (WP) files.
2. Technical writers import the word processor files into their desktop publishing (DTP) systems, aggregate the content from various contributors and illustrators, refine and enhance the content to meet the needs of the ultimate consumer, adjust copy and formatting to create attractive page layouts, produce master copies for printing, and send their electronic files to the Web publishing group.

3. The Web publishing group converts the DTP files to Web-
    friendly text and graphics, splits the files into smaller chunks,
    adds navigation aids, adjusts the appearance of the documents
    to make them more 'Webby', revises any print-specific content
    (for example, "see figure on the next page") and places the files
    on the Web server.

27.1.2 *Revisions and updates*

Most vital business information eventually requires revisions and updates.
The revision process starts when the contributors revise their original word
processor files and send them to the technical writers

The technical writers must either rebuild their DTP documents from
scratch or, more likely, ask the contributors to mark up hard copies of the
existing DTP documents instead of changing their word processing documents (Figure 27-2).

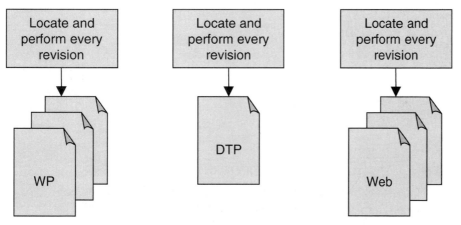

Figure 27-2   Revisions must be made independently to each separate file.

Since information tends to proliferate during the publishing process
through "copy/paste" to multiple locations and multiple documents, the
technical writers must find and modify every instance where the revised
information appears.

When the technical writers have finished their revisions, they send the revised documents to the Web publishing group. The Web group then faces a dilemma: Do they repeat the labor-intensive effort (step 3) that they invested in the original, or refer to the contributors' hand-written revisions and revise only the Web content that has changed? Either way, it's a costly manual process.

The cost and effort to revise content can be many times the cost of creating that content in the first place. Several factors aggravate the cost and effort further:

- Multiple languages (e.g., French and Japanese)
- Personalized versions (e.g., versions for specific audiences such as employees, partners and customers)
- Additional media (e.g., CD-ROM)
- High frequency of change

Most organizations find themselves caught in a dilemma. As the pace of change spirals higher, their ability to keep their information fresh, relevant and accessible falls increasingly behind.

27.2 | How to make the process efficient

Through modern, XML-based content management, the problems of today's systems can be addressed.

27.2.1 *Dealing with file conversions*

There are two key points in the process where files must be converted:

1. When WP files are transferred from the contributors to the technical writers (step 2).
2. When the DTP files are transferred to the Web publishers (step 3).

Each of these conversions requires a different solution.

27.2.1.1 WP to DTP

There are several strategies for making this conversion (Figure 27-3) efficiently.

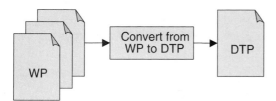

Figure 27-3 Converting from word processing files to desktop publishing files.

One approach is to force contributors and writers to use the same tools, either the same word processing software or the same desktop publishing software. This strategy is often impractical because word processing tools lack long document support and desktop publishing software tends to be more expensive and less familiar.

Another potential solution is to use separate WP and DTP tools, but to use tools that work with a common file format.

Other approaches are possible when the technical writers use XML-based *content management (CM) systems*, such as Arbortext's *Epic*, instead of DTP software. WP and DTP files are normally renditions, which means that the abstract information content is mixed with style information. XML files, in contrast, can keep the two from mixing; normally, in fact, they don't contain any style information to begin with. This distinction between rendered and abstract representations is especially vital in the DTP-to-Web conversion step that we'll look at next, but it also enables some interesting strategies for this step.

For example, the CM product (*Epic* is one) could provide editing capabilities in two versions, one for contributors (such as subject matter experts) and the other for authors (such as technical writers). Both create and edit the same XML abstractions, but the contributor version does so through a familiar word-processing interface while the author version adds support for high-volume and long document publishing. This strategy makes the functionality illustrated in Figure 27-4 possible.

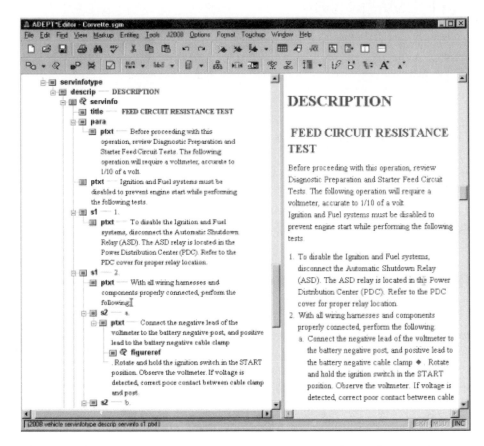

Figure 27-4   Structural and word processing views for authors and contributors in *Epic*.

Finally, XML CM systems can provide a form of automatic conversion to and from *Microsoft Word* that allows contributors to continue using their word processing software. The conversion is possible if contributors carefully follow some basic rules (usually supported by Word templates and macros) that cause them to create abstractions in the word processor.

27.2.1.2   DTP to Web

This conversion (Figure 27-5) involves more than simple rendition format changes. Even with a "perfect" conversion, someone would have to restructure the resulting documents to make them Web-friendly.

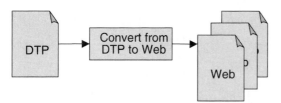

Figure 27-5   Converting from desktop publishing files to Web files.

So far, the most successful approach to this conversion problem has been to capture information in a representation that is *independent* of print or Web formatting and presentation, and then *automatically* produce the print *and* Web versions from that single source. That representation, of course, is an XML abstraction. When properly designed, it enables a system like *Epic* to automate extensively.

■ By automatically balancing page "fullness" with the need to keep related elements together, the system produces attractive printed pages with no need for manual intervention or inspection. In addition, it automatically generates tables of contents, indexes, cross references, and lists of figures, equations, and tables.

■ The system can ensure that documents conform to legal requirements such as the formatting of safety warnings. For example, it may be a requirement that safety warnings appear in their entirety and on the same page as the text to which they're related. A warning is issued if compliance is not possible (if, for example, the safety warning exceeds the size of the page).

■ Authors are freed from the responsibility of adjusting content and formatting and creating appropriate page breaks, which can consume as much as one-third of an author's time with WP or DTP tools. With a system like *Epic*, optimum page layouts are automatic, freeing authors to focus on the task for which their expertise is required: content creation.

■ Revisions and updates are streamlined because only the XML source information must be revised. If formatting is fully automatic, it's never necessary to make the same revisions multiple times in different media.

27.2.2 *Preventing duplicate content proliferation*

The proliferation of content through "copy/paste" represents another profound problem in today's businesses.

The solution seems easy: Maintain only one instance of a component of information and incorporate it *by reference* wherever it's needed. When the component is changed, all of the documents that refer to it should change automatically.

Most word processing and desktop publishing tools enable reuse of information components by reference, but these tools typically present several significant barriers which XML-based CM systems such as *Epic* can overcome with the capabilities described here.

27.2.2.1 Component viewing in context

With most tools, to revise a reusable component of information the author must open that component by itself in a separate window. Highly granular levels of reuse - where objects may be as tiny as table cells - create an undue burden on authors. XML CM systems, however, can display collections of document components within the context in which each is used.

27.2.2.2 Component-level access control

The system can ensure that the author changes only those components for which the author is permitted to make changes and that are not currently under revision by another author at that time. In fact, several users could have the same "compound document" (document comprised of a number of reusable components) open for viewing at the same time. Since "permissions" and "checkout" are enforced at the component level, a user is specifically restricted to editing the components he or she has checked out. This means that in a workgroup environment, contributors can simultaneously edit their portions of a document while viewing that portion in the context of the full document.

27.2.2.3 Component-level rendition

In a rendition-oriented WP or DTP system, a component cannot be reused by reference with a different display format. The author must copy the component, paste it where it's needed, and apply different formatting. That's because the rendition of the component is part of the document representation.

On the other hand, when the document representation is an XML abstraction, the same component can be rendered differently based on where and how it is used. Revisions to the original content automatically apply everywhere that content is used, regardless of how that content is formatted in each use.

27.2.2.4 Browsing support for reusable components

Word processing and desktop publishing tools do not provide navigation aids for browsing the components within a document or within the document repository. Navigation becomes especially difficult in those environments when aiming for high levels of reuse, because of the likelihood that reusable components will be nested within other reusable components, potentially to as many as 30 levels.

Epic allows navigation among components within the document as well as within the entire repository (Figure 27-6).

27.2.3 *Personalized delivery*

In a print-oriented world, we accept the fact that a single printed document may have to serve the needs of many diverse groups. For instance, it's common to see operating manuals that span many different product variations. An automobile owner's manual is a well-known example.

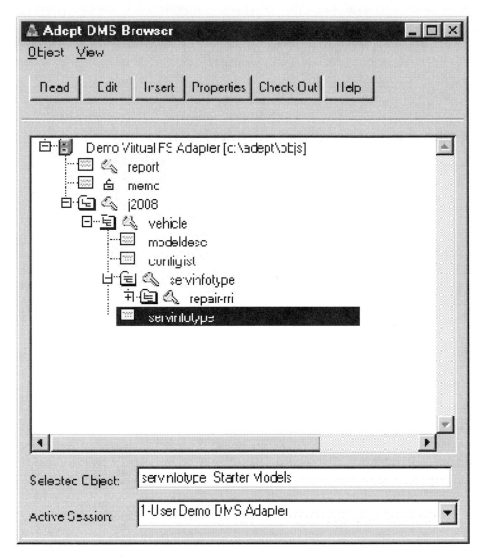

Figure 27-6   Component browsing in *Epic*

In the Web world, consumers expect to receive all the information they need, but only what they need, at the time of need and in the form that they prefer.

Tailoring information to specific audiences is the ultimate efficiency afforded by XML content management. Arbortext's *Epic*, for example, allows profiles to be defined that represent a combination of such criteria as audience personal characteristics, delivery media, and operating system. A component with an applied profile can be viewed only if the criteria are satisfied. Profiles can be applied to components at three stages (Figure 27-7):

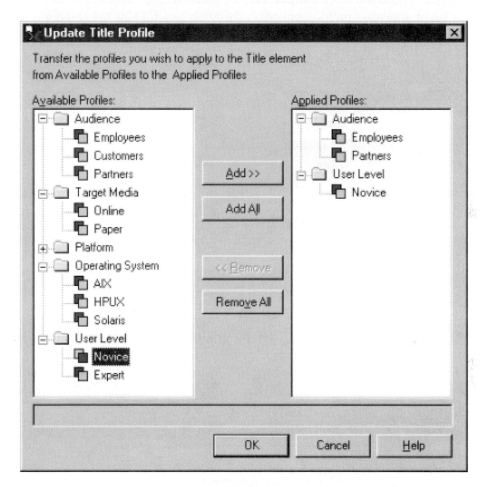

Figure 27-7   Authors can apply profiles to components with *Epic*

Create

Components can be written with a specific profile in mind. For example, some sections may be for internal distribution while others may apply only to a single product model.

Publish

The author can specify any combination of profiles and the system will omit any components that do not match them.

Access

The information consumer can be allowed to choose profiles when accessing the document on the Web or a CD-ROM (Figure 27-8).

Figure 27-8   Consumers can select profiles when viewing on the Web or CD-ROM.

27.3 | Conclusion

Efficient content management can be attained with XML-based content management systems like *Epic*. Such systems enable organizations to create, manage and present their vital business information in a variety of media formats. The efficiencies these systems offer are dramatic, including the ultimate efficiency of delivering personalized information to the constituents who rely on that vital business information.

Tip   Arbortext has provided atrial version of its software on the CD-ROM.

Document storage and retrieval

▌ Dispersed storage vs. integral storage

▌ XML Path Language (XPath)

▌ Searching without knowing the document structure

Sponsor: IXIASOFT, http://www.ixiasoft.com

Contributing experts: IXIASOFT staff and Bob DuCharme

An abstract XML document can contain rich information about the structure and other properties of its content data. A content management system can let you exploit that information to access the documents you need — even when you don't know their structure!

T he key to content management is being able to find the content you want when you want it. How easily and effectively you can do so depends on two things: how your documents are stored, and the tools available for retrieving them.

28.1 | Storage strategies

Although content management systems use a variety of techniques for storing XML documents, they boil down to combinations and variations of just two approaches: dispersed and integral.

Dispersed storage

Dispersed storage typically involves parsing the document and storing the parsed data content, attribute values, and other components in multiple fields of a database. Both relational and object databases have been used successfully for this purpose, as well as hybrid object-relational databases. Indexes and maps are used to maintain the relationship between the element structure of the document and the underlying database schema. A variation of this approach stores the components as unparsed text.

Integral storage

Integral storage normally keeps the unparsed document intact and stores it in a single field of a database or as a file in a file system. The document is parsed, however, in order to build indexes that facilitate searching the document base and locating individual components within their documents.

Caution   Integral storage is sometimes called "document-centric", in contrast to either "data-centric" or "component-centric", depending on the context. Those terms can be confusing because "document-centric" has a different implication in each context. Moreover, data and components aren't distinct from documents, they are part of them.

28.1.1 *Selection criteria*

Both dispersed and integral storage are being applied successfully in the real world, so choosing between them is not a cut-and-dried decision. Like many high-tech issues, it depends on a mix of technical, practical, and quasi-theological criteria, such as:

- Are your documents stable or in a constant state of revision?
- How large are they? Do you work with pieces or with the whole thing at once?
- How many documents are there? How many users? Proponents of integral storage claim that dispersed storage does not scale well. They say that adding documents makes the database structure grow in complexity – not just in size – which slows performance.
- What are your passionate beliefs about the "rightness" of keeping XML documents in their official standardized representation, or the value of keeping all information in a managed, centralized (relational or object) data store?

- How much does your management care about your passionate beliefs?
- Do the products you are evaluating work well with your existing systems? Do they work at all?
- Can your staff cope with the complexity of the proposed solution? How will their passionate beliefs affect their efficiency?
- What is the cost of the solution?

28.1.2 *An integral storage example*

We discuss dispersed systems in detail in other chapters, so here we'll consider the characteristics of an integral storage system, illustrated by IXIA-SOFT's *TEXTML Server*.

With *TEXTML Server*, storing documents is akin to using a file system in several important respects:

- All document representations (file formats) are tolerated.
- The integrity of the original document is preserved.
- Properties of the documents can be kept.

The integral storage strategy allows large volumes of documents to be stored without compromising performance. Users report document base sizes in the millions.

A lock mechanism is available to allow document check-in and check-out. Additions, deletions and modifications are reflected dynamically in the indexes as they occur.

Administrators can design and index the document base with no need to optimize a mapping onto an underlying database schema. The design can be based solely on the structure of the documents themselves. As we'll see shortly, this simplicity can also have a positive effect on the user's ability to search the document base.

28.2 | Indexing and retrieval

In any document management system, documents can be addressed, and therefore retrieved, by properties of the document as a whole. Such properties typically include a unique document identifier (e.g. a catalog number or ISBN) or a location (e.g. a file identifier or URL).

In component management systems, as we have seen, addressing and access are possible at the level of individual elements or other components.

However, even when documents are stored and accessed as whole objects, addressing the document need not be based solely on properties of the whole document. Most systems allow searches on the text of a document, for example. Plain text and word processing documents can be searched in this way (although spurious hits can occur if the system doesn't understand – and ignore – the word processing markup).

When a document is represented in XML, an XML-aware system can support addressing of properties of the whole document or any part of it. The XPath specification provides a standardized notation for expressing those properties. It is very powerful, as we shall see, as it is the basis for XSL Transformations, extended linking, and other sophisticated accessing of XML documents.

Many XML content management systems offer their own query languages, often with simpler addressing schemes designed for the expected uses of the system. We'll look at one of those as well.

28.2.1 *XML Path Language (XPath)*

XPath is a notation for addressing information within a document. That information could be:

- An "executive summary" of a longer document.
- A glossary of terms whose definitions are scattered throughout a manual.
- The specific sequence of steps, buried in a large reference work, needed to solve a particular problem.
- The customized subset of information that a particular customer subscribes to.
- All the sections and subsections of a book that were written by a particular author or revised since a specific date.

- For documents holding information from relational databases, all the typical queries made of relational databases: a particular patient's medical records, the address of the customer with the most orders, the inventory items with low stock levels, and so on.

- For documents that are containers for document collections, all the typical queries made in a library catalog or on a website: articles about Abyssinian cats, essays on the proper study of mankind, prospectuses of Internet IPOs with positive earnings, etc.

A programmer working with an XML-aware programming or scripting language could write code to search the document for the information that meets the specified criteria. The purpose of XPath is to automate this searching so that a non-programming user can address the information just by writing an expression that contains the criteria.

28.2.1.1 Location paths

In order to retrieve something, you need to know where to find it – in other words, its *address*. Addresses in XML documents – whether used in a search query, an XSL template rule, or an XPointer – all can be represented in a similar format, called an *XPath expression*. An expression can address a single thing, or several things at the same time.

The most important form of XPath expression is called a *location path*. If you use UNIX or Windows, you may already be familiar with location paths because they are used to address files by specifying the path from the file system's root to a specific subdirectory. For example, the path `/home/bob/xml/samples` identifies a particular one of the four `samples` subdirectories shown in Figure 28-1.

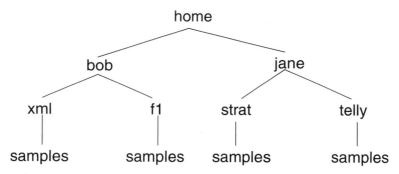

Figure 28-1   File system directory structure

28.2.1.2   Addressing multiple objects

A location path is capable of addressing multiple objects. For example, the expression in Example 28-1 addresses all `caption` elements within `figure` elements that are within `chapter` elements within `book` elements.

Example 28-1. Location path

```
/book/chapter/figure/caption
```

In the book whose structure is shown in Figure 28-2, the expression in Example 28-1 would address the first two `caption` elements, because they are children of `figure` elements. It would not address the third, which is the child of an `example` element.

Example 28-2 shows the XML representation of the book.

28.2.1.3   Children and descendants

The `/book/chapter/figure/caption` expression addresses two elements with no children other than data. The expression `/book/chapter/figure`,

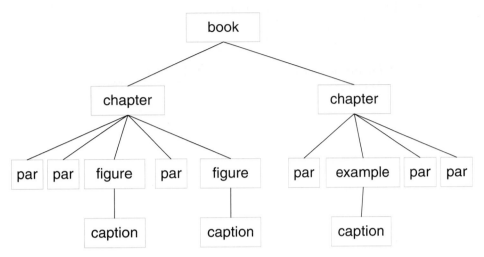

Figure 28-2   Document structure

Example 28-2. A short book in XML

```
<?xml version="1.0"?>
<book>
  <chapter>
    <par author="bd">First paragraph. <emph>Really.</emph></par>
    <par author="cg">Second paragraph.</par>
    <figure picfile="one.jpg">
      <caption>The first figure's caption</caption>
    </figure>
    <par>Third paragraph.</par>
    <figure picfile="two.jpg">
      <caption>The second figure's caption.</caption>
    </figure>
  </chapter>
  <chapter>
    <par author="pp">Chapter 2, first paragraph.</par>
    <example>
      <caption>The first example.</caption>
    </example>
    <par>Chapter 2, second paragraph.</par>
    <par author="bd">Chapter 2, third paragraph.</par>
  </chapter>
</book>
```

however, addresses the `figure` elements with their `caption` children, as shown in Example 28-3.

Example 28-3. Figure elements with their caption children

```
<figure picfile="one.jpg">
  <caption>The first figure's caption</caption>
</figure>
<figure picfile="two.jpg">
  <caption>The second figure's caption.</caption>
</figure>
```

The location path `/book` addresses the entire document.

In a location path, the slash character (/) means "child of." A double slash (//) means "descendant of," which is more flexible as it includes children, grandchildren, great-grandchildren, and so on. For example, `/book//caption` addresses any `caption` element descended from a `book` element. In the book shown in Figure 28-2 it would address the `example` element's `caption` from the book's second chapter along with the figure elements' two `caption` elements:

Example 28-4. Caption elements descended from the book element

```
<caption>The first figure's caption</caption>
<caption>The second figure's caption.</caption>
<caption>The first example.</caption>
```

28.2.1.4   Attributes

An address in XML document navigation is not a storage address like a file system path, despite the similarity in syntax. An XPath expression locates objects by their position in a document's structure and other properties, such as the values of attributes.

A diagram like Figure 28-2 should not present an attribute's information as a child of the element exhibiting the attribute. To do so would be incorrect, because attributes are not siblings of subelements. For this reason, XPath uses `/@` to show the element/attribute relationship.

For example, the expression in Example 28-5 addresses all the values of the `par` elements' `author` attributes.

Example 28-5. Expression with an attribute

```
/book//par/@author
```

Example 28-6. Objects addressed by Example 28-5

```
bd
cg
pp
bd
```

28.2.1.5 Predicates

A *predicate* is an expression that changes the group of objects addressed by another expression that precedes it. A predicate expression is delimited by square brackets and is either true or false. If true, it adds to the objects addressed; if false, it removes objects.

For example, the expression in Example 28-7 addresses all chapters that have a `figure` element in them.

Example 28-7. Addressing chapters with a `figure` element

```
/book/chapter[figure]
```

The predicate expression `figure` is true for any `chapter` that contains a `figure`. If true, that `chapter` is included among the addressed objects. Note that the `figure` itself is not among the objects addressed (although it is contained within the addressed `chapter` object).

A predicate expression can be a comparison. For example, `.=` lets you address an element by comparing its content data to a specific character string. Example 28-8 uses this technique to address all the `par` elements that have "Second paragraph." as their content data.

Example 28-8. Addressing `par` elements with specific content data

```
/book//par[.="Second paragraph."]
```

Example 28-9. Objects addressed by Example 28-8

```
<par author="cg">Second paragraph.</par>
```

Tip   An advanced tutorial on XPath can be found in Chapter 54, "XML Path Language (XPath)", on page 800.

28.2.2 *A simple XML query language*

Not all situations require the power of XPath addressing. In many document retrieval applications, the users have little or no knowledge of the structure of the documents in the document base. Without such knowledge, they cannot formulate queries with location paths.

Moreover, the document base might contain documents with a wide variety of structures. And the users might not care about the detailed structure of the documents in the first place; consider searching the Web, for example. However, even in a Web search the ability to restrict the context in which a search argument appears can reduce the overwhelming volume of irrelevant hits.

Let's take a look at a query language that is built on these principles. It is part of IXIASOFT's *TEXTML Server.*

28.2.2.1   The document base

In Chapter 20, "XMLNews: A syndication document type", on page 276 we took a close look at the *XMLNews-Story* document type, a streamlined subset of the News Industry Text Format (NITF) standard. For this example, we will use an excerpt from a document conforming to the full `nitf` document type.

The example is shown in Example 28-10. It is a portion of an article about an Irish emigrant to Australia in the 19th century. The article is stored in an archive of news stories.

Example 28-10. Excerpt from an `nitf` document

```
<?xml version ="1.0" encoding="UTF-8"?>
<!DOCTYPE nitf SYSTEM "nitf.dtd">
<nitf>
 <body>
  <body.head>
   <hedline>
    <hl1>ON THE MARCO POLO</hl1>
    <hl2>Irish immigration and life aboard a ship in the 19th
century</hl2>
   </hedline>
  </body.head>
  <body.content>
   <block>
    <p>An Irish emigrant describes life aboard the Marco Polo.</p>
    <p> ... </p>
    ... ...
   </block>
   <block>
    <photo-inst>
     <photo>
      <photo.caption>
       <caption>On the Marco Polo, the trip from Britain to
Australia in 77 days</caption>
      </photo.caption>
     </photo>
    </photo-inst>
   </block>
   <block>
    ... ...
   </block>
  </body.content>
 </body>
</nitf>
```

28.2.2.2   The search

A user consults the news story archive to retrieve information regarding
Irish immigration to Australia. He does not know or care about the structure of the documents in the archive, but of course cares about their subject.

The query interface offers two search fields: "Document Title" and
"Document Text". He specifies these as "Irish immigration" and "Australia",
respectively. This search locates all documents that – conceptually at least –

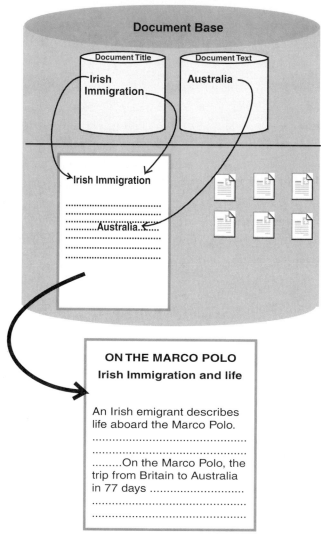

Figure 28-3 Searching without structural knowledge

include "Irish immigration" in the title and "Australia" anywhere in the data content (see Figure 28-3).

The *TEXTML Server* returns the document in Example 28-10. Note that it does not have an actual `DocumentTitle` element. The element whose data satisfied the query was actually a secondary headline (`hl2`), as shown in Example 28-11:

Example 28-11. Data in secondary headline

```
  <hedline>
   <hl1>ON THE MARCO POLO</hl1>
   <hl2>Irish immigration and life aboard a ship in the 19th
century</hl2>
   </hedline>
```

Similarly, there is no literal `DocumentText` element. "Australia" occurs in the data content of a photo caption, as shown in Example 28-12:

Example 28-12. Data in photo caption

```
    <photo>
     <photo.caption>
      <caption>On the Marco Polo, the trip from Britain to
Australia in 77 days</caption>
     </photo.caption>
     </photo>
```

28.2.2.3 Indexing strategy

In the upper part of the Document Base in Figure 28-3, there are two disk drive icons labeled "Document Title" and "Document Text". These represent indexes that were created by the document base administrator.

Each index pertains to a subject that is deemed relevant to users of the document base, here "Document Title" and "Document Text". A set of element types is associated with each index subject by means of an XML document containing `index` elements, as shown in Example 28-13:

Example 28-13. Index definition document

```
<Index NAME = "Document Title"
       TYPE = "Full Text"
       ELEMENTS = "hedline"/>
<Index NAME = "Document Text"
       TYPE = "Full Text"
       ELEMENTS = "p, caption"/>
```

When a user searches for documents with a specific "Document Title", it is actually the data content of `hedline` elements and their children (`hl1` and `hl2`) that is being tested. The relationship is depicted graphically in Figure 28-4.

An index subject can also be associated with multiple element types, as shown for "Document Text" and the `p` and `caption` elements.

The user, of course, is unaware of these relationships. He can frame his query solely in terms of the index subjects, with no knowledge of the document structure.

28.3 | Conclusion

For some content management situations there is a compelling logic to leaving the content where you found it – in an integral XML document – and letting the indexing schema provide addressability to the components.

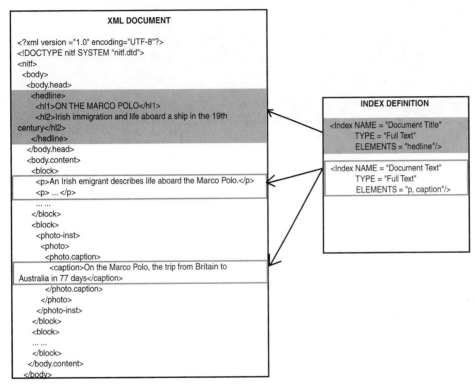

Figure 28-4   Index definition in *TEXTML Server*

Such indexes can be simple enough to allow users to formulate meaningful queries without knowing the structure of the documents.

Tip   There is a free light version of TEXTML Server on the XML Handbook CD-ROM.

Enterprise data management

▌ Enterprise data management requirements

▌ Mapping XML to databases

▌ Internet file system

▌ Complete data integration

Sponsor: Oracle Corporation, http://www.oracle.com/xml

Contributing expert: Oracle Corporation staff

Scratch the surface of a content management
system and underneath you'll find a database. The
same is true for middle-tier servers, portals,
integration servers, and publishing systems. In this
chapter we get below the surface for a close look at
how databases deal with XML.

Today's enterprises are connected as never before, and their applications show it.

E-commerce applications connect organizations with their partners and
suppliers, and integrate business processes for supply chain and sales force
automation. Other e-business applications analyze Web data to better
understand customer behavior, and aggregate legacy and current data to
support enterprise portals.

This activity presents a significant challenge. The enterprise's applications accumulate data at an incredible rate – a rate that is only increasing
thanks to the growth in Internet-deployed applications.

And this data is not homogeneous: It comes in different datatypes, representations, and protocols. Application developers must find efficient ways
to integrate all this data, store it, and use it within their applications.

XML helps by providing a universal representation of data for inter-
application information exchange. However, it does not address the issues
of how to store and administer the data, nor how to leverage existing data.
And it does not eliminate the need for other views of data, such as object,
relational, or the traditional file system view.

Let's look at the data management needs of the enterprise and the requirements these applications impose on database support for XML. Then we'll see how those requirements are addressed by an actual database product – *Oracle8i*.™

29.1 | Applications and XML

Every enterprise of any size has applications that automate a series of business processes, including finance, sales force automation, order processing, warehouse management, etc. Most enterprises use several such applications, often from different vendors.

These applications frequently need to be connected to Internet-based applications that collect or disseminate data for them, as well as to one another, and to the corresponding applications of business partners.

Application developers are using XML in these situations for two main reasons:

- Data sharing and communication between different applications
- Customized presentation of data

29.1.1 *Data sharing and communication*

As we have seen, in order to achieve the promise of integrated e-commerce, an organization needs to bridge its "islands of automation". For example, its order processing application must be able to pass information to the inventory management system. And both of them must be able to access the existing customer accounts database.

Businesses do not have to convert their existing databases and applications to XML databases to satisfy this need. Instead, they can "XML-enable" the data and systems they already have. In other words, XML can provide an open application communication framework for message transport between applications, while each application continues to operate on its own private data store and data model.

These XML messages can be highly structured, ranging from simple single-element documents to complex, multi-level structures. Efficient facilities must therefore be provided to convert enterprise data into XML form and parse XML messages into a data model on which applications can easily operate.

29.1.2 *Customized presentation of data*

The technologies available for end-users to view information are evolving rapidly. Information presentation must now be optimized for different browsers or for other devices, such as Personal Digital Assistants (PDAs) and cell phones.

An XSL processor, either on the client or server, can transform an XML document into an appropriate form for any given client. It can thereby insulate the business application from the means of data delivery and consumption. Transforming information and generating it in multiple forms is key to the effective management of data.

29.2 | Requirements for enterprise data management

We will discuss four categories of requirements:

- Data storage and management
- Data views and interchange
- Query facilities
- Integration with existing systems

29.2.1 *Data storage and management*

The requirements for data storage and management are discussed in this section.

29.2.1.1   Management of structured data

Databases must be able to "read" and "write" XML without losing the structure of the data. Data stored in relational form is structured as a table, and can be mapped to tree-structured XML documents. Likewise, simple XML documents can be mapped to a relational schema, although more complex XML structures may require the use of object-relational technology to fully represent all the data relationships.

29.2.1.2   Performance, reliability, availability and scalability

A datastore that is to be used by enterprise Internet applications must meet very high standards of performance, reliability, availability, and scalability. It should be developed to run 24x7x365 under heavy loads and come with a broad set of management tools. These should include, for example, transparent application failover with no loss of performance even in the event of hardware failure.

29.2.1.3   Rich datatypes

XML document types are, in fact, custom datatypes. As they can be made up of atomic typed data, character text, multimedia, etc., the storage system must be able to support all these datatypes and optimally provide a single location for their storage and management.

Oracle8i, for example, handles character text, images, audio and video natively. It also provides an extensible framework that includes interfaces to management capabilities, including type management, storage management, indexing, and optimization. These interfaces allow users to:

- Define arbitrarily complex datatypes.
- Plug them into the database.
- Define their own indexing, sort and search algorithms for the data.
- Leverage the data management and transaction facilities of the database.

29.2.1.4   Security and data integrity

Applications that are accessed by large numbers of people require the type of access security, transaction management, locking and concurrency control that is typical of modern databases.

29.2.2   *Data views and interchange*

A datastore should be able to satisfy these requirements for supporting renditions and interchange.

29.2.2.1   Multiple clients

A datastore for enterprise data should be able to easily exchange XML documents with a variety of clients, including browsers, email clients, enterprise messaging systems, FTP clients, cell phones, PDAs, and server-to-server communication (via HTTP).

29.2.2.2   Rendition and conversion

An XML datastore should provide facilities to *render* business data for presentation to an end-user. It should also be able to *convert* business data into the appropriate XML messages for interchange with applications. Both requirements can be met by running an XML parser and an XSL processor on the server and/or the client.

29.2.2.3   Persistent messaging

As XML becomes widely used for inter-enterprise communication, developers will want to store, track, and audit XML message information. Therefore, the enterprise datastore must provide integrated persistence facilities for XML messages. Since the raw data for the XML messages is being held in the database, it is simple to provide an audit trail for inter-application and inter-enterprise messages.

29.2.3 *Query facilities*

For querying, an enterprise datastore must meet two important requirements:

29.2.3.1   Universal query domain

An enterprise datastore must be able to perform complex queries over data from multiple sources. For example, providing book recommendations based on subject classification or keyword, availability, price, or previous purchases requires the integration of information from multiple systems into one delivery system. As all data may be integrated into a single datastore, queries may be run against all datatypes and sources.

29.2.3.2   Query performance and scalability under load

Applications often need to execute queries quickly across large datasets. Moreover, performance must remain high even when large numbers of concurrent users access the system, which requires an efficient and fine-grained locking model.

29.2.4 *Integration with existing systems*

In deploying XML for enterprise data management, a difficult tradeoff must be made between deploying completely new systems and XML-specific datastores, or extending existing systems and databases with XML capabilities. For the latter option to be viable, the existing database must have suitable tools for working with XML.

29.3 | XML database operations

In the preceding sections, we have discussed the requirements for enterprise data management and where XML can be of benefit. As most of these requirements rely on the ability to efficiently "read" and "write" XML to and from a database, let's look at the tools and techniques used by *Oracle8i* to accomplish these tasks. We'll also look briefly at indexing and searching, as searches frequently accompany reading and writing.

First, some definitions:

- *Read XML from a database*: Export database objects or schemas and represent them as XML documents.
- *Write XML into a database*: Parse an XML document and store its components in a database without losing the metadata that describes the properties of the components and the relationship among them.

29.3.1 *Reading XML from a database*

The ability to represent a database object in XML requires infrastructure components that can use SQL to request the object and transform it into an XML document.

Figure 29-1 depicts an insurance claim form stored as an object in a database using the relational tables shown.

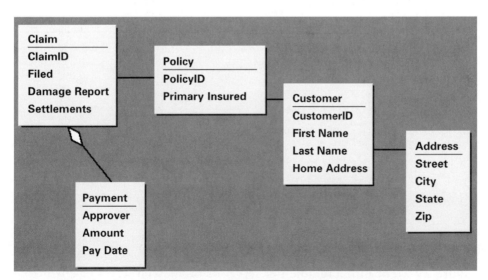

Figure 29-1   An insurance claim form in a relational database

This object can be represented as the XML document shown in Example 29-1, which preserves the data relationships set up by the database schema. The document was produced using the *Oracle XSQL Servlet for Java*.

Example 29-1. XML representation of an insurance claim form

```xml
<?xml version="1.0"?>
<CLAIM>
  <CLAIMID>123456</CLAIMID>
  <FILED>1999-01-01 12:00:00.0</FILED>
  <CLAIMPOLICY>
    <POLICYID>8895</POLICYID>
    <PRIMARYINSURED>
      <CUSTOMERID>1044</CUSTOMERID>
      <FIRSTNAME>John</FIRSTNAME>
      <LASTNAME>Doe</LASTNAME>
      <HOMEADDRESS>
        <STREET>123 Cherry Lane</STREET>
        <CITY>San Francisco</CITY>
        <STATE>CA</STATE>
        <ZIP>94100</ZIP>
      </HOMEADDRESS>
    </PRIMARYINSURED>
  </CLAIMPOLICY>
  <DAMAGEREPORT>
    The driver lost control of the vehicle.
    This was due to <CAUSE>faulty brakes</CAUSE>.
  </DAMAGEREPORT>
  <SETTLEMENTS>
    <PAYMENT id="0">
      <PAYDATE>1999-03-01 09:00:00.0</PAYDATE>
      <AMOUNT>7600</AMOUNT>
      <APPROVER>JCOX</APPROVER>
    </PAYMENT>
  </SETTLEMENTS>
</CLAIM>
```

29.3.1.1 Oracle XSQL Servlet for Java

The *XSQL Servlet* is a component of the *Oracle XML Developer's Kits* that generates XML documents from one or more SQL database queries. It can be loaded into a database that supports *Java*, such as *Oracle8i* (as shown in Figure 29-2), or into a middle-tier server or other Web server or client that supports servlets.

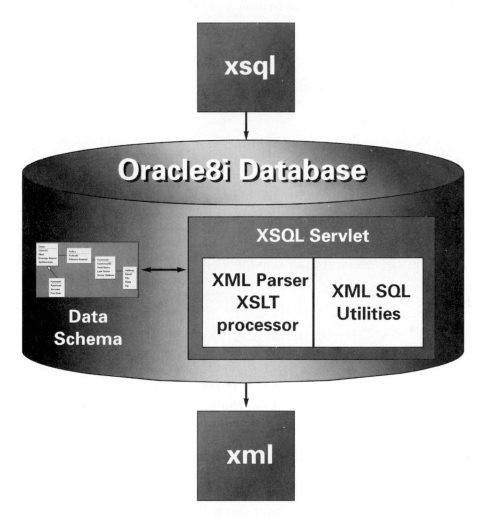

Figure 29-2 Structure of the *XSQL Servlet*

The SQL statement is included in a document of type query, an instance of which is shown in Example 29-2. That document contains an SQL statement that searches for insurance claims submitted by Mr. Doe. Note that the query may be written as regular SQL or, as in this case, using object dot notation.

Example 29-2. An XML document containing an SQL search for insurance claims

```
<?xml version="1.0"?>
<?xml-stylesheet type="text/xsl" href="claim.xsl"?>
<query connection="xmldemo">
  select value(c) as Claim from insurance_claim_view c
  where c.claimpolicy.primaryinsured.lastname = 'Doe'
</query>
```

The servlet uses the *XML Parser* to parse this file and passes any XSL processing statements to the *XSLT Processor*. It also passes the attributes and data content of the `query` element to the *XML SQL Utilities*.

The query results are received either as an XML document or a JDBC `ResultSet` object. If necessary, the query results may be parsed with the parser and/or transformed using the *XSLT Processor*.

The parser can also be loaded independently into the *Java* virtual machine in *Oracle8i*, run from a middle-tier server, or run on the client as a *JavaBean*.

29.3.1.2   XSLT transformations

XML documents can also be used as messages to transport data between heterogeneous databases, with XSLT providing the translation from one message format to the other. This capability is particularly useful for e-commerce and enterprise application integration.

XSLT can also be used to render documents in HTML. The process is driven by a template consisting of an HTML page with appropriate XSL statements at the locations where the XML data is to be displayed.

For example, using the insurance claim document in Example 29-1, we can create an HTML page to render selected data elements. While developing the template, we initially use dummy data as page formatting placeholders. Once the HTML is satisfactorily formatted, the dummy data is replaced with XSL processor statements, as follows:

JCOX

```
<xsl:value-of
select="claim/settlements/payment/approver"/>
```

7600

```
<xsl:value-of
select="claim/settlements/payment/@amount"/>
```

123456

```
<xsl:value-of select="claim/@claimid"/>
```

29.3.2 *Writing XML into a database*

The *Oracle XDK* and Oracle's *XML SQL Utility* offer two ways to store an XML document: as a single object with its markup intact; or distributed across a set of tables.

It is also possible to combine these two approaches using views.

Storage of the intact document is a good strategy when the data is static or will be updated only by replacing the entire document.

Distributing across tables maps XML data into the relational schema, which allows individual data elements to be accessed and revised. An XSL stylesheet determines the appropriate SQL insert and update statements for storing the parsed data.

For the claim document in Example 29-1, for example, the stylesheet fragment shown in Example 29-3 could create the entry for the PAYMENT table.

Example 29-3. Stylesheet fragment

```
insert into PAYMENT values
    ('<xsl:value-of
select="claim/settlements/payment/approver"/>',
    <xsl:value-of
select=""claim/settlements/payment/@amount">,
    <xsl:value-of
select="claim/settlements/payment/@paydate"/>);
```

Oracle8i offers other storage techniques as well.

29.3.3 *Indexing and searching*

For documents that are stored intact, facilities are available for searching for data content of elements and attribute values. Documents that are mapped onto relational tables can be searched with SQL.

For example, using the insurance claim in Example 29-1 as the search domain, the SQL statement in Example 29-4 searches for all settlements approved by JCOX. It uses the CONTAINS SQL function to find those where "faulty brakes" were the cause.

Example 29-4. SQL statement

```
SELECT SUM(Amount)
   FROM Claim_Header ch, Claim_Settlements cs,
        Claim_Settlement_Payments csp
WHERE csp.Approver = 'JCOX'
AND CONTAINS(DamageReport,'faulty brakes WITHIN cause')>0;
```

29.4 | Internet file system

We point out in Chapter 3, "The XML usage spectrum", on page 54 that XML documents are an alternative representation for abstract data, one that is independent of the application or database that created it. The ubiquitous practice on the World Wide Web, of serving HTML documents that are constructed dynamically in response to queries, shows that documents can be representations of rendered data as well.

Such documents have no persistent existence as files in a file system. In fact, they suggest that for an enterprise with a sufficiently capable database, such as *Oracle8i*, it may make sense to avoid the traditional file system even for persistent files. *Oracle Internet File System*™ utilizes the XML infrastructure in a more general way, for the storing and generating of documents in any representation, not just XML.

The system parses incoming documents with an appropriate parser and inserts the data into a database schema. Documents are then generated from database tables on demand, looking like normal file system files. The file view from *Windows Explorer* is shown in Figure 29-3.

This facility makes data available to both relational and file-oriented applications as required. Although documents can be viewed and retrieved

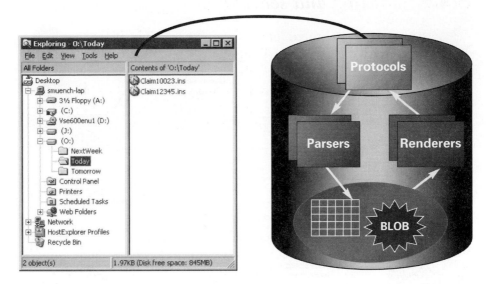

Figure 29-3   File view from *Windows Explorer*

as if they were files in the file system, they may also be updated directly in the database. And, because their content is stored in the database, they can also participate in searches over a unified domain of data and documents.

29.5 | An e-commerce example

Let's see how the XML facilities of a database can support a B2B integrated e-commerce transaction among heterogeneous systems. In Figure 29-4 a *Retailer* captures customer orders and sends them to a *Supplier* by means of a *Message Broker* middle-tier server. Each system uses a different database.

The transaction begins when a customer of *Retailer* places an order through a browser, PDA, or cell phone. The business logic associated with the creation of the order is encapsulated and the order is inserted into *Retailer*'s database.

An XML message document reflecting the insert is sent to *Message Broker* (Example 29-5).

Message Broker uses XSLT to transform the incoming message to the document type required by *Supplier*. The stylesheet for the transformation is

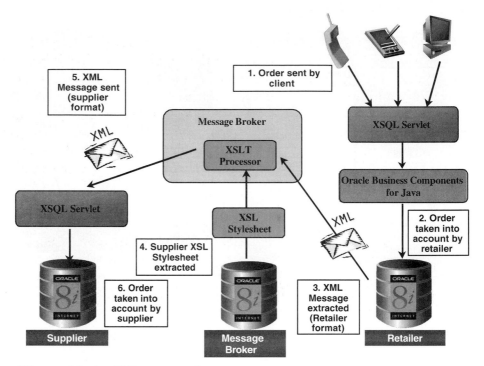

Figure 29-4   B2B integrated e-commerce transaction

Example 29-5. New order message

```
<message>
<origin>Retailer</origin>
<destination>Supplier</destination>
<purpose>New order</purpose>
<items>
  <item>Red widget</item>
  <item>Blue widget</item>
</items>
</message>
```

chosen based on the data of the `origin`, `destination`, and `purpose` elements. The transformed result document is sent to *Supplier*'s system, which parses it and generates an insert into *Supplier*'s database.

The same process could be used in reverse so that *Supplier*, for example, could update the order status in *Retailer*'s database.

29.6 | Conclusion

Over the past 15 years, enterprises have overwhelmingly chosen relational databases as the infrastructure to support their applications. This is because of the flexibility and broad applicability of the technology. XML is now becoming popular for largely the same reasons.

Databases such as *Oracle8i*, by providing XML interchange, styling, and support facilities, can allow enterprises to adopt XML without changing their existing systems or databases. They are able to include XML – along with object, relational, and file system – in the list of supported alternative views of the same managed data.

 Tip   You can obtain the Oracle XDK and its associated utilities described in this chapter from `http://technet.oracle.com`.

Content Acquisition

- Creating abstract XML documents directly
- Converting legacy documents
- Large-scale conversion
- Accessing transactional data

Part Eight

Content is king!

Yes, we said that before, but now we can tell the whole truth.

Actually, content is a royal family. There is *persistent information*, which you find in documents, and *transactional data*, which is a by-product of business processes. Ideally, we want the documents to be unrendered abstractions, represented in XML, just as we want the data to be in sharable enterprise databases.

But much of the time, the documents are *legacy documents* – either rendered or not XML (or both!) – and the data is *legacy data*, usable only by the application that created it.

In this part, we look closely at the different ways of acquiring usable abstract content for XML systems: creating it directly in XML, converting legacy documents, and accessing transactional data.

First, we look at the problem of creating new content for multiple unknown uses. We also look at techniques of converting rendered document files to abstractions.

We then consider the formidable task of converting vast quantities of legacy documents to XML, both the detailed planning that is needed and the facilities required. Finally, we see how XML can make legacy data an integral part of the enterprise's information resources.

Developing reusable content

Application Discussion

▌ The content developer's dilemma

▌ Content development strategy

▌ Editing XML abstractions

▌ Linking and navigation

Sponsor: Adobe Systems Incorporated, http://www.adobe.com

Contributing expert: Doug Yagaloff and Lani Hajagos

How do you develop content when you have no idea how it will be used? When you create a rendered document with a word processor, what you see is all you've got, but at least you've got something you can see! When you create an XML abstraction, you've got a lot more, but only if you've done it right. This chapter will show you how.

I n the wonderful way that often occurs with high-tech solutions, XML has become a requirement in its own right for content developers. As a result, authors and publishing groups find themselves rushing to implement XML in their writing and delivery solutions, often without clear objectives and requirements for XML use. This tendency can throw a content development plan into a tailspin, as developers chase ever-changing and poorly defined requirements.

30.1 | The content developer's dilemma

Have you ever been involved in a construction project? The excited anticipation of the first step – clearing the ground for the foundation – can easily blur the details of the steps that must follow. If you have mapped out all of the steps before you begin, you will forge ahead with confidence. If not, you may find your project faltering after that first step.

Many content developers have had similar experiences with their XML projects. The anticipation of developing and deploying an XML-based publishing solution is so great that only after completing the first few steps do they take time to fully understand the complexity of the project.

The first component of the solution – content creation – is easy to plan, since it is the primary function of the content developer. The second component – determining who will use the information and making it suitable for their intended uses – may be difficult or impossible to accomplish.

30.1.1   *What do solution developers want from XML?*

XML is deployed in a wide range of application solutions involving the control and delivery of data, from simple online help systems to complex integrated e-commerce systems. You've been getting some idea of the scale and diversity from this book, but XML is undoubtedly being put to use in still more ways even as you read this.

These applications may be conceived and defined independently of the developers of the content, usually without consideration of writing workflow constraints or packaging of content deliverables. This singular focus on deployment can create conflict between the needs of the XML-using solution developer and the requirements of the content creator.

30.1.2   *What do content creators need from XML?*

Content creators look to XML to improve the process of writing and managing content from the beginning of a writing project to the delivery. They rely on specific XML facilities:

- *Schemas and DTDs*, which define rules for organizing and validating information content.
- *Attributes*, which provide a means of annotating the information content with descriptive metadata.
- *Abstraction preservation*, which allows the information content to be kept separate from rendition style so that the information can be reused in multiple ways.

The attention of the content creator is on creation and management, not necessarily deployment – which can create a conflict with the solution developer's requirements.

30.1.3 *Creation and deployment requirements may not conform*

In addition to the differing goals and needs of the content creator and the solution developer, there are other reasons why the requirements for creation and deployment may conflict:

- The content creator and solution developer may have little or no interaction.
- The requirements for the content creator may not be known, or may not even exist, when the solution is being developed.
- The requirements for the solution may not be known, or even exist, when the content is being created.
- The requirements for each may be affected by differing business objectives and constraints.

These factors can hinder the content creator from implementing a development strategy that delivers reusable XML abstractions. He will be hard put to deliver anything but well-defined renditions, like printed pages, HTML pages, or online help files.

To overcome these hindrances, the content creator needs a strategy for reusable content development, the ability to create abstract XML documents, and facilities for creating portable and reusable hyperlinks and other navigation aids. We'll discuss these points in the next few sections.

30.2 | Content development strategy

For the content creator, the basic development strategy of design, create, validate, and deploy has worked well for delivering renditions (Figure 30-1). The process is easy to manage and the deployment expectations are well-defined. If the rendition requirements change, the process can easily be modified. The representation of the information can be optimized for the particular rendition because it will not be reused for other purposes.

Figure 30-1   The basic content development strategy

Today's deployment requirements affect each of these stages, making the process more dynamic and complex. The process must utilize tools and methods that allow the development of content that can be reused and processed by tools and applications unknown to the content creators.

30.2.1 *Beyond the basic*

As the deployment requirements of solution developers are ever-changing, there must be a step added to the current content development process (Figure 30-2).

Figure 30-2   The basic content development strategy extended

The more detailed a document's structure and the richer its set of attributes, the more likely that applications will have the data they need. However, as each data point adds development cost, and as it is impossible to predict all future deployment requirements, it is important to design for future extensibility.

Consider the following suggestions:

- Design DTDs and schemas that can be expanded. Identify and document aspects of the design that you know cannot possibly be complete until deployment requirements are defined. Return to these areas periodically to determine when and if they can be completed.

- Expect that information created and maintained today may never be "rich" enough for some future deployment requirements. Regularly survey users to help anticipate requirements.

- Research current and developing XML facilities like namespaces, topic maps, extended linking, and XSL stylesheets. Consider whether and how those facilities might improve your content development strategy. There are tutorials on all of them, and others, in this book.

There are also specific techniques to employ in schemas and DTDs that will enhance reusability by improving both the quality of the content and the extensibility of the schema:

- Provide attributes that are solely for management and classification: keywords, references, purpose, source, etc.
- Design element types that can be extended with newly-developed subelements.
- Provide "annotation" element types for describing the context and content of other elements. The descriptions could occur in the attributes or data content of the annotation elements.
- Model schemas with a database to identify relationships, expose limitations, and test reusability.
- Be clear and precise regarding the naming and usage of element types and attributes.
- Create a well-defined syntax for complex attribute values and a parser for extracting their data. Better yet, express complex properties as multiple attributes (perhaps in "annotation" subelements) and let XML do the parsing.

30.3 | Editing XML abstractions

Writing and editing an abstract XML document is different from creating a rendered document in a word processor. You are capturing a lot more information that will maximize the potential uses of the document, but you can't normally see this information in a rendition and so you lack the conventional visual confirmation that it is being created accurately.

Fortunately, XML editing tools offer capabilities to overcome these difficulties, and to take advantage of the strengths of abstract documents. We'll discuss a few of the key points and illustrate them with Adobe *FrameMaker+SGML*, an integrated XML editing and composition product.

The tool is designed to shield the user from the technicalities of XML and to support a workgroup environment. It includes a robust composition capability that can handle complex page layouts with a high degree of automation, even such professional graphic arts requirements as spot and process color separations.

30.3.1 *Guided editing*

Guided editing features help authors create documents that conform to the rules for a document type. In Figure 30-3, the element-type catalog shows which element types are valid for the current location in the document. The interactive structure view lets the author manipulate the structure of the document. It graphically advises whether a proposed move will invalidate the structure. These devices make it possible to create and manipulate the structure of the document without ever working directly with, or even looking at, a markup tag.

30.3.2 *Editing non-valid documents*

When creating type-valid XML documents, an editing tool might require that the document be valid at all times, even if that means putting in empty elements when information is not yet available. Maintaining validity in this way means that the author has to start at the beginning of the document, and write everything in order, not skipping any required elements.

However, this isn't what happens in the real world. All too often, the information a writer needs simply isn't available. So the writer may skip some parts of the document and write others out of order. As more and more of the information becomes available, the gaps are filled in and eventually the document is complete. This is easy to do in a word processor, but difficult if your editing tool insists that validity must be maintained.

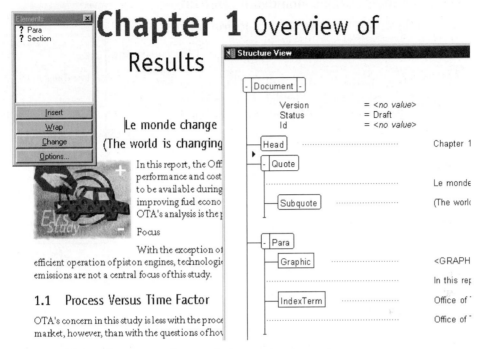

Figure 30-3   Structure view and element-type catalog.

Some editors address this requirement by allowing information to be entered in any order and allowing required information to be skipped. The document can be saved as a work in progress even if it is not valid. The software keeps track of what is missing and what is in the wrong place, and helps the writer fix things. So the end result is a valid, complete document, without the hassle of having to fight with an inflexible editing tool.

With *FrameMaker+SGML*, when working in the guided editing mode, the element-type catalog shows only those element types valid at the current location in the document. However, as shown in Figure 30-4, the element-type catalog can also be set to display all element types, or any element type that may be valid within a parent element, even further down in the hierarchy. The valid element types are indicated by a checkmark.

This facility is also helpful when editing merely well-formed XML documents.

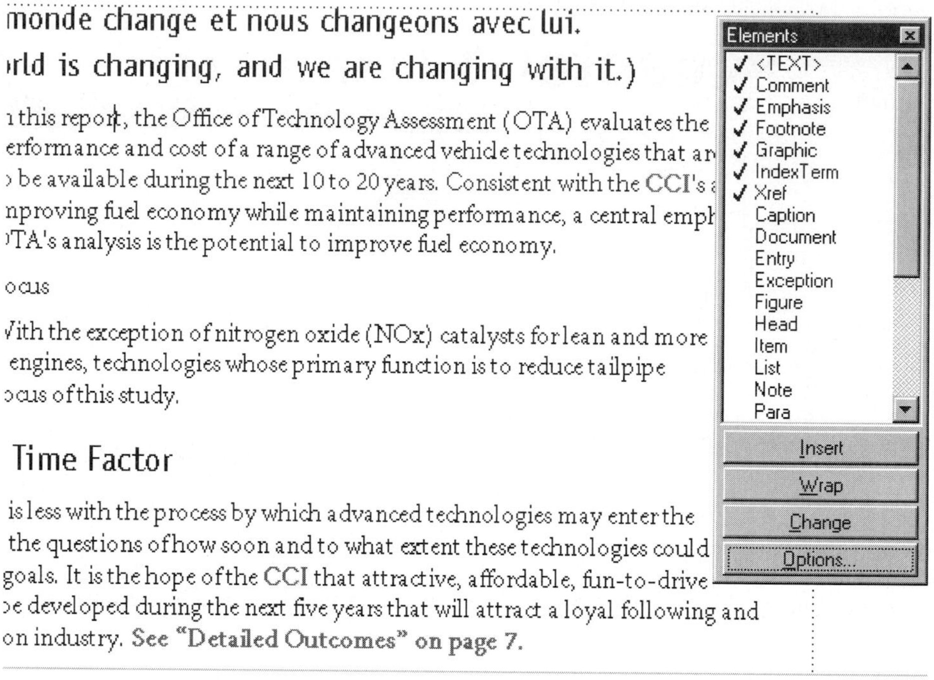
monde change et nous changeons avec lui.
rld is changing, and we are changing with it.)
ı this report, the Office of Technology Assessment (OTA) evaluates the
erformance and cost of a range of advanced vehicle technologies that ar
› be available during the next 10 to 20 years. Consistent with the CCI's
nproving fuel economy while maintaining performance, a central emph
)TA's analysis is the potential to improve fuel economy.
ocus
Vith the exception of nitrogen oxide (NOx) catalysts for lean and more
engines, technologies whose primary function is to reduce tailpipe
ocus of this study.
Time Factor
is less with the process by which advanced technologies may enter the
the questions of how soon and to what extent these technologies could
goals. It is the hope of the CCI that attractive, affordable, fun-to-drive
be developed during the next five years that will attract a loyal following and
on industry. See "Detailed Outcomes" on page 7.
Elements
✓ <TEXT>
✓ Comment
✓ Emphasis
✓ Footnote
✓ Graphic
✓ IndexTerm
✓ Xref
Caption
Document
Entry
Exception
Figure
Head
Item
List
Note
Para
Insert
Wrap
Change
Options...

Figure 30-4 Element-type catalog displaying all element types; valid ones are checked.

30.4 | Linking and navigation

In an XML document, the links and indexes can be developed as abstractions, which enhances their reusability. They can even be developed on the principles of topic maps, which can make them extensible and portable as well.

30.4.1 *Abstract links*

A link is a representation of a relationship. Let's look at two of the most common kinds and see how an XML editor can support them as abstractions. We'll again use *FrameMaker+SGML* to illustrate.

30.4.1.1   Cross-references

The cross-reference tool makes it easy to link pieces of information, either within a document or across documents, using standard XML methodology. The user inserts a cross-reference element, and selects a target element type from a list. The tool (Figure 30-5) shows all the instances of that element type in the document.

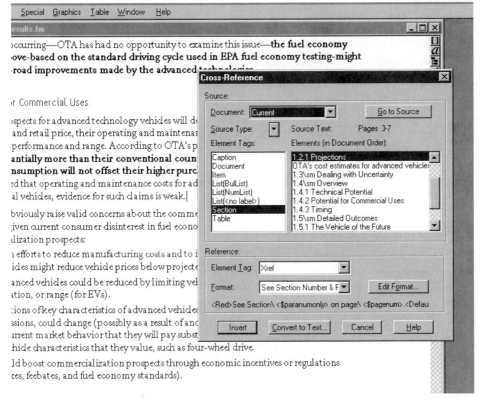

Figure 30-5   Cross-reference interface.

The user selects the appropriate element and the format of the generated text (e.g., "see table 5 on page 23"), and the generated string is placed in the displayed rendition of the document. For the XML markup, a unique ID value is automatically generated and placed in the ID attribute of the target element, as well as in the IDREF attribute of the referencing element.

Users can control the generated text by editing the cross-reference format in the stylesheet. As table, paragraph, and page numbers are similarly generated only for rendition, they are automatically updated in the display as content is inserted into or removed from the document.

30.4.1.2   Indexing

An index is a form of topic map that links subjects to page numbers. Think of it as a bunch of cross-references, taken out of context and sorted alphabetically. As with cross-references, the page numbers are generated automatically when the document is rendered.

FrameMaker+SGML can handle complex, multi-level indexes like the following example:

Example 30-1. Multi-level index entry

Continental drift
  Fossil evidence, 57
  Rock structures, 62, 80

Users enter index entries in proximity to occurrences of the subject in the document. Doing so also implicitly associates the entries with the numbers of the pages on which the subjects will occur when the document is rendered. These entries are used to compile the indexes automatically, either for a single document or a group of documents.

30.4.2   *Extensible and portable links*

Because all possible deployments of a document cannot be predicted, content developers are not always able to determine all of the links they need at the time they are developing the content. There are several reasons for this:

- The scope of references (i.e., the set of potential anchors) cannot be determined until the document is rendered and deployed.
- The actual addresses of anchors are subject to change, even after deployment, as websites move or cease to be.

Nevertheless, the relationships that the links will represent can be defined during content development. It is just the related objects that are unknown. Topic maps, which are described in Chapter 43, "Topic maps: Knowledge navigation aids", on page 606, are a generalized application of this principle.

The links, like the cross-references and index entries we have already seen, are forms of metadata. They are represented by element types and attributes that are defined for a given document type. For each link, a set of queries is developed that will address all available objects that are anchors of the link.

When a document is deployed, the queries are executed and the addresses of the result set objects are obtained. These are inserted in the deployed document in the form of XPointers.

30.4.3 *Extensible tools*

In order for your content development strategy and your content to be extensible, your tools should be extensible as well. For example, you might want to provide support for creating the extensible and portable links just described.

XML editing and composition products may offer scripting or programming languages for this purpose. A proprietary language usually offers the advantage of product-specific functions, while a standard language can be utilized more easily by a large body of developers who are already familiar with it.

For example, further customizing or extending the functions of *FrameMaker+SGML* can be accomplished by developing a "plug-in" using a C-based application programming interface (API). The API is accessed through a developers kit that provides an application development environment incorporating a library of function calls and makefiles. It was used to create the *Knowledge Chain™ Builder* plug-in shown in Figure 30-6.

The plug-in uses document properties such as content data strings to help users construct links. At deployment time, it parses the XML docu-

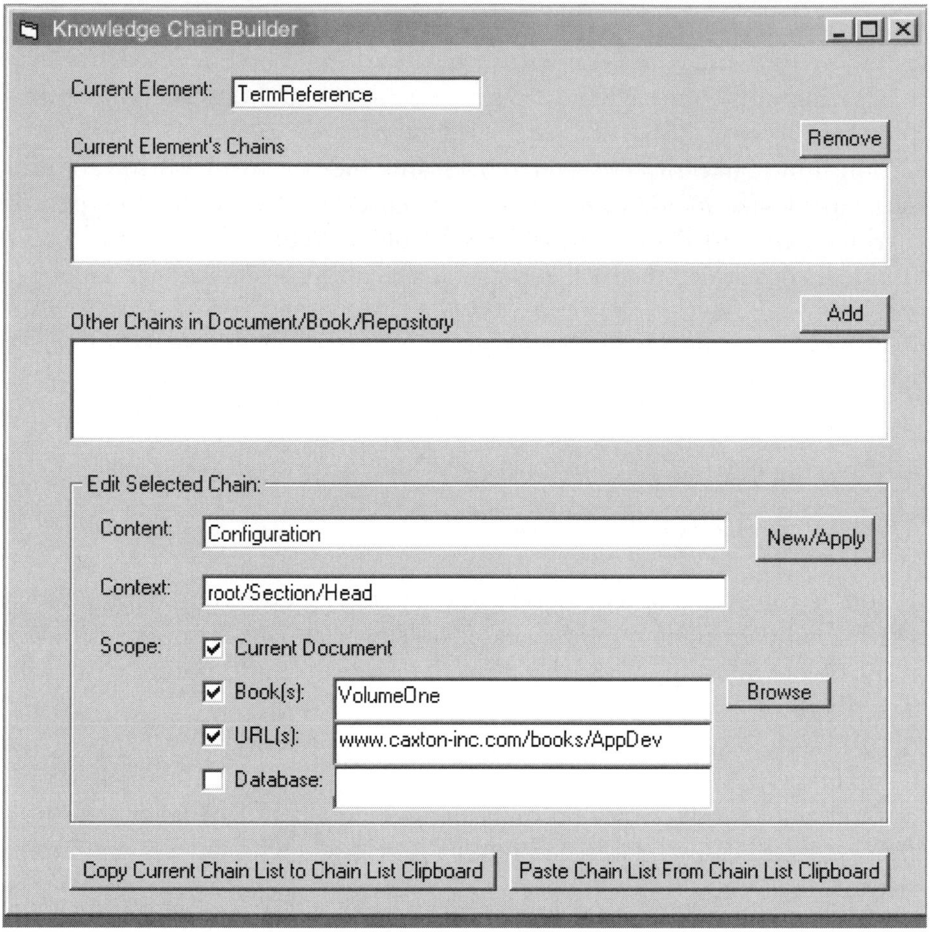

Figure 30-6   *Knowledge Chain Builder* plug-in

ment and builds the queries for locating potential link anchors. It also validates the anchors and constructs the XPointers that address them.

Analysis Here's an interesting contradiction. One of the most important aspects of XML is that it can preserve data in the abstract; that is, it won't accidentally intermingle your data with rendition information. On the other hand, the style of a rendition is important, because that is what makes communication of the data effective.

This chapter illustrated an approach to XML editing that seeks to resolve that contradiction. The product is structure-driven, but provides a WYSIWYG rendered view and sophisticated graphic arts functionality. Other XML editors make different tradeoffs. Understanding them all will help you determine your own requirements more accurately.

Converting renditions to abstractions

Application Discussion

- Document conversion concepts

- Style and structure

- Tools for XML conversion

Sponsor: Quark, Inc., http://www.quark.com

Contributing expert: Trevor Alyn

Chapter

31

Word processing and publishing document file formats faithfully record how data should look, but they are useless as reliable sources for processing that data. That's why so many of those documents need to be converted to XML. Portals and similar middle-tier data aggregators need to convert them dynamically, and content developers need to do it as part of the editing process. This chapter explains what's involved.

Transformations between abstract data and rendered documents are at the heart of XML processing. We've already seen a variety of applications that go from abstraction to rendition automatically, by applying style to content based on the content's structure. But what if you need to go the other way – from rendition to abstraction?

31.1 | Concepts of document conversion

An XML document consists of data intermixed with markup. The purpose of the markup is to describe the data: its meaning, structure, and other properties.

31.1.1 *Starting with abstractions*

When data originates in a database, as in many middle-tier applications, it is straightforward to incorporate it in an XML document. That is because a database keeps data in an *abstract* state; it isn't mixed up with reports, entry forms, or other rendition information. Moreover, the database schema knows how to associate meaning with the data – meaning that is easily represented as element types and attributes when creating the XML document.

Creating an XML document is also straightforward with an XML structured editing system. Such systems, like databases, keep the data in an abstract state internally even if they present a rendered view to the author.

31.1.2 *Starting with renditions*

But the real garden variety word processors, beloved of authors and typists the world over, have no concept of data. They exist solely to create renditions and will happily mingle formatting commands with data, given the slightest opportunity.

Despite that fact, many XML-savvy organizations use word processors regularly to create XML documents. They prefer not to invest in the retraining and process changes that switching editing environments requires.

A similar situation exists in the publishing world, where content is often developed in a format designed for printed pieces. Publishers create books, newspapers, and magazines, using long-established publishing tools that focus on formatting and style. When they want to move that content to the Web (or elsewhere), they must convert the formatted content to an abstract representation such as XML offers.

Which is why XML conversion tools were invented. Many of them are essentially programming languages with varying degrees of XML-awareness. (There are some on the CD-ROM accompanying this book.) They often require a programmer's skills to create rules for parsing word processing formats, and they don't provide visual feedback.

31.1.3 *Two key concepts*

We'll see a different approach later in this chapter, but first we need to look at two key concepts: *data rescue* and *style serves meaning*.

31.1.3.1   Data rescue

Converting a word processing document to XML typically involves more than just changing from one representation ("file format") to another. Instead of simply translating the document's formatting characteristics and content, it is necessary to isolate the real information content – the abstract data and its structure – from the style information. In other words, the data must be rescued from the rendered form, and stored in a notation – XML – that is capable of preserving structured data as an abstraction.

Data rescue restores rendered content so that it can be deployed for many uses in a variety of delivery environments.

31.1.3.2   Style serves meaning

The basic principle behind data rescue is that the purpose of the style in word processing documents is to help convey the meaning of the data. In other words, as an example, the reason for using a particular set of formatting instructions (such as bold, centered, 18 point type) is to show that the data in that style is a "title".

By taking advantage of this principle, it is possible to transform word processing styles to XML markup.

31.1.4 *Style and structure*

The tags in an abstract XML document and the styling in a rendered print document do the same thing – they just do it differently. XML communicates structure literally, using element types and nesting. Print publications communicate structure visually, using formatting and arrangement.

Our brains perceive the structure in a print document by decoding visual styling. Is a particular chunk of text large, bold, and at the beginning? It's probably a headline. Is it beneath a graphic and different from the surrounding text? Most likely it's a caption. By noting the positioning of headlines and subheadings within an article, we create a mental outline of that article; by noting that certain words are always bold, we determine that those words fall into the same class.

Since the structure of a document is already inherent in the styling of a rendition, converting a rendition of a document to an XML abstraction shouldn't be a matter of *imposing* a structure on that document; it should be a matter of *perceiving* and *interpreting* the existing structure as expressed in terms of style.

The next section explains this process. It is illustrated with Quark's *avenue.quark*, a tool that operates on rendered documents created by the *QuarkXPress* publishing system.

31.2 | The conversion process

Avenue.quark employs a process called *rule-based tagging* to recognize stylistic structures and convert them into XML abstractions. The process of tagging a document has three basic steps:

1. Choosing a DTD and root element type
2. Creating tagging rules
3. Tagging content

31.2.1 *Choosing a DTD and root element*

The first step in rule-based tagging is to specify the desired result; that is, the document type definition to which the abstract document will conform. Doing so identifies the element types that may be used in the tagging process.

This step is accomplished by choosing a DTD and root element type (document element type), as seen in Figure 31-1.

31.2.2 *Creating tagging rules*

The next step is to open a document and create *tagging rules*.

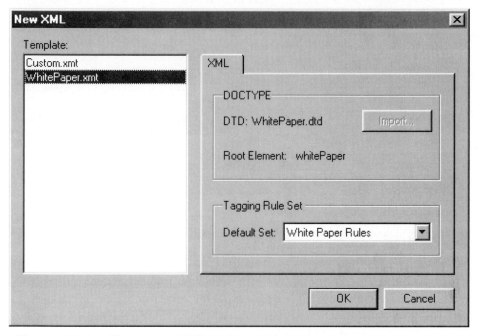

Figure 31-1 Choosing a DTD and root element type

Tagging rules are a form of mapping; when you create a tagging rule, you associate an element type with one or more stylistic properties. Then content with those stylistic properties can automatically be marked with the tag for the associated element type.

Tagging rule creation is shown in Figure 31-2.

The document you choose for the development of tagging rules should be a good representative of the class of documents you wish to convert. In that way the tagging rules can be reused for the other members of the class.

31.2.2.1 Tagging rules based on styles

Experienced publishing professionals have known for years that the best way to control formatting in large periodical publications is with styles.

A *style* is a named group of formatting properties.[1]

For example, a style named "Headline" might specify bold, 36-point Futura text with an indent and extra space above. You can apply the "Head-

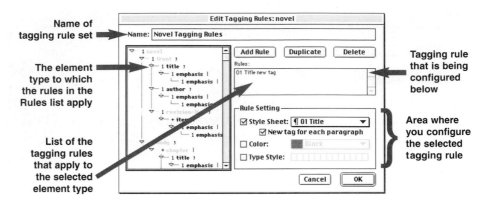

Figure 31-2   A tagging rule

line" style to a paragraph with one click, and that paragraph instantly becomes bold, 36-point Futura with an indent and extra space above.

Styles also make global formatting changes much easier; rather than changing the font of all of your headlines individually, you can simply change the font of the "Headline" style.

Most systems allow styles to be defined both for blocks of text ("paragraph styles") and for character strings ("character styles").

Styles make the conversion to XML a lot easier. For example, if you've applied the "Title" style to all of your headlines, you can create a tagging rule that simply maps that style to the `title` element.

31.2.2.2   Tagging rules based on other formatting

In *avenue.quark*, tagging rules are not restricted to styles. You can also associate other kinds of formatting with element types.

For example, you can map italic text to an `emphasizedText` element type. You can also map different-colored text to different element types.

---

1. Quark actually calls the group a "style sheet". We use "style" to avoid confusion with an XSL stylesheet, and because that's what most word processors and publishing systems call such a group.

31.2.2.3   Context-sensitive tagging rules

Tagging rules can be constrained to apply only when the specified formatting occurs in specific contexts.

For example, consider an article in which italic text indicates different things depending on where it occurs: In body text it indicates emphasis, and in a bibliography entry it indicates the name of a book.

You can accommodate this situation with a single context-sensitive rule. It associates italic text in a paragraph that uses the "Body Text" style with the `emphasizedText` element type, and italic text in a paragraph with the "Bibliography Entry" style with the `bookName` element type.

31.2.2.4   Multiple tagging rules for an element type

You can also define multiple tagging rules for a single element type.

For example, if formatting constraints require you to use one style for the first element in a bulleted list and another style for the rest of the items, you can map both of those styles to the `listItem` element type.

31.2.2.5   Conflict resolution

It is possible for a number of tagging rules to be applicable to the same text.

For example, you may have a tagging rule that maps the "Body Text" style to the `paragraph` element type, and another tagging rule that maps bold text to the `UIelement` element type. Bold text in a paragraph that uses the "Body Text" style matches both rules; how should it be tagged?

avenue.quark handles such situations by applying varying "weights" to different kinds of rules. For example, a rule that applies to local formatting (in this case, bold text) has a higher weight than a rule for a paragraph style; therefore, the rule applicable to bold text is used.

More specific rules have higher weights. A rule that applies to both a paragraph style *and* a kind of local formatting – for example, the "Caption" style *and* bold text – has a higher weight than a rule that applies only to one or the other.

If you prefer, you can bypass rule weighting altogether and manually choose which rule to apply when a conflict occurs. You can also assign your own weights to your tagging rules to suit your particular needs.

31.2.3 *Tagging content*

avenue.quark provides a graphical interface for tagging called the *XML Workspace*, shown in Figure 31-3 along with a rendered *QuarkXpress* document. The applicable tagging rule set is specified in the drop-down box at the top of the window.

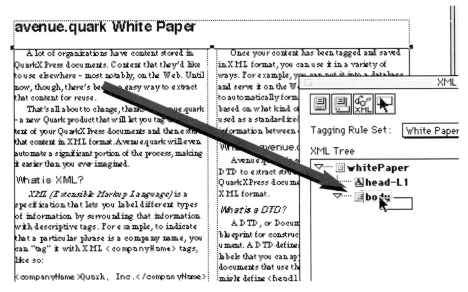

Figure 31-3   Tagging content with *avenue.quark*

After automatic tagging, the *XML Workspace* appears as in Figure 31-4.

Elements and attributes are displayed in the left pane in a directory-style tree structure; the start of their data is shown opposite in the right pane. The full data is available in the *Content* pane at the bottom, where it can be viewed and edited.

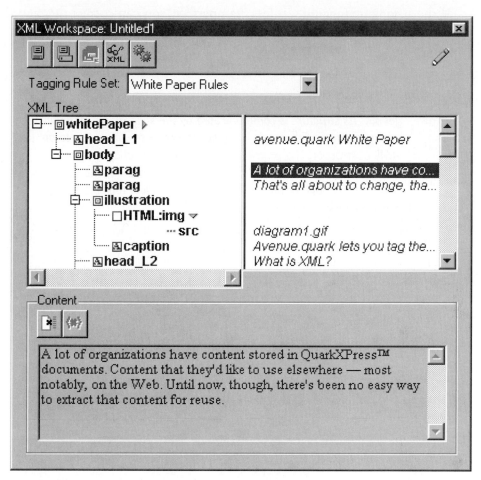

Figure 31-4 The *XML Workspace* after tagging

If the automatic tagging was less than perfect, you can correct the tagged text manually. The end result is a valid XML document, which you can then save and use anywhere you like.

Analysis   In every rendition there is an abstraction yearning to get out! Its structure is communicated by the style of the rendition, and awareness of that style is the key to accurate conversion to an XML abstraction. The principles described in this chapter should help you with those conversions, whether you do them with a scripting language or have the help of a graphical tool like avenue.quark.

Planning for document conversion

Application Discussion

- **▍** Methodology for large-scale conversion projects
- **▍** Concept and planning
- **▍** Proof-of-concept
- **▍** Analysis, design and engineering
- **▍** Production

Sponsor: Data Conversion Laboratory, http://www.dclab.com

Contributing experts: Mark Gross and John Lynch

Chapter

32

Legacy document conversion is a jungle, and the next best thing to a personal guide through it is an accurate map made by someone who's been over the ground many times. This chapter provides such a map for you.

Whether you're building an e-commerce site with an online catalog containing 1,000,000 products, publishing journals online or on CD-ROM, or maintaining a huge legal citation database, it is highly likely that the existing documents you wish to use are renditions. That means the real data in your files is mixed in with style information and can't be processed reliably.

The solution, of course, is to make this legacy content useful by converting it to XML.

But simply converting those files to XML syntax will not gain the benefits you are seeking. To be useful, your converted XML documents must preserve the integrity of the abstract information that the renditions are trying to convey; that is, the real data and its structure.

As we have seen, there are techniques available to assist with extracting data from renditions. However, the effectiveness of those techniques tends to vary with the consistency of the rendition files. Effectively, the more control over their creation and the more discipline used, the greater the chance that simple rule-based conversions will do the job.

Legacy documents, however, are often amassed over a period of many years and written by multiple authors. There can be huge volumes of materials, produced in a multitude of electronic formats. Worse still, they may include mountains of pre-computer paper documents as well.

In this kind of an environment, on this kind of scale, mastering the technical aspects of the conversion is only part of the job. For the project to be successful requires a disciplined methodology, which is what this chapter is about.

The methodology we will describe was developed by Data Conversion Laboratory, based on its experience with more than 25,000 projects, converting some 50 million pages. With it you can hope to avoid pitfalls like that shown in Figure 32-1.

Figure 32-1   It is easy to underestimate a large-scale conversion project.

32.1 | The Data Conversion Laboratory methodology

While you might build a tool shed without a blueprint, it is not likely that you would construct a 20-story building without one. Large conversion efforts are quite similar to large construction projects and many of the techniques to ensure that the final product meets the end-user's needs are common to both.

No matter how well you think it's going to go, a conversion project has many unknowns. By following the phased approach shown in Figure 32-2, there will be specific checkpoints at which you can reconsider the project in terms of new information and redirect the project appropriately.

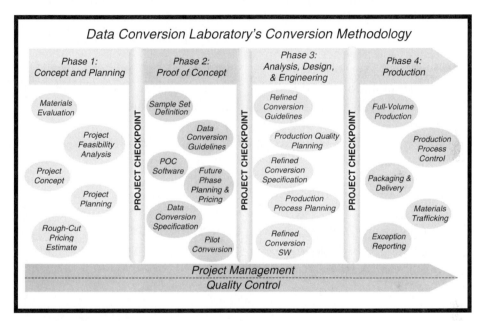

Figure 32-2 A phased approach to document conversion

Phase 1: Concept and planning

The purpose of this phase is to get everyone to agree to a common definition of what the project is. You'll want to lay out the project objectives and expectations, define the success criteria, lay out a preliminary approach, identify the risk areas, estimate approximate cost ranges, and define a preliminary budget.

Phase 2: Proof-of-concept

The purpose of this vital step is to test your approach on a limited scale, paying particular attention to the areas identified as potential risk areas. The results of this phase will help you arrive at a more detailed plan, while further fleshing out functional requirements. Based on the results of the test, preliminary software is prepared, and cost projections are fine-tuned.

Phase 3: Analysis, design, and engineering
This is the critical step where all the details get worked out and the project is prepared for volume production. Specifically, keying and conversion specifications are finalized, cleanup and review guidelines are defined, and final production costs are confirmed. More generally, the entire conversion process is finalized and tested, and production ramp-up begins.

Phase 4: Production
This is the objective that was planned for in the other phases: data flowing smoothly at 500 or 50,000 pages a week. If the preceding phases were done well, this phase can focus on monitoring quality and productivity with an eye towards improvement.

In addition to the four phases, there are two other important aspects to this methodology. These are the disciplines shown as two stripes at the bottom of Figure 32-2. As in any large project, management and quality control are critical and apply to every phase. Ideally, a single dedicated person will oversee both disciplines in order to guarantee cooperation.

32.2 | Phase 1: Concept and planning

Although it is an important step, this can be a pretty short one if you've carefully thought through exactly what you want to happen. It may just be a day or two, though it's more likely to be several weeks. The major elements of this phase are described below.

32.2.1 *Project concept*

Everybody needs to be in complete agreement.

The first step is to define the project clearly, and to get an agreement that people's various expectations are the same. You simply cannot meet a goal that you don't know about in advance. At this point, the project concept is discussed at a high level, without getting bogged down in detail. The following are the critical questions that need to be answered honestly:

- What do you need to do, and how quickly do you need to do it?
- Do you have a technical approach in mind?
- What are the goals and what are the success criteria?
- What's critical and what's nice to have?
- What's the expected budget and what are the estimated costs?
- Where are the tradeoffs in time, budget, and functionality?

The end result of this analysis is a project concept document.

32.2.2 *Materials evaluation*

While a detailed inventory of materials does not usually get done until the proof-of-concept phase, it is critical to get an early understanding of the project's scope. Design and implementation decisions on where best to focus resources will be based on this information. This is illustrated by the chart in Figure 32-3. While the specific questions will vary from project to project, typical questions are:

- *How big is the project?* You need to quantify in terms you're used to thinking in – pages, books, journal issues, products, etc.
- *How much source variation is there?* Materials may have been produced in a multitude of electronic formats, on different computer operating systems, or by different typesetters. Some of it may even live as paper, under dust, in huge warehouses.
- *How much format variation is there?* How often has the rendition style changed over the years? Invariably, different authors choose different styles. While it would be nice to have a strictly enforced template, if you're dealing with legacy documents, you're bound to find a lot of formatting inconsistency.

■ *What are the special issues?* Tables, formulas, cross-referencing and graphics are all areas that need special attention in the planning process.

All of these critical issues will differ slightly from project to project; it's a good idea to lay them out explicitly in a format like Figure 32-3.

Materials Evaluation Worksheet			
Document Set	% of Total	Average Frequency of Elements Per Page	Other Special Issues
FrameMaker	25%	Characters = 3,023 Tables = .92 Equations = None X-Refs = 5 Images = .28	Text Boxes, Complex Tables, Cross Refs
WordPerfect	12%	Characters = 4,009 Tables = 1.2 Equations = 2.2 X-Refs = 7 Images = .5	Equations, Complex Tables
Ventura	30%	Characters = 3,540 Tables = 1.1 Equations = None X-Refs = 5 Images = 1.4	Multiple Authors, No Stylesheet Used, Poorly Formatted
Quark	13%	Characters = 5,806 Tables = .05 Equations = None X-Refs = 2 Images = 1.27	Mac Files, Text Boxes,TIFF Images
Paper	20%	Characters = 3,877 Tables = .3 Equations = .51 X-Refs = 8 Images = .2	Old - Not Suitable For OCR, Equations, Tables

Figure 32-3   Materials evaluation sheet

32.2.3 *Rough-cut pricing estimate*

Usually, there is not enough information available this early in the process to allow an accurate prediction of the project's overall production costs. There are simply too many variables that will not be finalized until well into Phase 2. However, it is possible (and useful) to start assembling rough-cut costing parameters.

You can use a chart like the one shown in Figure 32-4 to lay out what the major tasks in the production process are. Alongside each task, indicate its historic cost range.

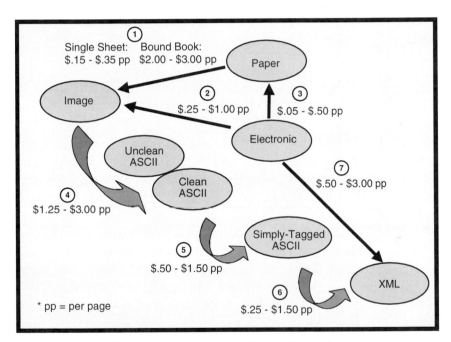

Figure 32-4   Rough-cut cost ranges for major tasks

You now have a guide for both feasibility analysis ("I didn't know we were talking about a $2,000,000 project!") and sensitivity analysis ("If we didn't have to do that step we could save $2.00 per page"). If budgeting has not yet been done for your project, these ranges will also prove to be useful guides for setting budgets.

32.2.4 *Project feasibility analysis*

While the information collected so far is fairly sketchy, this is an early opportunity to assess, based on those broad parameters, whether the project is still feasible. You'll typically need to answer questions like the following:

- If this is a $1-$2 million project, does it still make good business sense to proceed?
- If it's way over budget can you redefine the project's scope? Is there another way to do this?
- Can you do without certain elements in order to bring down the cost? If so, does the project make sense at a reduced level?
- And most importantly, does it make sense to go on with Phase 2?

32.3 | Phase 2: Proof-of-concept

So Phase 1 has told you that the project may actually be worth pursuing. You've got the rough-cut estimate, and even your CFO admits that it sounds like a pretty sound business model. Most importantly, everyone is agreed on what the broad strokes of the project are. The next step is the proof-of-concept.

The purpose of the proof-of-concept phase is to test your planned approach on a limited scale. This will be your opportunity to test out the areas that were identified as being particularly risky, and to test on a small scale the hypothesis developed in Phase I. The results of this phase will provide a more detailed plan, including fleshed-out functional requirements, preliminary software development, a converted sample set, and more finely-tuned cost projections.

Returning to the building analogy again, this is the step where the preliminary design is laid out, and a model built so that everyone can get an idea of what the building will look like. Additionally, a test boring is done to ensure that the soil will be able to support the building.

Figure 32-5 shows a typical project timeline for this phase. For a significantly larger project, this phase might take up to ten weeks. Let's look at the key stages and deliverables.

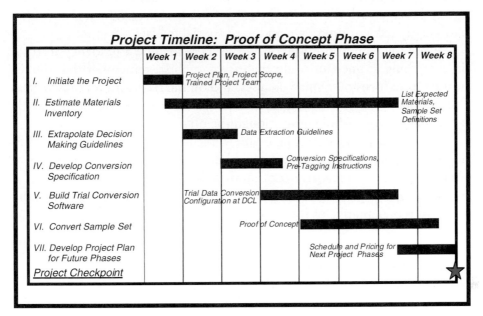

Figure 32-5 Project timeline for proof-of-concept phase

32.3.1 *Project initiation*

You always need a project kickoff meeting. One of the main purposes of this meeting is to make sure that everyone on the expanded team has the same understanding of the project concept. The team should include a project manager, a domain expert, a data analyst, a programmer and a senior editor.

The project initiation is also where the detailed task plan is created and reviewed. The task plan will help ensure that everyone understands his role and responsibilities as a member of the team.

32.3.2 *Sample set definition*

Important questions need to be answered in order to define the proof-of-concept. Be patient here; you probably won't be ready after the kickoff meeting.

Ask yourself the following questions: What's intended to be proven? How big should the sample be? Which project elements are known technology and therefore don't need to be part of this exercise? Which elements are particularly risky or unknown and need special focus?

Beware the common mistakes. While there may be a tendency to try to do everything at once, or to do the easy parts first, remember that the real purpose is to focus on a small data set, and on the risky and unknown areas. Fail to identify where your project's critical challenges are now, and the hypothesis of your whole project might be off.

With this in mind, it may be better to focus on 10 pages of difficult bibliographic references or complex tables, rather than 100s of pages of straightforward or repetitive text. And if there are 20 major variations of material, don't try to analyze them all. Instead, pick the two or three that are most representative of the issues.

32.3.3 *Inventory materials*

This task invariably provokes groans, but someone has to do it. You need to have a good idea of how big the pile of documents is, and a clear understanding of the variation contained within the pile. The exact methodology you use to collect this information will vary depending on the project.

While it would seem ideal to get a detailed list of everything that needs to be done, that's not usually the case. What you are trying to do at this stage is get an understanding of how much of each type of material there might be. That's because each type of material will probably require its own programming and conversion process. And while building conversion software to help automate much of the conversion makes sense, you don't want to invest lots of programming time automating for a particularly difficult type of material when you only have 10 pages of it.

32.3.4 *Data conversion guidelines*

This is usually the heart of the proof-of-concept phase. The extent to which you can develop rules and guidelines for transforming your source materials into "properly tagged data" will be the most important determinant of the final cost of this project. In other words, the development must be done with care.

The domain expert and the data analyst should work closely together here, to try to generalize the rules and condense them into as small a set as possible. What you are trying to do at this stage is build a functional set of rules. Don't make the mistake of turning this into a programming exercise: That will just bog you down.

Equally importantly, don't give up too early. While the usual tendency is to think there are no rules – "it's just common sense and you either know it or you don't" – that's rarely the case.

32.3.5 *Data conversion specification*

It is useful at this stage to organize the guidelines derived to this point into a single document. The conversion specification document will become the primary repository of project information; it will be continually consulted and reviewed by the end user, the domain expert, the analyst, and the programmer.

This document expands the previously established guidelines into a set of rules that can be programmed for. It also identifies areas that are ambiguous or difficult to define. These areas will then need to be reviewed by the domain expert.

The conversion specification document typically circulates among the various parties involved, and becomes the central discussion document until issues are resolved. Remember that it is also the document that defines the programming efforts.

32.3.6 *Software and pilot conversion*

O.K., the conversion specification document is written. Hopefully it addresses all the major issues of the conversion. Now it's time to see if you can really use those guidelines and specifications to convert anything.

As in the project initiation phase, you need to be cautious here. While most successful conversion projects combine automation with manual effort, programming should be done sparingly at this point. There simply isn't time during the proof-of-concept phase to program for everything you'd like to. In addition, there will be a tendency to program for the easy things first.

The best approach is to select a few complex areas which people doubt can be converted in an automated manner. For these areas, invest time testing out programmatic approaches to the unique problems. This learning process will be invaluable and will help tremendously when you move on to Phase 3.

For the rest of the sample set, however, it probably makes sense for people to follow the conversion specification manually, rather than investing heavily in writing and testing programs.

The end result of this phase should give you a good feel for what can and should be automated, and what will need to be done manually. It will also yield some valuable timings for the likely labor elements of the project.

32.3.7 Pricing

If all has gone well thus far, you'll now be able to estimate the project's costs more closely and lay out a realistic timeframe in which it can be done. As more materials are tested and converted in the next phase, these estimates will be further refined.

Keep in mind that programming costs will rise in the next phase as you start to expand your efforts toward automation. However, if the materials you initially selected for the sample are truly representative, and you've taken into account people's learning curves as they started working with your sample data, your estimate at this point should be pretty accurate.

32.3.8 Go/no-go decision

This phase is also the checkpoint at which to determine whether the project still makes sense. You'll be able to address these issues:

Time to market
> You'll have a realistic estimate of how long this project will take, as well as your options for speeding it up.

Quality
> You'll be able to demonstrate expected results while there's still time to make modifications.

Cost

You'll have an understanding of the project costs and what the tradeoffs are.

Scalability

You'll understand the extent to which the size of the project can scale.

32.3.9 *Planning for future phases*

By now, you will have a clear understanding of what you want to achieve from this conversion. The proof-of-concept has yielded valuable clues as to where and how to refine the conversion guidelines. Mistakes have been identified and concepts proven.

More than anything else, the proof-of-concept should land the entire conversion team on the same page and become the foundation upon which the remainder of the project will be built. You now have:

- Improved conversion guidelines.
- Refined conversion specification.
- Refined conversion software.
- More finely-tuned cost projections.

32.4 | Phase 3: Analysis, design and engineering

Phase 3 is primarily a matter of refining the various deliverables produced from the conversion sample, for the fuller set of materials. Additionally, you now program for all the things you did not have time for (or did not need to prove) during the proof-of-concept phase. Planning for gradual ramp-up and full volume production processing will also be done in this phase.

A typical project timeline for this phase is shown in Figure 32-6. For the typical larger project, this phase will likely take 6-10 weeks. Let's take a look at the key tasks.

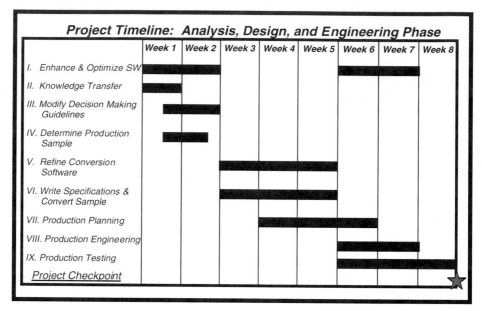

Figure 32-6   Timeline for the analysis, design, and engineering phase

32.4.1 *Production process planning*

Integrating the various elements of the conversion process is too often an afterthought. That can be an expensive mistake. The most mundane things, such as agreeing upon filename conventions and basic data trafficking procedures, are too often not properly planned in advance.

Typically, a large conversion effort consists of some 30 to 50 independent steps, requiring multiple skills and often multiple vendors. There are also time dependencies that need to be integrated in order to ensure a smooth production flow.

In planning the production process, there are also a number of important logistical considerations:

- How many pages a week can each step in the process handle?
- What's the weak link in the chain?
- Can you keep up with reviewing and inspecting converted materials as they're delivered?

- Technical questions will arise; will there be a dedicated point of contact for them?
- How will materials be transported back and forth?

Another important question to ask is "How much time will it take?" If you already have, or can contract, an ongoing production facility that handles thousands of pages a day, you still need to allow 4-6 weeks for the integration to take place. You'll therefore need to start early in Phase 3. And if you're going to be building a process from scratch, you should allow at least 6 months.

32.4.2 *Production quality planning*

Many of the standard quality control processes apply to a conversion project, but conversion is unique in one respect. Your favorite cookie baker may make the best cookies, but he'll attribute it to using the choicest chocolate chips and the finest flour. Unlike a cookie factory, you can't really control the quality of ingredients coming into your machine.

No matter how well you select your samples and trial materials, you are unlikely to find every significant variation. Therefore, it is expecting too much to hope to account for all the possibilities in advance. The documents will typically have been written by many individuals, at several different locations, in many different editing packages, over a long period of time, and on a variety of systems. So, like the people who made them, the documents will have personalities. And, like people, their behavior may not always be exemplary.

Ensuring quality control in this environment means building feedback loops at each step of the process. These checkpoints are designed to report when things are not meeting expectations, and provide guidelines, rather than rules, to the people inspecting the results. Information needs to flow back and forth easily in order to allow refinement of this process. You'll also need to collect statistics in order to tell how much sampling will be needed as the process improves.

32.4.3 *Production ramp-up*

Just as we advised in Phase 1, caution is critical at this stage. The best approach is usually to plan for a few weeks of low-volume production through the initial production process. This will help to identify any weaknesses in the process.

The entire production team needs to be aware that the purpose of the first weeks of production is to provide feedback in order to help engineer a smoother process. This is not yet the time to put dozens of people to work, but rather a time to assign a select few individuals who are capable of figuring out where improvements can be made.

32.5 | Phase 4: Production

You're there at last, but you do need to monitor results continually and make sure that quality and productivity stay where you expect them to be.

Full-volume production

Even after the production ramp-up stage, it is not necessarily prudent to plan for full production volume immediately. Increase volume gradually, thereby allowing ample time for people to be trained and come fully up to speed.

Production process control

You need a method to track production through the various phases. For smaller projects, spreadsheets may be sufficient. But for larger projects, you probably need a project management program. At a minimum you need to know where in the process each batch of materials is, how long it is taking a batch to go through, and how much material is awaiting each phase of processing.

Materials trafficking

It is very rare that you have everything that needs conversion ready in a pile at the beginning of a project. More likely, materials will be readied gradually as the project progresses. In order to avoid slowdowns, someone needs to be in charge of trafficking the materials, making sure that materials are ready and complete, and forwarding them appropriately.

Process improvement feedback

The process certainly won't be perfect when you first go into production. You will need a method to formally collect information on exceptions and on what's not working properly. This method will need to be quite flexible as different parts of the process will report exceptions at different times.

Exception reporting

You'll also have to allow for exception reporting. Exception reports are delivered to the end-user along with the converted documents. Because of the wide variance and inconsistencies of the materials being converted, there will inevitably be materials that need special handling by the recipient. And it would seem wise to have a mechanism more sophisticated than yellow stickers to deal with this.

Packaging and delivery

This may seem obvious, but you need to get the finished materials to the right person! The right materials! Otherwise frustration can set in. This is also a convenient point at which to do some final quality checking, and to document any specific procedures the person you're delivering to needs to follow.

32.6 | Conclusion

Data Conversion Laboratory's methodology for large-scale conversion is highly detailed, as would be expected from an organization that's been through so many conversions. But there are some major principles that stand out and can be kept in mind:

- Don't just do it. Figure out exactly what you want to accomplish before you start planning, then plan it before you do it. (Don't be the company in Figure 32-7).

Figure 32-7   Maybe everyone involved should read this chapter.

- Project management and quality assurance are key. To ensure that the project proceeds properly and on time, you'll need a dedicated team. Don't think of this as a part-time job; your critical team members need to be dedicated to the project.
- Communications are vital. The domain expert, the technical expert, and management all need to be in complete agreement.
- Select your sample set carefully. It is better to pick 200 truly representative pages than 5000 random ones.
- Plan the production process. Work through the details before you ramp up to volume processing.
- Be sure that it's working. Build feedback loops into every step to monitor, control and continually improve the production process.

XML mass-conversion facility

Tool Discussion

▌ XML content: why it is different

▌ Automating for markup consistency

▌ Value-added editorial services

Sponsor: Innodata Corporation, http://www.innodata.com

Contributing expert: J. Sperling Martin and John Chelsom

33

In the musical *Ragtime*, Henry Ford sings "Speed up the belt, speed up the belt!" He refers to what is arguably the first complex mass-production system – his automobile assembly line. In today's XML conversion assembly lines, the system is equally complex but the "belt" is virtual and the control methods are a lot more sophisticated.

The demands of e-business and Web publication are creating an overwhelming demand for XML conversion and enrichment services. For many projects, the volumes are such that results can only be achieved by systematized mass-production facilities.

In other words, there is a requirement for a very special category of tool – the high-volume XML conversion facility. As an example of the scale involved, consider Innodata's dedicated facility for XML conversion, which it calls its *XML Content Factory.*™ It is a 54,000 square foot building with 2,500 computer workstations networked to a fully-clustered system of data center servers.

If this "tool" were packaged like most of the others in this book, it would need 142,833 square feet of shrink wrap!

33.1 | The challenge

Of course document conversion – even mass conversion – is nothing new. But creating XML content presents a very special challenge.

33.1.1 *Why XML is different*

Before generalized markup, document conversion was either from a paper rendition to a machine-processable rendition, or from one machine-processable rendition to another.

In creating XML data, however, a conversion facility is undertaking what are conceptually two different tasks. The first task is the classical one of capturing the text in digital form.

The second task is the difficult one: metadata must be associated with the captured textual data in the form of XML markup, distinguishing the style information from the real information content. Unlike conventional data conversion, XML conversion requires separating the true abstract data and its structure from the rendered form.

Performing this second task in a mass production environment is where the challenge arises. Let's look at some of the issues involved.

33.1.2 *Tagging consistency*

Large-scale projects that seek maximum value from XML are typically driven by complex DTDs. Project specs therefore call for richly-structured metadata and detailed hyperlinking.

Given the scale of the effort required for such large volumes, and the inherently subjective nature of operator-level decision-making, the many operators involved in complex tagging would likely compromise internal consistency. A conversion facility needs to overcome this problem.

33.1.3 *Diversity of project types*

Because XML applications are expanding into every sphere of business, a conversion facility must be able to handle a wide variety of project types. The facility must be able to build everything from e-commerce catalogs to electronic libraries, and anything else that can benefit from XML. There is diversity in all aspects, from the type of content, to the varying input data formats, to the set of output products produced.

The workflow for an XML conversion facility therefore needs to be independent of project type, yet capable of seamlessly integrating a variety of highly specialized content editors into the production process.

33.1.4 *Text accuracy*

XML conversion projects almost invariably produce abstractions, rather than renditions. That is because the data is intended for processing by computers, rather than simply being presented to humans.

As a result, the conversion facility must be capable of producing output that conforms to the highest industry standards for character accuracy. Producing 99.995% accurate data means one error in 20,000 characters.

33.2 | The solution

Meeting the challenge of mass-producing complex metadata requires a conversion facility whose design reflects the experience of conventional conversion projects, plus a technology-driven workflow that incorporates processes optimized for XML.

33.2.1 *Applicable lessons from the past*

Experience shows you can never have enough storage, planning, or quality assurance.

33.2.1.1   Employ large scale, fully redundant data storage

As enterprises embrace e-business they generate massive data conversion requirements. Such projects require equally massive data storage in the conversion facility.

The *XML Content Factory*, for example, was designed for a monthly output capacity of 15 gigabytes. To accomplish this, its 2,500 workstations are connected to a fully-clustered system of data center servers. To achieve high levels of redundancy as well as performance, each data center server has parallel CPUs and redundant storage and is connected to a fiber-optic backbone network.

33.2.1.2   Planning precedes production!

All projects should undergo detailed requirements analysis, proof-of-concept, analysis, design, and engineering before going into production. This ensures, to the greatest extent possible, that all kinks are worked out of the process well in advance of the project going into full production.

33.2.1.3   Employ ISO-compliant quality assurance methodologies

ISO-compliant quality assurance methodologies should be fully integrated, including methodologies in respect of statistically valid sampling and auditing. In addition, quality circles should be integrated into the assembly line, with automated quality gates installed after each major phase in the production process.

33.2.2   *Technology-driven workflow*

To meet the throughput demands of mass conversion while at the same time applying metadata accurately requires a technology-driven workflow that incorporates processes optimized for XML.

Figure 33-1 illustrates a workflow for document conversion. It shows just seven processes, at a high level and quite generic. In contrast, the real-world workflow of the *XML Content Factory*, for example, involves over 45 distinct concurrent and serial processes, including six separate quality gates.

Nevertheless, we can use Figure 33-1 to show the basic sequence of processing, and to show where some of the optimization for XML takes place.

Before we do, however, let's take a quick refresher course in workflow.

33.2.2.1   Workflow explained

A business process that is organized or automated by a computer system is called a workflow. The software that defines and controls a workflow is called a workflow management system. A typical workflow can be decomposed into a set of sub-processes which may themselves consist of further sub-processes.

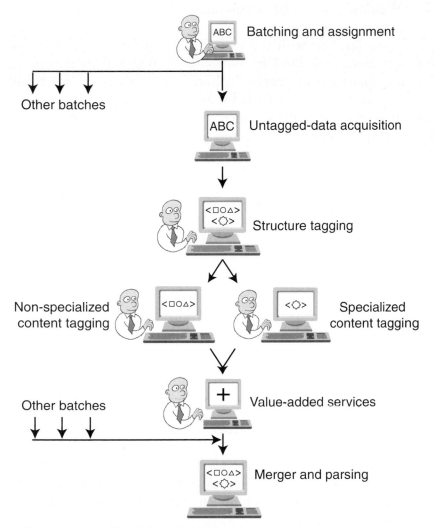

Figure 33-1   Workflow for high-volume conversion

At the lowest level, a process consists of an activity performed by one of the participants in the workflow. The overall process can therefore be thought of as a set of activities, and is complete when all the activities have been completed successfully.

An activity can be manual (performed by one or more humans) or automated, in which case one or more software applications are invoked to perform it. Of course these applications may or may not involve manual intervention.

A participant interacts with the workflow management system to find the list of activities assigned to him. When he selects an activity to perform, the workflow management system "acquires" the activity on his behalf, thereby removing it from the activity list of all the other participants in the workflow. It then delivers the required data to the participants desktop, launches any applications that are needed to perform the activity, and monitors the status of the activity until it is complete.[1]

33.2.2.2   Batching and assignment

In this, the first step of the workflow in Figure 33-1, a project begins. In the *XML Content Factory*, a project is broken into "batches" for assignment to different departments. There are two considerations in the batching decisions:

load balancing
> Batches are created and assigned based on available capacity in order to maximize throughput.

content-based routing
> Batches reflect the nature of the tagging that is required and are routed to content editors who possess the necessary skills.

The workflow system tracks the exact status of each batch, allowing bottlenecks to be identified early. Production managers know the upcoming load for each workgroup. Capacity is therefore deployed in an optimal way.

33.2.2.3   Untagged-data acquisition

There are several ways that untagged data can be acquired. Hardcopy documents can be scanned to produce images. The images are processed by

---

1. This description of workflow used the terminology of the Workflow Management Coalition (WfMC), a vendor-sponsored body set up in 1993 to develop industry standards for workflow management products.

rules-based optical character recognition (OCR) software and then edited to produce untagged character data.

Other paths to this point are possible. For example, some OCR software is capable of using page-layout patterns as a basis for automatic tagging.

Data can also be acquired from word processing files or other forms of legacy electronic data. Their rendition markup can be stripped, or else partially converted to XML tags by automated means.

33.2.2.4   Structure tagging

The workflow differentiates "structure" tagging from "content" tagging – more precisely, "element-content" tagging from "mixed-content" tagging. The principal reason for the distinction is that it is only when the higher levels of a document are tagged that a context is established for the mixed-content tagging.

Another reason is that different skills are required for the two. It is easier to train operators to perform element-content tagging, while mixed-content tagging often requires knowledge of the document's subject matter.

33.2.2.5   Content tagging

This step is divided into two paths because even at the mixed-content level, varying skills are required. Non-specialized mixed content only requires the ability to recognize citations, emphasized phrases, and other generic element types.

Specialized mixed content, on the other hand, can require domain knowledge. That requirement varies widely, depending on the specific project, from training in recognizing a few phrases that occur in specific element types, to detailed, substantive knowledge of the subject area.

In both cases, the mixed-content tagger is also the one to flag text that needs value-added services such as enriched indexing or the application of links. We discuss these shortly.

We now consider some aspects of tagging to keep in mind for both element content and mixed content.

33.2.2.5.1   Prevent data modification

One risk of XML conversion is that of inadvertently modifying the data when adding markup. The system should be able to take measures to prevent this.

For example, in the *XML Content Factory*, as a safety measure, the software does not allow the content editors to delete or modify data when their assignment is to add tags.

33.2.2.5.2   Assisted markup

The editing software can assist the operator by using its knowledge of the DTD and the partially-tagged structure to propose only valid tags at any given point in the document.

This capability is more complex than it might seem, given that the batching and assignment process makes only a portion of the document available. For example, `<book>` will only occur in the first batch and `</book>` will only occur in the last. As a result, the workflow system must generate a DTD fragment that applies to the portion of the document that is the subject of the operator's assignment.

The editing software can suggest the most likely markup for specific words and phrases in the data. The suggestions are motivated by rules created when the project content was analyzed and serve to minimize errors of contextual interpretation.

Markup accuracy can be checked during assisted markup by means of a validating parser. Doing so allows errors to be caught while an individual batch is being processed and the error is easier to isolate and correct.

The workflow system can supplement assisted markup by invoking processes that apply markup automatically.

33.2.2.6   Value-added services

Conversion to XML presents an excellent opportunity to add value to documents through editorial processes. As part of the conversion planning, documents will be given careful scrutiny and analysis, which will help in defining the value-adds. It should also prove less expensive to do the editorial work at the same time as markup is added, as the document will need to be processed only once.

Typical value-added services are indexing, creating abstracts, classification with a taxonomy or thesaurus, attaching multimedia content, imbedding hyperlinks, developing topic maps, and so on.

Innodata's *XML Content Factory* extends the concept to include a full-service professional services section that works with clients on-site or at their locations to build DTDs and perform other data architecture-related services. There is even a research and development team that keeps current on XML developments and tools.

Let's take a look at an example of value-added services.

33.2.2.6.3   A converted document

Example 33-1 shows a document that has been converted to XML. The workflow system has delivered it to a value-added editing workstation.

Example 33-1. XML document extract

```
<data>
<recordset rowcount="3"
           fieldnames="Results-url, Test-ID, Index">
  <field name="Results-url">
    <string>http://**********</string>
    <string>http://**********</string>
    <string>http://**********</string>
  </field>
  <field name="Test-ID">
    <string>95-002367A</string>
    <string>95-008856H</string>
    <string>97-017834C</string>
  </field>
  <field name="Index">
    <string>DAB, DAJ</string>
    <string>DA, DBA, DAHA</string>
    <string>DAAB, DBB, DC</string>
  </field>
</recordset>
</data>
```

The document has three `field` elements with different `name` attributes:

Results-url
> The `string` subelements each contain a URL for test data details posted on the document owner's intranet.

Test-ID

The `string` subelements identify motor vehicle brake test reports.

Index

These `string` subelements are initially empty. They are to be completed as part of the value-added processing.

33.2.2.6.4   Data gathering and indexing

The workflow system presents the operator with two windows: the document in Example 33-1 and the taxonomy shown in Example 33-2.

Example 33-2. Taxonomy extract

```
D Testing -- Evaluation
  DA . Vehicle testing
    DAA. . Brake systems tests
      DAAA . . Effectiveness of systems tests
      DAAB . . . Fade/recovery tests
      DAAC . . . Spike stops
      DAAD . . . Parking brake tests
    DAB. . Durability testing during vehicle tests
    DAC. . Brake component tests
    DAD. . Procedures for performing brake tests
    DAE. . Assembly line testing -- brakes
    DAF. . Hydraulic brake systems
    DAG. . Skid checks
    DAH. .Testing of safety vehicles
      DAHA . . . Evaluation of safety vehicle principles
    DAJ. . Vehicle inspections/test by local governments
  DB . Laboratory testing of brakes
    DBA. . Dynamometer brake tests
    DBB. . Bench tests of brake components
    DBC. . Durability testing in laboratory
    DBD. . Procedures for laboratory tests
  DC . .Test methods
```

The operator first gathers the three motor vehicle brake test reports identified in the `Test-Id` field. As part of his training for the project, he has been taught enough about the subject area to recognize the contextual cues and other indicators that will dictate which taxonomy codes apply to each report. He enters those codes in the `string` elements of the `Index` field.

33.2.2.7   Merger and parsing

This is the final step, in which the separate batches are recombined into a single document and parsed and validated. As the workflow system created the batches in the first instance, and has been tracking them through the conversion process, this step can be automated.

33.3 | Conclusion

Converting vast amounts of information to XML requires a new kind of "tool" – the high-volume XML conversion facility. Such a facility must do more than apply techniques that worked for other kinds of conversion, because XML has unique requirements.

Content that fully exploits XML usually has complex DTDs, which means that operators must apply significant editorial judgment. With ultra-large projects, maintaining consistency can be a challenge.

Automated mass-conversion facilities, such as Innodata's *XML Content Factory*, meet the challenge with technology-driven workflows that combine experience from conventional conversions with processes optimized for XML.

These "tools" may not lend themselves well to shrink-wrap, but they can undertake large XML tagging projects without compromising consistency or production speed.

Integrating legacy data

Application Discussion

■ Legacy data defined

■ Profiting from the Y2K problem

■ Legacy data flow

Sponsor: XMLSolutions Corporation, http://www.xmls.com

Contributing expert: Sowmitri Swamy

34

The infamous Y2K problem had a secret good side. Because of the efforts made to solve it, enterprises have better knowledge of their legacy data than ever before. This chapter shows how that knowledge can produce valuable XML data and metadata.

T he overwhelming fact of legacy data is that there is a lot of it, and it is critical to the operations of the enterprises that own it. It has been a dominant theme in this book, as we have examined the task of dynamic data acquisition in the context of middle-tier servers, e-commerce, portal systems, and publishing.

34.1 | What is legacy data?

Simply put, *legacy data* is data that is generated and used by specific business processes and that is not directly available to other processes. The shared data in enterprise databases is *not* legacy data, although it is business process data.

Caution   Legacy data is not the same thing as legacy documents, which are documents that are either renditions, or are not represented in XML, or both. However, legacy documents usually contain legacy data, which is why there is such interest in converting them to XML abstractions.

34.1.1 *Unlocking legacy data*

Legacy data is a critical revenue-generating asset in many corporations, but for reasons that are largely historical and technological, it is not easily accessed by any application but the one that created it.

Web-enabling of legacy applications and data is a goal of many companies, who look forward to leveraging their legacy data assets by migrating to a Web-based communication paradigm. However, although Web-enabling provides access, it does not necessarily provide knowledge of what the data means. Knowing what the data means leads to methods to transform and use it effectively.

The correct enterprise goal should be to *unlock* legacy data – not only provide access, but also an idiomatic understanding of the data for both human and computer use. Synergy is achieved when legacy data can be accessed, understood and utilized throughout the enterprise in a timely manner.

34.1.2 *The benefit of Y2K*

Such sharing of legacy data as exists in an enterprise is often in a specific context, such as a report, memo, or other document. Documents, however, are usually summaries or extracts from larger data sources and they tend to be formatted to suit the reporting context. Extracting complete data from a rendered document is often difficult or impossible. When it is possible, the data may not be current because of the lead time to produce and distribute the document.

So the only completely reliable means of utilizing legacy data is to go directly to the data itself, which in effect means analyzing the legacy applications that understand its structure and semantics. Fortunately, as a result of the otherwise completely unfortunate Year 2000 (Y2K) bug, enterprises have recently expended vast resources to do just that.

This valuable knowledge is being applied a second time – to making legacy data a sharable enterprise resource through the use of XML. Consultants with extensive Y2K backgrounds, such as XMLSolutions Corporation, are leveraging their Y2K experience to offer a systematic approach to legacy data integration. Their model, called *legacy data flow*, provides conceptual underpinnings and heightened potential for dynamic data acquisition and EDI (see Chapter 13, "XML and EDI: Working together", on page 194).

34.2 | E-commerce with legacy data

Unlocking legacy data for use in e-commerce is valuable for business growth because it provides timely information on products, pricing, policy, and availability. Let's examine some e-commerce applications with an eye towards developing a model of automated legacy data flow.

Figure 34-1 provides a capsule view of the enabling architecture. Two legacy applications are interfaced to an XML-based e-commerce network implementation through special modules, identified in the figure as *metadata engines*.

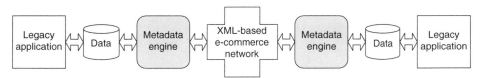

Figure 34-1   XML-based e-commerce integrates legacy data

The e-commerce network uses XML to convey data and metadata between two XML servers anchoring the e-commerce implementation at either end (represented by the two stubs protruding from the e-commerce box).

The roles played by the metadata engines are critical in the proper functioning of the scheme because their role is to convert between XML metadata and legacy data so that the legacy applications can perform their normal processing.

We will use three simple examples to illustrate the functionality of the metadata engine: Year 2000 compliant dates, euro currency conversion, and inventory part numbers. In all three examples, legacy data is changed in an anonymous manner. That means the legacy applications process data in the formats that they are familiar with; they are unaware of the intermediate transformations into and out of XML.

34.2.1 Y2K-compliant date exchange

The solution for bringing legacy systems into Year 2000 compliance involves two major techniques: date expansion and windowing. The "expansion" part of the solution involves prefixing the two-digit year with a two-digit century whenever a date is accessed; the "windowing" part determines which century. A common window is "1930-2029", meaning that two-digit years lower than 30 are treated as occurring in the 21st century.

Note that the "compliance" occurs dynamically in the application software. The storage representation of the date is still two digits.

Consider the case of two compliant insurance applications with different internal date representations that need to communicate with one another. One application uses a flat file to store a policy record with the date in MMDDYY format, as shown in Example 34-1.

Example 34-1. Date stored in legacy flat file

```
...052998...
```

This application is written in Cobol. The code declares the date in the POLICY-ISSUED field of the POLICY-RECORD structure that is partly shown in Example 34-2.

Example 34-2. Legacy Cobol structure for date

```
01 POLICY-RECORD
   ....
   05 POLICY-ISSUED
      10 MM PIC 9(2)
      10 DD PIC 9(2)
      10 YY PIC 9(2)
   ....
```

The two applications interchange dates using the XML representation shown in Example 34-3.

Example 34-3. XML representation of Y2K-compliant date

```
<POLICY>
  ....
  <ISSUE_DATE FORMAT="ISO-8601">19980529</ISSUE_DATE>
  ....
</POLICY>
```

Example 34-4 shows the transformation rules by which the Cobol application's metadata engine produces the date in Example 34-3 from the Cobol record, prior to its transmittal over the XML-based e-commerce network. Note that CC refers to the calculated century prefix.

Example 34-4. Semantic transformation rules

```
<POLICY-ISSUED> => <ISSUE_DATE>
<FORMAT ISO-8601> <= CC&&YY&&MM&&DD
```

The metadata engine for the other application uses similar rules (not illustrated) to convert the XML data into a representation that its legacy application can process.

34.2.2 *International invoicing*

With the advent of the euro, a fourth reserve currency has been added to the current three widely-used reserve currencies: the dollar, the pound sterling and the yen. The XML-based techniques we have been examining can be used to enable legacy applications to handle e-commerce in euros.

Consider a U.S. vendor that must invoice a French customer. In addition to the normal conversion between legacy data and XML, the French metadata engine must convert to euros and add French value-added tax (VAT). The scenario would proceed as follows.

The metadata engine for the U.S. invoicing application converts the legacy invoice to the XML document partly shown in Example 34-5, prior to sending it over the e-commerce network.

Example 34-5. U.S. invoice in XML

```
<INVOICE>
....
<INVOICE_DATE format="ISO-8601">19990621</INVOICE_DATE>
<AMOUNT currency="USD">12000</AMOUNT>
<AMOUNT_DUE currency="USD">12000</AMOUNT_DUE>
....
</INVOICE>
```

The metadata engine for the French accounts payable application first transforms the U.S. XML invoice into the French XML invoice shown in Example 34-6 by applying the following semantic transformations:

- Convert U.S. dollars to euros.
- Compute French VAT tax payable.
- Calculate the total amount due in euros.

Example 34-6. Invoice created by French metadata engine

```
<INVOICE>
....
<INVOICE_DATE format="ISO-8601">19990621</INVOICE_DATE>
<AMOUNT currency="EURO">12600</AMOUNT>
<VAT country="FR" currency="EURO">2520</VAT>
<AMOUNT_DUE currency="EURO">15120</AMOUNT_DUE>
....
</INVOICE>
```

The French metadata engine then converts the French invoice data in Example 34-6 into legacy form (not shown) by applying other transformations, similar to those in Example 34-4.

34.2.3 *Automated bid response*

In this e-commerce scenario, a customer puts forth a list of parts on which it invites suppliers to bid. A vendor chooses from the list only those items that it can supply and submits bids on them.

Example 34-7 shows excerpts from the customer's consolidated list of bid requests. It requests bids on three different sizes of the part numbered "12T20-2".

Example 34-7. Customer's bid request

```
<BID_REQUEST>
<UNIT>MD-STLOUIS</UNIT>
<DEPARTMENT>EN</DEPARTMENT>
<CONTACT>J.DOE</CONTACT>
<TEL>8001111111</TEL>
<EMAIL>JDOE@MD-STLOUIS.COM</EMAIL>
<BID_OOB format="ISO-8601" >19990821</BID_OOB>
....
<ITEMNO>24</ITEMNO>
  <PARTNUM dimension="124">12T20-2</PARTNUM>
  <QUANTITY>2000</QUANTITY>
....
<ITEMNO>52</ITEMNO>
  <PARTNUM dimension="28">12T20-2</PARTNUM>
  <QUANTITY>3000</QUANTITY>
<ITEMNO>53</ITEMNO>
  <PARTNUM dimension="52">12T20-2</PARTNUM>
  <QUANTITY>3000</QUANTITY>
</BID_REQUEST>
```

The vendor's metadata engine extracts the PARTNUM content and dimension attribute value of each item to determine the part numbers and sizes requested. It queries the legacy application to determine which ones the vendor can supply. The application's response is used to prepare the XML bid document shown in Example 34-8.

The vendor uses the same BID document type for all its bids to all its customers, which allows it to use the bid data effectively. As a result, some ele-

Example 34-8. Vendor's bid document

```
<BID>
<CUST>MD-STLOUIS</CUST>
<DEPARTMENT>EN</DEPARTMENT>
<ATTN>J.DOE</ATTN>
<TEL>8001111111</TEL>
<EMAIL>JDOE@MD-STLOUIS.COM</EMAIL>
<DUE_DATE format="ISO-8601" >19990821</DUE_DATE>
<ITEMNO>52</ITEMNO>
  <PARTNUM dimension="28">12T20-2</PARTNUM>
  <QUANTITY>3000</QUANTITY>
<ITEMNO>53</ITEMNO>
  <PARTNUM dimension="52">12T20-2</PARTNUM>
  <QUANTITY>3000</QUANTITY>
</BID>
```

ments that appear in both the bid request and the bid have a different element-type name in each. For this reason, before sending the bid to the customer, the vendor's metadata engine will translate the element-type names CUST, ATTN, and DUE_DATE to UNIT, CONTACT, and BID_OOB, respectively.

34.3 | Legacy data flow

Legacy data flow is a concept that underlies much of the promise of XML, and therefore much of what you have been reading about in this book. It is the notion of making legacy data speedily available wherever it is needed in the enterprise, and in a form that is suitable for use at that point.

Specifically:

- Data flows from *data generation points* to *data use points* through the enterprise network.
- Data use points determine the usage of the data. The term "usage" includes aggregation, transformation, rendition, and presentation. Therefore, the same data may be used in different ways at different use points.
- *Data semantics* – the meaning assigned to data – determines its usage. Therefore, a data use point may ascribe its own semantics to the data it receives.

■ Data flow is autonomous.

There are many advantages implicit in this concept.

■ First and most importantly, it provides a conceptual framework in which enterprise data is truly integrated and thereby becomes a competitive advantage.

■ Second, it refutes the notion that an enterprise monoculture in terminology, acronyms, etc., is essential to its success. Data is made available to all groups, and each group interprets it in ways that is useful to its process or task. There is a kind of data ubiquitousness that may prove to be the key ingredient of success.

■ Third, data use points may use data in multiple ways: to generate documents as input to their applications, for external use such as e-commerce databases, or for statistical purposes such as data mining.

■ Fourth, the concept embraces a full range of data atomicity, structure, and type. For example, data atomicity may range from a single product id to a departmental organizational chart; data structures may range from lists, tables, and tree structures to entire documents; and datatypes may range from conventional numeric data to complex non-numeric data such as company logos.

34.3.1 *Usage scenarios*

In the legacy data flow model, the traditional role of documents as collators and interpreters of data is not diminished; rather it is enhanced. Legacy data flow will simply make documents and enterprise communication more precise, and enterprise processes run faster and less prone to errors or delays. The usage scenarios described below illustrate these points.

Catalog generation

The enterprise product catalog generation process speeds up due to quicker data updates and less need for manual editing and error checking. The "busy-wait" periods in data exchange between enterprise departments are eliminated.

E-commerce server

The enterprise e-commerce server database can better reflect product availability and pricing changes. This is especially true when complex product configurations or multiple pricing models are involved. Human data entry errors, catalog maintenance delays, and other factors that bedevil product databases are reduced.

Corporate merger

A corporate merger can be consummated more efficiently if both corporations' legacy data are organized on legacy data flow principles. Disruption in either partner's operations during the initial days of the merger can be reduced by initially providing bridges between the two data flows. Later, the best practices of each enterprise can be incorporated in the merged organization by retaining the corresponding data flows.

Data event reporting

A tripwire reporting facility based on the occurrence or non-occurrence of data events may be implemented. Examples include triggers based on critical parts availability, financial flows, personnel issues, etc. More sophisticated versions may provide a data filtering mechanism based on the semantic content of data such as email.

34.3.2 *XML-based legacy data flow*

XML provides the ideal technology framework for implementing the legacy data flow concept. XML, through its tagged data and metadata structure, provides the means to "describe" the data to each use point. Two items of essential metadata are needed for legacy data to work. XML can be used to describe both. They are:

- Context metadata
- Semantic property metadata

Context is key because the same data may be interpreted differently in different contexts. A use point may therefore use or ignore data depending on context. Context includes such information as the means by which the data was generated (legacy application name, for example), the data generation point, generation date, time, etc. It would also contain the name of a larger data structure of which it is a part.

Semantic property information on the other hand is metadata that is intrinsic to the data itself; and may therefore remain unchanged in different contexts. Put in the context of legacy data flow, it is the interpretation of the data according to the data generating point.

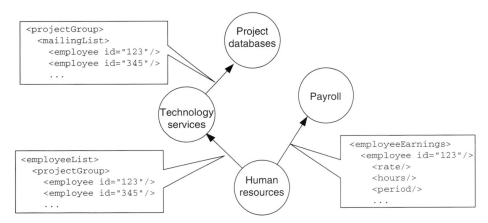

Figure 34-2   XML-based legacy data flow for employee data

Figure 34-2 depicts a simplified partial data flow of employee information between four departments in a corporation: the Human Resources (HR) department, the Technology Services department, the Payroll department, and the Project Group. Each arc represents data flow between its end points. On each arc, the context and semantic property metadata are shown as callouts; the actual data is not illustrated.

The information channel can be implemented as a centralized Information channel. The actual flows that occur may occur at different times: possibly bi-weekly between HR and Payroll, and at unscheduled times between Technical Services and Project Group. Generally, we can expect today's processes to implement efficient data flow when it is regularly scheduled, as between HR and Payroll. However, unscheduled data flows are rarely as successful.

34.3.3 *XML communication server*

One way to implement the concept of legacy data flow is to start with a preliminary list of data elements around which individual flows are then constructed. These flows will be multi-point data flows, unlike the e-commerce examples that we discussed earlier.

Moreover, each data element will have its own individual data flow tree or graph. In addition, we need to decide the mode of initiation of each flow: time-triggered or event-triggered.

To manage these flows simultaneously, we define an *XML communication server*. The XML communication server processes XML metadata just like the metadata engine, so it should not be surprising that many of the functions of the two overlap. Among these are homonymic and synonymic transformations of metadata, data formatting, aggregation, and extraction.

However, managing the individual data flows still remains the most important task handled by the XML communications server. In doing so, it must construct one or more contexts for a given data element at the generation point. Similarly, at each use point, the XML communication server must first evaluate the context, decide the course of action (accept or ignore), extract data and other related information, and then perform the metalanguage transformations necessary to insert the data in the use center's database.

34.3.4 *Data repositories*

The legacy application data repository is a source of information regarding data relationships. Many such repositories were constructed during the analysis phase of Y2K compliance projects. In particular, the data dictionaries are the starting points for building legacy data flows.

Each legacy application has its own data dictionaries, which are relatively isolated from other data dictionaries. In the legacy data flow implementation, care must be taken to ensure that these repositories are not modified in a manner that leaves them incompatible with the legacy applications they serve.

The bridge between these legacy data repositories is the XML communications server metadata repository. This repository consists of one or more metadata dictionaries spanning multiple legacy applications. Data element descriptions, semantic property descriptions, context specifications, and metadata transformation grammars are some of the objects in the metadata repository.

34.4 | Legacy data challenges

Despite the name, legacy applications are not frozen in time, but are continuously evolving. The challenge is therefore in being able to maintain compatibility between legacy data changes and the metadata descriptions of legacy data. Sometimes these changes are very subtle.

For example, the windowing technique described earlier for Y2K fixes involves no change in the structure of the application data, but only in its interpretation. A metadata repository must be able to interpret this change, perhaps at the level of individual date elements.

Another example is where apparently irrelevant data (e.g. Cobol record FILLERS) is interpreted as meaningful data by the legacy application, due to new application enhancements.

High-throughput online transaction-oriented legacy systems may pose another challenge. It may be difficult to design XML modules that will provide metadata transformation synchronized to the transaction rate.

Such examples are not rare scare stories, but rather common occurrences in the world of legacy applications. They are the outcome of a requirement to maintain compatibility with "old" legacy data and the systems that rely on it.

Tip   XMLSolutions Corporation, sponsor of this chapter, has provided a free copy of its Apache-based ExeterXML Server on the CD-ROM.

Schemas

- Schema development
- Schema management
- Vocabulary development
- Survey of public vocabularies

Part Nine

Nature abhors a schema-less database equally as much as she abhors a vacuum. Create a data table in a spreadsheet and the program will immediately search for field names, and supply them even if you fail to.

Although XML will let you create a document without an explicit formally-written schema definition (also known as a "document type definition", or DTD), the benefits of having one are enormous. These chapters will provide insight into schemas, whether you write them using XML DTD declarations, or one of the proposed new schema definition languages.

We start with a hands-on introduction to schema design, focusing on concepts rather than syntax. We then consider the issues of schema management and the enormous impact it can have on your business.

Vocabularies – sets of named element types and attributes – are the building blocks of schemas. Since the vocabulary determines the information that will be available at your portal and for use by your applications, you ultimately have to develop your own. We show you two ways to get started: with the data already in use by your company, and with public vocabularies developed by your industry.

Building a schema for a product catalog

Friendly Tutorial

- Schema design considerations
- Step-by-step schema design
- DTD declarations and schema notations
- Datatypes

Sponsor: Extensibility, Inc., http://www.extensibility.com

Contributing expert: Lee Buck

Chapter

35

The better your schema, the better your data! In the case of product catalogs, you could add: And the better your business! In this chapter we will walk you through the analysis and design of a schema for an online product catalog.

The online catalog is in many respects the heart of electronic commerce. With XML, it can provide a standard and platform-independent way of exchanging information between resellers, manufacturers and customers.

Such exchanges can be thought of as information flows between the various organizations. We'll look at one such flow between manufacturers and the folks at a fictitious website called www.we-sell-everything.com.

We'll use a schema to define what information may exist in the flow, where it may appear and how it should be used. This schema establishes a vocabulary by which we can exchange information and a contract that ensures that the information conforms to our expectations. It must reflect the requirements of our product catalog application.

35.1 | Online catalog requirements

Online catalogs have no bounds. Electronic catalogs provide resellers and manufacturers the opportunity to personalize the customer's experience. Rather than merely publishing a conventional print based catalog on the

Internet, our catalog example will use XML to build part of the framework for a catalog application. This application will build upon existing information resources to provide enriched content interaction and access.

Because XML objects are processable both as documents and as data, the catalog can include not only blocks of descriptive text but also database information. The two will allow our site to provide the user with flexible presentation of the information as well as powerful comparison facilities. This content may be in the form of character text and audio and video files.

The components of our online catalog will enable personalized product pricing for prospects and customers. By including promotional codes and rebate information, the reseller and manufacturer gain added pricing flexibility. Additionally, the catalog will link complementary products to create dynamic solution offerings.

By creating an online catalog, results of customer buying habits can be determined quickly. Using the appropriate approach for schema design, changes to the catalog can be deployed quickly, further enhancing results.

35.2 | Design considerations

Schema design involves a number of issues.

Validation

XML 1.0, using DTDs, provides a strong foundation for ensuring that all the necessary pieces of information are present at the right places in a document (i.e. required elements are included, inappropriate ones are not, attributes are supplied when required, etc.). DTDs can also offer some help in constraining the value of a particular attribute or data content of an element. (See 35.3, "Datatypes", on page 502.) The XML Schema Definition Language (XSDL) is a more comprehensive language that also offers these facilities.[1]

---

1. And lots of other facilities as well. See the advanced tutorial in Chapter 59, "XML Schema (XSDL)", on page 908.

Modularity

Modular schemas are one of the best means to build a flexible and reusable schema repository. A modular approach to schema creation delivers application flexibility and component reuse. Libraries of modular schemas can facilitate e-commerce in heterogeneous environments. Taking a modular approach to schema design is an important goal for our little project. In our case it will mean pulling out the notion of an address and placing it into a budding corporate standards schema which will contain such often repeated element types.

Relationship modeling

Schemas provide several facilities to model the relationships between pieces of information. One is the structure of the document: the context in which an element appears. Another is ID/IDREF relationships. These permit all kinds of relationships to be modeled independently of the structure of the document. In our example we'll use these two facilities to model the relationships involved.

Collaboration

Collaborative schema design efforts help ensure schemas reflect diverse corporate needs. Schemas will be shared between organizations to help ensure successful e-commerce applications. Resellers and manufacturers will want to collaborate on schemas to establish mutually agreeable rules for data interchange.

Elements vs. attributes

Many pieces of information which we want to model could be represented either as elements or as attributes. While each has its own strengths and limitations, the choice between them is often a matter of style. In our case we'll tend to use attributes for atomic data with a corresponding datatype and use elements for organizing concepts and for representing structures of data items.

Iterative design and schema flexibility

Schemas are living documents that must change as business requirements change. When such change occurs, two sets of compatibility issues arise: a) can existing XML documents be validated against the new schema and b) can existing processes handle documents conforming to the new schema? Careful design can maximize the potential for answering "yes" to both. For our example, we'll design the `promotion` element type to accommodate new kinds of promotions in the future.

35.3 | Datatypes

A *datatype* is a category of information, usually the kind that comes in small pieces and is used to build bigger ones. The examples in Table 35-1 will convey the idea better than any formal definition. They are a subset of those defined in the W3C Datatypes spec (Chapter 58, "Datatypes", on page 894).

Table 35-1   Common datatypes

string	decimal	IDREFS
boolean	float	date
uriReference	integer	time

It is good for a schema to be able to identify and enforce the use of datatypes because it strengthens the contract between the producer and the consumer of an XML document. In e-commerce applications such as our catalog, we need to assure the integrity of the information to the maximum extent possible at the earliest moment. We'll want to specify datatypes for the attribute values in our schema.

35.4 | The design

Our catalog is to come from one or more manufacturers. It needs to contain information about each manufacturer, the products available and any special promotions available for the products.

To build the schema we'll use *XML Authority*™. A trial version is provided on the CD-ROM. To follow along, install and open the program and click "New Schema."

35.4.1 *The catalog*

We'll model a catalog as the root element of the document. It contains a repeatable sequence of elements which provide information about each of the concepts: manufacturer, product, and promotion. Our model is as shown in Figure 35-1.

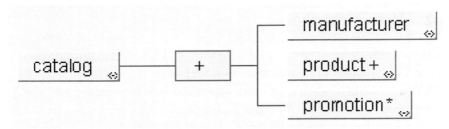

Figure 35-1   Catalog's content model: (manufacturer, product+, promotion*)+

Figure 35-1 is produced by *XML Authority*. It provides a concise visualization of the structure of our schema. A brief explanation of its symbology:

- Square brackets represent a sequence of elements
- Angled brackets represent a choice between elements
- Occurrence symbols alone represent grouping of elements
- The icons at the right of an element represent what an element may contain: other elements, untyped character data, or typed data.

A catalog element will need various bits of housekeeping information like its effective date and its expiration date. More robust implementations might well contain routing information, authentication and other bells and whistles but we'll keep it simple. We'll model the dates as attributes as shown in Figure 35-2:

☐ Attribute Type	Element	Data Type
date.expires	catalog	date
date.issued	catalog	date

Figure 35-2   Catalog's attributes

Figure 35-2 illustrates an attributes table in *XML Authority*. If you are following along, bring up the window by clicking "Attribute Types" in the toolbar and enter the information as shown above.

35.4.2 *Manufacturer*

A manufacturer element will contain name and address information, as shown in Figure 35-3. The former we'll model as an ID attribute type since we need it to uniquely identify a particular manufacturer (see Figure 35-4).

The address information provides a simple example of a powerful concept in schema design: modularization. It enables us to build an inventory of reusable chunks that can be referenced from multiple schemas. The address model shown is rather limited and inappropriate to our global audience. By separating it out into its own schema, we'll be able to isolate the necessary enhancements from our design efforts (as long as they are done in a compatible way).

35.4.3 *Product*

The product element type provides basics like name, SKU (essentially its bar-code), and SRP (standard retail price). These we'll model as attributes. Importantly, we'll model SKU as an ID attribute so we can refer to it later from within a promotion. We can then also use SKUs in a `complements` attribute to refer to other products that are complementary to this product (i.e. taken as a whole they comprise a complete solution). We want to be able to include a picture or other such media about the product so we'll define a media attribute that locates such media.

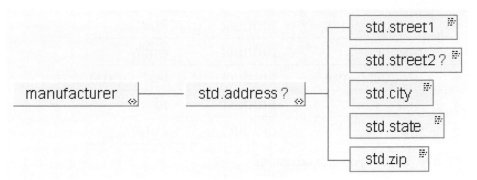

Figure 35-3   Manufacturer's content model: (std.address?) std.address':
(std.street1, std.street2?, std.city, std.state, std.zip)

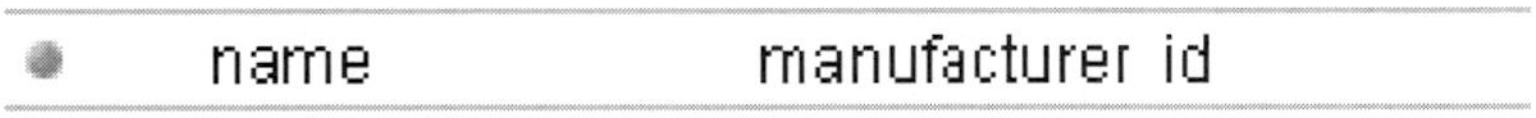

●	name manufacturer id

Figure 35-4   Manufacturer's attributes

We'll also include a mixed element type for a product description that permits portions of the description to be marked as a feature or a benefit (see Figure 35-5 and Figure 35-6). This simple refinement of the description enables a much richer set of presentation possibilities on our website. More advanced designs would include a much richer set of potential markup here, providing maximum flexibility to our website designers to present the information in various ways.

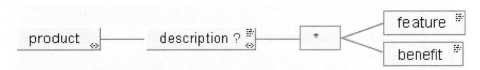

Figure 35-5   Product's content model: (description?) description's:
(feature | benefit)*

◆ complements	product	idrefs
◆ media	product	entity
◆ product.name	product	text (cdata)
◆ sku	product	id
◆ srp	product	currency

Figure 35-6   Product's attributes

35.4.4 *Promotion*

Finally we have the promotion element type. A promotion element may contain information about two different types of price reduction: bundle, which provides for a lower price for a particular product when one or more other products are purchased at the same time, and discount, which provides volume-based pricing (see Figure 35-7 and Figure 35-8). In the future, as shown in Figure 35-7, rebate could be added without affecting existing documents.

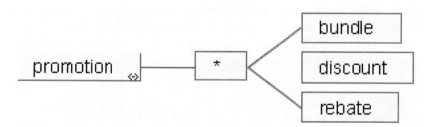

Figure 35-7   Promotion's content model after adding rebate: (bundle | discount | rebate)*

35.4.5 *The big picture*

We did it. Taken as a whole our schema's structure looks like Figure 35-9.

❧ other.skus	bundle	idrefs
❧ sku	bundle	id
❧ price	bundle	currency
❧ sku	discount	id
❧ min.qty	discount	integer
❧ pct.off	discount	float

Figure 35-8   Attributes of promotion's subelements

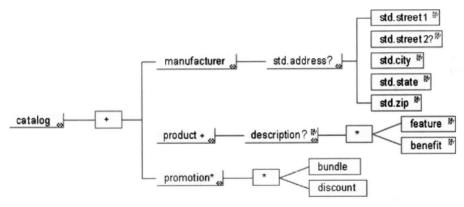

Figure 35-9   Document structure

35.5 | Schema definition notations

We designed our schema at a conceptual level, using a tool that presented a visualization of the schema definition. Software, however, requires a character string representation of the schema definition. We show several examples in this section. (With *XML Authority*, you can export your schema definition in a variety of notations by choosing "Export" from the File menu.)

35.5.1 *XML 1.0 DTD declarations*

In Example 35-1 we can take a look at part of the schema expressed as DTD declarations. Notice the use of a-dtype fixed attributes to specify the datatype for various attributes.

Example 35-1. Schema excerpt expressed as DTD declarations

```
<!ELEMENT catalog   (manufacturer , product+ , promotion* )>
<!ATTLIST catalog   date.issued  CDATA     #IMPLIED
                    date.expires CDATA     #IMPLIED
                    a-dtype      NMTOKENS #FIXED 'date.issued date
                                                 date.expires date'>
<!ELEMENT manufacturer  (std.address? )>
<!ATTLIST manufacturer  name     ID        #IMPLIED >
<!ELEMENT product (description? )>
<!ATTLIST product sku          ID        #REQUIRED
                  product.name CDATA     #IMPLIED
                  srp          CDATA     #REQUIRED
                  complements  IDREFS    #IMPLIED
                  media        ENTITY    #IMPLIED
                  a-dtype      NMTOKENS #FIXED 'srp currency'>
<!ELEMENT promotion  (bundle | discount | rebate )*>
<!ELEMENT bundle   EMPTY>
<!ATTLIST bundle   price        CDATA     #REQUIRED
                   complements  IDREFS    #REQUIRED
                   sku          ID        #REQUIRED
                   a-dtype      NMTOKENS #FIXED 'price currency'>
<!ELEMENT discount EMPTY>
<!ATTLIST discount min.qty      CDATA     '1'
                   pct.off      CDATA     #REQUIRED
                   sku          ID        #REQUIRED
                   a-dtype      NMTOKENS #FIXED 'min.qty integer
                                                 pct.off float'>
```

A single a-dtype names the datatypes for all of an element type's attributes that need them. In order to link each datatype name with its attribute, the a-dtype value is a list of pairs, each attribute name being followed by its datatype name.[2]

---

2. a-dtype is defined in the W3C Note at http://www.w3.org/TR/dt4dtd and is explained in 58.3.2, "XML DTDs", on page 905. The CD-ROM contains open source software that lets programmers support a-dtype with both the DOM and SAX interfaces.

35.5.2 *W3C XML Schema Definition Language (XSDL)*

Example 35-2 shows the XSDL version of most of the element types defined in Example 35-1. The XSDL definition is an XML document. Note that the datatype is specified individually for each attribute definition, using the `type` attribute.

35.5.3 *Microsoft XML-Data*

The `manufacturer` element type, expressed in the Microsoft XML-Data schema definition language, appears in Example 35-3. As with XSDL, the schema definition is an XML document. The datatype is specified individually for each attribute type definition, using the `dt:type` attribute.

35.6 | A sample document

A sample document that conforms to the schema looks like Example 35-4. (In *XML Authority*, you can get a head start on such a sample document by choosing `Export->Example XML Document` from the File menu. It will create a template for you to populate.)

35.7 | Conclusion

Our catalog schema provides the foundation for building an e-commerce website. By formulating and expressing our information flows using XML schemas we are assured that we can connect with our business partners no matter what type of technical infrastructure they may have. We can maxi-

Example 35-2. Schema excerpt expressed in XSDL

```
<element name = "catalog">
  <complexType content = "elementOnly">
    <sequence minOccurs = "1" maxOccurs = "unbounded">
      <element ref = "manufacturer"/>
      <element ref = "product" minOccurs="1" maxOccurs="unbounded"/>
      <element ref="promotion" minOccurs="0" maxOccurs="unbounded"/>
    </sequence>
    <attribute name = "date.expires" type = "date"/>
    <attribute name = "date.issued" type = "date"/>
  </complexType>
</element>
<element name = "manufacturer">
  <complexType content = "elementOnly">
    <sequence>
      <element ref = "std.address" minOccurs = "0" maxOccurs = "1"/>
    </sequence>
    <attribute name = "name" type = "ID"/>
  </complexType>
</element>
<element name = "product">
  <complexType content = "elementOnly">
    <sequence>
      <element ref = "description" minOccurs = "0" maxOccurs = "1"/>
    </sequence>
    <attribute name = "complements" type = "IDREFS"/>
    <attribute name = "media" type = "ENTITY"/>
    <attribute name = "product.name" type = "string"/>
    <attribute name = "sku" type = "ID"/>
    <attribute name = "srp" type = "currency"/>
  </complexType>
</element>
<element name = "promotion">
  <complexType content = "elementOnly">
    <choice minOccurs = "0" maxOccurs = "unbounded ">
      <element ref = "bundle"/>
      <element ref = "discount"/>
    </choice>
  </complexType>
</element>
```

Example 35-3. Manufacturer expressed in XML-Data

```
<ElementType name="manufacturer" content="eltOnly" order="seq">
  <element type = "s:std.address" minOccurs="0" maxOccurs="1"/>
  <AttributeType name = "name" dt:type = "ID"/>
  <attribute type = "name"/>
</ElementType>
```

Example 35-4. Sample catalog document

```
<catalog date.issued = "5-31-2001" date.expires = "6-30-2001">
<manufacturer name = "Stuff-o-rama">
   <std.address>
      <std.street1>127 Walking Way</std.street1>
      <std.city>Chapel Hill</std.city>
      <std.state>NC</std.state>
      <std.zip>27514</std.zip>
   </std.address>
</manufacturer>

<product sku = "12-3783-23" product.name = "foozle" srp = "29.99">
<description>
The foozle is the finest in plastic oven-ware.
Its <feature>patented melt-away containment
</feature>means that <benefit>you'll never have
to wash another dish.</benefit>
</description>
</product>

<product sku = "12-2412-23" product.name = "singey" srp = "19.99">
<description>
The singey aluminum oven mitts are ideal for
accessories for any kitchen. Available in three
sizes with convenient <feature>teflon
coating</feature> to <benefit>ensure a steady
grip.</benefit>
</description>
</product>

<promotion>
   <bundle sku="12-2412-23" price="14.99" other.skus="12-3783-23"/>
   <discount sku = "12-2412-23" min.qty = "10" pct.off = "10" />
   <discount sku = "12-2412-23" min.qty = "20" pct.off = "15" />
   <discount sku = "12-2412-23" min.qty = "50" pct.off = "20" />
</promotion>
</catalog>
```

mize the business impact of the information and respond quickly to new opportunities as they emerge.

Tip   You can get started with schema development using the free trial of XML Authority on the CD-ROM that accompanies this book.

Schema management at Major Bank

Case Study

- Centralized schema repository
- Schema development standards
- Cooperative development and reuse

Sponsor: XMLSolutions Corporation, `http://www.xmls.com`

Contributing expert: Priscilla Walmsley

Data is precious, and the companies with a lot of it, know it. For them, data format design is solely for the ordained, who are skilled and devoted champions of efficiency through standardization and reuse. But now, thanks to XML, anyone with a text editor can create data formats and the cats are out of the bag. Here's how one company herded them all in the same direction.

T he flexibility and extensibility of XML make it a powerful tool for information exchange. But this flexibility can result in chaos if it isn't carefully managed. The Data Management group at Major Bank took a close look at the way XML document types were defined in their organization and did not like what they saw...

36.1 | The situation

Banking is a highly competitive industry where providing customers with accurate, up-to-date information is crucial. Major Bank is involved in a number of cutting-edge XML projects, including online banking, instant credit approval, consolidation of customer statements, and an online concierge service for premier customers.

The document types for these projects, which are highly complex, are mostly developed internally. However, some come from industry standards (e.g. OFX/IFX), business partners, customers, and specific technologies (e.g. MQSeries). Most projects are currently using DTDs, although some are experimenting with XSDL.

Data Management at Major Bank is responsible for overall IT standards and architecture. Their main objective is to protect and manage the information assets of the company, and to reduce the costs and risks associated with developing and maintaining information structures.

The Data Management team decided to take a look at the current projects involving XML to determine what types of standards and services would be useful in this area. What they found was a mixed bag of independent XML efforts that were in various stages of development. They had already begun to build "legacy" XML systems!

36.1.1 *Inconsistent, incompatible efforts*

Six different business units were independently defining XML document types. As a result, many element types were defined redundantly, and in some cases incompatibly. For example, there were four different definitions for the element type address.

This redundancy was a problem for several reasons:

- It will be unnecessarily difficult for these applications to exchange data in the future.
- Extra effort was expended to design the same components twice.
- The groups that developed them did not have the benefit of one another's expertise.
- Redundant or overlapping definitions cause confusion and increase the maintenance effort and learning curve associated with the applications.

36.1.2 *Lack of understanding of existing schemas*

The individual projects had all created DTDs that were stored as plain text files in a variety of places, including various file systems, Web servers, and source code management systems. In many cases, the DTDs were stored redundantly in multiple locations and no definitive version was identified.

Several projects had modularized their DTDs, which is good design, but it was difficult to tell how the pieces related to one another. If a developer modified the contents of one file, he had only a vague understanding of how that impacted the other DTD files in the set.

The documentation for these DTDs was equally elusive. It existed in a variety of formats, including *Word* documents, HTML, PDF, and comments distributed throughout the DTD itself. Some projects had no documentation at all, while others had documentation that was too general to shed light on the individual declarations in the DTD.

36.1.3 *Dramatic variations in vocabulary and style*

The only consistency in the document types defined by the individual project teams was that they all used more-or-less correct DTD syntax. The individual DTDs were designed very differently. Some were highly modularized, while others had hundreds of declarations in the same DTD file. Some made heavy use of attributes, while others used none at all.

Most importantly, the vocabulary used in the various DTDs was not consistent. One group's definition of `Customer` was the same as another group's `Applicant`. Abbreviations for the same term varied by DTD. Some used user-friendly names, while others used COBOL-like names such as `PROD-ORD-NUM`.

There were stylistic differences, too. Capitalization varied from uppercase to lowercase to "camel case", even within the same DTD. The use of namespaces was unpredictable at best.

36.1.4 *Versions, versions everywhere*

Although most of the company's XML projects were in their initial phases, they already had several versions of DTDs in use. The number of versions was expected to increase dramatically as they went live with more projects and added more business partners.

In many cases, these versions would need to be managed simultaneously on an ongoing basis, in order to support different sets of customers. For example, in one project an individual personalized relationship was set up with each customer, which necessitated customized (and not necessarily mutually compatible) extensions for each of them.

In addition, the projects anticipated ongoing changes to all schemas, whether they were developed internally, designed by an industry standards group, or provided by a business partner. The rapid growth of the scope of e-commerce and normal progression in business processes made this instability inevitable.

36.2 | Schema management as a solution

After assessing the situation, the Data Management team determined that they needed a centralized repository to store and manage their XML schemas and DTDs. They decided to use XMLSolutions' *Schema Central* for this schema management function (Figure 36-1).

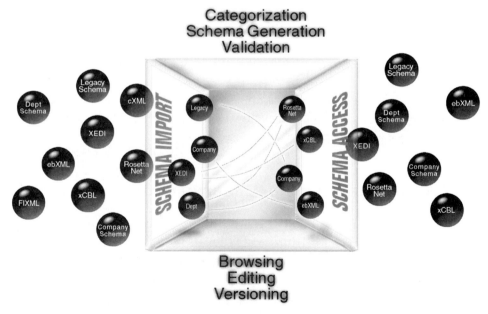

Figure 36-1   Schema management

Data Management identified several benefit areas that they expected from this solution.

36.2.1 *Schema categorization and documentation*

The immediate primary objective was to encourage reuse of schema components among project teams. In order to encourage new projects to use existing DTDs, these DTDs would have to be well documented and highly accessible to interested parties.

The team first deployed *Schema Central* as a tool for user-friendly viewing of existing DTDs, especially very large ones. The tool included the ability to search for DTDs by subject area and keywords. The existing documentation was also incorporated into the schema repository.

36.2.2 *Schema relationships*

One of the most significant benefits of a centralized schema repository is the ability to see how schemas relate to one another. The Data Management team felt that it was essential to cross-reference element types among multiple schemas, a function provided automatically by *Schema Central*. This ability allowed a user to immediately assess the impact of changing an element type on schemas throughout the organization.

Data Management also needed a facility for documenting synonym relationships among element types with different names. Many schemas used by the organization did not conform to the standard vocabulary, especially the industry standard schemas and "legacy" schemas. Keeping track of the relationships among synonymous element types would further the ability to assess the impact of a change.

The synonym relationships also provided the foundation for more complex transformation relationships among schemas and element types. One project generated XML documents from DB2 and VSAM legacy sources, combined them, and transformed the result into a different XML document that conformed to a schema defined by a credit bureau.

In this case, *Schema Central* served as a place to define the relationships among these schemas, including the transformation information required to convert documents from one to another. The XSLT for the transformations could then be generated automatically from that information.

36.2.3 *Version control*

Because of the growing web of versions, the Data Management team determined that a centralized approach to schema management would have to include support for versioning. They wanted not only to store multiple versions of a schema, but also to understand exactly what the differences were between them, and whether backward compatibility was maintained.

In many cases, several different versions of a schema would be used in production at the same time by different business partners. These multiple versions of schemas needed to be managed simultaneously.

36.2.4 *Schema standardization*

Another objective of centralized schema management was to encourage consistent style in the many DTDs and schemas that were developed internally. People throughout an organization can more quickly understand DTDs and their conforming XML documents when all schema definitions use the same element type names, with the same capitalization and hyphenation. This consistency in turn reduces maintenance time and costs, allowing the organization to adapt to change more quickly.

It was also expected that standardizing schema creation would help to encourage good schema design practices. Schema designers were likely to mimic the examples of well-designed schemas found in the repository. Additionally, centralized management would give Data Management an opportunity to review the schemas that were submitted to ensure that they were designed well.

36.3 | The plan of attack

After familiarizing themselves with the existing projects and the types of DTDs and schemas that were likely to be created, the Data Management team was ready to define the services and procedures necessary to manage the organization's XML environment.

36.3.1 *Create standards and guidelines*

The Data Management team had no desire to become a roadblock to fast-paced, mission-critical projects. They simply wanted to provide guidance and assistance to those projects. Accordingly, they set up a procedure to perform a design review each time a new schema was submitted to the repository.

A set of design criteria were incorporated into *Schema Central* against which schema definitions could optionally be evaluated. Violations are provided in a report. Let's look at the criteria.

36.3.1.1 Documentation

Is the schema definition properly documented? Could a user who is not familiar with this DTD understand it by reading the documentation?

36.3.1.2 Modularity

Is the schema definition designed as a set of modular, reusable components?

36.3.1.3 Reuse

Does the schema definition reuse existing, approved components wherever possible?

36.3.1.4 Style

Is the style of the schema definition consistent with organizational standards?

- Capitalization: Are element-type names mixed case, starting with a capital letter?

- Special characters: Hyphens are permitted in names; underscores are not.
- Have namespaces been omitted?
- Do any names exceed the 32-character limit?

36.3.1.5   Extensibility

Does the schema definition allow for future extensions? For example, is there a data item defined as an attribute that should be an element type because it may be broken down further in the future?

36.3.1.6   Accuracy

Does the schema definition accurately describe the business rule? The schema designer may not be a DTD expert and may misuse, for example, choice or sequence separators.

36.3.1.7   Wider applicability

There is a temptation to create schemas that are useful only for a specific application purpose. In some cases this may be appropriate. However, there are other times when it is better to create a schema that has broader applicability.

For example, a business unit that handles only domestic accounts might fail to define a Country element type as part of an address. They should consider defining it as an optional element for the purposes of consistency and future usability.

36.3.2   *Define a corporate e-commerce vocabulary*

Major Bank had already developed an approved glossary of terms designed to encourage consistent vocabulary in production systems. The glossary, which consisted of data element names, abbreviations, and definitions, was referenced during the creation of databases, program code, and other information structures.

For example, the glossary dictated that all data structures should use the term `customer`, abbreviated as `cust`, instead of `client` or `account_holder`.

The Data Management group determined that this same glossary should also apply to the creation of XML schemas and DTDs, ensuring consistent use of terms. As a result, they extended the *Schema Central* product to allow links to their online glossary.

36.3.3 *Create reusable building blocks*

There is no one "super-schema" that can satisfy the requirements of every group in an organization. Different business units often have conflicting definitions of even the most basic terms, like `account`, `transaction`, and `customer`. Trying to force them to model their data the same way is costly and results either in over-engineered models that try to capture everything, or overly simplistic models that cover only the lowest common denominator.

Therefore, instead of trying to design a universal model for their e-commerce data, the Data Management team decided to think smaller. They determined that the most reusable components were the most atomic, so they set out to build small units that could easily be popped into new applications.

Element types like `Address`, and `ContactInfo` were among the first developed. For the most part, these element types were defined using existing corporate entity-relationship models, and in some cases legacy systems. The models were converted automatically into markup declarations and loaded into *Schema Central* with XMLSolutions' *Vocabulary Builder* (see Chapter 37, "Building youre-commerce vocabulary", on page 524).

Schema components in the repository are tracked according to their life cycle stage. The glossary-derived element type definitions were identified as being at the "approved" stage, which allowed them to be reused in new projects. Project teams were not forced to use approved element types, but were encouraged to do so and notified when their DTDs missed an opportunity.

36.3.4   *Populate the schema repository*

Data Management next set out to populate the repository fully. They imported all of the DTDs in use in the company into the repository in order to evaluate them against the established design criteria. That enabled them to identify areas where the existing DTDs did not conform to the new company standards. Documentation for the DTDs was imported as well.

Several subject area categories were defined, and each of the existing DTDs was placed into one or more of those categories. This allowed users who were interested in finding and reusing schema components to search for them by subject area. The documentation could also be used as the basis for searching.

36.3.5   *Organize for future growth*

The Data Management team realizes that the use of XML in Major Bank will explode in the next several years. Therefore, they set out to organize roles and responsibilities to support this future growth.

The roles include a schema administrator who maintains the contents of the schema repository, a trainer who provides general XML courses, and a subject matter expert in schema design. The team also developed detailed procedures for the use of *Schema Central* in a complex, multi-version environment.

36.4 | Conclusion

Data Management's strategy was to become a service provider. They had neither the authority nor the desire to force project teams to conform to their standards. The fast-paced environment in which systems are developed today would not allow that.

Instead, the group established itself as a resource for the design, reuse, and understanding of Major Bank's schemas. In doing so, they created an XML environment that is less costly to maintain and expand, better integrated into the organization's business processes, and easier to tailor to individual customer needs.

Building your e-commerce vocabulary

Tool Discussion

- Creating a schema

- Capturing business semantics

- Reuse for e-commerce

Sponsor: XMLSolutions Corporation, `http://www.xmls.com`.

Contributing expert: Priscilla Walmsley

37

Your computers may walk the walk, but can they talk the talk? In today's e-commerce, just as in human discourse, vocabulary is vital. Your computer and those of your business partners might speak the same language – XML, of course – but do they attach the same meaning to the words? Let this chapter be your guide to straight talk!

T he people in your company have a vocabulary that they use when talking about your business. Words like part, adjustment, and transaction have a specific meaning when used in the context of your organization, and they're not just meaningful to people.

37.1 | Why do you need an e-commerce vocabulary?

Your specialized company vocabulary might have developed initially as purely human discourse, but information systems have since influenced it and made it more structured and precise. While developing those systems, users, programmers, and data analysts have painstakingly documented the terms and data elements used in your business. They have described what the words mean, how they relate to one another, what type of data they represent, and how to determine that data's validity.

Now e-commerce challenges us to share data with external business partners, customers, and suppliers. That means all parties must be using the same words to ensure that they understand each other. In XML terms, they must agree on schemas that define those words: the corporate e-commerce vocabulary.

37.2 | Where do schemas come from?

Sorry to say, the stork doesn't bring them. You either have to build them or borrow them.

37.2.1 *Building a new schema*

In some cases, your organization will have the luxury of defining the schemas that are to be used for data interchange with your trading partners. This may be the case if you are a large organization with many small trading partners.

We call this a luxury because there are lots of ways to model data. It is certainly convenient if you have the opportunity to use a vocabulary and data structure that closely match your own.

Consider two possible variations in something as elemental as telephone contact information, for example.

1. One way to model the phone number would be to allow for two specific phone numbers: day and evening. Many systems are currently designed this way.
2. Other systems may be designed to allow an unlimited number of phone numbers, with a description for each (e.g. "home", "mobile", "office", "pager", etc.).

To complicate things further, a different vocabulary might be used in each of these models. One may use the term "business phone" to represent what the other system calls "office number". Neither of these approaches is necessarily better, just different.

Being the creator of the schema reduces the amount of work required to convert your existing data structures to XML documents. For example, if you used the second model in your database and you had to use someone else's schema that was based on the first model, you would need to search through your data for each "home" phone number and convert it to "evening". Although this task may seem trivial taken alone, hundreds of these minor conversions require time to analyze and process.

Another benefit of owning the vocabulary is that the people in your organization will understand it intuitively and find it easier to assess the impact of a change. Also, if you eventually open up your schema to competing companies, they will have the extra task of converting their vocabulary to match yours.

37.2.2 *Borrowing an existing schema*

In many cases, you will not be creating the schemas you will use for interchange with other parties. Instead, you will be using schemas defined by an industry standards group, trading partner, or vendor. In this case, it may seem that capturing your own corporate vocabulary is less important, since a vocabulary is already provided for you. This is a fallacy.

It is essential to understand the interface between your own systems and the data you share with your trading partners. You won't be revising your internal systems to conform to the interchange schemas. Rather, you will be converting data back and forth between your internal systems and the external ones, and all the schemas will be subject to change over time.

Developing your internal vocabulary for e-commerce allows you to split the problem into two independent parts:

1. Capturing your existing data and metadata in its original format and translating it to XML using a vocabulary you understand; and
2. Translating the semantic meanings from one XML schema to another.

37.3 | Capturing existing business semantics

You may recall that we said earlier that, while developing your systems,

... users, programmers, and data analysts have painstakingly documented the terms and data elements used in your business. They have described what the words mean, how they relate to one another, what type of data they represent, and how to determine that data's validity.

That's the good news!

The bad news is that your corporate vocabulary is probably not neatly documented in a single place, but rather embedded in legacy systems on various platforms. These legacy systems are often cryptic, but they contain the key to understanding the data that will be exchanged.

A vast resource of information about your business processes exists embedded in your legacy systems and models. The reason for building an e-commerce vocabulary is to expose this system information, or metadata, and thereby allow it to be used easily in e-commerce applications.

Fortunately, there's more good news: Computers can be trained to scan existing systems and models and unify them in a common, tree-structured XML-based model. Let's see how that is done, using *Vocabulary Builder* from XMLSolutions as the illustrative software.

37.3.1 *Relational databases*

A large percentage of the data that is to be used in e-commerce applications currently resides in relational databases. These databases were designed by database administrators and developers who understood the business logic behind the data.

The catalogs of relational databases precisely describe the data they contain. From an ODBC data source, *Vocabulary Builder* can extract relational database information, including table layouts, table and column descriptions, datatypes and primary and foreign keys, as shown in Figure 37-1.

37.3.2 *Electronic Data Interchange (EDI)*

The EDI standard dictionaries provide a semantically rich model for e-commerce. If your organization is using EDI, chances are many of your existing processes use the EDI vocabulary, or at least understand it.

Much of the semantics of the EDI standards can be leveraged for use in XML-based e-commerce systems. For example, EDI defines thousands of

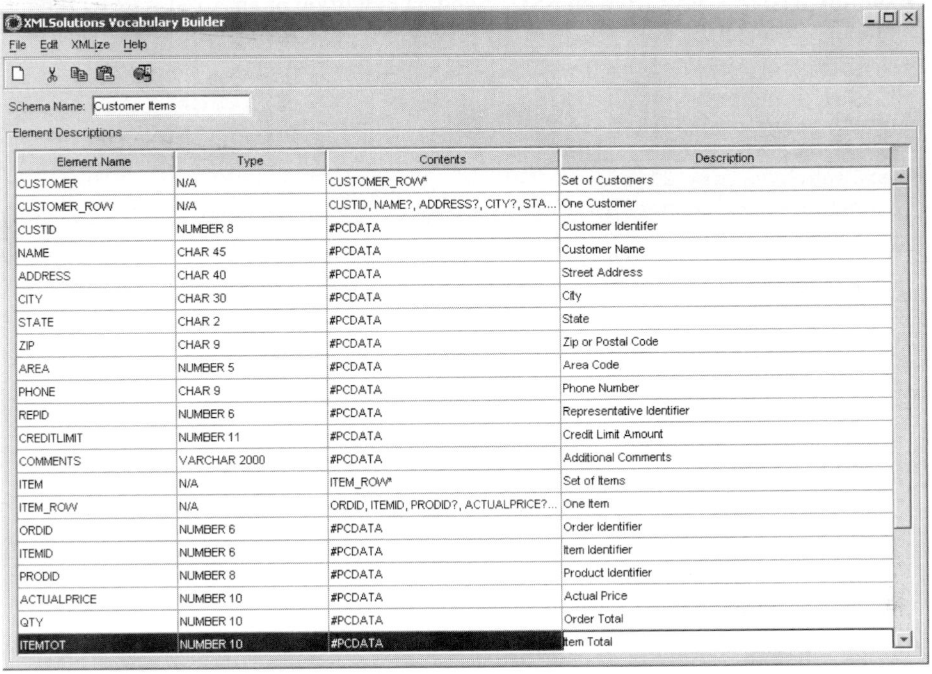

Element Name	Type	Contents	Description
CUSTOMER	N/A	CUSTOMER_ROW*	Set of Customers
CUSTOMER_ROW	N/A	CUSTID, NAME?, ADDRESS?, CITY?, STA...	One Customer
CUSTID	NUMBER 8	#PCDATA	Customer Identifer
NAME	CHAR 45	#PCDATA	Customer Name
ADDRESS	CHAR 40	#PCDATA	Street Address
CITY	CHAR 30	#PCDATA	City
STATE	CHAR 2	#PCDATA	State
ZIP	CHAR 9	#PCDATA	Zip or Postal Code
AREA	NUMBER 5	#PCDATA	Area Code
PHONE	CHAR 9	#PCDATA	Phone Number
REPID	NUMBER 6	#PCDATA	Representative Identifier
CREDITLIMIT	NUMBER 11	#PCDATA	Credit Limit Amount
COMMENTS	VARCHAR 2000	#PCDATA	Additional Comments
ITEM	N/A	ITEM_ROW*	Set of Items
ITEM_ROW	N/A	ORDID, ITEMID, PRODID?, ACTUALPRICE?...	One Item
ORDID	NUMBER 6	#PCDATA	Order Identifier
ITEMID	NUMBER 6	#PCDATA	Item Identifier
PRODID	NUMBER 8	#PCDATA	Product Identifier
ACTUALPRICE	NUMBER 10	#PCDATA	Actual Price
QTY	NUMBER 10	#PCDATA	Order Total
ITEMTOT	NUMBER 10	#PCDATA	Item Total

Figure 37-1 Capturing relational metadata in *Vocabulary Builder*

atomic data elements in detail, including lengthy lists of valid values for each one. There is no need to throw this information away and start from scratch.

Example 37-1 shows how XML can represent EDI semantics.

Vocabulary Builder can understand the metadata of EDI, including the valid value lists, for both standard and customized EDI dictionaries.

37.3.3 *Program data structures*

Large mainframe files contain most of the production data that is not stored in relational databases. Programmers have written complex *copybooks* to represent this data, including names and datatypes for the elements in these files, and valid values in some cases. *Vocabulary Builder* can parse a copybook and match it to a corresponding XML tree structure.

Example 37-1. Excerpt from an XSDL schema definition of an ANSI X12 EDI data element

```
<simpleType name="element-482" base="string">
<annotation>
  <documentation>Payment Action Code</documentation>
</annotation>
<maxlength value="2" />
  <enumeration value="AJ">
    <annotation>
      <documentation>Adjustment</documentation>
    </annotation>
  </enumeration>
  <enumeration value="ER">
    <annotation>
      <documentation>Evaluated Receipts Settlement</documentation>
    </annotation>
  </enumeration>
  <enumeration value="FL">
    <annotation><documentation>Final</documentation></annotation>
  </enumeration>
  <enumeration value="NS">
    <annotation>
      <documentation>Not Specified</documentation>
    </annotation>
  </enumeration>
  <enumeration value="PA">
    <annotation>
      <documentation>Payment in Advance</documentation>
    </annotation>
  </enumeration>
  <enumeration value="PO">
    <annotation>
      <documentation>Payment on Account</documentation>
    </annotation>
  </enumeration>
  <enumeration value="PP">
    <annotation>
      <documentation>Partial Payment</documentation>
    </annotation>
  </enumeration>
</simpleType>
```

37.3.4 *Logical models*

Your company may have logical models of your business systems and processes. These models have additional descriptive information to supplement your corporate e-commerce vocabulary.

For example, a database administrator may have created an ERWin entity-relationship model of a database for an accounting system. The model contains detailed information about each column in the database, including use cases, examples, and valid values. *Vocabulary Builder* can incorporate such models into your e-commerce vocabulary.

37.3.5 *Repositories*

Some organizations have already put a lot of effort into capturing and managing their corporate metadata. These organizations have built metadata repositories, which centrally store system information such as database layouts, copybook structures, and logical models. *Vocabulary Builder* can leverage these efforts by extracting metadata from commercially available repository products.

37.3.6 *Customized sources*

Many organizations have metadata stored in proprietary or less-common formats. For example, some systems may be documented in customized HTML files. A business semantics gathering tool should be extensible to handle these situations.

For example, *Vocabulary Builder* is designed so that users can plug in modules that understand unsupported data formats.

37.4 | Reuse for e-commerce

After capturing the existing semantic business definitions, the next step is to make them useful for e-commerce systems.

37.4.1 *Editing and refining*

Because descriptive data is often incomplete, or is merged from many sources, some manual refinement might be required. It is helpful if your semantics gathering tool allows editing of the descriptive information in the new XML data definitions.

37.4.2 *Schema generation*

After the descriptive information has been refined, users can generate DTDs and XSDL schema definitions that incorporate the new vocabulary. These DTDs might represent only fragments of complete document types.

For example, a schema generated from a DB2 table may contain customer header information only. This is desirable, since schemas are more likely to be used and reused if they are modular. An XML document could contain data from many different subject areas (e.g. customer information, sales data, and product information), and several XML documents might use the same customer information.

37.4.3 *Managing the vocabulary*

Capturing your existing vocabulary and preparing it for e-commerce is an important initiative. However, the bulk of the effort is wasted if that vocabulary languishes in text files somewhere and is never reused.

It is important to provide access to the corporate e-commerce vocabulary so that it can be understood and reused freely. *Vocabulary Builder* works with XMLSolutions' *Schema Central* product to perform this function. Using the two together, you can create your e-commerce vocabulary, publish it to your entire organization, and store and manage the definitions centrally at a detailed level (Figure 37-2).

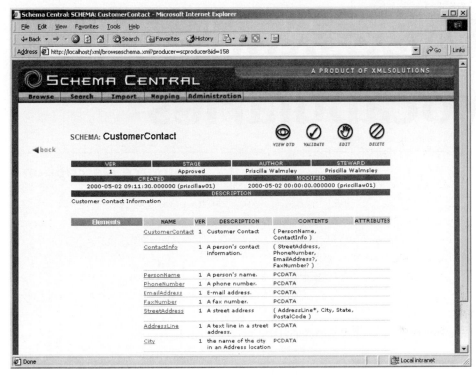

Figure 37-2   Publishing an e-commerce vocabulary in *Schema Central*

Repositories and vocabularies

Resource Description

- Schemas, DTDs and other specifications

- Vertical and cross-industry

- Repositories

- Industry vocabularies

Sponsor: Documentum, http://www.documentum.com

Contributing expert: Lilia Prescod

Chapter

38

There are so many XML specifications out there that it can be hard to find the ones that apply to you. Here's a guide.

here are so many vocabularies being developed, seemingly several for every industry and application, that It can be difficult to find the ones that will apply to your situation. This guide should help by listing many of the vocabularies that are available at the time of printing.

The list is not totally comprehensive. There is not yet a single home for all industry vocabularies and therefore no way to find them all reliably. In other words, there is not yet a comprehensive schema *repository*.

38.1 | Repositories

There is so much happening in the XML world that it can be hard to find the work that has already been done. In particular, it can be tricky to find out if there is a DTD, schema or standard that applies to the problem you are trying to solve. It would be helpful if there were an official place to find all XML-related schemas and specifications.

A list of these specifications is known as a *registry*. The good news is that registries exist. The bad news is that there are several of them and none of them has complete coverage yet. Still, searching three or four websites for an applicable specification is better than searching the entire Web!

Over time, the backers of these registries would like them to become Internet backbone technologies like the Domain Name Service or the IP number allocators. This eventuality will require the sites to move beyond a role as simple yellow pages and into a more sophisticated role of schema server and integrator: not just registry but also repository.

The path from here to there is not entirely clear. But it is clear that there is a lot at stake. The owner of the Internet's "XML Schema Server" will have a lot of influence on uses of XML.

38.1.1 *xml.org*

xml.org, `http://www.xml.org`, is a project of the Organization for the Advancement of Structured Information Standards (OASIS). Its site incorporates a *Documentum 4i eBusiness Edition* content management system, which allows the site to serve as both a registry (search engine) and a repository (storage site) for DTDs, schemas and other standards documents. Groups and individuals who create such documents can store them at the xml.org site.

xml.org is considered a resource for "XML specifications, schemas and vocabularies". At this point, the repository does not require any particular schema language or adherence to a particular framework. It is framework and technology neutral. This is good in that it maximizes contributor freedom and opportunity to innovate. The downside is that all of these specifications may not work together nicely because there are no published guidelines for making them work together.

OASIS wants xml.org to become more than a standalone repository. It should also become an index to a variety of other, technically compatible repositories. In other words, it should one day be able to delegate queries to affiliated repositories run by other companies.

38.1.2 *BizTalk repository*

The BizTalk repository, `http://www.biztalk.org`, is for schemas that are compatible with the BizTalk framework. Although the repository is run primarily by Microsoft there is also an "advisory board" made up of outsiders.

BizTalk schemas will need to pass a verification test. Once again, this is a double-edged sword. In theory, these tests can impose some level of quality control and interoperability requirements. This could help independently created schemas to work together. These tests will inevitably reject some schemas or specifications that are useful despite the fact that they do not adhere to the BizTalk framework specifications.

Whether you prefer the BizTalk or xml.org repositories will likely depend, in the long run, on whether you want to build on BizTalk or on some other framework. xml.org also has the advantage of vendor neutrality whereas BizTalk has the advantage of being run by one of the computer industry's dominant players. There is also opportunity for cooperation between the two. For instance BizTalk could become an official xml.org affiliate. We live in interesting times!

38.1.3 *Unofficial registries*

xml.org and BizTalk dream of being the backbone of the Web's XML infrastructure but some individuals are interested primarily in being a yellow pages for existing schemas hosted on other sites. These sites are older than the repositories and in some domains they are more complete.

The first such site was Robin Cover's, `www.oasis-open.org/cover`. Robin has cataloged markup-related information since the earliest SGML days, before there was even a Web as we know it. His Web pages have come to be known as the "Cover pages" (get it)?

Robin's pages are more than a schema repository and also less. They are more than a schema repository because they track software, Web pages, printed books and everything else pertaining to XML and SGML. The Cover pages are one-stop shopping for consumers of XML news and information. On the other hand, the pages do not actually store the schemas in question and cannot serve them to client software on demand.

Our Australian friend, James Tauber, runs another schema index with the imaginative name "schema.net", `http://www.schema.net`. Well, okay, the name itself is rather obvious; the imagination was in grabbing the domain name before anyone saw the importance of schemas!

38.2 | Public vocabularies

We use the catch-all term *vocabulary* to refer to all sorts of element-type and attribute specifications. Some are DTDs, some use one of the new schema definition languages, and some use informal English prose.

Some vocabularies define complete, self-contained document types, both POP-like and for messages. Some define only parts of the document because their designers expect them be augmented by other vocabularies that define the other parts.

In the following list, we've grouped the vocabularies into 49 categories, which are in turn grouped into five super-categories. For each project, there is a URL. For your convenience, the list is also available on a page on the CD-ROM so you can let your browser link directly to the project sites.

38.2.1 *Business systems*

Advertising

adXML
`http://www.adxml.org/`
NAA Classified Advertising Standards Task Force and DTD
`http://www.naa.org/technology/clsstdtf/`

Application integration

Open Applications Group Interface Specification (OAGIS)
`http://www.openapplications.org`
Portal Markup Language (PML)
`http://www.datachannel.com/schemas/`

Catalog

eCatalog XML (eCX)
`http://www.ecx-xml.org/`
Open Catalog Format (OCF)
`http://www.martsoft.com/docs/ocf/ocf.htm`
Open Catalog Protocol (OCP)

http://www.martsoft.com/ocp/
Product Data Markup Language (PDML)
http://www.pdml.org/pdmlintro.html

Commerce

Business Rules Markup Language (BRML)
http://www.research.ibm.com/rules/commonrules-overview.html
CommerceXML (cXML)
http://www.cxml.org/home/
Common Business Library (xCBL)
http://www.commerceone.com/xml/cbl/cblfaq.html
eCo Framework
http://www.commerce.net/projects/currentprojects/eco/
Electronic Business XML Initiative (ebXML)
http://www.ebxml.org/geninfo.htm#what
Internet Open Trading Protocol (OTP)(Trade)
http://www.ietf.org/html.charters/trade-charter.html
Network Trade Model (NTM)
http://www.sungard.com/h_ntm.htm
RosettaNet
http://www.rosettanet.org
Trading Partner Agreement Markup Language (tpaML)
http://www-4.ibm.com/software/developer/library/tpaml.html
Universal Commerce Language and Protocol (UCLP)
http://www.w3.org/TR/NOTE-uclp/
Visa XML Invoice Specification
http://www-s2.visa.com/ut/dnld/spec.ghtml

Customer information

Customer Profile Exchange Network (CPExchange)
http://www.cpexchange.org/
Unified Customer Reporting (UCR)
http://www.haifa.il.ibm.com/projects/sysapps/ucr.html

Data mining

Predictive Model Markup Language (PMML)
`http://www.dmg.org/public/techreports/pmml-1_0.html`

Edi

ACORD EDI (AL3)
`http://www.acord.org/`
Electronic Data Interchange for Documents (EDIDOC)
`http://www.sgmltech.com/projects/edidoc.htm`
XEDI
`http://www.xedi.org/about.html`
XML/EDI (Electronic Data Interchange)
`http://www.geocities.com/WallStreet/Floor/5815/`

Finance

Annotated Digital Receipt
`http://www.valicert.com/html/solutions.html`
Bank Internet Payment System (BIPS)
`http://www.fstc.org/projects/bips/`
Extensible Business Reporting Language (XBRL)
`http://www.xfrml.org/`
Financial Information eXchange (FIX)
`http://www.fixprotocol.org/cgi-bin/rbox/Welcome.cgi`
FinXML
`http://www.finxml.org/`
FpML (Financial products Markup Language)
`http://fpml.org/`
Interactive Financial eXchange (IFX)
`http://www.ifxforum.org/`
Open Financial Exchange (OFX)
`http://www.ofx.net/ofx/`

Forms

Extensible Forms Description Language (XFDL)
`http://www.w3.org/TR/1998/NOTE-XFDL-19980902`

XML Forms Architecture (XFA)
`http://www.xfa.com/`

Human resources

Human Resources Markup Language (hrml)
`http://www.hrml.com/`
Human Resources XML (HR-XML)
`http://www.hr-xml.org/`
JOB markup language (JOB)
`http://www.tapestry.net/xmlstand.html`
Resume
`http://www.hr-xml.org/schema.html`

Industrial automation

Machinery Information Management Open Systems Alliance (MIMOSA)
`http://www.mimosa.org/`
Virtual Instruments Meta Language (VIML)
`http://nacimiento.com/VIML/`

Systems administration

Directory Services Markup Language (DSML)
`http://www.dsml.org/about.html`
DirXML
`http://www.novell.com/products/nds/dirxml/quicklook.html`
DMTF Common Information Model (CIM)
`http://www.dmtf.org/spec/cims.html`
Signed Document Markup Language (SDML)
`http://www.w3.org/TR/1998/NOTE-SDML-19980619/#SECTION00200`

Workflow

Simple Workflow Access Protocol (SWAP)
`http://www.ics.uci.edu/~ietfswap/`
Workflow Management Coalition (WfMC)
`http://www.aiim.org/wfmc/standards/index.htm`

38.2.2 *Content creation, maintenance, and distribution*

Alternative delivery device

NISO Digital Talking Books (DTB)
http://www.loc.gov/nls/niso/dtd.htm
Open eBook
http://www.openebook.org/specification.htm
SyncML
http://www.syncml.org/
Wireless Markup Language (WML)
http://www.wapforum.org/

Content management

HTTP Distribution and Replication Protocol (DRP)
http://www.w3.org/TR/NOTE-drp-19970825.html
Portable Site Information (PSI)
http://www.xml.com/pub/2000/03/22/psi/index.html
WEBDAV
http://www.ics.uci.edu/~ejw/authoring/
XML Catalog
http://www.ccil.org/~cowan/XML/XCatalog.html

Content syndication

Information & Content Exchange (ICE)
http://www.icestandard.org/
NewsML
http://www.iptc.org/NMLIntro.htm
NITF (News Industry Text Format)
http://www.nitf.org/
Open Content Syndication
http://internetalchemy.org/ocs/
RDF Site Summary (RSS)
http://www.oreillynet.com/topics/rss/rss
XMLNews-Meta

`http://www.xmlnews.org/docs/xmlnews-meta.html`
XMLNews-Story
`http://www.xmlnews.org/docs/xmlnews-story.html`
Channel Definition Format (CDF)
`http://www.w3.org/TR/NOTE-CDFsubmit.html`

Hypertext

HyTime
`http://www.hytime.org/`
ibtwsh: Itsy Bitsy Teeny Weeny Simple Hypertext DTD
`http://www.ccil.org/~cowan/XML/`
Virtual HyperGlossary (VHG)
`http://www.vhg.org.uk/home/index.html`
XML Bookmark Exchange Language (XBEL)
`http://www.python.org/topics/xml/xbel/`

Metadata

BiblioML
`http://www.culture.fr/BiblioML/`
Common Warehouse Metadata Interchange (CWMI)
`http://www.omg.org`
Dublin Core
`http://purl.org/dc/`
Encoded Archival Description (EAD)
`http://cidc.library.cornell.edu/xml/`
MAchine Readable Cataloging (MARC)
`http://lcweb.loc.gov/marc/marc.html`
Meta Content Framework Using XML (MCF)
`http://www.w3.org/TR/NOTE-MCF-XML.html`
Resource Description Framework (RDF)
`http://www.w3.org/RDF/`
Structured Graph Format (SGF)
`http://www.isl.hiroshima-u.ac.jp/projects/SGF/index.html`
XMLMARC
`http://xmlmarc.stanford.edu/`

Multimedia

HyTime
`http://www.hytime.org/`
Synchronized Multimedia Integration Language (SMIL)
`http://www.w3.org/AudioVideo/Activity.html`

Music

ChordML
`http://www.cifranet.org/xml/ChordML.html`
FlowML
`http://wendy.vub.ac.be/~bschiett/saol/FlowML.html`
Music Markup Language (MML)
`http://is.up.ac.za/mml/index.htm`
MusicML
`http://195.108.47.160/3.0/musicml/`
Standard Music Description Language (SMDL)
`http://www.oasis-open.org/cover/smdlover.html`

Tables

CALS table
`http://www.oasis-open.org/html/tm9901.htm`

Technical publishing

DocBook DTD
`http://www.oasis-open.org/docbook/`
eFirst XML for Scholarly Articles
`http://www.openly.com/efirst/`
Question and Answer Markup Language (QAML)
`http://www.ascc.net/xml/en/utf-8/qaml-index.html`
Text Encoding Initiative (TEI)
`http://www.uic.edu/orgs/tei/`

Translation

OpenTag Format

```
http://www.opentag.com/
```
Translation Memory Exchange (TMX)
```
http://www.lisa.org/tmx/tmx.htm
```

Vector graphics

Extensible 3D (X3D)
```
http://www.vrml.org/x3d.html
```
Precision Graphics Markup Language (PGML)
```
http://www.w3.org/TR/1998/NOTE-PGML
```
Scalable Vector Graphics (SVG)
```
http://www.w3.org/Graphics/SVG/Overview.htm8#intro
```
Vector Markup Language (VML)
```
http://www.w3.org/TR/NOTE-VML
```

Voice

Java Speech Markup Language Specification (JSML)
```
http://java.sun.com/products/java-media/speech/forDevelopers/J
SML/
```
SSML: A Speech Synthesis Markup
```
http://www.cstr.ed.ac.uk/projects/ssml_details.html
```
Voice eXtensible Markup Language (VoiceXML)
```
http://www.voicexml.org/forum_1.html
```
VoxML
```
http://www.voxml.com/voxml.html
```

38.2.3 Math and science

Astronomy and instruments

(Astronomical) Instrument Markup Language (IML/AIML)
```
http://pioneer.gsfc.nasa.gov/public/aiml/
```
Astronomical Markup Language (AML)
```
http://monet.astro.uiuc.edu/~dguillau/these/
```
Spacecraft Markup Language (SML)
```
http://www.interfacecontrol.com/sml/
```

Biology

Bioinformatic Sequence Markup Language (BSML)
`http://www.intl-pag.org/pag/7/abstracts/pag7792.html`
BIOpolymer Markup Language (BIOML)
`http://www.bioml.com/BIOML/index.html`
Gene Expression Markup Language (GEML)
`http://www.rii.com/geml/`

Math

Mathematical Markup Language (MathML)
`http://www.w3.org/Math/`
OpenMath
`http://www.openmath.org/`

Other science

Chemical Markup Language (CML)
`http://www.xml-cml.org/`
eXtensible Data Format (XDF)
`http://tarantella.gsfc.nasa.gov/xml/XDF_home.html`
Extensible Scientific Interchange Language (XSIL)
`http://www.cacr.caltech.edu/SDA/xsil/`
Molecular Dynamics Language
`http://violet.csa.iisc.ernet.in/~modl/`
Weather Observation Definition Format (OMF)
`http://zowie.metnet.navy.mil/~spawar/JMV-TNG/XML/OMF.html`

Social science

EcoKnowMICS ML
`http://www.ecoknowmics.com/prod01.htm`
GedML: Genealogical Data in XML
`http://users.iclway.co.uk/mhkay/gedml/`
Geography Markup Language (GML)
`http://feature.opengis.org/rfc11/GMLRFCV1_0.html`

38.2.4 *Software development*

Artificial intelligence

OML/CKML
`http://www.ontologos.org/`

Components

Bean Markup Language (BML)
`http://www.davecentral.com/7746.html`
Koala Bean Markup Language (KBML)
`http://www-sop.inria.fr/koala/kbml/kbmltech.html`
Open Software Description (OSD)
`http://www.w3.org/TR/NOTE-OSD.html`
Open Software Description (OSD)
`http://msdn.microsoft.com/workshop/delivery/osd/overview/osd.a`
`sp`
Software Component Documentation DTD
`http://www.componentregistry.com/`

Documentation

JavaDox
`http://www.creativepro.com/story/news/2953.html`

Logging

XLF (Extensible Log Format)
`http://www.docuverse.com/xlf/index.html`

Middleware

MIX - Mediation of Information Using XML
`http://www.npaci.edu/DICE/MIX/`
Simple Object Access Protocol (SOAP)
`http://www.microsoft.com/mind/0100/soap/soap.asp`
WebBroker: Distributed Object Communication on the Web
`http://www.w3.org/TR/1998/NOTE-webbroker/`

Web Distributed Data eXchange (WDDX)
`http://www.wddx.org/DTD.htm`
Web Interface Definition Language (WIDL)
`http://www.w3.org/TR/NOTE-widl`
XML-RPC (Remote Procedure Calling)
`http://www.xmlrpc.com/stories/storyReader$7`
XML-RPC Specification
`http://www.xmlrpc.com/stories/storyReader$7`

Modelling

CDIF XML-Based Transfer Format
`http://www.eigroup.org/cdif/intro.html`
Open Information Model (OIM)
`http://www.mdcinfo.com/OIM/index.html`
UML eXchange Format (UXF)
`http://www.yy.cs.keio.ac.jp/~suzuki/project/uxf/`
UML-Xchange
`http://www.cam.org/~nrivard/uml/umlxchng.html`
XML Metadata Interchange Format (XMI)
`http://www-4.ibm.com/software/ad/standards/xmi.html`

User interface

Extensible User Interface Language (XUL)
`http://www.mozilla.org/xpfe/xptoolkit/xulintro.html`
User Interface Markup Language (UIML)
`http://uiml.org/index.html`

38.2.5 Vertical industry

Architecture, engineering, and construction

Architecture, Engineering, and Construction XML Working Group
(aecXML Working Group)
`http://www.aecxml.org/index2.htm`

Automotive

DCS Automedia
`http://www.automedia.co.uk/`
MSR
`http://www.msr-wg.de/`
XML for the Automotive Industry - SAE J2008
`http://www.xmlxperts.com/sae.htm#over`

Cycling

BikeXML
`http://www.bikexml.org/`

Education

IMS Metadata Specification
`http://www.imsproject.org/metadata/index.html`
Learning Material Markup Language (LMML)
`http://daisy.fmi.uni-passau.de/projects/PaKMaS/LM2L/`
Net Quest
`http://www.ilrt.bris.ac.uk/netquest/about/lang/`
Schools Interoperability Framework (SIF)
`http://www.siia.net/sif/`

Food services

Document Encoding and Structuring Specification for Electronic Recipe
Transfer (DESSERT)
`http://www.formatdata.com/dessert/index.htm`

Healthcare

Health Level 7 (HL7)
`http://www.hl7.org/`

Hospitality

Hospitality Industry Technology Integration Standards (HITIS)
http://www.hitis.org/

Insurance

iLingo
http://www.ilingo.org/
Life (XMLife)
http://www.acord.org/standards/xml/life.htm

Legal

Legal XML
http://www.legalxml.org/
XrML (eXtensible rights Markup Language)
http://www.contentguard.com/newcontentguard/press_ecertain_042
700.htm

Petrochemical

WellLogML
http://www.posc.org/ebiz/WellLogML
WellSchematicML
http://www.posc.org/ebiz/WellSchematicML/index.shtml

Real estate

Real Estate Information Standards (REIS)
http://www.dataconsortium.org/
Real Estate Listing Management System (OpenMLS)
http://www.openmls.com/OpenMLS_Demo/description.htm
Real Estate Listing Markup Language (RELML)
http://www.4thworldtele.com/public/design/rsdtds.html
Real Estate Transaction Specification
http://www.rets-wg.org/docs/

Retail

First Retail Mark-up Language (frml)
`http://www.frml.org/`
Retail Enterprise Data in XML (REDX)
`http://www.nrf-arts.org/redx.htm`

Stylesheets

- Styles
- Behaviors
- Website design considerations

Part Ten

Style is the dress of thought.

Lord Chesterfield said that over a century ago, but he might have had XML in mind. He knew that the way you present your ideas is important – too important to mix up with the ideas themselves. Different audiences require different presentation styles, so you had better keep your data as an undressed abstraction until you know exactly where you want it to go today.

When you do, it is the stylesheet that spells out how to dress each part of the content – the colors, fonts, flow rules, etc. – and, increasingly, how that part should act as well (what programmers call "behaviors").

In this part we'll first look at the role of stylesheets and how they work, with an emphasis on traditional style specifications. Then we'll see how stylesheets are used for developing interactive tutorials, including the specification of behaviors and formatting for online and offline renditions. Finally, we'll examine the tradeoffs that affect stylesheet design in real-world Web applications.

The role of stylesheets

- Intelligent publications

- Template rules

- Specifying processing

Sponsor: Enigma, Inc., http://www.enigma.com

Contributing experts: Enigma, Inc. staff

Abstract XML documents make it easier to build robust intelligent electronic publications without programming. Instead, designers can specify presentation with declarative stylesheets, often aided by stylesheet design tools. This chapter shows how.

XML publishing systems are distinguished by their ability to deliver intelligent publications; that is, electronic publications with live tables of contents, hyperlinking, topic searching, and other navigation aids.

Stylesheets play a critical role in delivering these capabilities, from two standpoints:

- Stylesheets aren't just limited to specifying style for renditions (fonts, layout, color, etc.). They are really generalized "specification sheets" that can also control behaviors, such as interactivity, navigation, data processing, and so on. So the word "style" in their name shouldn't be taken too literally.
- Styles are applied to components of an XML document in accordance with *template rules*. The language for creating such rules can be quite powerful and allow for highly-granular application of the styles.

39.1 | The need for intelligent publications

The business need for delivering intelligent publications – such as mainte-nance and parts information or commercial reference publications – has always existed. The publications too have always existed, even in paper for-mat, with elaborate multiple indexes, various types of lists of illustrations, detailed running headers and footers, and extensive cross-referencing.

However, both the need and the opportunities for more effective imple-mentation, have significantly increased with the advent of corporate intra-nets. This infrastructure enables content providers to make their intelligent publications more useful, and more widely available. And with the ability to interconnect these publications with ERP and e-commerce systems, con-tent providers and end-users alike are improving productivity and increas-ing after-market revenues, as we have seen in other parts of this book.

Among the XML systems that have been developed to support this need is Enigma's *INSIGHT* electronic publishing software. It produced the intel-ligent document shown in Figure 39-1. Note the two panes. The left con-tains navigation aids and the right shows the material that is accessed by selecting a navigation aid. The bottom part of the left pane is a "live" table of contents that can be collapsed and expanded. The upper part is a list of search items.

In this case, the search item called "Visual Access" has been selected in the left pane, and an exploded graphic is shown on the right. Navigation can also be initiated within the right pane by hyperlinking. Here, any of the call-outs can be clicked in order to access more information about the parts they identify.

39.2 | Creating a stylesheet

We will use *INSIGHT* in this chapter to illustrate the concept of stylesheets and a selection of their capabilities. In order to make use of abstract XML content, a stylesheet must be created that specifies how the content should be presented.

In the terms used in the Extensible Stylesheet Language (XSL), a stylesheet for XML is a set of template rules. A template rule has two parts:

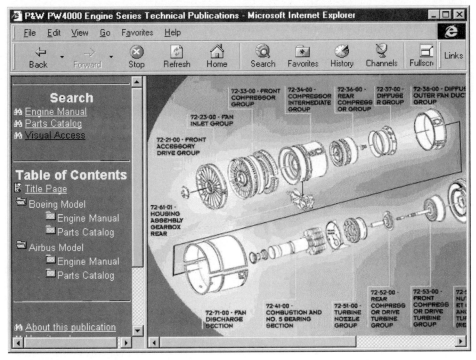

Figure 39-1 Intelligent publication with live navigation aids

- A *pattern*, which selects the content portions to which a rule applies.
- A *template*, which specifies the rendition style, behavior, and/ or other processing to be applied to the selected content.

INSIGHT provides a stylesheet editor to assist in defining these rules. It is illustrated in Figure 39-2.

In the left pane, the document type structure is presented in an expandable tree view. Alternatively, a list of element types could be shown by selecting the appropriate tab.

In the upper-right pane, there is a set of tabbed dialogs for the available style and behavior specifications. The illustrated dialog allows the selected content to be numbered and boilerplate text to precede or follow it. The lower-right pane shows a preview of the applied specification.

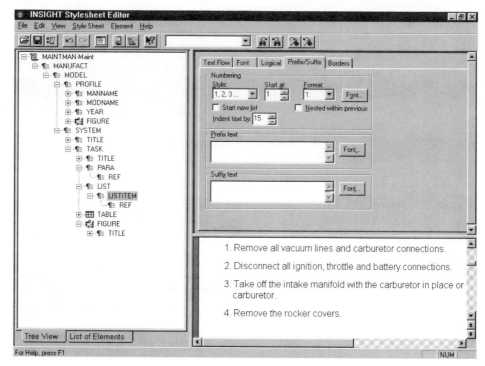

Figure 39-2   Stylesheet editor

39.2.1   *Associating processing with document components*

Let's look at *INSIGHT*'s facilities for applying template rules.

39.2.1.1   Pattern specification

There are several ways to specify a pattern (called a "match-pattern" in the *INSIGHT* product):

element type occurring anywhere
   An example would be: any PARA element, no matter where it occurs.

element type in hierarchical context

An example would be: any TITLE element that is the child of a TASK element.

qualified by attribute value

Patterns of the above types can be further qualified by attribute values. For example: Any PARA element that has a PERIL attribute whose value is DANGER.

39.2.1.2   Rule inheritance

It is not necessary to specify individual template rules for every element type in the document. If no rule applies specifically to an element, it inherits the rule that applies to its parent.

This principle is applied independently to each of the dialogs in Figure 39-2. For example, if you specify only font properties in the rule for an element, it will inherit all prefix, text flow and border properties from its parent.

39.2.2   *Specifying processing*

INSIGHT's facilities for the "template" portion of a template rule include both styling and behaviors.

39.2.2.1   Rendition style

A range of style properties can be specified in a template rule, including:

- Font information (e.g. font, size, bold/italic)
- Text flow (e.g. space before/after, justification)
- Borders and shading
- Prefix/suffix and list numbering
- Table type (CALS, HTML table, user-defined)
- Image/multimedia display (scaling, inline/iconized)

Attribute values can be included in the style specifications (e.g. as a prefix or suffix). Such uses are independent of whether the attribute was used to qualify the rule's pattern specification.

39.2.2.2   Behaviors

In addition to style properties, the following behaviors can be specified for the selected content:

- Search item in the navigation pane
- Table of Contents entry and hierarchy level
- Hyperlink rules (based on ID/IDREF, XPointer, attribute values, or data content)

39.3 | Delivering the results

After the stylesheet is defined, the entire publication is packaged for delivery to the end-user. The publication can be installed on a public Web server, delivered to the owner to be installed on a local intranet, or sent as a stand-alone or networked CD-ROM publication. *INSIGHT* provides a wizard to attend to the details (Figure 39-3).

Note that the source documents that are included in the publication are not restricted to XML or SGML. Rendered documents from common word processors and desktop publishing systems can also be included in the delivered publication, with their content hyperlinked and searchable.

Normally, the document and the stylesheet are served to the end-user and the stylesheet is applied dynamically on the client side. However, for

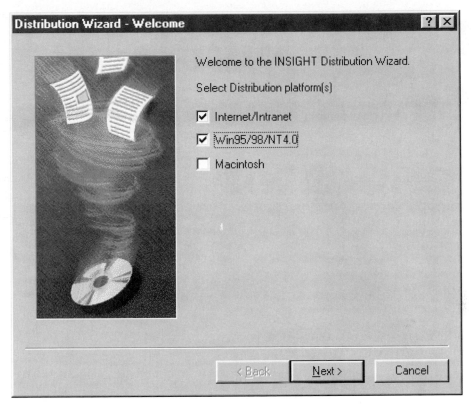

Figure 39-3   *INSIGHT* distribution wizard

browsers that do not support XML, HTML can be generated on the server and delivered to the browser.

 Tip   *A free personal-use version of INSIGHT is available on the CD-ROM that accompanies this book.*

A stylesheet-driven tutorial generator

Case Study

▌ XML tutorial document type

▌ Generated renditions for Web, offline, and print

▌ Automatic navigation aids

Sponsor: IBM Corporation, http://www.ibm.com/xml

Contributing experts: Doug Tidwell, Leah Ketring, Christine Stackel, Janet Willis, and Caroline Newsome.

Chapter

40

What do you call a tool that creates Web tutorials from XML documents, using XSLT stylesheets to automatically generate the needed HTML, JPEG, PDF, and ZIP files? We call it "awesome". IBM calls it *Toot-O-Matic*. Here's how it works.

The developerWorks website operated by IBM (`http://www.ibm.com/developerWorks`) supports the developer community, with an emphasis on standards-based, cross-platform technology. One of the services of developerWorks is its library of free tutorials; in fact, it is by far the most popular content on the site.

So when IBM sought a way to automate the development of new courseware, it was only natural to practice what it preaches. The course content is in XML, the transform specifications are in XSL, and the code is in Java.

IBM calls its automatic tutorial generator *Toot-O-Matic*. While you chuckle over that, let's look at what it does and how it does it.

40.1 | Touring a tutorial

The tutorial screen types are called "panels". A tutorial begins with a menu panel, as shown in Figure 40-1. It lists the sections of the tutorial.

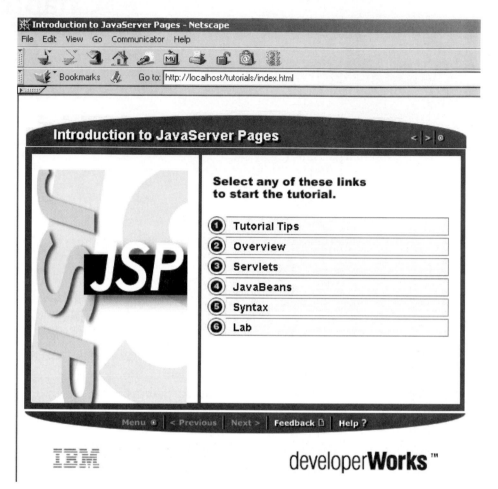

Figure 40-1   Menu panel

Clicking on one of the six section titles takes you to the first information panel in that section. Figure 40-2 shows the first information panel in the "Overview" section.

Most of the panels in a tutorial use this design. The uppermost section is called the "masthead". It contains the title of the tutorial and appears on every panel.

Below the masthead is a bar with the section title. It appears on every panel in the section. Below that is the body of the panel, with an image in the left column and text in the right.

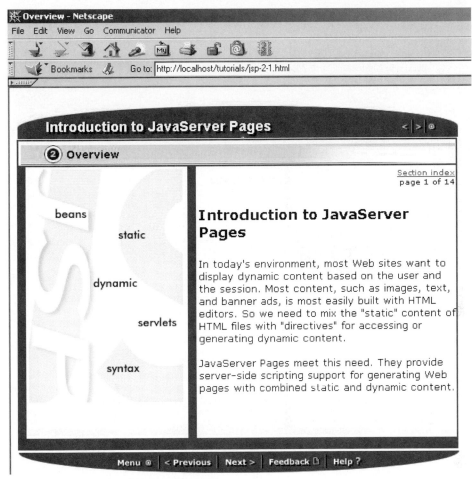

Figure 40-2 Information panel

Notice that the text column header identifies the panel as "page 1 of 14" in its section, and also contains a link to the section index. Clicking on that link displays the titles of all the pages in the section, as shown in Figure 40-3.

You can click on any of the page titles in the section index to go directly to its information panel.[1]

---

1. The tutorials also include panel types for quizzes and for additional information, but they are not discussed in this chapter.

Figure 40-3   Section index panel

40.2 | The tutorial XML document

Example 40-1 shows the start of the XML document that represents the tutorial we've just toured.

The root element of the document is the `tutorial` element. The value of its `prefix` attribute is a short string used to generate file names; more on this later. A `tutorial` contains a `title` and some number of `section` elements.

Example 40-1. tutorial document excerpt

```
<tutorial prefix="jsp">
<title>Introduction to JavaServer Pages</title>
<section><title>Overview</title>
<panel><title>Introduction to JavaServer Pages</title>
<body>
<image-column img="images/overview.gif"/>
<text-column>
<p>In today's environment, most Web sites want to display dynamic
content based on the user and the session.  Most content, such
as images, text, and banner ads, is most easily built with
HTML editors.  So we need to mix the "static" content of HTML
files with "directives" for accessing or generating dynamic
content.</p>
<p>JavaServer Pages meet this need.  They provide server-side
scripting support for generating Web pages with combined
static and dynamic content.</p>
</text-column>
</body>
</panel>
...
```

Each `section` in turn contains a `title` and some number of `panel` elements.

Each `panel` contains a `title` and a `body`. The `body` may contain an `image-column`, an empty element that identifies the graphic used in the panel.

The `body` typically also contains a `text-column`. That in turn contains some number of HTML element types: paragraphs, ordered and unordered lists, emphasized text, and a few others.

40.3 | Generating the tutorial

The *Toot-O-Matic* tool that the IBM team wrote is a single Java program. The tool processes the XML document to produce a number of outputs.

1. An HTML file that contains a menu of links to the different sections of the tutorial (Figure 40-1).
2. An HTML file for each information panel of the tutorial (Figure 40-2).

3. A number of HTML section indexes, each of which lists the titles of all panels in a given section (Figure 40-3). Each panel title is displayed as a link to its panel.

4. A file of XSL Formatting Objects (XSL-FO) that describe how the text and graphics of the tutorial should be rendered for printing (Example 40-7).

5. A number of JPEG files for the section headings and menu items, each of which contains text from the XML document (Figure 40-4).

6. A ZIP file that contains all of the generated HTML files, all of the generated graphics, and any resources referred to in the XML document. This file is a convenient package for downloading the tutorial for offline use.

7. A Portable Document Format (PDF) file based on the XSL-FO file created earlier (Figure 40-6).

The first four outputs are produced using XSLT stylesheets; Java libraries are used to create the JPEG, ZIP, and PDF files. We'll discuss each of the seven steps in the following sections.

40.3.1 *Main menu panel*

The main menu panel (Figure 40-1) consists of a standard header and footer, with a list of all the sections of the tutorial in between. Clicking on any of the section titles takes you to the first panel in that section.

To enhance the visual appeal of the panel, generated graphics and mouseover effects are used to display the panel title. The graphics are generated by Java code that retrieves the section title from the XML source document. (See 40.3.5, "JPEG files", on page 571 for more information.)

A stylesheet controls generation of the list of sections. The header and footer are generated from boilerplate text; the list of sections is generated with an `xsl:for-each` element, as shown in Example 40-2.[2]

---

2. For brevity, generation of some other attributes is omitted from the example.

Example 40-2. Generator for menu panel links

```
<xsl:for-each select="section">
  <a>
  <xsl:attribute name="href">
    <xsl:value-of select=
      "concat($fn, '-', position(), '-1.html')"/>
  </xsl:attribute>
  ...
  <img width="335" height="26" border="0">
    ...
    <xsl:attribute name="src">
      <xsl:value-of select=
        "concat('imagemaster/menu-', position(), '.jpg')"/>
    </xsl:attribute>
  </img>
  </a>
</xsl:for-each>
```

For the first section (`position()=1`), the stylesheet generates the HTML in Example 40-3. All of the "1"s (except for the second "1" in `jsp-1-1.html`) were generated by the XPath `position()` function.

Example 40-3. Generated menu panel link

```
<a href="jsp-1-1.html" onMouseOut="iOut('menu1');"
  onMouseOver="iOver('menu1'); self.status=menu1blurb;
  return true;">
  <img border="0" height="26" name="menu1"
      src="imagemaster/menu1.jpg" width="335"/>
</a>
```

40.3.2 *Information panels*

The header and footer of the panels are generated by boilerplate, and most of the tags in the body of the panel are virtually identical to their HTML counterparts. The most interesting thing about generating the individual panels is the use of an XSLT extension to redirect the output of the transformation into different files.

The Apache XML Project's *Xalan* stylesheet engine provides the extension, which must be declared in the `xsl:stylesheet` element (the root element of the stylesheet), as shown in Example 40-4.

Example 40-4. Stylesheet extension declaration

```
<xsl:stylesheet xmlns:xsl="http://www.w3.org/1999/XSL/Transform"
   version="1.0"
   xmlns:redirect="org.apache.xalan.xslt.extensions.Redirect"
   extension-element-prefixes="redirect">
```

In this example, `org.apache.xalan.xslt.extensions.Redirect` is the name of the Java class that implements the extension, and `redirect` is the namespace prefix that is used to invoke it. The extension allows output to be piped to different files and XPath expressions can be used to generate the file names, as shown in Example 40-5.

Example 40-5. Stylesheet extension invocation

```
<redirect:write select="concat($fn, '-',
                                $sectionNumber, '-',
                                position(), '.html')">
...
</redirect:write>
```

To streamline processing, the prefix attribute of the `tutorial` element is stored in the variable `fn`, and the `position()` of the current `section` is stored in the variable `sectionNumber`. So, for example, if the prefix were `jsp`, and the page was the fourth page in the fifth `section`, the XPath `concat` function would create the file name `jsp-5-4.html`.

Throughout the document, link anchors and references are all generated automatically. Doing so ensures that references remain correct and consistent as the source document changes.

40.3.3 *Section indexes*

To generate the section index, Example 40-6 creates an HTML file with an ordered list of all of the `panel` elements in the `section`. Because the file names are generated dynamically, hyperlinks to all of the panels can be created as well.

Example 40-6. Generator for a section index

```
<ol>
<xsl:for-each select="panel"><li><a>
  <xsl:attribute name="href">
    <xsl:value-of select=
      "concat($fn, '-', $sectionNumber, '-', position(), '.html')"/>
  </xsl:attribute>
  <xsl:value-of select="title"/>
</a></li></xsl:for-each>
</ol>
```

The `concat` function call generates the filename, as in Example 40-5. Here is it is used as the value of the `href` attribute in the a tag. `xsl:value-of` retrieves the `title` of the current panel to be the content of the a element.

40.3.4 *XSL-FO file*

The print layout consists of the graphics and text from the tutorial, combined with page numbers, headers, and footers to create high-quality printed output.

Example 40-7 shows the formatting objects generated from the *panel* in Example 40-1.

The formatting objects are converted into flowed text. (See 40.3.7, "PDF file", on page 575 for a discussion of that process.)

40.3.5 *JPEG files*

JPEG graphic files are generated for the masthead and for the section title. Let's look at the process for each of them.

40.3.5.1   Masthead graphics

A `masthead.jpg` file is shown in Figure 40-4.

Example 40-7. Formatting objects generated from Example 40-1

```
<fo:block font-size="8pt" line-height="10pt"
  text-align-last="end" space-after.optimum="8pt">
  page 1 of 14
</fo:block>
<fo:block font-size="16pt" line-height="19pt" font-weight="bold"
space-after.optimum="12pt">
  Introduction to JavaServer Pages
</fo:block>
<fo:block space-after.optimum="6pt">
  In today's environment, most Web sites want to display dynamic
  content based on the user and the session.  Most content, such
  as images, text, and banner ads, is most easily built with
  HTML editors.  So we need to mix the "static" content of HTML
  files with "directives" for accessing or generating dynamic
  content.
</fo:block>
<fo:block space-after.optimum="6pt">
  JavaServer Pages meet this need.  They provide server-side
  scripting support for generating Web pages with combined
  static and dynamic content.
</fo:block>
```

Brain Surgery for Young People

Figure 40-4   Generated masthead graphic

Creating it involves two steps:

1. Extracting the title text from the XML document.
2. Overlaying the title text onto a blank graphic.

40.3.5.1.1 *Extracting the title text*

The text of the masthead comes from the `title` element of the tutorial (Example 40-8). It is extracted with the aid of an XSLT stylesheet.

Example 40-8. Tutorial `title` element

```
<tutorial>
  <title>Brain Surgery for Young People</title>
```

40.3.5.1.2   Overlaying the title onto a blank graphic

Java code is used to read the blank graphic shown in Figure 40-5 onto a blank canvas and to draw the title text over it. The result is then written out to a JPEG file.

Figure 40-5   Blank masthead graphic

Example 40-9 shows the bulk of the Java code that does the work.

Example 40-9. Code to generate JPEG files

```
FileInputStream fis =
  new FileInputStream("master" + File.separator +
                      "masthead.jpg");
JPEGImageDecoder northDecoder =
    JPEGCodec.createJPEGDecoder(fis);
BufferedImage bi = northDecoder.decodeAsBufferedImage();
Graphics g = bi.getGraphics();
g.setFont(tutorialTitleFont);
g.setColor(Color.black);
g.drawString(titleText, 39, 50);
g.setColor(Color.white);
g.drawString(titleText, 36, 47);
String outputFilename = "imagemaster" + File.separator +
                        "masthead.jpg";
FileOutputStream fos = new
    FileOutputStream(outputFilename);
JPEGImageEncoder encoder =
    JPEGCodec.createJPEGEncoder(fos);
encoder.encode(bi);
fos.flush();
fos.close();
```

40.3.5.2   Section title graphics

Three graphics are generated for the `title` of each `section` of the tutorial:

- A graphic for the section title that appears at the top of each panel in the section.
- A normal color graphic for the section item in the menu panel.
- A highlighted graphic for the menu panel item when the mouse is hovering over it.

As with the masthead graphic, the section title graphics are based on a blank JPEG image, onto which the appropriate text is drawn before the combined image is written to a file.

40.3.6 ZIP file

Each file that makes up the complete tutorial is added to the ZIP archive using the classes in the `java.util.zip` library. Example 40-10 shows the code that adds the file `imagemaster/masthead.jpg` to the archive.

Example 40-10. Code to build a ZIP file

```
zipOut = new ZipOutputStream(new
            FileOutputStream(getZipFilename()));

if (zipOut != null
{
  byte[] buffer = new byte[4096];
  int bytes_read;

  File graphicsFile = new File("imagemaster" +
      File.separator + "masthead.jpg");
  FileInputStream fis = new FileInputStream(graphicsFile);
  ZipEntry graphicsEntry =
    new ZipEntry(graphicsFile.getPath());
  zipOut.putNextEntry(graphicsEntry);
  while ((bytes_read = fis.read(buffer)) != -1)
    zipOut.write(buffer, 0, bytes_read);
}
```

The ZIP file is useful for users who want to download the entire tutorial to their machines, enabling them to view the tutorial without an Internet connection.

40.3.7 *PDF file*

The PDF file is generated from the XSL-FO file that was created by the XSL transformation described in 40.3.4, "XSL-FO file", on page 571. The Apache XML Project's *Formatting Objects to PDF (FOP)* tool was used.[3]

Example 40-11 shows the heart of the code that does this work.

Example 40-11. Converting XSL Formatting Objects to PDF

```
Driver driver = new Driver();
driver.setRenderer(
  "org.apache.fop.render.pdf.PDFRenderer", version);
driver.addElementMapping(
  "org.apache.fop.fo.StandardElementMapping");
driver.setWriter(new PrintWriter(new FileWriter(pdffile)));
driver.buildFOTree(parser, foInputStream);
driver.format();
driver.render();
```

The result is illustrated in Figure 40-6. Notice that the running header contains the titles of both the section and the tutorial, and that the graphics, text, and other items from the HTML page have found their way into the PDF.

40.4 | Conclusion

The *Toot-O-Matic* tool illustrates the wide range of outputs that can be generated from a single XML document. The metadata captured in the document structure and markup informs a number of different transformations, all of which work together to deliver a single piece of content in a variety of interesting and useful ways.

The tool has shortened and streamlined IBM's development process, making it easier, faster, and cheaper to produce their tutorials. Moreover,

---

3. The actual source was an XSLTInputSource created during the transform, which is more efficient than writing the XSL-FO stream out to disk, then reading it back in and parsing it.

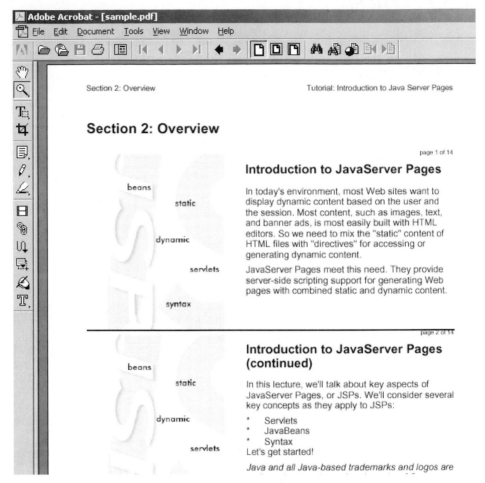

Figure 40-6   Generated PDF file

the tool is based on open source software and open standards and works on any Java-enabled platform.

Tip   *There are twenty free XML tools from IBM on the CD-ROM for your use.*

Designing website stylesheets

Application Discussion

- IE5 XML Sports demo
- Server delivery strategy
- Navigation in large mixed document sets
- Using XSL for data processing
- Presentation in non-traditional media

Sponsor: Microsoft, http://msdn.microsoft.com/xml

Contributing expert: Charles Heinemann

Chapter

41

XSL offers immense creative possibilities to website developers, far beyond the simple generation of HTML renditions. But real-world conditions relating to a given application and its data can affect your stylesheet design. These issues are explored in this chapter.

Website stylesheets can't be designed in a vacuum. Although modular design and reuse of stylesheet components is a desirable goal, the more specifically a stylesheet focuses on particular documents and their implications for the client/server relationship, the more efficient the stylesheet will be.

The *XML Sports Demo*, which was released with Microsoft *Internet Explorer 5*, demonstrates different techniques for building websites that exploit the XML technology of the browser.

The demo site is data-driven. It hosts a large interconnected set of news stories and statistical information for teams and players in several major American sports. The demo is elaborated in sufficient detail to raise – and resolve – a number of the issues that affect practical stylesheet design.

We will discuss several of those issues in this chapter.[1] They are:

- Server delivery strategy
- Navigation in large mixed document sets
- Using XSL for data processing
- Presentation in non-traditional media

---

1. The full demo is available on the CD-ROM for further examination.

The discussion assumes knowledge of *Active Server Pages* (ASP), which were explained in Chapter 8, "Building an online auction website", on page 120.

41.1 | Server delivery strategy

The *XML Sports Demo* is an example of a data-driven website. This means that the site offers large amounts of data to the client. The goals of the demo in that respect were to:

1. Provide access to all the data needed by the user.
2. Serve up that data in the most efficient manner.

41.1.1 *Accessing all the data*

Achieving the first goal requires the website to have access to a large amount of data. In the case of the *XML Sports Demo*, this does not create a significant performance problem because all of the necessary files are located on the same server.

The results would be different, however, if the data were stored on other servers somewhere else on the Web. It could take some time to download a large XML document containing, for instance, the statistical information concerning yesterday's Major League Baseball box scores

It is difficult to get around the fact that the user simply must wait for data to be downloaded. However, a Web developer can help the situation by making that wait more palatable. Web surfers have come to accept the initial time hit when a Web page is first loading. However, they soon grow impatient if the website takes a long time to respond to their subsequent actions.

The *XML Sports Demo* solves this problem by loading and parsing most of the XML necessary to drive the website before it sends the user interface HTML page to the client. This means that the user has to wait a little longer for the user interface to appear, but by the time it does, the site that sent it will have all of the data ready in parsed form.

The user's experience begins with the display of the user interface HTML page. The page is generated dynamically by an ASP file. That file also loads and parses the large XML documents that contain all of the data for the demo. To simplify our discussion (but without loss of generality), we will speak as though there were two such documents: one containing all the basketball stories, and another containing statistics on all the basketball teams that are mentioned in any of the stories.

The `XMLDOMDocument` objects that result from parsing the XML documents are assigned to `Application` variables that are instantiated and initialized in `Global.asa`, a file that executes when an ASP file is called in the same directory.

The ASP script that does these things is shown in Example 41-1.

Example 41-1. ASP script to load, parse, and save an XML document

```
var oSource = Server.CreateObject("Microsoft.FreeThreadedXMLDOM");
oSource.async = false;
oSource.load("http://localhost/xmlsports/stry_xml.asp");
Application("xmlsportsXML")=oSource;
```

Once an `Application` variable is set, the server can access it throughout the session. There is no need to reload and reparse the document every time a user needs it.

41.1.2 *Serving the data efficiently*

Although each complete XML document is parsed and ready on the server, it would not be efficient to send them in their entirety to the client. By performing some processing on the server, it is possible to deliver to the client only the information that the user needs.

For example, when the ASP file constructs the user interface, it can create a menu with the headlines in it, as shown in Example 41-2. That by itself doesn't cause any part of the document to be downloaded, other than the headlines in the menu.

A story is delivered only when the user clicks on one of the headlines, which causes the client-side function in Example 41-3 to be executed. The function changes the color of the headline as an acknowledgment of the user's request.

Example 41-2. Script to create a menu from the story headlines

```
oHeadlines = oSource.selectNodes(
            "stories/story[sport='" + sSport + "']/headline"
            );
for (i=0; i < oHeadlines.length; i++)
{
  if (i>0)
    sHeadlines += '<hr color = "ffffff">';
  sHeadlines += '<SPAN CLASS="link" ID="oHead"
                + onClick="fnFillStory(this.innerHTML);">'
            + oHeadlines.item(i).text + '</span>';
}
oTDHeadlines.innerHTML = sHeadlines;
```

Example 41-3. Requesting the specific story

```
function fnFillStory(headline)
{
  var oStory = new ActiveXObject("Microsoft.XMLDOM");
  oStory.async = false;
  // Grab the story with the selected headline
  oStory.load("getStory.asp?headline=" + headline);
  divStory.innerHTML =
    oStory.documentElement.transformNode(oStyle.documentElement);
  // Color this story's headline
}
```

When `oStory.load` in Example 41-3 executes, the server invokes the ASP file `getStory.asp` and passes it the value of the `headline` variable. The ASP file executes the script shown in Example 41-4.

Example 41-4. Selecting the requested story element from a document containing all of them

```
headline = Request.QueryString("headline");
oSource = Application("xmlsportsXML");
oStory = oSource.selectSingleNode("stories/story[headline='" +
        headline + "']");
Response.write(oStory.xml);
```

The script returns an XML document that consists of just the requested story. By extracting only a portion of the comprehensive XML document, the server spares the user from waiting for uninteresting data.

41.2 | Designing document types for navigation

In the *XML Sports Demo*, when the user's mouse pointer hovers over a team name in a story, the statistics for that team are displayed in a pop-up window. Figure 41-1 demonstrates what this looks like to the user.

Figure 41-1   A window pops up with team statistics.

This bit of magic is accomplished by designing cross-references into the documents.

41.2.1 *Cross-referencing*

Each of the stories made available on the site contains references to elements in other documents that contain team statistics. For example, let's look at the `story` element in Example 41-5, which was downloaded in response to a headline click.

Note the `team` element in the second `paragraph`. It references an element with the ID `team78`. In this case, the statistics element with that ID is

Example 41-5. Story document

```
<story>
  <sport>NBA</sport>
  <headline>NBA coaches not enjoying lockout</headline>
  <image>281073.jpg</image>
  <city>null</city>
  <storybody>
<paragraph>IT'S A WORKING stiff's fantasy - even rich
working stiffs and yet, most NBA coaches are finding that no
work and all pay makes for a dull lifestyle. When you're a
basketball junkie and you're used to getting an adrenaline
high 82 times a season and you suddenly find yourself
separated from the source of your competition, well, it's
hard to kick the habit.</paragraph>
<paragraph>"The coaching staff has been working hard
twiddling our thumbs," <team ref="team78">Miami Heat</team>
coach Pat Riley said recently. It must be weird for Riley to
have no players to yell at right now. "I actually miss
them," Riley said, apparently surprised at the
thought.</paragraph>
  </storybody>
</story>
```

also a `team` element, but as it exists in a different XML document there is no conflict between the element type names.

The XML document containing the referenced `team` statistics element is shown in Example 41-6.

Example 41-6. Team statistics document

```
<team id="team78">
  <city>Miami</city>
  <name>Heat</name>
  <Conference>Eastern</Conference>
  <Division>Atlantic</Division>
  <record>55-27</record>
</team>
```

Because of the cross-referencing between the XML document that contains the story and the XML document that contains the team statistics, we can easily navigate from the story to the statistics. This frees us from having to incorporate all of the statistics repeatedly in every story, and having to download statistics that the user might not ever access.

41.2.2 *Traversing to referenced nodes*

Traversal from a team reference to the team statistics that it references is done using the services of the XML Document Object Model (DOM).

A story is processed under the control of an XSL stylesheet that causes the team reference elements to be rendered in the form of HTML elements, like that shown in Example 41-7.

Example 41-7. HTML rendition of a team reference element in a story

```
<SPAN style="color:#333399;cursor:hand" onmouseout="fnChuckInfo()"
  onmouseover="fnGetInfo('team78')">Miami Heat</SPAN>
```

The fnGetInfo function calls the nodeFromID method on the team statistics XML document. The string team78 is passed as a parameter and the function returns the team statistics element with that id value. The statistics element is rendered as a pop-up window, as we saw in Figure 41-1.

41.2.3 *Defining an ID attribute*

In XML, as we have seen, cross-references can be represented by ID and IDREF attributes. An element with an ID reference attribute is one anchor of a link; an element with an ID attribute is the other.

The attribute of the team statistics element in Example 41-7 that is named id has to be defined to be of type "id". The name alone has no significance to the XML processor. The attribute definition is included in the definition of the document type schema.

When the demo site processes an XML document, any element exhibiting an id attribute is indexed by the attribute value, which allows the element to be located quickly.

41.2.3.1 Using DTD declarations

If the document type were defined using DTD declarations, the relevant fragment would be that shown in Example 41-8.

Unfortunately, this approach is not available to the *XML Sports Demo* in its present form. That's because in a valid XML document, the value of an

Example 41-8. Markup declaration for `id` attribute of `team`

```
<!ATTLIST team id ID #REQUIRED>
```

ID reference (i.e., an attribute of type "IDREF") must be an ID of an element in the same document. In the demo, the team statistics elements are in a separate document from the story elements.

The easy solution would be to change the element type name of `team` in the story document to something like `teamref` and combine the two documents into one. Validity of the combined large document would be checked by the parser during the site initialization in Example 41-1.

41.2.3.2   Using a schema definition language

The *XML Sports Demo* actually addresses the problem by using a schema definition in the XML-Data schema definition language, the relevant fragment of which is shown in Example 41-9.

Example 41-9. XML-Data definition for `id` attribute of `team`

```
<AttributeType
 name="id"
 xmlns:dt="urn:schemas-microsoft-com:datatypes"
 dt:type="id"
/>
<ElementType name="team">
  <attribute type="id"/>
</ElementType>
```

Note that with a schema definition language, unlike DTD declarations, the document is not valid and therefore an ID reference need not be to an ID of an element in the same document.[2]

---

2. As schema definition languages are still in development, there are still many unanswered questions. One of them concerns the scope of extra-document references. The XML Sports Demo defines that scope to be the demo website, but this is a processing decision that is not reflected in the documents themselves. It works, but it is not a general solution for portable self-describing XML documents.

41.3 | Filtering with XSL

In Example 41-1 we saw that a comprehensive XML document containing all of the statistics for all of the teams is parsed and loaded onto the server when the client requests the initial Web page. The user, however, from that initial user interface page, can select the sports that are of interest. That selection enables the server to filter the comprehensive document so that extraneous data is not served.

The filtering is accomplished under control of an XSL stylesheet that is generated from an ASP file. This custom stylesheet applies templates only to those nodes of the parsed comprehensive document that have data concerning the user's selected sports.

The line of code in Example 41-10 comes from the ASP file that generates the XSL stylesheet. Recall that an XSL stylesheet is itself an XML document, and that XSL components are therefore elements.

Example 41-10. ASP script to generate XSL filtering element

```
<xsl:for-each select="root/sport<%=sMySports%>">
```

When the ASP file executes it substitutes the user's selected value into the XSL pattern. For example, `[@name='NBA']` might be inserted in place of `<%=sMySports%>`. The script would then generate the XSL filtering element shown in Example 41-11.

Example 41-11. XSL filtering element generated by the ASP script in Example 41-10

```
<xsl:for-each select="root/sport[@name='NBA']">
```

The generated XSL stylesheet element selects only those elements in the statistics document that match the pattern `root/sport[@name='NBA']`. Therefore, MLB and NFL statistics and others that don't concern basketball will be ignored. Only the statistics that fit the criteria selected by the user will be displayed.

It is important to note that when an ASP file generates an XSL stylesheet or other XML document, only the generated XML is seen by the parser. All of the ASP code completes execution before the XML or XSL is parsed.

41.4 | Rendering XML documents as speech

An interesting application of XSL in the *XML Sports Demo* produces a sort of *social interface* by using the IE5 agent feature. The demo allows a user not only to view the statistics of interest, but to have them read aloud by the agent of his choice.

The same XML that is rendered as HTML for viewing is transformed under control of an XSL stylesheet into simple lines of text. As in Example 41-10, the XSL stylesheet itself is generated from an ASP file. The generated stylesheet is shown in Example 41-12.

Example 41-12. XSL stylesheet to render simple text for speech synthesis

```
<xsl:stylesheet xmlns:xsl="uri:xsl">
  <xsl:template match="/">
    <xsl:for-each select="root/sport[@name='NBA' $or$ 'MLB']">
    <!-- Write a different bit for each sport -->
      <xsl:if match="root/sport[@name='NBA']">
        In hoops:
  </xsl:if>
  <xsl:if match="root/sport[@name='MLB']">
    Baseball action this week saw:
  </xsl:if>
  <xsl:if match="root/sport[@name='NFL']">
    On the gridiron:
  </xsl:if>
  <xsl:for-each select=
    "game[hometeam/name='Rangers' $or$ awayteam/name='Rangers']"
  >
    The <xsl:value-of select="hometeam/name" /> played the
      <xsl:value-of select="awayteam/name" />.
    The score was <xsl:value-of select="hometeam/name" />
      <xsl:value-of select="hometeam/score" />,
    the <xsl:value-of select="awayteam/name" />
      <xsl:value-of select="awayteam/score" />.
  </xsl:for-each>
    </xsl:for-each>
  </xsl:template>
</xsl:stylesheet>
```

The stylesheet in Example 41-12 could generate the text in Example 41-13, which would then be passed to a text-to-speech engine to generate an audible presentation.

Example 41-13. Text to be passed to the agent's text-to-speech engine

```
Baseball action this week saw: The Rangers played the
Tigers. The score was Rangers 5 the Tigers 1.
```

Although the transformation of XML to plain text is a relatively simple one, it serves to illustrate an important way to think about utilizing XSL. XSL is not simply a language for rendering XML as HTML. XSL is a means of processing XML documents, not just for traditional rendition, but for data processing and alternative renditions as well.

41.5 | Conclusion

The *XML Sports Demo* demonstrates techniques of website construction using the XML support in *Microsoft Internet Explorer 5*. In particular, it illustrates uses of XSL that go beyond merely generating HTML renditions. The demo reveals real-world issues related to managing very large data collections, navigation among multiple documents, data processing, and audio rendition. These considerations affect the design of optimal stylesheets, and ultimately affect user satisfaction with your website.

Navigation

- Extended linking
- Topic maps tutorial
- Distributed programming with topic maps

Part Eleven

There are only two ways to get there from here: go directly, or go someplace else and then go there.

Or to put it in terms of Web navigation, you can either type in a URL, or keep clicking on links until you reach your destination.

The second kind of navigation is called *link traversal*; the first is a form of query ("Find the Web page whose URL is ..."). Either can operate in physical space, topical (information) space, or a mix.

As practiced on the Web today, both kinds are primitive. The direct access query uses physical addresses (URLs), as do hyperlink anchors. Although the links themselves represent topical associations, there is no hint of the *reason* why things might be linked. Of course there are search engines that operate in topical space, but they are totally undisciplined and routinely return thousands of irrelevant pages.

This part shows how XML can be used today to cure these problems. Extended linking supports meaningful relationships. And topic maps can organize the Web's information space so you can use topical querying and addressing and never get lost.

In fact, we'll see that you can use topic maps to organize *any* information space – even integrating your applications!

Extended linking

Application Discussion

- Extended linking defined
- XLink applications
- XPointers
- Strong link typing

Sponsor: DataChannel, Inc., http://www.datachannel.com

Contributing expert: Steven R. Newcomb of TechnoTeacher, Inc., http://www.techno.com, co-editor of the HyTime International Standard (ISO/IEC 10744)

42

Extended linking and strong link typing will let the Web traverse to locations where it has never been. Those concepts are explained simply and clearly in this chapter.

Future generations of Web browsers and editors will reduce the effort required to keep our personal affairs organized and our corporate memories up to the minute. The productivity of many kinds of work will be enhanced, and in many ways. It's all going to happen basically because of two simple enhancements to the Web paradigm.

The W3C's draft XLink "extended link" facility proposes to give all of us the ability to annotate documents, and to share those annotations with others, even when we cannot alter the documents we are annotating. In other words, we won't have to change a document in order to supply it with our own annotations – annotations that a browser can make appear as though they were written right into the annotated document.

42.1 | The shop notes application

As an example, consider a technician's set of online maintenance manuals. These are electronic books that the technician is not (and should not be) authorized to change. With the Web's existing HTML hyperlinks, the technician cannot write a note in a manual that can take future readers of that manual, including himself, to his annotations. Nor can the technician's annotations be displayed in their proper context – the parts of the manual that they are about.

42.1.1 *What is extended linking?*

By using *extended linking*, when the technician makes an annotation, he does so purely by editing his own document; no change is made to the read-only manual document that he is annotating.

The big difference between "extended" linking and present-day HTML linking is this. With an HTML (or "simple") link, traversal can only begin at the place where the link is; traversal cannot begin at the other end. With an "extended" link, however, you can click on any of the link's anchors, and traverse to any other anchor, regardless of where the link happens to be.

Tip   Extended linking allows the starting anchor of a link to be different from the link itself. Instead of HTML's "A" tagged element that is linked to one other element, you can have (say) an "L" tag that links two or more other elements to one another.

A simple link (top of Figure 42-1) is always embedded ("inline") in (for example) the InstallLog text from which it provides traversal; the link cannot be traversed by starting at the target anchor (for example, the Installation procedure document).

An extended link (bottom of Figure 42-1) can appear in a separate document, and provide traversal between the corresponding parts of two other documents: for example, the technician's shop notes document ("TechLog") and the read-only installation manual. Because the location of this particular link is not the same as any of its anchors, it is said to be "out-of-line" (not embedded).

In our example, an annotation takes the form of just such an extended link element.

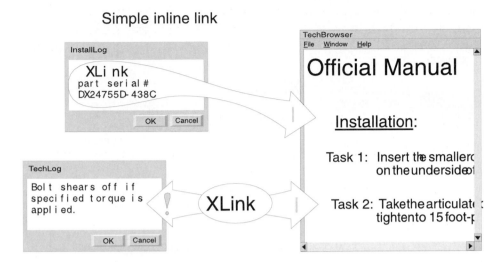

Figure 42-1   Simple vs. extended linking.

42.1.2 *Displaying extended links*

One way to realize the benefits of extended links is to display an icon at each anchor that indicates something about the other anchor. (The mechanism that supports this is discussed in greater detail under "Strong link typing", below.)

For example, as shown in Figure 42-2, a reader of the installation manual on the right will know that, if he clicks on the exclamation point displayed near Task 2, he will see a shop note about that task. If he clicks on the pound sign, he will be shown the serial number of a part that was installed according to the procedure, recorded in an "InstallLog" document.

Similarly, a reader of the annotation in the shop notes document ("TechLog") will know that clicking on the "I" icon will bring him to the installation instruction that the annotation discusses.

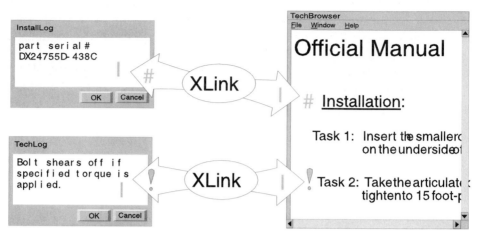

Figure 42-2   The exclamation point icon near Task 2 indicates that a shop note is available.

42.1.3 *Notes survive to new versions of manuals*

The technician's annotations – his "shop notes" – accumulate over time, and they represent a valuable asset that must be maintained. If the technician were to write shop notes inside each manual, when a new version of a manual is received it would be a chore to copy annotations from the old manual to the new manual.

With extended linking, however, the annotations are not in the old version; they are in a separate document. Therefore, the shop notes don't disappear when an annotated manual is replaced by a newer version.

That is because each link is equipped with "pointers" – pieces of information that can tell a browser where (for example) clickable icons should be rendered that indicate the availability of an annotation. Each such "XPointer" (as it is called) can point at anything in any XML document.

In our technician's shop, when a manual is replaced by a new version, the XPointers keep on working, even with the new manual, so the new manual is instantly and automatically equipped with the old manual's annotations.

In most cases, the XPointers don't have to be changed, because they continue to point at the right things, even in the new manual. If, because of differences between the old and new versions of the manual, some XPointers in the shop notes don't still point at the right things (or perhaps have nothing to point at any more), certain techniques can be used to detect each such situation. By dealing with these problem spots, the maintainers of the shop notes can minimize their efforts.

Moreover, XPointers and extended links enhance the potential for achieving high levels of quality and consistency, even when there are voluminous shop notes that annotate many manuals.

42.1.4 *Vendors can use the notes*

Some shop notes may also have value to the vendors of the manuals they annotate; they may beneficially influence subsequent versions of the manual. An editor of the manual can load (i.e., make his browser aware of) all the shop notes of many repair shops; this has the effect of populating the manual with icons representing the annotations of all the shops. The most common trouble spots in the manual will be made obvious by the crowds of annotation icons that they appear to have accumulated (Figure 42-3).

The fact that the shop notes take the form of interchangeable XML documents that use standardized extended links makes the task of sharing internal shop notes with manual vendors as easy as sending them any other kind of file. There is no need to extract them from some other resource, or to format them in such a way that they can be understood by their recipients. They are ready to work just as they are, in the tradition of SGML, HyTime, HTML, and now XML.

42.2 | Other applications of extended linking

The above "shop notes" example is just a sample of the kinds of enhancements that extended linking will bring to our interactions with information resources. Some of the broader implications are a bit more startling.

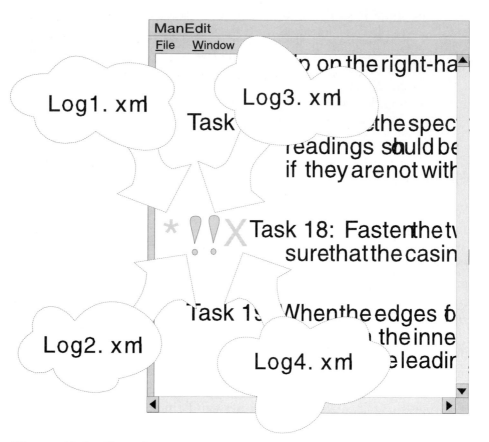

Figure 42-3   Task 18 evidently prompted three kinds of annotations in four different shop logs.

42.2.1 *Public resource communities of interest*

For example, many web sites today contain HTML links to public resources. One is the U.S. Government's online service for translating any U.S. postal code into its corresponding Congressional district and the name of its current incumbent Representative (http://www.house.gov/zip/ZIP2Rep.html).

However, if those HTML links were to become XLink extended links, an XLink-enabled browser could render this U.S. government Web page in such a way as to add to it a catalog of the activists and lobbying organizations who refer readers of their websites to this particular U.S. government resource. The "marketplace of ideas" represented by the aggregate of such organizations is thus revealed in a new and interesting way.

42.2.2 *Guidance documents*

Another startling possibility is the association of browser-controlling metadata with any and all Web resources.

In this scenario, a document of annotations (or a set of such documents) can be a user's companion during excursions on the Web. These annotations might make suggestions to users as to where to find more recent material, or they might even take control of the browser's link traversal ability in order to protect children from disturbing material.

While the latter XLink-enabled possibility may sound inimical to the freedom of speech, in fact it enhances liberty. It provides a new public medium for free speech: documents that censor the Web and/or otherwise provide guidance to Web travelers in the form of annotations that appear only in their designated contexts.

Of course, no adult is required to use any such guidance document, just as no one is required to read any particular book, but it's easy to predict that many will pay for the privilege of using many kinds of such "guidance documents".

More importantly, everyone will have the tools to write such guidance documents, so the technical ability to provide guidance (and, yes, even to provide censorship services) will be widely distributed, rather than being dangerously concentrated in a few generalized rating services. The creation and maintenance of guidance documents may well become a thriving cottage industry. Anyone can be a critic.

In the case of electronic commerce, it's easy to imagine that vendors will attempt to provide guidance documents designed to annotate the online sales catalogs of their competitors. In response, some providers of online sales catalogs will take steps to render the pointers in these kinds of guidance documents invalid and unmaintainable.

Regardless of all this, the overall impact on electronic commerce will certainly be positive; increasing the meaningful interconnectedness of the Web will help more people find exactly what they're looking for.

And it may turn out to be a mistake, in many cases, for catalog owners to attempt to render the pointers used to annotate their catalogs invalid, because similar pointers could be used, for example, by impartial consumer testing organizations to attach "best buy" recommendations to certain products. The guidance documents of consumer testing organizations will probably be quite popular, and well worth the cost of using them.

42.2.3 *Computer-augmented memory*

Extended linking has the potential to make radical improvements in our ability to keep track of what we are doing. Someday, we can expect to automatically annotate each piece of information we work with in such a way that, in effect, it refers future readers to the work we did with respect to it.

In other words, practically everything we do can be usefully seen as an annotation of one or more other pieces of work. If everything we do is, in some sense, an annotation of one or more other things, everything we do can all be found far more easily, starting from any piece of work anywhere in the "chain" (or, more likely, "tree" or "graph") of relevant information.

This is because extended linking allows all links to be bidirectional. (Or, rather, "n-directional", to account for extended links with more than two ends.) All of the connections among our affairs can then be tracked more or less automatically, so that each of us can enjoy a radical reduction in filing, cross-indexing, and other organizational chores, and with vastly increased ability to find what we're looking for quickly and easily.

Obviously, this same idea is even more significant in the realm of corporate memory. Even with today's behemoth enterprise integration technologies, it's still too hard to figure out what has happened, who is doing what, how various plans and projects are going to integrate, and where the relevant paperwork can be found.

Going a step further, there is an International Standard (ISO/IEC 13250) that seeks to exploit extended linking in such a way as to create living, easily explored and maintained "topic maps" of sets of information resources (see Chapter 43, "Topic maps: Knowledge navigation aids", on page 606). This goal sounds almost insanely ambitious, but extended linking, in combination with strong link typing (see below), should make it practical and achievable.

The topic maps paradigm elegantly solves consistency and usability problems faced by people who must collaborate in developing indexes and glossaries, or who must merge multiple indexes into master indexes. When applied to the Web, topic maps are analogous to the Global Positioning System provided by earth-orbiting satellites, allowing Web users to determine their current locations in a multidimensional "topic space".

42.2.4 *Intellectual property management*

The advent of extended linking also offers interesting new possibilities for the management and exploitation of intellectual property.

For example, metadata regarding the licensing policies of owners of Web resources could be associated with those resources by means of extended links. Such metadata could be changed when the resources are sold or licensed, without requiring any changes to the assets themselves.

This method greatly reduces the likelihood of inadvertent damage to the assets, and greatly increases the ease with which ownership and/or management policies can change. There is already an official, internationally-ratified ISO standard for using extended linking for exactly this purpose (see `http://www.ornl.gov/sgml/wg8/document/n1920/html/clause-6.7.html#clause-6.7.3`).

Such activity policies, and the means by which they are associated with online assets, could well become a source of private law that will strongly influence the development of intelligent agents (see `http://www.hytime.org/papers/higgins1.html`).

42.3 | Strong link typing

With the XLink extended link facility, there is no limit to the number of links that can be traversed from a single point in a single document. Many different documents can contain links to the very same anchor, with the result that, theoretically, at least, an unlimited number of traversals are possible, starting from a single point. In addition, there are no limits on the kinds of annotations that can be made, nor on the purposes to which such annotations may be put.

Therefore, it makes sense to provide some easy way to sort the annotations (i.e., the links) into categories. For example, some kinds of annotations will be made in order to provide "metadata" about the document, and these will often take effect in some way other than by rendering an icon on the display screen. Some kinds of annotations are interesting only for specialized purposes.

42.3.1 *Hiding the installation log*

Going back to our earlier example, the technician can create an annotation that indicates the serial number of a new part that he installed in accordance with a particular maintenance procedure. The fact that such an annotation is available would be of interest only to someone who was auditing the installation of parts; it probably wouldn't appear even to the technician, despite the fact that it was he who created the annotation.

The technician's installation log annotation can be hidden from most people because it is "strongly typed": it has been clearly and unambiguously labeled as to its intended meaning and purpose, so all browsers can see what kind of link it is. In effect, the link says, "I am a Part-Installation-Log-Entry". People who aren't interested in part installation records can arrange for their browsers to hide them.

42.3.2 *Why do we need strong link typing?*

People may still choose to be made aware of other kinds of annotations made by our technician. For example, other technicians may wish to read our technician's accounts of any special situations that he has experienced when attempting to follow a particular instruction, or about successful and unsuccessful experiments with substitute parts.

The notion of "strong link typing" is virtually absent from HTML links. Basically, in HTML, the browser software knows where the user can go, but not why the author of the document being browsed thought the user might like to go there. The human reader can usually divine something from the context about the material that will be shown if the "anchor" hyperlink is traversed, but the browser itself is basically unable to help the user decide whether to click or not to click, so it can't hide any available traversals.

To be able to hide the availability of unwanted kinds of links can save a lot of time and effort. So the draft W3C XLink recommendation also provides for the addition of strong typing features, not only to extended links, but also to the "simple" links that closely resemble the familiar HTML "anchor" (<a>) element. Thus, browsers can start supporting strong link typing promptly, even before they can handle extended linking.

42.3.3 *Anchor role identification*

The notion of strong link typing includes the notion of "anchor role" designation.

For example, the simple link at the top of Figure 42-1 characterizes its target anchor as an installation instruction; in the diagram, this is indicated by the "I" icon in the arrowhead. Similarly, the extended link at the bottom of Figure 42-1 characterizes one of its anchors as a shop note (the exclamation point) and the other anchor as an installation instruction (another "I" arrowhead).

Thus, a link can do more than just identify itself by saying, for example, "I am a Part Installation Log Entry". It can also specify which of its anchors fulfill which roles in the relationship it expresses.

For example, our Part Installation Log Entry link can say, in effect, "I signify that part [pointer to entry in parts catalog or inventory record] was installed in [pointer to information that identifies the unit being maintained] in accordance with maintenance directive [XPointer to instruction in manual]".

In other words, the log entry link is a three-ended link whose anchor roles might be named "replacement-part" (indicated with a "#" icon), "maintained-unit" ("@" icon), and "maintenance-directive" ("I" icon) (Figure 42-4).

The fact that an anchor plays some specific role in a relationship often determines whether the relationship is interesting or even relevant in a given application context.

42.4 | Conclusion

It is easy to see that the impact of extended linking will be significant, and that technical workers and electronic commerce will be early beneficiaries. Extended linking will enhance the helpfulness and usefulness of the Web environment. The burden of many kinds of paperwork will be very substantially mitigated.

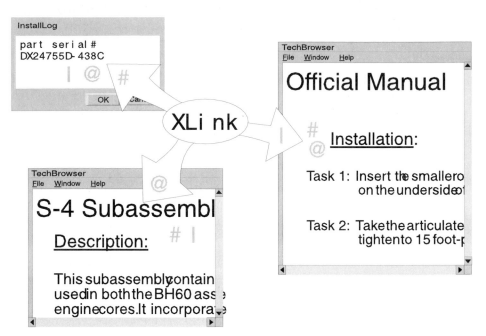

Figure 42-4   Link with two traversal possibilities at each anchor, distinguishable because of anchor role identification.

On the horizon, there appears to be serious potential for significant improvements in the availability of all kinds of knowledge, due to the possibility of creating and interchanging topic maps. Intellectual property management, and the Web-based utilization of intellectual property, will become easier and more orderly.

All of these benefits, and probably many more, emanate from two very simple enhancements of the Web paradigm in the draft XLink and XPointers recommendations of the World Wide Web Consortium:

- Allowing the starting anchor of a link to be different from the link itself; and

■ Strong link typing, in which links plainly exhibit the kind of relationship they represent, and the roles their anchors play in that relationship.

Tip   *For more on XLink, see Chapter 57, "XML Linking Language (XLink)", on page 874. The text of the XLink and XPointer drafts are on the CD-ROM.*

Topic maps: Knowledge navigation aids

Friendly Tutorial

- Topic maps in a nutshell
- Indexes, glossaries, and thesauri
- Topic map applications
- Tools for topic maps

Sponsor: XCare.net, http://www.ontopia.net

Contributing experts: Hans Holger Rath and Steve Pepper, of the ISO topic map standards group (ISO/IEC JTC1/SC34/WG3)

Chapter

43

True story: Charles was searching an online shopping site for a CD by the doo-wop greats, the Flamingos. He was offered a pink neon sculpture. That site needs topic maps! This chapter explains why, and might lead you to think that yours does too.

Ever want to fire your Web search engine for bringing you thousands of useless pages? Or to navigate from one Web page to another on the same subject when there is no link between them? Then you want topic maps.

When you ask your Web browser to search for "Mozart", that composer is the "topic" of your search and you hope to find Web pages that are in some way devoted to it. The browser might actually find such pages, but they will probably be lost among the thousands of pages in which "Mozart" is simply a word that occurs in passing and in no way the main topic of the page.

Similarly, when you look up "Mozart" in the index of a book, you hope to find the pages whose topic is Mozart.

So topics are a familiar concept, one that we work with all the time. What then are topic maps and why do we need them?

Well, suppose you want to find out about operas composed by German composers that were influenced by Mozart. There is no way to formulate such a query in a Web search engine. You can try to use a set of relevant keywords such as "opera + Germany + composer + Mozart", but you are guaranteed to get an enormous number of useless hits. You are also guaranteed to miss some of the most interesting pages. More importantly, even if the search were extremely accurate, you would still have to wade through all the resulting documents simply to find the names of the works you are interested in.

How much easier if you could simply query your index for all *operas* "written by" *composers* associated with *Germany* ("born in" or "lived in") and with *Mozart* ("influenced by")!

The key difference between the two approaches is that the former simply uses a full text index built from the raw content of a set of information resources. The latter, however, utilizes an index that encapsulates the structure of the underlying knowledge.

The latter solution is actually an example of a *topic map*; that is, a structured network of hyperlinks above an information pool. Each node in the network represents a named topic (e.g. Germany, Mozart, Wagner). The links connecting the nodes express the associations between the nodes (e.g. written by, lived in, influenced by).

From this it should be clear that indexes are actually very simple forms of topic maps. So, too, are glossaries and thesauri. This chapter will explain the basic concepts of topic maps, how they relate to the kinds of navigational aids we are already familiar with, what additional benefits they provide, and how to create and use them. We'll also look at some applications and consider requirements for topic map tools.

43.1 | Topic maps in a nutshell

A topic map is an XML or SGML document whose element types represent topics, occurrences of topics, and associations between topics. The document conforms to the International Standard ISO/IEC 13250, which also standardizes the conceptual model for topic maps.

The key concepts are:

- topic and topic type
- topic occurrence and occurrence role
- topic association and association type

Other concepts, which extend the expressive power of the topic map model, are:

- scope
- public subject
- facets

43.1.1 *Topic and topic type*

In the context of an encyclopedia, a *topic* might represent subjects such as "Germany", "Bavaria", "Munich", the king "Ludwig II", or the opera "Lohengrin" by the composer "Richard Wagner": anything that might have an entry (or indeed a mention) in the encyclopedia.

The subject represented by a topic can be any "thing" whatsoever – a person, an entity, a concept, really *anything*, regardless of whether it exists or has any other specific characteristics, about which anything whatsoever may be asserted by any means whatsoever. Exactly what one chooses to regard as topics in any particular application will vary according to the needs of the application, the nature of the information, and the uses to which the topic map will be put.

A topic can have a number of characteristics. First of all, it can have a *name* – or more than one. The standard provides an element form for *topic name* which consists of at least one *base name*, and optional *display* and *sort* names.

A topic also has a *topic type* – or perhaps multiple topic types. Thus, Germany would be a topic of type "country", Bavaria a topic of type "state", Munich and Würzburg topics of type "city", Ludwig II a topic of type "king", etc. In other words, topic types express typical *class-instance* relationships or the *is a* relation (see Figure 43-1).

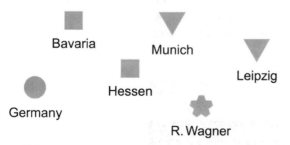

Figure 43-1   Topic names and types (represented by different symbols)

Topic types are themselves defined as topics. In order to use them for typing, you have to explicitly declare "country", "state", "city", etc. as topics in your topic map, and this then allows you to say more about them using the topic map model itself.

43.1.2 *Topic occurrence and occurrence role*

A topic can have one or more *occurrences*. An occurrence of a topic is a link to an information resource (or more than one) that is deemed to be somehow relevant to the subject that the topic represents. It could be an article about the topic in an encyclopedia, a picture or video depicting the topic, a simple mention of the topic in the context of something else, a commentary on the topic, or any of a host of other forms in which an information resource might have some relevance to a given subject.

Such resources are generally outside the topic map document itself, and they are "pointed at" using whatever addressing mechanisms the system supports, typically XPointer or HyTime.

Occurrences may be of any number of different types (we gave the examples of "article", "illustration", "mention" and "commentary" above). Such distinctions are supported in the standard by the concept of the *occurrence role* (see Figure 43-2). As with topic types, occurrence roles are themselves formally considered to be topics, although the actual occurrences are not.

43.1.3 *Indexes and glossaries*

As described so far, topics and occurrences provide a model for explicitly stating which subjects a pool of information pertains to and how. That is basically what an index also does.

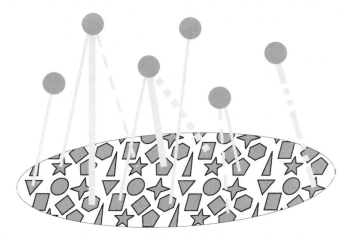

Figure 43-2   Occurrences of topics in an information pool and their various occurrence roles (represented by different line types).

In Example 43-1, the index terms are topics and the page numbers are their occurrences.

Example 43-1. An index is a simple form of topic map.

Germany 17, 77
Mozart 72
Wagner 49
Würzburg 22

But topic maps offer more. Through the concept of *occurrence roles*, they generalize and extend the conventions used to distinguish different kinds of references from one another.

In Example 43-2 the use of different typefaces indicates different *roles* played by the occurrences on pages 17 and 77 (perhaps a *main description* and a *mention*).

Example 43-2. An index with occurrence roles

Germany **17**, 77

Some books contain more than one index (index of names, index of places, etc.). *Topic types* provide the same facility, but extend it in several directions to enable the creation of multiple, dynamic, user-controlled indexes organized as taxonomic hierarchies.

Glossaries, too, can be implemented using just the bare bones of the topic map standard that has been described so far. Like an index, a glossary is also a set of topics and their occurrences, ordered by topic name. Here, though, the occurrence role is "definition".

Example 43-3. A glossary is a topic map.

Federal Republic of Germany: see *Germany.*

...

Germany: Federal republic in the northern part of central Europe, population (1998) approx. 82 million.

...

Würzburg: City in Bavaria, Germany on the river Main, 90 km south-east of Frankfurt. 128.000 inhabitants (1998).

Note that "Federal Republic of Germany" does not have a definition. It is just another topic name for the topic that also has the name "Germany", and in this map there can be only one definition per topic.

The definitions in Example 43-3 are instances of just one kind of occurrence – those that play the role of "definition". With a topic map it is easy to create and maintain much more complex glossaries than this; for example, ones that use multiple kinds of definitions (perhaps suited to different kinds of users).

43.1.4 *Topic association and association type*

Topic maps don't stop here, however. They go far beyond just providing a mechanism for creating more robust and powerful indexes and glossaries. The key to their true potential lies in their ability to model *relationships* between topics, and for this the topic map standard provides a construct called the *topic association*.

A topic association is (formally) a link element that asserts a relationship between two or more topics. Examples might be as follows:

- Munich *is in* Bavaria.
- Bavaria *is in* Germany.
- Wagner was *born in* Leipzig.
- Lohengrin was *composed by* Wagner.
- Wagner was *influenced by* Mozart.

43.1.4.1   Association role

Just as topics can be grouped according to type (country, state, city, etc.) and occurrences according to role (definition, article, illustration, commentary, etc.), so too can associations between topics be grouped according to their type. The *association types* of the five relationships in the list above are "is in", "born in", "composed by" and "influenced by" (see Figure 43-3). As with most other constructs, association types are themselves regarded as topics.

Each topic that participates in an association has a corresponding *association role* which states the role played by that topic in the association. In the case of the relationship "Wagner was born in Leipzig" those roles might be "person" and "birthplace"; for "Lohengrin was written by Wagner" they might be "opera" and "composer".

Like topic types, association roles must be declared as topics in order to be used.

43.1.4.2   Association topology

In the topic map model, associations do not have a direction; that is, they are not one-way (or "unilateral"). The "born in" relationship between Wagner and Leipzig implies what might be called a "fostered" relationship between the city and the composer ("Leipzig fostered Wagner"), and the "composed by" relationship between Lohengrin and Wagner is also a "composed" relationship between the composer and his opera ("Wagner composed Lohengrin").

Sometimes associations are *symmetrical*, in the sense that the nature of the relationship is the same whichever way you look at it. For example, the corollary of "Wagner was a friend of Ludwig II" would be that "Ludwig II was a friend of Wagner". Sometimes the association roles in such symmetrical relationships are the same (as in this case: "friend" and "friend"), sometimes they are different (as in the case of the "husband" and "wife" roles in a "married to" relationship).

Other association types, such as those that express superclass/subclass and some part/whole relationships, are *transitive*: If we say that Munich is in Bavaria, and that Bavaria is in Germany, we have implicitly asserted that Munich is in Germany and any topic map search engine should be able to draw the necessary conclusions without the need for making the assertion explicitly. Much of the real power of topic maps results from using transitive relations between topics, types, and roles for querying the map.

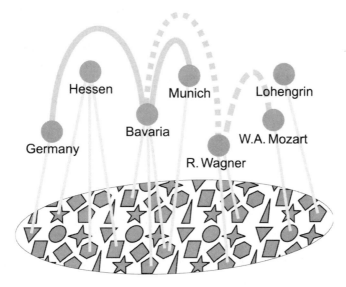

Figure 43-3   Associations of various types between topics (represented by different line types)

43.1.5 *Thesauri and semantic networks*

Typed topic associations extend the power of topic maps to the modeling of thesauri and other networks of information and knowledge.

A *thesaurus* is a network of interrelated terms (along with their definitions, examples, or whatever) within a particular domain. There exist various standards for thesauri that predefine relationship types, such as "broader term", "narrower term", "used for", and "related term", all of which correspond directly to association types in a topic map. Other thesaurus constructs, such as "source", "definition", and "scope note" would be modeled as occurrence roles in a topic map.

One advantage of applying the topic map model to thesauri is that it becomes possible to create hierarchies of association types that extend the thesaurus schema without deviating from accepted standards (for example, by subclassing "used for" as "synonymous for", "abbreviation for", and "acronym for"). Further advantages would be gained from using the facilities for scoping, filtering and merging described in the next three sections.

"Semantic networks", "associative networks" and "knowledge" (or "conceptual") "maps" are terms used within the fields of semantics and artificial intelligence to describe various models for representing knowledge structures within a computer. Many of these already correspond closely to the topic/association model. Adding the topic/occurrence axis provides a means for "bridging the gap" between these fields and the field of information management, thereby establishing a basis for true knowledge management.

43.1.6 *Scope*

When I refer to "Paris", you know immediately that I am talking about the capital city of France. Or do you? How do you know that I'm not talking about the town of the same name in Texas or the hero of Troy? Presumably because you are assuming a *scope* set by some form of context, whether it be a particular subject area under discussion or a generally accepted default.

The concept of scope is important for avoiding ambiguities like this and for increasing the precision with which assertions can be made. In topic maps, any assignment of a characteristic to a topic, be it a name, an occurrence or a role in an association, is considered to be valid within certain limits, which may or may not be specified explicitly. The limit of validity of such an assignment is called its *scope*; scope is defined in terms of *themes*, and themes are modeled as topics.

So, in topic maps where the scope is defined by the themes "France", "USA", and "Greek mythology", the name "Paris" could be used unambiguously. Similarly the association expressing the assertion that "Leipzig *is in* East Germany" could be qualified by giving it the scope "1949-90".

43.1.7 *Public subject*

Sometimes the same subject is represented by more than one topic. This can be the case when two topic maps are merged. In such a situation it is necessary to have some way of establishing the identity between seemingly disparate topics.

This can be done in either of two ways:

■ Explicitly, by specifying *identity attributes* of the topic elements that address the same *public subject;* or

■ Implicitly, through the *topic naming constraint*, which states that any topics that have the same name in the same scope refer to the same subject.

43.1.8 *Facets*

The final feature of the topic map standard to be considered in this introduction is the concept of the *facet.* Facets basically provide a mechanism for assigning property-value pairs to information resources. A facet is simply a property (such as "language" or "security level"); its values are called *facet values.* Facets are typically used for applying metadata which can then be used for filtering the information resources.

43.2 | Applications of topic maps

We will consider two applications. They both involve publishing, but topic maps have broad applicability in other areas as well.

43.2.1 *Reference work publishing*

In the age of digital information all commercial publishers face major new challenges, but perhaps none more so than publishers of reference works, especially encyclopedias and dictionaries. Not only has the advent of the World Wide Web finally forced all such publishers to think seriously about moving into electronic publishing; it has also turned out to be perhaps their biggest and most threatening competitor.

The reason for this, of course, is that the raw material from which reference works are fashioned consists for the most part of "hard facts" that cannot be owned. The knowledge that Wagner was born in Leipzig or that the population of Germany is about 82 million cannot be copyrighted. Almost every piece of information to be found in any modern, commercial encyclopedia can be found somewhere on the Internet for free. So how is a reference work publisher to compete?

43.2.1.1   Adding value

Paradoxically, the answer lies in the fact that most users today do not need more information – if anything, they need less, because they are already drowning in enormous quantities of it. At the very least, they need the ability to be able to find their way to relevant information as quickly as possible and to be able to filter out the "noise" created by all the information for which they have no use. They also need to be able to trust the information they receive, to know that it is reliable and up-to-date. Thus, two of the most important "value-adds" that commercial publishers can provide are

- tools and methods for finding the required information in a timely manner; and
- the confidence that the information so found can be trusted.

Topic maps can greatly assist the discovery of relevant information. In addition, the topic paradigm turns out to provide an *organizing principle* for many kinds of information that helps ensure its timeliness and accuracy.

43.2.1.2   A typical topic map

Encyclopedia articles are – at a very abstract level – about persons, geographical objects, history, culture, and science. These are the main *topic types*. Existing classification systems list further subclasses of these topic types, such as:

- historic person (monarch [emperor, king, queen], politician, [president, chancellor], explorer), artists (writer [novelist, poet], painter, sculptor, composer, musician), scientists (mathematician, physicist, chemist, biologist, physician);

■ country, state, landscape, city/town, river, mountain, island.

The *occurrence roles* point to the resources of an encyclopedia publisher. Typical data assets are articles, definitions, mentions of the topic in an article, pictures/images, audio, and video clips.

Even more interesting (because of the value added to the publication) are the *association types* that are used to structure the mass of cross-references normally found in such works. Obvious examples are: ruled over, conquered, painted, composed, wrote, played, discovered, invented, parent of, child of, located in, larger than, took place, before, after, discovered by, conquered by, founded by, invented by, etc.

Some of these are simply different names for the same association type viewed from different perspectives (e.g. conquered/conquered by, parent of/child of). Others exhibit the important property of transitivity (e.g. located in, larger than).

It is a good idea to identify transitive relationships like these because the topic map engine can use this information to generate more intelligent answers to the queries of the user.

43.2.2 *Technical documentation*

Technical documentation for a complex product could consist of thousands of pages, or megabytes of textual data. Corporate publishers have to manage and publish the documentation for different product versions and product variants. More ambitious corporate publishers add reader-related information to the publications ("skill level" is the typical example) or publish different views of the same material ("Overview", "Reference Manual", "Questions and Answers", etc.).

Versions, variants, and views require a more complex organization of the text than the sequential ordering of printed book. XML alone does not meet these requirements; publishers must also change the information management paradigm.

43.2.2.1   Text modules

Modularization of the text is the first step towards an appropriate solution. The existing chapter-section-subject structure of book-oriented technical documentation is split up into hundreds or thousands of separate text modules (information objects). The modules consist of "self-contained" text about a given subject (e.g. "Installation"). Hyperlinks connect the modules.

Hierarchical subject codes – assigned as metadata – allow quick access when querying the database containing the modules.

These two characteristics (self-contained text, hierarchical subject codes) indicate a class of technical documentation that is an ideal candidate for a topic map application.

43.2.2.2   A typical topic map

The identification of *topic types* can be based on the subject code classification. If this is not available, the technical design of the product or semantic markup in the documentation will give the necessary hints. In software documentation for example, the topic types might consist of "program block", "command group", "command", "macro", "parameter", "error", etc.

The *occurrence roles* would relate to existing modularized material. Data modules, functional diagrams, tables, screen shots, error messages, and syntax examples are among the possibilities.

Finally, *association types* can be derived from knowledge of the relationships between the topic types already identified: "command group A *consists of* commands X, Y, and Z", "command X *has parameters* P and Q", etc.

43.3 | Tool support for topic maps

Possibilities for tool support exist at each phase of the topic map life cycle.

43.3.1   *Topic map design*

The design of topic maps is an incremental process. The definition of the various types and roles and sub-/super-classes of them should be done under the control of a topic map design tool. Doing so will help ensure the consistency of the map.

Outside the scope of the topic map standard, but nevertheless very useful, are constraining conditions that can drive consistency checks. They make it possible to check whether transitive associations are used correctly, whether the types of topics in an association correspond to the respective association roles, etc.

Another part of the topic map design is the generation of all the topics, associations, and occurrences. In a large application these can be numbered in the thousands or even millions. The design tool has to offer an easy access to all these objects of the map.

As in a content management system, user access rights play an important role in a topic map design tool. Permission for creating, changing, and deleting parts of the map could be assigned to different user groups with different responsibilities, and the system has to take care that these rules are enforced.

43.3.2 *Creation and maintenance*

The boundary between the design and the creation of a topic map is fluid. Only the initial design will distinguish the declaration of types and roles on the one hand, and the topics, associations, and occurrences on the other. During the maintenance of the map these will be done concurrently – maybe by different user groups.

The editors (designer, author) of the topic map need a visualization tool besides the consistency checker. The visualization tool produces a rendition of the map that is similar to the one the end-users will see. The querying possibilities should also be similar.

The initial creation of the map out of an existing information pool can probably be supported by an automatic rule-based process. This process can be compared to the conversion of word processor files to XML abstractions. Both add structure to "flat" data.

A conversion for topic maps takes as its input information objects in which the topics and associations exist only implicitly, and produces a linked and structured knowledge base as output.

43.3.3 *Exchange of topic maps*

The publication of topic maps will be done electronically, since paper-based presentations of any but the simplest of topic maps are to all intents and purposes impossible. The topic map document architecture defined in the standard is the interface between topic map design and creation tools, and the topic map browser – the rendition and navigation tool of the end-user.

Note that this interchange standard does not address application-specific semantics such as the "association topology" properties described earlier. Eventual de facto acceptance of such semantics may cause them to be supported by topic map tools.

43.3.4 *Navigating a map*

There are two ways to navigate a topic map: by traversing the links or by directly addressing the nodes through queries.

Traversal of a large link network – possibly consisting of millions of nodes and links – requires an easy-to-use and easy-to-understand user interface. Very sophisticated colorful graphical user interfaces with nodes and edges that move in accordance with physical laws (like magnetism or gravity) might be eye-catchers.

However, a familiar interface like a Web search engine might prove to be practical. Figure 43-4, for example, shows Ontopia's *Atlas Navigator*, which is built on top of its *Atlas Topic Map Engine*. The left pane allows the user to navigate within the topic map. By clicking on an occurrence, he can see the appropriate resource presented in the right pane (in this case, an opera synopsis).

Querying a topic map requires a query language covering the concepts of the topic map standard and desirable application-specific semantics (associations, transitivity). The user needs additional support when defining a query – the information available in the map can be offered to the user by the query interface, e.g. in a menu-like style.

There should also be the possibility to "build-in" the knowledge that, say, the (virtual) topic type "clarinetist" is in fact a synthesis of all topics of type "person" that are connected via a "player of" association with the topic "clarinet". This will allow the user to work in a very intuitive manner and ensure very precise query results.

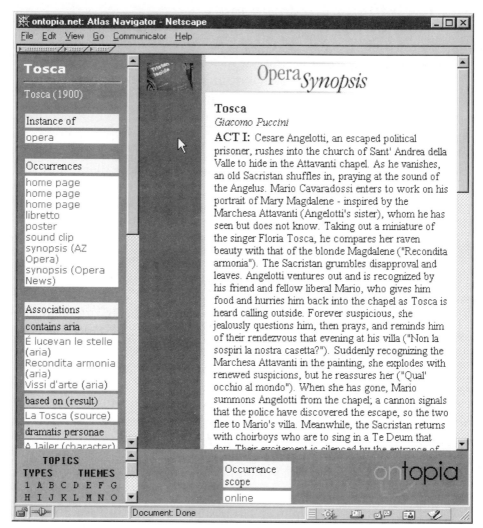

Figure 43-4   Ontopia's *Atlas Navigator*

43.3.5 *As we think ...*

The human brain always remembers previously recognized things in context. Association is the main way we think. A topic map browser can support our way of thinking by offering related topics when the user looks at a given topic. The related topics can be dynamically calculated just by following the various "links" of the map. The relevancy of a related topic depends on its "distance" to the current one – where the distance could be the number of links to follow from one topic to the other. The "associative navigation" makes topic maps very powerful.

43.4 | Conclusion

The topic map standard provides a limited but complete and implementable set of concepts for organizing and navigating large and continuously growing information pools. The combination of the concepts opens up a wide variety of applications.

Topic maps are information assets in their own right, irrespective of whether they are actually connected to any information resources or not. Also, because of the separation between the information resources and the topic map, the same topic map can be overlaid on different pools of information, just as different topic maps can be overlaid on the same pool of information to provide different views to different users.

Furthermore, this separation provides the potential to be able to interchange topic maps among publishers and to merge one or more topic maps. Because of this, topic maps can stimulate a new business: An "Information Broker" can design topic maps, sell them separately to the information owner (e.g. publisher), or link the topics to resources from contracted information providers and sell both map and resource access to the end-users.

Analysis   The ability to apply multiple topic maps to arbitrary information pools has enormous potential for the World Wide Web. Website owners and independent third parties can develop and apply topic maps to collections of websites, thereby providing an overall information context for them. Instead of relying solely on physical addresses, which have no information context, a surfer could check his location in an applicable topic map to see where he is in an information space. In other words, topic maps can act as the Global Positioning System (GPS) for the World Wide Web.

Application integration using topic maps

Application Discussion

- ▍ Distributed objects
- ▍ Workflow topic maps
- ▍ Application integration architecture

Sponsor: XCare.net, http://www.xcare.net
Contributing expert: Suriya Narayanan

44

It's midnight ... do you know where your applications are? There was a time when the answer was "wrapped in a rubber band in my desk drawer", but that time is gone forever. Today's Web applications are composed of a multitude of cooperating components. You might not even know *what* they are, let alone where they are. Unless, of course, you've got a topic map!

L ong, long ago, in a data processing center far, far away, applications were implemented as monolithic programs. Today, with the evolution of the Web and the driving forces behind it, distributed object computing has become the prevailing architecture for developing applications.

44.1 | Distributed objects

Just about any application can be modeled and developed as a collection of objects in a network, collaborating to accomplish what the application is expected to accomplish. The network where the applications run can span the globe or be limited to a single computer's internal bus.

An object has an *interface* that exposes its *methods* – operations performed on the object. Objects can invoke one another's methods while collaborating, in order to perform the application functionality.

Even a legacy application that was developed back in that ancient data processing center can participate. It can be *wrapped*, using an appropriate *object wrapper*, to provide an object-oriented interface and object-oriented access to its functionality.

44.1.1 *Navigating the object ocean*

What if we treated the operations on the distributed objects as topics in a topic map?[1] More precisely, we want to treat the methods defined in the classes as topics, and the methods on specific instances of the classes – the objects – as the corresponding topic occurrences.

Recall that associations are relationships between topics. The fact that the topic "method A" is calling the topic "method B" is an *association* between the two topics. The *association roles* that the topics – the methods – play in that association would be `caller` and `callee`.

44.1.2 *Mapping control flow*

What happens when you navigate a topic map that represents the methods of distributed objects? As the *control flow* – the logic – of the application is captured in the topic map, the application executes as those methods are called during the navigation.

This is an important notion.

Programmers have customarily included the control flow in the code. After all, this is a good part of what programming is all about and is actually fun to do! Is it even feasible, let alone desirable, to move control flow out of the code in this way?

The answer lies in the granularity of the objects and methods that we choose to model in the topic map.

At the micro, physical data structure level, encapsulating the control flow in the code is unavoidable. Although in principle even this control flow could be represented in a topic map, that map would be too large, too focused on the physical aspects, and too detailed to serve any useful purpose.

---

1. If you aren't certain of what that means, take a few moments to read the tutorial in Chapter 43, "Topic maps: Knowledge navigation aids", on page 606.

However, if the objects and methods being modeled as a topic map are at a sufficiently high level – representing abstractions of real-life business objects – then the topic map of the object interactions is immediately meaningful. Such topic maps are useful for integration because they model the workflow of the business.

44.1.3 *Workflow*

Workflow is a discipline for modeling real-life systems as a sequence of tasks, with the ability to make some branching decisions along the way.

For example the processing of a sales order in a business can be modeled as a workflow. A workflow could also describe how a patient is handled when visiting the physician's office. You can see a workflow illustrated in Figure 44-1; we'll discuss it in detail later on.

A well-designed workflow is *loosely-coupled*, meaning that the components that implement the individual tasks know nothing about one another's internals or data formats, only about their formally-defined interfaces. In contrast, traditional applications (including the components themselves) are termed *tightly-coupled* because their internal objects do have intimate knowledge of one another.

44.1.3.1 Topic maps and workflow

As we have seen, a topic map can model interactions of meaningful high-level business objects. As those interactions represent the workflow of the business, we are effectively modeling business workflow with topic maps.

Given tools to define and manage distributed object topic maps, and a runtime platform for map navigation, topic maps could become vehicles for application integration without heavy-duty programming.

44.1.3.2 Content and workflow

Business objects return business data, which has formally-defined semantics and a known format. It is the same sort of data found in relational databases and spreadsheets.

Enterprises also have large amounts of free-form creative data, such as reports, plans, procedures, and similar documents. Chapter 43, "Topic maps: Knowledge navigation aids", on page 606 explained how to navigate around such content using topic maps.

Suppose that in addition to business objects, a workflow were to include distributed objects that generated free-form content from a topic map. That content topic map would be distinct from the distributed object topic map, although as both are topic maps they could be stored and managed in the same topic map database, using the same access mechanisms.

However, the distributed object topic map could model the operations of the content-generation objects together with the operations on the application business objects. Doing so would facilitate tighter integration of free-form content with business process data.

Let's look at an architecture that could support such workflows.

44.2 | Architecture for application integration

Figure 44-1 illustrates an architecture for application integration by means of topic maps. It is based on an actual implementation of a topic-based integration platform developed by XCare.net.

The architecture provides for application business objects and content generation objects. Their behavior is controlled by topic maps of their interactions and topic maps of the content.

The primary components of the architecture are the three managers: the context manager, the semantic manager, and the service manager. These components essentially act as brokers, by connecting a client browser service request to an appropriate server component.

44.2.1 *Context manager*

The context manager is responsible for managing the session and maintaining its state. As the user navigates the information space described by the topic map, the context manager maintains the state across the navigations and makes session-level data available to the other components.

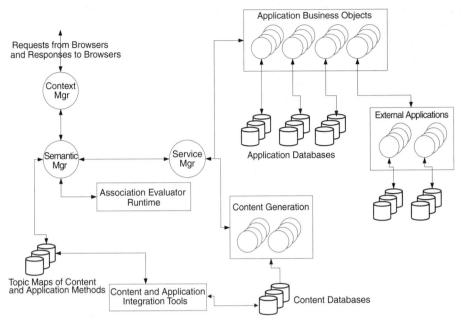

Figure 44-1 Application integration architecture using topic maps

44.2.2 *Semantic manager*

The semantic manager has the most to do of all the managers. Its role is to navigate the topic maps that model the interactions of the application business objects. The semantic manager also manages the topic maps database.

44.2.2.1 Topic maps

The semantic manager understands workflows that are represented as `topicmap` XML documents, like the one shown in Example 44-1.

44.2.2.2 Association evaluators

The semantic manager evaluates the associations defined in the topic maps by running *association evaluators (AEs)* that are included in the association definitions. In XCare.net's implementation, AEs are snippets of Java code that have access to the context in which they are running.

The runtime context for AEs consists of:

- the user's security principal,
- the state data managed by the context manager,
- the object instances of the classes that are defined as topics in the topic map, and
- the specific set of HTTP request parameters that the browser sent.

The semantic manager provides the runtime environment for the AEs.

44.2.3 *Service manager*

The service manager's primary responsibility is to bridge the connections among the application objects, the content generation objects, and the external systems. It is essentially a specialized directory service for locating those things.

The service manager isn't fundamental to the architecture, but it helps draw the line between those software components that are responsible for the integration and those that need to be integrated.

44.3 | A simple workflow example

Let's look at a simple example of a workflow topic map.

Suppose you decide to take your spouse out on a surprise date to dinner, followed by a show or a movie. This "system" can be modeled using the workflow in Figure 44-2.

The topic map representing this workflow model is in Example 44-1. It begins with a bit of housekeeping in which it defines the "types" of things that occur in the map, then topics for the complete workflow (SurpriseDate) and for the exit from it (GoHome).

The map then defines the HaveDinner, EnjoyTheShow and EnjoyTheMovie topics.

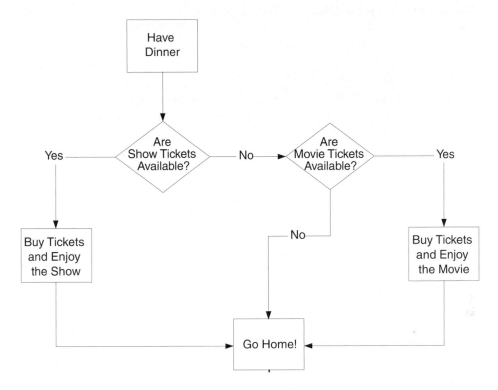

Figure 44-2   Simple workflow for a surprise date

These topics represent class-methods of objects, not their specific instances. The instances will not be determined until a runtime instantiation of the workflow is made. Associations representing paths through the workflow are defined. They associate the topics that represent the workflow steps.

Example 44-2 shows a topic map representing such a runtime instantiation. Again, housekeeping topics occur, as do the class-method topics `HaveDinner`, `EnjoyTheShow` and `EnjoyTheMovie`. This time, however, the latter three topics have occurrences, which are references to object-methods.

The workflow instance topic map inherits from the workflow definition topic map the associations that define the flow of control.

Example 44-1. Simple workflow definition topic map

```
<topicmap>
<!-- "Types" for categorizing topics and associations -->
<topic id="class-method"/> <!-- For topics -->
<topic id="control-flow"/> <!-- For control flow -->
<topic id="caller"/>  <!-- Calling object in association -->
<topic id="callee"/>  <!-- Called object in association -->
<topic id="AE"/>      <!-- Association evaluator -->
<!-- Topics -->
<topic id="SurpriseDate" types="class-method">
  <topname><basename>SurpriseDate</basename></topname>
</topic>
<topic id="GoHome" types="class-method">
  <topname><basename>GoHome</basename></topname>
</topic>
<topic id="HaveDinner" types="class-method">
  <topname><basename>HaveDinner</basename></topname>
</topic>
<topic id="EnjoyTheShow" types="class-method">
  <topname><basename>EnjoyTheShow</basename></topname>
</topic>
<topic id="EnjoyTheMovie" types="class-method">
  <topname><basename>EnjoyTheMovie</basename></topname>
</topic>
<!-- Associations -->
<assoc type="control-flow">
  <assocrl type="caller" href="SurpriseDate"/>
  <assocrl type="callee" href="EnjoyTheShow"/>
  <assocrl type="AE"     href="AreShowTicketsAvailable()"/>
</assoc>
<assoc type="control-flow">
  <assocrl type="caller" href="SurpriseDate"/>
  <assocrl type="callee" href="EnjoyTheMovie"/>
  <assocrl type="AE"     href="AreMovieTicketsAvailable(Cabaret)"/>
</assoc>
<assoc type="control-flow">
  <assocrl type="caller" href="SurpriseDate"/>
  <assocrl type="callee" href="GoHome"/>
  <assocrl type="AE"     href="Always()"/>
</assoc>
</topicmap>
```

44.4 | A compound workflow example

Real life workflows are more complex than the simple workflow defined above. But the complexity usually derives from the repetition of simple

Example 44-2. Simple workflow instance topic map

```
<topicmap>
<!-- "Types" for categorizing topics -->
<topic id="class-method"/> <!-- For topics -->
<!-- Topics and occurrences -->
<topic id="SurpriseDate" types="class-method">
  <topname><basename>SurpriseDate</basename></topname>
  <occurs type="object-method" href="OurDate"/>
</topic>
<topic id="HaveDinner" types="class-method">
  <topname><basename>HaveDinner</basename></topname>
  <occurs type="object-method" href="BonesSteakHouse"/>
</topic>
<topic id="EnjoyTheShow" types="class-method">
  <topname><basename>EnjoyTheShow</basename></topname>
  <occurs type="object-method" href="Ragtime"/>
</topic>
<topic id="EnjoyTheMovie" types="class-method">
  <topname><basename>EnjoyTheMovie</basename></topname>
  <occurs type="object-method" href="Cabaret"/>
</topic>
<topic id="GoHome" types="class-method">
  <topname><basename>GoHome</basename></topname>
  <occurs type="object-method" href="OurHome"/>
</topic>
</topicmap>
```

workflows in various combinations. In other words, the supposedly complex workflow is actually a compound one, consisting of a hierarchy of simple workflows with relatively straightforward logic relating them.

Topic maps lend themselves well to representing compound workflows because they are easily combined. Any of the topics in a topic map can be a topic map in its own right.

Suppose we complicate the SurpriseDate workflow in Figure 44-2. Let's say that the kids need to be taken care of before the surprise date with your spouse can begin.

The new workflow, shown in Figure 44-3, is conceptually more complex, but actually simpler than Figure 44-2 in practice, as it is built on top of the SurpriseDate workflow. Its topic map is shown in Example 44-3.

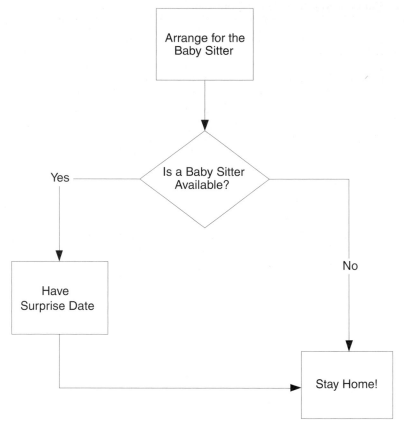

Figure 44-3   Compound workflow

44.5 | Conclusion

We have seen many examples in this book of using XML for data sharing among disparate applications. XML workflow topic maps offer an elegant technique for coordinating the execution of those applications. Industries, such as healthcare, where there is currently a serious lack of effective integration among systems, could especially benefit from topic-based integration.

Example 44-3. Compound workflow topic map

```
<topicmap>
<!-- "Types" for categorizing topics and associations -->
<topic id="class-method"/> <!-- For topics -->
<topic id="control-flow"/> <!-- For control flow -->
<topic id="caller"/>  <!-- Calling object in association -->
<topic id="callee"/>  <!-- Called object in association -->
<topic id="AE" />     <!-- Association evaluator -->
<!-- Topics -->
<topic id="KidlessDate" types="class-method">
  <topname><basename>KidlessDate</basename></topname>
</topic>
<topic id="GoHome" types="class-method">
  <topname><basename>GoHome</basename></topname>
</topic>
<topic id="ArrangeBabySitter" types="class-method">
  <topname><basename>ArrangeBabySitter</basename></topname>
</topic>
<topic id="SurpriseDate" types="class-method">
  <topname><basename>SurpriseDate</basename></topname>
</topic>
<!-- Associations -->
<assoc type="control-flow">
  <assocrl type="caller" href="KidlessDate"/>
  <assocrl type="callee" href="ArrangeBabySitter"/>
  <assocrl type="AE"     href="IsBabySitterAvailable()"/>
</assoc>
  <assocrl type="caller" href="KidlessDate"/>
  <assocrl type="callee" href="SurpriseDate"/>
  <assocrl type="AE"     href="DoesWorkflowExist()"/>
</assoc>
<assoc type="control-flow">
  <assocrl type="caller" href="KidlessDate"/>
  <assocrl type="callee" href="GoHome"/>
  <assocrl type="AE"     href="Always()"/>
</assoc>
</topicmap>
```

Infrastructure

- Programming technology
- Rich-media digital asset management
- XML in low-level system functions

Part Twelve

So far in this book, any mention of "infrastructure" was in the context of XML being a vital part of the infrastructure provided by information distribution and electronic business applications.

In the following chapters, however, we dig down a lot further and see the role that XML plays in the infrastructure that supports those very applications.

We've seen throughout the book how products support XML for content management and data integration, and in this part we'll see how programming technology supports many of those products.

We'll also look at how a powerful platform for XML-based multimedia applications is developed, and how XML figures in the development.

Finally, we'll get a glimpse into a future where XML is ubiquitous, even finding its way into low-level system functions and specialized hardware.

Java technology for XML development

Tool Discussion

- Tools for tool-building

- SAX and DOM APIs

- Middleware development services

Sponsor: Sun Microsystems, http://java.sun.com/xml

Contributing experts: Sun Microsystems staff

Chapter

45

When the definitive history of gastronomical influences on technological development is written, it may well record that Sun Microsystems had more to do with satisfying the coffee cravings of programmers than Starbucks. Certainly, if you sniff around the software that supports XML applications, you're bound to smell the Java!

S everal of the products that we've used to illustrate the chapters of this book have something in common: They are written in the Java™ programming language. If they support EDI or other forms of application integration, they may also use the Java 2 Platform, Enterprise Edition (J2EE).

But we don't say much about these common characteristics in those chapters. For one thing, we'd be repeating ourselves a lot if we did.[1] But more importantly, we'd be getting off-topic.

The chapters in which those products appear occur in application-oriented parts of the book. For that reason, we focus on *what* the products do with XML, rather than *how* they accomplish it. In contrast, the purpose of this chapter is to provide – in a single place – a look at some of the *Java* technology that influences a product's ability to process XML.

Some might argue that the main influence is metaphysical: there is a profound *rightness* about using XML and *Java* together in that both were designed for the Web, both are internationalized (because they support Unicode), and both are designed for portability.

---

1. We repeat ourselves a lot as it is, but we generally restrict the repetition to emphasizing important XML concepts.

More than portability! They are designed to *let information be free*, to liberate it from the bonds of operating systems, to let it travel unhindered throughout the network that is the computer ...

Right.

Metaphysics notwithstanding, in this chapter we'll focus strictly on technical capabilities. We'll look at implementations of the SAX and DOM interfaces, and services for developing XML middleware.

 Note   In 2.10, *"Programming interfaces and models"*, on page 46, we covered some basic concepts that are necessary for this chapter: parsing, APIs, DOM, and SAX.

45.1 | SAX and DOM implementations

An XML parser must ensure that the XML document is *well-formed*, which means (in a nutshell) that the tags are properly constructed, every start-tag has an associated end-tag, and the elements they identify are always nested properly, one within the other.

Proper nesting means that the `title` element, for example, is always fully inside or fully outside the `chapter` element, not overlapping. The `title` element can't start outside the `chapter`, and then finish inside it.

When validating, a parser goes even further and verifies that the XML document lives up to the restrictions and specifications declared in the document's DTD (or schema definition). If there is no document type declaration, the document is not valid.

All XML parsers must be able to check for well-formedness. Those that can also validate are known as (surprise!) *validating parsers*. Either kind can be used with the SAX and DOM APIs.

45.1.1 *The SAX API*

You can think of this interface as "serial access" for XML.

Recall from 2.10, "Programming interfaces and models", on page 46 that SAX is "event-driven". The parser reads through an XML document once, from start to finish. At each parsing event, such as recognizing the start or end of an element, it notifies the application. It also provides the information associated with the event, such as the element-type name, attributes and their values, or content data characters.

The SAX API is fast and it uses little memory, which recommends it for server applications and simple programs that only read data or make only small changes to it.

The basic outline of the SAX parser is shown in Figure 45-1. First the `ParserFactory` generates an instance of the parser. The XML text is shown coming into the parser from the left. As the parser runs, it invokes the appropriate operations (called "methods"), which are organized into the four groups (called "interfaces") shown on the right.

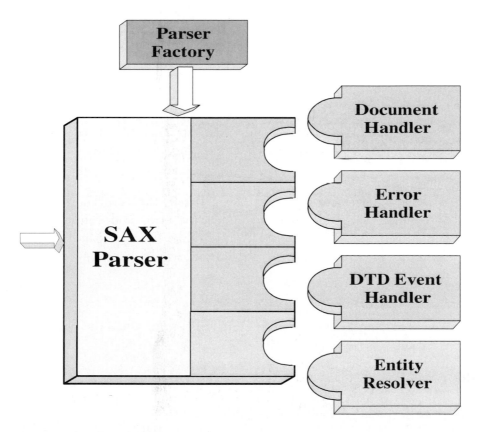

Figure 45-1   SAX API

What those methods actually do is determined by the application programmer, who might not even implement all of them. A typical application provides at least the DocumentHandler methods. A robust one will implement the ErrorHandler interface as well.

Here is a summary of the major SAX functions, grouped by the interfaces in which they are defined:

ParserFactory

The ParserFactory class defines the makeParser() method, which lets the user determine which parser to use at runtime. For example, the user might choose to use a parser from a different vendor, or choose a validating parser rather than a nonvalidating parser.

Parser

The parser reads the XML text and recognizes parsing events, as described above.

DocumentHandler

The information about the events the parser recognizes is sent to the DocumentHandler for processing. This is where the application developer puts the code that processes the data.

ErrorHandler

When the parser encounters an error, it tells the ErrorHandler. Sometimes the application can ignore the error and continue. Sometimes the error makes it impossible for the parser to continue, in which case the application would issue an error message.

DTDHandler

The DTDHandler takes care of events that occur when the DTD is parsed.

EntityResolver

The resolveEntity method is invoked when the parser must access text that is outside the document entity.

45.1.2 *The DOM API*

You can think of this interface as "random access" for XML, because you can access any part of the data at any time.

The Document Object Model is a collection of objects in your program. You can manipulate the object model in any way that makes sense. You can modify data, remove it, or insert new data. When your application is through making changes, it can then write the structure out as an XML document. Interactive applications can use the DOM API to maintain the parsed document while displaying a rendition for users to read and edit.

While the SAX API is fast, it is only good for reading data. You can't use it to write XML, or to modify an XML document that has been parsed. The DOM API fills those needs.

On the other hand, the DOM can't be used to read XML. For that it uses SAX, so SAX and DOM work together hand-in-hand.

Figure 45-2 shows how Sun's *Java* XML libraries implement the Document Object Model.

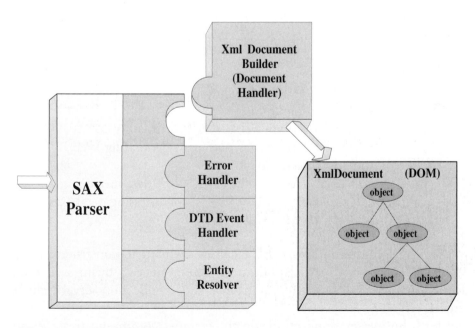

Figure 45-2   DOM API

The `XmlDocumentBuilder` class is just an elaborate SAX `DocumentHandler`. As event information arrives from the parser, the XML-DocumentBuilder uses it to construct a DOM representation of the parsed document.

The DOM API hides the intricacies of the SAX API, and provides a relatively familiar tree structure of objects. It also provides a framework to help generate an XML document from the object tree.

On the other hand, constructing the DOM requires reading the entire XML document and holding the object tree in memory, so it is much more CPU and memory intensive. For that reason, the SAX API may be preferable for server-side applications and data filters that do not require an in-memory representation of the entire document at once.

Implementations of both APIs, together with sample application code, can be found on the CD-ROM.

45.2 | XML middleware services

The *Java 2 Platform, Enterprise Edition* is a set of middleware services for developing enterprise applications. XML is supported in J2EE as a standardized data representation for information interchange.

J2EE includes such technologies as:

- *Enterprise JavaBeans™* (EJB) technology, for server-centric component-based programming
- *Java Servlets*, for extending web server functionality
- *JavaServer Pages™* (JSP), for dynamically generating Web content, including XML documents
- *Java Message Service*, for asynchronous XML data messaging.
- *Java Database Connectivity* (JDBC™), for accessing databases and other tabular data sources

Figure 45-3 illustrates how J2EE facilities are used to construct a business-to-business e-commerce application. There are two businesses, each with its own secure intranet of database servers, application servers, client systems, etc.

In both businesses, applications on the intranet communicate across an internal firewall to the company's Web server, using JSP and/or Servlets.

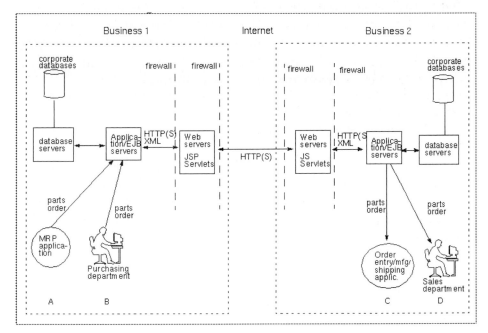

Figure 45-3 Business-to-business e-commerce application

The communication protocol is HTTP(S) and the data is represented in XML.

An external firewall protects the Web server from the Internet. Other businesses can communicate with the Web server only by using HTTP(S) to cross the external firewall.

45.2.1 *Business 1*

Business 1 is an end-product manufacturer. It runs a Materials Resource Planning (MRP) application on its intranet that calculates when to order parts, and in what quantities. It also has a purchasing department that places special orders interactively.

45.2.1.1 Automated parts ordering

Area A of Figure 45-3 illustrates the automated ordering process.

The MRP application generates order data, which is converted to a "parts order" document represented in XML using techniques like those described in Part [no number], "E-commerce" of this book. The parts order is transmitted to an EJB server, then to the Web server, and eventually across the Internet to a parts supplier, such as Business 2.

45.2.1.2   Interactive parts ordering

The interactive purchasing process is shown in area B of Figure 45-3.

Purchasing personnel interact with a browser-based application, similar to those described in Part [no number], "Middle-tier Servers" of this book. JSP pages are used to collect the purchasing data and generate "parts order" XML documents that are sent to the parts supplier over the Internet.

45.2.2   *Business 2*

Business 2 is an OEM parts manufacturer. It runs an order-entry, manufacturing, and shipping application on its intranet that automatically books and processes e-commerce orders. However, its application server is programmed to route non-routine orders, such as very large orders and rush orders, to the sales department for interactive processing.

45.2.2.1   Automated sales processing

Area C of Figure 45-3 depicts the automated sales processing. It is essentially the inverse of Business 1's automated order processing and uses similar techniques.

The parts order document is parsed and its data is incorporated in a sales order in the form accepted by the order entry application. That application enters the order into the manufacturing system. It also generates and sends a confirmation of the order to Business 1, including pricing and shipping dates.

45.2.2.2   Interactive sales processing

Interactive sales processing is shown in area D of Figure 45-3.

The parts order XML document is rendered on the client under the control of an XSL stylesheet, using techniques like those discussed in Part [no number], "Stylesheets". Sales personnel review and approve the order and enter it into the system.

Tip   *Sun has provided some free Java software for you on the CD-ROM.*

Building a rich-media digital asset manager

Application Discussion

- **|** System architecture

- **|** Object-oriented messaging

- **|** Scripting with XML

- **|** Element structure and storage structure

- **|** XML-based rich-media distribution

Sponsor: Artesia Technologies, http://www.artesiatech.com

Contributing experts: Dipto Chakravarty and Roger Medlin

Chapter

46

Hollywood and Silicon Valley are converging, promising universal on-demand access to the multimedia resources of the planet – business data *and* Baywatch. And the software that manages those digital assets will run on XML as well as deliver it.

T he Web is rapidly maturing into a major distributor of rich media – not just words and pictures, but audio and video files and streams.[1] Digital media represent an increasingly important part of an enterprise's information assets. Like other digital assets, they have to be managed.

46.1 | Architecture of a rich-media digital asset manager

Figure 46-1 illustrates the architecture of a rich-media digital asset manager (DAM). It has the familiar three-tier structure that was introduced in Part [no number], "Middle-tier Servers":

1. Information presentation, constituting the user interface.

---

1. Sounds like an outdoors magazine for multimedia ... Cover story in this month's Files and Streams: How I caught a 300MB video download on a 28.8KB line!

2. Information administration, governed by business rules and procedures incorporated into application servers.
3. Information storage and retrieval, generally provided by a database management system.

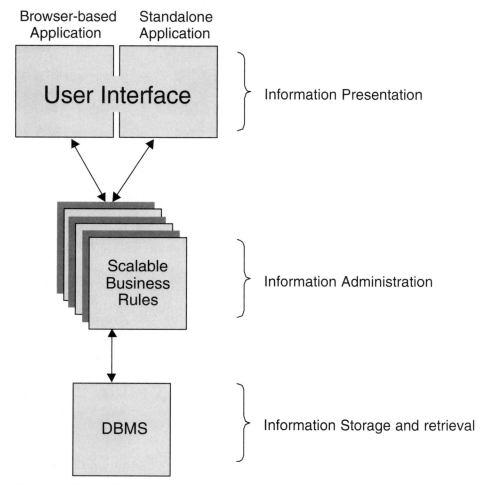

Figure 46-1   Three-tier architecture for digital asset management

Massively scalable, enterprise-level digital asset management systems, such as the TEAMS™ system from Artesia Technologies, are designed and implemented upon architectural underpinnings such as this. However, despite the similarity to other information systems at the architectural level, rich media poses a set of unique challenges.

- There are myriad data types, whose size, behavior, and access methods vary across a wide spectrum.
- Rich media almost always require specialized presentation aids at the user interface – such as renderers, viewers, and players – in order to complete the personalized experience.
- Rich media make enormous demands on bandwidth and transport facilities. It is difficult to move such data around on a local or wide area network without degrading performance.

XML can play an important role in building a DAM that can meet these challenges. Let's look at some of the considerations involved.

46.2 | Object-oriented messaging

In the MOM application discussions in this book – e-commerce, portals, etc. – XML is presented as a *data integration* enabler: It allows data from disparate sources, such as databases, ERP systems, and legacy business applications, to be combined into a single XML document for processing and/or rendition.

But there is another way to look at the very same behavior. Because XML is enabling disparate programs to work in combination, it is really (also) a *distributed programming* enabler. In programming terms, it is an object-oriented *component model* and its implementation is a *component framework*.

Object-oriented system behavior is ultimately governed by the messages that are passed between objects. The means by which objects are implemented is considerably less important.

What *is* important is the way a message is *serialized* – converted to a string of bits or characters that can be interchanged among different platforms – and the means by which it will ultimately be processed. XML and its derivative standards offer a framework that addresses both these points effectively.

46.2.1 *Neutral serialization*

XML-based messaging enables programs to communicate across disparate programming environments, irrespective of operating system, language, or compiler. Processes in each environment need only understand the common XML messaging format and protocol. This common neutral message format can eliminate a great deal of grief caused by other techniques.

Consider that messages are intrinsically just data structures, which can be serialized in a variety of ways. In Example 46-1 we have a C++ data structure, an array of four integers:

Example 46-1. A C++ array

```
int array[4] = {-9,0,-2,1};
```

Logically, the data structure exists in storage as shown in Table 46-1.

Table 46-1   Logical view of the data structure of Example 46-1

Array size	Index_0 value	Index_1 value	Index_2 value	Index_3 value
4	-9	0	-2	1

However, physically, on an 8-bit machine, the actual bits are stored as seen in Table 46-2.

Table 46-2   8-bit storage of Example 46-1

Array size	Index_0 bits	Index_1 bits	Index_2 bits	Index_3 bits
00000100	11110111	00000000	11111110	00000001

If this array is passed in a message, special care must be taken to assure that the receiving object's view of the data is identical to the sending object's, which is by no means a certainty.

For example, an integer may be defined on the receiving machine as unsigned, in which case the logical view of the data structure would be as seen in Table 46-3.

Table 46-3   The array in Example 46-1 as unsigned integers

Array size	Index_0 value	Index_1 value	Index_2 value	Index_3 value
4	247	0	254	1

Furthermore, on other platforms integers may be multibyte, 16-bit, 32-bit, or 64-bit. Add to this bit-ordering uncertainties (high-order first or low-order?), and quickly one realizes that message serialization had better not depend on language, compiler, or platform characteristics.

The XML serialization of the array in Example 46-1, shown in Example 46-2, presents none of these problems.

Example 46-2. XML serialization of the array in Example 46-1

```
<array size='4'>
  <integer value='-9'/>
  <integer value= '0'/>
  <integer value='-2'/>
  <integer value= '1'/>
</array>
```

Among the numerous industry standards that exist for the XML serialization of objects are the following:

- Bean Markup Language (BML)
- XML BeanMaker
- XML-CORBA Link (XORBA)
- Koala Object Markup Language (KOML)
- Coins, an XML-based alternative to *JavaBeans*

In addition, for rich-media digital asset management, Artesia Technologies has defined the XML Persistent Interchange Syntax for Assets (PISA). All of these XML representations can readily be transported using such protocols as RPC, RMI, and HTTP.

46.2.2 *Cost-effectiveness*

The software engineering discipline has come to recognize that initial development of code represents but a small fraction of the actual life-cycle costs. Code maintenance will inevitably account for the vast majority of outlays. For this reason, organizations should seek to acquire standards-based software for integration rather than writing proprietary, in-house solutions.

For example, consider a data structure for a message transmitting a number of digital assets, each of which contains metadata and content. This message could be represented using a plain text proprietary format, as in Example 46-3.

Example 46-3. Proprietary digital asset transmission format

```
[ASSET/METADATA]
NAME=Daytona 500
DATE=February, 2001

[ASSET/CONTENT]
FILE=daytona.jpg
```

With this approach, the application developer is responsible for parsing the messages. His code will need to check things like:

- Where does one field end and the next begin?
- Where does one field grouping end and the next begin?
- How is containment defined?
- What white-space is significant, and how should the end of each line be treated?
- What represents a recoverable error when parsing the data?

Once he parses the message and finds the individual data element fields, he will also have to write code to validate the field data:

- Is it a date field? If so, is the date specified valid (no February 31st allowed)?
- Is the field numeric? If so, what is the prescribed range of values?
- Is the field variable character data? If so, is there a restriction on its length?
- Is the field an enumerated type? If so, what are the valid values?

By employing a standards-based approach such as XML, the standards themselves answer these questions. With fundamental design decisions having been answered, the software developer can focus attention on implementing the application solution.

46.3 | Scripting with XML

Returning to the initial goal of function shipping, what is ultimately necessary is a ubiquitous practice to describe and process data. The actual logic, encapsulated within components or objects, must be shippable; however, the runtime code itself need not be when the logic controllers are data driven. XML provides a ubiquitous way to process data that can be employed to govern system behavior.

Consider the fundamentals of digital asset management. These naturally involve a specialized set of CRUD (Create, Read, Update, Delete) operations that can be performed on assets, each of which constitutes a specific behavior. The following list categorizes these CRUD operations.

Create
Import Version Checkin

Read
Search Export Checkout

Update
Replace Delete

Delete
Purge

From an object-oriented perspective, many operations are specializations of others. For example, in the **create** category, `version` is a specialization of `import`. In both cases a new digital asset is created, but for `version` the previous copy of the asset is kept and the new asset receives a later version number.

Similarly, the `check-in` operation is a specialization of `version`, with the added step of releasing the software "lock" that was set when the asset was checked-out to be revised.

46.3.1 *An* `AssetProcessor` *class*

Artesia Technologies' XML Persistent Interchange Syntax for Assets (PISA) defines a data structure that is composed of N digital assets, where in actual practice, the upper bound of N can sometimes literally be in the hundreds of thousands. With an XML document that can measure gigabytes in size, the DOM cannot sensibly be employed – the memory required to so would be immense. Hence, Artesia Technologies' DAM, *TEAMS*, utilizes SAX instead, with the transaction level being per asset.

To aggregate the components of a digital asset expressed within a PISA file using SAX, the default document handler must be subclassed, coded specifically for the PISA format. Because the CRUD operations enumerated above and the transaction level are per asset, a generic `AssetProcessor` class can be defined from which all operations on an asset are derived; hence, all operations are by definition `AssetProcessor`(s).

When an XML end-tag for an asset is encountered, the document handler will have completed the construction of the in-memory data structure representing that asset. Therefore, it can subsequently initiate a call to the process method of an `AssetProcessor` for that asset.

Which `AssetProcessor` is applied can vary depending upon the actual type passed to the constructor of the document handler, usually governed by a specific callback intended to invoke an asset-level operation. Therefore, by writing just a single XML document handler, all asset operations can be made available as bulk operations in the digital asset management system.

This implementation approach is referred to as a *design pattern*. It simplifies the design, implementation and maintenance of the XML processing, as there is need for only a single data format (PISA) and a single document handler.

46.3.2 *Batching assets for processing*

Selection of an AssetProcessor via a specific callback has a singular drawback: the processor type is fixed for the duration of the process. This would stop us from queueing processing of a series of assets, each of which might have a distinct per asset operation.

To process this queue as a single batch job, it is necessary for the XML document to be coded so that an event can be fired indicating a change of AssetProcessor. To accomplish this, the PISA format incorporates an embedded scripting language. The language employs XML processing instructions to syntactically enumerate the control of system behaviors, such as which AssetProcessor is currently active.

Beyond requiring a target, the XML constraints on a processing instruction are minimal. They don't prevent us from representing data using the syntax of attribute specifications, as shown in Example 46-4.

Example 46-4. Data represented as attribute specifications

```
<?PITarget attr1='some value' attr2='another value'?>
```

The SAX event for handling processing instructions conveniently dissects a processing instruction into its target name and its remaining data. Parsing the attribute specification syntax requires writing only a minimalist document handler that will tranform the processing instruction into an empty-element tag, as in Example 46-5, and submit it to an XML parser.

Example 46-5. Processing instruction transformed into empty-element tag

```
<PITarget attr1='some value' attr2='another value'/>
```

The SAX event for handling start element returns a list of attribute values sorted by attribute name. These facilities allow us to employ processing instructions as a scripting language that can easily be processed in a consistent manner, employing the XML parser as an application framework.

By using XML in this way, one can readily build a data-driven, event-based system capable of providing services previously accessible only through programmer-level APIs.

46.4 | Element structure and storage structure

Digital asset management systems provide application services at the middle architectural tier that must be able to push and pull data from the persistent storage layer. That layer is generally proprietary – specific to the database management and/or operating system. Utilizing XML as an application framework, it is possible to construct a DAM that can rapidly be redeployed to new persistent storage platforms.

This portability stems from the fact that XML separates its logical and physical data representations: its *element structure* and *storage structure*.

Logically, a digital asset is comprised of a `metadata` element and a `content` element; however, physically, the data of these two elements may be stored in any number of ways. This is where the XML concept of entities is useful. Entities can isolate the logical view of the asset from the physical storage, as shown in Example 46-6:

Example 46-6. Entities for digital assets

```
<!DOCTYPE digital-asset [
  <!ENTITY metadata
          PUBLIC "-//TEAMS//TEXT digital asset metadata//EN"
                 "metadata.ent">
  <!ENTITY content
          PUBLIC "-//TEAMS//TEXT digital asset content//EN"
                 "content.ent" >
]>
<digital-asset>
<metadata>&metadata;</metadata>
<content>&content;</content>
</digital-asset>
```

As the XML parser encounters the entity references, it looks to the entity declaration to locate the actual entity data. The resolution of an entity reference through its declaration is handled by an entity manager. As entity management is distinct from parsing, numerous underlying physical storage schemes can be supported, simply by substituting different entity managers.

The most basic persistent storage mechanism for the metadata of a digital asset would be a file system. The entity manager would need only map the PUBLIC identifier for the metadata to a specific host, path, and file-name.

The same data could also be stored within relational or object-oriented databases, SGML/XML component managers, or proprietary data storage schemes. Because no one specific implementation can be optimal for all situations, in terms of price, performance or other variables, the DAM system must be easily configurable to facilitate any of these persistent storage systems.

As an entity manager can be written to retrieve data using any conceivable storage strategy, XML can serve as a level of indirection between persistent storage and the business logic. As entities are resolved, pulling data from persistent storage, the information can, again, be serialized as XML and passed to other middle-tier application services for processing. The whole constitutes a ubiquitous mechanism for processing the data independently of the plethora of known and unknown methods by which the data can be warehoused.

46.5 | XML-based rich-media distribution

The same XML notation that is so useful in constructing a high-quality, completely scalable, enterprise digital asset management system is also useful for pushing rich media content and its associated metadata downstream to a variety of distribution channels.

As digital assets are accessed from a repository or a directory, XML serves as the data glue binding metadata and content. Thereafter, one or more transformation programs can be applied to enhance and filter the metadata and to convert content from one data representation to another.

Subsequently, the digital assets can be aggregated and distributed to various publication vehicles, such as page layout programs, CD mastering tools, or website management software (Figure 46-2).

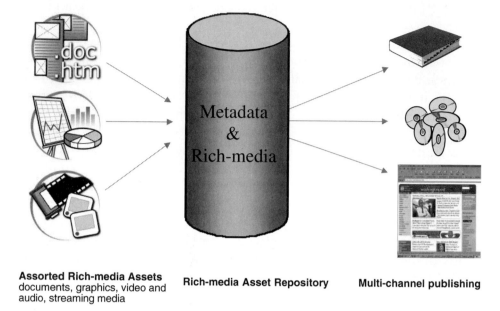

Assorted Rich-media Assets
documents, graphics, video and
audio, streaming media

Rich-media Asset Repository

Multi-channel publishing

Figure 46-2   Rich-media data distribution

New directions for XML applications

Application Discussion

- Performance analysis
- XML does television
- Load balancing and routing

Sponsor: Intel Corporation, `http://www.intel.com/eBusiness`

Contributing experts: Walter Shands, Murali Rajappa, John Abjanic, and Randy E Hall

XML is going where no markup language has gone before. Thanks to a company that really knows about bits and bytes, XML is now in low-level, performance-oriented applications. You can even find it on television – or at least in the computer that provisions your television!

I n the 30-year history of markup languages, we have seen several major trends in application emphasis:

- The first wave, using GML and SGML, was large-scale industrial publishing on paper.
- The second wave, using HTML, was (and is) online information presentation.
- The third wave, using XML, is electronic business and application integration.

And now XML is starting to make inroads in performance-oriented areas that were never before open to an "inefficient" text-based interchange representation. Let's see how Intel Corporation is leading XML into the 21st century.

47.1 | Performance analysis

For a long time a debate raged – and in some quarters is still raging – about the wisdom of using XML for messaging in distributed systems. Despite the many obvious benefits of platform neutrality, human readability, self-description, standardized support, and the rapid deployment and inexpensive maintenance that goes with such characteristics, there is always the last resort of the nay-sayers – resources. After all, the anti-XML argument goes, with an overhead of 300% in a message like `<price>10.00</price>`, XML is clearly an unacceptable drain on performance.

So there is a delicious irony in the fact that one of Intel's envelope-stretching XML applications is ... (fanfare) ... performance analysis!

47.1.1   *Remote data collection*

The company's *VTune* performance analyzer helps developers identify program hot spots and provides advice on how to remedy them. To do that, it needs to collect and present data from distributed machines running on *Microsoft Windows* or *Linux* operating systems. Windows supports remote data collection via Distributed Component Object Module (DCOM), but DCOM is not available on the Linux operating system

47.1.2   *A clean solution ... with SOAP!*

The solution lay in the use of XML requests formatted according to the Simple Object Access Protocol (SOAP). The SOAP specification defines rules for representing both messaging data and remote method invocation requests within a document.

Each request consists of a mandatory header, optional application-specific data conforming to the HTTP Extension Framework, and an envelope. XML schemas provide support for multiple namespaces and ensure that datatype fidelity is maintained across process and server boundaries.

The remote data collection process in *VTune* works as shown in Figure 47-1:

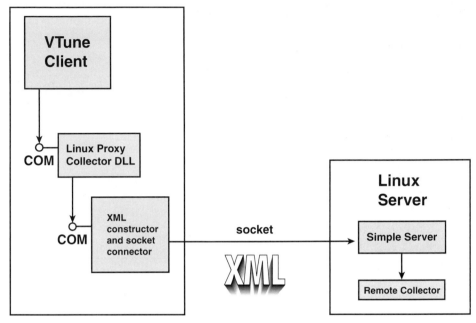

Figure 47-1   Remote data collection in *VTune*

Example 47-1. SOAP request

```
POST  ... HTTP/1.1
Host: ###.###.###.###
Content-Type: text/xml
Content-Length: ###
SOAPMethodName: urn:SamplingCollector:IVTCollector#DoStart
<Envelope>
  <Body>
    <m:DoStart xmlns:m='urn:SamplingCollector:IVTCollector'>
    </m:DoStart>
  </Body>
</Envelope>
```

1. The *VTune* client, which runs on the *Microsoft Windows* platform, makes a Component Object Model (COM) call to a remote collection proxy object.
2. The remote collection proxy collector opens a socket connection to the *Linux* machine.

3. The remote collection proxy collector formats a SOAP request containing a collector name, interface name, method name to execute, and parameter data (Example 47-1).

4. The remote collection proxy collector sends the request to the *Linux* machine.

5. A stub collector on the *Linux* machine either invokes an executable or makes a method call to a sample collector implemented in a C programming language driver.

6. The stub collector collects data and constructs a SOAP response (Example 47-2).

7. The stub collector sends the XML response back to the *VTune* client application.

Example 47-2. SOAP response

```
200 OK
Content-Type: text/xml
Content-Length: ###
<Envelope>
  <Body>
    <m:DoStartResponse
      xmlns:m='urn:SamplingCollector:IVTCollector'>
      <result>OK</result>
    </m:DoStart>
  </Body>
</Envelope>
```

The current SOAP specification is focused on requests and responses over HTTP. XML, however, can be layered on top of other protocols – including SMTP and WAP – making remote data collection possible from cellular phones and other hand-held devices. The SOAP capabilities in the *VTune* performance analyzer support remote data collection on non-*Windows* machines in a way that could permit adding protocols in the future.

47.2 | Coming soon to a television near you ...

XML-TV?

Not exactly, but XML provides such a clean and predictable way to exchange data between disparate systems that it's a natural for an application where no errors can be tolerated. For this reason XML is being deployed in the distribution of digital television (DTV) programming, for consumers to view via DTV-enabled PCs, digital TV sets, and set-top boxes.

Such programming, for example, enables viewers to check an electronic program guide, send electronic greeting cards, take interactive quizzes, watch movie trailers, check sports statistics, and more – all on demand.

47.2.1 Distribution system design

In one set-top box system, the content served includes regular television channels, interactive programming in which the user becomes an active participant, and Web-based media.

Service providers are organized in a hub configuration, wherein a Primary Network Operations Center (PNOC) supports multiple Franchised Network Operations Centers (FNOCs) located in different cities. The PNOC broadcasts content that is cached locally and redistributed by the FNOCs. This approach conserves PNOC/FNOC bandwidth and reduces content delivery latency when serving Web pages.

Subscriber data for specific services resides at both the PNOC and FNOC sites, with the PNOC owning the master record. To ensure that customers receive the services they request, the PNOC subscription center's information must be replicated to the FNOC.

Because the PNOC and FNOC most likely have different subscriber database implementations, the data must be exchanged in a format that disparate systems can easily understand. In the current implementation, the PNOC's master subscriber database is implemented using Oracle database products running on Microsoft *Windows NT* servers. At the FNOC, *Linux* servers host databases for local data storage of customer subscription data.

47.2.2 Adding a subscriber

A document type definition is used to describe the subscriber data to be exchanged. In this case, the DTD acts as a contract between the PNOC and the FNOC so the data elements from the customer document, shown in Example 47-3, are correctly mapped to database columns in tables.

Example 47-3. New account request

```
<Action RefNo="999999999999" Actiontype="Add Record">
  <IP_Address>192.168.2.7</IP_Address>
  <MAC_Address>00:D0.B7:1C:B7:5D</MAC_Address>
  <FNOC_ID>FNOC1</FNOC_ID>
  <Hostname>fnoc1.cn.now.com</Hostname>
  <LoginId>carmen</LoginId>
  <Password>password</Password>
  <ActiveService><Service>modem</Service></ActiveService>
</Action>
```

The process for adding a new subscriber is illustrated in Figure 47-2. It is described as follows:

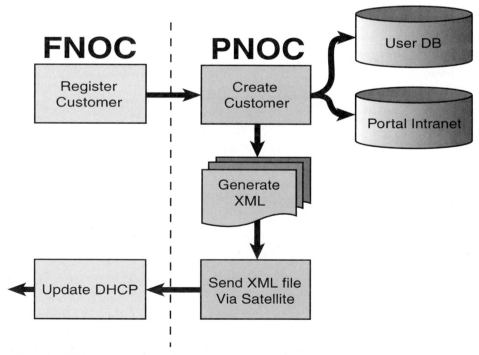

Figure 47-2   Adding a subscriber

1. The FNOC sends a new account request to the PNOC.
2. Subscriber information is inserted into the PNOC customer database.
3. The PNOC customer database generates an XML document containing subscriber information.
4. The system transmits the XML subscriber record document via satellite to the FNOC.
5. The FNOC receives the data and inserts it into its local database.
6. The FNOC configures the subscriber's set-top box for the requested services.

Subscriber updates and deletions are handled in a similar fashion.

As this example makes clear, XML can be used to represent data exchanged between components of a multi-vendor and multi-platform system. With XML, best-of-breed products can be packaged in new and innovative ways to provide services that otherwise would require porting all pieces to a common operating system.

47.3 | Performance enhancement

Remember the raging debate about the wisdom of using XML in distributed systems because it is supposedly such a drain on performance?

Well, here is another delicious irony: Intel is using XML in specialized networking hardware to ... (fanfare) ... enhance performance!

47.3.1 *Load balancing and routing*

One way to guarantee that network transactions are processed in a reliable and expedient manner is to build an infrastructure of high-end servers that can support unpredictable traffic loads. In industries where demand is volatile or difficult to predict, this option could prove to be expensive and could limit the ability to respond to the rapid pace of change.

A more economical and flexible alternative is to offload certain capabilities from the main application processing servers onto specialized devices. A single such "accelerator" or "director" can serve multiple application servers and improve their performance by several means.

The devices operate in domains that system designers call *load balancing* and *routing*. Let's look at what they do.

47.3.1.1   Offload routine tasks

An accelerator can perform such routine tasks as decoding an encrypted message before forwarding it to an application server for fulfillment. It can also encrypt the reply before sending it to the client.

47.3.1.2   Route requests for best response time

On busy websites, several application servers perform the same task. A network device can enhance client response times by routing each request to the server that can fulfill it most quickly. The device typically needs to know (or calculate) the speed of each server and the number of messages enqueued on it.

47.3.1.3   Route requests based on message content

This technique is used for websites that perform multiple services and use different application servers for each. It requires a device that acts like a bank receptionist who decides whether to send you to the loan officer or the new account representative. The device looks at the incoming message to make the routing decision.

For example, URI references can be analyzed to distinguish content requested by clients performing online transactions, from content typically requested by casual surfers. In this way, users performing online transactions can be given higher priority access to server resources (and better response times) than other users.

The choice of server for fulfillment of a request is determined by a table that associates pattern-matching expressions with server names. Possible expression types might include:

- Filetype expressions, such as `*.asp` or `*/order.htm`

- Path expressions, such as `/home/*` or `/home/images/*` or `/home/ images/a*`
- Unique file expressions, such as `/index.html`
- Wildcard expressions, such as `*`
- Negations of the other expression types, such as `!*.gif` or `!*/index.html`

47.3.2 *XML content matching*

The phenomenal growth in the use of XML for e-commerce and other applications suggests that a richer source of information might be available for routing: the data and metadata in XML messages.

As an example of a device that indeed uses that richer source, let's look at the Intel *NetStructure 7280 XML Director*. It incorporates a rules-based XML engine that can identify and classify incoming XML requests based on data within the XML object.

Once classified, the device can then transparently prioritize and direct the "most important" XML transactions, according to predefined business rules. Those could be transactions from key trading partners, those with a high dollar value, or perhaps those that are considered time-sensitive.

47.3.2.1 How the rules-based engine works

How can the *XML Director* route XML transactions to application servers based on business parameters such as "all orders over $50,000 *and* from the Western region"?

Rules, in the form of expressions using a subset of the XPath abbreviated syntax, are associated with specific servers. If a message satisfies a rule, it is routed to the associated server.

One application of the rules engine is to identify the XML framework, if any, used by a message, such as *BizTalk* or *RosettaNet* (see 5.1, "Commerce frameworks", on page 84). The message can then be directed to the appropriate back-end server for processing.

47.3.2.2   An XML-based routing scenario

For example, Figure 47-3 illustrates an implementation that uses three groups of servers:

- Set 1 for high-value transactions of the *RosettaNet* framework.
- Set 2 for high-value transactions of the *BizTalk* framework.
- Set 3 for medium and low-value transactions of both *RosettaNet* and *BizTalk* frameworks, plus regular HTTP traffic that may at times contain XML messages.

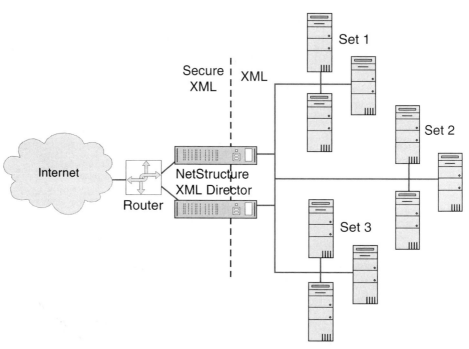

Figure 47-3   *NetStructure 7280 XML Director* configuration

All three server sets can handle any transaction; the dedication to specific frameworks is strictly to increase performance for the high-value transactions.

The *XML Director* can be configured so that if the traffic volume becomes too great for Set 1, either of the other sets can temporarily be enlisted.

47.3.3 *Other XML Director capabilities*

As Figure 47-3 shows, the *XML Director* is installed inline between the router and the XML servers. No changes to the existing XML implementation are needed.

The product enables businesses to offload Secure Sockets Layer (SSL) encryption and decryption processing from the server, offering up to 150 times faster processing for secure transactions. The decryption is a prerequisite for inspecting the data packets for their XML tags; it reduces server workloads as a by-product. The device can handle up to 1200 new SSL connections per second.

The *XML Director* can also use URI reference analysis, port number, and virtual IP address as routing criteria.

The device is capable of detecting failing or overloaded XML servers and resubmitting the requests to another server for processing. High availability is supported via a serial cable connection to a backup *XML Director*; if the primary device goes offline, the backup will automatically pick up the load.

Analysis   The dominant use of XML today is for e-business, squarely at the MOM end of the application spectrum. Most of the original thinking about XML, however, has appeared to be at the POP end, where ideas like extended linking and topic maps promise to revolutionize our whole approach to information. So it may have come as a surprise to see that originality is occurring in the mundane, message moving arena as well. Intel's XML applications defy conventional notions of the "appropriate" places to use markup technology.

XML Tutorials

- Basic XML markup
- Document type definitions
- Entities
- Advanced features
- How to read the W3C XML Recommendation
- Full spec on CD-ROM

Part Thirteen

This part continues the XML tutorial that we began in Part One. If you haven't read Part One in its entirety, please go back and do so, as we introduced some critically important ideas there.

In this part, you'll learn every useful detail of the XML 1.0 language. At the end you'll be able to read the markup of both DTDs and document instances.

The part is intended to be read in order, with one exception. As you read the first four chapters you'll notice that here and there we've included excerpts from the XML 1.0 specification. The tutorials are written so that *you can skip the spec excerpts*. They are not required for continuity; they are there so that the hard-core techies among you can get down with the deepest details.

But they need a little tutorial of their own to be read, which is why we have Chapter 52. Dig into that when – and if – you decide to read the spec excerpts in Chapters 48-51, or to tackle the full spec itself, which is on the CD-ROM.

XML basics

- Syntactic details

- The prolog and the document instance

- XML declaration

- Elements and attributes

X ML's central concepts are quite simple, and this chapter outlines the most important of them. Essentially, it gives you what you need to know to actually create XML documents. In subsequent chapters you will learn how to combine them, share text between them, format them, and validate their structure.

Before looking at actual XML markup (don't worry, we'll get there soon!) we should consider some *syntactic* constructs that will recur throughout our discussion of XML documents. By *syntax* we mean the combination of characters that make up an XML document. This is analogous to the distinction between sounds of words and the things that they mean. Essentially, we are talking about where you can put angle brackets, quote marks, ampersands, and other characters and where you cannot! Later we will talk about what they mean when you put them together.

After that, we will discusses the components that make up an XML document instance[1]. We will look at the distinction between the prolog (information XML processors need to know about your document) and the instance (the representation of the real document itself).

---

1. Roughly, what the XML spec calls the "root element".

48.1 | Syntactic details

XML documents are composed of characters from the *Unicode* character set. Any such sequence of characters is called a *string*. The characters in this book can be thought of as one long (but interesting) string of text. Each chapter is also a string. So is each word. XML documents are similarly made up of strings within strings.

Natural languages such as English have a particular *syntax*. The syntax allows you to combine words into grammatical sentences. XML also has syntax. It describes how you combine strings into well-formed XML documents. We will describe the basics of XML's syntax in this section.

48.1.1 *Case-sensitivity*

XML is *case-sensitive*. That means that if the XML specification says to insert the word "ELEMENT", it means that you should insert "ELEMENT" and not "element" or "Element" or "ElEmEnT".

For many people, particularly English speaking people, case-insensitive matching is easier than remembering the case of particular constructs. For instance, if a document type has an element type named img English speakers will often forget and insert IMG. They confuse the two because they are not accustomed to considering case to be significant. This is also why some people new to the Internet tend to TYPE IN ALL UPPER CASE. Most applications of SGML, including HTML, are designed to be case-insensitive. They argue that this eliminates case as a source of errors.

Others argue that the whole concept of case-insensitivity is a throwback to keypunches and other early text-entry devices. They also point out that case-sensitivity is a very complicated concept in an international character set like Unicode for a variety of reasons.

For instance, the rules for case conversion of certain accented characters are different in Quebec from what they are in France. There are also some languages for which the concept of upper-case and lower-case does not exist at all. There is no simple, universal rule for case-insensitive matching. In the end, internationalization won out in XML's design.

So mind your "p's" and "q's" and "P's" and "Q's". Our authoritative laboratory testing by people in white coats indicates that exactly 74.5% of all XML errors are related to case-sensitivity mistakes. Of course XML is also spelling-sensitive and typo-sensitive, so watch out for these and other by-products of human fallibility.

Note that although XML is case-sensitive it is not case-prejudiced. Anywhere that you have the freedom to create your own names or text, you can choose to use upper- or lower-case text, as you prefer. So although you must type XML's keywords exactly as they are described, your own strings can mix and match upper- and lower-case characters however you like.

For instance, when you create your own document types you will be able to choose element type names. A particular name could be all upper-case (SECTION), all lower-case (section) or mixed-case (SeCtION). But because XML is case-sensitive, all references to a particular element type would have to use the same case. It is good practice to create a simple convention such as all lower-case or all upper-case so that you do not have to depend on your memory.

48.1.2 *Markup and data*

The constructs such as tags, entity references, and declarations are called *markup*. These are the parts of your document that are supposed to be understood by the XML processor. The parts that are between the markup are typically supposed to be understood only by other human beings. That is the *character data*. Spec Excerpt 48-1 reports what the XML specification says on this issue.

Spec Excerpt (XML) 48-1. Markup

Markup takes the form of start-tags, end-tags, empty-element tags, entity references, character references, comments, CDATA section delimiters, document type declarations, and processing instructions.

We haven't explained what all of those things are yet, but they are easy to recognize. All of them start with less-than (<) or ampersand (&) characters. Everything else is character data.

48.1.3 *White space*

There is a set of characters called *white space* characters that XML processors treat differently in XML markup. They are the "invisible" characters: space (Unicode/ASCII 32), tab (Unicode/ASCII 9), carriage return (Unicode/ASCII 13) and line feed (Unicode/ASCII 10). These correspond roughly to the `spacebar`, `tab`, and `Enter` keys on your keyboard.

When the XML specification says that white space is allowed at a particular point, you may put as many of these characters as you want in any combination. Just as you might put two lines between paragraphs in a word processor to make a printed document readable, you may put two carriage returns in certain places in an XML document to make your source file more readable and maintainable. When the document is processed, those characters will be ignored.

In other places, white space will be significant. For instance you would not want the processor to strip out the spaces between the words in your document! Thatwouldmakeithardtoread. So white space outside of markup is always preserved in XML and white space within markup may be preserved, ignored, and sometimes combined in weird, and wonderful ways. We will describe the combination rules as we go along.

48.1.4 *Names and name tokens*

When you use XML you will often have to give things names. You will name logical structures with element type names, reusable data with entity names, particular elements with IDs, and so forth. XML names have certain common features. They are not nearly as flexible as character data. See Spec Excerpt 48-2 for more information.

Spec Excerpt (XML) 48-2. Names

A Name [begins] with a letter or one of a few punctuation characters, and [continues] with letters, digits, hyphens, underscores, colons, or full stops, together known as name characters. Names beginning with the string "xml", [matched case-insensitively] are reserved for standardization in this or future versions of this specification.

In other words, you cannot make names that begin with the string "xml" or some case-insensitive variant like "XML" or "XmL". Letters or underscores can be used anywhere in a name. You may include digits, hyphens and full-stop (.) characters in a name, but you may not start the name with one of them. Other characters, like various symbols and white space, cannot be part of a name.

There is another related syntactic construct called a *name token*. Name tokens are just like names except that they *may* start with digits, hyphens, full-stop characters, and the string XML.

Spec Excerpt (XML) 48-3. Name tokens

An Nmtoken (name token) is any mixture of name characters.

In other words every valid name is also a valid name token, but Example 48-1 shows some name tokens that are not valid names.

Example 48-1. Name tokens

```
.1.a.name.token.but.not.a.name
2-a-name-token.but-not.a-name
XML-valid-name-token
```

Like almost everything else in XML, names, and name tokens are matched case-sensitively. Names and name tokens do not allow white space, most punctuation or other "funny" characters. The remaining "ordinary" characters are called *name characters*.

48.1.5 *Literal strings*

The data (text other than markup) can contain almost any characters. Obviously, in the main text of your document you need to be able to use punctuation and white space characters! But sometimes you also need these characters *within* markup. For instance an element might represent a hyperlink and need to contain a URL. The URL would have to go in markup, where characters other than the name characters are not usually allowed.

Literal strings allow users to use funny (non-name) characters within markup, but only in contexts in which it makes sense to specify values that might require those characters. For instance, to specify the URL in the hyperlink, we would need the slash character. Example 48-2 is an example of such an element.

Example 48-2. Literal string in attribute value

```
<REFERENCE URL="http://www.documents.com/document.xml"/>
```

The string that defines the URL is the literal string. This one starts and ends with double quote characters. Literal strings are always surrounded by either single or double quotes. The quotes are not part of the string. See Spec Excerpt 48-4 for more information.

Spec Excerpt (XML) 48-4. Literal data

Literal data is any quoted string not containing the quotation mark used as a delimiter for that string. Literals are used for specifying the content of internal entities, the values of attributes, and external identifiers.

You may use either single (') or double (") quotes to mark (*delimit*) the beginning and end of these strings in your XML document. Whichever type of quote the string starts with, it must end with. The other type may be used within the literal and has no special meaning there. Typically you will use double quotes when you want to put an actual single-quote character in the literal and single quotes when you want to embed an actual double quote. When you do not need to embed either, you can take your pick. For example see Example 48-3.

Example 48-3. Quotes within quotes

```
"This is a double quoted literal."
'This is a single quoted literal.'
"'tis another double quoted literal."
'"And this is single quoted" said the self-referential example.'
```

The ability to have quotes within quotes is quite useful when dealing with human speech or programming language text as in Example 48-4.

Example 48-4. Quoted language

```
"To be or not to be"
'"To be or not to be", quoth Hamlet.'
"'BE!', said Jean-Louis Gassee."
'B = "TRUE";'
```

Note that there *are* ways of including a double quote character inside of a double-quoted literal. This is important because a single literal might (rarely) need both types of quotes.

48.1.6 *Grammars*

Natural language syntax is described with a *grammar*. XML's syntax is also. Some readers will want to dig in and learn the complete, intricate details of XML's syntax. We will provide grammar rules for them as we go along. These come right out of the XML specification. If you want to learn how to read them, you should skip ahead to Chapter 52, "Reading the XML specification", on page 776. After you have read it, you can come back and understand the rules as we present them. Another strategy is to read the chapters without worrying about the grammar rules, and then only use them when you need to answer a particular question about XML syntax.

You can recognize grammar rules taken from the specification by their form. They will look like Spec Excerpt 48-5.

Spec Excerpt (XML) 48-5. An example of a grammar rule

```
xhb ::= 'a' 'good' 'read'
```

We will not specifically introduce these rules, because we do not want to interrupt the flow of the text. They will just pop up in the appropriate place to describe the syntax of something.

48.2 | Prolog vs. instance

Most document representations start with a header that contains information about the real document and how to interpret its representation. This is followed by the representation of the real document.

For instance, HTML has a HEAD element that can contain the TITLE and META elements. After the HEAD element comes the BODY. This is where the representation of the real document resides. Similarly, email messages have "header lines" that describe who the message came from, to whom it is addressed, how it is encoded, and other things.

An XML document is similarly broken up into two main parts: a *prolog* and a *document instance*. The prolog provides information about the interpretation of the document instance, such as the version of XML and the document type to which it conforms. The document instance follows the prolog. It contains the actual document data organized as a hierarchy of elements.

Spec Excerpt (XML) 48-6. Document production

```
document ::=  prolog element Misc*
```

48.3 | The logical structure

The actual content of an XML document goes in the document instance. It is called this because if it has a DTD, it is an instance of a class of documents defined by the DTD. Just as a particular person is an instance of the class of "people", a particular memo is an instance of the class of "memo documents". The formal definition of "memo document" is in the memo DTD.

Here is an example of a small XML document.

Example 48-5. Small XML Document

```
<?xml version="1.0"?>
<!DOCTYPE memo SYSTEM "memo.dtd">
<memo>
<from>
   <name>Paul Prescod</name>
   <email>papresco@prescod.com</email>
</from>
<to>
   <name>Charles Goldfarb</name>
   <email>charles@sgmlsource.com</email>
</to>
<subject>Another Memo Example</subject>
<body>
<paragraph> Charles, I wanted to suggest that we
<emphasis>not</emphasis> use the  typical memo example in
our book. Memos tend to be used anywhere a small, simple
document type is needed, but they are just
<emphasis>so</emphasis> boring!
</paragraph>
</body>
</memo>
```

Because a computer cannot understand the data of the document, it looks primarily at the *tags*, the markup between the less-than and greater-than symbols. The tags delimit the beginning and end of various elements. The computer thinks of the elements as a sort of tree.

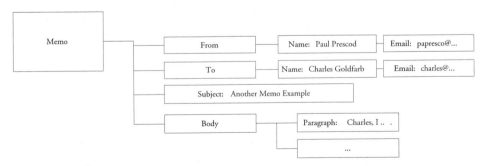

Figure 48-1   The memo XML document viewed as a tree

Figure 48-1 shows a graphical view of the logical structure of the document. The MEMO element is called either the *document element* or the *root element*.

The document element (memo) represents the document as a whole. Every other element represents a component of the document. The from and to elements are meant to indicate the source and target of the memo. The name elements represent people's names. Continuing in this way, the logical structure of the document is apparent from the element-type names.

Experts refer to an element's real-world meaning as its *semantics*. In a particular DTD, the semantics of a P element might be "paragraph" and in another it might mean pence.

If you find yourself reading or writing markup and asking: "But what does that *mean*?" or "What does that look like?" then you are asking about semantics.

Computers do not know anything about semantics. They do not know an HTTP protocol from a supermodel. Document type designers must describe semantics to authors some other way. For instance they could send email, write a book or make a major motion picture (well, maybe some day). What the computer does care about is how an element is supposed to look when it is formatted, or how it is to behave if it is interactive, or what to do with the data once it is extracted. These are specified in *stylesheets* and computer programs.

48.4 | Elements

XML elements break down into two categories. Most have content, which is to say they contain characters, elements or both, and some do not. Those that do not are called *empty elements*. Elements within other elements are called *subelements*.

Example 48-6 is an example of an element with content.

Example 48-6. Simple element

```
<title>This is the title</title>
```

Most elements have *content*. Elements with content begin with a start-tag and finish with an end-tag. The "stuff" between the two is the element's content. In Example 48-6, "This is the title" is the content.

Spec Excerpt (XML) 48-7. Element with content

```
[39] element ::=   start-tag content End-tag
```

XML start-tags consist of the less-than (<) symbol ("left angle bracket"), the name of the element's type, termed a *generic identifier* (*GI*), and a greater-than (>) symbol ("right angle bracket"). Start-tags can also include attributes. We will look at those later in the chapter. The start-tag in Example 48-6 is `<title>` and its generic identifier is "title".

Spec Excerpt (XML) 48-8. Start-tag

```
[40] STag ::=   '<' Name (S Attribute)* S? '>'
```

XML end-tags consist of the string "</", the same generic identifier (or *GI*) as in the start-tag, and a greater-than (>) symbol. The end-tag in Example 48-6 is `</title>`.

You must always repeat the GI in the end-tag. This helps you to keep track of which end-tags line up with which start-tags. If you ever forget one or the other, the processor will know immediately, and will alert you that the document is not well-formed. The downside of this redundancy is that it requires more typing. Some people like belts and some prefer suspenders. The XML Working Group likes belts *and* suspenders.

Spec Excerpt (XML) 48-9. End-tag

```
[42] ETag ::=   '</' Name S? '>'
```

Note that less-than symbols in content are always interpreted as beginning a tag. If the characters following them would not constitute a valid tag, then the document is not well-formed.

Caution   Use the word "tag" precisely.
Many people use the word "tag" imprecisely. Sometimes they mean "generic identifier", sometimes "element-type name", sometimes "element type" and sometimes they actually mean "tag". This leads to confusion. In XML, tags always start with less-than symbols and end with greater-than symbols. Nothing else is a tag. Tags are not defined in DTDs; element types are defined in DTDs.

It is possible for an element to have no content at all. Such an element is called an *empty element*. One way to denote an empty element is to merely leave out the content. But as a shortcut, empty elements may also have a different syntax. Because there is no content to delimit, they may consist of a single empty-element tag. That looks like this: <EmptyTag/>.

The slash at the end indicates that this is an empty-element tag, so there is no content or end-tag coming up. The slash is meant to be reminiscent of the slash in the end-tag of an element with both tags.

Spec Excerpt (XML) 48-10. Empty-element tag

```
[44]    EmptyElemTag ::=   '<' Name (S Attribute)* S? '/>'
```

Usually empty elements have *attributes*. Occasionally an empty element without attributes will be used to flag a particular location in a document. Example 48-7 is an example of an empty element with an attribute.

Example 48-7. Empty element with attribute

```
<EMPTY-ELEMENT ATTR="ATTVAL"/>
```

In summary, elements are either empty or have content. Elements with content are represented by a start-tag, the content, and an end-tag. Empty elements can either have a start-tag and end-tag with nothing in between, or a single empty-element tag. An element's type is always identified by the generic identifiers in its tags.

The reason we distinguish element types from generic identifiers is because the term "generic identifier" refers to the syntax of the XML document – the characters that represent the real document. The term "element type" refers to a property of a component of the real document.

48.5 | Attributes

In addition to content, elements may have *attributes*. Attributes are a way of attaching characteristics or properties to elements of a document. Attributes have *names*, just as real-world properties do. They also have *values*. For instance, two possible attributes of people are their "shoe size" and "IQ" (the attributes' names), and two possible values are "12" and "12" (respectively).

In a DTD, each attribute is defined for a specific element type and is allowed to exhibit a certain type of value. Multiple element types could provide attributes with the same name and it is sometimes convenient to think of them as the "same attribute" even though they technically are not.

Attributes have semantics also. They always *mean* something. For example, an attribute named `height` might be provided for `person` elements (allowed occurrence), exhibit values that are numbers (allowed values), and represent the person's height in centimeters (semantics).

Here is how attributes of `person` elements might look:

Example 48-8. Elements with attributes

```
<person height="165cm">Dale Wick</person>
<person height="165cm" weight="165lb">Bill Bunn</person>
```

As you can see, the attribute name does not go in quotes, but the attribute value does.

Spec Excerpt (XML) 48-11. Attributes

```
[41]  Attribute ::=  Name Eq AttValue
[25]  Eq ::=  S? '=' S?
```

Like other literals (see 48.1.5, "Literal strings", on page 681), attributes can be surrounded by either single (') or double (") quotes. When you use one type of quote, the other can be used within that attribute value. As we discussed earlier, this makes it convenient to create attribute values that have the quote characters within them. This is shown in Example 48-9.

Example 48-9. Attribute values can have quotes in them

```
<PERSON HEIGHT='80"'> ... </PERSON>
<PERSON QUOTE="'To be or not to be'">...</PERSON>
```

There are other ways of getting special characters into attribute values and we will discuss them in 51.2, "Character references", on page 763.

A DTD constrains an attribute's allowed occurrence and values. One possibility is to require an attribute to be specified for all elements. For example, a military document might require section elements to have a security attribute with the value unclassified, classified, or secret. Example 48-10 demonstrates.

Example 48-10. Security attribute declaration

```
<!ATTLIST SECTION
          SECURITY (unclassified | classified | secret) #REQUIRED >
```

The attribute would need to be specified for each section element as shown in Example 48-11.

Example 48-11. Security attribute specification

```
<SECTION SECURITY="unclassified">...</SECTION>
```

It would be a validity error to create a section element without a security attribute.

Usually empty elements have attributes. Sometimes an element with sub-elements can be modeled just as well with an empty element and attributes. Example 48-12 shows two ways of modeling a person element in an email message.

Yet another way to do it would be to let the person's name be data content as shown in Example 48-13.

Example 48-12. Alternative person element

```
<FROM><NAME>Paul Prescod</NAME>
      <EMAIL>"papresco@prescod.com"</EMAIL>
</FROM>
vs.
<FROM NAME="Paul Prescod" EMAIL="papresco@prescod.com"/>
```

Example 48-13. Another alternative person element

```
<FROM><PERSON EMAIL="papresco@prescod.com">Paul Prescod
      </PERSON>
</FROM>
```

As you can see, there can be many different ways to represent the same construct. There is no one right way to do so. In the case of person, the last version shown is the most typical because the character data of a document generally represents what you would expect to see in a "print-out".

But that is not a hard and fast rule (after all, renditions vary widely). Because there are so many ways to represent the same thing, it is advisable to use a DTD. The constraints in a DTD can maintain consistency across a range of documents, or even within a single large document. There may be many ways to represent a particular concept, but once you choose one, let the DTD help you stick to it.

48.6 | The prolog

XML documents should start with a prolog that describes the XML version ("1.0", for now), document type, and other characteristics of the document.

The prolog is made up of an *XML declaration* and a *document type declaration*, both optional. Though an author may include either, neither, or both, it is best to try to maximize the amount of prolog information provided. This will make later processing more reliable.

The XML declaration must precede the document type declaration if both are provided. Also, comments, processing instructions, and white space can be mixed in among the two declarations. The prolog ends when the first start-tag begins.

Example 48-14 is a sample prolog as a warm-up.

Example 48-14. A simple prolog

```
<?xml version="1.0"?>
<!DOCTYPE book SYSTEM "http://www.oasis-open.org/.../docbookx.dtd".
```

This DTD says that the document conforms to XML version 1.0 and declares adherence to a particular document type, book.

Spec Excerpt (XML) 48-12. Prolog

```
[22]  prolog ::=  XMLDecl? Misc* (doctypedecl Misc*)?
[27]  Misc ::=  Comment | PI | S
```

48.6.1 *XML declaration*

The XML declaration is fairly simple. It has several parts and they fit together one after another.

Spec Excerpt (XML) 48-13. XML declaration

```
[23]  XMLDecl ::=  '<?xml' VersionInfo EncodingDecl? SDDecl? S? '?>'
```

A minimal XML declaration looks like this:

Example 48-15. Minimal XML declaration

```
<?xml version="1.0"?>
```

Example 48-16 is a more expansive one, using all of its parts.

Example 48-16. More expansive XML declaration

```
<?xml version="1.0" encoding="UTF-8" standalone="yes"?>
```

There is one important thing to note in the last example. It looks like a start-tag with attributes, but it is *not*. The different parts of the XML declaration just happen to look like attributes. Well, not quite "just happen": it could have had a completely different syntax, but that would have been harder to memorize. So the parts were chosen to look like attributes to reduce the complexity of the language. One important difference between XML declaration parts and attributes is that the parts are strictly ordered whereas attributes can be specified in any order.

48.6.1.1 Version info

The *version info* part of the XML declaration declares the version of XML that is in use. It is required in all XML declarations. At the time of writing, the only valid version string is "1.0". But if you always use the version string, you can be confident that future XML processors will not think that your document was meant to conform to XML version 2.0 or 3.0 when and if those languages become available. Since they do not exist yet, you cannot know if your documents will be compatible with them.

In fact, the only reason that the XML declaration is optional is so that some HTML and SGML documents can be used as XML documents without confusing the software that they usually work with. You can imagine that an older browser would not react nicely to an HTML document with an XML declaration. But this "backwards compatibility" consideration is only temporary. Future versions of XML may require the XML declaration.

The XML version information is part of a general trend towards information representations that are *self-identifying*. This means that you can look at an XML document and (if it has the declaration) know immediately both that it is XML and what version of XML it uses. As more and more document representations become self-identifying, we will be able to stop relying on error-prone identification schemes like file extensions.

48.6.1.2 Encoding declaration

An XML declaration may also include an *encoding declaration*. It describes what character encoding is used. This is another aspect of being self-identifying. If your documents are encoded in the traditional 7-bit-ASCII used on most operating systems and with most text editors, then you do not need to worry about the encoding-declaration. 7-bit-ASCII is a subset of a Unicode encoding called *UTF-8* which XML processors can automatically detect and use. If you use 7-bit ASCII and need to encode a character outside of 7-bit-ASCII, such as the trademark sign or a non-English character, you can do so most easily by using a numeric character reference, as described in 51.2, "Character references", on page 763.

Spec Excerpt (XML) 48-14. Encoding declaration

```
[80]EncodingDecl::= S 'encoding'
                  Eq ('"' EncName '"' | "'" EncName "'" )
[81]EncName::= [A-Za-z] ([A-Za-z0-9._] |'-')*
```

48.6.1.3   Standalone document declaration

An XML declaration can include a *standalone document declaration*. It declares what components of the document type definition are necessary for complete processing of the document. This declaration is described in 51.5, "Standalone document declaration", on page 771.

48.6.2   *Document type declaration*

Somewhere after the XML declaration (if present) and before the first element, the *document type declaration* declares the document type that is in use in the document. A "book" document type, for example, might be made up of chapters, while a letter document type could be made up of element types such as ADDRESS, SALUTATION, SIGNATURE, and so forth.

The document type declaration is at the heart of the concept of *structural validity*, which makes applications based on XML robust and reliable. It includes the markup declarations that express the *document type definition (DTD)*.

The DTD is a formalization of the intuitive idea of a document type. The DTD lists the element types available and can put constraints on the occurrence and content of elements and other details of the document structure. This makes an information system more robust by forcing the documents that are part of it to be consistent.

48.7 | Markup miscellany

This section contains information on some more useful markup constructs. They are not as important or as widely used as elements, attributes and the XML declaration, but they are still vital parts of a markup expert's toolbox.

48.7.1 *Predefined entities*

Sometimes when you are creating an XML document, you want to protect certain characters from markup interpretation. Imagine, for example, that you are writing a user's guide to HTML. You would need a way to include an example of markup. Your first attempt might be to create an `example` element and do something like this Example 48-17.

Example 48-17. An invalid approach to HTML examples in XML

```
<p>HTML documents must start with a DOCTYPE, etc. etc. This
is an example of a small HTML document:
<sample>

  <!DOCTYPE HTML PUBLIC "-//W3C//DTD HTML 3.2 Final//EN">
  <HTML>
  A document's title
  <H1>A document's title</H1>
  </HTML>

</sample>
```

   This will not work, however, because the angle brackets that are supposed to represent HTML markup will be interpreted as if they belonged to the XML document you are creating, not the mythical HTML document in the example. Your XML processor will complain that it is not appropriate to have an HTML DOCTYPE declaration in the middle of an XML document! There are two solutions to this problem: predefined entities and CDATA sections.

   Predefined entities are XML markup that authors use to represent characters that would otherwise be interpreted as having a special meaning, such as a start-tag or an entity reference. There are five *predefined* ("built-in") entities in XML. These were included precisely to deal with this problem. They are listed in Table 48-1.

Table 48-1   Predefined entities

Entity reference	Character
&amp;	&
&lt;	<
&gt;	>
&apos;	'
&quot;	"

Why these specific five characters?

Spec Excerpt (XML) 48-15. Predefined entities

The ampersand character (&) and the left angle bracket (<) may appear in their literal form only when used as markup delimiters, or within a comment, a processing instruction, or a CDATA section. [...] If they are needed elsewhere, they must be escaped using either numeric character references or the strings "&" and "<" respectively.

Spec Excerpt (XML) 48-16. Attribute values

To allow attribute values to contain both single and double quotes, the apostrophe or single-quote character (') may be represented as "'", and the double-quote character (") as """.

An entity for the right angle bracket is also provided because it is sometimes useful to avoid putting a special string called *CDEnd* (discussed later) into your document. But you do not have to use this entity in most cases.

We can use references to the predefined entities to insert these characters, instead of typing them directly. Then they will not be interpreted as markup. Example 48-18 demonstrates this.

Example 48-18. Writing about HTML in XML

```
<p>HTML documents must start with a DOCTYPE, etc. etc. This
is an example of a small HTML document:
<sample>
   &lt;!DOCTYPE HTML PUBLIC "-//W3C//DTD HTML 3.2 Final//EN">
   &lt;HTML>
   &lt;HEAD>
   &lt;TITLE>A document's title
   &lt;/TITLE>
   &lt;/HEAD>
   &lt;/HTML>
</sample>
```

When your XML processor parses the document, it will replace the entity references with actual characters. It will not interpret the characters it inserts as markup, but as "plain old data characters" (character data).

48.7.2 CDATA sections

While predefined entities are convenient, human beings are not as good at decoding them as computers are. Your readers will get the translated version, so they will be fine. But as the author, you will spend hours staring at character entity references while you are editing your XML document. You may also spend hours replacing special characters with character entity references. This can get annoying.[1]

Another construct, called a *CDATA section*, allows you to ask the processor not to interpret a chunk of text as containing markup: "Hands off! This isn't meant to be interpreted." CDATA stands for "character data". You can mark a section as being character data using this special syntax as shown in Example 48-19.

Example 48-19. CDATA section

```
'<![CDATA[' content ']]>'
```

Example 48-20 and Example 48-21 are other examples.

---

1. This is especially nasty when you are writing an XML book, where examples tend to contain many angle brackets.

Example 48-20. Writing about HTML in a CDATA section

```
<![CDATA[
<HTML>
This is an example from HTML for Dumbbells!
<p>It may be a pain to write a book about HTML in HTML,
but it is easy in XML!
</HTML>
]]>
```

Example 48-21. Java code in a CDATA section

```
<![CDATA[
if( foo.getContentLength() < 0  && input = foo.getInputStream() )
    open = true;
]]>
```

As you can see, it does not usually matter what you put in CDATA sections because their content is not scanned for markup. There is one obvious exception (and one not-so-obvious corollary). The string that ends the CDATA section,]]> (known as *CDEnd*), cannot be used inside the section. Use Example 48-22 as a cautionary tale.

Example 48-22. Illegal CDATA usage

```
<![CDATA[
 Javascript code: if( a[c[5]]> 7 ) then...
]]>
```

The first occurrence of CDEnd in the middle of the Javascript expression will terminate the section. You simply cannot use a CDATA section for content that includes CDEnd. You must end the section and insert the character as in Example 48-23.

Example 48-23. Legal CDATA usage

```
<![CDATA[
 Javascript code: if( a[c[5]]]>><![CDATA[ 7 ) then...
]]>
```

This is quite painful and can cause a problem for embedding programming languages. But even in those languages, CDEnd is probably a fairly rare character string, so you should just keep an eye out for it.

The non-obvious corollary is:

Caution   CDEnd (]]>) *should only be used to close CDATA sections. It must not occur anywhere else in an XML document.*

This is an absolute requirement, not just a recommendation. Because of it you can easily check that you have closed CDATA sections correctly by comparing the number of CDEnd strings to the number of sections. If you do not close a CDATA section correctly, some of your document's markup may be interpreted as character data. Since (]]>) is not something that typical documents contain, this restriction is rarely a problem.

With all of these warnings, CDATA sections may sound tricky to use, but they really aren't. This book, for example, has several hundred. Mistakes involving CDATA sections are usually quite blatant, because either markup will show up in your rendered document, or data characters will be interpreted as markup and probably trigger an error message.

Predefined entities and CDATA sections only relate to the interpretation of the markup, not to the properties of the real document that the markup represents.

48.7.3 *Comments*

Sometimes it is useful to embed information about a document or its markup in a manner that will be ignored by computer processes and renditions of the document. For example, you might insert a note to yourself to clean up the wording of a section, a note to a co-author explaining the reason for a particular section of the document, or a note in a DTD describing the semantics of a particular element. This information can be hidden from the application in a *comment*. Comments should never be displayed in a browser, indexed in a search engine, or otherwise processed as part of the data of the real document. They may, however, be treated as metadata.

Example 48-24. A comment

```
<!-- This section is really good! Let's not change it. -->
```

Comments consist of the characters "<!--" followed by almost anything and ended by "-->". The "almost anything" in the middle cannot contain the characters "--". This is a little bit inconvenient, because people often use those two characters as a sort of dash, to separate thoughts. This is another point to be careful of, lest you get bitten.

Spec Excerpt (XML) 48-17. Comment

```
[15]   Comment ::= '<!--'((Char - '-')|('-'(Char - '-')))*'-->'
```

Comments can go just about anywhere in the instance or the prolog. However, they cannot go within declarations, tags, or other comments. Example 48-25 is a document using some comments in several correct places.

Example 48-25. Comments all over the place

```
<?xml version="1.0"?>
<!-- There is no other version yet! -->
<!-- Now on to the doctype -->
<!DOCTYPE SAMPLE [
  <!-- This is a comment in the
  doctype declaration internal subset! -->
  <!ELEMENT SAMPLE (#PCDATA)>
  <!-- This is a very simple DTD. -->
]> <!-- Here comes the "root" or "document" element. -->
<SAMPLE>This is some character data.
<!-- That was some character data. -->
</SAMPLE>
<!-- That's all folks -->
```

Markup is not recognized in comments. You can put less-than and ampersand symbols in them, but they will not be recognized as the start of elements or entity references.

Comments are a good place to describe the semantics of element types and attributes. So you might use a comment to tell other DTD maintainers and authors that an element type with a cryptic name like p is actually intended to model paragraphs and not (for example) British currency. Comments are not just about being helpful to other people. After all, even expert document type designers have a limited and imperfect memory. Some day even you will wonder exactly what it was you meant by a particular element-type name. The DTD comments will help. The job that you are saving might be your own!

48.8 | Summary

An XML document is composed of a prolog and a document instance. The prolog is optional, and provides information about how the document is structured both physically (where its parts are) and logically (how its elements fit together). Elements and attributes describe the logical structure. Entities describe the physical structure. To use a rough analogy, the entities are like a robot's body parts, the elements are his thoughts, and stylesheets and software provide his behavior.

Creating a document type definition

- Document type declaration
- Element type declarations
- Attribute list declarations

Chapter

49

Creating your own document type definition or schema definition is like creating your own markup language. If you have ever chafed at the limitations of a language with a fixed set of element types, such as HTML or TEI, then you will embrace the opportunity to create your own language.[1] DTDs are XML's built-in markup-language definition language.

Another way of expressing your ideas formally is by creating a schema definition using XSDL, which we discuss in Chapter 59, "XML Schema (XSDL)", on page 908. Schema definitions allow even more power (and complexity!) than DTDs, so they are also important to learn.

We should note again that it is possible to keep a document type definition completely in your head rather than writing the declarations for a DTD or schema. Sometimes DTD designers do that while they are testing out ideas. Usually, though, you actually commit your ideas to declarations so that a validating processor can help you to keep your documents consistent.

We feel that it is important for serious XML users to understand both. Because schema definitions employ DTD concepts, learning one will help

---

1. With its own set of limitations!

you learn the other. Indeed, *XML Schema* datatypes, covered in Chapter 58, "Datatypes ", on page 894, can even be used in conjunction with DTDs.

Note also that, for the present, we are maintaining the distinction, discussed in 6.3, "Document type, DTD, and markup declarations", on page 96, between a document type, the XML markup rules for it (DTD), and the markup declarations that declare the DTD. Those *DTD declarations* are connected to the big kahuna of markup declarations – the *document type declaration*.

49.1 | Document type declaration

A document type declaration for a particular document might say "This document is a concert poster." The document type definition for the document would say "A concert poster must have the following features." As an analogy: in the world of art, you can *declare* yourself a practitioner of a particular movement, or you can *define* the movement by writing its manifesto.

The XML spec uses the abbreviation DTD to refer to document type definitions because we speak of them much more often than document type declarations. The DTD defines the allowed element types, attributes and entities and can express some constraints on their combination.

A document that conforms to its DTD is said to be *valid*. Just as an English sentence can be ungrammatical, a document can fail to conform to its DTD and thus be *invalid*. That does not necessarily mean, however, that it ceases to be an XML document. The word valid does not have its usual meaning here. An artist can fail to uphold the principles of an artistic movement without ceasing to be an artist, and an XML document can violate its DTD and yet remain a well-formed XML document.

As the document type declaration is optional, a well-formed XML document can choose not to declare conformance to any DTD at all. It cannot then be a valid document, because it cannot be checked for conformance to a DTD. It is not invalid, because it does not violate the constraints of a DTD.

XML has no good word for these merely well-formed documents. Some people call them "well-formed", but that is insufficiently precise. If the document were not well-formed, it would not be XML (by definition). Saying that a document is well-formed does not tell us anything about its conformance to a DTD at all.

For this reason, we prefer the terms used by the ISO for full-SGML: *type-valid*, meaning "valid with respect to a document type", and *non-type-valid*, the converse.

Example 49-1 is an XML document containing a document type declaration and document type definition for mailing labels, followed by an instance of the document type: a single label.

Example 49-1. XML document with document type declaration

```
<!DOCTYPE label[
    <!ELEMENT label (name, street, city, state, country, code)>
    <!ELEMENT name (#PCDATA)>
    <!ELEMENT street (#PCDATA)>
    <!ELEMENT city (#PCDATA)>
    <!ELEMENT state (#PCDATA)>
    <!ELEMENT country (#PCDATA)>
    <!ELEMENT code (#PCDATA)>
]><label>
<name>Rock N. Robyn</name>
<street>Jay Bird Street</street>
<city>Baltimore</city>
<state>MD</state>
<country>USA</country>
<code>43214</code>
</label>
```

The document type declaration starts on the first line and ends with "]>". The DTD declarations are the lines starting with "<!ELEMENT". Those are *element type declarations*. You can also declare attributes, entities and notations for a DTD. The element type declarations that contain #PCDATA (parsed character data) allow textual data content.

Recall from 2.4, "Entities: The physical structure", on page 34 that an XML document can be broken up into separate objects for storage, called "entities".[1] The document type declaration occurs in the first (or only) entity to be parsed, called the "document entity".

In Example 49-1, all of the DTD declarations that define the label DTD reside within the document entity. However, the DTD could have been partially or completely defined somewhere else. In that case, the document type declaration would contain a reference to another entity containing those declarations.

---

1. Loosely, an entity is like a file.

A document type declaration with only external DTD declarations looks like Example 49-2.

Example 49-2. Document type declaration with external DTD declarations

```
<?xml version="1.0"?>
<!DOCTYPE label SYSTEM "http://www.sgmlsource.com/dtds/label.dtd">
<label>
...
</label>
```

They keyword SYSTEM is described more completely in 50.9.1, "System identifiers", on page 756. For now, we will just say that it tells the processor to fetch some resource containing the external information. In this case, the external information is made up of the declarations that define the label DTD. They should be exactly the ones we had in the original label document. The big difference is that now they can be reused in hundreds, thousands, or even millions of label documents. Our simple DTD could be the basis for the largest junk mailing in history!

All document type declarations start with the string "<!DOCTYPE". Next they have the name of an element type that is defined in the DTD. The root element in the instance (described in 48.4, "Elements", on page 686) must be of the type declared in the document type declaration. If any of the DTD declarations are stored externally, the third part of the document type declaration must be either "SYSTEM" or "PUBLIC". We will cover "PUBLIC" later. If it is "SYSTEM", the final part must be a "URI" pointing to the external declarations. A URI is, for all practical purposes, a URL. URIs are discussed in 56.2, "Uniform Resource Identifiers", on page 862.

Spec Excerpt (XML) 49-1. DOCTYPE declaration

```
[28] doctypedecl ::= '<!DOCTYPE' S Name (S ExternalID)? S? ('['
                     (markupdecl | PEReference | S)* ']' S?)? '>'
[75] ExternalID ::=  'SYSTEM' S SystemLiteral
                     | 'PUBLIC' S PubidLiteral S SystemLiteral

[29] markupdecl ::= elementdecl | AttlistDecl | EntityDecl
                    | NotationDecl | PI | Comment
```

49.2 | Internal and external subset

In Example 49-1, the DTD declarations were completely *internal*. They were inside of the document type declaration. In Example 49-2, they were completely external. In many cases, there will be a mix of the two. This section will review these options and show how most XML document type declarations combine an internal part, called the *internal subset* and an external part, called the *external subset*.

From now on, as we'll almost always be writing about DTD declarations, we'll refer to them as "the DTD". We'll resort to the finer distinctions only when necessary for clarity.

We will start with an example of a DTD in Example 49-3.

Example 49-3. Garage sale announcement DTD.

```
<!ELEMENT GARAGESALE (DATE, TIME, PLACE, NOTES)>
<!ELEMENT DATE (#PCDATA)>
<!ELEMENT TIME (#PCDATA)>
<!ELEMENT PLACE (#PCDATA)>
<!ELEMENT NOTES (#PCDATA)>
```

These markup declarations would make up an ultra-simple DTD for garage sale announcements.[1] As you may have deduced, it declares five element types. We will get to the syntax of the declarations soon. First we will look at how they would be used. These could reside in a separate file called `garage.dtd` (for instance) and then every document that wanted to conform to them would declare its conformance using a document type declaration. This is shown in Example 49-4.

Instead of a complete URL, we have just referred to the DTD's file name. Actually, this is still a URL. It is a *relative URL*. That means that in a standard Web server setup, the XML document entity and its DTD entity reside in the same directory. You could also refer to a full URL as we do in Example 49-5.

The relative URL is more convenient while you are testing because you do not need to have a full server installed. You can just put the two entities

---

1. A garage sale is where North Americans spend their hard-earned money on other people's junk, which they will eventually sell at their own garage sales.

Example 49-4. Conforming garage sale document.

```
<!DOCTYPE GARAGESALE SYSTEM "garage.dtd">
<GARAGESALE>
<DATE>February 29, 1998</DATE>
<TIME>7:30 AM</TIME>
<PLACE>249 Cedarbrae</PLACE>
<NOTES>Lots of high-quality junk for sale!</NOTES>
</GARAGESALE>
```

Example 49-5. Specifying a full URL

```
<!DOCTYPE GARAGESALE SYSTEM
          "http://www.tradestuff.com/stuff.dtd">
<GARAGESALE>
...
</GARAGESALE>
```

in the same directory on your hard drive. But your DTD and your instance can get even more cozy than sharing a directory. You can hoist your DTD into the same entity as the instance as in Example 49-6.

Example 49-6. Bringing a DTD into the same entity as the instance

```
<!DOCTYPE GARAGESALE
[
<!ELEMENT GARAGESALE (DATE, TIME, PLACE, NOTES)>
<!ELEMENT DATE (#PCDATA)>
<!ELEMENT TIME (#PCDATA)>
<!ELEMENT PLACE (#PCDATA)>
<!ELEMENT NOTES (#PCDATA)>
]>
<GARAGESALE>
...
</GARAGESALE>
```

The section between the square brackets is called the *internal subset* of the document type declaration. For testing, this is very convenient! You can edit the instance and the DTD without moving between entities. Since entities usually correspond to files, this means that instead of moving between two files, you need only edit one.

Although this is convenient, it is not great for reuse. The DTD is not available anywhere but in this file. Other documents cannot conform to this DTD without copying the declarations into their internal subset.

Often you will combine both approaches. Some of the DTD declarations can go in an external entity where it can be reused, and some of it can go in the same entity as the instance. Often graphic entities (see 50.6, "Unparsed entities", on page 747) would be declared in the internal subset because they are specific to a document. On the other hand, element type declarations would usually be in the *external subset*, the external part of the document type declaration. Example 49-7 demonstrates.

Example 49-7. Reference to an external subset

```
<!DOCTYPE GARAGESALE SYSTEM "garage.dtd"[
<!ENTITY LOGO SYSTEM "logo.gif">
]><GARAGESALE> ... </GARAGESALE>
```

The declarations in the internal subset are processed before those in the external subset. This gives document authors the opportunity to override[1] some kinds of declarations in the shared portion of the DTD.

Note that the content of both the internal subset and the external subset makes up the DTD. `garage.dtd` may have a `.dtd` extension but that is just a convention we chose to emphasize that the file contains DTD declarations. It is *not* necessarily the full set of them. The full set of DTD declarations is the combination of the declarations in the internal and external subsets.

Caution   Many people believe that the file containing the external subset is "the DTD". Until it is referenced from a document type declaration and combined with an internal subset (even an empty one) it is just a file that happens to have markup declarations in it. It is good practice, however, when an external subset is used, to restrict the internal subset to declarations that apply only to the individual document, such as entity declarations for graphics.

It is often very convenient to point to a particular file and refer to it as "the DTD" for a given document type. As long as the concepts are straight

---

1. Actually, preempt.

in your mind, it does seem a trifle simpler than saying "the file that contains the markup declarations that I intend to reference as the external subset of the document type declaration for all documents of this type".

49.3 | Element type declarations

Elements are the foundation of XML markup. Every element in a valid XML document must conform to an element type declared in the DTD. Documents with elements that do not conform could be well-formed, but not valid. Example 49-8 is an example of an element type declaration.

Example 49-8. Element type declaration.

```
<!ELEMENT memo (to, from, body )>
```

Element type declarations must start with the string "<!ELEMENT", followed by the name (or *generic identifier* of the element type being declared. Finally they must have a *content specification*. The content specification above states that elements of this type must contain a `to` element followed by a `from` element followed in turn by a `body` element.

Spec Excerpt (XML) 49-2. Element type declaration

```
<!ELEMENT' S Name S contentspec S? '>'
```

Element type names are XML *names*. That means there are certain restrictions on the characters allowed in them. These are described in 48.1.4, "Names and name tokens", on page 680. Each element type declaration must use a different name because a particular element type cannot be declared more than once.

Caution   Unique element type declaration. Unlike attributes and entities, element types can be declared only once.

49.4 | Element type content specification

Every element type has certain allowed content. For instance a document type definition might allow a `chapter` to have a `title` in its content, but would probably not allow a `footnote` to have a `chapter` in its content (though XML itself would not prohibit that!).

There are four kinds of content specification. These are described in Table 49-1.

Table 49-1   Content specification types

Content specification type	Allowed content
EMPTY content	May not have content. They are typically used for their attributes.
ANY content	May have any content at all.
Mixed content	May have character data or a mix of character data and subelements specified in mixed content specification.
Element content	May have only subelements specified in element content specification

49.4.1 *Empty content*

Sometimes we want an element type that can never have any content. We would give it a content specification of `EMPTY`. For instance an image element type like HTML's `img` would include a graphic from somewhere else. It would do this through an attribute and would not need any subelements or character data content. A cross-reference element type might not need content because the text for the reference might be generated from the target. A reference to an element type with the title "More about XML" might become "See *More about XML* on page 14".

You can declare an element type to have empty content by using the EMPTY keyword as the content specification. See Example 49-9.

Example 49-9. Empty element type

```
<!ELEMENT MY-EMPTY-ELEMENT EMPTY>
```

49.4.2 *ANY content*

Occasionally, you want an element type to be able to hold any element or character data. You can do this if you give it a content spec of ANY as in Example 49-10.

Example 49-10. Element type with ANY content

```
<!ELEMENT LOOSEY-GOOSEY ANY>
```

This is rarely done. Typically we introduce element type declarations to express the structure of our document types. An element type that has an ANY content specification is completely unstructured. It can contain any combination of character data and subelements. Still, ANY content element types are occasionally useful, especially while a DTD is being developed. If you are developing a DTD for existing documents, then you could declare each element type to have ANY content to get the document to validate. Then you could try to figure out more precise content specifications for each element type, one at a time.

49.4.3 *Mixed content*

Element types with *mixed content* are allowed to hold either character data alone or character data with child elements interspersed. A paragraph is a good example of a typical mixed content element. It might have character data with some mixed in emphasis and quotation subelements. The simplest mixed content specifications allow data only and start with a left parenthesis character ("("), followed by the string #PCDATA and a final close parenthesis (")"). Example 49-11 demonstrates.

Example 49-11. Data-only mixed content

```
<!ELEMENT emph (#PCDATA)>
<!ELEMENT foreign-language ( #PCDATA ) >
```

You may put white space between the parenthesis and the string #PCDATA if you like. The declarations above create element types that cannot contain subelements. Subelements that are detected will be reported as validity errors.

In other words, these elements do not really have "mixed" content in the usual sense. Like the word "valid", XML has a particular meaning for the word that is not very intuitive. Any content specification that contains #PCDATA is called mixed, whether subelements are allowed or not.

We can easily extend the DTD to allow a mix of elements and character data. This is shown in Example 49-12.

Example 49-12. Allow a mix of character data and elements

```
<!ELEMENT paragraph (#PCDATA|emph)*>
<!ELEMENT abstract (#PCDATA|emph|quot)*>
<!ELEMENT title ( #PCDATA | foreign-language | emph )* >
```

Note the trailing asterisk. It is required in content specifications that allow a mix of character data and elements. The reason it is there will be made clear when we study content models. Note also that we can put white space before and after the vertical bar ("|") characters.

These declarations create element types that allow a mix of character data and subelements. The element types listed after the vertical bars ("|"), are the allowed subelements. Example 49-13 would be a valid title if we combine the declarations in Example 49-12 with those in Example 49-11.

Example 49-13. Sample data

```
<title>this is a <foreign-language>tres gros</foreign-language>
       title for an <emph>XML</emph> book</title>
```

The title has character data ("This is a"), a foreign-language subelement, some more character data ("title for an"), an emph subelement and some final character data "book". We could have reordered the emph and foreign-language elements and the character data however we wanted.

We could also have introduced as many (or as few) `emph` and `foreign-language` elements as we needed.

49.5 | Content models

The final kind of content specification is a "children" specification. This type of specification says that elements of the type can contain only child elements in its content. You declare an element type as having *element content* by specifying a content model that has only element type names, instead of a mixed content specification or one of the keywords described above.

A content model is a pattern that you set up to declare what subelement types are allowed and in what order they are allowed. A simple model for a `memo` might say that it must contain a `from` followed by a `to` followed by a `subject` followed by a `paragraph`. A more complex model for a `question-and-answer` might require `question` and `answer` elements to alternate.

A model for a `chapter` might require a single `title` element, one or two `author` elements and one or more `paragraphs`. When a document is validated, the processor would check that the element's content matches the model.

A simple content model could have a single subelement type as in Example 49-14.

Example 49-14. A single subelement

```
<!ELEMENT WARNING (PARAGRAPH)>
```

This says that a WARNING must have a single PARAGRAPH within it. As with mixed content specifications, you may place white space before or after the parentheses. We could also say that a WARNING must have a TITLE and then a PARAGRAPH within it as in Example 49-15.

Example 49-15. Two subelements

```
<!ELEMENT WARNING (TITLE, PARAGRAPH)>
```

The comma (",") between the "TITLE" and "PARAGRAPH" GIs indicates that the "TITLE" must precede the "PARAGRAPH" in the "WARNING" element. This is called a *sequence*. Sequences can be as long as you like (Example 49-16).

Example 49-16. Longer sequence

```
<!ELEMENT MEMO (FROM, TO, SUBJECT, BODY)>
```

You may put white space before or after the comma (",") between two parts of the sequence.

Sometimes you want to have a *choice* rather than a sequence. For instance Example 49-17 shows a declaration for an element type that allows a FIGURE to contain either a GRAPHIC element (inserting an external graphic) or a CODE element (inserting some computer code).

Example 49-17. Allowing choice

```
<!ELEMENT FIGURE (GRAPHIC|CODE)>
```

The vertical bar character ("|") indicates that the author can choose between the element types. We say that this is a *choice* group. You can put white space before or after the vertical bar. You may have as many choices as you want:

Example 49-18. Multiple Choices

```
<!ELEMENT FIGURE (CODE|TABLE | FLOW-CHART| SCREEN-SHOT)>
```

You may also combine choices and sequences using parenthesis. When you wrap parenthesis around a choice or sequence, it becomes a *content particle*. Individual GIs are also content particles. You can use any content particle where ever you would use a GI in a content model:

Example 49-19. Content particles

```
<!ELEMENT FIGURE (CAPTION, (CODE|TABLE|FLOW-CHART|SCREEN-SHOT) )>
<!ELEMENT CREATED ((AUTHOR | CO-AUTHORS), DATE )>
```

The content model for FIGURE is thus made up of a sequence of two content particles. The first content particle is a single element type name. The second is a choice of several element type names. You can break down the content model for CREATED in the same way.

You can make some fairly complex models this way. But when you write a DTD for a book, you do not know in advance how many chapters the book will have, nor how many paragraphs each chapter will contain. You need a way of saying that the part of the content specification that allows captions is *repeatable* – that you can match it many times.

Sometimes you will also want to make an element optional. For instance, some figures may not have captions. You may want to say that part of the specification for figures is optional.

XML allows you to specify that a content particle is optional or repeatable using an *occurrence indicator*. Table 49-2 shows the three occurrence indicators.

Table 49-2   Occurrence indicators

Indicator	Content particle is...
?	Optional (0 or 1 time).
*	Optional and repeatable (0 or more times)
+	Required and repeatable (1 or more times)

Occurrence indicators directly follow a GI, sequence or choice. The occurrence indicator cannot be preceded by white space.

Example 49-20 illustrates how we can make captions optional on figures:

Example 49-20. Captions are optional.

```
<!ELEMENT FIGURE (CAPTION?, (CODE|TABLE|FLOW-CHART|SCREEN-SHOT))>
```

We can allow footnotes to have multiple paragraphs:

Example 49-21. Footnotes have multiple paragraphs

```
<!ELEMENT FOOTNOTE (P+)>
```

Because we used the "+" indicator, footnotes must have at least one paragraph. We could also have expressed this in another way:

Example 49-22. Multiple paragraphs: the sequel

```
<!ELEMENT FOOTNOTE (P, P*)>
```

This would require a leading paragraph and then 0 or more paragraphs following. That would achieve the same effect as requiring 1 or more paragraphs. The "+" operator is just a little more convenient than repeating the preceding content particle.

We can combine occurrence indicators with sequences or choices:

Example 49-23. Occurrence indicators and sequences

```
<!ELEMENT QUESTION-AND-ANSWER (INTRODUCTION,
                              (QUESTION, ANSWER)+,
                              COPYRIGHT?)>
```

It is also possible to make all of the element types in a content model optional:

Example 49-24. Optional content

```
<!ELEMENT IMAGE (CAPTION?)>
```

This allows the IMAGE element to be empty sometimes and not other times. The question mark indicates that CAPTION is optional. Most likely these IMAGE elements would link to an external graphic through an attribute. The author would only provide content if he wanted to provide a caption.

In the document instance, empty IMAGE elements look identical to how they would look if IMAGE had been declared to be always empty. There is no way to tell from the document instance whether they were declared as empty or are merely empty in a particular case.

49.5.1 *Mixed content models*

We have already talked about mixed content but we should look at it a little more in light of our new understanding of content models. They say that a little knowledge can be a dangerous thing. It's true! Now that you know about content models, you can interpret the syntax for mixed content a little bit better.

Example 49-25. Mixed content again

```
<!ELEMENT abstract (#PCDATA|emph|quot)*>
```

Take a look at Example 49-25 We can see now that this model is similar to element-only content models. What it really says is that you can have a mix of as many parsed characters and elements (emph and quot, in this example) as you like.

First you could select to add some data characters (choosing the #PCDATA branch of the choice group) and then the asterisk would allow you to select from the group again. You could select a quot and then select again and so forth. In this manner you would build up a list of character data, emph elements and quot elements.

Here is where this knowledge becomes a little dangerous. You might think that you could use #PCDATA however and wherever you want in a content model. That is not true. You must use it in the exact pattern we have shown you. The #PCDATA must be the first token in the group. The group must always be a choice, never a sequence. The other components must be element type names, never parenthesized groups. The symbol at the end must always be an asterisk ("*"). It can never be a plus ("+"). You can only omit the asterisk if the mixed content model allows character data but no elements, as in Example 49-26.

It is somewhat confusing to call the model in Example 49-26 "mixed" because it only allows character data. Nevertheless, that is the correct terminology. If it helps, you can remember that it is always possible to mix char-

Example 49-26. Mixed content with no elements

```
<!ELEMENT abstract (#PCDATA)>
```

acter data with character references, entity references, processing instructions and other kinds of markup. Really, the only markup that is prohibited in an element like that is subelement markup.

49.6 | Attributes

Attributes allow an author to attach extra information to the elements in a document. For instance a `code` element for computer code might have a `lang` attribute declaring the language that the code is in. On the other hand, you could also use a `lang` subelement for the same purpose. It is the DTD designer's responsibility to choose a way and embody that in the DTD. Attributes have strengths and weaknesses that differentiate them from subelements so you can usually make the decision without too much difficulty.

The largest difference between elements and attributes is that attributes cannot contain elements and there is no such thing as a "sub-attribute". Attributes are always either text strings with no explicit structure (at least as far as XML is concerned) or simple lists of strings. That means that a `chapter` should not be an attribute of a `book` element, because there would be no place to put the titles and paragraphs of the chapter. You will typically use attributes for small, simple, unstructured "extra" information.

Another important difference between elements and attributes is that each of an element's attributes may be specified only once, and they may be specified in any order. This is often convenient because memorizing the order of things can be difficult. Elements, on the other hand, must occur in the order specified and may occur as many times as the DTD allows. Thus you must use elements for things that must be repeated, or must follow a certain pattern or order that you want the XML parser to enforce.

These technical concerns are often enough to make the decision for you. But if everything else is equal, there are some usability considerations that can help. One rule of thumb that some people use (with neither perfect success nor constant abject failure) is that elements usually represent data that is the natural content that should appear in every print-out or other rendition, Most formatting systems print out elements by default and do not print out attributes unless you specifically ask for them. Attributes represent data that is of secondary importance and is often information about the information (*"metadata"*).

Also, attribute names usually represent properties of objects, but element-type names usually represent parts of objects. So given a `person` element, subelements might represent parts of the body and attributes might represent properties like weight, height, and accumulated karma points.

We would advise you not to spend too much of your life trying to figure out exactly what qualifies as a part and what qualifies as a property. Experience shows that the question "what is a property?" ranks with "what is the good life?" and "what is art?". The technical concerns are usually a good indicator of the philosophical category in any event.

49.6.1 *Attribute-list declarations*

Attributes are declared for specific element types. You declare attributes for a particular element type using an *attribute-list declaration*. You will often see an attribute-list declaration right beside an element type declaration:

Example 49-27. My first ATTLIST

```
<!ELEMENT PERSON (#PCDATA)>
<!ATTLIST PERSON EMAIL CDATA #REQUIRED>
```

Attribute declarations start with the string "<!ATTLIST". Immediately after the white space comes an element type's generic identifier. After that comes the attribute's *name*, its *type* and its *default*. In the example above, the attribute is named `EMAIL` and is valid on `PERSON` elements. Its value must be *character data* and it is required – there is no default and the author must supply a value for the attribute on every `PERSON` element.

Spec Excerpt (XML) 49-3. Attribute-list declarations

```
[52]   AttlistDecl ::=  '<!ATTLIST' S Name AttDef* S? '>'
[53]   AttDef ::=  S Name S AttType S DefaultDecl
```

You can declare many attributes in a single attribute-list declaration.[1]

Example 49-28. Declaring multiple attributes

```
<!ATTLIST PERSON EMAIL CDATA #REQUIRED
                 PHONE CDATA #REQUIRED
                 FAX CDATA #REQUIRED>
```

You can also have multiple attribute-list declarations for a single element type:

Example 49-29. Multiple declarations for one element type

```
<!ATTLIST PERSON HONORIFIC CDATA #REQUIRED>
<!ATTLIST PERSON POSITION CDATA #REQUIRED
                 ORGANIZATION CDATA #REQUIRED>
```

This is equivalent to putting the declarations altogether into a single attribute-list declaration.

It is even possible to have multiple declarations for the same attribute of the same element type. When this occurs, the first declaration of the attribute is binding and the rest are ignored. This is analogous to the situation with entity declarations.

Note that two different element types can have attributes with the same name without there being a conflict. Despite the fact that these attributes have the same name, they are in fact different attributes. For instance a SHIRT element could have an attribute SIZE that exhibits values SMALL, MEDIUM and LARGE and a PANTS element in the same DTD could have an attribute also named SIZE that is a measurement in inches:

Example 49-30. Two size attributes

```
      <!-- These are -->
<!ATTLIST SHIRT SIZE (SMALL|MEDIUM|LARGE) #REQUIRED>

      <!-- two different attributes -->
<!ATTLIST PANTS SIZE NMTOKEN #REQUIRED>
```

---

1. That's why it is called a list!

It is not good practice to allow attributes with the same name to have different semantics or allowed values in the same document. That can be quite confusing for authors.

49.6.2 *Attribute defaults*

Attributes can have *default values*. If the author does not specify an attribute value then the processor supplies the default value if it exists. A DTD designer can also choose not to supply a default.

Specifying a default is simple. You merely include the default after the type or list of allowed values in the attribute list declaration:

Example 49-31. Default values

```
<!ATTLIST SHIRT SIZE (SMALL|MEDIUM|LARGE) MEDIUM>
<!ATTLIST SHOES SIZE NMTOKEN "13">
```

Any value that meets the constraints of the attribute list declaration is legal as a default value. You could not, however, use "***" as a default value for an attribute with declared type NMTOKEN any more than you could do so in a start-tag in the document instance.

Sometimes you want to allow the user to omit a value for a particular attribute without forcing a particular default. For instance you could have an element SHIRT which has a SIZE attribute with a declared type of NMTOKEN. But some shirts are "one size fits all". They do not have a size. You want the author to be able to leave this value out and you want the processing system to *imply* that the shirt is "one size fits all". You can do this with an *impliable* attribute:

Example 49-32. Impliable attribute

```
<!ATTLIST SHIRT SIZE NMTOKEN #IMPLIED>
```

The string "#IMPLIED" gives any processing program the right to insert whatever value it feels is appropriate. This may seem like a lot of freedom to give a programmer, but typically implied attributes are simply ignored. In the case of our SHIRT, there is no need to worry about "one size fits all" shirts because anybody can wear them. Authors should only depend upon the implied value when they do not care or where there is a well-defined convention of what the lack of a value "really" means. This is again a case of semantics and would be communicated to the author through some other document, DTD comment or other communication mechanism.

It is easy for an author to not specify a value for an attribute that is not required: just do not mention the attribute. Note that specifying an attribute value that is an empty string is *not* the same as not specifying an attribute value:

Example 49-33. Empty versus non-existent

```
<SHIRT>          <!-- This conforms to the declaration above. -->
<SHIRT SIZE=""> <!-- This does *not* conform to the declaration. -->
```

The opposite situation to providing a default is where a document type designer wants to force the author to choose a value. If a value for an attribute is important and cannot reliably be defaulted, the designer can require authors to specify it with a *required* attribute default:

Example 49-34. Required attribute

```
<!ATTLIST IMAGE URL CDATA #REQUIRED>
```

In this case, the DTD designer has made the URL attribute required on all IMAGE elements. This makes sense because without a URL to locate the image file, the image element is useless.

It may be surprising, but there are even times when it is useful to supply an attribute value that cannot be overridden at all. This is rare, but worth knowing about. Imagine, for instance, that an Internet directory maintainer like *Yahoo*™ decides to write a robot [1] that will automatically extract the first section title of every document indexed by the directory. The difficulty is that different DTDs will have different element-type names for titles. HTML-like DTDs use H1 etc. DocBook-like DTDs use title. TEI-like DTDs use head. Even if the robot knows about these DTDs, what about all of the others? There are potentially as many DTDs in existence as there are XML documents! It is not feasible to write a robot that can understand every document type.

---

1. A robot is an automatic Web information gatherer.

The vendor needs to achieve some form of standardization. But it cannot force everyone to conform to the same DTD: that is exactly what XML is supposed to avoid! Instead, they can ask all document creators to label the elements that perform the *role of* section titles. They could do this with an attribute, such as `title-element`. The robot can then use the content of those elements to generate its index.

Each DTD designer thinks through the list of element types to add the attribute to. They specify what their element types mean in terms of the indexing system understood by the robot. They may not want authors changing the value on an element by element basis. They can prevent this with *fixed* attributes:

Example 49-35. Fixed attributes

```
<!ATTLIST H1 TITLE-ELEMENT CDATA #FIXED "TITLE-ELEMENT">

<!ATTLIST HEAD TITLE-ELEMENT CDATA #FIXED "TITLE-ELEMENT">

<!ATTLIST TITLE TITLE-ELEMENT CDATA #FIXED "TITLE-ELEMENT">
```

Now all of the appropriate elements are marked with the attribute. No matter what else is in the DTD, the robot can find what it is looking for.

49.6.3 *Attribute types*

An important feature of attributes is that attributes have *types* that can enforce certain *lexical* and *semantic* constraints. *Lexical* constraints are constraints like "this attribute must contain only numerals". Semantic constraints are along the lines of "this attribute must contain the name of a declared entity". These constraints tend to be very useful in making robust DTDs and document processing systems.

However, it is vital to remember that *the value of an attribute is not necessarily the exact character string that you enter between the quotation marks.* That string first goes through a process called *attribute-value normalization* on its way to becoming the attribute value. Since attribute types apply to the *normalized value*, we had better digress for a moment to master normalization.

49.6.3.1 Attribute value normalization

XML processors normalize attribute values to make authors' lives simpler. If it were not for normalization, you would have to be very careful where you put white space in an attribute value. For instance if you broke an attribute value across a line:

Example 49-36. Normalization

```
<GRAPHIC ALTERNATE-TEXT="This is a picture of a penguin
    doing the ritual mating dance">
```

You might do this merely because the text is too long for a single line in a text editor.

This sort of thing is normalized by the XML processor. The rules for this are a little intricate, but most times they will just do what you want them to. Let's look at them.

All XML attribute values are entered as quoted strings. They start and end with either single-quotes ("'") or double-quotes ("""). If you want to embed a single-quote character into an attribute value delimited by single quotes or a double-quote character into an attribute value delimited by double quotes, then you must use an entity reference as described in 48.7.1, "Predefined entities", on page 695.

The first thing the XML parser does to prepare for normalization is to strip off the surrounding quotes.

Then, character references are replaced by the characters that they reference. As we discussed earlier, character references allow you to easily insert "funny" characters.

Next, general entity references are replaced. This is important to note. While it is true that entity references are not allowed in markup, unnormalized attribute values are *text* – a mixture of markup and data. After normalization, only the data remains.[1].

If the expansion for an entity reference has another entity reference within it, that is expanded also, and so on and so forth. This would be rare in an entity used in an attribute value. After all, attribute values are usually

---

1. Philosophically, attribute values are metadata, but it is an article of faith in the XML world that metadata is data.

very short and simple. An entity reference in an attribute value cannot be to an external entity.

Newline characters in attribute values are replaced by spaces. *If* the attribute is known to be one of the tokenized types[1] (see below), then the parser must further remove leading and trailing spaces. So "   token   " becomes "token". It also collapses multiple spaces between tokens into a single space, so that "space   between" would become "space between".

Caution   The distinction between unnormalized attribute value text and normalized attribute value data trips up even the experts. Remember, when reading about attribute types, that they apply to the normalized data, not the unnormalized text.

49.6.3.2   CDATA and name token attributes

The simplest type of attribute is a *CDATA* attribute. The CDATA stands for "character data". The declaration for such an attribute looks like this:

Example 49-37. CDATA Attributes

```
<!DOCTYPE ARTICLE[
<!ELEMENT ARTICLE>
<!ATTLIST ARTICLE DATE CDATA #REQUIRED>
...
]>
<ARTICLE DATE="January 15, 1999">
...
</ARTICLE>
```

Character data attribute values can be any string of characters. Basically anything else is legal in this type of attribute value.

Name token (NMTOKEN) attributes are somewhat like CDATA attributes. The biggest difference is that they are restricted in the characters that name

---

1. If, in other words, attribute-list declarations were provided and the processor is either a validating processor or a non-validating processor that decides to read them.

tokens allow. Name tokens were described in 48.1.4, "Names and name tokens", on page 680. To refresh your memory, they are strings made up of letters, numbers and a select group of special characters: period ("."), dash ("-"), underscore ("_") and colon (":").

Example 49-38. Name token attribute type

```
<!DOCTYPE PARTS-LIST[
...
<!ATTLIST PART DATE NMTOKEN #REQUIRED>
...
]>
<PARTS-LIST>
...
<PART DATE="1998-05-04">...</PART>

</PARTS-LIST>
]>
```

An empty string is not a valid name token, whereas it would be a valid CDATA attribute value.

Name tokens can be used to allow an attribute to contain numbers that need special characters. They allow the dash, which can be used as a minus sign, the period, which can be a decimal point, and numbers. These are useful for fractional and negative numbers. You can also use alphabetic characters to specify units.

Name tokens can also be used for naming things. This is similar to how you might use variable names in a programming language. For instance, if you used XML to describe the structure of a database, you might use name tokens to name and refer to fields and tables. The restrictions on the name token attribute type would prevent most of the characters that would be illegal in field and table names (spaces, most forms of punctuation, etc.). If there is a reason that all fields or record names must be unique, then you would instead use the *ID* attribute type discussed in 49.6.3.4, "ID and IDREF attributes", on page 729.

If it is appropriate to have more than one name token, then you can use the NMTOKENS attribute type which stands for "name tokens". For instance Example 49-39 shows how you might declare a DTD representing a database.

Example 49-39. Name tokens attribute type

```
<!DOCTYPE DATABASE [
...
<!ELEMENT TABLE EMPTY>
<!ATTLIST TABLE NAME NMTOKEN #REQUIRED
               FIELDS NMTOKENS #REQUIRED>
...
]>
<DATABASE>
...
<TABLE NAME="SECURITY" FIELDS="USERID PASSWORD DEPARTMENT">
...
</DATABASE>
```

One other difference between CDATA attributes and NMTOKEN attributes is in their *normalization*. This was discussed in 49.6.3.1, "Attribute value normalization", on page 725.

49.6.3.3   Enumerated and notation attributes

Sometimes as a DTD designer you want to create an attribute that can only exhibit one of a short list of values: "small/medium/large", "fast/slow"; "north/south/east/west". *Enumerated attribute types* allow this. In a sense, they provide a choice or menu of options.

The syntax is reminiscent of choice lists in element type declarations:

Example 49-40. Choice lists

```
<!ATTLIST OPTIONS CHOICE (OPTION1|OPTION2|OPTION3) #REQUIRED>
```

You may provide as many choices as you like. Each choice is an XML *name token* and must meet the syntactic requirements of name tokens described in 48.1.4, "Names and name tokens", on page 680.

There is another related attribute type called a *notation* attribute. This attribute allows the author to declare that the element's content conforms to a declared notation. Here is an example involving several ways of representing dates:

Example 49-41. Different date representations

```
<!ATTLIST DATE TYPE NOTATION (EUDATE|USDATE|ISODATE) #REQUIRED>
```

In a valid document, each notation allowed must also be declared with a notation declaration.

49.6.3.4   ID and IDREF attributes

Sometimes it is important to be able to give a name to a particular occurrence of an element type. For instance, to make a simple hypertext link or cross-reference from one element to another, you can name a particular section or figure. Later, you can refer to it by its name. The target element is labeled with an *ID* attribute. The other element refers to it with an *IDREF* attribute. This is shown in Example 49-42.

Example 49-42. ID and IDREF used for cross-referencing

```
<!DOCTYPE BOOK [
...
<!ELEMENT SECTION (TITLE, P*)>
<!ATTLIST SECTION MY-ID ID #IMPLIED>
<!ELEMENT CROSS-REFERENCE EMPTY>
<!ATTLIST CROSS-REFERENCE TARGET IDREF #REQUIRED>
...
]>
<BOOK>
...
<SECTION MY-id="Why.XML.Rocks"><TITLE>Features of XML</TITLE>
...
</SECTION>

...
If you want to recall why XML is so great, please see
the section titled <CROSS-REFERENCE TARGET="Why.XML.Rocks"/>.
...
</BOOK>
```

The stylesheet would instruct browsers and formatters to replace the cross-reference element with the name of the section. This would probably be italicized and hyperlinked or labeled with a page number if appropriate.

Note that we made the section's MY-ID optional. Some sections will not need to be the target of a cross-reference, hypertext link or other reference and will not need to be uniquely identified. The TARGET attribute on CROSS-REFERENCE is required. It does not make sense to have a cross-reference that does not actually refer to another element.

IDs are XML names, with all of the constraints described in 48.1.4, "Names and name tokens", on page 680. Every element can have at most one ID, and thus only one attribute per element type be an ID attribute. All IDs specified in an XML document must be unique. A document with two ID attributes whose values are the same is invalid. Thus "chapter" would not be a good name for an ID, because it would make sense to use it in many places. "introduction.chapter" would be a logical ID because it would uniquely identify a particular chapter.

IDREF attributes must refer to an element in the document. You may have as many IDREFs referring to a single element as you need. It is also possible to declare an attribute that can potentially exhibit more than one IDREF by declaring it to be of type IDREFS:

Example 49-43. IDREFS attribute

```
<!ATTLIST RELATED-CHAPTERS TARGETS IDREFS #REQUIRED>
```

Now the TARGETS attribute may have one or more IDREFs as its value. There is no way to use XML to require that an attribute take two or more, or three or more, (etc.) IDREFs. You will recall that we could do that sort of thing using content models in element type declarations. There is no such thing as a content model for attributes. You could model this same situation by declaring RELATED-CHAPTERS to have content of one or more or two or more (etc.) CHAPTER-REF elements that each have a single IDREF attribute (named TARGET in Example 49-44).

As you can see, element type declarations have the benefit of having content models, which can define complex structures, and attributes have the benefit of attribute types, which can enforce lexical and semantic constraints. You can combine these strengths to make intricate structures when this is appropriate.

Example 49-44. IDREF attributes

```
<!DOCTYPE BOOK[
...
<!ELEMENT RELATED-CHAPTERS (CHAPTER-REF+)>
<!ELEMENT CHAPTER-REF EMPTY>
<!ATTLIST CHAPTER-REF TARGET IDREF #REQUIRED>
...
]>
<BOOK>
...
<RELATED-CHAPTERS>
<CHAPTER-REF TARGET="introduction.to.xml">
<CHAPTER-REF TARGET="xml.rocks">
</RELATED-CHAPTERS>
...
</BOOK>
```

49.6.3.5 ENTITY attributes

External unparsed entities are XML's way of referring to objects (files, CGI script output, etc.) on the Web that should not be parsed according to XML's rules. Anything from HTML documents to pictures to word processor files fall into this category. It is possible to refer to unparsed entities using an attribute with declared type *ENTITY*. This is typically done either to hyperlink to, reference or include an external object. This is shown in Example 49-45.

Example 49-45. Entity attribute type

```
<!DOCTYPE BOOK[
<!ATTLIST BOOK-REF TARGET ENTITY #REQUIRED>
...
<!ENTITY another-book SYSTEM
        "http://www.buyOurBooks.com/TheOtherBook.html" NDATA HTML>
...
]><BOOK>
...
<BOOK-REF target="another-book">
...
</BOOK>
```

You can also declare an attribute to be of type *ENTITIES*, in which case its value may be the name of more than one entity. It is up to the application or stylesheet to determine whether a reference to the entity should be treated as a hot link, embed link or some other kind of link. The processor merely informs the application of the existence and notation of the entity. You can find information on unparsed entities and notations in Chapter 50, "Entities: Breaking up is easy to do", on page 736 and 49.7, "Notation Declarations", on page 732.

49.6.3.6 Summary of attribute types

There are two *enumerated* attribute types: *enumeration* attributes and NOTATION attributes.

Seven attribute types are known as *tokenized* types because each value represents either a single token (ID, IDREF, ENTITY, NMTOKEN) or a list of tokens (IDREFS, ENTITIES, and NMTOKENS).

The final type is the CDATA string type which is the least constrained and can hold any combination of XML characters as long as "special characters" (the quote characters and ampersand) are properly entered. Table 49-3 summarizes.

49.7 | Notation Declarations

Notations are referred to in various parts of an XML document, for describing the data content notation of different things. A data content notation is the definition of how the bits and bytes of class of object should be interpreted. According to this definition, XML is a data content notation, because it defines how the bits and bytes of XML documents should be interpreted. Your favorite word processor also has a data content notation. The notation declaration gives an internal name to an existing notation so that it can be referred to in attribute list declarations, unparsed entity declarations, and processing instructions.

The most obvious place that an XML document would want to describe the notation of a data object is in a reference to some other resource on the web. It could be an embedded graphic, an MPEG movie that is the target of a hyperlink, or anything else. The XML facility for linking to these data resources is the entity declaration, and as we discussed earlier, they are

Table 49-3 Summary of attribute types

Type	Lexical constraint	Semantic constraint
CDATA	None	None
Enumeration	Name Token	Must be in the declared list.
NOTATION	Name	Must be in the declared list and a declared notation name.
ID	Name	Must be unique in document.
IDREF	Name	Must be some element's ID.
IDREFS	Names	Must each be some element's ID.
ENTITY	Name	Must be an unparsed entity's name.
ENTITIES	Names	Must each be unparsed entity's name.
NMTOKEN	Name Token	None
NMTOKENS	Name Tokens	None

referred to as *unparsed entities*. Part of the declaration of an unparsed entity is the name of a declared notation that provides some form of pointer to the external definition of the notation. The external definition could be a public or system identifier for documentation on the notation, some formal specification or a helper application that can handle objects represented in the notation.

Example 49-46. Notations for unparsed entities

```
<!NOTATION HTML SYSTEM "http://www.w3.org/Markup">
<!NOTATION GIF SYSTEM "gifmagic.exe">
```

Another place that notations arise are in the notation attribute type. You use this attribute type when you want to express the notation for the data content of an XML element. For instance, if you had a date element that used ISO or EU date formats, you could declare notations for each format:

Example 49-47. Notations for data content

```
<!NOTATION ISODATE SYSTEM "http://www.iso.ch/date_specification">
<!NOTATION EUDATE SYSTEM "http://www.eu.eu/date_specification">
<!ELEMENT TODAY (#PCDATA)>
<!ATTLIST TODAY DATE-FORMAT NOTATION (ISODATE|EUDATE) #REQUIRED>
```

Now the DATE-FORMAT attribute would be restricted to those two values, and would thus signal to the application that the content of the TODAY element conforms to one or the other.

Note   You can specify datatypes more precisely for data content and attribute values by using the facilities described in Chapter 58, "Datatypes", on page 894.

Finally, notations can be used to give XML names to the targets for processing instructions. This is not strictly required by XML, but it is a good practice because it provides a sort of documentation for the PI and could even be used by an application to invoke the target.

This seems like a good way to close this chapter. DTDs are about improving the permanence, longevity, and wide reuse of your data, and the predictability and reliability of its processing. If you use them wisely, they will save you time and money.

Tip   Learning the syntax of markup declarations so that you can write DTDs is important, but learning how to choose the right element types and attributes for a job is a subtle process that requires a book of its own. We suggest David Megginson's Structuring XML Documents, also in this series (ISBN 0-13-642299-3).

Entities: Breaking up is easy to do

Tad Tougher Tutorial

- Parameter and general
- Internal and external
- Parsed and unparsed

50

X ML allows flexible organization of document text. The XML constructs that provide this flexibility are called entities. They allow a document to be broken up into multiple storage objects and are important tools for reusing and maintaining text.

50.1 | Overview

In simple cases, an entity is like an abbreviation in that it is used as a short form for some text. We call the "abbreviation" the *entity name* and the long form the *entity content*. That content could be as short as a character or as long as a chapter. For instance, in an XML document, the entity dtd could have the phrase "document type definition" as its content. Using a reference to that entity is like using the word DTD as an abbreviation for that phrase – the parser replaces the reference with the content.

You create the entity with an *entity declaration*. Example 50-1 is an entity declaration for an abbreviation.

Entities can be much more than just abbreviations. There are several different kinds of entities with different uses. We will first introduce the differ-

Example 50-1. Entity used as an abbreviation

```
<!ENTITY dtd "document type definition">
```

ent variants in this overview and then come back and describe them more precisely in the rest of the chapter. We approach the topic in this way because we cannot discuss the various types of entity entirely linearly. Our first pass will acquaint you with the major types and the second one will tie them together and provide the information you need to actually use them.

Another way to think of an entity is as a box with a label. The label is the entity's name. The content of the box is some sort of text or data. The entity declaration creates the box and sticks on a label with the name. Sometimes the box holds XML text that is going to be *parsed* (interpreted according to the rules of the XML notation), and sometimes it holds data, which should not be.

If the content of an entity is XML text that the processor should parse, the XML spec calls it a *parsed entity.* The name is badly chosen because it is, in fact, unparsed; it will be parsed only if and when it is actually used.

If the content of an entity is data that is not to be parsed, the XML spec calls it an *unparsed entity.* This name isn't so great either because, as we just pointed out, an XML text entity is also unparsed.

We'll try to minimize the confusion and to avoid saying things like "a parsed entity will be parsed by the XML parser". But we sure wish they had named them "text entity" and "data entity".

The abbreviation in Example 50-1 is a parsed entity. Parsed entities, being XML text, can also contain markup. Example 50-2 is a declaration for a parsed entity with some markup in it.

Example 50-2. Parsed entity with markup

```
<!ENTITY dtd "<term>document type definition</term>">
```

The processor can also fetch content from somewhere on the Web and put that into the box. This is an *external* entity. For instance, it could fetch a chapter of a book and put it into an entity. This would allow you to reuse the chapter between books. Another benefit is that you could edit the chapter separately with a sufficiently intelligent editor. This would be very useful if you were working on a team project and wanted different people to work on different parts of a document at once. Example 50-3 demonstrates.

Example 50-3. External entity declaration

```
<!ENTITY intro-chapter SYSTEM "http://www.megacorp.com/intro.xml">
```

Entities also allow you to edit very large documents without running out of memory. Depending on your software and needs, either each volume or even each article in an encyclopedia could be an entity.

An author or DTD designer refers to an entity through an *entity reference*. The XML processor replaces the reference by the content, as if it were an abbreviation and the content was the expanded phrase. This process is called *inclusion*. After the operation we say either that the entity reference has been *replaced* by the entity content or that the entity content has been *included*. Which you would use depends on whether you are talking from the point of view of the entity reference or the entity content. The content of parsed entities is called their *replacement text*.

Example 50-4 is an example of a parsed entity declaration and its associated reference.

Example 50-4. Entity Declaration

```
<!DOCTYPE MAGAZINE[
...
<!ENTITY title "Hacker Life">
...
]>
<MAGAZINE>
<TITLE>&title;</TITLE>
...
<P>Welcome to the introductory issue of &title;. &title; is
geared to today's modern hacker.</P>
...
</MAGAZINE>
```

Anywhere in the document instance that the entity reference "&title;" appears, it is *replaced* by the text "Hacker Life". It is just as valid to say that "Hacker Life" is *included* at each point where the reference occurs. The ampersand character starts all general entity references and the semicolon ends them. The text between is an entity name.

Spec Excerpt (XML) 50-1. General entity reference

```
[68]   EntityRef ::=   '&' Name ';'
```

We have looked at entities that can be used in the creation of XML documents. Others can only be used to create XML DTDs. The ones we have been using all along are called *general* entities. They are called general entities because they can generally be used anywhere in a document. The ones that we use to create DTDs are called *parameter* entities.

We would use parameter entities for most of the same reasons that we use general entities. We want document type definitions to share declarations for element types, attributes and notations, just as we want documents to share chapters and abbreviations. For instance many DTDs in an organization might share the same definition for a paragraph element type named *para*. The declaration for that element type could be bundled up with other common DTD components and used in document type definitions for memos, letters and reports. Each DTD would include the element type declaration by means of a parameter entity reference.

Unparsed entities are for holding data such as images or molecular models in some data object notation. The application does not expect the processor to parse that information because it is not XML text.

Although it is an oversimplification, it may be helpful in your mind to remember that unparsed entities are often used for pictures and parsed entities are usually used for character text. You would include a picture through an unparsed entity, since picture representations do not (usually!) conform to the XML specification. Of course there are many kinds of non-XML data other than graphics, but if you can at least remember that unparsed entities are used for graphics then you will remember the rest also. Example 50-5 demonstrates.

Example 50-5. Unparsed entity declaration

```
<!ENTITY picture SYSTEM "http://www.home.org/mycat.gif" NDATA GIF>
```

We use unparsed entities through an entity attribute. A processor does not expand an entity attribute, but it tells the application that the use occurred. The application can then do something with it. For instance, if the application is a Web browser, and the entity contains a graphic, it could display the graphic. Entity attributes are covered in 49.6.3.5, "ENTITY attributes", on page 731.

50.2 | Entity details

 Caution   Like other names in XML, entity names are case-sensitive: &charles; refers to a different entity from &Charles;.

It is good that XML entity names are case-sensitive because they are often used to name letters. Case is a convenient way of distinguishing the upper-case version of a letter from the lower-case one. "Sigma" would represent the upper-case version of the Greek letter, and "sigma" would be the lower-case version of it. It would be possible to use some other convention to differentiate the upper- and lower-case versions, such as prefixes. That would give us "uc-Sigma" and "lc-Sigma".

Entities may be declared more than once (Example 50-6), but only the first declaration is *binding*. All subsequent ones are ignored as if they did not exist.

Example 50-6. Contradicting entity declarations

```
<!ENTITY abc "abcdefghijklmnopqrst"> <!-- This is binding. -->
<!ENTITY abc "ABCDEFGHIJKLMNOPQRST"> <!-- This is ignored. -->
<!ENTITY abc "AbCdEfGhIjKlMnOpQrSt"> <!-- So is this.       -->
```

Declarations in the internal DTD subset are processed before those in the external subset, as described in Chapter 49, "Creating a document type definition", on page 702. In practice, document authors can override parameter entities in the external subset of the DTD by declaring entities of the same name in the internal subset.

Entities are not difficult to use, but there are several variations and details that you should be aware of. We have already covered the major varieties, but only informally.

There is one special entity, called the *document entity* which is not declared, does not have a name and cannot be referenced. The document entity is the entity in which the processor started the current parse. Imagine you download a Web document called `catalog.xml`. Before a browser can display it, it must start to parse it, which makes it the document entity. It may include other entities, but because parsing started with `catalog.xml`, those others are not the document entity. They are just ordinary external entities.

If you click on a link and go to another XML Web page, then the processor must parse that page before it can display it. That page is the document entity for the new parse. In other words, even the simplest XML document has at least one entity: the document entity. The processor starts parsing the document in the document entity and it also must finish there.[1]

The document entity is also the entity in which the XML declaration and document type declaration can occur.

You may think it is strange for us to call this an entity when it is not declared as such, but if we were talking about files, it would probably not surprise you. It is common in many computer languages to have files that include other files. Even word processors allow this. We will often use the word entity to refer to a concept analogous to what you would think of as a file, although entities are more flexible. Entities are just "bundles of information". They could reside in databases, zip files, or be created on the fly by a computer program.

50.3 | Classifications of entities

There are many interesting things that you can do with entities. Here are some examples:

- You could store every chapter of a book in a separate file and link them together as entities.

---

1. To put it mystically: it is the alpha and the omega of entities.

- You could "factor out" often-reused text, such as a product name, into an entity so that it is consistently spelled and displayed throughout the document.
- You could update the product name entity to reflect a new version. The change would be instantly visible anywhere the entity was used.
- You could create an entity that would represent "legal boilerplate" text (such as a software license) and reuse that entity in many different documents.
- You could integrate pictures and multimedia objects into your document.
- You could develop "document type definition components" that could be used in many document type definitions. These would allow you to reuse the declarations for common element types (such as paragraph and emphasis) across several document types.

Because XML entities can do so many things, there are several different varieties of them. But XML entities do not break down into six or eight different types with simple names. Rather, you could think of each entity as having three properties that define its type. This is analogous to the way that a person could be tall or short and at the same time male or female and blonde or brunette.

Similarly, entities can be *internal* or *external*, *parsed* or *unparsed* and *general* or *parameter*. There is no single word for a short, male, brunette, and there is similarly no single word for an internal, parsed, parameter entity.

Caution   Some combinations of entity types are impossible. Obviously an entity cannot be both internal and external, just as a person could not be both blonde and brunette. It turns out that due to restrictions on unparsed entities, there are five combinations that are valid and three that are not.

Most of the rest of this chapter will describe the five types of entities in greater depth. We will use one convention that might be confusing without this note. In a section on, for instance, internal parsed general entities, we may describe a constraint or feature of all general entities. When we do so, we will use the word "general entity" instead of "internal general entity". This convention will allow us to avoid repeating text that is common among entity types. We will refer back to that text from other sections when it becomes relevant.

50.4 | Internal general entities

Internal parsed general entities are the simplest type of entity. They are essentially abbreviations defined completely in the document type declaration section of the XML document.

All internal general entities are parsed entities. This means that the XML processor parses them like any other XML text. Hence we will leave out the redundant word "parsed" and refer to them simply as internal general entities.

The content for an internal general entity is specified by a string literal after the entity's name. The string literal may contain markup, including references to other entities. An example is in Example 50-7.

Example 50-7. Internal general entity

```
<?xml version="1.0"?>
<!DOCTYPE SAMPLE SYSTEM "sample.dtd"[
    <!ENTITY xml "Extensible Markup Language">
]>
<SAMPLE>
    &xml;
</SAMPLE>
```

Internal general entities can be referenced anywhere in the content of an element or attribute value, including an attribute default value (in the DTD). They can also be referenced in the content of another general entity. Because they are general entities, they cannot be used to hold markup declarations for expansion in the DTD. They can only hold element or attribute content. Because of this, Example 50-8 is not well-formed. The only contexts in which general entities can occur in a DTD are entity replacement values and attribute default values.

The grammar rules for internal general entities are described in Spec Excerpt 50-2.

Example 50-8. Illegal: General entity cannot contain markup declarations

```
<?xml version="1.0"?>
<!DOCTYPE SAMPLE[
    <!ENTITY xml "Extensible Markup Language">
    &xml;
]>
```

Spec Excerpt (XML) 50-2. Internal general entities

```
[70]   EntityDecl ::=  GEDecl | PEDecl
[71]   GEDecl ::=  '<!ENTITY' S Name S EntityDef S? '>'
[73]   EntityDef ::=  EntityValue | (ExternalID NDataDecl?)
[9]    EntityValue ::=  '"' ([^%&"] | PEReference | Reference)* '"'
                     |  "'" ([^%&'] | PEReference | Reference)* "'"
```

50.5 | External parsed general entities

Every XML entity is either internal or external. The content of internal entities occurs right in the entity declarations. External entities get their content from somewhere else in the system. It might be another file on the hard disk, a Web page or an object in a database. Wherever it is, it is located through an *external identifier*. Usually this is just the word SYSTEM followed by a URI (see 56.2, "Uniform Resource Identifiers", on page 862).

In this section, we are interested specifically in external parsed general entities. Example 50-9 is an example of such an entity.

Example 50-9. External parsed general entity

```
<!ENTITY ent SYSTEM "http://www.house.gov/Constitution.xml">
```

It is the keyword SYSTEM that tells the processor that the next thing in the declaration is a URI. The processor gets the entity's content from that URI. The combination of SYSTEM and the URI is called an external identifier because it identifies an external resource to the processor. There is another kind of external identifier called a PUBLIC identifier. It is denoted by the keyword PUBLIC. External identifiers are described in 50.9, "External identifiers", on page 755.

External parsed general entities can be referenced in the same places that internal general entities can be – the document instance and the replacement text of other general entities – except not in the value of an attribute.

50.5.1 *External parsed entity support is optional*

XML processors are allowed, but not required, to validate an XML document when they parse it. The XML specification allows a processor that is not validating a document to completely ignore declarations of external parsed entities (both parameter and general). There is no way to control this behavior with the standalone document declaration or any other XML markup.

The reason for this is improved Web surfing performance. The XML working group thought that it was important for processors to be able to download the minimum amount of data required to do their job and no more. For instance, a browser could display unresolved external parsed entities as hypertext links that the user could click on to receive. Because the entity would only be downloaded on demand, the original page might display faster.

Unfortunately this is very inconvenient for authors, because it means that external parsed entities are essentially unreliable in systems that you do not completely control (e.g. the Internet vs. an intranet).

Caution   External parsed entity processing is optional
XML processors can ignore external parsed entities. If you use them to store parts of your documents, those parts will only show up at the browser vendor's option.

In practice this probably means that you should not put documents that use external entities on the Web until a pattern for browser behavior emerges. In the meantime, tools like James Clark's *sgmlnorm* can read an XML document that uses external entities and expand all of the entities for you.[1] We hope that future versions of the XML specification will make external entity inclusion mandatory.

50.6 | Unparsed entities

Every XML entity is either an *unparsed* entity or a *parsed* entity. Unparsed entities are external entities that the XML processor does not have to parse. For example a graphic, sound, movie or other multimedia object would be included through an unparsed entity. You can imagine the number of error messages you would get if an XML processor tried to interpret a graphic as if it were made up of XML text!

It is occasionally useful to refer to an XML document through an unparsed entity, as if it were in some unparsable representation. You might embed a complete letter document in a magazine document in this way. Rather than extending the magazine DTD to include letter elements, you would refer to it as an unparsed entity. Conceptually, it would be handled in the same way a picture of the letter would be handled. If you refer to it as an unparsed entity, the processor that handles the magazine does not care that the letter is actually XML.

All unparsed entities are external entities because there is no way to express non-XML information in XML entities. They are also all general entities because it is forbidden (and senseless) to embed data in XML DTDs. Hence, the term "unparsed entity" implies the terms "general" and "external".

Syntactically, declarations of unparsed entities are differentiated from those of other external entities by the keyword NDATA followed by a *notation* name.

Spec Excerpt (XML) 50-3. Non-XML data declaration

```
NDataDecl ::=  S 'NDATA' S Name
```

The name at the end is the name of a declared notation. Notation declarations are described in 49.7, "Notation Declarations", on page 732. The

---

1. sgmlnorm is on the CD-ROM.

processor passes this to the application as a hint about how the application should approach the entity.

If the application knows how to deal with that sort of entity (for instance if it is a common graphics notation) then it could do so directly. A browser might embed a rendition of the entity. It might also make a hyperlink to the entity. If it needs to download or install some other handler such as a Java program or Active-X control, then it could do so. If it needs to ask the user what to do it could do that also. The XML specification does not say what it must do. XML only expects processors to tell applications what the declared notation is and the applications must figure out the rest.

In the rare case that the entity is an XML document, the application might decide to process it, create a rendition of it, and then embed it. Alternatively, it might decide to make a hyperlink to it.

50.7 | Internal and external parameter entities

XML entities are classified according to whether they can be used in the DTD or in the document instance. Entities that can only be used in the DTD are called *parameter* entities. For instance, you might want to wrap up a few declarations for mathematical formulae element types and reuse the declarations from DTD to DTD.

The other entities can be used more generally (throughout the entire document instance), and are called *general* entities. Authors can use general entities as abbreviations, for sharing data among documents, including pictures, and many similar tasks.

There is an important reason why the two types are differentiated. When authors create documents, they want to be able to choose entity names without worrying about accidently choosing a name that was already used by the DTD designer. If there were no distinction between entities specific to the DTD and general to the document instance, according to XML's rules, the first declaration would win. That means that either the author would accidently take the place of ("clobber") a declaration that was meant to be used in the DTD, and thus trigger a cryptic error message, or the DTD designer's entity would clobber the entity that was meant to go in the document instance, and a seemingly random string of DTD-text would appear in the middle of the document! XML prevents this by having two different types of entities with distinct syntaxes for declaration and use.

Parameter entities are distinguished from general entity declarations by a single percent symbol in their declaration, and by a different syntax in their use. Example 50-10 is an example of a parameter entity declaration and use.

Example 50-10. Parameter entity

```
<!DOCTYPE SAMPLE[
    <!-- parameter entity declaration -->
<!ENTITY % sample-entity "<!ELEMENT SAMPLE (#PCDATA)>">
    <!-- parameter entity use -->
%sample-entity;
]>
<SAMPLE>
</SAMPLE>
```

This entity is declared with a syntax similar to that of general entities, but it has a percent sign between the string <!ENTITY and the entity's name. This is what differentiates parameter entity declarations from general entity declarations. If you want a general entity you just leave the percent character out.

The entity contains a complete element type declaration. It is referenced on the line after it is declared. Parameter entity references start with the percent-sign and end with the semicolon. The parser replaces the entity reference with the entity's content. In Example 50-10, the processor replaces the reference with the element type declaration "<!ELEMENT SAMPLE (#PCDATA)>". It then parses and interprets the element type declaration as if it had occurred there originally. The element type *is* declared and so the example is valid.

Spec Excerpt (XML) 50-4. Parameter Entity Declaration

```
[72]   PEDecl ::=  '<!ENTITY' S '%' S Name S PEDef S? '>'
[74]   PEDef ::=  EntityValue | ExternalID
[75]   ExternalID ::=  'SYSTEM' S SystemLiteral
            | 'PUBLIC' S PubidLiteral S SystemLiteral
[69]   PEReference ::=  '%' Name ';'
```

Parameter entities can be external, just as general entities can be. But they can never be unparsed. Parameter entities exist to provide building blocks for reusing markup declarations and making DTDs more flexible. It would not make sense to tell the XML processor not to process one! An example of an external parameter entity is in Example 50-11.

Example 50-11. External parameter entity

```
<!DOCTYPE SAMPLE[
    <!-- parameter entity declaration -->
<!ENTITY % sample-entity SYSTEM "pictures.ent">
    <!-- parameter entity use -->
%sample-entity;
]>
<SAMPLE>
</SAMPLE>
```

Parameter entities cannot be referenced in the document instance. In fact, the percent character is not special in the document instance, so if you try to reference a parameter entity in the instance, you will just get the entity reference text in your data, like "%this;".

Entities can only be referenced after they have been declared. General entities may appear to be referenced before they are declared but that is a mere trick of the light.

Example 50-12. General entity usage

```
<!ENTITY user "This entity uses &usee;.">
<!ENTITY usee "<em>another entity</em>">
```

Example 50-12 is legal because the entity replacement for &usee; does not take place until the point where the user entity is *referenced*.

With one exception (described below), general entities can only be expanded in the document instance. So the fact that user refers to usee is recorded, but the replacement is not immediately done. Later, in the document instance, the author will refer to the user entity using the general entity reference, &user;. At that point, the inclusion of its replacement text will trigger the expansion of the &usee; entity reference and the inclusion of its replacement text.

The exception is general entity references in default attribute values. These must be expanded immediately – in the DTD so that they can be checked for validity. These general entities must have been declared before they are used. Whether this exception is important or not depends on how much you use general entities in default attribute values.

Note that the text of a general entity can contain references to other general entities that are declared after it, while the text of a parameter entity cannot reference later-declared parameter entities. That is because parameter entity references are resolved when an entity declaration containing them is *parsed* (i.e., at declaration time). In contrast, general entity references are not resolved until the entity whose declaration contains them is *referenced*, which usually occurs in the document instance, after all DTD declarations have been processed. Referencing can also occur in a default value of an attribute declaration, after all relevant general entity declarations have been processed.

50.8 | Markup may not span entity boundaries

Parsed entities may contain markup as well as character data, but elements and other markup must not span entity boundaries. This means that a particular element may not start in one entity and end in another. If you think of entities as boxes, then an element cannot be half in one box and half in another. Example 50-13 is an example of illegal entity use:

Example 50-13. Elements spanning entity boundaries.

```
<!DOCTYPE SAMPLE[
    <!ENTITY start "<title>This is a">
    <!ENTITY finish "title</title>">
]>

&start;&finish;
```

This document is not well-formed. When the entity references are replaced with their text, they create a title element. This element spans the entities.

Other markup cannot span entities either. Declarations, comments, processing instructions and entity references must all finish in the entity in which they started. This applies to the document entity as much as any other. Markup strings and elements may not start in the document entity and finish in an included entity. This is a subtle but important rule. Documents which fail to conform are not well-formed.

In Example 50-14, entities are used in ways that are illegal. They are all illegal because they start markup without finishing it or finish it without starting it.

Example 50-14. Illegal entities

```
<!DOCTYPE TEST[
    <!ENTITY illegal1 "This will soon be <em>illegal">
    <!ENTITY illegal2 "This will too <em>">
    <!ENTITY illegal3 "This will also </em>">
    <!ENTITY illegal4 "And so will <!-- this">
    <!ENTITY illegal5 "And this &too;">
    <!-- note that none of these are illegal yet. -->
...
]><TEST>
<!-- These references are all illegal -->
&illegal1; <!-- Start-tag in entity with no end-tag there. -->
&illegal2; <!-- Start of tag in entity -->
&illegal3; <!-- End-tag in entity with no start-tag there. -->
&illegal4; <!-- Comment start but no end in entity. -->
&illegal5; <!-- Entity reference starts in entity. -->
</TEST>
```

The entities in Example 50-15 can be used legally or illegally. They do not necessarily represent the start or end of elements or markup, because they do not contain the strings that are used to start a tag ("<"), comment ("<!--"), general entity reference ("&") or other markup. Entity content is interpreted as markup if the replacement text would be interpreted as markup in the same context. In other words, the processor expands the entity and then looks for markup. If the markup it finds spans entity boundaries, then it is illegal.

In this case, it is not the declared entities themselves that are causing the problem, but the fact that elements, entities and markup started in the document entity must end there, just as in any other entity. The context of an entity reference is very important. That is what decides whether it is legal or illegal.

This is true even of entities that hold *complete* tags, elements, comments, processing instructions, character references, or entity references. References to those entities are legal anywhere their replacement text would be

Example 50-15. Sometimes legal entities

```
<?xml version="1.0"?>
<!DOCTYPE TEST[
<!ELEMENT TEST (#PCDATA)>
<!ENTITY maybelegal1 "em>"> <!-- May not be part of tag -->
<!ENTITY maybelegal2 "-->"> <!-- May not be comment delimiter -->
<!ENTITY maybelegal3 "ph>"> <!-- May not be part of tag -->
]>
<TEST>
&maybelegal1; <!-- Legal: Interpreted as character data -->
&maybelegal2; <!-- Legal: Interpreted as character data -->
&maybelegal3; <!-- Legal: Interpreted as character data -->

<&maybelegal1; <!-- Illegal: Markup (tag) spans entities -->
<!-- &maybelegal2; Ignored: entity ref ignored in comment -->
<em&maybelegal3;    <!-- Illegal: Markup (tag) spans entities -->
</TEST>
```

legal. The same applies to *validity* (conformance to a document type definition). Example 50-16 is well-formed, but not valid, because the fully expanded document would not be valid. Validity is covered in Chapter 49, "Creating a document type definition", on page 702.

Example 50-16. Well-formed but not valid

```
<?xml version="1.0"?>
<!DOCTYPE TEST[
  <!ELEMENT EVENT (TIME, DESCRIPTION)>
  <!ELEMENT TIME (#PCDATA)>
  <!ELEMENT DESCRIPTION (#PCDATA)>
  <!ENTITY accident "<ERROR>Error</ERROR>">
]>
<EVENT>&accident;</EVENT>
```

The document in the example is well-formed. Both the EVENT and ERROR elements start and end in the same entity. It meets all of the other rules required for it to be well-formed. But it is not valid, because accident's replacement text consists of an ERROR element which is not valid where the entity is referenced. (in the EVENT element).

Conceptually, validation occurs after all entities have been parsed.

Spec Excerpt (XML) 50-5. General entity definition

```
[70]  EntityDecl ::=  GEDecl | PEDecl
[71]  GEDecl ::=  '<!ENTITY' S Name S EntityDef S? '>'
[73]  EntityDef ::=  EntityValue | (ExternalID NDataDecl?)
[72]  PEDecl ::=  '<!ENTITY' S '%' S Name S PEDef S? '>'
[74]  PEDef ::=  EntityValue | ExternalID
```

50.8.1 *Legal parameter entity reference*

Neither general entities nor parameter entities may span markup boundaries, but parameter entities have other restrictions on them. There are precise places that parameter entity references are allowed. Within the internal subset, the rules are simple: parameter entities can only be expanded in places where full markup declarations are allowed. For them to be legal in these contexts they must always contain one or more markup declarations.

Example 50-17. Multiple markup declarations in one parameter entity

```
<!ENTITY % several-declarations
               "<!ELEMENT FOO (#PCDATA)>
               <!ELEMENT BAR (#PCDATA)>
               <!ELEMENT BAZ (#PCDATA)>">
%several-declarations;
```

Because of the way XML handles white space, the replacement text for the entity declaration in Example 50-17 is parsed as it would if the entity declaration had occurred on a single line. In this case we have defined the literal entity value over several lines to make the DTD more readable. When we refer to the parameter entity "several-declarations", the three element types are declared.

The rules for parameter entities in the external subset are much more complex. This is because parameter entities in the external subset are not restricted to complete markup declarations. They can also be parts of a markup declaration. XML restricts parameter entities in the internal subset to full declarations because the internal subset is supposed to be very easy to process quickly by browsers and other processors. The external subset allows more complex, powerful parameter entity references. For instance, in the external subset, Example 50-18 would be a legal series of declarations.

Example 50-18. Entities in the external subset

```
<!ENTITY % ent-name "the-entity">
<!ENTITY % ent-value "This is the entity">
<!ENTITY %ent-name; "%ent-value;">
```

Both the name and the replacement text of the final entity declaration are specified through parameter entity references. Their replacement texts become the entity's name and replacement text.

The tricky part is that there are only particular places that you can use parameter entity references in markup declarations. You might wonder, for instance, if you could replace the string "<!ENTITY" with a parameter entity reference. You might guess that this is impossible because XML does not allow a markup declaration to start in one entity and end in another. You would guess correctly. It would be harder to guess whether you could use an entity reference to fill in the string "ENTITY" which follows the "<!" It turns out that this is illegal as well.

To be safe, we would advise you to stick to using parameter entities only to hold full markup declarations and portions of another entity's replacement text until you are familiar with the text of the XML specification itself. The specification relies on knowledge of grammatical tokens to constrain the places that parameter entity replacement is allowed in the external subset. Those token boundaries are only described in the complete grammar.

50.9 | External identifiers

External identifiers refer to information outside the entity in which they occur. There are two types. System identifiers use URIs to refer to an object based on its location. Public identifiers use a publicly declared name to refer to information.

Spec Excerpt (XML) 50-6. External identifier

```
[75]   ExternalID ::=   'SYSTEM' S SystemLiteral
                      | 'PUBLIC' S PubidLiteral S SystemLiteral
```

50.9.1 *System identifiers*

The *SystemLiteral* that follows the keyword SYSTEM is just a URI. Example 50-19 is another example of that.

Example 50-19. System identifier

```
<!ENTITY ent SYSTEM "http://www.entities.com/ent.xml">
```

You can also use relative URIs to refer to entities on the same machine as the referring entity. A relative URI is one that does not contain a complete machine name and path. The machine name and part of the path are implied from the context. Example 50-20 demonstrates.

Example 50-20. Local external general entity

```
<!ENTITY local SYSTEM "local.xml">
```

If this were declared in a document at the URI http://www.baz.org/, then the processor would fetch the replacement text from http://www.baz.org/local.xml.

These URIs are relative to the location of the referring entity (such as an external parameter entity or the external subset of the DTD) and not necessarily to the document entity. If your document entity is on one machine, and it includes some markup declarations from another machine, relative URIs in the included declarations are interpreted as being on the second machine.

For example, your document might be at http://www.myhome.com. It might include a DTD component with a set of pictures of playing cards from http://www.poker.com/cards.dtd. If that DTD component had a

URI, `4Heartss.gif`, it would be interpreted relative to the poker site, not yours.

50.9.2 *Public identifiers*

It is also possible to refer to a DTD component or any entity by a name, in addition to a URI. This name is called a "public identifier". If a few entities become widely used in XML circles then it would be inefficient for everyone to fetch the entities from the same servers. Instead, their software should come with those entities already installed (or else it should know the most efficient site from which to download them, perhaps from a corporate intranet). To enable these smarter lookup mechanisms, you would refer to those DTDs by public identifiers, as shown in Example 50-21.

Example 50-21. Referencing a DTD by public identifier

```
<!DOCTYPE MEMO PUBLIC "-//SGMLSOURCE//DTD MEMO//EN"
              "http://www.sgmlsource.com/dtds/memo.dtd">
<MEMO> </MEMO>
```

The public identifier is a unique name for the entity. It should be unique world-wide. Usually they contain corporate or personal names to make them more likely to be unique. If the software knows how to translate the public identifier into a URI, it will do so. If not, it will use the system identifier.

Right now, the translation from public identifier to URI is typically either hard-wired into a processor or controlled through files called "entity catalogs". Entity catalogs list public identifiers and describe their URIs, in the same way that phone books allow you to look up a name and find a number. Documentation for XML software should mention the format of the catalogs it supports, if any.

In the future there may be intranet- and Internet-wide systems that will look up a public identifier and download the DTD from the site that is closest to you. The Web's designers have been promising this feature for years and XML is ready when they deliver. In the meantime, the system identifier following the public identifier will be used.

50.10 | Conclusion

As you can see, XML separates issues of logical structure from those of the physical storage of the document. This means that document type designers do not have to foresee every possible reasonable way of breaking up a document when they design the document type. This is good, because that sort of decision is best made by those who know their system resource limits, bandwidth limits, editor preferences, and so forth. The document type designer, in contrast, takes responsibility for deciding on a good structure for the document.

Advanced
features of XML

Friendly Tutorial

- Conditional sections
- Character references
- Processing instructions
- Standalone declaration

The features in this chapter are advanced in the sense that only advanced users will get around to reading them. They do not require advanced degrees in computer science or rocket science to understand. They are just a little esoteric. Most XML users will get by without ever needing to use them.

51.1 | Conditional sections

Conditional sections can only occur in the external subset of the document type declaration, and in external entities referenced from the internal subset. The internal subset proper is supposed to be quick and easy to process. In contrast, the external subset is supposed to retain some of the full-SGML mechanisms that make complicated DTDs easier to maintain. One of these mechanisms is the conditional section, which allows you to turn on and off a series of markup declarations.

Like the internal and external subsets, conditional sections may contain one or more complete declarations, comments, processing instructions, or nested conditional sections, with optional white space between them.

A conditional section is turned on and off with a keyword. If the keyword is INCLUDE, then the section is processed just as if the conditional section markers did not exist. If the keyword is IGNORE, then the contents are ignored by the processor as if the declarations themselves did not exist, as in Example 51-1

Example 51-1. Conditional sections

```
<![INCLUDE[
 <!ELEMENT magazine (title, article+, comments* )>
 ]]>
<![IGNORE[
 <!ELEMENT magazine (title, body)>
]]>
```

This is a useful way of turning on and off parts of a DTD during development.

The real power in the feature derives from parameter entity references. These are described in 50.7, "Internal and external parameter entities", on page 748.

If the keyword of the conditional section is a parameter entity reference, the processor replaces the parameter entity by its content before the processor decides whether to include or ignore the conditional section. That means that by changing the parameter entity in the internal subset, you can turn on and off a conditional marked section. In that way, two different documents could reference the same set of external markup declarations, but get slightly (or largely) different DTDs. For instance, we can modify the example above:

Example 51-2. Conditional sections and parameter entities

```
<![%editor[
 <!ELEMENT magazine (title, article+, comments* )>
 ]]>
<![%author[
 <!ELEMENT magazine (title, body)>
]]>
```

Now editors will have a slightly different DTD from authors. When the parameter entities are set one way, the declaration without comments is chosen:

Example 51-3. Internal subset of a document type declaration

```
<!DOCTYPE MAGAZINE SYSTEM "magazine.dtd"[
   <!ENTITY % editor "IGNORE">
   <!ENTITY % author "INCLUDE">
]>
```

Authors do not have to worry about `comments` elements that they are not supposed to use anyway. When the document moves from the author to the editor, the parameter entity values can be swapped, and the expanded version of the DTD becomes available. Parameter entities can also be used to manage DTDs that go through versions chronologically, as an organization's needs change.

Conditional sections are also sometimes used to make "strict" and "loose" versions of DTDs. The loose DTD can be used for compatibility with old documents, or documents that are somehow out of your control, and the strict DTD can be used to try to encourage a more precise structure for future documents.

51.2 | Character references

It is not usually convenient to type in characters that are not available on the keyboard. With many text editors, it is not even possible to do so. XML allows you to insert such a character with a *character reference*. If, for instance, you wanted to insert a character from the "International Phonetic Alphabet", you could spend a long time looking for a combination of keyboard, operating system and text editor that would make that straightforward. Rather than buying special hardware or software, XML allows you to refer to the character by its *Unicode number*.

Here is an example:

Example 51-4. Decimal character reference

```
<P>Here is a reference to Unicode character 161: &#161;.</P>
```

Unicode is a character set. The character numbered 161 in Unicode happens to be the inverted exclamation mark. Alternatively, you could use the *hex* (hexadecimal) value of the character number to reference it:

Example 51-5. Hex character reference

```
<P>Here is a different reference to Unicode character 161: &#xA1;.
```

Hex is a numbering system often used by computer programmers that translates naturally into the binary codes that computers use. The *Unicode Standard book* uses hex, so those that have that book will probably prefer this type of character reference over the other (whether they are programmers or not).

Here are the specifics on character references from the XML spec:

Spec Excerpt (XML) 51-1. Character reference

```
CharRef ::=  '&#' [0-9]+ ';'
  | '&#x' [0-9a-fA-F]+ ';'
```

Spec Excerpt (XML) 51-2. Interpreting character references

If the character reference begins with "&#x", the digits and letters up to the terminating ; provide a hexadecimal representation of the character's code point in ISO/IEC 10646. If it begins just with "&#", the digits up to the terminating ; provide a decimal representation of the character's code point.

ISO/IEC 10646 is the Borg of character set standards. It seemingly includes every character from every other character set and leaves room for characters not yet created. Unicode is an independently developed industry-standard character set that is identifiable as a subset of ISO/IEC 10646. For XML purposes, there's no real need to distinguish them.

Note that character references are not entity references, though they look similar to them. Entities have names and values, but character references only have character numbers. In an XML document, all entities except the predefined ones must be declared. But a character reference does not require a declaration; it is just a really verbose way to type a character (but often the only way).

Because Unicode numbers are hard to remember, it is often useful to declare entities that stand in for them:

Example 51-6. Entity declaration for a Unicode character

```
<!ENTITY inverted-exclamation "&#161;">
```

Most likely this is how most XML users will refer to obscure characters. There will probably be popular character entity sets that can be included in a DTD through parameter entity references. This technique will free users from learning obscure character numbers and probably even from learning how to use character references.

51.3 | Processing instructions

XML comments are for those occasions where you need to say something to another human being without reference to the DTD, and without changing the way the document looks to readers or applications. Processing instructions are for those occasions where you need to say something to *a computer program* without reference to the DTD and without changing the way that the document is processed by other computer programs. This is only supposed to happen rarely.

Many people argued that the occasions would be so rare that XML should not have processing instructions at all. But as one of us said in *The SGML Handbook*: "In a perfect world, they would not be needed, but, as you may have noticed, the world is not perfect." It turns out that processing instruction use has changed over the years and is not as frowned upon as it was in the early days of SGML.

Processing instructions are intended to reintroduce software-specific markup. You might wonder why you would want to do that. Imagine that you are creating a complex document, and, like a good user of a generalized markup language, you are concentrating on the structure rather than the formatting. Close to the deadline you print the document using the proprietary formatting system that has been foisted on you by your boss. There are many of these systems, some of which are of fantastic quality and others which are not.

Your document looks reasonable, but you need a way to make the first letter of each paragraph large. However, reading the software's manual, you realize that the formatter does not have a feature that allows you to modify the style for the first letter of a word. The XML Purist in you might want to go out and buy a complete formatting system but the Pragmatist in you knows that that is impossible.

Thinking back to the bad-old days of "What You See is All You Get" word processors, you recall that all you really needed to do is to insert a code in the beginning of each paragraph to change the font for the first letter. This is not good "XML Style" because XML Purists do not insert formatting codes and they especially do not insert codes specific to a particular piece of software – that is not in the "spirit" of generalized markup. Still, in this case, with a deadline looming and stubborn software balking, a processing instruction may be your best bet. If the formatter has a "change font" command it may be accessible through a processing instruction:

Example 51-7. Processing instruction

```
<CHAPTER>The Bald and the Dutiful
<P><?DUMB-FORMATTER.FONT="16PT"?>N<?DUMB-FORMATTER.END-FONT?>ick
took Judy in his arms</P>
```

If you find yourself using many processing instructions to specify formatting you should try to figure out what is wrong with your system. Is your document's markup not rich enough? Is your formatting language not powerful enough? Are you not taking advantage of the tools and markup you have available to you? The danger in using processing instructions is that you can come to rely on them instead of more reusable structural markup. Then when you want to reuse your information in another context, the markup will not be robust enough to allow it.

Processing instructions start with a fixed string "<?". That is followed by a name and, after that, any characters except for the string that ends the PI, "?>".

Here are the relevant rules from the XML specification:

Spec Excerpt (XML) 51-3. Processing Instruction

```
[16]   PI ::=   '<?' PITarget (S (Char* - (Char* '?>' Char*)))? '?>'
[17]   PITarget ::=  Name - (('X' | 'x') ('M' | 'm') ('L' | 'l'))
```

This name at the beginning of the PI is called the *PI target*. This name should be standardized in the documentation for the tool or specification. After the PI target comes white space and then some totally proprietary command. This command is not processed in the traditional sense at all. Characters that would usually indicate markup are totally ignored. The command is passed directly to the application and it does what it wants to with it. The command ends when the processor hits the string "?>". There is absolutely no standard for the "stuff" in the middle. Markup is not recognized there. PIs could use attribute syntax for convenience, but they could also choose not to.

It is possible that more than one application could understand the same instructions. They might come from the same vendor or one vendor might agree to accept another vendor's commands. For instance in the early days of the Web, the popular NCSA (National Center for Supercomputing Activities) Web Server introduced special commands into HTML documents in the form of special HTML comments. Because the NCSA server was dominant in those days, many servers now support those commands.

Under XML we would most likely use processing instructions for the same task. The virtue of XML processing instructions in this case is that they are explicitly instructions to a computer program. In our opinion, one of the central tenets of generalized markup is that it is important to be *explicit* about what is going on in a document. Reusing markup constructs for something other than what they were intended for is not explicit.

For instance, since comments are meant to be instructions to users, an ambitious Web Server administrator might decide to write a small script that would strip them out to save download time and protect internal comments from being read by others. But if instructions to software (like the NCSA server commands) were hidden in comments, they would be stripped out as well. It would be better to use the supplied processing instruction facility, which was designed for the purpose.

Better still (from a purist's point of view) would be a robust XML-smart mechanism for accomplishing the task. For instance, one thing that the NCSA servers do is include the text of one HTML file into another. XML's entity mechanism (see Chapter 50, "Entities: Breaking up is easy to do", on page 736) can handle this, so you do not need processing instructions in that case.

If you want to insert the date into a document, then you could connect the external entity to a CGI[1] that returns the date. If you want to insert information from a database then you could have software that generates XML entities with the requested information.

Sometimes, though, the processing instruction solution may be the most expedient. This is especially the case if your application vendor has set it up that way. If your document is heavily dependent on a database or other program, then it is not very "application independent" in any case. If a document is inherently dependent on an application then you may decide that strictly adhering to generalized markup philosophy is just too much work. In the end you must choose between expediency and purity. Most people mix both.

Processing instructions are appropriate when you are specifying information about a document that is unrelated to the actual structure of the document. Consider, for instance, the problem of specifying which stylesheets go with which XML documents on a web site. Given enough money and time you could erect a database that kept track of them. If you already had your XML documents in a text database then this would probably be the most efficient mechanism. If you did not have a text database set up, then you could merely keep the information in a flat text file. But you would have to keep that external information up-to-date and write a program to retrieve it in order to do formatting. It would probably be easier to simply stick the information somewhere in the file where it is easy to find (such as at the beginning).

You could add a STYLESHEET element or attribute to each document, but that could cause three problems. First, it would violate the XML Purist principle that elements should represent document components and not formatting or other processing information. Second, if you are using DTDs with your documents then you must add the element or attribute to each DTD that you will be using. This would be a hassle.

The third reason to use processing instructions instead of elements is the most concrete: you may not be able to change those DTDs. After all, DTDs are often industry (or international!) standards. You cannot just go monkeying around with them even if you want to. Instead, you could put a processing instruction at the start of each document. Processing instructions are not associated with particular DTDs and they do not have to be declared. You just use them.

---

1. CGI is the "Common Gateway Interface", a specification for making Web pages that are generated by the server when the user requests them, rather than in advance.

As we described in 55.10, "Referencing XSL stylesheets", on page 857), XML provides a processing instruction for associating stylesheets:

Example 51-8. Stylesheet PI

```
<?xml-stylesheet
          href="http://www.sgmlsource.com/memo.xsl"
          type="text/xsl"?>
```

Note that the stylesheet processing instruction does not really add anything to the content or structure of the document. It says something about how to *process* the document. It says: "This document has an associated stylesheet and it is available at such and such a location." It is not always obvious what is abstract information and what is merely processing information. If your instruction must be embedded in documents of many types, or with DTDs that you cannot change, then processing instructions are typically your best bet.

The XML *encodingPI* is an example of another processing instruction. It says what character encoding the file uses. Again this information could be stored externally, such as in a database, a text file or somewhere else, but XML's designers decided (after weeks of heated discussion) that it would be most convenient to place it in the XML document itself rather than require it to be stored (and transmitted across the Internet) externally.

If you go back to 48.6.1, "XML declaration", on page 692 you will also notice that the XML declaration has the same prefix ("<?") and suffix ("?>") as processing instructions do. Formally speaking, the XML declaration is a special form of processing instruction. From an SGML processor's point of view, it is a processing instruction that controls the behavior of a particular class of software: XML processing software. Software that treats XML as just another kind of SGML will ignore it, as they do other types of processing instructions.

To summarize: PIs (processing instructions) were invented primarily for formatting hacks but based on our experience with SGML we know that they are more widely useful. There are already predefined processing instructions in the XML specification for some kinds of processing. Processing instructions will probably be used for other things in the future. Everything that can be accomplished with PIs would be accomplished by other means in a perfect world of pure generalized markup, but in the real world they are often convenient.

51.4 | Special attributes and newlines

There are two attribute names that the XML specification treats as special whenever it encounters them. If a document is to be valid then it must have declarations for these attributes but if it is well-formed but not valid then it may just use them undeclared, as it would any other attribute.

The attribute `xml:lang` is an convention for stating the language of the content of an element. This is language not in some esoteric computer sense but in the normal, human languages sense. The attribute's value is typically a language code like "`en`" for English and "`fr`" for French.

It is also common to follow the language code with a dash and a country code to indicate a more precise dialect. The country codes are the same ones used in Internet domain names: "uk", "us", "ca" etc. If you do serious internationalization work you should check the XML specification for the full details.

The attribute `xml:space` is a hint to an application about how it should handle whitespace in an element. For instance, an XML editor might use the attribute to know whether it is appropriate to collapse several spaces into a single one or to convert newline characters into spaces. The two valid values are `default` and `preserve`. Default means that an application should do whatever it usually does with whitespace – collapse, delete, preserve or anything. Preserve means that the application should not change the whitespace in any way.

Both of these attributes are *inherited*. That means that an attribute applies to the element and all descendants unless some descendant has a conflicting value for it. In that case the descendant's attribute value would be in effect for that element and *its* descendants, but the ancestral value would again be in effect after that element ends.

Regardless of the value of these attributes, XML processors must always convert end-of-line markers to a single Unix-style newline character. It does not matter what platform (e.g. Windows, Macintosh, Unix) the document is processed on nor what platform it was created on. The various end-of-line conventions are all converted automatically to the Unix convention before the application sees the data. This means that software programs can behave in exactly the same way on all platforms and documents.

51.5 | Standalone document declaration

We should start by saying that the standalone document declaration is only designed for a small class of problems, and these are not problems that most XML users will run into. We do not advise its use. Nevertheless, it is part of XML and we feel that you should understand it so that you can understand why it is seldom useful.

A DTD is typically broken into two parts, an external part that contains declarations that are typically shared among many documents, and an internal part that occurs within the document and contains declarations that only that document uses (see Chapter 49, "Creating a document type definition", on page 702). The external part includes all external parameter entities, including both the external subset of the document type declaration and any external entities referenced from the internal subset.

The DTD describes the structure of the document, but it can also control the interpretation of some of the markup and declare the existence of some other entities (such as graphics or other XML documents) that are required for proper processing. For instance, a graphic might only be used in a particular document, so the declaration that includes it (an *entity declaration*) would usually go in the internal subset rather than the external one.

Processors that validate a document need the entire DTD to do so. A document is not valid unless it conforms to both the internal and external parts of its DTD. But sometimes a system passes a document from program to program and it does not need to be validated at each stage. For instance, two participants in an electronic data interchange system might agree that the sender will validate the document once, instead of having both participants validate it.

Even though the receiving processor may not be interested in full validation, it may need to know if it understands the document in exactly the same way that the sender did. Some features of the DTD may influence this slightly. Documents with defaulted attributes would be interpreted differently if the attribute declarations are read rather than ignored. Entity declarations would allow the expansion of entity references. Attribute values can only be normalized according to their type when the attribute declarations are read. Some white space in content would also be removed if the DTD would not allow it to be interpreted as text.

If a process can reliably skip a part of the DTD dedicated exclusively to validation, then it would have less data to download and process and could let the application do its work (browsing, searching, etc.) more quickly. But it would be important for some "mission critical" applications to know if they are getting a slightly different understanding of the document than they would if they processed the entire DTD.

The *standalone document declaration* allows you to specify whether a processor needs to fetch the external part of the DTD in order to process the document "exactly right." The Standalone document declaration may take the values (case sensitive) of yes and no.

A value of yes says that the document is *standalone* and thus does not depend on the external part of the DTD for correct interpretation. A value of *no* means that it either depends on the external DTD part or it might, so the application should not trust that it can get the correct information without it. You could always use no as the value for this attribute, but in some cases applications will then download more data than they need to do their jobs. This translates into slower processing, more network usage and so forth.

Example 51-9. A standalone document declaration that forces processing of the internal subset.

```
<?xml version="1.0" standalone="no"?>
<!DOCTYPE MEMO SYSTEM "http://www.sgmlsource.com/memo.dtd" [
<!ENTITY % pics SYSTEM "http://www.sgmlsource.com/pics.ent">
 %pics;
]>
<MEMO></MEMO>
```

Example 51-9 will tell the application that unless the processor fetched the pictures, the application might get a different understanding of the document than it would if it processed the whole document. For instance, the MEMO element might have defaulted attributes.

But if the value is *yes*, the receiving application may choose not to get the external part of the DTD. This implies that it will never know what was in it. Still, it needs to be able to trust the accuracy of the declaration. What if the security level for a document is set in an attribute and the default level is top-secret? It would be very bad if a careless author could obscure that with a misleading standalone document declaration. In the scenario we outlined, the sender has already validated the document. So the sender has enough information to check that the information is correct. The XML specification requires a validating processor to do this (see Spec Excerpt 51-4).

Spec Excerpt (XML) 51-4. Standalone document declaration

The standalone document declaration must have the value "no" if any external markup declarations contain declarations of:

- attributes with default values, if elements to which these attributes apply appear in the document without specifications of values for these attributes, or
- entities (other than amp, lt, gt, apos, quot), if references to those entities appear in the document, or
- attributes with values subject to normalization, where the attribute appears in the document with a value which will change as a result of normalization, or
- element types with element content, if white space occurs directly within any instance of those types.

The last one is very likely to happen. Often people use white space between tags to make the source XML document readable, but that can slightly change the interpretation of the document. Validating processors will tell applications that there are some contexts where character data is not legal, so the white space occurring in those places must be merely formatting white space (see 49.5, "Content models", on page 714). If an application that does not want to validate a document is to get exactly the same information out of the document, it must know whether there are any elements where white space should be interpreted just as source formatting. We say that this sort of white space is *insignificant*.

The standalone document declaration warns the application that this is the case so that mission critical applications may download the DTD just to get the right information out of the document, even when they are not interested in validating it.

The standalone document declaration is fairly obscure and it is doubtful if it will get much use outside of a few mission critical applications. Even there, however, it is safest to just get the external data and do a complete validation before trusting a document. You might find that it had been corrupted in transit.

51.6 | Is that all there is?

We've pretty much covered all the details of XML, certainly all that are likely to see extensive use. There are some things we didn't touch on, such as restrictions that must be observed if you are using older SGML tools to process XML. As the generalized markup industry is retooling rapidly for XML, such restrictions will be short-lived and, we felt, did not warrant complicating our XML tutorial.

In any case, you are now well-prepared – or will be after reading Chapter 52, "Reading the XML specification", on page 776 – to tackle the XML spec yourself. You'll find it in the XML SPECtacular section of the CD-ROM that accompanies this book.

Tip   We can also recommend Bob DuCharme's *XML:The Annotated Specification,* which is published in this series (ISBN 0-13-082676-6). It is extensively annotated and has over 170 new usage examples.

Reading the XML specification

Tad Tougher Tutorial

- **Grammars**
- **Rules**
- **Symbols**

T he XML specification is a little tricky to read, but with some work you can get through it by reading and understanding the glossary and applying the concepts described so far in this book. One thing you'll need to know is how to interpret the production rules that make up XML's grammar. This chapter teaches how to read those rules.

When discussing a particular string, like a tag or declaration, we often want to discuss the parts of that string individually. We call each part of the string a *token*. Tokens can always be separated by white space as described above. Sometimes the white space between the tokens is required. For instance we can represent the months of the year as tokens:

Example 52-1. Tokens

```
JANUARY  FEBRUARY  MARCH    APRIL       MAY        JUNE
```

White space between tokens is *normalized* (combined) so that no matter how much white space you type, the processor treats it as if the tokens were separated by a single space. Thus the example above is equivalent to the following:

Example 52-2. Tokens after normalization

```
JANUARY FEBRUARY MARCH APRIL MAY JUNE
```

Whenever we discuss strings made up of tokens, you will know that you can use as much white space between tokens as you need and the XML processor will normalize it for you.

52.1 | A look at XML's grammar

There are two basic techniques that we could use to discuss XML's syntax precisely. The first is to describe syntactic constructs in long paragraphs of excruciatingly dull prose. The better approach is to develop a simple system for describing syntax. In computer language circles, such systems are called *grammars*. Grammars are more precise and compact. Although they are no less boring (as you may recall from primary school), you can skip them easily until you need to know some specific detail of XML's syntax.

As a bonus, once you know how to read a grammar, you can read the one in the XML specification and thus work your way up to the status of "language lawyer".[1] As XML advances, an ability to read the specification will help you to keep on top of its progress.

The danger in this approach is that you might confuse the grammar with XML markup itself. The grammar is just a definitional tool. It is not used in XML applications. You don't type it in when you create an XML document. You use it to figure out what you *can* type in. Before "the new curriculum", students were taught grammar in primary school. They would be taught parts of speech and how they could combine them. XML's grammar is the same. It will tell you what the parts of an XML document are, and how you can combine them.

Grammars are made up of production *rules* and *symbols*. Rules are simple: they say what is allowed in a particular place in an XML document.

---

1. You too can nitpick about tiny language details and thus prove your superiority over those who merely use XML rather than obsess over it.

Rules have a symbol on the left side, the string "::=" in the middle and a list of symbols on the right side:

Example 52-3. A Rule

```
people ::= 'Melissa, ' 'Tiffany, ' 'Joshua,' 'Johan'
```

If this rule were part of the grammar for XML (which it is not!) it would say that in a particular place in an XML document you could type the names listed.

The symbols on the right (the names, in the last example) define the set of allowed values for the construct described by the rule ("people"). An allowed value is said to *match*. Rules are like definitions in a dictionary. The left side says what is being defined and the right side says what its definition is. Just as words in a dictionary, are defined in terms of other words, symbols are defined in terms of other symbols. Rules in the XML grammar are preceded by a number. You can look the rule up by number. If an XML document does not follow all of the XML production rules, it is not *well-formed*.

52.2 | Constant strings

The most basic type of symbol we will deal with is a *constant string*. These are denoted by a series of characters in between single quote characters. Constant strings are matched case-sensitively (as we discussed earlier). Here are some examples:

Example 52-4. Matching constant strings

```
AlphabetStart ::= 'ABC'
Example1 ::= '<!DOCTYPE'
```

This would match (respectively) the strings

Example 52-5. Matches

```
ABC
<!DOCTYPE
```

When we are discussing a constant string that is an English word or abbreviation, we will refer to it as a *keyword*. In computer languages, a keyword is a word that is interpreted specially by the computer. So your mother's maiden name is not (likely) a keyword, but a word like `#REQUIRED` is.

Symbols in XML's grammar are separated by spaces, which means that you must match the first, and then the second, and so on in order.

Example 52-6. Representing sequence

```
AlphabetStartAndEnd ::= 'ABC' 'XYZ'
NumbersAndLetters ::= '123' 'QPZ'
```

These would match:

Example 52-7. Sequence matches

```
ABCXYZ
123QPZ
```

Note that a space character in the grammar does not equate to white space in the XML document. Wherever white space can occur we will use the symbol "S". That means that wherever the grammar specifies "S", you may put in as much white space as you need to make your XML source file maintainable.

Example 52-8. Whitespace

```
SpacedOutAlphabet ::= 'ABC' S 'XYZ'
```

matches:

Example 52-9. Matching whitespace

```
ABC XYZ
ABC     XYZ
ABC               XYZ
```

This is the first example we have used where a single rule matches multiple strings. This is usually the case. Just as in English grammar there are many possible verbs and nouns, there are many possible strings that match the rule SpacedOutAlphabet, depending on how much white space you choose to make your XML source file maintainable.

Obviously XML would not be very useful if you could only insert pre-defined text and white space. After all, XML users usually like to choose the topic and content of their documents! So they need to have the option of inserting their own content: a *user defined string*. The simplest type of user defined string is *character data*. This is simply the text that isn't markup. You can put almost any character in character data. The exceptions are characters that would be confused with markup, such as less-than and ampersand symbols.

52.3 | Names

The XML specification uses the symbol "Name" to represent names. For example:

Example 52-10. Names

```
PersonNamedSmith :: = Name S 'Smith'
```

When we combine the name, the white space and the constant string, the rule matches strings like these:

Example 52-11. Matching names

```
Christina Smith
Allan      Smith
Michael    Smith
Black        Smith
Bla_ck         Smith
_Black         Smith
```

52.4 | Occurrence indicators

Sometimes a string is *optional*. We will indicate this by putting a question mark after the symbol that represents it in a rule:

Example 52-12. Optional strings

```
Description ::= 'Tall' S? 'dark'? S? 'handsome'? S? 'person'
Tall person
Tallperson
Tall handsomeperson
Tall dark person
Talldarkhandsomeperson
```

Notice that optionality does not affect the order of the tokens. For example, dark can never go before tall. We can also allow a part of a rule to be matched multiple times. If we want to allow a part to be matched one or more times, we can use the plus symbol and make it *repeatable*.

Example 52-13. Repeatable parts

```
VeryTall ::= 'A' S ('very' S)+ 'tall' S 'person.'
A very tall person.
A very very tall person.
A very very very tall person.
```

An asterisk is similar, but it allows a string to be matched zero or more times. In other words it is both repeatable and optional.

Example 52-14. Both repeatable and optional

```
VerySmall ::= 'A' S ('very' S)* 'small' S 'person.'
A small person.
A very small person.
A very very small person.
A very very very small person.
```

Symbols can be grouped with parentheses so that you could, for instance, make a whole series of symbols optional at once. This is different from making them each optional separately because you must either supply strings for all of them or none:

Example 52-15. Grouping with parentheses

```
Description2 ::= 'A' S ('tall' S 'dark' S 'handsome' S)? 'man.'
```

This rule matches these two strings (and no others):

Example 52-16. Matching groups

```
A tall dark handsome man.
A man.
```

We will sometimes have a choice of symbols to use. This is indicated by separating the alternatives by a vertical bar:

Example 52-17. Optional parts

```
Description3 ::= 'A' S ('short'|'tall') S
                ('fair'|'tan'|'dark') S ('man'|'woman') '.'
A tall dark man.
A short fair woman.
A short tan man.
A tall dark woman.
```

Note that we broke a single long rule over two lines rather than having it run off of the end of the page. This does not in any way affect the meaning of the rule. Line breaks are just treated like space characters between the symbols.

We can combine all of these types of symbols. This allows us to make more complex rules.

Example 52-18. Combining types of symbols

```
Book ::= (('Fascinating'|'Intriguing') S ('XML'|'SGML') S 'Book')
                | ('Yet another HTML' S 'Book')
Fascinating XML Book
Yet another HTML Book
Intriguing SGML Book
```

So in this case, you should treat the first large parenthesized expression (saying good things about SGML and XML books) as one option, and the second (saying not as good things about HTML books) as another. Inside the first set, you can choose different adjectives and book types, but the ordering is fixed and there must be white space between each part.

52.5 | Combining rules

Finally, rules can refer to other rules. Where one rule refers to another, you just make a valid value for each part and then put the parts together like building blocks.

Example 52-19. Combining rules

```
FunnyDate ::= Month S Day ',' Year
Month ::= 'Jan'|'Feb'|'Mar'|'Apr'|'May'|'Jun'
                |'Jul'|'Aug'|'Sep'|'Oct'|'Nov'|'Dec'
Day ::= ('1'|'2'|'3')?
                ('1'|'2'|'3'|'4'|'5'|'6'|'7'|'8'|'9'|'0')
Year ::= '1998'|'1999'|'2000'|'2001'|'2002'
```

This would match strings such as:

Example 52-20. Matching strings

```
Jan 21,1998
May 35,2000
Sep 2,2002
```

As you can see, this is not quite a strict specification for dates, but it gets the overall form or *syntax* of them right.

52.6 | Conclusion

We've explained the bulk of what is needed to understand XML's production rules. There are a few more details that you can find in section 6 of the XML spec itself. It is included in the XML SPECtacular on the CD-ROM.

Related Tutorials

- Namespaces
- XML Path Language (XPath)
- XML Stylesheet Language (XSL and XSLT)
- XML Pointer Language (XPointer)
- XML Linking Language (XLink)
- Datatypes
- XML Schema definition language (XSDL)
- Full specs on CD-ROM

Part Fourteen

This part covers seven core XML-related specifications from the World Wide Web Consortium, in varying stages of development. You'll need a pretty firm grasp of the material in Part Thirteen before you tackle any of these.

But unlike Part Thirteen, it isn't necessary to read these chapters in order unless you are trying to sop up all the good technical stuff that you can. Here's a roadmap in case you are only interested in specific subjects.

Namespaces are an approved Recommendation and are seeing a lot of use. You need to know something about them before reading the other chapters in this part, but you don't need to cover everything.

XPath is a prerequisite for both stylesheets and XPointers, but again you don't need to master all the details before moving on.

XSL and XPointer aren't prerequisites for anything else, although understanding XPointer will add to your appreciation of the power of XLink. XLink isn't a prerequisite either.

Datatypes is a prerequisite for XML Schemas, but here too only the basics are needed.

Namespaces

- Unique names
- URI-based namespaces
- Namespaces and DTDs

T he Namespaces in XML specification is an extension to XML that answers the burning question: Are we talking about the same subject?

Using namespaces it is possible to create elements with the generic identifier para in two different documents, with two different document types (or no explicitly-declared document types at all) and write software and queries that recognize that both represent a paragraph. This might not seem like much of a feat, but consider that in a third document an element with that element-type name might represent a paramedic (consider an employment record from the television show "ER"), a paranormal encounter (in a document from the FBI's "X-Files") or a paralegal (court records).

Even a fully spelled-out word can be ambiguous. A list can be a list of items or the angle of list (tilt) of a seagoing vessel. Besides, if two different people invented two different document types, they might use the words "list" and "para" to mean the same basic thing but their underlying model of paragraphs and lists might be different. One might expect elements of type "list" to be ordered. The other might want to allow lists to have a header.

Everyone in the world is allowed to invent document types, so we need to be clear about the origin of our element types. If you have a document database containing both ship records and technical manuals, a database-wide query needs to be able to figure out which list is which – even if the documents do not have DTDs.

Despite the general agreement on the need for this sort of *disambiguation*, we should mention that the XML namespaces concept is not universally embraced as the best solution. In fact XML namespaces are downright controversial. After reading this chapter you can make up your own mind.

Nevertheless, namespaces are already in widespread use. World Wide Web Consortium specifications already build upon the namespace mechanism and will do so in the future. Microsoft's *Office 2000* document types also use them. Namespaces look like they are here to stay.

53.1 | Problem statement

Namespaces are easiest to understand if we work in the realm of well-formed documents without DTDs. We will address the relationship to DTDs later on.

You may be familiar with email programs that can recognize and visually highlight URLs and email addresses. This works nicely in the program, but when the email is saved to disk or forwarded to a less intelligent email program, that highlighting is lost. It might be better if the program could actually introduce markup representing the highlighting. That way other applications could get the benefit of the email program's analysis and recognition. We could use web and email element types to capture this information.

Our system would work fine for a while, but the time would come when people would want to send XML documents (remember, well-formed but DTD-less XML documents) through email. We might want to allow our system to continue to work on these documents. The problem is that it is a bad idea for us to presume that any element with an element type name of web or email was meant to refer to our element types.

Perhaps an XML document will come through the email with a web element that is meant to represent spider webs or knowledge webs. Perhaps the web elements really do represent URLs, but they use an attribute to hold the address instead of content. Then we have the same meaning but a different internal structure.

What we need to do is clearly separate our names from other people's names. We need to have different so-called `namespaces`. We do this in the real world all of the time.

What would you do if you needed to refer to a particular John Smith without confusing him with any other John Smith. You qualify the name: "John Smith from London." That sets up a namespace that separates Londoners from everyone else.

If that isn't sufficient then you further qualify the namespace: "John Smith from East London". That makes a namespace that separates Easterners from everyone else. You could narrow it down even more: "John Smith from Adelaide Street in East London." The trick is qualifying names in order to separate them from other names. The separate groups of names are known as "namespaces."

53.2 | The namespaces solution

Given that what we want to do is qualify names, the most obvious idea is to have a prefix that does the qualification. `myEmailProgram:web` or `myEmailProgram:email`. This seems to work at first, but eventually two people will make program names that clash. In fact, there will be a strong tendency to use three-letter acronyms. There are only so many of these acronyms!

In the real world people constantly choose names that other people also choose. Even city names can clash: consider how many there are named "Springfield"! If people are allowed to choose names without any central authority then they will eventually choose names that clash.

The World Wide Web Consortium could set up a registry of these acronyms and names. But that would require a great deal of effort both in setting up the registry and in registering individual namespaces.

A better mechanism would be to use a registry that already exists. One such registry is the domain name registry. We could use prefixes like: `mycompany.com:email`. We would call "mycompany.com" the *namespace* and "email" a particular name in that namespace.

This solution is getting much closer but it still is not as democratic as we would like. The problem is that domain names cost $70.00 USD and applying for them is a difficult process. What if an ordinary America

OnLine (AOL) user wants to develop a namespace? Does he have to register a domain name?

Every AOL user has a little bit of space to put files and assign a URL such as `http://www.aol.com/EmailAppGuy`. If we could use that as the basis for a namespace identifier, then we would open up the namespace-creating process to a larger number of people.

This idea also works for organizations other than Internet Service Providers. Consider a big company like General Electric. Various parts of the company may develop XML namespaces. The company probably already has a mechanism for delegating Web URLs. It makes sense to re-use that mechanism for XML namespaces. Example 53-1 shows what URL-based namespace prefixes might look like.

Example 53-1. Mythical (illegal!) URL-based namespace prefix

```
<http://www.aol.com/EmailAppGuy:email>email@machine.com
</http://www.aol.com/EmailAppGuy:email>
```

There are two problems with these prefixes. First, they are not legal XML names because of all of the funny characters such as slashes and dots. Second, they are plug-ugly and incredibly verbose. We need a way to set up a local abbreviation. The XML *Namespaces* specification defines the mechanism for setting up such abbreviations.

53.2.1 *Namespace prefixes*

The *Namespaces* specification defines a rule that attributes that start with the prefix `xmlns:` should be interpreted as prefix-defining attributes. The name immediately following the prefix is a local abbreviation for the namespace.

The attribute value is a URI. You can use any URI (typically a URL) that you would normally have control over. Throughout the element exhibiting that attribute, the prefix stands for the namespace identifier. Example 53-2 demonstrates.

The actual prefix you use is not relevant. It is just a stand-in for the URI. So, for example, when creating an XSL stylesheet you do not need to use the `xsl:` prefix for names defined in the XSL spec. Doing otherwise might be confusing, but it is totally legal.

Example 53-2. Using XML namespaces

```
<eag:email xmlns:eag="http://www.aol.com/EmailAppGuy">
  email@machine.com
</eag:email>
```

Note that the details of the URI are not relevant either. It does not matter whether there is a document at that location or whether the client machine is Internet-connected. There is no need to connect to the Internet to check the contents of the document at that address.

The data (or lack of data) at the other end of the URI is absolutely irrelevant to the namespaces design. Its only goal is to have a long, globally unique string to use in comparisons.

That's an important point! Namespaces work with broken URIs because namespaces only disambiguate names, they don't define names. The URIs therefore don't have to address the definitions of the names in the namespace (although they may).

The only requirement is that you really do control the URI that you use. It is your responsibility to guarantee that nobody else (your spouse?) will accidently but legitimately use the same URI and mean something different by it.

53.2.2 *Scoping*

The prefix scheme is still pretty verbose, but it is some improvement. It looks better when you realize that namespace declarations are *scoped* by their declaring elements. That means that they apply to the element, its children, and the children's children and so forth unless some child has a declaration that specifically overrides the first declaration. Therefore you could declare namespaces in the document (root) element and have them apply throughout the entire document! Example 53-3 demonstrates.[1]

We can minimize the impact even more by removing some of the prefixes. There is a special namespace called the *default namespace*. This namespace is defined without a prefix, so element-type names in the scope of the definition that have no prefix are considered to be in this namespace.[2] If you expect to use many elements from a particular namespace, you can make it the default namespace for the appropriate

---

1. Note that .con is the new high-level domain for Internet scams.

Example 53-3. XML namespace scope

```
<html:html
    xmlns:eag="http://www.aol.com/EmailAppGuy"
    xmlns:html="http://www.w3.org/TR/WD-HTML40"
    xmlns:math="http://www.w3.org/TR/REC-MathML/">
 <html:title>George Soros Personal Wealth Page</html:title>
 <html:h2>Counting My Cash</html:h2>
 <html:p>As you know, my cash rivals the gross national
 product of some small countries. Consider the following
 equation:
 <math:reln>
   <math:eq/>
   <math:ci>wealth</math:ci>
   <math:ci>gnp</math:ci>
 </math:reln>
 If you have any ideas of how I could spend
 this money. Please contact
 <eag:email>georges@aol.con</eag:email>.
</html:p>

</html:html>
```

scope. In fact, you can even have a document in which the namespaces correspond cleanly to the elements and there are no prefixes at all, as Example 53-4 demonstrates.

Example 53-4. Two default namespaces: HTML and MathML

```
<html
    xmlns="http://www.w3.org/TR/WD-HTML40">
 <title>George Soros Personal Wealth Page</title>
 <h2>Counting My Cash</h2>
 <p>As you know, my cash rivals the gross national
 product of some small countries. Consider the following
 equation:
 <reln xmlns="http://www.w3.org/TR/REC-MathML/">
   <eq/>
   <ci>wealth</ci>
   <ci>gnp</ci>
 </reln>
 If you have any ideas of how I could spend
 this money.</p>
</html>
```

---

2. You can think of the default namespace as having a null prefix, if that helps
    any.

Note that the default namespace is HTML both before and after the `reln` element. Within the `reln` element the default namespace is MathML. As you can see, we can eliminate many of the prefixes but still keep the relationship between the element-type names and the namespaces.

We can also establish a scope in which namespaces aren't in use and all names are local, by using an empty URI. In Example 53-5, `notes` and `to-do` are not in the MathML namespace.

Example 53-5. A scope for local names

```
<reln xmlns="http://www.w3.org/TR/REC-MathML/">
  <eq/>
  <ci>wealth</ci>
  <ci>gnp</ci>
  <notes xmlns="">
    <todo>check the math</todo>
  </notes>
</reln>
```

53.2.3 *Attribute names*

Attribute names can also come from a namespace, which is indicated in the usual way by prefixing them with a namespace prefix. For instance, the current working draft of XLink uses the namespace mechanism to allow XLink attributes to appear on elements that themselves come from some other namespace. Example 53-6 shows such attributes.

Example 53-6. Attributes in XLink namespace

```
<myLink xmlns:xlink="http://www.w3.org/XML/XLink/0.9"
  xlink:type="simple">
...
</myLink>
```

It does not matter what the namespace of the element type is. The XLink attributes are in the XLink namespace even when they are exhibited by an element type that is not in the XLink namespace.

In fact, even attributes without prefixes are not in the same namespace that their element type is in. Nor are they in the default namespace. Attributes without prefixes are in no namespace at all.[3]

From a processing standpoint, the lack of a namespace doesn't matter. The attribute name can still be specified in a stylesheet pattern or utilized by the template for the element type's template rule.

In other words, an `html:img` element could have an `href` attribute and that attribute could be processed properly even though it is not formally part of the `html` namespace. Any application that knows how to handle `html:img` will know what to do with an `href` attribute.[4]

From a data modeling standpoint, unprefixed attributes are normal. They are defined by the semantics of their specific element types. In contrast, prefixed attributes have semantics that apply to the class of all element types. XLink is a good example because, in principle, any element can be linked.

53.3 | Namespaces and DTDs

You read about DTDs and type-validation in Chapter 49, "Creating a document type definition", on page 702 and might have wondered why that chapter had no mention of namespaces. That's because namespaces were invented after DTDs.[5] Therefore, type-validation does not behave as you would expect it to behave had it been designed with namespaces in mind.

In fact, the base XML language has no inherent knowledge of namespaces. There is no special part of an element-type name or attribute name called the prefix. The name is all one string that, when name spaces are used, just happens to have a colon in it. The colon could just as easily be an underscore, dot or happy face character from the XML point of view. It is not a special character.

----

3. From the syntactic standpoint of the Namespaces spec, that is. All names have to be in some namespace or they couldn't function as names. An unprefixed attribute is in a (non-syntactic) namespace that is defined by its element type, which, as we said, is not the same as the namespace that its element type itself is in. The `href` attribute of `html:img`, for example, is in the (non-syntactic) `html:img` namespace, while its element type, `img`, is in the (syntactic) `html` namespace.
4. That's because, as we saw in the last footnote, `href` is in the `html:img` namespace.
5. About 30 years after, but who's counting.

You might think, from learning about namespaces, that it would be possible to have two different `list` element types in the same DTD. However, you can only do that if you give them different prefixes. But in DTDs, prefixes must be *hard-wired onto the names*. They are not namespace prefixes and you cannot depend on the default namespace: XML 1.0 allows only one element type declaration for the element type `list`.

Declaring `my:list` and `your:list` would be fine. XML 1.0 sees these as no more the same than `my_list` and `your_list` or `my.list` and `your.list`. But once you define the element types this way, you cannot default them or change the prefix. XML 1.0 would not recognize `list` as a synonym for `my:list`. These are no more related than `list` and `my_list` or `foo` and `bar`.

Therefore, when you create a DTD that uses namespaces, you must declare every `prefix:name` combination individually, exactly as you would if the `:` were just another name character (which it is!).

Example 53-7 illustrates declarations for two different `email` element types. The prefixes disambiguate them, but not in the same way that namespace prefixes would. As far as XML 1.0 is concerned, these are two nine-letter element-type names that differ in their first three letters.

Example 53-7. Disambiguating two `email` element types

```
<!ELEMENT eag:email ...>
<!ATTLIST eag:email
    xmlns:eag CDATA #FIXED "http://www.aol.com/EmailAppGuy">
<!ELEMENT cmp:email ...>
<!ATTLIST cmp:email
    xmlns:cmp CDATA #FIXED "http://www.compuserve.com/email">
```

Note that the `xmlns` attributes are fixed. That is because the prefixes are hard-wired to the names; they can't be changed in a valid document instance regardless of what the *Namespaces* spec says. If authors try to act otherwise, the document will become invalid.

Defining each namespace attribute with a fixed value protects against such mistakes. The parser will issue an error message if an author tries to specify a different namespace value in the document instance.

Fixing namespace attributes enforces markup practices that make a document both type-valid and namespace compatible. It is the sensible thing to do.[6]

A DTD can also simulate scoping and default namespaces, as shown in Example 53-8.

Example 53-8. Scoping and default namespaces in a DTD

```
<!ELEMENT music ...>
<!ATTLIST music
    xmlns CDATA #FIXED "http://www.ihc.org/smdl">
<!ELEMENT math ...>
<!ATTLIST math
    xmlns CDATA #FIXED "http://www.w3.org/TR/REC-MathML/">
```

However, remember that the declared names in a valid document are the *only* names. Example 53-8 works only when the subelement types of `music` and `math` have different names from one another.

One final example to drive home the point: In Example 53-9, the first namespace prefix has no effect. The two element-type names are different in a valid document, even though they are the same according to the *Namespaces* spec.

Example 53-9. `rap:music` isn't `music`

```
<!ELEMENT music ...>
<!ATTLIST music
    xmlns CDATA #FIXED "http://www.rude-noises.go">
<!ELEMENT rap:music ...>
<!ATTLIST rap:music
    xmlns:rap CDATA #FIXED "http://www.rude-noises.go">
```

Remember: The rule is that colons and namespace declarations are not relevant or special to a DTD validator. Always define fixed values for your namespace attributes and your documents should be able to get the best of both worlds.

---

6. In fact, it makes so much sense that it probably should have been a requirement of the Namespaces spec. The XML implementation in Internet Explorer 5 enforces it as though it were.

53.4 | Are namespaces a good thing?

We said in the introduction to this chapter that namespaces are controversial. We've seen how namespace prefixes cause clutter and how redefining them causes confusion. Why then were they considered so vital that they were rushed to Recommendation status almost as soon as XML was approved?

And why does the spec allow all that flexibility in their use?

As the application parts of this book show, the predominant use for XML on the Web is data integration. In those applications, a middle-tier server may aggregate XML fragments from many sources into a single well-formed (but not valid) document and send it to a client for processing.

Because only computers ever see those documents, prefix clutter doesn't matter. It adds to the overhead somewhat, but it could also aid in debugging.

And reusing prefixes for different namespaces doesn't matter in those applications either, since the software can base its processing strategy on the full URI, rather than the short nickname.[7]

Furthermore, there are cases where namespace prefixes cause less clutter than alternative approaches might have. In XSL specifications, for example, the prefixes disambiguate the markup that controls the XSL processing from the markup of the generated text in the templates.

But more than that, namespaces provide a mechanism for universal vocabularies of element type names that can be used in all document types. Namespaces provide a way to define element types so that their names are unique throughout the world. As long as everyone adheres to the namespaces convention there can be no confusion about whether element types with identical names belong to one vocabulary or another.

---

7. In fact, when the W3C schema language is eventually defined, it will probably support validation based on the full URI as well.

XML Path Language (XPath)

Tad Tougher Tutorial

- XPath applications
- XPath data model
- Location expressions

Contributing expert: G. Ken Holman of Crane Softwrights Ltd., http://www.CraneSoftwrights.com, **author of** _Practical Transformation Using XSLT and XPath_

ll XML processing depends upon the idea of addressing. In order to do something with data you must be able to locate it. To start with, you need to be able to actually find the XML document on the Web. Once you have it, you need to be able to find the information that you need within the document.

The Web has a uniform solution for the first part. The XML document is called a *resource* and *Uniform Resource Identifiers* are the Web's way of addressing resources. The most popular form of Uniform Resource Identifier is the ubiquitous Uniform Resource Locator (URL).

The standard way to locate information *within* an XML document is through a language known as the *XML Path Language* or *XPath*. XPath can be used to refer to textual data, elements, attributes and other information in an XML document.

XPath is a sophisticated, complex language. We will cover its most commonly used features, most of which are available using an abbreviated form of its syntax.

54.1 | XPath applications

Over the next few years, XPath is likely to become a basic building block of XML systems. Let's look at just a few possible applications of XPath.

54.1.1 *User scenarios*

Consider the process of stylesheet creation. A paragraph of text in one chapter may refer to another chapter through a cross-reference. During style application it makes sense to fetch the title of the referenced chapter and its chapter number. The stylesheet could then insert those pieces of information into the text of the cross-reference. For example, the marked-up phrase "`Please see <crossref refid="introduction.chapter">`" might be rendered as "Please see 'Chapter 1, Introduction'." XPath can be used within XSLT to find the appropriate chapter, find its title and locate the text of the title.

Now consider an e-commerce application. It might receive a purchase order from another system. In order to do accounting it would need to know the prices of the purchased items. In XPath notation it would locate "`/po/item/price`", meaning all of the prices in all of the items in the current purchase order document.

Finally, imagine an ordinary Web surfer of the near future. He might be reading his favorite recipes Web page. Unbeknownst to him, the page is written in XML (this is the near future, after all!). As he scrolls through, he finds a recipe that he would really love to share with his brother-in-law. He clicks the right mouse button at the beginning of the recipe. One of the choices in the popup menu might be: "email this address."

The menu item would instruct the browser to email a string of characters, termed a *URI reference* to a particular email address. The URI reference would uniquely identify not just the Web page but also the particular `recipe` element. The first part of the string would be an ordinary URI, pointing to the Web page. The last part would be an *XPointer*. XPointers are a customization of XPath for use in URI references.

As you can see, XPath is going to be a valuable tool in all sorts of XML processing.

54.1.2 *Specifications built on XPath*

XPath was developed when the groups responsible for XSLT and XPointer realized that they had to provide many of the same functions and could develop a shared solution.

These two World Wide Web Consortium specifications depend upon XPath today. XPointer uses XPath to build Web addresses (URI references) that reference parts of XML documents. URI references can address individual points and elements, as in our recipe example. They can also address lists of elements, attributes or characters.

The XSL Transformations language (XSLT) uses XPath for transformation and style application. As in our cross-reference example, XPath can be used to retrieve information from somewhere else in the document. XPath can also be used to declare that certain XSLT style rules apply to particular elements in the input document.

XPath's syntax was carefully chosen. XPath is used by XPointer in URI references and by both XPointer and XSLT in attribute values of XML documents. XPath needed to easily fit into attribute values, browser URL fields and other places where XML's element within element syntax would be too verbose. Accordingly, XPath's syntax is very concise and does not depend on an XML parser.

XPath is designed to be extensible. W3C specifications and other XPath applications can create extensions specific to the application's problem domain. XPointer and XSLT already extend XPath.

54.1.2.1 An XLink example

Example 54-1 shows an XLink with an `xlink:href` attribute. The attribute value contains a URI reference. The reference contains an XPointer (starting with the string `xpointer`). The characters within the parentheses are an XPath expression.

Example 54-1. XLink use of XPath

```
<A xlink:type="simple"
   xlink:href="info.xml#xpointer(id('smith')/info[@type='public'])">
   Mr. John Smith
</A>
```

To summarize, Example 54-1 contains an XLink which contains a URI reference which contains an XPointer which in turn contains an XPath expression. Don't worry. We will take you through each part gently!

54.1.2.2   An XSLT example

An example of the XSLT use of the same XPath expression is the `select` attribute of Example 54-2.

Example 54-2. XSLT selecting based on XPath

```
<xsl:apply-templates select="id('smith')/info[@type='public']"/>
```

This `select` attribute finds the element identified `smith` and identifies the `info` subelements with the attribute `type` having the value "`public`". It then processes each of those `info` elements with an XSLT *template rule.* The applicable rule is found by matching each element against an XSLT pattern in the template's match attribute. Example 54-3 demonstrates.

Example 54-3. XSLT use of XPath

```
<xsl:template match="info[@type='public']">
    ...
</xsl:template>
```

54.2 | The XPath data model

It is only possible to construct an address – any address – given a model. For instance the US postal system is composed of a model of states containing cities containing streets with house numbers. To some degree the model falls naturally out of the geography of the country but it is mostly artificial. State and city boundaries are not exactly visible from an airplane. We give new houses street numbers so that they can be addressed within the postal system's model.

Relational databases also have a model that revolves around tables, records, columns, foreign keys and so forth. This "relational model" is the basis for the SQL query language. Just as SQL depends on the relational model, XPath depends on a formal model for the logical structure and data in an XML document.

54.2.1 *Sources of the model*

You may wonder if XML really needs a formal model. It seems so simple: elements within elements, attributes of elements and so forth. It *is* simple but there are details that need to be standardized in order for addresses to behave in a reliable fashion. The tricky part is that there are many ways of representing what might seem to be the "same" information. We can represent a less-than symbol in at least four ways:

- a predefined entity reference: `&lt;`
- a CDATA section: `<![CDATA[<]]>`
- a decimal Unicode character reference: `&#60;`
- a hex Unicode character reference: `&#x3c;`

We could also reference a text entity that embeds a CDATA section and a text entity that embeds another text entity that embeds a character reference, etc. In a query you would not want to explicitly search for the less-than symbol in all of these variations. It would be easier to have a processor that could magically *normalize* them to a single model. Every XPath-based query engine needs to get exactly the same data model from any particular XML document.

The XML equivalent of the relational model is termed, depending on the context, either a *grove*, an *information set* or a *data model*. The *grove* concept comes from ISO and is thus important when you are working with International Standards like HyTime, Topic Maps and DSSSL.

The XML Information Set is another model of the important information in an XML document. W3C specifications are built on top of the Information Set. Whereas the grove is generalized and can include both XML and non-XML data notations, the information set is specific to XML. XPath is a W3C specification and is only for addressing into XML documents, so its data model is derived from the W3C XML Information Set.[1]

---

1. Perhaps one day a grove-based XPath might be invented. It might allow querying arbitrary information types based on topic metadata.

The XPath specification does not use the Information Set directly. The Information Set takes a more liberal view of what is "important" than XPath does. Therefore XPath has a concept of a *data model*: an Information Set with some XPath-irrelevant parts filtered out.

For instance the Information Set says that it may be important to keep track of what entity each element resides within. The XPath developers chose not to care about that information and it is not, therefore, part of the XPath data model.

54.2.2 *Tree addressing*

The XPath data model views a document as a tree of nodes, or *node tree*. Most nodes correspond to document components, such as elements and attributes.

It is very common to think of XML documents as being either families (elements have child elements, parent elements and so forth) or trees (roots, branches and leaves). This is natural: trees and families are both hierarchical in nature, just as XML documents are. XPath uses both metaphors but tends to lean more heavily on the familial one.[2]

XPath uses genealogical taxonomy to describe the hierarchical makeup of an XML document, referring to children, descendants, parents and ancestors. The parent is the element that contains the element under discussion. The list of ancestors includes the parent, the parent's parent and so forth. A list of descendants includes children, children's children and so forth.

Insofar as there is no culture-independent way to talk about the first ancestor, XPath calls it the "root". The root is not an element. It is a logical construct that holds the document element and any comments and processing instructions that precede and follow it.[3]

Trees in computer science are very rarely (if ever) illustrated as a natural tree is drawn, with the root at the bottom and the branches and leaves growing upward. Far more typically, trees are depicted with the root at the top just as family trees are. This is probably due to the nature of our writing systems and the way we have learned to read.[4] Accordingly, this chapter

---

2. Politicians take note: in this case, family values win out over environmentalism!

3. In the full Information Set, the root is called the document information item and it also contains information about the document's DTD.

refers to stepping "down" the tree towards the leaf-like ends and "up" the tree towards the root as the tree is depicted in Figure 54-1. One day we will genetically engineer trees to grow this way and nature will be in harmony with technology.

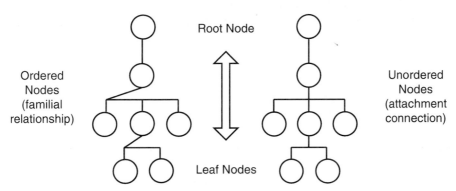

Figure 54-1   Vertical tree depictions

54.2.3 *Node tree construction*

A *node tree* is built by an XPath processor after parsing an XML document like that in Example 54-4.

Example 54-4. Sample document

```
<?xml version="1.0"?>
<!--start-->
<part-list><part-name nbr="A12">bolt</part-name>
<part-name nbr="B45">washer</part-name><warning type="ignore"/>
<!--end of list--><?cursor blinking?>
</part-list>
<!--end of file-->
```

In constructing the node tree, the boundaries and contents of "important" constructs are preserved, while other constructs are discarded. For example, entity references to both internal and external entities are expanded and character references are resolved. The boundaries of CDATA

---

4. To do: rotate all tree diagrams for Japanese edition of The XML Handbook.

sections are discarded. Characters within the section are treated as character data.

The node tree constructed from the document in Example 54-4 is shown in Figure 54-2. In the following sections, we describe the components of node trees and how they are used in addressing. You may want to refer back to this diagram from time to time as we do so.

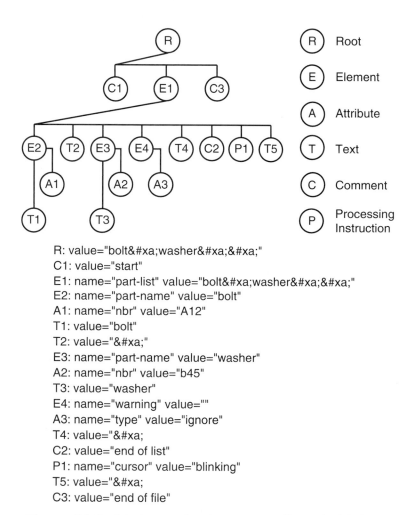

R: value="bolt
washer

"
C1: value="start"
E1: name="part-list" value="bolt
washer

"
E2: name="part-name" value="bolt"
A1: name="nbr" value="A12"
T1: value="bolt"
T2: value="
"
E3: name="part-name" value="washer"
A2: name="nbr" value="b45"
T3: value="washer"
E4: name="warning" value=""
A3: name="type" value="ignore"
T4: value="

C2: value="end of list"
P1: name="cursor" value="blinking"
T5: value="

C3: value="end of file"

Figure 54-2   Node tree for document in Example 54-4

54.2.4 *Node types*

The XPath data model describes seven types of nodes used to construct the node tree representing any XML document. We are interested primarily in the root, element, attribute and text node types, but will briefly discuss the others.

For each node type, XPath defines a way to compute a *string-value* (labeled "value" in Figure 54-2). Some node types also have a "name".

54.2.4.1   Root node

The top of the hierarchy that represents the XML document is the root node.

It is important to remember that in the XPath data model the root of the tree representing an XML document is *not the document (or root) element of the document*. A root *node* is different from a root *element*. The root node *contains* the root element.

The nodes that are children of the root node represent the document element and the comments and processing instructions found before and after the document element.

54.2.4.2   Element nodes

Every element in an XML document is represented in the node tree as an element node. Each element has a parent node. Usually an element's parent is another element but the document element has as its parent the root node.

Element nodes can have as their children other element nodes, text nodes, comment nodes and processing instruction nodes.

An element node also exhibits properties, such as its name, its attributes and information about its active namespaces.

Element nodes in documents with DTDs may have unique identifiers. These allow us to address element nodes by name. IDs are described in 49.6.3.4, "ID and IDREF attributes", on page 729.

The string-value of an element node is the concatenation of the string-values of all text node descendants of the element node in the document order. You can think of it as all of the data with none of the markup, organized into one long character string.

54.2.4.3   Text nodes

The XML 1.0 Recommendation describes character data as all text that is not markup. In other words it is the textual data content of the document and it does not include data in attribute values, processing instructions and comments.

 *Caution   The word "text" means something different in XPath from its meaning in the XML Recommendation (and the rest of this book!). We'll try to minimize the confusion by always saying "text node", even when the context is clear, reserving "text" as a noun for its normal meaning.*

XPath does not care how a character was originally represented. The string "<>" in an XML document is simply "<>" from the data model's point of view. The same goes for "&60;&62;" and "<![CDATA[<>]]>". The characters represented by any of these will be grouped with the data characters that precede and follow them and called a "text node." The individual characters of the text node are not considered its children: they are just part of its value. Text nodes do not have any children.

Remember that whitespace is significant. A text node might contain nothing else. In Figure 54-2, for example, nodes T2, T4, and T5 contain line feed characters, represented by hexadecimal character references.

54.2.4.4   Attribute nodes

If an element has attributes then these are represented as attribute nodes. These nodes are not considered children of the element node. They are more like friends that live in the guest house.

An attribute node exhibits name, string-value, and namespace URI properties. Defaulted attributes are reported as having the default values. The data model does not record whether they were explicitly specified or merely defaulted. No node is created for an unspecified attribute that had an #IMPLIED default value declared. Attribute nodes are also not created for attributes used as namespace declarations.

Note that an XML processor is not required to read an external DTD unless it is validating the document. This means that detection of ID attributes and default attribute values is not mandatory.

54.2.4.5   Other node types

Namespace nodes keep track of the set of namespace prefix/URI pairs that are in effect at a particular point in a document. Like attribute nodes, namespace nodes are attached to element nodes and are not in any particular order.

Each comment and processing instruction in the XML document is instantiated as a comment or processing instruction node in the node tree. The string-value property accesses the content of these constructs, as you can see in Figure 54-2.

54.3 | Location paths

An instance of the XPath language is called an *expression*. XPath expressions can involve a variety of operations on different kinds of operands. In this chapter we will focus on two operand types: function calls and location paths.

A *location path* is the most important kind of expression in the XPath notation. Its syntax is similar to the familiar path expressions used in URLs and in Unix and Windows systems to locate directories and files.[5]

54.3.1   *Basic concepts*

A location path has a starting point, which XPath calls its *context node*. In a file system path, it might be a computer, a disk drive, or a directory. In an

---

5. There is an illustrated tutorial on path expressions in 28.2.1, "XML Path Language (XPath)", on page 394.

XPath location path it could be, for example, the document element node or some other element node.

The purpose of the location path is to select nodes from the document by locating the desired nodes relative to the initial context node.

Arguably, the simplest location path is "/". This selects the root node (not the document element node).

54.3.1.1   Stepping down the hierarchy

We can extend this location path to select the document element node instead of the root node. "/mydoc" will select a document element node named "mydoc". The name of an element node is the element-type name of the element it represents.

Note   *From now on, as long as we are discussing node trees, we'll often just say "element" instead of "element node".*

We have taken a step "down" the tree. We can take another step: "/mydoc/section". This will select every section element that is a child of the mydoc element.

Each slash-separated (/) path component is a *step*.

Any amount of whitespace can be present between the parts of a location path. Steps can be written across a number of lines or spaced apart to be more legible to a reader.

54.3.1.2   Predicates

So far we have seen how to build single and multi-level location paths based on element-type names. However, the type name is not the only thing that is interesting about an element. For example, we might want to filter out elements that have (or do not have) particular attributes with particular values. Or we may be interested in the first or seventh element, or just the even-numbered ones.

We can express these constraints with qualifiers called *predicates*. Any step can be qualified. The location path in Example 54-5, for example, selects the seventh paragraph from each `section` with a `security` attribute whose string-value is "`public`".

Example 54-5. Selecting the seventh para from each public `section`

```
/mydoc/section[@security="public"]/para[7]
```

54.3.1.3   Selection

Note that we use the word *select* carefully. We could say that the expression *returns* certain nodes but that might put a picture in your head of nodes being ripped out of the tree and handed to you: "Here are your nodes!"

Rather, what you get back is a set of locations – pointers to the nodes. Imagine the result of a location path as a set of arrows pointing into the node tree, saying: "Your nodes are here!"

54.3.1.4   Context

The context node keeps changing as we step down the path. As each step is evaluated, the result is a set of nodes – in XPath talk, a *node-set*. The node-set could have one or more nodes, or it could be empty.

The next step is then evaluated for each member of that node-set. That is, each member is used as the context node for one of the evaluations of the next step. The node-sets selected by each of those evaluations are combined (except for any duplicates) to produce the result node-set.

Consider what happens in Example 54-5.

1. The XPath processor first evaluates the "`/`". The root node becomes the initial context node.
2. Next it looks for every child of the context node with the name "`mydoc`". There will be only one member of that node-set because XML allows only a single root element. It becomes the context node for the next step, which is evaluated only once.
3. Next the processor looks for all of the `section` children in the context of the `mydoc` element that have the appropriate attribute value and returns their node-set. The next step will

be evaluated once for each selected `section` node, which is the context node for that evaluation.

4. We're almost done. The processor looks for the seventh `para` several times, once for each `section` in the node-set. It puts the selected `para` nodes together into the final node-set and returns a set of pointers to them: "Your nodes are here!".

The initial context does not always have to be the root node of the document. It depends on the environment or application. Whatever application (e.g. database or browser) or specification (e.g. XSLT or XPointer) is using XPath must specify the starting context.

In XSLT there is always a concept of the *current node*. That node is the context node for location paths that appear in XSLT transforms. In XPointer, the starting context is always the root node of the particular document, selected by its URI. In some sort of document database, we might be allowed to do a query across thousands of documents. The root node of each document would become the context node in turn. XPath itself does not have a concept of working with multiple documents but it can be used in a system that does.

In addition to the current node, an application could specify some other details of the context: it could supply some values for variables and functions that can be used in the XPath expression. It could also include namespace information that can be used to interpret prefixed names in a location path.

54.3.1.5   Axes

But wait. That's not all! Up to now we've always stepped down the tree, to a child element. But we can also step *up* the tree instead of down and step many levels instead of one.

We can step in directions that are neither up nor down but more like sideways. For example we can step from elements to attributes and from attributes to elements.

We can also step from an element directly to a child of a child of a child (a descendant).

These different ways of stepping are called *axes*.

For example, the *descendant axis* (abbreviated `//`) can potentially step down all the levels of the tree. The location path "`/mydoc//footnote`" would select all footnotes in the current document, no matter how many levels deep they occur.

The *parent axis* uses an abbreviated syntax (`..`) that is similar to that for going up a directory in a file system. For instance we could select all of the elements *containing* a footnote like this: "`/mydoc//footnote/..`".

The *attribute axis* (abbreviated "`@`") steps into the attribute nodes of an element.

The *namespace axis* is used for namespace information associated with an element node.

There are a number of less commonly used axes as well. You can find out more about them in the XML specification.

54.3.1.6 Node tests

The attribute and namespace axes each have only one type of node, which is (necessarily!) its principal node type.

The other axes, however, have element as the principal node type but have comment, processing instruction, and text node types as well. We'll refer to such an axis as a *content axis* and its nodes as *content nodes*.

A step normally selects nodes of the principal type. In the case of content axes, a node test can be used to select another type. For example, the node test `text()` selects text nodes.

54.3.2 *Anatomy of a step*

We've now seen enough of the basics to take a formal look at the parts of a location step. There are three:

- An axis, which specifies the tree relationship between the context node and the nodes selected by the location step. Our examples so far have used the child axis.
- A node test, which specifies the node type of the nodes selected by the location step. The default type is element, unless the axis is one that can't have element nodes.
- Zero or more predicates, which use arbitrary expressions to further refine the set of nodes selected by the location step. The expressions are full-blown XPath expressions and can

include function calls and location paths. In Example 54-5 the first predicate is a location path and the second uses an abbreviation for the `position()` function.

In this tutorial, we've only been using abbreviated forms of the XPath syntax, in which common constructs can often be omitted or expressed more concisely. Example 54-6 shows the unabbreviated form of Example 54-5. Note the addition of explicit axis names (`child` and `attribute`) and the `position()` function call.

Example 54-6. Unabbreviated form of Example 54-5

```
/child::mydoc/child::section[attribute::security="public"]
                /child::para[position()=7]
```

In the remainder of the chapter, we'll take a closer look at each of the three parts: node tests, axes, and predicates.

54.3.2.1   Node tests

Some node tests are useful in all axes; others only in content axes.
Node tests for all axes are:

`*`

any node of the principal type; i.e., element, attribute, or namespace.[6]

`node()`
any node of any type

Node tests solely for content axes are:

`text()`
any text node

---

6. The asterisk cannot be used as a prefix (`"*ara"`) or suffix (`"ara*"`) as it is in some regular-expression languages.

```
comment()
```
> any comment node

```
processing-instruction()
```
> any processing-instruction node, regardless of its target name

```
processing-instruction(target-name)
```
> any processing-instruction node with the specified target name

Here are some examples of node tests used in a *content* axis:

```
processing-instruction(cursor)
```
> all nodes created from a processing instruction with the target name "cursor"

```
part-nbr
```
> all nodes created from an element with the element-type name `part-nbr`

```
text()
```
> all text nodes (contrast below)

```
text
```
> all nodes created from an element with the element type name `text`

```
*
```
> all nodes created from elements, irrespective of the element-type name

```
node()
```
> all nodes created from elements (irrespective of the element-type name), contiguous character data, comments or processing instructions (irrespective of the target name)

54.3.2.2   Axes

The most important axes are described here.

54.3.2.2.1   Child

The default axis is the child axis. That means that if you ask for "/section/ para" you are looking for a para in a section. If you ask merely for "para" you are looking for the para element children of the context node, whatever it is.

54.3.2.2.2   Attribute

When using the symbol "@" before either an XML name or the node test "*", one is referring to the attribute axis of the context node.

The attribute nodes are attached to an element node but the nodes are not ordered. There is no "first" or "third" attribute of an element.

Attribute nodes have a string-value that is the attribute value, and a name that is the attribute name.

Some examples of abbreviated references to attribute nodes attached to the context node are:

@type

  an attribute node whose name is "type"

@*

  all attributes of the context node, irrespective of the attribute name

54.3.2.2.3   Descendant

We can use the double-slash "//" abbreviation in a location path to refer to the descendant axis.[7] This axis includes not only children of the context node, but also all other nodes that are descendants of the context node.

This is a very powerful feature. We could combine this with the wildcard node test, for example, to select all elements in a document, other than the document element, no matter how deep they are: "/doc//*".

Some examples:

---

7. You may read in the XPath spec that the axis referred to by the abbreviation is actually the descendant-or-self axis. However, that is merely a technical device to enable the abbreviation to have the desired effect of referencing all descendants. The formal expansion of the abbreviation introduces another step, which would otherwise have caused children of the context node to be excluded. We refer to "//" as standing for the descendant axis because that's the way it acts.

`/mydoc//part-nbr`

> all element nodes with the element-type name `part-nbr` that are descendants of the `mydoc` document element; that is, all of the `part-nbr` elements in the document

`/mydoc//@type`

> all attribute nodes named `type` attached to any descendant element of the `mydoc` document element; i.e., all of the `type` attributes in the document

`/mydoc//*`

> all elements that are descendants of the `mydoc` document element; i.e., every element in the document except the `mydoc` element itself

`/mydoc//comment()`

> all comment nodes that are descendants of the `mydoc` document element

`/mydoc//text()`

> all of the text nodes that are descendants of the `mydoc` document element; i.e., all of the character data in the document!

We do not have to start descendant expressions with the document element. If we want to start somewhere farther into the document we can use "`//`" in any step anywhere in the location path.

We could also begin with "`//`". A location path that starts with "`//`" is interpreted as starting at the root and searching all descendants of it, including the document element.

54.3.2.2.4   Self

The self axis is unique in that it has only one node: the context node. This axis can solve an important problem.[8]

---

8. In fact, we suspect it was invented for that purpose only. It is another ingenious hack, like the one in the previous footnote, for enabling convenient abbreviations to be mapped onto a coherent normalized form.

For instance in an XSLT transformation we might want to search for all descendants of the current node. If we begin with "`//`" the address will start at the root. We need a way to refer specifically to the current node.

A convenient way to do this is with an abbreviation: a period (.) stands for the context node.[9]

So "`.//footnote`" would locate all footnote descendants of the context node.

54.3.2.2.5 Parent

The parent axis (`..`) of a content node selects its parent, as the axis name suggests. For a namespace or attribute node, however, it selects the node's attached element.

You could therefore search an entire document for a particular attribute and then find out what element it is attached to: "`//@confidential/..`". You could go on to find out about the element's parent (and the parent's parent, etc.): "`//@confidential/../..`".

54.3.2.2.6 Ancestor

There is also a way of searching for an ancestor by name, but it does not have an abbreviated syntax. For example, "`ancestor::section`" would look for the ancestor(s) of the context node that are named "`section`".

This location path locates the titles of sections that contain images: "`//image/ancestor::section/title`".

54.3.3 *Our story so far*

Here are some examples of location paths using features we have covered so far:

`item`
> `item` element nodes that are children of the context node

---

9. This "dot-convention" also comes from the file system metaphor. Unix and Windows use "." to mean the current directory.

`item/para`

> `para` element nodes that are children of `item` element nodes that are children of the context node; in other words, those `para` grandchildren of the context node whose parent is an `item`

`//para`

> `para` element nodes that are descendants of the root node; in other words, all the `para` element nodes in the entire document

`//item/para`

> `para` element nodes that are children of all `item` element nodes in the entire document

`//ordered-list//para`

> `para` element nodes that are descendants of all `ordered-list` element nodes in the entire document

`ordered-list//para/@security`

> `security` attribute nodes attached to all `para` element nodes that are descendants of all `ordered-list` element nodes that are children of the context node

`*/@*`

> attribute nodes attached to all element nodes that are children of the context node

`../@*`

> attribute nodes attached to the parent or attached node of the context node

`.//para`

> `para` element nodes that are descendants of the context node

```
.//comment()
```
comment nodes that are descendants of the context node

 Tip   The XPath specification includes numerous other examples of location paths. You can find it on the CD-ROM.

54.3.4   *Predicates*

It is often important to filter nodes out of a node-set. We might filter out nodes that lack a particular attribute or subelement. We might filter out all but the first node. This sort of filtering is done in XPath through *predicates*. A predicate is an expression that is applied to each node. If it evaluates as false, the tested node is filtered out.

We'll discuss some common types of predicate expressions, then look at some examples.

54.3.4.1   Expression types

54.3.4.1.7   Node-sets

A location path expression can be used as a predicate. It evaluates to `true` if it selects any nodes at all. It is false if it does not select any nodes. So Example 54-7 would select all paragraphs that have a footnote child.

Example 54-7. Using a location path as a predicate
```
//para[footnote]
```

Recall that the evaluation of a step in the path results in a node-set, each member of which is a context node for an evaluation of the next step.[10]

One by one, each member of the result node-set, which in this case is every paragraph in the document, would get a chance to be the context

---

10. In other words, Example 54-7 is really an abbreviation for "`//para[./footnote]`".

node. It would either be selected or filtered out, depending on whether it contained any footnotes. Every paragraph would get its bright shining moment in the sun when it could be ".".[11]

A number of predicates can be chained together. Only nodes that pass all of the filters are passed on to the next step in the location path. For example, "`//para[footnote][@important]`" selects all paragraphs with `important` attributes and `footnote` children.

Like other location paths, those in predicates can have multiple steps with their own predicates. Consider the complex one in Example 54-8. It looks for `sections` with `author` child elements with `qualifications` child elements that have both `professional` and `affordable` attributes.

Example 54-8. A complex location path predicate

```
section[author/qualifications[@professional][@affordable]]
```

54.3.4.1.8   String-values

Not all predicates are location path expressions. Sometimes you do not want to test for the existence of some node. You might instead want to test whether an attribute has some particular value. That is different from testing whether the attribute exists or not.

Testing an attribute's value is simple: "`@type='ordered'`" tests whether the context node has a `type` attribute with value "`ordered`".

In XPath, every node type has a string-value. The value of an element node that is the context node, for example, is the concatenation of the string-values from the expression: "`.//text()`". In other words, it is all of the character data content anywhere within the element and its descendants.

So we can test the data content of a section's `title` child element with "`section[title='Doo-wop']`" and both of the sections in Example 54-9 would match.

---

11. Unfortunately, the moment is brief and the price of failure is exclusion from the selection set.

Example 54-9. Matching sections

```
<section><title>Doo-wop</title>
...
</section>

<section><title>Doo-<emph>wop</emph></title>
...
</section>
```

54.3.4.1.9   Context position

There is more to the context in which an expression is evaluated than just the context node. Among the other things is the node's *context position*, which is returned by a function call: `position()=number`.

In practice, an abbreviation, consisting of the number alone, is invariably used. A number expression is evaluated as `true` if the number is the same as the context position.

Context position can be a tricky concept to grasp because it is, well, context sensitive. However, it is easy to understand for the most common types of steps.

In a step down the child axis (`a/b`) the context position is the position of the child node in the parent node. So "`doc/section[5]`" is the fifth section in a `doc`. In a step down the descendant axis (`a//b[5]`) it still refers to the position of the child node in its *parent node*, not its numerical order in the list of matching nodes.

XPath also has a function called "`last()`". We can use it to generate the number for the last node in a context: "`a//b[last()]`". We can also combine that with some simple arithmetic to get the next-to-last node: "`a// b[last()-1]`".

54.3.4.2   Predicate examples

Here are some examples, using the predicate types that we've discussed:

`item[3]`
> third `item` element child of the context node

`item[@type]/para`
> `para` element children of `item` elements that exhibit a `type` attribute and are children of the context node

//list[@type='ordered']/item[1]/para[1]

> first para element child of the first item element child of any list element that exhibits a type attribute with the string-value "ordered"

//ordered-list[item[@type]/para[2]]//para

> para elements descended from any ordered-list element that has an item child that exhibits a type attribute and has at least two para element children (whew!)

This last example is illustrated in Figure 54-3.

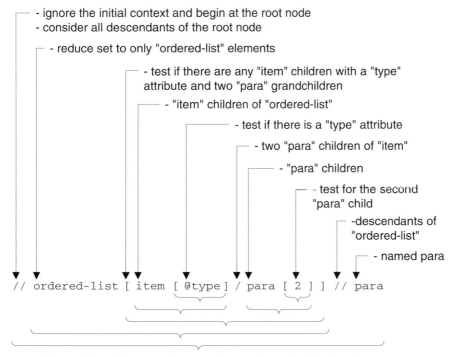

all "para" element nodes that are descendents of all "ordered-list" element nodes of the entire document node tree that have at least two "para" element node children of an "item" child that has a "type" attribute specified or defaulted

Figure 54-3   Evaluating multiple steps

The XPath spec includes numerous other examples of using predicates. XPath is a powerful expression language, including operators and functions that operate on node-sets, numbers, strings, and booleans.

54.4 | ID function

The most common high-level expression in XPath is the location path, which we have explored in some detail. And, as we have seen, a location path can also be used at lower levels – as a predicate expression, for example.

Another form of expression that returns a node-set is a function call to the id(string) function. The main use of the function is to select the element node whose ID is the same as the string. For example, "id('final')". selects the element node whose unique identifier is "final".

An ID function and a location path can be used in the same expression. One way is to create the union of the two, as in Example 54-10. The result node-set is the element whose ID is "final", plus all para elements descended from ordered-list elements.

Example 54-10. Union expression

```
id('final') | /ordered-list//para
```

Another way to combine the two is to use the ID function as the initial context node of a location path, to create a path expression like that in Example 54-11. It locates the title child of the element whose ID is "A12345".

Example 54-11. Path expression

```
id('A12345')/title
```

Instead of a literal string, the argument could be a node whose string-value would be used, as in "id(@IDREF)". This expression locates the element referenced by the IDREF attribute of the context node.

54.5 | Conclusion

XPath is an extremely powerful language and is destined to be as important in the XML world as SQL is in the relational world. Although XPath has depths that we could not address in a friendly tutorial, we have covered all of the most common features.

With all these features one can very powerfully address the nodes of the XML data model. XPath is already in use in both XPointer and XSLT. Microsoft has added XPath support to their DOM through a function called "selectNodes". Future versions of the DOM may have XPath support as a standard feature. In short, XPath seems on track to become a central part of many XML systems.

Extensible Stylesheet Language (XSL)

Friendly Tutorial

- XSL Transformations (XSLT)
- Template rules
- Patterns
- Templates
- Formatting objects

The Extensible Stylesheet Language (XSL) is a specification under development within the World Wide Web consortium for applying formatting to XML documents in a standard way. Over time a part of XSL called the XSL Transformations (XSLT) has evolved into an independently useful language for transforming one XML document to another. It is now the first part of the standard. The second part defines the semantics of formatting, in the form of a catalog of formatting objects.

Under the covers, XSL borrows from two other specifications: *DSSSL* and *CSS*. DSSSL, Document Style Semantics and Specification Language is a very powerful International Standard from ISO. DSSSL provides the transformational template application paradigm that XSLT uses. CSS, the Cascading Stylesheet Language, is a popular World Wide Web Consortium specification. CSS provides much of XSL's formatting model. Although XSL borrows concepts from both of these languages, XSL stylesheets do not look like either DSSSL or CSS. XSL looks like XML! In fact, XSL is an XML vocabulary made up of two XML namespaces.

Tip   XSLT needs a dedicated book to be covered in its entirety. A preview excerpt of just such a book, Practical Transformation Using XSLT and XPath (Eighth Edition - ISBN 1-894049-05-5), is included on the CDROM.

The most important thing to take from this chapter is a feeling for how XML documents are actually processed by XSLT. We have seen where XSL is used at a high level in the application chapters, now we'll look at the details of how it works.

XSLT's processing model is very similar to that of many XML processing tools. Unlike general purpose programming languages, XML-aware tools can take care of some of the tedious parts of processing so that you can concentrate on your application needs. If you understand XSLT then you will be able to use other languages and systems much more effectively.

55.1 | Transformation vs. rendition

XSL is designed to apply style to XML documents by transforming them into XSL formatting object rendition documents using XSLT. These *source* documents will usually be marked up entirely according to their abstract structure without (in theory) markup specifically tailored for style application or any other particular kind of processing. Thus XSL is the "missing link" between the abstract data that is intended for computer processing and the formatted rendition required for comfortable reading. In technical terms an XSLT processor *transforms* a document from an abstraction to a rendition.

In this context the word "transforms" has a completely general meaning. Simple stylesheet languages such as CSS help documents to put on a little make-up. XSL allows them to get a complete make-over. XSLT can reorder duplicate, suppress, sort and add elements. It can move end-notes to the end of a document. It can duplicate the title of a chapter so that appears in the chapter, in the header and in the Table Of Contents. It can suppress a corporation's internal annotations and metadata. It can sort the names in a phone directory. It can also add boilerplate text such as a copyright or corporate logo. In fact, XSLT does not so much apply a makeover as a complete Cher-style plastic surgery.

There are many applications where these sorts of *transformations* would be useful. Style processing is a very important one but there are others. Consider an electronic commerce application where many companies must communicate. Each of their internal systems may use similar but different document types. To communicate they need to translate their various document types into a common one. An XSLT transformation provides a sophisticated but simple way to do so.

In fact, XSLT goes even further to support arbitrary processing through customized extensions (the "X" in "XSLT") supported by an XSLT processor. The XSLT language has a mechanism that allows you to call into a component written in any programming language. You could refer to a *Java* class file, Python program, Perl script or an ActiveX control. You could even embed a small script from a scripting language such as *Javascript* or *Python*. The function can be defined right in your stylesheet!

In order to allow these general uses, the XSL specification defines style application as a two-part process. The first part is a transformation from XML into some other kind of XML. The result XML could either be a rendition represented as XSL formatting object elements, or something unrelated to rendition, such as an e-commerce document type.

If the result of the first part conforms to the formatting object vocabulary then the XSL processor may display it on a screen, print it out or convert it to some other formatted representation such as PDF, PostScript, Microsoft's RTF, or even voice synthesis! If it conforms to some other document type then the XSL processor can do whatever it thinks is appropriate. Typically it will generate the document so that it may be saved to a file or transmitted over the network.

To summarize: name notwithstanding, XSL is more than just a style language. It has two stages. The first part is a generally useful transformation language called XSLT. The second part is a vocabulary of formatting objects for rendering documents.

Some applications will use only the transformation language. Other applications will use the transformation language to create formatting object elements that can be displayed, printed or saved as renditions in XML or some other representation.

55.2 | Formatting objects

The second part of XSL defines a large and very sophisticated set of formatting objects. If your goal is style application (and not just transformation) then you can use these formatting objects so that the renderer will know what to display.

Caution   The formatting object part of XSL is not finalized and could still change. We will cover the high-level concepts that are not likely to change radically.

Imagine taking an XML "manuscript" and typing it into a word processor. You would have to use the constructs provided by the word processor, such as paragraphs, bulleted lists, hypertext links and so on. In XSL terms, those constructs are the formatting objects. XSL stylesheets will typically contain block, display graphic, display rule (for horizontal rules), table formatting objects and so forth. A table formatting object might itself contain blocks. The blocks would contain characters, and also "sequence" formatting objects that would apply formatting like italics and bold to sequences of characters.

Conceptually, these objects form a tree. The page (or Web page) is the root. Paragraphs, tables, sequences and other "container" objects are the branches, and characters, graphics and other indivisible objects are the leaves. The tree of formatting objects is called the "formatting object tree." XML documents also describe a tree so it is logical that the formatting tree should also be an XML document.

Every formatting object has *properties*. The exact set of properties that a formatting object exhibits depends on its *class*. For example, blocks may specify the space before and after the block, clickable links may specify their destinations, characters may specify their font sizes, and pictures may specify their heights and widths.

At the time of writing, the formatting object vocabulary is still changing. Implementing a robust formatting engine is quite difficult so there are very few implementations of the experimental objects. We expect this situation to change once they stabilize.

55.3 | In the meantime

While we wait for the formatting objects to be designed and implemented we still need to get our jobs done.

Many XSLT implementations allow transformations from XML into HTML. This is good for serving to today's mainstream browsers (4.x) and the legacy (2.x, 3.x) browsers that most websites must still support. It also takes advantage of many Web designers' knowledge of HTML. If you format a document using element types from HTML instead of from the formatting object vocabulary it will look to a browser as if it had been created in HTML directly. You can think of this process as a conversion from XML markup to HTML markup. Internet Explorer 5.0 can actually do this conversion right in the browser.

So that you can start using XSL immediately we will use these element types in most of our examples instead of the formatting object element types. We will restrict our usage to only a few of them, namely:

- `h1` and `h2` element types for top-level and second-level headings,
- `p` element type for paragraphs
- `body` element type to contain the document's content; and the
- `em` element type to emphasize a series of characters.

For clarity of the stylesheet itself, we will use XML Namespaces to label these elements with an `html` prefix. (See Chapter 53, "Namespaces", on page 788 for more information.)

There is a subtlety in how this transformation works. The XSLT transformation language typically converts XML to XML. An XML document could look very much like an HTML document if it used HTML element types.[1] However, this is still not quite what older browsers understand as HTML.

---

1. Recall the discussion of XHTML in Chapter 4, "Better browsing through XML", on page 66.

For instance "legacy HTML" uses a different syntax for empty elements. Most XSLT processors can generate "legacy HTML", suitable for processing with older browsers. You can invoke this feature with the `xsl:output` instruction. Processors will also invoke this feature automatically when they recognize that the transformation result's document (or root) element is HTML.

55.4 | XSL stylesheets

Most XSL looks more or less like "ordinary" XML. Simple XSL stylesheets are merely a specialized form of XML markup designed for specifying the formatting of other XML documents. You can think of XSL as just another document type. The XSL language defines element types and attributes, constrains them to occurring in particular places, and describes what they should look like. However, because of its heavy use of XML namespaces it is not possible in general to use a validating parser to ensure that an XSL document conforms to the XSL specification.

A stylesheet that uses the XSL formatting objects would have a root element that looks like Example 55-1.

Example 55-1. XSL stylesheet using formatting objects

```
<xsl:stylesheet xmlns:xsl="http://www.w3.org/1999/XSL/Transform"
                xmlns:fo="http://www.w3.org/1999/XSL/Format"
                version="1.0">
   <!-- template rules go here -->
</xsl:stylesheet>
```

The `xsl:stylesheet` element is usually the root element of XSLT stylesheets. You can also call this element `xsl:transform`. There is no difference in the processing of the element. `xsl:transform` is merely a synonym.

The `xsl:stylesheet` or `xsl:transform` element must have a namespace declaration for `xsl`. It makes sense to use the same declaration and `xsl:` prefix every time. You can also specify the output method to be used by the processor, choosing between XML, HTML and text.

The declarations in Example 55-1 are appropriate for XSL formatting object vocabulary output. The declarations for HTML look like Example 55-2.

Example 55-2. XSL stylesheet using HTML elements

```
<xsl:stylesheet xmlns:xsl="http://www.w3.org/1999/XSL/Transform"
                version="1.0">
<xsl:output method="html"/>
    <!-- template rules go here -->
</xsl:stylesheet>
```

The `xsl:stylesheet` element is usually filled with template rules. The template rules describe how to format elements in the source document. Of course almost every element type could be formatted differently from every other element type so there are many rules in an XSLT stylesheet. Particular elements could even be formatted differently if they share a type but have different attributes or occur in a different context.

55.5 | Rules, patterns and templates

In the application sections of this book, we looked at many products that mapped parts of a source document into a result document. They did so to convert from a word processor format to XML, to create stylesheets, to convert from XML to a legacy data format, etc. Often, they used a graphical interface to allow the user to define the transformation and generated XSLT or some earlier or variant version of it, or proprietary equivalent.

In this chapter, we look at the actual XSLT stylesheet that such products might generate to specify those mappings. Of course, because it is an XML document, it could also be created by means other than application-specific or proprietary product interfaces.

In XSLT, the mapping construct is called a *template rule*. During XSLT processing every element, character, comment and processing instruction in an XML document is processed by some template rule. Some of them will be handled by template rules that the stylesheet writer created. Others are handled by *built-in* template rules that are hard-coded into every XSLT processor.

Template rules consist of two parts, the *pattern* and the *template*. Be careful with the terminology: a template is not a template rule. The pattern describes which source nodes (elements, textual data strings, comments or processing instructions) should be processed by the rule. The template describes the XML structure to generate when nodes are found that match the pattern.

In an XSLT stylesheet, a template rule is represented by an `xsl:template` element.[2] The pattern is the value of the `xsl:template` element's `match` attribute, and the template proper is the element's content.

Template rules are simple. You do not have to think about the order in which things will be processed, where data is stored or other housekeeping tasks that programming languages usually require you to look after. You just declare what you want the result to look like and the XSLT processor figures out how to make that happen. Because everything is done through declarations we say that XSL is a *declarative* language. One important benefit of declarative languages is that they are easy to *optimize*. Implementors can use various tricks and shortcuts in order to make them execute quickly.

55.6 | Creating a stylesheet

XSLT's processing model revolves around the idea of *patterns*. Patterns are XPath expressions designed to test nodes. Patterns allow the XSLT processor to choose which elements to apply which style rules to. XSLT's pattern language is basically XPath with a few extensions and restrictions. Patterns are used in the `match` attribute of template rules to specify which elements the rule applies to.

XPath expressions are also used in XSLT template rules to select other elements (and other nodes) so that the stylesheet can process them also.

55.6.1 *Document-level template rule*

Consider a document with a `book` element type which can contain `title`, `section` and `appendix` element types. `section` and `appendix` elements can

---

2. It would have been clearer had they called it an `xsl:template-rule` element, but they didn't.

contain `title`, `para` and `list` subelements. Titles contain `#PCDATA` and no subelements. Paragraphs and list items contain `emph` and `#PCDATA`. Example 55-3 is a DTD that represents these constraints and Example 55-4 is an example document.

Example 55-3. DTD for book example

```
<!ELEMENT book (title, (section|appendix)+)>
<!ELEMENT section (title, (para|list)+)>
<!ELEMENT appendix (title, (para|list)+)>
<!ELEMENT title (#PCDATA)>
<!ELEMENT para (#PCDATA|emph)*>
<!ELEMENT emph (#PCDATA)>
<!ELEMENT list (item)+>
<!ELEMENT item (#PCDATA|emph)*>
```

Example 55-4. Book document instance

```
<book>
    <title>Chicken Soup for the Chicken's Soul</title>
    <section>
        <title>Introduction</title>
        <para>I've always wanted to write
              this book.</para>
    </section>
</book>
```

First the XSLT processor would examine the root element of the document. The XSLT processor would look for a rule that applied to books (a rule with a *match pattern* that matched a `book`). This sort of match pattern is very simple. Example 55-5 demonstrates.

Example 55-5. Simple match pattern

```
<xsl:template match="book">
  <!-- describe how books should be formatted -->
</xsl:template>
```

We can choose any basic structure for the generated book. Example 55-6 shows a reasonable one.

The template in this template rule generates a `body` to hold the content of the document. The tags for the body element are usually omitted in

Example 55-6. Generated book structure

```
<xsl:template match="book">
  <body>
    <h1><!-- handle title --></h1>
    <!-- handle sections -->
    <hr/> <!-- HTML horizontal rule -->
    <h2>Appendices</h2>
    <!-- handle appendices -->
    <hr/>
    <p>Copyright 2000, the establishment.</p>
  </body>
</xsl:template>
```

HTML but we will want to add some attributes to the element later. The body is called a *literal result element*.

55.6.2 *Literal result elements*

The XSLT processor knows to treat body as a *literal result element* that is copied into the output because it is not an XSLT instruction (formally, it is not in the XSLT namespace). Elements in templates that are not part of the XSLT namespace are treated literally and copied into the output. You can see why these are called templates! They describe the form of the result document both by ordering content and by generating literal result elements. If the XSLT processor supports legacy HTML output, and the HTML output method is being used to serialize the result, then it will know to use legacy HTML conventions.

The h1, h2 and hr elements are also literal result elements that will create HTML headings and horizontal rules. The stylesheet is represented in XML so the specification for the horizontal rule can use XML empty-element syntax. Finally the document has a literal result element and literal text representing the copyright. XSLT stylesheets can introduce this sort of *boilerplate* text.

55.6.3 *Extracting data*

The template also has comments describing things we still have to handle: the document's title, its sections and the appendices.

We can get the data content from the `title` element with the `xsl:value-of` instruction. It has a `select` attribute which is a pattern. If this pattern names a simple element type then it will match a subelement of the *current* element.

In this case the current element is the `book` element. That is the element matched by the `match` attribute. Example 55-7 shows what that would look like.

Example 55-7. Extracting data from a subelement

```
<h1><xsl:value-of select="title"/></h1>
```

55.6.4 *The* `apply templates` *instruction*

The next step is to handle sections and appendices. We could do it in one of two ways. We could either create a new template rule for handling sections or we could handle sections directly in the `book` template rule.

The benefit of creating a new rule is that it can be used over and over again. Before we create the new rule we should ensure it will get invoked at the right point. We will use a new instruction, `xsl:apply-templates`. Example 55-8 shows this instruction.

Example 55-8. The `xsl:apply-templates` instruction

```
<xsl:apply-templates select="section"/>
```

The `xsl:apply-templates` instruction does two important things.

1. It finds all nodes that match the `select` attribute pattern.
2. It processes each of these in turn. It does so by finding and applying the template rule that matches each node.

This important principle is at the heart of XSLT's processing model.

In this case, the *select* pattern in the `xsl:apply-templates` element selects all of the book's subelements of type `section`. The `xsl:apply-templates` instruction always searches out the rule that is appropriate for each of the selected nodes. In this case the `xsl:apply-templates` instruction will search out a rule that applies to sections. The expanded template is in Example 55-9.

Example 55-9. Handling section elements

```
<xsl:template match="book">
  <body>
    <h1><xsl:value-of select="title"/></h1>
    <xsl:apply-templates select="section"/>
    <hr/>
    <h2>Appendices</h2>
    <xsl:apply-templates select="appendix"/>
    <p>Copyright 2000, the establishment</p>
  </body>
</xsl:template>
```

55.6.5 *Handling optional elements*

Our sample document does not have appendices but the stylesheet should support anything that the DTD allows. Documents created in the future may have appendices.

Our stylesheet generates the title element followed by section elements (in the order that they occurred in the document) followed by appendix elements (also in *document order*).

If our DTD allowed more than one title subelement in a book element then this stylesheet would generate them all. There is no way for a stylesheet to require that the document have a single title. These sorts of constraints are specified in the DTD.

Our DTD does permit documents to have no appendices. Our title and horizontal rule separating the appendices from the sections would look fairly silly in that case. XSLT provides an instruction called `xsl:if` that handles this situation. We can wrap it around the relevant parts as shown in Example 55-10.

Example 55-10. Using `xsl:if`

```
<xsl:if test="appendix">
  <hr/>
  <h2>Appendices</h2>
  <xsl:apply-templates select="appendix"/>
</xsl:if>
```

The `xsl:if` instruction goes within a template. We could drop it into our `book` template as a replacement for our current appendix handling.

The instruction also contains another template within it. The contained template is only instantiated (generated) if there is some element that matches the pattern `appendix` exhibited by the `test` attribute.

As with the `select` attribute, the context is the current node. If there is no node that matches the pattern in the `test` attribute then the entire contained template will be skipped.

There is another instruction called `xsl:choose` that allows for multiple alternatives, including a default template for when none of the other alternatives match.

55.6.6 *Reordering the output*

If the DTD had allowed titles, sections and appendices to be mixed together our stylesheet would reorder them so that the title preceded the sections and the sections preceded the appendices.

This ability to reorder is very important. It allows us to use one structure in our abstract representation and another in our rendition. The internal structure is optimized for editing, validating and processing convenience. The external structure is optimized for viewing and navigation.

Reordering is easy when you know exactly the order in which you want elements of various types to be processed. In the case of the body, for example: titles before sections before appendices. But within a section or appendix, reordering is somewhat trickier because we don't know the complete output order.

That is, we need to format titles before any of the paragraphs or lists, but we cannot disturb the relative order of the paragraphs and lists themselves. Those have to be generated in the document order.

We can solve this fairly easily. In DTD syntax the vertical bar (|) character means "or". It means the same in XPath pattern syntax. So we can make a rule like the one in Example 55-11.

Example 55-11. The section rule

```
<xsl:template match="section">
    <h2><xsl:value-of select="title"/></h2>
    <xsl:apply-templates select="para|list"/>
</xsl:template>
```

This rule forces titles (in our DTD there can be only one) to be handled first and paragraphs and lists to be processed in the order that they are found. The rule that we already defined for paragraphs will automatically be selected when paragraphs appear.

55.6.7 *Sharing a template rule*

Next we can handle appendices. If we wrote out the rule for appendices we would find it to be identical to sections. We could just copy the rule but XSLT has a more elegant way. We can amend our rule for appendices to say that the rule applies to sections *or* appendices. Example 55-12 demonstrates.

Example 55-12. Handling sections and appendices

```
<xsl:template match="section|appendix">
    <h2><xsl:value-of select="title"/></h2>
    <xsl:apply-templates select="para|list"/>
</xsl:template>
```

55.6.8 *Data content*

Next we can handle paragraphs. We want them each to generate a single HTML element. We also want them to generate their content to populate that element in the order that the content occurs, not in some pre-defined template order.

We need to process all of the paragraph's *subnodes*. That means that we cannot just handle emph subelements. We must also handle ordinary character data. Example 55-13 demonstrates this.

Example 55-13. Paragraph rule

```
<xsl:template match="para">
    <p><xsl:apply-templates select="node()"/>
    </p>
</xsl:template>
```

As you can see, the rule for paragraphs is very simple. The `xsl:apply-templates` instruction handles all of the bookkeeping parts for us. The `select` attribute matches all nodes: element nodes, text nodes, etc. If it encounters a text node it copies it to the result; that is a *default* rule built into XSLT. If it encounters a subelement, it processes it using the appropriate rule.

XSLT handles much of the complexity for us but we should still be clear: transformations will not always be this easy. These rules are so simple because our DTD is very much like HTML. The more alike the source and result DTDs are the simpler the transformation will be. It is especially helpful to have a very loose or flexible result DTD. HTML is perfect in this regard.

55.6.9 *Handling inline elements*

`emph` follows the same basic organization as paragraph. Mixed content (character-containing) elements often use this organization. The HTML element-type name is `em` (Example 55-14). Note that in this case we will use an abbreviated syntax for the `xsl:apply-templates` element: Because the `select` attribute defaults to `node()`, we can leave it out.

Example 55-14. Handling emphasis

```
<xsl:template match="emph">
    <em><xsl:apply-templates/></em>
</xsl:template>
```

List items also have mixed content, so we should look at the rules for lists and list items next. They are in Example 55-15.

Example 55-15. List and item rules

```
<xsl:template match="list">
    <ol>
        <xsl:apply-templates/>
    </ol>
</xsl:template>
<xsl:template match="item">
    <li><xsl:apply-templates/></li>
</xsl:template>
```

The rules in Example 55-14 and Example 55-15 work together. When a `list` is detected the literal result element is processed and an `ol` element is generated. It will contain a single `li` element for each `item`. Each `li` will in turn contain text nodes (handled by the default rule) and `emph` (handled by the `emph` rule).

55.6.10 *Final touches*

We now have a complete stylesheet but it is rather basic. We might as well add a background color to beautify it a bit. HTML allows this through the `bgcolor` attribute of the `body` element. We will not go into the details of the HTML color scheme but suffice to say that Example 55-16 gives our document a nice light purple background.

Example 55-16. Adding a background color

```
<xsl:template match="book">
  <body bgcolor="#FFDDFF">
    <title><xsl:value-of select="title"/></title>
    <h1><xsl:value-of select="title"/></h1>
    <xsl:apply-templates select="section"/>
    <xsl:if test="appendix">
      <hr/>
      <h2>Appendices</h2>
      <xsl:apply-templates select="appendix"/>
    </xsl:if>
    <p>Copyright 2000, the establishment</p>
  </body>
</xsl:template>
```

There is also one more detail we must take care of. We said earlier that the more flexible a document type is the easier it is to transform to. Even though HTML is pretty flexible it does have one unbreakable rule. Every document must have a `title` element. We've handled the `title` element from the source as a heading but HTML has different concepts of heading and title. The title shows up in the window's title bar, in the bookmark list and in search engine result lists. We need the document's title to appear as both the HTML title and as a heading element. Luckily XSLT allows us to duplicate data.

With these additions our stylesheet is complete! It is shown in Example 55-17.

Example 55-17. Complete stylesheet

```
<?xml version="1.0"?>
<xsl:stylesheet xmlns:xsl="http://www.w3.org/1999/XSL/Transform"
                version="1.0">
<xsl:output method="html"/>

<xsl:template match="book">
  <body bgcolor="#FFDDFF">
    <title><xsl:value-of select="title"/></title>
    <h1><xsl:value-of select="title"/></h1>
    <xsl:apply-templates select="section"/>
    <hr/>
    <xsl:if test="appendix">
      <hr/>
      <h2>Appendices</h2>
      <xsl:apply-templates select="appendix"/>
    </xsl:if>
    <p>Copyright 2000, the establishment</p>
  </body>
</xsl:template>

<xsl:template match="para">
    <p><xsl:apply-templates/></p>
</xsl:template>

<xsl:template match="section|appendix">
    <xsl:apply-templates select="title"/>
    <xsl:apply-templates select="para|list"/>
</xsl:template>

<xsl:template match="emph">
    <em><xsl:apply-templates/></em>
</xsl:template>

<xsl:template match="list">
    <ol>
        <xsl:apply-templates/>
    </ol>
</xsl:template>

<xsl:template match="item">
    <li><xsl:apply-templates/></li>
</xsl:template>
</xsl:stylesheet>
```

As you can see, simple XSLT transformations can be quite simple – evidence of XSLT's good design. The important thing for you to recognize is that the basic XSLT processing model is based on template rules, patterns and templates. Flow of control between rules is handled by special instructions. In fact this processing model is ubiquitous in XML processing.

55.7 | Top-level instructions

XSLT also allows you to do more complex things. It supports all of XPath, sophisticated selections, stylesheet reuse and many other advanced features. We will introduce a few of these in this section, but remind you that the preview book on the CD goes into much more detail.

Top-level instructions are those that go directly in the `xsl:transform` or `xsl:stylesheet` elements. They do not apply to any particular template but rather declare behaviors, variables and other things that affect the entire stylesheet. Except for `xsl:import` instructions, the order of top-level statements is not important. As the XSLT specification says: "Users are free to order the elements as they prefer, and stylesheet creation tools need not provide control over the order in which the elements occur."

55.7.1 *Stylesheet combination*

The `xsl:include` instruction includes another stylesheet. Stylesheets may not include themselves directly or indirectly. The instructions in an included stylesheet are treated exactly as if they had been typed directly in the including stylesheet. They are not second-class in any sense. Example 55-18 demonstrates the inclusion of other stylesheets through both absolute and relative URL references.

Example 55-18. Including another stylesheet

```
<xsl:include href="http://.../currency.xsl"/>
<xsl:include href="bonds.xsl"/>
```

Importing is a little bit different from *including*. Just as in the real world, things that are imported get taxed! In the XSLT context that means that they are second class. Imported rules only take effect when no rule in the main stylesheet matches. Also, import statements earlier in the document take precedence over later ones.

Import instructions *must* go at the top of a stylesheet, before other instructions in the `xsl:stylesheet` or `xsl:template` element. A stylesheet must not directly or indirectly import itself. Example 55-19 demonstrates the importation of other stylesheets through both absolute and relative URL references.

Example 55-19. Importing another stylesheet

```
<xsl:import href="http://.../stocks.xsl"/>
<xsl:import href="credit-cards.xsl"/>
```

55.7.2 *Keys*

Keys allow you to look up elements based on names, but they let you decide what attributes or subelements serve as the names. XML has a built-in element naming construct – the ID attribute – but it has several not appropriate for all naming tasks.

Consider this case: every person in your company has a unique userid. Therefore it makes sense to use the "userid" attribute as a unique identifier for "person" elements. You do that by declaring its attribute type to be "ID".

Perhaps your company also has elements for machines and machine names. You might think it a good idea to declare "machinename" to have the attribute type "ID" as well.

But don't!

The software that generates userids and machine names probably has nothing to do with XML. It may be an ancient mainframe program or a brand new directory server. Either way, it has no reason to ensure that userids of people never clash with machinenames of machines.

If such a clash ever happens, XML will complain that a "userid" attribute value conflicts with a "machinename" attribute. The problem is that XML has a single, document-wide namespace for unique element names. It has no idea that you are trying to name real-world objects, not just XML elements.

Caution   The name of an individual element – its unique identifier – is not the name that occurs first in the element's start-tag. That name is the element-type name, which is shared by all elements of that type. It is not the element name. Unfortunately, even people who should know better are guilty of using this, er, misnomer!

There are ways to avoid this difficulty. The most common technique is just to not use XML's ID feature for the conflicting attributes. Instead, declare the attribute's type to be "NMTOKEN" (or some other type) in the DTD or schema.

Another approach is to use "keys". *Keys* allow a stylesheet author to tell XSLT that the "userid" attribute can serve as a "key" to the "person" elements. The word key is used in the database sense: it is a unique value that can be used to identify individual objects.

In this sense, "person name" is a key in a phone book. Actually that is not strictly true – two people can have the same name. That is why most phone books also publish addresses. The name and the address can be used together to form a key. XSLT keys allow this also. Two or more attributes, subelements, or other values can be combined using XPath string combination functions. Then they can be used together as a key.

You can also index a single element by multiple keys. For instance, person elements could be indexed in one context by userids and in another context by social-security numbers, depending on what you are trying to accomplish. We will not go into detail but we will give an example to give you a feeling for the flavor of declaring XSLT attributes. Example 55-20 shows a sample document.

In the sample document, employees are uniquely identified both by employee IDs and social security numbers. We will not presume that their names are unique because in large companies they are typically not.

Names are only useful if they are referenced somewhere. Elsewhere in the input document there is a description of departments. Departments are composed of references to employees by their employee ID (Example 55-21).

Example 55-20. Sample input for the stylesheet

```
<employees>
<employee employeeID="e98302">
  <social-security>000-00-0000</social-security>
  <name>Anthony Sobers</name>
</employee>
<employee employeeID="e02322">
  <social-security>111-11-1111</social-security>
  <name>Mossy Rock</name>
</employee>
</employees>
```

Example 55-21. Referring to employee elements

```
<department>
  <person empid="e98302" />
  <person empid="e02322" />
</department>
```

Keys are not declared in the XML file nor in the DTD or schema. They are declared in the XSLT stylesheet. Example 55-22 demonstrates.

Example 55-22. Declaring keys

```
<xsl:stylesheet ...>

...

    <xsl:key name="employees-by-id"
            match="employee"
            use="@employeeID"/>
    <xsl:key name="employees-by-ss"
            match="employee"
            use="social-security"/>

...

</xsl:stylesheet>
```

Every key has a name. There must only be one key with a particular name. Each key has a `match` attribute. It defines what nodes (typically elements) are addressed by the key. The `use` attribute says what value to use as the key value. In one case we are using an attribute of the element named `employeeID`. In the other case we are using the content of a subelement named `social-security`.

When we refer to the key we will use the `key` function. We supply the key name and a value. The XSLT processor computes a value for each node matched by the `match` attribute based on the `use` attribute. One and only one node should have the value we are looking for. That node will be returned. Example 55-23 demonstrates key use in a portion of an XSLT stylesheet.

Example 55-23. Using keys

```
<xsl:value-of select='key("employees-by-id","e98302")/name'/>
<xsl:value-of select='key("employees-by-ss","000-00-0000")/name'/>
```

It would be quite rare to use explicit employee IDs or numbers into a stylesheet (unless the employee is very important!). More likely you would use a rule that processes `person` elements within `department` elements, based on `empid` attributes, as in Example 55-24.

Example 55-24. Using keys without explicit numbers

```
<xsl:template match="person">
Name: <xsl:value-of
          select='key("employees-by-id",@empid)/name'/>
Social: <xsl:value-of
          select='key("employees-by-id",@empid)/social-security'/>
</xsl:template>
```

55.7.3 *Whitespace handling*

In machine-to-machine applications, whitespace nodes are usually irrelevant. Even in POP-oriented applications, some whitespace is not important for processing. A new line between two section elements is just intended to make the source XML easier to read. It is not intended to affect what is seen by the ultimate readers of the rendered document.

As we saw in Figure 54-2, whitespace nodes are ordinary text nodes that happen to have only whitespace (tab, space, newline) characters in them. Nodes T2, T4, and T5 in that figure are examples.

XSLT has a feature that allows you to strip out these whitespace-only nodes based on what element they are contained within. The `xsl:strip-space` instruction strips space from elements of specified types in the source document. Example 55-25 shows how you would strip space from address and date elements.

Example 55-25. Stripping space

```
<xsl:strip-space elements="address date"/>
```

In some vocabularies, all element types are space-stripping. You can accomplish this by using an asterisk in the `xsl:strip-space` instruction. (Example 55-26)

Example 55-26. Strip space from all elements

```
<xsl:strip-space elements="*"/>
```

If a vocabulary has only a few non-whitespace stripping elements (*whitespace-preserving elements*), you can selectively override the blanket stripping statement with the `xsl:preserve-space` instruction. By default, whitespace is preserved.

55.7.4 *Output descriptions*

The `xsl:output` instruction sets various options that control what the stylesheet should generate as output. The main attribute in the instruction is the `method` attribute, which typically takes a value like "xml", "html" or "text".

"xml" is appropriate for (surprise!) generating XML; it is the default. "html" uses html conventions for empty-elements, processing instructions and similar constructs. The "text" output is useful when you want to generate raw text without the XSLT processor representing special characters like less-than signs ("<") as < and so forth.

Other attributes can control whether the output is indented for "pretty printing", what character encoding to use, whether to add an XML declaration and/or document type declaration and other (even more obscure) output options. Most XSLT stylesheets will not need to change these options.

But if you find that the output of your stylesheet is not quite what you would expect, then `xsl:output` may have the answer for you.

55.7.5 *Numeric formats*

The `xsl:decimal-format` instruction allows you to describe how decimal numbers will be printed by your stylesheet. For instance, you can use this to change the character that is used to separate the "decimals" from the integral part of the number. Using this feature you could set that option to "." for North Americans and "," for Europeans.

Other options allow you to change the "grouping separator" between the billions, millions and thousands and to choose characters or strings to represent "infinity", "minus", "percent", "per-mille" (per thousand), "the zero digit" and "Not a number" (NaN). The latter is used for error handling.

55.7.6 *Attribute sets*

`xsl:attribute-set` allows you to define a reusable set of attributes. If you have several different types of images that must share certain attributes then it is more efficient to define those in an attribute set than to repeat them all in each template rule. Example 55-27 demonstrates the basic idea.

Example 55-27. Reusable set of attribute values

```
<xsl:attribute-set name="big-image">
    <xsl:attribute name="width">500px</xsl:attribute>
    <xsl:attribute name="height">500px</xsl:attribute>
</xsl:attribute-set>
<xsl:attribute-set name="small-image">
    <xsl:attribute name="width">100px</xsl:attribute>
    <xsl:attribute name="height">100px</xsl:attribute>
</xsl:attribute-set>

... in a template ...
<img xsl:use-attribute-sets="big-image">
```

55.7.7 *Namespace alias*

Just as `xsl:output` helps you to solve the problem of how to have a less-than sign that is treated as "just a less-than sign", `xsl:namespace-alias` helps you to treat a namespaced literal result element as just a literal result element, even if the namespace happens to be XSLT! This sounds strange but it could happen if you were writing an XSLT stylesheet that generates an XSLT stylesheet. Needless to say, this is not a common situation so we will not dwell on it further.

55.8 | Variables and parameters

XSLT variables and parameters are closely related. A variable is a value that a stylesheet creator "stores away" for use in some other part of the stylesheet. A top-level variable is one defined outside of any template. The value is automatically available for use in any template. For instance a variable could hold the company name. The value that the variable holds could even be extracted from the input XML document. Example 55-28 demonstrates.

Example 55-28. Defining a variable

```
<xsl:variable name="company-name" select="/doc/creator/company"/>
```

Variables can be referred to in XPath instructions by preceding the variable name with a dollar-sign ("$"). Example 55-29 demonstrates.

Example 55-29. Referencing a variable

```
<xsl:value-of select="$company-name"/>
```

A parameter is just like a variable except that the value can be "overridden." How it would be overridden depends on your XSLT implementation. Command-line XSLT transformation engines typically use command-line options. Graphical environments might use options in a graphical user interface. In other words, parameters are "user options" that change the stylesheet's behavior. They are declared and referenced just as variables are. Example 55-30 demonstrates.

Example 55-30. Defining a parameter

```
<xsl:param name="company-name" select="/doc/creator/company"/>
```

The `select` attribute of a parameter is used as a *default value*. If the user chooses not to supply a parameter (or forgets), the default value is used.

It is also possible to have templates and parameters within templates. In that case, they are only available within that template. Parameters for a particular template are passed not from the user, but from other templates. For instance a template for a chapter might use a parameter to pass the chapter number to a template for a section. That way the section number could be derived from the chapter number easily (e.g. Section 5.4).

There are many more interesting features in the XSLT language but XSLT is only part of the picture. The other part is XSL formatting objects: a bold new approach to formatting documents online.

55.9 | XSL formatting objects

As we described earlier, Part Two of the XSL specification defines a set of formatting objects. Those are based primarily upon CSS. When you use these you use both parts of the XSL specification and you need an implementation that supports both parts of it. That implementation could be a command line utility, a browser or a desktop publishing program. XSL supports both online and print publishing.

Let's start simply and consider a stylesheet that would say that "Paragraphs should use a 12pt font" and "Titles should be 20 point and bold-faced."

Example 55-31 contains a stylesheet with two rules to apply font styles to titles and paragraphs.

The rules say that whenever the XSLT processor encounters a PARA or TITLE element in an XML document, it should create a `fo:block` element. Because the result uses the formatting object vocabulary, an XSL processor should proceed to render the document. A renderer could also be a separate software component or program, such as a word processor or Web browser.

The renderer (word processor, browser etc.) generates a block (`fo:block`) of text on the screen which is separated from the text above and below it. This makes sense. Visually a paragraph is just a text block set off from other text. The `fo:block` element has an attribute called `font-size`. This attribute is also defined by the XSL specification and will be properly interpreted by the XSL processor in the rendition stage. Similarly, this stylesheet will look for `title` elements and make them bold and 20pt.

Example 55-31. XSL formatting objects

```
<?xml version="1.0"?>
<xsl:stylesheet xmlns:xsl="http://www.w3.org/1999/XSL/Transform"
                xmlns:fo="http://www.w3.org/1999/XSL/Format"
                version="1.0">
<xsl:output method="xml"/>

    <xsl:template match="PARA">
        <fo:block font-size="12pt">
            <xsl:apply-templates/>
        </fo:block>
    </xsl:template>

    <xsl:template match="TITLE">
        <fo:block font-size="20pt" font-weight="bold">
            <xsl:apply-templates/>
        </fo:block>
    </xsl:template>

</xsl:stylesheet>
```

The `fo:root` is the root element and contains everything else. Within the root you can have one or more `fo:page-sequence` elements. Each represents a series of pages – either print pages or Web pages. The main content of the document goes into `fo:flow` elements. There are several different types of "block-level" objects that are allowed to go into the `fo:flow`. A few of these are listed next.

fo:block
     The `fo:block` element type holds a block of text. It can be used for paragraphs, titles, block quotations and so forth. Blocks have a huge number of properties for changing the background color, background image, font size, padding (space around block), orphans (handling of page breaks) and so forth.

fo:external-graphic
     The `fo:external-graphic` element type allows you to create a graphic that is formatted inline (between characters). You could use that for icons. The image is specified through a URI.

`fo:leader`

The `fo:leader` element type creates a horizontal or vertical line. It has properties for changing the color, length, width and style (solid, dotted, dashed).

`fo:table`

The `fo:table` element type is used for tables. It has a *table model* similar to (but not identical to) that used by HTML.

`fo:list-block`

The `fo:list-block` element type represents a list. It can contain a sequence of `fo:list-item` elements, representing the list items, which are pairs of `fo:list-item-label`, `fo:list-item-body` elements. The label/item pairs could be used for a dictionary; the words would be the labels and the definitions would be the items. The labels could also be used for bullets or numbers in unordered and ordered lists.

`fo:simple-link`

The `fo:simple-link` element type allows you to create hypertext clickable links to a destination specified by a URI or to another element in the formatting object tree. This element type allows XLinks to be rendered.

`fo:page-number`

The `fo:page-number` element type generates a page number for printed documents.

55.10 | Referencing XSL stylesheets

There is a W3C Recommendation that specifies how XML documents should refer to their stylesheets. Here is the relevant text:

Spec Excerpt (XML-SS) 55-1. The `xml-stylesheet` processing instruction

The `xml-stylesheet` processing instruction is allowed anywhere in the prolog of an XML document. The processing instruction can have pseudo-attributes `href` (required), `type` (required), `title` (optional), `media` (optional), `charset` (optional).

These are called "pseudo-attributes" instead of attributes. Although they use attribute syntax, they do not describe properties of an element. In real XML terms, only elements can have attributes. The only real syntactic difference between pseudo-attributes and attributes is that you must use pseudo-attributes in the order they are defined. You can use attributes in any order.

The most important pseudo-attributes for this processing instruction are `href`, which supplies a URI for the stylesheet, and `type`, which says that the stylesheet is in XSL and not DSSSL, CSS, or some other stylesheet language. You can also supply a `title` that the browser might use when offering a list of stylesheet choices. The `media` option allows you to specify what medium the stylesheet is for. You could, for example, have different stylesheets for print (with footnotes and page breaks), online (with clickable links), television (large text and easy scroll controls) and telephone (read aloud using inflection to render emphasis). XSL is not powerful enough yet to handle all of these media equally well, but it will be one day.

Example 55-32 is an example stylesheet processing instruction (PI).

Example 55-32. Stylesheet PI

```
<?xml-stylesheet href="http://www.xmlbooks.com/memo.xsl"
                 type="text/xsl"?>
```

You can also provide multiple PIs to allow for choice by media, title or stylesheet language. Example 55-33 demonstrates this.

Example 55-33. Alternative stylesheets

```
<?xml-stylesheet rel=alternate
                 href="mystyle1.xsl"
                 title="Fancy"
                 type="text/xsl"?>
<?xml-stylesheet
                 rel=alternate
                 href="mystyle2.css"
                 title="Simple"
                 type="text/css"?>
<?xml-stylesheet
                 rel=alternate
                 href="mystyle2.aur"
                 title="Aural"
                 type="text/aural"?>
```

55.11 | Conclusion

XSL is at one time a work in progress and also a runaway success. The industry support for the XSLT part of XSL clear but the support for the formatting side will take shape only after the specification is finished. Even then, it make take time for tools to embrace the new spec. The XSL formatting object vocabulary will be much more sophisticated, but also more complicated, than the HTML vocabulary that is so popular as a transformation target today.

XML Pointer Language (XPointer)

Friendly Tutorial

- Uniform Resource Identifiers (URI)

- URI references

- ID references with XPointers

56

X Pointer is an extension and customization of XPath. XPointer allows XPath expressions to be used as parts of URIs (including URLs). Using the XPointer extension it is possible to make references deep into an XML document. That means that you can link to an element, or even a span of elements, based on things like position, element type and ID – all of the usual XPath features.

> *Caution*   XPointers are still under development. We will only cover the concepts that we consider most stable.

56.1 | XPointers: The reason why

There are many times when it is necessary to refer not just to another document but to a particular part of that document. We can use a simple URI to refer to another document. Once we have a document it is possible to refer to a particular node or set of nodes using XPath. The XPointer specification allows the URI and the XPath to be combined into a *URI reference*. This combination of document and node addressing is very powerful.

An XPointer-containing URI reference can be used almost anywhere that an ordinary URI can be used. Not only can you put them in hypertext links – you can also put them on the sides of buses and in previews for movies! You can type the URI reference into a Web browser and have the browser jump directly to a particular place in the document. In some situations either the browser or the server could use an XPointer to actually restrict your view to a particular section of the document.

Inter-document addressing is vital for linking. Using XPointer it is possible to link a single element in an XML document to a single character in another. The full power of XPath is available in XPointer. So it is also possible to link a set of nodes (e.g. element nodes) in one document to one or more nodes (e.g. attribute nodes) in another document.

Although XPointers are important in linking it is also important to remember that they can be used outside of XLink. You might see an XPointer in a URI reference in the newspaper or in an email; it would represent the address of some XML nodes, but there would be no XLink.

In fact URIs are so common today that you can even use them to represent hypertext links in MS Word or PDF documents. In the future it will be possible to use URI references with XPointers in these contexts. That will mean that it will be possible to link from deep in a Word document or PDF file to the middle of an XML document.

Let's take a closer look at URIs before we start tacking XPointers onto them.

56.2 | Uniform Resource Identifiers

The basic form of address on the Web is a *URI*, which stands for *Uniform Resource Identifier*. It comes in two flavors:

URL
Today's most important form of URI is the ubiquitous *URL* or *Uniform Resource Locator*.

URN

A new form of URI, *Universal Resource Name (URN)*, isn't location-dependent and perhaps will reduce the number of broken links. However, it has yet to catch on because it requires more sophisticated software support.

URLs are uniform, in that they have the same basic syntax no matter what specific type of resource (e.g. Web page, newsgroup) is being addressed or what mechanism is described to fetch it. They describe the locations of Web resources much as a physical address describes a person's location. URLs are hierarchical, just as most physical addresses are. A land mail address is resolved by sending a letter to a particular country, and from there to a local processing station, and from there to an individual. URLs are similar.

The first part of a URL is the *protocol*. It describes the mechanism that the Web browser or other client should use to get the resource. Think of it as the difference between Federal Express, UPS, and the other courier services. The most common such protocol is `http` which is essentially the "official" protocol of the World Wide Web. The `ftp` file transfer protocol is also widely used, chiefly for large downloads such as new browser versions.

After the protocol, there is a *hostname* and then a *datapath*. The datapath is broken into chunks separated by slash (/) characters, as you have no doubt seen in hundreds of URLs. Technically, a URL ends at that point. Since URLs are just the most common form of URI, it is also safe to say that the URI ends here.

56.3 | URI references

There is another term that is confusingly similar to URI: *URI reference*. A URI reference as the combination of a URI (which could be a URL) and an optional *fragment identifier*. For instance you may have seen links into HTML documents that look like Example 56-1.

Example 56-1. Reference into HTML

```
http://www.megabank.com/banking#about
```

In the example, #about is a fragment identifier. It refers to a particular HTML element. XPointers are the form of fragment identifier appropriate for XML documents. They are much more flexible than HTML fragment identifiers. Essentially, XPointers are an extension to URIs (i.e., a fragment identifier syntax) to allow you to point not just *to* an XML document, but into the content of one.

For instance, on today's Web, if you wanted to quote a particular paragraph out of another document, you would go to that document and cut and paste the text into yours. If, in the future, the text on the Web changes, yours does not. If that is what you want, that is fine. But an XPointer and XLink-smart application might allow you to construct a "living document" that quotes and refers to the very latest version of the paragraph.

56.4 | ID references with XPointers

The simplest form of XPointer allows you to refer to a particular element named with an ID. This is also the most robust form of XPointer, because it does not at all depend on the location of the referenced text within its document. Consider the XML document in Example 56-2.

Example 56-2. Example document

```
<?xml version="1.0"?>
<!DOCTYPE HEATWAVES SYSTEM "heatwaves.dtd">
<HEATWAVES>
<WAVE ID="summer_92_info">
    <DURATION><FROM>July 22</FROM><TO>August 2</TO></DURATION>
    <TEMPERATURE>101 Degrees</TEMPERATURE>
</WAVE>
<WAVE ID="summer_94_info">
    <DURATION><FROM>July 12</FROM><TO>July 18</TO></DURATION>
    <TEMPERATURE>100 Degrees</TEMPERATURE>
</WAVE>
<WAVE ID="summer_96_info">
    <DURATION><FROM>June 15</FROM><TO>July 18</TO></DURATION>
    <TEMPERATURE>103 Degrees</TEMPERATURE>
</WAVE>
</HEATWAVES>
```

If this document resides at `http://www.hotdays.com/heatwave.xml`, then we could refer to the second `WAVE` element with the URI in Example 56-3.

Example 56-3. URI with XPointer

```
http://www.hotdays.com/heatwave.xml#xpointer( id("summer_94_info") )
```

The XPointer is the last little bit of the URI, after the pound-sign (#). The text "`xpointer`" starts the XPointer. Inside the outer parentheses we have an XPath. Typically the XPath will be just like those defined in Chapter 54, "XML Path Language (XPath)", on page 800, but sometimes they will use extensions that are defined in the XPointer specification.

We are not restricted to XPath's `id` function. IDs are the most robust way to refer to elements but we can also refer to elements that do not have IDs. This is especially important if we do not control the document that we are referencing. Any XPath can be used.

If you use a namespace prefix in an XPointer, it is taken as a reference to the namespace bound to that prefix in the context of the XML element that contains the XPointer. The prefix and bindings in the target document are irrelevant. If an XPointer is used in a context other than an XML document then it cannot use namespace prefixes. The XPointer recommendation suggests using the more verbose form shown in the second line of Example 56-4. Assume that there is a namespace declaration in scope in the first case and it looks like `xmlns:ex="http://example.com/foo`.

Example 56-4. Short and long form namespace references

```
xpointer(//ex:y)
xpointer(//*[local-name()='y' and
            namespace-uri()='http://example.com/bar'])
```

56.5 | XPointer abbreviations

The usual syntax for XPointer is called the "full syntax". There are also two abbreviations that save some typing for common XPointer uses.

The first shortcut is for referring to elements by their IDs. You can do this by using the ID as the whole XPointer. You can replace the keyword "xpointer" and everything else. This abbreviation is called a *bare name*.

Example 56-5 demonstrates equivalent XPointers.

Example 56-5. Equivalent XPointers

```
http://www.hotdays.com/heatwave.xml#xpointer( id("summer_96_info") )
http://www.hotdays.com/heatwave.xml#summer_96_info
```

You can use IDs more concisely with this abbreviation. IDs are an excellent way to refer to an element because they are impervious to minor changes such as re-ordering or adding elements to a document.

The other abbreviation is called a *child sequence*. With a child sequence you can refer to a child or descendant element of some particular element based on its position. For instance to refer to the first child of the summer_96_info element we would add a slash after the bare name and follow that by an integer. Example 56-6 demonstrates.

Example 56-6. Child sequence

```
http://www.hotdays.com/heatwave.xml#summer_96_info/1
```

This example refers to the first subelement of the WAVE element called summer_96_info. In our sample document, this is a DURATION element. We can also refer to a subelement of a subelement (or subelement of a subelement of a subelement ... you get the picture) by adding slash-separated numbers to the end. Example 56-7 addresses all of the elements within the element with ID summer_96_info and its children.

Example 56-7. Deeper child sequences

```
http://www.hotdays.com/heatwave.xml#summer_96_info/1
http://www.hotdays.com/heatwave.xml#summer_96_info/1/1
http://www.hotdays.com/heatwave.xml#summer_96_info/1/2
http://www.hotdays.com/heatwave.xml#summer_96_info/2
```

These XPointers refer (respectively) to DURATION, FROM, TO and TEMPERATURE elements.

Rather than referring to an element by ID, you can refer to it by its position relative to the start of the document by starting the abbreviated XPointer with "/1". The "/1" refers to the root (or document) element. The next number (if any) refers to one of its children. The number after that (if any) refers to a child of that child and so on. Example 56-8 refers again to the elements that are within the element with ID `summer_96_info`.

Example 56-8. Rooted child sequences

```
http://www.hotdays.com/heatwave.xml#/1/3/1
http://www.hotdays.com/heatwave.xml#/1/3/1/1
http://www.hotdays.com/heatwave.xml#/1/3/1/2
http://www.hotdays.com/heatwave.xml#/1/3/2
```

The `"/1"` refers to the root (document) element HEATWAVES. The "/3" in each XPointer refers to the third child element of HEATWAVES, the WAVE with ID `summer_96_info`. The trailing numbers are as before.

It is important to understand that these abbreviations are used only in XPointers, and only instead of the traditional XPath syntax. You cannot mix them with ordinary XPaths.

56.6 | Extensions to XPath

XPointer extends the XPath model to support two new concepts: *points* and *ranges*. Since a range is defined as the area between two points, we'll examine the point concept first.

XPath normally returns nodes, which represent actual pieces of a document. If you think of a row of boxes on a piece of graph paper, nodes are the boxes and points occur at the vertical blue lines that separate the boxes.

XPointer takes things even further, though. In addition to allowing points before and after a node, it also allows points between the characters of a text node.

Ranges represent an area that a user might select in a document. Just like a user interface selection, it starts at one point (between two characters of a text node or between two elements or other nodes) and goes to another point.

56.6.1 *Ranges*

Ranges can be addressed with a variety of functions introduced by XPointer's extensions to XPath.

56.6.1.1   range-to

The `range-to` function takes two XPaths and addresses a range from the point preceding the first XPath to a point following the second. For instance, if you had an element with ID "summer_92_info" and wanted to create a range that contained that element, an element named "summer_96_info", and everything in between, you could do so with the XPointer in Example 56-9.

Example 56-9. range-to

```
xpointer(id("summer_92_info")/range-to(id("summer_96_info")))
```

56.6.1.2   string-range

The `string-range` function searches for a string in the text nodes representing the data content of an element or a set of elements, or in the values of any other node set.

The simplest form of this function takes an XPath as its first parameter and a string as its second parameter. It finds occurrences of the string in the values of the nodes and returns them as a list of ranges.

The XPath to address all title elements in a document is "//title". If we wanted to find all occurrences of the string "Extensible Markup Language" in the titles, we would do it through the XPath in Example 56-10.

Example 56-10. string-range

```
something.xml#xpointer(
   string-range( //title, "Extensible Markup Language" ))
```

You can also refer to a particular item in the list by appending an ordinary XPath predicate (Example 56-11).

Example 56-11. 11th occurrence

```
something.xml#xpointer(
  string-range( //title, "Extensible Markup Language" )[11])
```

Sometimes you want to address only a portion of long string. Perhaps you want to select the word "Markup" but only in the context of "Extensible Markup Language". To do this you would count into the string and find that the "M" in "Markup" is the twelfth character in the complete string.

In Example 56-12, we use "12" as the third argument to `string-range`. The final argument says how much of the string to select beyond the "M". The word "Markup" has six letters so we use "6" as the fourth parameter.

Example 56-12. range-slice

```
something.xml#xpointer(
  string-range( //title, "Extensible Markup Language", 12, 6 ))
```

These last two parameters are optional. If you do not specify them then you select the entire string. If you leave out the last parameter then you select to the end of the requested string.

56.6.1.3   range-inside and range

The `range-inside` function addresses a range that starts just inside the beginning of an element or other node or a set of nodes (including sets of elements) and goes to just inside the end.

For instance `range-inside(/book/title)` will select a range that includes everything inside of the `title` but does not include the `title` itself. If you visualize this in terms of the XML document string, it selects the content of the `title` element but not the `title` start- and end-tags.

A related function selects the content and the tags together. It is simply called `range`. This function is used to select an entire node or to address a set of ranges for a set of nodes. For instance `range(//title)` would select the ranges of each `title` element. If you visualize this in terms of the XML document string, it selects the ranges for the content and the tags of the elements.

Note the difference between `range(//title)` and `//title`. In the range case, the result is a list of ranges. In the straightforward XPath case, the result is a list of nodes.

56.6.2 *Point functions*

XPointer can also select points without addressing a range. This capability could be used, for example, to position a cursor between characters or elements in a document.

The `start-point` function selects the point just before an element or range. For instance to create a point just before the string "XML" in a title you could use an expression like that in Example 56-13.

Example 56-13. start-point

```
foo.xml#xpointer(start-point(string-range(//title, "XML")[1]))
```

This would select the point just before the first occurrence of the string "XML" in any `title` in the document. If we change the function from `start-point` to `end-point` then we would select the point just after the "L" in "XML".

If you pass a node (typically an element) or list of nodes to the `start-point` function then it will select the first point within the node or in each of the nodes. Similarly, the `end-point` function will select the last point in the node or each of the nodes. If you want to select the point just before or after a node (not inside it) then you can combine one of these functions with the `range` function.

56.6.3 *Other extension functions*

XPointer adds some other functions to XPath which are unrelated to the new concepts of point and range.

The first new function is called `here`. It returns the node that contains the actual XPointer text, if the XPointer is in an XML document. This might be useful to find some other information that might be useful in computing the XPointer. For instance, an attribute of the same element in the XPointer source XML document might contain a string that should be matched in the target XML document.

The second new function is called `origin`. This function is useful only when XPointers are used with XLink. Outside of the hyperlinking context, `origin` is not meaningful and not legal.

`origin` returns the element that was used to start traversal in an XLink. In the case of out-of-line (extended) links, this is not necessarily the element that contains the XPointer.

The final XPointer extension function is called `unique`. It is just a convenience function that checks that an XPointer selects one and only one node. This allows an XPointer creator to express the intention that the XPointer select only a single node, range or point. If the document changes so that the XPointer returns more than one location then the XPointer will break and the author can be alerted and can fix it.

56.6.4 *Multiple XPointer parts*

It is possible to string together several full (not abbreviated) XPointer parts to allow the system to attempt multiple addressing strategies. All you need to do is concatenate multiple strings starting with "xpointer(" and ending in ")". Each of these is called an XPointer part. You may separate them with whitespace if you wish.

For instance, you could start with an ID-based XPointer because they are the most robust. This strategy might fail if the ID was deleted or renamed or if the processor did not support ID processing. Then you could try a string-search strategy. This would work unless the document had been edited to delete or change the target string. You could fall back from there to a positional strategy.

Example 56-14 demonstrates (on multiple lines for clarity).

Example 56-14. Multiple XPointers in one URI

```
foo.xml#xpointer(id('summer_96_info'))
        xpointer(string-range('103 Degrees')/../..)
        xpointer( /HEATWAVES/WAVE[3] )
```

With each strategy you are less and less sure that you have addressed the thing that you wanted to address, but it may be better to take that risk than to just give up as soon as the document changes. In a Web surfing situation, users may well tolerate the occasional mistake in exchange for fewer broken links overall.

56.7 | The role of XPointers

You could say that an XPointer is mostly just a shell for an XPath, but the shell is very important. The XPointer is the glue between the URI that precedes the pound-sign and the XPath in the parentheses.

An important thing to note is that an XPointer does not *do* anything. It refers to something. Whether the object is included, hyperlinked, or downloaded depends completely on the context of the reference.

It is just like referring to a person by name. The act of referring to him doesn't really accomplish anything. You have to refer to someone before you can tell somebody to do something to him (hopefully something nice), but the reference is not the action.

For instance, you could use the XPointer in an XLink to create a hyperlink to something, or in a browser address window to download and display a particular element. It is also up to the software to decide whether the referenced element is returned alone, or in the context of its document.

For instance, if you use an XPointer in a browser window, it would probably present the whole document and highlight the referenced element. But if you use it in an inclusion link to include a paragraph, it would probably take that paragraph out of its context and present it alone in the new context. The specific behavior depends on your link processor and stylesheet.

56.8 | Conclusion

XPointer is an extension and customization of XPath. XPointer allows XPath expressions to be used as parts of URIs (including URLs). Using the XPointer extension it is possible to make references deep into an XML document. This will allow new forms of commentary, annotation and information reuse.

XML Linking Language (XLink)

- Linking and addressing
- Simple links
- Extended links

57

H ypertext links are the backbone of the World Wide Web. Documents were shuffled around the Internet long before today's
Web existed, but it was the ease of moving from page to page
with hypertext links that made the Web into the mass market phenomenon it is today.

However, despite their centrality, Web links have many weaknesses. The
linking system that we use today is essentially unchanged from the earliest
version of the Web. Unfortunately, market inertia has prevented anything
more powerful from coming along ... until now.

The XML-family hyperlinking specification is called XLink. It allows
links that go far beyond those provided by HTML. XLinks can have multi-

ple end points, be traversed in multiple directions, and be stored in databases and groups independently of the documents they refer to.

Caution   XLink is still not quite there yet. Although there are partial implementations in several products, they are not mainstream. The current version of XLink is a working draft and will change before it is completed. The basic concepts are well understood and will not change, but the specifics may change between now and then. However, the parts we cover here are those that appear to be relatively stable.

57.1 | Basic concepts

The most important (and sometimes subtle) distinction in any discussion of hyperlinking is that of *linking* versus *addressing*. Linking is simply declaring a relationship between two (or more) things. If we say "George Washington and Booker T. Washington share a last name" then we have linked those two people in some way.

Addressing, on the other hand, is about describing how to find the two things being linked. There are many kinds of addresses, such as mail addresses, email addresses and URLs. When you create a link in XLink, you declare a relationship between two objects referred to by their addresses (URI References). We refer to these objects as *resources*. We discuss the addresses more in 56.2, "Uniform Resource Identifiers", on page 862.

When you follow a link one way or another, we say that you have *traversed* the link. We call the process of doing so *traversal*.

The action that starts the traversal is called its *actuation*. The ringmaster lights the fuse that *actuates* the human cannonball's *traversal* across the circus arena to a vital net resource.[1]

If you have created Web pages before, you are probably familiar with HTML's simple A element. Whether or not you are familiar with HTML, that link is a good starting point for understanding hyperlinking in general.

The A stands for *anchor*. Anchor is the hyperlinking community's term for what the XLink spec calls a *participating resource*. An HTML link has

---

1. A 404 error would mean that more than the link was broken!

two ends, termed the *source* and *destination*. When you click on the source end, (designated with an A element and href attribute), the Web browser transports you to the other end. Example 57-1 shows how this works.

Example 57-1. An HTML (not XLink) link

```
<a href="http://www.mysite.com">Go to my site!</a>
```

In this case, the a element itself describes a link, and its href attribute points to one of the resources (the destination). As we know, links connect resources, so there must be at least one more resource involved. The other resource, the source, is actually the content of the a element itself! The XLink spec calls this a *local resource*. As we will see, XLink *simple* links also use the content of the linking element as one of the resources.

There is another pervasive type of link in HTML documents. Consider the HTML markup to embed an image (Example 57-2).

Example 57-2. HTML (not XLink) image-embedding link

```
<IMG SRC="http://www.hotpics.com/jalapeno.gif">
```

That may not seem like a link but it is.[1] It declares a relationship between the containing document and the embedded image: "that picture goes in this document." HTML element types that use href attributes to address Java applets and plug-in objects are also forms of link.

Note that the destination of a link does not necessarily know that it is a destination. If you want to link to the Disney home page, you do not need to inform Disney. If a particular document has fifty a elements with href attributes, then you know that it has fifty links out. But the Web provides no way to know how many links into it there are.

In the more general *extended* link case, we will link two things such that *neither* end will "know" that the two are being linked. The link exists in some third location. This is intuitive if you go back to the definition of linking as defining a relationship. In a real-world sense, I can "link" Jenny Jones and Oprah Winfrey just by speaking of them in the same sentence.

---

1. What it isn't is a navigational link. You don't click on it to go somewhere else. Instead, its traversal is actuated automatically, as we'll see later in this chapter.

Unless they are interested in careers as XML experts, they will probably never know. XLink provides a standardized way to express this relationship in markup.

We might even want to link something that is not explicitly labeled. For instance, we might want to link the third paragraph of the fourth sub-point of the second section of a legal document to the transcript of a relevant court case.

This is analogous to the real world situation where you can either send something to a labeled location ("Please take this to the White House.") or you can give directions to the destination. In hyperlinking terms, we would consider either one of these to be an "address." Obviously there must be some way of locating a resource from a link, but it could be either an address, a label or a combination of the two: "The building is 5 blocks down the street from the White House."

57.2 | Simple links

Although XLink allows more flexible links than does HTML, it also offers simple links that are not much more complicated than HTML's links are. This sort of link is referred to as a *simple link*. A simple link has two ends, a source and a destination, just like an HTML link. One end represents a resource (usually the source) and it refers to the other end through a URI as in Example 57-3.

Example 57-3. XLink simple link

```
. . . for more information, consult
<citation xlink:type="simple"
          xlink:href="http://www.uw.ca/paper.xml">
Biemans(1997)
</citation>
```

The biggest difference between this link and the HTML link is that this element is not designated a link by its element-type name. It is not called a or any special element-type name specified in the XML or XLink specification. You can call your linking elements whatever you want to. This is an important feature, because it allows you to have many different types of linking elements in a document, perhaps with different declarations, attributes and behaviors. Just as XML allows you to use any element-type name for paragraphs or figures, XLink allows you flexibility in your linking element-type names.

The link is actually designated an XLink link by its `xlink:type` attribute. The `xlink:type` attribute describes what kind of link is being described. In this case, it is a *simple* link. The `xlink:` prefix indicates that this attribute's allowed values and semantics are defined by the XLink specification.

Formally speaking, the attribute lives in the `xlink:` namespace. Namespaces are discussed in Chapter 53, "Namespaces", on page 788. This namespace should be declared in your document: probably in the document (i.e., root) element as shown in Example 57-4.

Example 57-4. Namespace declaration in root element

```
<yourdoc xmlns:xlink="http://www.w3.org/1999/xlink">
...
</yourdoc>
```

For type-valid documents, it is best to declare the `xmlns:xlink` attribute in the DTD as a fixed attribute of the root element type, as shown in Example 57-5.

Example 57-5. Namespace declaration in DTD

```
<!ATTLIST yourdoc xmlns:xlink CDATA
                  #FIXED "http://www.w3.org/1999/xlink">
```

Note   All of the examples in this chapter assume that the linking element is in the scope of a namespace declaration that sets up the `xlink:` namespace prefix.

57.2.1 *Link roles*

In HTML, link resources are either sources or destinations. The linking element is always the source. The resource referred to is always the destination. In XML, this rigid distinction is not hard-wired. An application can make either or both resources into sources or destinations.

Consider, for instance, if a Web browser made it possible to create notes about someone else's Web site and "stick" them on to it like Post-It notes. These *annotations* might be represented as XLink *extended* links as in Example 57-6.

Example 57-6. XLink annotations

```
<annotation xlink:type="extended"
       xlink:href="http://www.mynewspaper.com">
As usual, your editorial is filled with the kind of claptrap and
willywag that gives me the heebie-jeebies!
</annotation>
```

In this case, we actually want the application to make some form of clickable "hotspot" at the *other* end, on the newspaper's Web page. Of course we don't want them to have control of the actual linking element, or else they might just choose not to show our link. So we want the link to exist in one spot and create a "hotspot" at another. This is the opposite of traditional HTML links.

In order to reverse linking roles, we must somehow tell the application that we want it to do so. One way would be to use an element-type name that the application is hard-coded to understand as having that semantic. For instance an "annotation server" might only deal with `annotation` elements, or perhaps a few different variants, and would thus know exactly how to handle it.

Another way would be to use some form of stylesheet. But you would still need to have something special in the document that would differentiate annotations from other links (perhaps the annotation element-type name). The stylesheet would provide an extra level of translation to allow your private element-type names to be interpreted as annotations by software.

Yet another way to solve this problem would be to provide an attribute that describes the role of the link in the document and hypertext system.

Any of these are valid approaches, and the XLink specification provides a special `xlink:role` attribute to handle the last case. Example 57-7 is an example of that attribute in action.

Example 57-7. Role attribute

```
<hlink xlink:role="annotation"
    xlink:type="extended"
    xlink:href="http://www.mynewspaper.com">
As usual, your editorial is filled with the kind of claptrap and
willywag that gives me the heebie-jeebies!
</hlink>
```

In this case, the role designation has moved from the element-type name (now `hlink` instead of `annotation`) to the role attribute. Which is more appropriate will depend on your DTD, your software and your taste. XLink could perhaps dictate one style or the other, but real world usage is not that simple. For instance you might need to extend an industry standard DTD and thus have no control over element-type names. In another application, you might need to constrain the occurrence of certain kinds of linking elements, and thus need to use element-type names and content models.

57.2.2 *Is this for real?*

You might well ask whether all of this annotation stuff is likely to happen. After all, there are all sorts of social, technical and financial difficulties related to being able to annotate someone else's Web page. Imagine annotation spam: "Tired of reading this boring technical Web page? Click here for HOT PICS!!!"

It turns out that early versions of the pre-Netscape Mosaic browser allowed remote annotations (using a proprietary linking scheme), and you could share your annotations with friends or co-workers, but not with everybody on the Web. There are various other experimental services and products that provide the same ability for the modern-day Web. However, each uses a distinct link description notation so that they cannot share.

We may or may not get to the point where everybody can publish annotations to the whole world, but we already have the technology to create annotations that can be shared by other people we know. Unfortunately, this technology has never been widely deployed.[1] Perhaps when XLink is finalized and third-party annotation products are able to interoperate, Web pages will become generally annotatable and even more linkable than they are today.

So what can you do without a world-wide link database? Well let's say that your organization was considering buying a very expensive software product. You and your co-workers might agree to submit your opinions of the product specifications published on the vendor's Website. You could make a bunch of external links from the vendor's text to your comments on it and submit that to your organizational link database. When your co-workers go to see the page, their browsers can fetch your links and actually display them as if they were part of the original document. When your co-workers click on them, the browser will take them to your annotations.

In fact, with a reasonably large link database, you could annotate any Web page you came upon in this manner. When others from your organization came upon the page, they would see your annotations. In one sense, you are editing the entire Web! Of course, the bigger your organization is, the more points of view you can see on each page. On the other hand, sometimes you might not want to share all of your comments with the entire company, so you might have a smaller departmental database which is separate, and only shared by your direct co-workers. And of course at the opposite end of the spectrum, there might be a database for everyone on the Web (if we can make link database software that scales appropriately and find someone to run it).

External links can be useful even without a link database. Without such a database, there is no easy way to distribute your links to other people, so you must communicate the links' existence in some other way. For instance, you could include a critique of a Web page as an attachment to an email. You could also build a document full of links that annotated one of your own Web pages with links to glossary and bibliographic information. The XLink specification terms such a collection a *link base*. Depending on which link base the reader used, he would get either the glossary links or the bibliographic links or both sets of links overlapping. A link base is not a full database; it is an XML document that must be parsed before it can be used.

If it makes sense to "project" a link from your home computer onto an existing website, then surely it makes just as much sense to link two existing websites. For instance, we could make a link that is targeted towards mem-

---

1. One product that has recently taken another run at the problem is called Third Voice™.

bers of the SGML newsgroup that links the World Wide Web consortium's XML Web page to a related page we know about on the Web. This link would still have two ends, but both could be sources and destinations at the same time. If so, we would term that link *bidirectional,* because you could *traverse* it from either end. Because the link would exist on your Web site, but link two other pages, we would call it a *third-party* link. And if it makes sense to link two pages, then why not three, or four, or five? Extended links allow this.

57.2.3 *Link behaviors*

XML authors usually go out of their way to avoid putting information about formatting and other types of document behavior into XML documents. We've already been through all of the benefits of keeping your information "pure". As we have said, if you just mark up your documents according to their abstractions, you can apply formatting and other behavior through stylesheets.[1]

Even though it is usually best to put behavioral information in a stylesheet, XLink provides a more direct mechanism. There are some link behaviors that are so common – almost universal – that the XML working group decided that it should provide some attributes so that users could easily specify them. This facility removes a level of indirection and thereby makes hyperlinking a little bit easier. Still, one should think thrice about adding rendition attributes to abstract documents. The stylesheet is usually the best place to describe behavior and other presentational issues.

The most interesting type of link behavior is traversal. When you click on a hyperlink, you are traversing it. If a link is intended to embed information from one resource in another, then the process of actually accomplishing the embedding is a traversal.

The behavioral descriptions are still abstract enough to allow a variety of specific behaviors, depending on the situation. For example, a printer might interpret them differently from a Web browser. Although a printer might not seem like a machine that would care about hyperlinks, it might be use-

---

1. That is the theory, anyhow. At the time of writing, however, mainstream stylesheet languages did not support the recognition of XLinks or the execution of link behaviors. As we said in the introduction, XLinks are not quite there.

ful to have one that could directly print Web pages and their annotations, and that could access the images to print by traversing XLinks in the Web pages.

57.2.3.1   Show

As the name implies, the `xlink:show` attribute describes how the results of a link traversal should be shown. When you click on a Web link, that is a link traversal – one initiated by your click. On the other hand, if you have ever been to a site where a Web page comes up and says: "You will be forwarded to another page in just a few seconds", then that is a link traversal that is automatic. Typically on the Web, when a link is traversed (manually or automatically) it replaces the previous document in the Web browser window. XLink allows an author to request this behavior with the `replace` value of the `show` attribute:

Spec Excerpt (XLINK) 57-1. Replace

An application traversing to the ending resource should load the resource in the same window, frame, pane, or other relevant presentation context in which the starting resource was loaded.

For example see Example 57-8.

Example 57-8. A `replace` link

```
<A   xlink:type="simple"
     xlink:show="replace"
     xlink:href="http://www.gop.org/">
Click here to visit the GOP</A>
```

Occasionally you will also come across a link that actually opens a new window, so that after traversal there is a window for the new page in front

of the window for the old page. XLink allows this through the new value of
the show attribute.

Spec Excerpt (XLINK) 57-2. New

An application traversing to the ending resource should load it in a new
window, frame, pane, or other relevant presentation context.

Example 57-9 shows a link where the remote resource is launched into a
new window.

Example 57-9. A new link

```
<A xlink:type="simple"
   xlink:show="new"
   xlink:href="http://www.democrats.org/">
Click here to launch a new window and visit the the Dems.</A>
```

As we have seen, a link can represent *any* relationship. We discussed the
relationship between a document and an embedded graphic, but did not
discuss the XLink syntax for it yet. We can say that one resource should be
embedded in another using the embed option of the xlink:show attribute.
Example 57-10demonstrates.

Example 57-10. An embedded link

```
<MyEmbed xlink:type="simple"
   xlink:show="embed"
   xlink:href="http://www.democrats.org/platform.gif"/>
```

An embedded link can embed any datatype, not just graphics. You could
embed a movie, sound or even another XML document:

Example 57-11. An embedded XML document

```
<MyEmbed xlink:type="simple"
   xlink:show="embed"
   xlink:href="somedata.xml"/>
```

Note that this is not like embedding text using text entities. When you use text entities, the entire behavior of those entities is defined by the XML specification. The parser manages the expansion of entities according to well-defined rules. In the case of embed, the embedding rules are dictated by the application (which might delegate the decision to a stylesheet or configuration file). Valid behaviors might include textual inclusion (as with text entities), image-like embedding in a square box or something in between. The application could also decide whether the inclusion inherits font properties.

To summarize: the big difference between embed-style links and text entities is who controls the embedding. Text entities are expanded by the XML parser and the application has no control over it. Embedded links must be expanded by the application (browser, editor, B2B engine, video game, whatever).

There are two other values for xlink:show: other and none. In both cases, the author is telling the application that it is free to determine the behavior that will accompany the traversal. With other, however, the author is saying that other markup present in the link should guide that determination.

57.2.3.2   Actuate

The actuate attribute allows the author to describe when the link traversal should occur. For instance it could be user-triggered, such as by a mouse click or a voice command. Or else it could be automatic, such as the automatic embedding of a graphic, or an automatic forward to another Web page (e.g. "This page has moved. You will be directed to the new page momentarily.")

The onRequest value indicates that the traversal should be user-triggered. When it is combined with a a show attribute of replace, it is a typical, click-here-to-go-there link, at least in a graphical browser. On a text-based browser, it might be a type-this-number-to-go-there link. On a spoken-word browser it might be a say-this-number-to-go-there link.

When it is combined with a value of new it opens a new "context" (usually a browser window) at user command and leaves the old one open. When it is combined with a value of embed, the target resource is displayed embedded in the source, replacing the linking element.[1]

The `onLoad` value of the `actuate` attribute is used to specify that traversal should be done automatically when the document is loaded. For instance, most `show="embed"` links would specify automatic traversal. If you combine `show="new"` with `actuate="onLoad"`, then you can create a Web page that immediately opens another Web page. Perhaps with a stylesheet or other attribute, you could make them appear side by side. The final combination is `show="replace"` with `actuate="onLoad"`. You would use this to set up a "forwarding" link, such as the one we have described, and thus forward users from one page to another.

57.3 | Extended links

In this section, we will discuss more features of *extended links*. One that we have already discussed is the ability to specify them in third-party documents. Extended links also allow for more link ends, more advanced link roles, and other good stuff. We will also be able to re-describe the simple links that we have already seen in the terminology of the more general extended link system.

57.3.1 *Locator elements*

The first extension we will undertake is links with more than two link ends. Consider, for example, that you are redirecting users to several different interpretations of a text. For instance if there were two competitive schools of thought on a topic, each hotspot in the document might allow traversal to a different interpretation of the topic. Now you have three link ends, one for the source and one for each of the interpretations of it. Just as in real life, XLink allows you to make logical links among two or more concepts.

The first big difference between simple links and extended links is that we need to figure out how to specify the address of more than one destination link. We do this by putting *locator* subelements into the extended linking element. Example 57-12 demonstrates.

In this case, the three locators each address a resource. A sufficiently sophisticated browser displaying this document might represent each with

---

1. In hypertext terms, this is called a transclusion.

Example 57-12. Multi-ended link

```
<commentary xlink:type="extended">
   <locator xlink:type="locator"
            xlink:href="roberts.xml"
            xlink:role="analysis"/>
   <locator xlink:type="locator"
            xlink:href="beam.xml"
            xlink:role="rebuttal"/>
   <locator xlink:type="locator"
            xlink:href="goodwin.xml"
            xlink:role="precis"/>
<P>My fellow Americans, this speech will go down in history...</P>
</commentary>
```

an icon or supply a popup menu that allows access to each of the resources. It could even open a small window for each interpretation when the hotspot is selected. This could be controlled by a stylesheet or a behavior attribute. As you can see, each locator can have a different role, but they could also share roles. The role just specifies a semantic for processing the resource when processing the link, not some sort of unique identifier.

Locators can also have some other associated attributes. They can have titles, specified through a `xlink:title` attribute. These provide information for human consumption. The browser does not act on them. It merely passes them on to the human in some way, such as a popup menu, or text on the status bar. Locators can also have `show` and `actuate` behavior attributes with the same semantics as for a simple link. We will also show you how to use *arcs* to declare which resources can be the start of a traversable path and to which other resources the user can traverse.

Locators seem very similar to simple links because a simple link is a combination of a link, a locator, a resource and an arc. In fact, this is how they are defined in the XLink spec:

Spec Excerpt (XLINK) 57-3. Simple links

The purpose of a simple link is to be a convenient shorthand for the equivalent extended link. A single simple linking element combines the basic functions of an extended-type element, a locator-type element, an arc-type element, and a resource-type element.

A simple link automatically defines an arc between the local resource (the linking element) and the remote resource (the target of the `xlink:href` attribute). You do not need to add an arc-type element inside of it and in fact you are not allowed to.

It is both useful and convenient that simple links combine these things, but it means that we must be careful to keep the ideas separate in our heads. The link describes a relationship. The locators say what resources are being related. A simple link uses the linking element itself as one resource and the target of its `xlink:href` attribute as the other.

57.3.2 *Arcs*

An extended link can link many resources. You may not want to allow traversal from every resource to every other resource. In other words, you may want to restrict some *traversal paths*. XLink has a feature called arcs to allow this.

An arc defines an allowed traversal path. An arc is an element that exhibits a `xlink:type` attribute with the value `arc`. Arcs go directly within the content of the extended link element itself. If you have no arcs then all paths are traversable. If you have one, then only the paths defined by that one arc are traversable, and so forth.

If you have three resources in your link then you can have between zero and six arc elements. For instance, if your links are to Peter, Paul and Mary (or to their home pages!) then you may or may not want to allow traversal from (1) Peter to Paul, (2) Peter to Mary, (3) Paul to Peter, (4) Paul to Mary, (5) Mary to Peter and (6) Mary to Paul.

Of course, resources do not have names like Peter, Paul and Mary. Well, actually they can! We can give names to resources by putting an `xlink:label` attribute on the locators. This is shown in Example 57-13.

Now we can set up traversal paths between them. For instance if Peter and Paul have had a little fight, then they could both talk (traverse) to Mary but not to each other. Example 57-14 demonstrates.

It turns out that there is a shorter way to say the same thing. If we leave out the `xlink:from` attribute then an XLink processor is supposed to presume that all paths to the named resource are legal. See Example 57-15.

In this case traversal from both Peter and Paul to Mary is allowed. We might also want to allow the opposite. In that case we would use an arc with a `xlink:from` attribute with a value of "Mary" and no `xlink:to` attribute.

Example 57-13. Extended links with labels

```
<extendedlink xlink:type="extended">
  <loc xlink:type="locator"
       xlink:label="Peter"
       xlink:href="..."/>
  <loc xlink:type="locator"
       xlink:label="Paul"
       xlink:href="..."/>
  <loc xlink:type="locator"
       xlink:label="Mary"
       xlink:href="..."/>
</extendedlink>
```

Example 57-14. Peter and Paul traverse to Mary

```
<loc xlink:type="arc"
     xlink:from="Peter"
     xlink:to="Mary"/>
<loc xlink:type="arc"
     xlink:from="Paul"
     xlink:to="Mary"/>
```

Example 57-15. Abbreviated form of Example 57-14

```
<loc xlink:type="arc"
     xlink:to="Mary"/>
```

Just to round out our example, we might allow Peter to traverse to Paul but not the reverse. (Paul is a little sedentary). Example 57-16 shows what a complete extended link would look like in that case.

In this example, every path is traversable except Paul to Peter. You might wonder whether there is a more concise way to say this. For instance, you might expect an anti-arc element. There is no such thing. You always specify which paths are traversable. On the other hand, if you provide no arc elements at all, all paths are traversable.

57.4 | Linkbases

It is often useful to be able to process a group of hyperlinked documents all together. For instance, if one document contains some text and another contains a rebuttal of the text, the browser might want to show them "side

Example 57-16. Extended link with arcs

```
<extendedlink xlink:type="extended">
  <loc xlink:type="locator"
      xlink:label="Peter"
      xlink:href="..."/>
  <loc xlink:type="locator"
      xlink:label="Paul"
      xlink:href="..."/>
  <loc xlink:type="locator"
      xlink:label="Mary"
      xlink:href="..."/>
  <arc xlink:type="arc" xlink:from="Mary"/>
  <arc xlink:type="arc" xlink:to="Mary"/>
  <arc xlink:type="arc" xlink:from="Peter" xlink:to="Paul"/>
</extendedlink>
```

by side". It could also allow link traversals in one window to trigger the correct portion of the rebuttal in the other.

Such processing can only work if the browser knows about both documents at the same time. Linkbases allow you to tell the browser about all of the documents that should be processed together.

A *linkbase* element is an arc that associates one XML document with another XML document that serves as a linkbase. The linkbase is used as a source of links in addition to those in the original XML document.

Linkbases are distinguished from other arcs with an `xlink:arcrole` attribute. That attribute must have the value: `http://www.w3.org/1999/xlink/properties/linkbase`

We said before that simple links automatically define an arc. So the simplest way to declare a linkbase is with a simple link, as in Example 57-17.

Example 57-17. Reference to a linkbase

```
<xlink
  xlink:type="simple"
  xlink:arcrole="http://www.w3.org/1999/xlink/properties/linkbase"
  xlink:href="http://www.xxx.com/mylinks.xml" />
```

This will instruct an XLink processor that there are additional links to be found in the `mylinks.xml` file.

57.5 | Conclusion

XLink has the power to change the Web, and our lives, in unforeseeable ways. For more of the vision, see Chapter 42, "Extended linking", on page 592. For the current version of the spec, see the *XML SPECtacular* on the CD-ROM.

Datatypes

- ▌ Datatype requirements

- ▌ Built-in datatypes

- ▌ User-derived datatypes

- ▌ Using datatypes in DTDs

Contributing expert: Bob DuCharme, author of *XML: The Annotated Specification*, http://www.snee.com/bob/xmlann

P erhaps the most eagerly-awaited aspect of the W3C XML Schema project is the datatype work. It has been made a separate Part 2 of the XML Schema spec, with the intention "that it be usable outside of the context of XML Schema for a wide range of other XML-related activities".

In this chapter, we describe the basic concepts of XML datatypes and show how they can be used both in the XML Schema definition language (XSDL – Part 1 of the spec) and in one of those "other XML-related activities": XML 1.0 DTDs.

> *Caution*   XML Schema Datatypes are still under development. We present only the most basic and stable aspects in this chapter.

58.1 | Datatype requirements

Datatypes answer important questions about the description and validation of character data in element content or attribute values.

How do you say that a `date` element should contain content that conforms to the syntax `YYYY-MM-DD` or that an email address must be of the form `name@machine.domain.code`? How would you even say that a `description` element must not be empty?

A system to support datatypes must meet three requirements:

- First, you need a way for an application to know that an element type's content or an attribute's value is always supposed to be of a particular type. Ideally a programmer would not need to specially program knowledge about the datatypes into each application. Dates would just appear to the application code as date objects, integers as integer objects and so forth.
- Second, you need a way to validate that the data really conforms to the restrictions of the datatype. There should be no February 30 in a date, every email address needs an "@" symbol and so forth.
- Finally you need a way to define new datatypes. Just as XML allows you to define new element types, you would want to be able to define datatypes that are specific to your domain. A geographer might define a latitude/longitude notation. A mathematician might define a notation for matrices.

A datatype name is usually applied to both the conceptual object (the "abstract datatype") and its representation as a character string. That is, in markup language terms, datatypes are notations and XML's notation attribute type can be used to describe the datatype of an element's content.

However, there is no registry for data content notations so the full notation identifier for (e.g.) "real number" is not universally defined. Without that standardization, there is no way to create common software for validating real numbers in XML documents.[1]

---

1. Although techniques similar to mimetype and file extension associations are frequently used.

Furthermore, XML does not provide a language for defining new datatypes. You can refer to datatypes if you have a name for them but for all XML cares the "definition language" could be a regular expression, C++ code or Swahili. We need a standard for the definition language.

XML Schema Datatypes address these issues.

58.2 | XML Schema Datatypes

The DTD fragment in Example 58-1 shows the declaration for an attribute whose value is intended to be a year.

Example 58-1. Attribute declaration in a DTD

```
<!ATTLIST poem pubyear CDATA #IMPLIED>
<!-- Publication year should be four-digits -->
```

Although the pubyear value is supposed to represent a year, XML's set of attribute types cannot say that directly. All of the pubyear values in the start-tags shown in Example 58-2 would be valid.

Example 58-2. Legal pubyear CDATA values

```
<poem publisher="B and L" pubyear="1922">
<poem publisher="B and L" pubyear="0">
<poem publisher="B and L" pubyear="99999999999999999999999">
<poem publisher="B and L" pubyear="-3">
<poem publisher="B and L" pubyear="3.14159265">
<poem publisher="B and L" pubyear="1.0e+6">
<poem publisher="B and L" pubyear="Hello_World">
<poem publisher="B and L" pubyear=":">
<poem publisher="B and L" pubyear="----">
```

Wouldn't it be nice if the declaration for a pubyear attribute – or even for a pubyear element type –could specify that its value (or content) must be a four-digit number between 1000 and 2100?

This would make it easier to write robust applications that use that data. If your application must check whether this poem is in the public domain yet, it might add 75 to that pubyear value and compare the result with the current year to see if the poem is more than 75 years old.

You can only do this calculation reliably if you know that the value is an integer. You could do this by writing error-checking code, but one major goal of all schemas (including DTDs) is to reduce the need for custom error-checking code.

Programmers want to plug in an off-the-shelf, validating XML processor and have it check the mundane details of datatype conformance. When they get a weekly salary value out of a document they don't want to write code to make sure that it's a usable decimal floating point number before they subtract it from another number.

More importantly: end users want to be able to do the checks with off-the-shelf processors also. It is very common for programmers to forget or purposely leave out some checks. For instance you can make hundreds of mistakes in an HTML document and most browsers will load the HTML without a complaint! You can only find your mistakes by using an HTML validator.

Let's look at the datatypes the spec makes available so we can choose an appropriate one for the `pubyear` attribute.

58.2.1   *Built-in datatypes*

The XML Schema Datatypes spec defines two categories of datatype: primitive and derived. All of the former and several of the latter must be supported by every implementation of the spec; they are called *built-in datatypes* and are described in this section.

58.2.1.1   Primitive datatypes

The *primitive datatypes* are the building blocks of all others, as well as being useful themselves. The first four, which are shown in all uppercase letters below, come from XML.

- `ID`
- `IDREF`
- `ENTITY`
- `NOTATION`

The remaining XML attribute types are derived names and are discussed later.

Another important primitive datatype is based on the XML namespaces specification. It is called QName and stands for a namespace-qualified name. In other words, a QName is a name that may have a colon in it. If it does, the text before the colon should be a namespace prefix for a namespace that has been declared. If it does not, the names should be interpreted as belonging to the default namespace. See Chapter 53, "Namespaces", on page 788 for more information on namespaces.

The remaining primitive datatypes are common datatypes in most programming languages and database management systems.

string
> Equivalent to CDATA in a DTD.

boolean
> true and false values.

float
> Single precision 32-bit floating point numbers.

double
> Double precision 64-bit floating point numbers.

decimal
> arbitrary precision decimal numbers.

timeDuration
> Based on the SQL and ISO 8601 date format standards. It represents a length of time, such as "an hour" or "3.56 seconds". Durations can be represented with a precision of seconds or fractions of a second.

recurringDuration
> A timeDuration that recurs at a specific interval (also a timeDuration) starting from a specific time. For instance, a one-hour interview with a therapist, once a week, starting immediately after reading this.

binary
>   For non-textual data that has been encoded for representation in
>   XML. You could use a binary-containing element to embed a
>   bitmap image in an XML parsed (i.e., text) entity.

uriReference
>   Uniform Resource Identifier reference. These are a generalization
>   of the concept of URLs. See 56.2, "Uniform Resource Identifiers",
>   on page 862 for more information.

That is the complete list of primitive datatypes. All other datatypes
derive from these.

58.2.1.2   Derived datatypes

The *derived datatypes* are built from the primitive ones. The XML Schema
Datatypes spec defines some derived datatypes and provides facilities for
users to define their own.

The ones defined in the spec are listed below. They fall into a few categories. The first category is numeric types more specific than the primitive
types.

integer
>   Numbers with no fractional part.

positiveInteger
>   Numbers greater than zero

negativeInteger
>   Numbers less than zero.

nonPositiveInteger
>   Numbers less than one.

nonNegativeInteger
>   Numbers greater than negative one

byte
>   8-bit number (one between 127 and -128)

unsignedByte
    8-bit non-negative number (between 0 and 255)

short
    16-bit number (one between 32767 and -32768)

unsignedShort
    16-bit non-negative number (one between 0 and 65535)

int
    32-bit number (one between 2147483647 and -2147483649)

unsignedInt
    32-bit non-negative number (one between 0 and 4294967295)

long
    64-bit number (one between 9223372036854775807 and -9223372036854775808)

unsignedLong
    64-bit non-negative number (one between 0 and 18446744073709551615) (whew!)

These seemingly arbitrarily limited number sets are those that computers can handle with varying levels of efficiency. Everything from bytes to integers can be handled very efficiently on most modern computers. Longs can be handled efficiently on 64-bit computers and numbers bigger or smaller than longs are not very efficient to deal with (relatively speaking). If you can restrict your programs to dealing with efficient datatypes then you can *optimize* your program more easily.

Many of the other derived datatypes are based on times and dates.

timeInstant
    An instant of time.

time
    A time of day that recurs every day: "The bank opens at 10:30AM"

timePeriod

A period of time starting at one instant and continuing to another.

date

A `timePeriod` that starts at midnight of a specified day and lasts for 24 hours.

month

A `timePeriod` that starts at midnight on the first day of the month and lasts until the midnight that ends the last day of the month.

year

A `timePeriod` that starts at the midnight that starts the first day of the year and ends at the midnight that ends the last day of the year.

century

A `timePeriod` that starts at the midnight that starts the first day of the century and ends at the midnight that ends the last day of the century.

recurringDate

A date that recurs, such as your Mother's birthday (forgot, didn't you!)

recurringDay

A day of the month that recurs, such as payday (not likely to forget, are you!)

As we mentioned before, some derived types come from XML DTDs.

IDREFS

A list of IDREF values.

ENTITIES

A list of ENTITY values.

NMTOKEN
>A string with certain character constraints placed upon it.

NMTOKENS
>A list of NMTOKEN values.

Name
>An XML name, such as an element-type name or attribute name.

See 48.1.4, "Names and name tokens", on page 680 for more information on these XML names.

There is also a derived type called NCName. This stands for no-colon name which means (drum roll please...) a name with no colons in it. You can use this when you want to avoid namespace behavior in a datatype.

The final built-in derived datatype is language. It represents a spoken language. See 51.4, "Special attributes and newlines", on page 770.

58.2.2 *User-derived datatypes*

In addition to the built-in datatypes, the spec provides a means of creating *user-derived datatypes*.

Users derive a datatype by defining it in the XML Schema definition language. Usually they do so by adding constraints to an existing datatype.

For example, we can define a user-derived datatype to solve our pubyear problem, as shown in Example 58-3. The datatype element defines a pubYear datatype as a year that must fall between 1000 and 2100.

Example 58-3. Defining a restricted range integer datatype

```
<simpletype base="year" name="pubYear">
  <minInclusive value="1000"/>
  <maxInclusive value="2100/>
</simpletype>
```

You can also define a datatype as a named list of allowable values by using an enumeration element. In Example 58-4, we define a daysOfWeek datatype.

Note that in a datatype definition, the simpletype element has a base attribute which defines the base type. Here, the base type is a primitive

Example 58-4. Defining an enumerated datatype

```
<simpletype name="daysOfWeek" base="string">
  <enumeration>
    <literal>Monday</literal>
    <literal>Tuesday</literal>
    <literal>Wednesday</literal>
    <literal>Thursday</literal>
    <literal>Friday</literal>
    <literal>Saturday</literal>
    <literal>Sunday</literal>
  </enumeration>
</simpletype>
```

datatype (*string*), but it doesn't have to be – a user-derived type can be based on any datatype, whether it is primitive, derived or even user-derived.

58.3 | Using datatypes

Although XML Schema Datatypes were originally designed for use with XSDL, they can also be used with DTDs.

58.3.1 *XML Schema definition language (XSDL)*

XSDL is described in some detail in Chapter 59, "XML Schema (XSDL)", on page 908. It is sufficient for our purposes here to say that the spec defines how to represent a document type schema using another XML document.

In Example 58-5, the `pubYear` datatype is defined as it was in Example 58-3. A `pubyearattr` attribute is declared that uses that datatype.

Example 58-5. Defining and using a user-derived datatype

```
<simpletype base="year" name="pubYear">
  <minInclusive value="1000"/>
  <maxInclusive value="2100/>
</simpletype>

<attribute name="pubyearattr" required="false" type="pubYear/>
```

58.3.2 *XML DTDs*

Since XML Schema Datatypes were designed after DTDs[2], there is no built-in provision in DTD declarations for declaring the use of datatypes. Instead, users and software developers have adopted a convention for making the association.

Tip   This convention is supported by open source software available on the CD-ROM, and by the XML Authority schema editor described in Chapter 35, "Building a schema for a product catalog", on page 498, a trial version of which is also available on the CD-ROM.

The convention uses two reserved attribute names:

e-dtype

> The value of this attribute is the name of the datatype for the element's data content. The attribute is only declared if the element type has a datatype for its data content. In a valid document, it should be declared as a fixed attribute.

a-dtype

> The value of this attribute is the names of the datatypes for all the attributes that have datatypes. In order to link each attribute with its datatype, the a-dtype attribute value is a list of pairs, each attribute name being followed by its datatype name. The attribute is only declared if the element type has a datatype for one or more of its attributes. In a valid document, it should be declared as a fixed attribute.

If a datatype is not a built-in datatype, you can optionally declare a notation of the same name to reference its definition. An implementation can use that information to invoke the software program that checks and/or processes the data.

---

2. About 30 years after, but who's counting.

In Example 58-6, the `a-dtype` attribute declares the datatypes for the `pubyear` and `linecount` attributes. The datatype of `linecount` is built-in, but the datatype of `pubyear` is user-derived so there is a NOTATION declaration that references its definition.

Example 58-6. Declaring datatypes for attributes

```
<!NOTATION pubYear          SYSTEM "datatypeDefs.xml/pubYear">
<!ATTLIST  poem
           a-dtype   CDATA #FIXED "pubyear    pubYear
                                   linecount nonNegativeInteger"
           pubyear   CDATA #IMPLIED
           linecount CDATA #IMPLIED >
```

58.4 | Conclusion

The XML world has long awaited a standard for defining datatypes. XML Schema Part 2 finally provides this facility. These datatypes can be used in XSDL schema definitions and may also be referenced from DTDs.

XML Schema (XSDL)

Tad Tougher Tutorial

- ▌ Syntax and element declarations

- ▌ Complex types

- ▌ Other new capabilities

Contributing expert: Bob DuCharme, author of *XML: The Annotated Specification*, http://www.snee.com/bob/xmlann

X ML's Document Type Definition mechanism serves many important purposes in real XML systems. DTDs allow us to check XML documents for conformance to strict rules.

The DTD is a specific case of a more general concept called a schema definition. The dictionary defines schema as a "general conception of what is common to all members a class." A schema definition takes that "conception" and turns it into something concrete that can be used directly by a computer.

There are many types of schema in use in the computer industry, chiefly for databases. DTDs are unique in that the class for which they declare "what is common to all members" is a class of XML/SGML documents.

This chapter will review the roles of DTDs and other schemas and then discuss a new schema definition language being developed by the World Wide Web Consortium: XML Schema definition language (XSDL). People often use the word "schema" to mean a particular schema definition in this language. Sometimes they also mean a schema conforming to one of the early Microsoft schema languages, "XML-Data" or "XML Schema Reduced". Terminology is always tricky in evolving areas!

Caution   The XML Schema spec is still in development and is subject to change. This chapter only covers the high level concepts and not the details. It should be considered a preview of the main concepts and not a definitive reference.

59.1 | DTDs and schemas

DTDs allow "mere mortals" to define XML-based languages for representing documents of various types. The languages consist of a vocabulary of element type and attribute names and rules for their combination. Using DTDs, mortals can check XML representations of documents for conformance to those languages.

Were it not for DTDs, you would have to trust a particular piece of application software to tell you whether the data you created is conforming. For example only *MS Word* can say for sure whether a file is a legal *Word* document.

With DTDs ordinary users can consult a "neutral third party", a validating XML parser. The validating parser could be used on its own or as a component embedded in a software application.

It is common for the code for a single validating parser to be embedded in hundreds of different software products. This means that these parsers are usually very well tested. Even in the unlikely event that a parser has a bug, XML 1.0 and XML DTDs are so simple that you could easily check your data by hand.

We admit, it would be tedious. The important thing is that you could do it without special tools or a degree in rocket science. In a very real sense, you own your XML application's document types because you do not need to depend on a black box to validate for you. A document either conforms to a DTD or it does not, and DTDs are simple enough that we humans can check for ourselves.

59.1.1 *Next generation schemas*

But simplicity isn't the only virtue, especially among those who are trained to deal with complexity. The popularity of XML has brought SGML and DTDs to entirely new constituencies. The database experts and programmers who are taking to XML in droves are examining it from the standpoint of their own areas of expertise and familiar paradigms.

All of these creative folks have ideas about what could be done differently. Not everyone will agree what should be different but everyone has ideas. The World Wide Web Consortium is trying to incorporate these ideas into a design for an enhanced schema definition facility called the *XML Schema definition language (XSDL)*.[1]

XSDL addresses four major areas of potential improvement:

Datatypes

> Datatypes are now the subject of a separate Part 2 of the XML Schema spec and were discussed in Chapter 58, "Datatypes", on page 894.

Namespaces

> Namespaces were invented after DTDs[2] and are not fully supported by them. This subject was discussed in Chapter 53, "Namespaces", on page 788.

Syntax

> XML DTDs are represented in a dedicated notation that is a subset of SGML's DTD declarations. As XML documents are such an excellent vehicle for representing structured abstractions, many feel that schema definitions should be XML documents as well.

---

1. The name is often shortened to XML Schema, but we reserve that name for the W3C spec. We call the language XSDL so you'll know when we are referring to the "schema definition language" as opposed to a particular "schema definition" or a conceptual "schema". The words "XML schema", unfortunately, could refer to any of those four things.
2. About 30 years after, but who's counting.

Greater expressiveness
Schema definitions will be able to express constraints that are not supported by existing DTD declarations.

In this chapter we will discuss the two items not addressed elsewhere – syntax and expressiveness – in the context of XSDL. Expressiveness is by far the more interesting of the two, so let's get the syntax issue out of the way.

59.1.2 *XSDL syntax*

Many consider the DTD syntax to be too different from the rest of XML. People ask: "If XML elements and attributes can be used to represent any kind of information, why not use XML to represent XML schema definitions?" In other words, why not represent DTDs in an element-based syntax? You could have element types for element type declarations, element types for attribute declarations and so forth. Computer programmers really like this sort of recursion.

One virtue of this approach is that tools for manipulating XML elements automatically become tools for manipulating DTD declarations. One downside is that the schema definitions typically become much larger and (arguably) harder to read. There are other arguments both for and against this idea but for the time being they are moot. The recursionists have won and XSDL uses XML element syntax.

59.2 | A simple sample schema

We will explain schemas by introducing a sample DTD to use as a baseline, then developing an equivalent schema and comparing the two.

59.2.1 *Baseline DTD*

The sample DTD in Example 59-1 demonstrates how some of XML 1.0's most important features are used in a DTD. Comparing this DTD with the XSDL equivalent will give us a baseline to work from.

Example 59-1. Poem DTD

```
<!ELEMENT  poem  (title, picture, verse+)>
<!ATTLIST  poem
    publisher CDATA      #IMPLIED
    pubyear   NMTOKEN    #IMPLIED
    xmlns     CDATA      #FIXED "http://www.poetry.net/poetns"
>
<!ELEMENT  title    (#PCDATA)>
<!ELEMENT  verse    (#PCDATA)>
<!ELEMENT  picture  EMPTY>
<!ATTLIST  picture  href      CDATA #REQUIRED
                    a-dtype   CDATA #FIXED "href uriReference">
```

The DTD defines a `poem` element type that consists of a `title` element followed by a `picture` and one or more `verse` elements. The poem element type has two optional attributes: `publisher` and `pubyear`. The namespace is fixed in the DTD for reasons discussed in Chapter 53, "Namespaces", on page 788>.

The `picture` element type's required `href` attribute is declared as a CDATA attribute. We use the "Datatypes for DTDs" convention (58.3.2, "XML DTDs", on page 905) to require that the attribute always have a URL value. (This convention is only enforced by applications; open-source code for doing so is provided on the CD-ROM.)

Example 59-2. Poem document

```
<!DOCTYPE poem SYSTEM "poem.dtd">
<poem publisher="Boni and Liveright" pubyear="1922">
<title>The Waste Land</title>
<picture href="pic1.gif"/>
<verse>April is the cruellest month, breeding</verse>
<verse>Lilacs out of the dead land</verse>
</poem>
```

Example 59-2 shows a document that conforms to the DTD in Example 59-1.

59.2.2 *Declaring an element type*

Example 59-3 is an XSDL definition for the poem document type.

Example 59-3. XSDL definition

```
<schema xmlns="http://www.w3.org/1999/XMLSchema"
        xmlns:poem="http://www.poetry.net/poetns"
    targetNamespace="http://www.poetry.net/poetns">
  <element name="poem">
    <complexType>
      <sequence>
        <element ref="poem:title"/>
        <element ref="poem:picture"/>
        <element ref="poem:verse" maxOccurs="unbounded"/>
      </sequence>
      <attribute name="publisher" type="string"/>
      <attribute name="pubyear" type="NMTOKEN"/>
    </complexType>
  </element>
  <element name="title" type="string"/>
  <element name="verse" type="string"/>
  <element name="picture">
    <complexType content="empty">
      <attribute name="href" use="required" type="uriReference"/>
    </complexType>
  </element>
</schema>
```

The most noticeable thing about the example is that instead of using the syntax of XML 1.0 DTD declarations, it represents a schema definition as a well-formed XML document.

The root element type is named schema. It requires a namespace declaration for the schema namespace so that the elements can be recognized as belonging to that namespace. It requires a namespace declaration for the poetry namespace with the prefix poem so that elements from that namespace can be referred to in this schema. Finally it declares that the "target namespace" (the namespace of elements that can be validated by this schema) is the poetry namespace.

Just as our DTD example had four element-type declarations, the schema definition has four element elements: poem, title, verse and picture. These perform the same task: they declare the element types that can be used in documents conforming to this schema.

The title and verse declarations tell us that the content of elements of these types must conform to the string datatype (i.e., character data). You can see how datatypes and schemas work together: we can use datatypes both for element content and for attributes.

We saw the range of possibilities offered by the type attribute in Chapter 58, "Datatypes", on page 894. This includes user-derived types.

59.2.2.1 Content models

Consider the poem element-type declaration in Example 59-3. It represents the content model with a sequence element, which defines a poem element to contain a title, a picture, and one or more verse elements, in that order. The sequence element identifies these content element types by using element elements[1], which in this case refer to element types declared elsewhere in the schema.

Element elements are sometimes definitions and are sometimes references. In this case, they are references rather than declarations because they have ref attributes instead of name attributes. The reference for verse states that it may have multiple occurrences through its maxOccurs attribute. There is a corresponding minOccurs that defaults to "1" – meaning at least one is required by default.

There are other element types that can be used to define a content model. They also may have minOccurs and maxOccurs. Here is the full list:

- sequence (like XML ",")
- choice (like XML "|")
- any (like XML "ANY")
- group (no XML equivalent)
- all (like SGML "&")
- element (like referring to an XML element type)

The last three require more explanation. The group element allows a reference to a group of elements defined somewhere else in the document. This allows you to use content model constructs over and over in different parts of the schema.

all requires all of the elements within the model but allows them to be in any order. The all element type has no equivalent in an XML content model. It is one of the SGML facilities that was not included in the XML 1.0 design.

---

1. Yes, element elements.

We have already seen `element`. It is used to refer to element types defined elsewhere in the document or to define an element type.

Like `sequence`, a `choice` or `all` model can use `element` elements with `ref` attributes to refer to element types declared elsewhere in the schema. A content model group can also be defined in a stand-alone, top-level `group` element, and element type declarations can then refer to this named model group when defining their content models.

For more complex content models, content model groupings can be nested. For example, we can duplicate the XML 1.0 content model `(title,picture,verse+, (footnotes|bibliography))` with a `choice` element within a `sequence` element as shown in Example 59-4.

Example 59-4. Sequence with nested choice

```
<sequence>
  <element ref="poem:title"/>
  <element ref="poem:picture"/>
  <element ref="poem:verse" maxOccurs="unbounded"/>
  <choice>
    <element ref="poem:footnotes"/>
    <element ref="poem:bibliography"/>
  </choice>
</sequence>
```

59.2.2.2   Empty element types

The `picture` element type declared in Example 59-5 uses the `content="empty"` attribute declaration to declare that picture elements should all be empty.

Example 59-5. Picture declaration

```
<element name="picture" content="empty">
  ...
</element>
```

We can also declare an element to have content of `textOnly` (for only text), `elementOnly` (for only sub-elements) and `mixed` for a mix of both.

59.2.3 *Declaring attributes*

The poem and picture element type declarations both contain attribute declarations equivalent to those in our original DTD. Example 59-6 shows declarations for the poem element type's optional publisher and pubyear attributes.

Example 59-6. Attribute declarations

```
<attribute name="publisher" type="string"/>
<attribute name="pubyear" type="NMTOKEN"/>
```

They are optional because there is no use attribute in their definitions. You can also make them required with use="required", fixed with use="fixed" and defaultable with use="default".

As we saw in Chapter 58, "Datatypes", on page 894, available datatypes include not just the usual XML attribute types like NMTOKEN, ID, IDREF, ENTITY, and ENTITIES, but also traditional programming datatypes such as integer, real, date, boolean and string. Even better, we could include a precise datatype definition for pubyear.

Example 59-7. URI reference attribute

```
<attribute name="href" use="required" type="uriReference"/>
```

Example 59-7 shows the declaration of the href attribute of the picture element. This has a datatype of uriReference.

Attribute declarations can also be grouped into a stand-alone attributeGroup element. An element type declaration can then refer to a named attribute group when defining its own attributes.

59.2.4 *Declaring schema conformance*

How does an XML document tell a processor that it conforms to a particular XSDL schema definition? It doesn't!

That's because it is not a *valid* document, just *well-formed*, and there is no standardized means by which a merely well-formed document can identify its schema definition. This fact is true regardless of the schema definition syntax. Since the schema isn't identified, it could as well be a DTD as an XSDL document.

This is an important feature in a security-constrained application. It may be important for you to know that a document conforms to a particular DTD or schema in order to ensure that it does not crash your commerce server. That means you, as the document recipient, want to validate the document against your own trusted copy of the schema definition.

You can determine which DTD or schema definition to use from the document's namespace, root element type, filetype, or other cues.[1] The sender may also provide you with the name through an API, command line, or graphical interface. Eventually, a trusted repository may supply the schema or DTD, as we described in Chapter 38, "Repositories and vocabularies", on page 534.

59.3 | Additional capabilities

So far we have pretty much just taken concepts from a DTD and represented them as XML elements conforming to the schema document type. Schemas get more interesting when they allow us to do things that are difficult or impossible in XML DTDs. We'll now look at those additional functions.

59.3.1 *Locally-scoped element types*

Any element type in an XML DTD can be referenced in any other element type's content model. So if you define `title` you can use it in chapters, sections and anywhere else that you see fit to use it.

Once you have defined your DTD, authors can use the `title` element in each of the contexts that you have specified. In each of those contexts the element type is exactly the same: it has the same name, attributes and allowed content.

XSDL has a facility that allows you to say that titles in one context should have a different attribute set and content model from titles in

---

1. Even if the document is, in fact, valid, you can ignore any declarations that it contains or references.

another. In effect, you can declare two element types with the same name. The name is *bound* to a different element type definition in each context.

You can do this by declaring an element type within the declaration for another element type. Example 59-8 shows two different title element types declared within the same schema. They each use a different user-derived datatype.

Example 59-8. Two locally-scoped title declarations

```
<element name="book">
    <sequence>
      <element name="title">
        <attribute name="booktitle" use="required" type="string"/>
        <attribute name="ISBN" use="required" type="ISBNFormat"/>
      </element>
      <element ref="chapter"/>
    </sequence>
</element>
<element name="employee">
  <sequence>
    <element name="empId"/>
    <element name="title">
      <sequence>
       <element ref="jobtitle"/>
       <element ref="company"/>
      </sequence>
    </element>
  </sequence>
</element>
```

In documents conforming to this schema, a title element within a book element must conform to the title element type declared within the book element type declaration, complete with the required ISBN and booktitle attribute values.

A title element within an employee element, however, must conform to the title element type declared inside the example's employee element type declaration.

59.3.2 *Element types versus types*

In a DTD, element type declarations associate a name with an element type definition. In an XSDL schema definition, the element type definition either refers to a type through a `type` attribute (as with `title` in Example 59-3) or through a `complexType` or `simpleType` subelement of the `element` element itself.

There is a subtle distinction here. "Element types" are different from "types". A type becomes an element type only when it is associated with an element type name. In an XML DTD, a type is defined in the same declaration that associates it with an element type name. Therefore a type can't be used with more than one element type name.

In XSDL, though, types can be defined independently and associated with more than one element type name, even the same name in multiple different contexts. We will often do this for *complex types*: types that have multiple parts. For example an `address` type is a good example of a complex type because it has multiple parts: street, state, etc. You could have two element types `billingAddress` and `shippingAddress` that both have the same type.

The closest similar feature in a DTD is parameter entities (Chapter 50, "Entities: Breaking up is easy to do", on page 736), which allow you to reuse content model parts and attribute declaration text. The underlying mechanism is simple string substitution. However, the fact that part of a declaration comes from a parameter entity is merely syntactic; it is not part of the structural model of the DTD. Graphical DTD editors, for example, have a hard time representing models constructed in this way.

Types, in contrast, are an explicitly structured way to share content models and attribute declarations. This explicit structuring makes them easier to work with in graphical editors and other schema manipulation tools. More importantly, it provides better control over the use of the types themselves.

59.3.2.1   Reusable definitions

Example 59-9 shows the definition of an `address` type. It is so much like an element type declaration that if you replaced its `complexType` start- and end-tags with `element` ones it would still be perfectly valid.

Example 59-10 shows two element type declarations that use the independently-defined `address` type.

The `shippingAddr` and `billingAddr` element type declarations both refer to the `address` type as their *base type*. They also add something. Each adds a new attribute, making them customized versions of an address. The

Example 59-9. An address type

```
<complexType name="address">
   <sequence>
     <element ref="line1"/>
     <element ref="line2"/>
     <element ref="city"/>
     <element ref="state"/>
     <element ref="zip"/>
   </sequence>
   <attribute name="id" type="ID"/>
</complexType>
```

Example 59-10. Element type declarations with external type

```
<element name="shippingAddr">
  <complexType base="address">
    <attribute name="attn" use="required" type="string"/>
  </complexType>
</element>
<element name="shippingAddr">
  <complexType base="address">
    <attribute name="custID" use="required" type="ID"/>
  </complexType>
</element>
```

content models of these elements are identical, but they have different additional attributes.

This example shows some of the power of complex types: we can create structural definitions as re-usable units that make element declaration and maintenance easier. Types are similar to the virtual or abstract classes used in object-oriented programming environments.

Types do not define element types that will be used directly. You cannot create an address element in a document. Instead the type is a set of reusable constraints that can be used as building blocks in an element type declaration. Only elements whose element types are actually declared can appear in the document.

59.3.2.2   Type extension

We can take the object-oriented analogy even further. *type extension* describes the concept of creating a new type or element as a variation on an existing one (or a variation on a combination of several existing ones). This is much the way object-oriented classes inherit from other classes. The new type or element will have a content model that is an extension of the type's.

Example 59-11 shows a new complex type, `internationalAddress`. It adds a new child element, called `countryCode`, to the `address` type.

Example 59-11. One type extends another

```
<complexType name="internationalAddr"
             base="address"
             derivedBy="extension">
  <element ref="countryCode"/>
</complexType>
```

With this definition, an `internationalAddr` is just like an `address`, but after specifying the details of the `address` you must also specify a `countryCode`.

You can also derive a type by *restriction*. That means that you add constraints, such as making an attribute or subelement required when it was previously optional.

59.3.3 *Schema inclusion*

XML 1.0 DTDs can share text by means of external parameter entities. For example, the `common` parameter entity declared and referenced in Example 59-12 tells an XML processor to treat the DTD as if the two lines of Example 59-13 had been inserted at the fourth line.

Example 59-12. DTD with an external parameter entity reference

```
<!ELEMENT  book    (title,chapter+)>
<!ELEMENT  chapter (title,par+)>
<!ENTITY % common  SYSTEM "common.dtd">
%common;
```

Example 59-13. `common.dtd` file referenced in Example 59-12

```
<!ELEMENT title (#PCDATA)>
<!ELEMENT par   (#PCDATA)>
```

The *schema inclusion* facility works similarly. It allows a schema definition to treat another schema definition's contents as part of its own. Example 59-14 uses the `include` element to incorporate element type declarations from the schema in Example 59-15. The declarations are thenceforth treated as part of the `book.xsd` schema.

Example 59-14. `book.xsd` schema including declarations from `common.xsd`

```
<schema>
  <include schemaLocation="common.xsd"/>
  <element name="book">
    <sequence>
      <element ref="title"/>
      <element ref="chapter" maxOccurs="unbounded"/>
    </sequence>
  </element>
  <element name="chapter">
    <sequence>
      <element ref="title"/>
      <element ref="par" maxOccurs="unbounded"/>
    </sequence>
  </element>
</schema>
```

Example 59-15. *common.xsd* schema

```
<schema>
  <element name="title" type="string"/>
  <element name="par" type="string"/>
</schema>
```

59.3.4   *Other capabilities*

Several other capabilities are planned for XSDL but are not presently fully-defined.

59.3.4.1   Documentation

Schemas currently offer the same kind of commenting that you can put in DTDs: anything you put inside of `<!-- -->` is ignored by the processor. To publish external documentation for the schema, an automated process using the DOM or SAX interface (or even scanning the unparsed text) could find these comments easily enough. However, in the absence of an agreed convention, it would have no clue as to their purpose.

It is intended that schemas provide the opportunity to add structured documentation. This will probably come in the form of specialized element types, to be used within the various schema declaration elements, that describe supplemental information about the declarations. These might include their purpose, author, last date updated, and so forth. These documentation elements will allow an automated process similar to the *javadoc* program, to generate usable, formatted documentation from a schema definition.

59.3.4.2   Schema evolution

Once a schema – any kind of schema, whether for XML documents, a relational database, or an object-oriented database – is written and put into production, making efficient, backward-compatible changes to that schema can be difficult.

How difficult? Computer scientists do thesis work on it.

Addressing the potential problems of schema evolution in the W3C spec is an ambitious but eminently worthwhile objective.

59.3.4.3   Conformance

The conformance clause of the spec is where details are provided about the means of determining whether a schema conforms to the schema specification and whether a document conforms to a given schema. Among the issues are distinguishing fatal errors from non-fatal errors, the responsibilities of schema-aware processors, and the exact information that we can count on a schema to represent.

These are gory details to be sure, but crucial to a spec that hopes to provide a reliable basis for a range of software applications that plan on being compatible with each other.

Resources

- Software featured on the Covers
- Free IBM alphaWorks software
- Free XML software on the CD-ROM
- XML specifications on the CD-ROM
- Other XML-related books

Part Fifteen

On the back cover of the first edition of this book, an inspired copywriter wrote: "The accompanying CD-ROM brings together an amazing set of XML resources."

As authors, we of course don't engage in such hyperbole, except on behalf of technologies that excite us. However, we feel obligated to make the purely factual observation that the CD-ROM for this edition is far superior to the first. In fact, there are two of them!

There are over 175 free XML software packages, compared to 55 in the first edition. Please note that we use the word "free" very precisely. We mean genuinely free use, XML-centric, no time limit, uncrippled software, that is usable with your own documents.

In addition, there are 27 contributors to the Sponsor Showcase, compared to 14 in that edition. Their materials include more free software, plus trial versions of major commercial products for your evaluation, and white papers, live demos, and examples.

Plus there are XML-related standards and specs and clickable directories of Web sources for free software and more specifications.

And if you like to read actual books, this part includes a reader's guide to other books in this series.

Free resources on the CD-ROM

Resource Description

▌ Over 175 free software packages

▌ IBM alphaWorks XML software suite

▌ XML SPECtacular

Contributing experts: Lars Marius Garshol, David A. Epstein, and Daniel Jue

928

Do you really need 175 XML software packages? Not likely, but our two CD-ROMs will save a lot of download time while you decide which you do need. Most are described in this chapter, along with the specifications that are on the CDs.

The two CD-ROMs that supplement The XML Handbook contain a wide variety of resources. There is free trial software, genuine freeware with no time limit, demos, white papers, markup and code samples, product information from our sponsors, and the full text of the most important standards and specifications.

We describe most of the free software and specs in this chapter, but not all of it; you'll need to dig into the discs for the rest.

Enjoy!

60.1 | Software featured on the covers

In this section, we briefly describe the free software and trialware that our sponsors feature on the covers of the book. We specify the platforms supported and, if it is trialware, the time limit or other usage description.

60.1.1   *XMLSolutions Corporation free software*

XMLSolutions Corporation has provided two free XML products on the CD-ROM.

60.1.1.1   *ExeterXML Server*

The *ExeterXML Server* is an XML-capable Web server that can serve XML documents to any client software, regardless of whether or not the client understands XML. The product is the centerpiece of XMLSolutions' *ExeterXML* e-commerce software suite, where it is used to serve XML documents in business-to-business e-commerce transactions. However, it can also operate independently and owners of *The XML Handbook* may use it freely.

The CD contains a free binary distribution, ready to install on any *Solaris*™ 2.5.1, 2.6, or 2.7 platform, Linux, and Windows NT.

60.1.1.2   *XMLZip*

XMLZip reduces the size of XML files while retaining accessibility through the DOM API, thereby allowing applications to access the data in its compressed form. In addition, XMLZip is capable of selective compression and decompression of the files, allowing users to determine the DOM level at compression time.

The CD-ROM contains a free distribution, which runs on any operating systems that support JDK 1.1.8. It is ready to install on any Solaris 2.5.1 platform or higher, Linux Red Hat 5.2 with Kernel 2.0.36 or higher, and Windows NT.

60.1.2   *IBM alphaWorks XML software suite*

This suite of free software contains a wide variety of programs, most of which will run on any Java platform.

The programs are described in the next section of this chapter.

60.1.3 *Adobe FrameMaker+SGML XML/ SGML editor/formatter*

FrameMaker+SGML 6.0 is a tool for editing and formatting long, complex publications such as books, manuals, and catalogs. It can convert documents to XML, HTML, and PDF for publishing electronically and on the Web. The product offers both a WYSIWYG formatted interface and a document-tree structured interface; both can be used simultaneously.

The tryout version on the CD-ROM is fully functional, except that Save As is disabled and printing is not possible. There is no time limit. The tryout version is available for the Mac, Windows, HP-UX, and IBM AIX platforms. Also included is product information, customer case stories, tutorials, and other materials.

60.1.4 *eXcelon Stylus XSL stylesheet manager*

eXcelon *Stylus* is an integrated environment for creating, managing and maintaining XSL stylesheets. Stylus assists initial development with its built-in knowledge of XSL commands, and eases maintenance through various debugging techniques.

The trial version on the CD-ROM runs on Windows 2000 or NT with Internet Explorer 5.0 or later. It may be used for 30 days.

60.1.5 *Extensibility XML Authority schema editor*

XML Authority is a graphical development tool for creating and modifying XML schemas, and for converting other data structures to XML schemas. The product can support DTDs, and can export DTDs and such other schema notations as XML-Data, XDR, DCD, SOX, and DDML.

The trial version on the CD-ROM runs on Windows 95/98 and Windows NT. There is no time limit, but the trial is limited to ten uses of the product.

60.1.6 *infoShark ViewShark XML relational data viewer*

ViewShark allows you to examine, subset, and merge data from Oracle and Microsoft *SQL Server* databases, as well as XML files formatted in the CARD (Commerce Accelerated Relational Data) schema. Since a CARD XML file describes the database structure, *ViewShark* is able to read the data as if it were in a relational database. *ViewShark* can also export data in such formats as *Excel*, tab or CSV text, and HTML tables.

The trial version on the CD-ROM comes with a sample database of CARD files and can be installed in any Windows environment. It may be used for 30 days.

60.1.7 *Arbortext Adept Editor LE*

Epic Editor LE allows authors to write text, develop tables, place graphics, and create a wide variety of business and technical documents. It supports multiple levels of undo, cut and paste, drag-and-drop editing, split screen views and multiple windows. The in-line table editor supports HTML, CALS, OASIS and Arbortext table formats

The free trial runs in any Windows environment. It may be used for 30 days.

60.1.8 *Enigma INSIGHT XML publishing software*

INSIGHT is software for automating the electronic publishing process. It turns large-document collections into intelligent cross-indexed and hyperlinked publications that can be distributed on the Internet, on intranets, and on CD-ROM.

The personal version on the CD-ROM runs on Windows 95/98 and Windows NT. It has no time limit, but publications can be viewed only with the product; they cannot be distributed for viewing with Web browsers or on CD.

60.2 | IBM alphaWorks

IBM *alphaWorks* is a team dedicated to speeding emerging IBM technology to the marketplace, from fields as diverse as management and transaction functions, networking, security, and power management.

Its website operates on a unique premise.

60.2.1 *The alphaWorks idea*

The *alphaWorks* website is a focal point for bidirectional communication with early adopters of strategic emerging technologies. At the site, users can download "alpha-code" implementations of those technologies. More importantly, they can also access and provide feedback to IBM's top researchers and developers, through the site's technology discussion forums.

alphaWorks serves as one of IBM's primary channels for the distribution of XML technology. You can find several different categories of XML technology at the site.

1. One of the main categories, which fulfills one of *alphaWorks'* primary goals, is implementations that track the important W3C Recommendations and other related XML specifications. One of the objectives in providing these implementations is to have them available in a timely manner, often the same day that Recommendations (proposed and final, and early Notes) become public.

2. In addition to these implementations of the important XML specifications, the site also serves as a distribution point for example applications that make use of these specifications.

3. *alphaWorks* also serves as a proving ground in which experimental new XML technologies are introduced and evaluated. User feedback is monitored directly by the research and development staff, and updated according to the comments supplied by users.

4. Finally, the site offers a variety of tools and components that provide a bridge between the XML and Java spaces.

60.2.2   *XML at alphaWorks*

The list of emerging XML technologies on *alphaWorks* is already quite long and growing almost daily. Rather than try to list all of them, we'll briefly describe a representative selection. They are all included on the accompanying CD-ROM.

Bean Markup Language

Bean Markup Language (BML) is an XML-based component configuration (wiring) language for the JavaBean component model. BML is directly executable; i.e., processing a BML script results in a running application configured as described in the script. BML has elements for describing the creation of new beans, accessing of existing beans, configuration of beans by setting and getting their properties, binding of events from some beans to other beans, and calling of arbitrary methods in beans.

Dynamic XML for Java (DXMLJ)

This tool allows you to annotate an XML document dynamically. The namespace-based annotations can specify how a particular subtree in an XML document is to be interpreted or filled in.

Extensible Types (eTypes)

A Java component library that enables users to specify constraints and determine whether objects satisfy them. It can validate many of the datatypes defined by XML Schema Datatypes as well as several ISO standard datatypes. There is a command line tool for deducing XML Schema text-only types from XML documents or example strings.

LotusXSL

A Java implementation of an XSLT processor that tracks the W3C specification. It is designed to be used either as a stand-alone application, as a submodule of a larger application, or within an applet or servlet. In addition to supporting the standard DOM 1.0 API, it can also be configured to generate streaming SAX output.

SVGView

SVGView is a Java program that uses Java 2D and the XML Parser for Java to parse, process, and display SVG files on any XML-enabled Web browser.

Task Guide Viewer

An XML-based tool for creating wizards that break complicated tasks into a sequence of simple steps that can be performed using a graphical, user-friendly interface. Building and displaying wizards is as easy as creating and viewing HTML files; no programming languages are required.

Visual XML Tools

An experimental package for use with IBM JDK 1.2.2 or Sun JDK/JRE 1.2.2. It consists of Visual XML Builder, Visual DTD, Visual XML Creation, Visual XML Transformation, and Visual XML Query.

Voice XML

VoiceXML is an XML-based markup language for distributed vocal renditions, much as HTML is a language for distributed visual renditions. VoiceXML is designed for creating audio dialogs that feature synthesized speech, digitized audio, recognition of spoken and DTMF key input, recording of spoken input, telephony, and mixed-initiative conversations. The goal is to provide voice access and interactive voice response (e.g. by telephone, PDA, or desktop) to Web-based content and applications.

Xeena

A DTD-driven XML editor. Using a visual, tree-oriented editing paradigm coupled with a context-sensitive palette of elements, Xeena provides an intuitive, self-validating, mechanism for viewing and editing XML documents.

XSL Editor

This tool allows you to import, create, and save XSL style sheets and XML source documents. It supports stylesheet development with aids for generating XPath syntax from sample documents and writing select and match expressions. It runs transforms with or without tracing and breakpoints. The user interface features a collapsible tree view of the XML source document.

XML Generator

This tool creates "random" test cases for XML applications by generating them from a DTD. The cases can be stored as XML files, or accessed directly through the DOM API.

XML Lightweight Extractor (XLE)

XLE allows you to annotate a DTD to associate its components with data sources. You can then extract data from those sources and assemble it into XML documents conforming to that DTD. SQL need not be used, but is permitted.

XMI Toolkit

XMI specifies an open information interchange model that gives developers working with object technology the ability to exchange models and data over the Internet in a standardized way, regardless of which development tools they use. XMI includes the ability to generate and convert Java from Rational Rose and UML models.

XML Enabler

XML Enabler is a servlet that can execute XSL stylesheets. Users of various browser types can send data requests to the servlet, which formats the data in accordance with the stylesheet associated with the requestor's browser.

XML Master (XMas)

A tool for designing visual and non-visual beans to work with a particular XML document type. You use the tool to design the layout for an editor for the element types needed by your application. XMas generates the necessary Java code for the beans. It places them in a jar file that can be imported into an IDE, where they can be wired into applications.

XML Parser for C++ (XML4C)

A technology based on Apache's Xerces-C XML parser, which is a validating XML parser written in a portable subset of C++.

XML4C integrates the Xerces-C parser with IBM's International Components for Unicode (ICU) and extends the number of encodings supported to over 150. It consists of three shared libraries (two code and one data) that provide classes for parsing, generating, manipulating, and validating XML documents. XML4C is faithful to the XML 1.0 Recommendation and associated standards (DOM 1.0, SAX 1.0, DOM 2.0 etc). Source code, samples and API documentation are provided with the parser.

XML Parser for Java (XML4J)

A configurable XML parser written in *Java*, based on the Apache Xerces XML Parser Version 1.0.3. The package contains classes for parsing, generating, manipulating, validating, and emitting XML documents. The package is designed in a modular fashion so that a variety of specially configured parsers can be constructed.

XML Security Suite

A collection of XML security capabilities that provide, or can be used to build, additional protection to XML documents beyond that afforded by SSL. The current version of the suite also includes a reference implementation of the DOMHASH canonical digest value for XML documents, as well as sample applications that illustrate its use for digital signatures, element-wise encryption, and access control.

XML Translator Generator (XTransGen)

A tool that automatically generates specialized translators capable of converting XML documents from one DTD to another. It does not require you to write XSL scripts or program code. The translators are generated from instances of documents conforming to each of the DTDs. XTransGen can also be used to filter data from HTML documents into XML documents.

XML Viewer

This tool provides several linked views of an XML document: the source text, the DTD, and a tree view. You can traverse the tree and view the source of a node in the source view and its definition in the DTD view.

XSL Trace

XSL Trace allows you to visually "step through" an XSL transformation script, highlighting the transformation rules as they are fired. You can also view the XML source and the corresponding XML or HTML result in "real time". You can also set and remove "break points" on the style sheet and source document, as well as highlight all source nodes processed by each style rule.

Tip   *You can visit the alphaWorks site,* `http://www.alphaWorks.IBM.com`, *to engage IBM researchers and developers at the earliest stages of development and to download the latest software.*

60.3 | An eXtravagance of free XML software

To make this list, software has to be genuinely free, worthwhile XML software. That means:

- It must have substantial XML-oriented functionality; no graphics packages, file utilities, or other general-purpose filler.
- It must let you do useful processing of your own documents. If you are taking the trouble to install and learn it, you should get some benefit from it.
- It can't have a time limit on its use. As above: you should be the one to decide when it's no longer interesting.
- Most of all, it's got to be pretty good stuff! Some of it is proven code that rivals the best ever written for speed and stability. Other packages are promising newcomers.

You'll find fuller descriptions of everything on the CD-ROMs, along with hyperlinks to the vendor's website for the latest versions of the programs that you like. The descriptions here are just to give you the flavor and, of course, they apply only to the version on the CDs.

Caution   *This list is incomplete! The CD-ROMs have over 175 packages. Be sure to check them out for yourself.*

60.3.1   *Parsers and engines*

XML parsers, parsing toolkits, HyTime engines and DSSSL engines.

60.3.1.1   Architectural forms engines

XAF

XAF is an architectural forms engine which offers a SAX 1.0 interface to the transformed document. XAF can be used with any SAX 1.0 parser. Only a subset of architectural forms is supported and this release is at beta level.

xmlarch

xmlarch is an architectural forms engine written in Python that works with any SAX 1.0 parser and offers a SAX 1.0 interface to the processed documents. It is also possible to receive architectural document events for several architectures in one parse pass.

60.3.1.2   XLink/XPointer engines

XPath4XT

XPath4XT is an XPath implementation that can evaluate XPath expressions against a DOM tree. XPath4XT uses XT and comes with a special version of XT which has to be used. It also requires a DOM implementation. Java Project X is supported, but support for other DOM implementations can easily be added.

XML::XPath

XML::XPath is a Perl implementation of XPath. It can parse XPath expressions and resolve them against a document tree built by the XPath module from SAX events or the XML::Parser.

60.3.1.3   XSL engines

FOP

FOP is a Java application that takes an XML document conforming to the formatting half of the XSL 19990421 Working Draft and produces PDF output. This way it can be used with any SAX 1.0 parser to produce PDF from XML + XSL. FOP can be invoked from the command line and read from a file, or it can be given a DOM document or a SAX DocumentHandler at runtime.

Passive TeX

Passive TeX is a TeX implementation of the XSL March 2000 WD and MathML which reads XML documents containing XSL formatting objects and MathML elements and uses LaTeX to produce formatted output. This can be used to produce well-formatted PDF, DVI or PostScript, and even supports bookmarks in the PDF output.

REXP

REXP is an XSL:fo to PDF file converter, based on the source of FOP 0.9.2. It supports a bit more of XSL than FOP does. A tiny bit of support for SVG is also there, and there will probably be more in the future.

60.3.1.4   XSLT engines

SAXON

SAXON is a Java framework for processing XML documents optimized for XML to XML/SGML/HTML conversions. Essentially, it is an XSLT implementation (1.0 recommendation) which can also be used as a Java development framework. The

XSLT implementation is fast, fully conformant and provides many useful extensions. Through its API Java and XSLT code can be combined.

XT

XT is an XSLT engine that implements the final XSLT recommendation, as well as the XPath recommendation. It is officially of beta quality, but experience has shown it to be very fast, stable and conformant. It does not support the full recommendation, but does have some useful extensions. It can be used with any SAX 1.0 parser and also as a servlet.

4XSLT

4XSLT is an XSLT processor implemented in Python on top of 4DOM and 4XPath (both of which are bundled with 4XSLT). 4XSLT implements the entire XSLT recommendation, apart from extension elements and fallback. Note that 4XSLT does not work in JPython.

xslt-parser

xslt-parser is a budding XSLT engine written in Perl. It is of alpha quality and not yet complete nor bug-free, but work is progressing.

Xalan-Java

Xalan-Java is an XSLT processor written in Java. It implements the entire final XSLT recommendation, and can produce both SAX and DOM output, with support for Java and JavaScript extensions. Xalan-Java uses Xerces-Java for XML parsing.

Xalan-C++

Xalan-C++ is a C++ implementation of an XSLT processor, following the final XSLT recommendation. The implementation is not complete. The XML parser used is Xerces.

Unicorn XSLT Processor

The Unicorn XSLT Processor is an XSLT engine implemented in C++. The release is a binary-only release, and the processor only has a command-line interface. The underlying parser does not resolve external entities, and only UTF-8 and UTF-16 are supported.

Sablotron

The Sablotron is an XSLT processor written in C++ (as open source). The goal is to make the processor fast, compact and portable. The Sablotron has both a command-line and an API interface. Not all features of XSLT are currently implemented. The Sablotron uses expat for XML parsing.

60.3.1.5   DSSSL engines

Jade

Jade is James Clark's excellent DSSSL engine, which is really a general SGML tool for conversion from SGML to other SGML DTDs or to output formats like RTF and TeX. Jade can process XML documents and can also output XML. Jade uses SP to parse the SGML/XML input.

60.3.1.6   SGML/XML parsers

SP

SP is an SGML/XML parser, and is fast, complete, highly conformant and very stable. SP has been the parser of choice for most of the SGML community for many years and has been embedded in lots of other applications. SP supports architectural forms as well as SGML Open catalogs.

SPIN_py

SPIN is a C module that can be compiled into the Python interpreter to provide an interface to the SP SGML parser.

SPIN_tcl

SPIN is a C module that can be compiled into the tcl interpreter to provide an interface to the SP SGML parser.

60.3.1.7   XML parsers

LTXML

LTXML is a set of tools (including a parser) written in portable C. Included are: a program to strip out all XML markup, an XML normalizer (mainly useful for well-formedness checking), an ESIS outputter, an element occurrence counter, a tokenizer, a down-translation tool, a grep tool, a sorting tool, some linking tools as well as some other minor utilities. The executables are mainly intended to be pipelined to produce various kinds of output, but provide a C API that can be used to extend them for other purposes.

expat

expat is a non-validating parser written in C, and is the parser previously known as XMLTok. It is used in Mozilla 5.0 and in parser modules for several different scripting languages. It is very fast and highly conformant.

TclXML

This is a validating XML parser written entirely in tcl. The parser offers both event-based and tree-based interfaces, and with Tcl 8.1 it supports Unicode.

XP

XP is written to be fully-conforming and as fast as possible, with an emphasis is on server-side production use. There is no validation, only well-formedness checking. Even though 0.5 is a beta release it is stable, conformant and fast. A SAX 1.0 driver is included. XP supports several Unicode encodings.

xmlproc

xmlproc is a validating parser written in Python. It implements nearly all of the XML Recommendation, including XML namespaces. (The home page lists the deviations.) xmlproc provides access to DTD information and also offers a DTD parsing module. xmlproc supports SGML Open catalogs and XML Catalogs. xmlproc can report errors in Norwegian and English and can be extended to support other languages as well.

Windows Foundation Classes

WFC is a collection of C++ classes for Windows programming. Included are a non-validating XML parser as well as other tools for working with XML documents. The parser has been tested on Unix too.

TclExpat

TclExpat is the expat C XML parser wrapped as a Tcl module. Version 1.1 uses the final 1.0 version of expat, which supports XML namespaces.

Expat Module for Ruby

This module wraps the expat parser for access from within the Ruby interpreter. (Ruby is an object-oriented scripting language with similarities to Perl.) It also has a DOM 1.0 implementation and XPointer support.

XML Parser Component for Delphi

This is a validating XML parser written in Delphi that parses XML documents into a DOM element tree that can then be modified and traversed. The component also allows programs to build DOM trees and write them out as an XML document. The parser supports both 8-bit and 16-bit encodings.

libxml

libxml is a validating XML parser written in C (also known as gnome-xml). It has an event-based (SAX-like) interface and can also build an in-memory DOM-like tree of the parsed document. There is also a nearly full XPath implementation, and libxml supports namespaces. An HTML parser is also included.

fxp

fxp is a validating XML parser written in Standard ML, a functional programming language in the ML family. fxp has a programming interface, and comes with some example command-line applications. It has only been tested with the Standard ML of New Jersey compiler under Unix, but might well work elsewhere as well. fxp supports XCatalog and Unicode.

OpenXML

OpenXML is a validating XML parser written in Java, with DOM 1.0 and XCatalog support. It can also parse HTML and supports the HTML parts of the DOM. SAX is also supported. The Xerces HTML DOM implementation is bundled with OpenXML.

Microsoft XML Parser

The Microsoft XML Parser is a COM component that can be accessed from any COM-aware application in any programming language. The parser is validating and supports the DOM 1.0, XML namespaces, a subset of the XSLT (final recommendation), a subset of XPath, and XML schemas (XDR ones, that is). The parser requires Microsoft Internet Explorer 4.01 with SP1.

HaXml

HaXml is a collection of libraries for using XML in Haskell. This includes a non-validating XML parser, an HTML parser, a library for transforming XML documents (and generating HTML) and special modules for building Haskell data structures from XML documents and dumping them back out as XML. HaXml supports Unicode if the Haskell compiler does.

PXP

PXP is a complete validating XML parser written in Objective Caml, a functional programming language in the ML family with OO features. PXP has some advanced features for building customized XML document trees and also provides access to DTD information. It supports Unicode and can read documents in many different encodings.

Xerces Java

Xerces Java is a validating XML parser with support for the DOM level 1 and SAX 1.0. In addition, it also includes preliminary support for the DOM level 2, SAX 2.0 and the XML Schemas 19.Apr.00 working draft.

Xerces C++

Xerces C++ is a validating XML parser written in a portable subset of C++. It supports XML Namespaces, the DOM level 1 and SAX

1.0. Preliminary support for DOM level 2 and SAX 2.0 is also available.

Xerces Perl

Xerces Perl is the validating Xerces C++ parser wrapped as a Perl module. It supports the DOM level 1.

xml.expat

xml.expat is a Common Lisp wrapper for expat, allowing it to be used from Franz' Allegro Common Lisp compiler. The package basically exposes the raw expat API, and then adds some convenience macros and functions on top of that.

xmlparse

xmlparse is a validating XML parser written in C++ with full Unicode support. The parser has been tested on the OASIS conformance test suite and should be highly conformant (only 3 errors). It uses a SAX-like API and passes text to the application in UTF-8 encoding.

TinyXML

TinyXML is a non-validating parser written in Java which has been made as small as possible. It supports an event-based callback interface similar to SAX (with this the parser is only 16k), but also has a very simple tree interface.

UncommonXML

UncommonXML is more or less a Common Lisp port of the XP XML parser. It does not validate, but reads the DTD. It is currently of alpha quality.

60.3.1.8   DOM implementations

TclDOM

TclDOM is a 100% Tcl implementation of the DOM 1.0. The aim is to create a standard Tcl version of the DOM to be used with any DOM implementation/parser.

4DOM

4DOM is a Python implementation of the DOM 1.0 core and HTML features and most of the DOM 2.0 interfaces (core, HTML and traversal) that supports CORBA (but does not require you to use an ORB). 4DOM uses saxlib to parse XML files.

InDelv Smalltalk DOM

The InDelv Smalltalk DOM is a DOM 1.0 implementation written in Smalltalk, and comes with a non-validating Smalltalk XML parser with a SAX-like interface.

C++DOM

C++DOM is a C++ implementation of the DOM 1.0 core, built on top of expat. It reads and stores DTDs using DOM extensions, but does not validate. Also, some parts of the DOM 1.0 specifications have not been implemented.

DOM2

This is an implementation of the DOM level 2 Candidate Recommendation. It contains support for the XML, Events, MutationEvents and Traversal features of the DOM. It can't build DOM trees from XML source documents, but the XML Utilities can be used to do precisely that.

XDOM

XDOM is an open source XML parser with a DOM level 1 and level 2 (core and traversal) implementation written in Delphi. The implementation implements some convenience extensions and also deviates from the specification in a couple of places.

60.3.1.9   XML middleware

SAX

SAX 1.0 is now obsolete, and has been replaced by SAX 2.0.

XML::Grove

XML::Grove uses XML::Parse to build a tree structure from the parsed document that programs can access and change. Similar to DOM, that is, but non-standard.

DOMParser

The DOM Parser is a SAX 1.0-compliant parser that turns a DOM Document into a SAX event stream, instead of parsing an XML document.

tmproc

tmproc is a Python implementation of Topic Maps (ISO 13250), a standard for creating navigational indexes on large sets of documents. tmproc requires saxlib and can also be used with xmlarch if architectural processing is wanted.

XML::Writer

XML::Writer is a Perl module which makes it easier to generate correct XML output from Perl. It has intelligent support for XML namespaces and will automatically generate prefixes (although this can be controlled, if desired).

CGI::XMLForm

CGI::XMLForm is a Perl module that extends CGI.pm to create custom XML from HTML form input and can also create HTML form values based on XQL-like queries of XML data. CGI::XMLForm uses XML::Parser.

Python XML package

The Python XML package is a package of various Python XML tools that has been put together by the Python XML Special Interest Group, a group of volunteers led by Andrew M. Kuchling, for the convenience of Python XML developers.

Xml2Beans

Xml2Beans reads XML DTDs and generates a JavaBean for each element that can process XML according to the DTD. With specialized bean editors (not yet available) it will be possible to make application-specific editors for any DTD.

PyXPath

PyXPath is a Python implementation of the 9.Jul.99 XPath working draft. It can parse and evaluate XPath expressions, but currently cannot do matching. It requires PyDOM.

4XPath

4XPath is an XPath implementation (of the final recommendation) built on 4DOM that can select nodes in a DOM tree. 4XPath supports the entire XPath recommendation, except for the 'lang' function. Note that parts of 4XPath are implemented in C, and so do not work in JPython.

LT PyXML

LT PyXML is a Python interface to the LT XML package parser and API, which provides Python with access to a fast validating parser and a powerful API.

SAX in C++

This is a C++ port of the SAX 1.0 API for XML parsers, based on the Java implementation. This package includes an in-progress SAX driver for expat.

XML Utilities

This is a collection of various Java XML utilities, including SAX 2.0beta2 drivers (which of course also support SAX 1.0) for AElfred, the Sun parser, the Swing HTML parser, the Oracle parser and a DOM parser (that walks the DOM tree to fire events). Also included is an enhanced version of AElfred and an XML validator tool.

GPS

GPS is a general implementation of the grove data model (from the HyTime ISO-standard). It implements both groves and property sets, in two different implementations. One is an in-memory structure, the other uses the ZODB object database for persistence.

Pyxie

Pyxie is a powerful XML processing library written in Python which can be used to develop XML processing software which is event-driven, tree-based or event-driven with tree access. Pyxie requires the Python XML package.

SAX2

SAX is a simple event-based API for XML parsers. It is not an official standard, since it was developed by the participants of the xml-dev mailing list instead of a standards body. However, SAX is very much a de facto standard, since it is supported by most XML parsers and is used by lots of applications

xmlBlaster

xmlBlaster is a pure Java publish/subscribe MOM server (message-oriented middleware) which exchanges XML-encoded messages between publishers and subscribers. Communication with the server is based on CORBA (using JacORB), and subscribers can use XPath expressions to filter the messages they wish to receive.

Protege

Protege is a very advanced knowledge-based framework for developing domain-specific systems. It has been developed and used by the medical informatics community for years and has lately been extended with support for RDF. So Protege does much much more, but can also be used for generating editors for specific RDF applications. It understands both RDF and RDF schemas.

JDOM

JDOM is an API for representing the XML document tree structure similar to the DOM, but much simpler and designed specifically for Java using the collections API. JDOM structures can be built from XML files, DOM trees and SAX events and can be converted to the same.

TM4J

TM4J is an implementation of the topic map standard (ISO 13250). TM4J can read in topic maps encoded in XML using

SAX 1.0 or the DOM and also generate XML topic maps. It provides a general API for manipulating topic maps, but no functionality directed towards end-users.

60.3.1.10   RDF parsers

SiRPAC

SiRPAC is the W3C RDF reference implementation that parses the XML encodings of RDF into the triple data model, to be used in applications. SiRPAC can be run as a command-line tool or embedded in Java applications. SiRPAC uses SAX 1.0 to parse documents, which means that it can work with nearly any Java XML parser.

ICS-FORTH Validating RDF Parser

The ICS-FORTH VRP can parse RDF documents and validate them against an RDF Schema. It is intended to be embedded in other software as a library.

RDF Filter

RDF Filter is a event-based RDF parser built on top of SAX 2.0. It fires callback methods for RDF input events and is suitable for use with large RDF documents, since it does not build the full in-memory structure.

60.3.2 *Editing and composition*

Tools for interactive creation, modification and composition of XML documents.

60.3.2.1   XML editors

JUMBO2

JUMBO is an XML browser/editor which displays documents in several different ways without using a style sheet. It is meant to be a core which can be extended to support new XML-related standards. JUMBO is built on SAX 1.0 and can use any SAX-compliant parser.

XED

XED is a simple XML editor written in C, Python and Tk. It tries to ensure that the author cannot write a document that is not well-formed and reads the DTD in order to be able to suggest valid elements to be inserted at any point in the document.

Amaya

Amaya is the W3C testbed browser, and is an HTML and XHTML browser (and editing tool) with CSS support. It supports the MathML 2.0 XML DTD and can edit and display presentational MathML graphically. There is also support for simple XLinks. Amaya can read HTML documents written in XML, and save HTML documents as XHTML.

Emile

Emile is an XML editor that reads the DTD to provide short-cuts for the user during editing. Emile can export documents as HTML.

PECEL

PECEL is an XML data entry tool geared towards data applications more than document applications. It is tree-based, and uses a DTD to guide the user during document creation. PECEL also has a template function for creating document templates. PECEL uses XML4J for parsing.

Merlot

Merlot is an open source XML editor for data-oriented applications rather than document-oriented applications. It has a plugin API that allows the editing of some elements to be customized for specific DTDs.

60.3.3 *Control information development*

Tools for creating, modifying and documenting DTDs, XSL style sheets etc.

60.3.3.1 XSL editors

xslide

xslide is a major Emacs mode for editing XSL style sheets that has both syntax coloring, automatic completion and convenience functions to run XSL engines. xslide was tested in Emacs 20.3.1.

60.3.3.2 XSL checkers

XSL Lint

XSL Lint is a Perl script that checks XSLT style sheets for mistakes. It is of alpha quality.

60.3.3.3 DTD documenters

dtddoc

dtddoc is a Python tool that can be used to generate HTML and DocBook RefEntry documentation for XML DTDs. It reads the DTD (using xmlproc) and an XML documentation file (using SAX) and generates the documentation from that. The XML DTD for DTD documentation is available separately and is documented using dtddoc.

60.3.3.4 DTD parsers

DTDParse

DTDParse is a Perl module that can parse a DTD into an in-memory structure. This structure can then be used in various kinds of programs that need DTD information. It comes with several scripts that can produce DTD documentation using this module.

DTDParser

DTDParser is a Java module for parsing XML DTDs separately from any XML document. The parser can parse from any kind of stream and builds an object structure representing the DTD. This structure can then be accessed to extract information about the DTD and also be modified.

60.3.3.5   Schema converters

DTD2RELAX

DTD2RELAX converts a DTD into a RELAX schema module. The converter has both a command-line and a GUI interface. It uses xml4j 1.1.16 to parse the DTD. Output can be produced as SAX events.

60.3.4   *Conversion*

Tools for scripted creation and modification of XML documents.

60.3.4.1   General S-converters

X-Tract

X-Tract is an interpreter for XML Script, an XML transformation language with XML syntax. XML Script can be seen as a non-standard version of XSLT, with different syntax and based more on a traditional imperative programming model, rather than the functional model of XSLT.

MetaMorphosis

MetaMorphosis is a tree-based XML transformation tool that can be used to convert between SGML/XML applications, to publishing formats etc. MetaMorphosis has an architecture where several parsers and output generators are available (and more can be written in Visual Basic or C++ and plugged in).

Unicorn XML Processor

The Unicorn XML Processor is an ECMAScript interpreter which supports many extension objects designed for XML processing. Included are objects for working with a non-validating XML parser, a DOM level 1 implementation, an XML writer supporting the XSLT output methods and file objects for file input and output. The interpreter is implemented in C++, but is only available in binary form.

60.3.4.2   Specific N-converters

RTF2XML

RTF2XML (formerly known as RTF2SGML) reads RTF files and converts them to an XML document corresponding to an XML DTD that comes with RTF2XML. RTF2XML supports Unicode RTF. RTF2XML is written in OmniMark and so requires OmniMark to run.

XML::Edifact

XML::Edifact is a set of Perl scripts for converting EDIFACT into an XML representation that mimics the original EDIFACT structure in an XML syntax. A DTD called edicooked.dtd describes the XML structure.

60.3.4.3   General N-converters

Majix

Majix is an RTF-to-XML converter written entirely in Java. It can handle RTF styles and also lets you customize it to fit your own XML DTDs.

Tidy

Tidy is a tool that can read your XML and HTML markup and detect and to some extent also fix errors in it. This can be used to clean up bad HTML and XML and also to convert from poor HTML to XML. Tidy can also pretty-print your markup.

DB2XML

DB2XML is a tool for generating XML from database queries. It is a GUI-driven application written in Java, but can also be used as a servlet and as a command-line application. The XML generated is configurable, and metadata (types etc) can optionally be included, dates can be customized and currency representation can be localized. The generated XML can be processed with an XSLT stylesheet, using the embedded LotusXSL XSLT engine.

Java HTML Tidy

Java HTML Tidy is a reimplementation of Tidy in Java. JTidy, as it is also known, can parse non-conforming HTML documents into a DOM tree and convert them to valid HTML.

60.3.5 *Electronic delivery*

Tools for electronic delivery and display of XML documents.

60.3.5.1   XML browsers

Mozilla

This is version 5 of Netscape Navigator, which can display XML documents with CSS style. It also has some support for MathML. Please note that this is a beta release.

InDelv XML Client

The InDelv XML Client is an XML browser written in Java that uses XSLT stylesheets to display the documents. It can also be used to edit documents. The client also supports XPath and XPointer.

60.3.5.2   Web publishing

Cocoon

Cocoon is a Java servlet framework that can be used to publish XML on the web as HTML. It tries to establish a three-layer framework for this, with the three layers being content (ie: XML source documents), style (ie: XSL style sheets) and a so-called logicsheet.

60.3.6   *Document Storage and Management*

Tools for supporting document management, such as document databases and search engines.

60.3.6.1   XML document database systems

XML-DBMS

XML-DBMS is a Java library that can be used to move data from XML to a relational database and also back again. Through the use of a mapping document the structure of the original document is preserved.

60.3.6.2   XML search engines

XML::QL

XML::QL is a Perl implementation of the proposed XML-QL XML query language (note: this is not XQL), built directly on top of XML::Parser.

Xtract

Xtract is a document search tool for with a query language loosely based on XQL. Xtract can handle both HTML and XML documents, but is currently at beta level.

XSet

> XSet is an XML search engine oriented towards performance. It keeps its working set in memory (using paging to support large documents) and can be accessed through RMI. The query language is very simple.

60.4 | The XML SPECtacular

The CD includes a collection of the relevant standards and specifications that you can browse, search, and print. There is a brief description of each.

For each document, we've included a link to a website where you can learn more about the underlying project and obtain the latest version of the spec. Where copyright and production considerations allowed, we've also included a browseable copy on the CD-ROM.

In this listing, we've only included brief summaries of specs for which the full text exists on the CD.

60.4.1 *W3C base standards*

The following standards are either approved W3C Recommendations or are in development.

XML: Extensible Markup Language

> Here it is: the XML standard itself. For a standard it is mercifully short and readable, and nicely unambiguous. This is definitely recommended reading!

Namespaces in XML

> This standard enables XML element-type names to be globally unique. This can be used in many ways, such as to mix elements from different vocabularies in a single document, as RDF and XSL do.

DOM1: Document Object Model - level 1

> The DOM is an important XML standard that is often used to implement many of the others. It describes a standardized API for

accessing, manipulating and building XML and HTML document structures in memory, and is often the basis for implementations of XSL, XPointer, XQL and many other standards. It is also intended to be used by browsers and editors.

DOM2: Document Object Model - level 2

This DOM specification extends the DOM level 1 with constructs for handling namespaces, style sheets, events, filters and iterators and ranges.

RDF: Resource Description Framework - Model and Syntax Specification

RDF promises to become an important part of the infrastructure of the Web in the future. It provides a framework for describing resources on the Web and as such holds great promise of providing new means of navigation on the Web and better guidance for Web robots.

RDF: Resource Description Framework Schemas

This RDF specification builds on the RDF syntax and data model specification and provides a schema syntax for RDF models.

XPath: XML Path Language

XPath is a language for addressing and querying the content of XML documents. XPath is used in both XSLT and XPointer. It is a very important standard.

XLink: XML Linking Language

XLink is a crucial part of the XML standards family as it describes hyperlinking in XML documents and takes major steps beyond the hyperlinking provided by HTML.

XPointer: XML Pointer Language

XPointer is a companion standard to XLink that describes mechanisms for addressing a particular part of a document.

XML Fragment Interchange

This standard describes how to exchange fragments of XML documents while retaining interesting parts of the context of the fragment, such as the DTD reference, ancestor information for the fragment, etc.

XML Information Set

This standard is much more important than it may seem at first glance. The XML recommendation itself only describes a syntax for representing the data in XML documents, but an actual data model for XML documents is not provided there. And, when you think about it, the only reason we have the syntax is to enable us to exchange documents and then recreate the data described by the document inside our systems and programs. And this is what the XML Information Set provides: a formal data model for XML documents.

XML Schema Part 1: Structures

This is perhaps one of the most important standards in the set of XML-related standards. XML 1.0 already has DTDs, which can be used to define what particular types of XML documents can and cannot contain. Schemas go beyond the features offered by DTDs in order to offer functionality required in the many new areas where XML is currently being used.

XML Schema Part 2: Datatypes

This specification provides the features used to define the datatypes of element content and attribute values. This can be used to declare that an element contains dates or URLs, and similarly for attributes. Although datatypes are part of the work on schemas, they can also be used in DTDs. (There is open source software on the CD-ROM that supports such use.)

XSL: Extensible Stylesheet Language

This is another important standard which provides a means of rendering XML documents in a way that is optimized for end-users of the information. This can be as visually formatted documents or as aurally formatted documents destined for text-to-speech synthesis.

XSLT: XSL Transformations

XSLT is an XML-based language for describing transformations on XML documents. This can be used to convert between XML document types, to HTML or to XSL flow objects as described in the XSL standard.

Associating stylesheets with XML documents

This very simple standard describes how to reference a style sheet from an XML document in a stylesheet-language- and application-independent way. A necessary reference.

CSS2: Cascading Style Sheets - level 2

CSS is the style sheet standard that is implemented in browsers today and can be used right now. It is simple, but effective and elegant. Software that can support CSS-based display of XML is already here and more should be just round the corner.

60.4.2 *W3C XML applications*

These application standards are either approved W3C Recommendations or are in development.

SMIL: Synchronized Multimedia Integration Language

SMIL is an XML application that can be used to integrate a set of multimedia objects into a coherent presentation, complete with hyperlinks and synchronization.

MathML: Mathematical Markup Language

MathML is the long-awaited solution to a problem many scientists and teachers have struggled with: how to publish mathematical formulae on the Web. It also provides a solution for exchanging formulae between programs.

XHTML: The Extensible HyperText Markup Language

XHTML is a reformulation of HTML 4.0 in XML syntax, and is intended to be the basis for further work on HTML. This work is likely to consist of both a modularization of XHTML as well as extensions to it.

SVG: Scalable Vector Graphics

SVG is an XML application that can be used to describe two-dimensional vector graphics, text and raster images. This allows for styling images with style sheets, and hyperlinking into (and out of) images.

60.4.3 *Other specifications*

These standards are developed by industry consortia, collaborations of several vendors, or informal user groups.

SAX1: Simple API for XML 1.0

SAX is a general event-based API for XML parsers. Using SAX enables application programmers to write applications that are parser-independent.

XMLNews

XMLNews is a set of specifications for exchanging news items, and allows optional richness of markup. There are two specifications: XMLNews-Story which is a document type for news stories, and XMLNews-Meta which is a document type for news story metadata records.

XSA: XML Software Autoupdate

XSA is an XML-based system for automatically discovering new releases of software products. Software developers publish an XSA document which describes all their software products, and list maintainers and other interested parties poll these documents to discover new releases and address changes.

Other XML-related books

- Program development with XML

- DTDs and schemas

- XML reference

- An awesomely unique XML/SGML application

- Knowledge management

- Learning the foundations of XML

Chapter

61

This chapter was written by Charles, based on material from his website, *All the XML Books in Print*™, http://www.xmlbooks.com.

E d Mosher, Ray Lorie, and I invented the first structured markup language in 1969, IBM's Generalized Markup Language (GML). It led to SGML, HTML, XML, and countless applications and variations on the theme.

But strangely, considering that markup is for documents, for the first two decades in which the markup language concept was gaining its now universal acceptance, hardly any books were published on the subject. (Amazingly, a few survivors of that period are in Amazon.com's current retail database, including a few ancient IBM product manuals. I never tried to find out what would happen if someone actually attempted to order one.)

Well, the last two years have more than made up for the first two decades. When we went to press, my website, *All the XML Books in Print*, listed more than 65 titles. I won't repeat them all here, but I will describe the ones I recommend most highly.

These are the books from the *Open Information Management* series that I edit for Prentice-Hall PTR, and its *Definitive XML* sub-series, in which *The XML Handbook* appears.

XML isn't HTML with a capital X. It requires new ways of thinking about Web content. The authors of these books have gotten the message and know how to share it with you. I recruited them personally for my book series because I know they are genuine experts. We worked together to make their books accurate and clear, which is why I am able to recommend the books from personal knowledge.

Of course, the book you are now reading is my recommendation for an introduction to XML. It focuses on what XML is and what it can do for you, but it doesn't purport to tell you how to go about doing it. For that, there are more specialized books.

61.1 | Program development with XML

Contrary to misuse in the popular press, and by some experts who ought to know better, XML isn't a programming language. It is a markup language, of course, and that means it's a data description language. You use normal programming languages, including scripting languages, to develop XML applications. These books show you how.

XML by Example: Building E-Commerce Applications
Sean McGrath / 1998
Also published in Japanese and Portuguese.
This book will teach you XML application programming from the ground up, all the while developing a full-blown e-commerce application. Programmers can learn the XML language from this book as well.

Enterprise Application Integration with XML and Java
JP Morgenthal with Bill La Forge / 2000
There are few greater information technology imperatives for the enterprise today than integrating its legacy applications. Not only is it necessary for normal operations, but it is a prerequisite for integrated e-commerce with business partners. XML is the complement to Java that makes the integration possible, and this book shows you how to take advantage of both of them.

XML Processing with Python
Sean McGrath / 2000
There is a reason that Python is attracting the best programmers away from other scripting languages, and XML is part of it. This

book will teach you how to program in Python, and how to use its unique capabilities for processing XML. The software you'll need is on the CD-ROM.

61.2 | Websites and Internet

The Web is what XML was designed for, and these books will show you how to get up and running there.

Building Web Sites with XML
Michael Floyd / 2000
XML adds a whole alphabet soup of acronyms to the Web developer's lunch box: XSLT, DOM, SAX, schemas, and more. The founder of *Web Techniques* magazine shows you how to master these technologies, while systematically constructing an XML-based website. All the code is on the CD-ROM, to help you get your own website started.

Designing XML Internet Applications
Michael Leventhal, David Lewis, Matthew Fuchs / 1998
On the other hand, if you need to put an internet app together in a hurry – and the word "hack" doesn't offend you – here's your book.

61.3 | DTDs and schemas

Nature abhors a schema-less database equally as much as she abhors a vacuum. Create a data table in a spreadsheet and the program will immediately search for field names, and supply them even if you fail to. Although XML will let you create a document without an explicit formally-written schema (also known as a "document type definition", or DTD), the benefits of having one are enormous. These books make the job easy, whether you write out the DTD using XML markup declarations, or one of the proposed new schema languages.

Structuring XML Documents
David Megginson / 1998
Also published in Japanese.
This book covers the fundamentals of good DTD design, illustrated by popular industry DTDs. It also has full coverage of architectural forms, which allow object-oriented development of XML DTDs.

The XML and SGML Cookbook: Recipes for Structured Information
Rick Jelliffe / 1998
On the other hand, if you're looking for specific proven techniques for an enormous variety of DTD challenges, plus a definitive exposition on dealing with Asian languages, you'll want this book.

61.4 | XML reference

XML: The Annotated Specification
Robert Ducharme / 1999
Japanese translation in preparation.
After you've gotten a working knowledge of XML from our other books, you'll want this one on your shelf for referencing the details. It is an annotated edition of the official XML spec, with over 170 new usage examples.

61.5 | An awesomely unique XML/ SGML application

TOP SECRET Intranet: How U.S. Intelligence Built Intelink – The World's Largest, Most Secure Network
Frederick Thomas Martin / 1998
If you've wondered how spies would use XML, how they could share information securely on a vast international network – and how you could apply their techniques to your own – now you can

find out. This is the first book ever to describe an ongoing U.S. Intelligence operation.

61.6 | Learning the foundations of XML

XML is a proper subset of SGML and the XML Recommendation is much shorter than the SGML International Standard. But the subsetting isn't the only reason for the shorter document. The XML spec is written for parser implementors and deliberately doesn't discuss applications, philosophy, style, alternatives, and other usage issues. I don't claim that you need to learn SGML in order to use XML, but I think it would help you use it better.

The SGML Handbook
Charles F. Goldfarb / 1991 / Oxford University Press
On the other hand, if you really must know every detail of SGML, here is the official ISO Standard, annotated by yours truly (who is also the Project Editor of the Standard). I've added a structured overview of the complete language that introduces every term and concept in context. This book has been in print for nine years and was the essential reference used by the W3C Working Group when designing XML.

Tip   *You can find Charles' up-to-date list of All the XML Books in Print at* http://www.xmlbooks.com

Index

A

Abstractions 13, 17, 21, 40, 45, 72, 95, 117, 257, 292, 321, 325, 328-329, 382-383, 385, 418, 423, 427, 432, 439, 441-442, 448, 451, 484, 553, 556, 620, 627
   definition 440
   converting renditions to 442-448
   distinct from renditions 59-61, 94, 100-102, 381
   preservation
      definition 426
   represented by SGML and XML 14
   separate from renditions 246, 259, 374, 426, 472-473
   using XML notation 102
Active Server Pages
   See ASP (Active Server Pages)
ActiveX 130, 132
Adobe Systems Inc. 425-437
   FrameMaker+SGML 430-435
   Illustrator™ 5, 74
   Knowledge Chain™ Builder 435-436
   PageMaker 7
   Portable Document Format (PDF) 68
Aggregation 270-271, 290, 302, 334, 407, 490, 494, 656, 659
ANSI 180
Apache XML Project
   Formatting Objects to PDF (FOP) 575
   Xalan 570
API (Application Processing Interface) 48, 145, 205, 435
   definition 47
API (Application Programming Interface) 657
API (Applied Programming Interface) 640
Application integration 663
   architecture using topic maps 628-630
   association evaluators 629-630
   context managers 628, 630
   semantic managers 629-630
   service managers 630
Application Processing Interface
   See API (Application Processing Interface)

Applications 642
   legacy 485
Arbortext Inc. 341-388
   Epic 381-386, 388
Architectural models 325
Ariba 202
Artesia Technologies 649-660
   PISA (XML Persistent Interchange Syntax for Assets) 654, 656-657
   TEAMS™ 650, 656
ASCII 271
   delimited 344
ASP (Active Server Pages) 121, 124, 155, 212-215, 580
   files 124-125, 127-128, 135, 581-582, 587-588
      to generate XML documents 124
      using to generate XML documents 121
Attribute list declarations 720
Attribute types
   summary 732
Attribute value normalization 724-725
   unnormalized text vs. normalized data 726
Attributes 46, 73, 145, 398-399, 428-429, 435, 440, 446, 497, 508, 515, 559-560, 566, 570, 641, 657, 687-691, 719-732
   definition 31, 426, 719
   datatypes 897, 905-906
   declarations 917
   default values 722-724, 751
   elements vs. 719-720
   ENTITY 731, 741
   enumerated 728
   fixed 724
   ID 585-586
   ID/IDREF 729
   identity 616
   IDREF 585-586
   implied vs. required 722-723
   inherited 770
   names 657, 795
   notation 728

required 723
semantics 689
values 657, 689
Auction database 122, 126, 135
Auction Demo 121-136
Auction website 121-136
auction.asp 121, 125-129, 132-135
auction.xml 122, 126, 128-129, 132-133

B

B2B (Business to Business E-commerce) 25, 139, 141, 176, 199, 419-420, 644, 645
   definition 24
B2C (Business-to-Consumer) 139, 176
Batching 476, 657
   content-based routing 476
   load balancing 476
Berglund, Anders 20
Berners-Lee, Tim 20, 22, 49
Binary Large Objects
   See BLOBs (Binary Large Objects)
Binding declarations 741
Bioinformatic Sequence Markup Language 78
BIS (Business Integration Service) 257, 262
   definition 261
BLOBs (Binary Large Objects) 143
BPA (Business Process Automation) software 25
   definition 24
Branches 31
Browsers 247
Business Integration Services
   See BIS (Business Integration Services)
Business Process Automation software
   See BPA (Business Process Automation) software
Business process data
   compared to XML and word processing documents 101
Business rules 165, 174-175, 179, 186, 188, 520, 650
Business to business E-commerce
   See B2B (Business to business E-commerce)
Business-to-Consumer
   See B2C (Business-to-Consumer)

C

CALS 559
Cascading Style Sheets
   See CSS (Cascading Style Sheets)

Case-sensitivity 678
   entity names 741
CDA (Content Delivery Agent) 259-260
   definition 261
CDATA 805
   definition 697
CD-ROM 122
CDS (Content Delivery Service) 255, 257
   definition 259
CGI (Common Gateway Interface) 768
Character references 763-765
   character entity sets 765
   decimal 764
   entity references vs. 764
   hexadecimal 764
   in attribute value normalization 725
   Unicode 763-764
Characters 32, 99
   data 31, 781
      definition 679
   data encoding
      definition 32
   encoding
      definition 100
   protecting from markup interpretation 695
   set
      definition 32
      7 bit ASCII 32, 34
   strings 444
   white space 681, 713-714, 720, 725, 754, 761, 767, 771, 773, 777-778, 780, 781, 784, 810, 812
      definition 680
Chemical Markup Language
   See CML (Chemical Markup Language)
Client/server 579, 581, 587, 670
   model 107, 110-111
CML (Chemical Markup Language) 77
Cobol 487, 495, 515
COC (Customer Oriented Change) 357-361
Coding
   definition 100
Collaborations 209, 213-214, 216-217
   intensity 209
   intensity vs. intimacy 211
   intimacy 209
   loosely-coupled 210-212
   tightly-coupled 210-211, 215

COM (Component Object Model) 52, 143, 145, 258, 665
Comma-Separated Values text file
    See CSV (Comma-Separated Values) text file
Comments 699-701
    definition 699
CommerceNet 84, 202
    eCo Interoperability Framework 84-85
CommerceOne 202
Commercially available Off-The-Shelf
    See COTS (Commercially available Off-The-Shelf)
Common data representation 9-10
Common Gateway Interface
    See CGI (Common Gateway Interface)
Complex types
    definition 920
Component management 371, 372, 375
    systems 394
Component Object Model
    See COM (Component Object Model)
Components 17, 371, 373, 385, 387-388, 655-656, 669
    definition 370
    multimedia 30
    reusable 327, 384, 521-522
Conditional sections
    definition 761
Constant strings 779-781
Content 312, 361, 391, 403-404, 439-441, 471-472, 476, 571, 628, 654, 659, 667, 670
    acquisition 292
    aggregation 337
    and workflow 627-628
    creation requirements 427
    customized 360
    delivery 303
    development 425-426, 428, 435
    development strategy 427-429, 435
    development with XML 426
    distribution 254
    downloads 306, 308-315
    editing 360
    empty 711
    mixed 712
    sources 254
    syndication 77, 302-303
    tagging 477

Content Delivery Agent
    See CDA (Content Delivery Agent)
Content Delivery Service
    See CDS (Content Delivery Service)
Content management 365, 391, 404, 637
    and XML 367
    systems 381-382, 384, 391, 394, 536, 620
Content models 714-719, 915-916
    definition 714
    choice group 715
    sequence
        definition 715
Content specification 710
Control flow
    in a topic map 626
CORBA 52
Corel Corporation
    Corel Draw™ 5
    CorelDraw™ 74
    WordPerfect 9
COTS (Commercially available Off-The-Shelf) 327
Cross-platform requirements 324
Cross-referencing
    navigation for 583-584
CSS (Cascading Style Sheets) 22-23, 45, 81, 829-830, 854
CSV (Comma-Separated Values) text file 220
Customer Originated Change
    See COC (Customer Originated Change)

D

DaimlerChrysler Aerospace 357-362
    MTU-Maintenance division 357
DAM (Digital Asset Manager) 649-651, 654, 656, 658-659
    architecture of 649-650
Data 439, 446-477, 527, 645, 655-656, 659, 669
    abstract content 246
    conversion 473
    elements 525
    freeform 94
    heterogeneous 243
    integration 637
    integration enabler
        definition 651
    managed 241-244
        definition 242

multimedia 295
processing 589, 625
real-time delivery 293
remote collection 664-666
rescue
    definition 441
reuse 351
sources 242-243
streaming 289-290, 293
transmitting 245
unmanaged 241-244
untagged 477
Data conversion 460
specification 461-462
Data Conversion Laboratory 451-468
Data engine
    definition 143
Data extraction 294
Data hub
    definition 141
Data interchange representation
use of XML for 19
Data representation 290-292
Data semantics 490
    definition 490
Data sources 107
updating from client 134-136
Database Management System
    See DBMS (Database Management System)
Databases 651, 667
connectivity 175, 186, 188, 193, 337
management systems 650
relational 804
XML-aware 348
DataChannel Inc. 239-251, 593-605
RIO 249, 251
XML Generator 251
XMLBluePrint™ 248-249
XMLFramework™ 248, 251
Datastores 410-412
Datatypes 502, 787, 895-906
    definition 502
derived 900-902
names 896
primitive 898-900
requirements 896-897
standard 906
syntax 896

user-derived 903
DBMS (Database Management System) 164, 190
DCD (Document Content Description) 145
DCOM (Distributed Component Object Module) 664
Delivery
multiple formats 374
Descriptive data binding 130, 133
Desktop Publishing (DTP) 378-383, 385
DHTML (Dynamic HTML) 121-122, 130, 344
Digital Asset Manager
    See DAM (Digital Asset Manager)
Digital dashboards
    See EIP (Enterprise Information Portal)
Digital television (DTV) 667
Distributed Component Object Module
    See DCOM (Distributed Component Object Module)
Distributed objects 625, 627-628
on topic maps 626
Distributed programming 651
Distribution system
design 667-669
DOCTYPE (Document Type Declaration) 41-42, 640, 694, 704-706, 742
    definition 38
includes DTD 694
internal vs. external subset 707-710
Document Content Description
    See DCD (Document Content Description)
Document element
    See elements, root
Document entity 742
Document instance 684
Document management system 394
Document Object Model
    See DOM (Document Object Model)
Document representation 328
Document Type Declaration
    See DOCTYPE (Document Type Declaration)
Document Type Definition
    See DTD (Document Type Definition)
Document types 21, 23, 37-38, 42, 45, 61-62, 90, 98-99, 144, 146, 166-168, 174, 254, 283, 295, 307, 393, 410, 413-414, 426, 428-429, 499-501, 504, 506, 508-509, 513-522, 526-527, 532, 536-538, 557, 585, 615, 664, 909-924
    definition 16, 96

elements 37
navigation for 583
rules needed 9
Documents 31, 97, 328, 331, 346, 368-369, 377,
379-380, 383-385, 393, 395, 400-401, 405, 410,
418, 442-443, 460, 465, 484, 560, 583, 608, 646,
664, 668
   definition 30, 56
   compound
      definition 384
   computer representation 103
   conceptual 97, 99, 102
   content 360
   conversion 453-455, 460, 463-467, 471-472,
    474
   converted to XML 479-481
   digital representation of 30
   dispersed storage 391-392
   dispersed vs. integral storage 392-393
   distribution 337
   guidance 599-600
   hierarchical view 33
   identifiers 394
   instance 97, 684, 700-701
   integral storage 392-393
   legacy 451
   life cycle requirements 326
   logical structure vs. physical storage 758
   logical structure vs. physical structure 701
   management 326-327, 331-332, 335, 346
   physical storage vs. logical structure 758
   physical structure 35
   production 323
   prolog 684, 691, 692, 700-701
   real 97
   representation 393
   security level 772
   structure 354, 397-398, 451
   tree structure of 31, 491
   valid 896, 898, 917
      definition 704
   well-formed 688, 704, 770, 779, 790, 917
   well-formed vs. valid 710
   word processing 101
Documentum 535-551
   4i eBusiness Edition 536
DOM (Document Object Model) 48, 130, 132, 145,
250, 258, 585, 640, 644, 656
   definition 47
   API 644
   XPath support 827
DSSSL (Document Style Semantics and Specification
Language) 19, 23, 45, 805, 829-830
DTD (Document Type Definition) 16, 19, 21, 38-
41, 43, 46, 90, 97-99, 182, 188-189, 191, 269, 333,
346, 354, 428-429, 442-443, 472, 478-479, 481,
497, 500, 507, 513-522, 532, 535-536, 538, 640,
642, 667, 703, 909
   definition 16, 38, 96, 426, 694
   and namespaces 796
   and schemas 910
   declaration syntax 38
   declarations 508, 585-586
   external part 771
   internal part 771
   internal/external subset 741
   part of DOCTYPE 694
   sharing location with document instance 708
   using datatypes 905
DTD (Document Type Definition) declarations
   external 706
DTD (Document Type Definition) location
   relative vs full URL 707
Dynamic applications 246
Dynamic data 483
   acquisition 485
   extraction 271
Dynamic delivery 344
Dynamic HTML
   See DHTML (Dynamic HTML)

E

EAI (Enterprise Application Integration) 79, 141, 258
   definition 25
   importance of 25
E-books 80-81, 593
E-business 83, 86, 139, 239, 255, 471, 473, 663, 673
   applications 139-140, 142, 145, 407, 637
   knowledge management 140
   portals 253
   supply chain integration 141
   World Wide Web (WWW) catalogs 140
ebXML 86, 202
E-commerce 11, 15, 56, 83-84, 88, 171, 176, 186,
195-197, 199, 209-217, 231, 234, 296, 302, 337,

408, 416, 419-420, 426, 451, 472, 483, 485, 488-489, 491-492, 494, 501-502, 516, 520-521, 526-528, 531-533, 556, 599, 603, 644-646, 651, 671
   and legacy data 485
   and XML 485, 487, 528
   applications 407, 528
   collaboration intensity vs. intimacy 211
   collaborators 209
   future of 206
   reuse 531-532
   See also E-business
   vocabulary 525-533
E-commerce portals 198, 209, 211-215
   definition 197
EDI (Electronic Data Integration) 639
EDI (Electronic Data Interchange) 24-25, 141, 171, 174, 210, 213, 215, 231-232, 234, 301, 336, 485, 528-530
   definition 24, 173, 179
   (X12) 201, 203, 205
   and IEC (Integrated E-Commerce) 175
   and XML 175-177, 179-204, 233
   history of 179
   implementation 231
   new 185-186
      and Internet 185
      bidirectional 180
      data filtering 191
      Internet technologies 189-190
      XML data storage 191
   real-time information 178
   traditional 174, 176, 186, 193, 195, 233, 303
      compared to XML E-commerce 196-197, 200-203
      high costs 183
      implementation of 177, 180
      limited penetration 185
      non-standard standards 182
      problems of 181-185
      slow standards evolution 182
      transaction sets with business rules 179-184
   value of 189, 192-193
EDI (Electronic Data Interchange) parser
   as translator 205
EDIFACT 179, 201, 203
EIP (Enterprise Information Portal) 79, 237, 245-249, 254, 267, 270
   definition 237

Electronic books
   See E-books
Electronic business
   See E-business
Electronic commerce
   See E-commerce
Electronic Data Interchange
   See EDI (Electronic Data Interchange)
Element structure 658
Element type declarations 710, 749
Element types 21, 270, 307, 333, 404, 429, 431-432, 435, 440-445, 497, 504-506, 509, 514, 517, 521, 557-559, 608, 689
   definition 17
   declaration 918-920
   tag vs. 688
Elements 46, 73, 272, 280, 282, 370, 383, 396, 446, 458, 460, 494, 567, 583, 586, 640-641, 654, 657-658
   attributes 31
   attributes vs. 501, 719-720
   content 687
   empty 686, 688, 690, 717
   inline 284
   reusable 247
   root 31, 126-127, 132, 280, 442-443, 503, 566, 570, 686, 706
   subelements 31
   tags vs. 95
Element-type names 490, 584, 586, 641
   definition 95
Empty content 711
Empty elements 717
   definition 686
Encoding 281
   definition 281
Enigma Inc. 362
   INSIGHT 556-561
   Xtend 358
Enterprise Application Integration
   See EAI (Enterprise Application Integration)
Enterprise applications 410, 412, 644
   and XML 408, 409
   integration 416
Enterprise data 491
Enterprise data management 408-412
Enterprise information 242-247, 649

Enterprise Information Portal
    See EIP (Enterprise Information Portal)
Enterprise Resource Planning
    See ERP (Enterprise Resource Planning)
Entities 35, 39, 658
    definition 34
    attributes 741
    boundaries and markup 751-754
    catalogs 757
    classifications of 742
    content 737, 749
        internal vs. external 745
    declarations 737-739, 755
    external 34-35, 738-739, 807
    external and parameter always parsed 749
    external identifiers 755
    external parsed general 745-747
    general
        definition 748
    general vs. parameter 740
    in external subset 755
    inclusion vs. replacement 739
    internal 807
    internal and external parameter 748
    internal general 744-745
        definition 744
    know the location of document's pieces 34
    name vs. content 737
    names 34, 737-738, 740
    parameter
        definition 748
    parameter and general distinguished 749
    parsed 738, 740, 744
    predefined 695-697, 699
    public identifiers 757
    references 34, 658, 700, 725, 739, 749
        legal parameters 754
    replacement text 739
    unparsed 35, 738, 741, 747
        definition 747
        "general" and "external" implied 747
    unparsed vs. parsed 740
ENTITY attributes 731-732
ERP (Enterprise Resource Planning) 25, 141, 197,
    199, 230-231, 240, 243, 556, 651
eXcelon Corporation 139-148, 151-156
    Data Server 143-145
    eBusiness Information Server 143, 152

Explorer 146
Manager 147-148
Query Wizard 146-147
Studio 144-146
Toolbox 143-148, 154
Xconnects 143-145
Extended linking 673
Extensibility Inc. 499-511
    XML Authority™ 503-509, 511
Extensible HTML
    See XHTML (Extensible HTML)
Extensible Linking Language
    See XLink (Extensible Linking Language)
Extensible Markup Language
    See XML
Extensible Stylesheet Language
    See XSL (Extensible Stylesheet Language)
External entity declaration 739
External identifiers 745, 755
    definition 755
    public identifiers 756
    system identifiers 755
External parsed entities
    support is optional 746
External parsed general entities
    referencing 746
External subset
    entities in 755
External subsets 761
Extranet 339
    secure connection 273

F

Facets
    values 616
File conversions 380
File formats 9
File Transfer Protocol
    See FTP (File Transfer Protocol)
FNOC (Franchised Network Operations Center)
    667-669
Formats
    proprietary 290
Formatting markup 8
    definition 7
Formatting objects
    definition 832

Franchised Network Operations Center
    See FNOC (Franchised Network Operations
    Center)
Frank Russell Company Advanced Technology Labs
    319-339
Frequent-flyer website 109-118
FTP (File Transfer Protocol) 50

G

General entity references 740
    in attribute value normalization 725
Generalized markup 14, 22, 63, 79, 204, 472
    definition 13
    alternative to formatting markup 13
    to represent data 18
Generalized Markup Language
    See GML (Generalized Markup Language)
GI (Generic Identifier) 687, 689, 710
GIF (Graphics Interchange Format) 31, 35
Global economy
    and information 239-242, 251
GML (Generalized Markup Language) 19-23, 40,
    246, 663
Goldfarb, Charles 9, 19
Grammars
    definition 778
    production rules 778
    symbols 778
GUI (Graphical User Interface) 146, 269, 307-308, 621

H

Health Level Seven
    See HL7 (Health Level 7)
Health portal system 266-273
    definition 268
Hierarchy 31, 644, 685
HL7 (Health Level 7) 89-90, 166
HTML (Hypertext Markup Language) 14, 35, 37, 39,
    41, 45, 67, 70, 79, 99-111, 117, 130, 187, 204, 246,
    262, 280, 331, 343-345, 354, 416, 427, 515, 531,
    559, 561, 568-569, 575, 580, 588, 594, 597, 663
    and XML 67
    data 348
    development of 20
    element types 567
    elements 585
    files 567

hyperlinks 593
links 598, 602
    destinations 877
    sources 877
markup 344-345
renditions 589
single standard as 22-23
strengths from SGML (Standard Generalized
    Markup Language) 21
transformation from XML 833
Hyperlinking 43, 555, 560, 591
    linking vs. addressing 876
    within graphics 556
Hyperlinks 361, 427, 571, 602, 608, 619
Hypertext 34
Hypertext Markup Language
    See HTML (Hypertext Markup Language)
HyTime 19, 330, 597, 610
    as ISO standard 23

I

IBM Corporation 9, 563-576
    developerWorks 563
    Toot-O-Matic 563, 567, 575
ICE (Information and Content Exchange) 257, 296,
    305, 308-309
    definition 304
    capabilities 304
    implementation 305
    messages 307, 309, 312
    specification 77
ID/IDREF 560
IDR (Proprietary Receiver) 289
IEC (Integrated E-Commerce) 25, 176-177, 186,
    193, 196-199, 206, 209, 210, 232, 235, 408, 419-
    420, 426
    definition 24, 175
    future of 176
Indexes 434
    topic maps vs. 435, 608, 611-612
Information
    access limitation 244
Information and Content Exchange
    See ICE (Information and Content Exchange)
Information exchange 230
Information flow 232
    bidirectional 160-168

bidirectional processing 165-167
external 233-234
internal 233-234
Information interchange 5, 12
use of XML for 6
Information server 143
requirements 142
XML-based 139
Information systems 525
Information Technology
See IT (Information Technology)
infoShark Inc. 159-168
CARD (Commerce Accelerated Relational Data) schema 160-168
Infoteria Corporation 219-226
iCONNECTOR for Notes™ 225
iMESSENGER™ 223-226
iRuleGenerator™ 225
XML Solution Components 220-221
Infrastructures 669
Innodata Corporation 471-481
XML Content Factory™ 471, 473-479, 481
Instance 684, 706
Integrated E-Commerce
See IEC (Integrated E-Commerce)
Intel Corporation 663-673
NetStructure 7280 XML Director 671-673
VTune 664-666
Internal subsets 761
International Organization for Standardization
See ISO (International Organization for Standardization)
International Press Telecommunications Council (IPTC) 277, 295
Internet 241, 243, 290, 301, 500, 536, 574, 617, 645-646
email 220
services 175-176
Internet Service Provider
See ISP (Internet Service Provider)
Intranets 152-153, 197, 199, 219, 241, 479, 644-645
Intuit Corporation
Quicken 88, 199
IP (Internet Protocol) 245, 673
IPNet Solutions 212
eBizness Suite 212-217

ISO (International Organization for Standardization) 76, 601
(13250) 600, 608
(4217) 284
(629) 285
(8601) 284
(8879) 19
ISP (Internet Service Provider) 220-221
IT (Information Technology) 88, 240, 242-249, 514
ITEM element 124-127
Item table 122-125
IXIASOFT 391-405
TEXTML Server 393, 400, 403, 405

J

Java 143, 145, 563, 567, 570, 573, 576, 630
JavaScript 112
JScript 124
servlets 414-415
JPEG (Joint Photographics Experts Group) 31, 35, 99, 568, 571, 573-574
JTC1/SC34 19

K

Keys
declarations 849
Keywords
definition 780
ATTLIST 720
ENTITY 731
FIXED 724
ID 729
IDREF 729
IGNORE 762
IMPLIED 722
NDATA 747
NMTOKENS 727
PUBLIC 745
REQUIRED 723
STYLESHEET 768
SYSTEM 706, 745
Kinecta Corporation 301-315
Interact 305, 307
Interact Subscriber 306-315
Interact Syndicator 306-315
Knowledge management 327-328
system 152, 156
definition 336

L

Language
    xml:lang attribute 770
LaTeX 7-8
Lead tracking 221-225
Leaves 31
Legacy data 483-495
    definition 483
    and E-commerce 485
Legacy data flow 485, 490-493
    definition 490
Legacy document conversion 451-468
Legacy systems 231, 234, 242
Library of Congress 329
Links 435, 437, 567, 604
    definition 432
    as abstractions 432-434
    bidirectional 600
    database 44
    extended 591, 593, 595-597, 600-603
        definition 594
    extensible 434
    external 44
    HTML 594
    portable 434
    simple 602, 603
        definition 594
    simple vs. extended 594-595
    traversal 591, 599, 604
        definition 591
Linux 52, 664-667
Literal strings 681-683
    definition 682
Load balancing 669
    definition 670
Lorie, Ray 9, 19
Lotus Corporation
    Domino 223, 225-226
    Notes 225-226

M

makebid.asp 122, 134-136
Management Information Systems
    See MIS (Management Information Systems)

Markup 9, 62, 70, 285, 287, 292-293, 295, 298, 346, 354, 374, 417, 478, 521, 537, 575, 663, 673
    definition 36, 679
    assisted 478
    codes 8
    common language 10
    delimiters 37
    desired to be extensible 9
    generalized 370
    inline 283, 286, 293-294, 298
    languages 295
    richly-tagging 349
    software-specific 765
    tags 8
    to describe data 439
Markup declarations 754-755
    definition 96
    external 762
Markup languages 12, 94, 99, 124
    structured vs. unstructured 94-95
MathML (Math Markup Language) 77, 794
Message-Oriented Middleware
    See MOM (Message-Oriented Middleware)
Metadata 60-62, 75-77, 81, 94, 160, 162, 165-166, 175, 200, 203, 257, 290-291, 293-296, 298, 335, 343, 360, 435, 472-474, 486-490, 492-495, 527-529, 531, 575, 599, 601, 616, 619, 654, 658-659, 671, 700
    definition 74-75, 98, 413, 720
    Dublin Core 81
    news 277
    normalization 294
Metalanguage 494
    definition 99
Metcalfe's Law 175, 185, 189
Microsoft Corporation 121-136, 202
    BizTalk™ 86, 202, 205, 257, 536-537, 671-672
    Excel 168
    Internet Explorer 4.0 (IE 4.0) 121, 130-134
    Internet Explorer 5 (IE 5) 579, 588-589
    Money 88
    MSXML parser 130, 132
    Office 154
    Office 2000 50
    SQL Server 164-166
    Windows 2000 47
    Windows Explorer 418-419
    Windows NT 667

Windows™ 52, 664-665
Word 7, 9, 21, 154, 382, 515
    templates 382
    XML conversion to and from 382
    XML Sports Demo 579-589
Middle-tier 107, 109, 111-118, 122, 124-125, 127, 130, 133-134, 414, 419, 440, 646, 649, 659
Middle-tier servers 483, 799
Middleware 244, 640, 644
    definition 60
MIS (Management Information Systems) 242
Mixed content models 712, 718-719
    #PCDATA 718
MOM (Message-Oriented Middleware) 57, 60-61, 83, 93, 220, 223, 651, 673
    abstractions 61
    and POP (Presentation-Oriented Publishing) 61, 63-64
Mosher, Ed 9, 19
MPEG (Moving Pictures Experts Group) 31
Multimedia 317, 410, 479, 579, 649
    applications 637
    digital 649
    streaming 649

N

Name tokens 680-681
    definition 681, 727
Names 680-681
Namespaces 515, 570, 787, 865
    definition 791
    and DTD 796
    declaration 914
    default 793, 795
    in XML 250, 899
    prefixes 792, 797, 799
    scoping 793-795
Native language 30
Netscape Corporation 21, 39, 77
News Industry Text Format
    See NITF (News Industry Text Format)
Newspaper Association of America (NAA) 278, 295
NITF (News Industry Text Format) 277-279, 284, 287, 295, 400-401
Non-type-valid
    definition 705
Normalization 773

    semantic 290
    syntactic 290
Notation declarations 732-734
    definition 732
Notation name 747
Notations 35, 62, 99, 174, 415
    binary, data object 62
    character-based 62, 99

O

OASIS (Organization for the Advancement of Structured Information Standards) 85-86, 536
    ebXML 202
Object-oriented communication 52
Object-oriented messaging 651, 656, 659
    component framework 651
    component model 651
Object-oriented programming 921-922
Objects 51-52, 72-73, 655
    interface 625
    methods 625
    object wrapper 626
Occurrence indicators 716-718, 782-784
ODBC (Open Database Connectivity) 111, 122, 130, 269, 528
OFX (Open Financial Exchange) 6, 88-89
Online catalogs 171
    requirements 499-500
Ontopia
    Atlas Navigator 621-622
Open Buying Initiative (OBI) 203
Open eBook Forum 80-81
Open Financial Exchange
    See OFX (Open Financial Exchange)
Optical Character Recognition (OCR) 477
Oracle Corporation 160, 407-421, 667
    Internet File System™ 418
    Oracle8i™ 165-166, 408, 410, 413-418, 421
    XDK 417
    XML Developer's Kits 414
    XML SQL Utility 417
    XSQL Servlet for Java 414-415
Organization for the Advancement of Structured Information Standards
    See OASIS (Organization for the Advancement of Structured Information Standards)

P

Parameter entities 763
    external 762
    internal 762
Parsers 47, 62, 99, 249, 411, 418, 586-587, 642
    event-based 48
    validating 250, 478
Parsing 46, 61, 391, 409, 413, 416, 420, 429, 440,
    481, 580-581, 587, 640, 642, 644, 646, 654, 657-
    658
        definition 46
        creating conceptual objects 46
PC World Online 341-355
PDA (Personal Digital Assistant) 210, 254, 259, 304,
    409, 419
        client-side processing 354
        Palm Pilot 354
PDF (Portable Document Format) 35, 68, 325, 329-
    330, 335, 515, 568, 575-576
Persistence
    messaging 411
Persistent information
    definition 423
Personal Digital Assistant
    See PDA (Personal Digital Assistant)
Personalization
    definition 79
PICS (Platform for Internet Content Selection) 74-75
Pilot conversion 461
Platform for Internet Content Selection
    See PICS (Platform for Internet Content
        Selection)
Platform portability 328-329
Platforms 249, 324
PNOC (Primary Network Operations Center) 667,
    669
POET Software Corporation 173-193
POP (Presentation-Oriented Publishing) 57-61, 83,
    538, 673
        abstractions 61
        and MOM (Message-Oriented Middleware) 61-
        64
Portable Digital Assistant
    See PDA (Personal Digital Assistant)
Portable Document Format
    See PDF (Portable Document Format)
Portal servers 254-255, 257-261

    architecture of 255-256
    cluster servers 256
    integration agents 254, 262-263
    load balancing 258
    portal clusters 257
        definition 256
    receivers 257-258
    requirements 253-263
    senders 257-258
Portal sites
    definition 237
Portals 254, 257, 268-273, 407, 483, 651
    definition 78, 245
    framework 247-250
Predefined entities 695-697, 699
Predicate expressions
    definition 399
Predicates
    definition 822
Presentation-Oriented Publishing
    See POP (Presentation-Oriented Publishing)
Primary Network Operations Center
    See PNOC (Primary Network Operations
        Center)
Procedural scripts 130, 132-133
Processing 466
Processing instructions 679, 691, 696, 719, 732, 734,
    752, 765-769, 810, 817
        definition 765
        and XML declaration 769
        comments vs. 765, 767
        database access 768
        element markup vs. 768
        encodingPI for character encoding 769
        generalized markup vs. 765-766
        not associated with DTD 768
        stylesheets 768-769, 857
        syntax 767
Processors 250
Prolog 684
Proprietary
    format 654
Proprietary Receiver
    See IDR (Proprietary Receiver)
Protocols 85, 174, 212, 652
    definition 49
    Ethernet 49

FTP (File Transfer Protocol) 212-213, 258, 293, 411

HTTP 49, 203, 212-213, 258, 293, 411, 645, 654, 664, 666, 672

POP 49

RMI 654

RPC 654

SMTP 49, 258, 666

SOAP (Simple Object Access Protocol) 49, 664-666

TCP/IP 49, 338

WAP (Wireless Access Protocol) 666

WebDAV (Web-based Distributed Authoring and Versioning) 49

XML-RPC 49

Public identifiers 757
    definition 757

Publishing Requirements for Industry Standard Metadata (PRISM) 304

Python 47

Q

QIR (Quarterly Investment Review) 324, 327-328

Quark Inc. 343-344, 348, 439-448
    avenue.quark 442-448
    QuarkXPress 442, 446

Quarterly Investment Review
    See QIR (Quarterly Investment Review)

Queries
    complex, over data 412
    over large datasets 412

Query languages 400-403

R

RDF (Resource Description Framework) 75, 277

RDF Site Specification
    See RSS (RDF Site Specification)

RealPlayer G2™ 74

Registry 535-536, 607, 621

Relational model
    grove 805

Remote Procedure Call (RPC)
    See RPC (Remote Procedure Call)

Renditions 7, 9, 12-13, 40, 156, 210, 268, 272, 279, 328-329, 350, 354, 373, 383, 385, 411, 416, 418, 427-430, 434, 439, 440, 442, 448, 451, 455, 472,

477, 484, 490, 553, 555, 557, 560, 568, 585, 588-589, 598-600, 602, 621, 647, 651
    created from abstractions 14
    distinct from abstractions 59-61, 94, 100-102, 381
    generated from abstractions 102
    separate from abstractions 246, 259, 374, 426, 472-473
    using HTML (Hypertext Markup Language) 102

Replacement texts 34, 739, 753-755

Repository 535-537, 659

Representations 9

Resource Description Framework
    See RDF (Resource Description Framework)

Return On Investment (ROI) 231

Rich Text Format
    See RTF (Rich Text Format)

Rich-media data distribution 659-660

RosettaNet 87-88, 202, 205, 257, 304, 671-672
    Partner Interface Processes (PIPs) 87-88

Routing 669, 671
    definition 670

RPC (Remote Procedure Call) 51, 257
    definition 50

RSS (RDF Site Specification) 77

RTF (Rich Text Format) 7, 94, 99

Rule-based markup 15

Rules engines 272

S

SAX (Simple API for XML) 47, 640, 644, 656-657
    API 641, 644
    functions 642
    parsers 641

Scalability 324

Scalable Vector Graphics
    See SVG (Scalable Vector Graphics)

Schema definition 16, 38, 41, 532, 640, 703
    definition 98
    accuracy 520
    as well-formed document 914-917
    extensibility 520
    modular 519
    notations 507
    reuse 519
    See also DTD (Document Type Definition)
    style 519, 520

Schema definition language
    definition 911
schema.net 537
Schemas 16, 38, 62, 90, 144, 146, 254, 393, 413-414,
    499, 508-509, 526-527, 532, 536-537, 585, 615,
    664, 909-924
    definition 98, 426
    collaborative 501
    definition language 98, 538, 586
    design 500
    inter-schema sharing 166-168
    management 516-522
    modular 501, 504
    relational, mapping XML documents to 410
    See also document types
Scoping 615-616
    definition 76, 615
Scripting
    design pattern 656
        definition 656
    with XML 655-657
Search engine 536
    See also registry
Secure Sockets Layer (SSL) 673
Semantic checks
    definition 15
Semantics
    definition 686
Sequoia Software Corporation 265-273
    XML Portal Server (XPS)™ 260-263
    XML Portal Server™ 267, 269-270
Serialization 651
    definition 651
    industry standards 653
    neutral 652-653
SGML (Standard Generalized Markup Language) 6,
    14, 16, 19, 37, 39, 58, 79, 88, 187, 204, 325, 330,
    331, 335, 338, 537, 560, 597, 608, 663
    and HTML (Hypertext Markup Language) 21
    development of 6, 19
    International Standard Organization (ISO 8879) 19
    standard of 20
    XML as a subset of 6, 23
SGML Buyers Guide 328
Simple API for XML
    See SAX (Simple API for XML)
Simple Object Access Protocol
    See SOAP (Simple Object Access Protocol)

SMIL (Synchronized Multimedia Integration
    Language) 74
SOAP (Simple Object Access Protocol) 52-53, 83
    for asynchronous systems 53
SoftQuad Inc. 109-118
Software
    conversion 461
    focused 249
SQL (Structured Query Language) 271, 413, 415,
    417, 418, 804
SQL database queries
    as XML 414
Standard Generalized Markup Language
    See SGML (Standard Generalized Markup
    Language)
Storage site 536
    See repository
Storage structure 658
Strings
    definition 678
    user defined 781
Strong link typing 602-603, 605
    definition 602
    anchor role identification 603-604
Structure tagging 477
Structured Query Language
    See SQL (Structured Query Language)
Styles 444
    definition 443
Stylesheets 17, 41, 45, 59, 61, 68, 70-71, 79, 100,
    214, 272, 354, 419, 553, 555-561, 568-570, 572,
    579, 589, 686, 796, 802
    definition 14
    applied with template rules 555
    creating 836-846
    creation 556
    DSSSL(Document Style Semantics and
        Specification Language) for creation of 19
    imported 846-847
    in E-commerce 15
    included 846
    keys 847-850
        definition 848
Subelements 398, 429
    definition 686
Sun Microsystems 639-647
    Java™ 639
        Enterprise JavaBeans™ (EJB) 644, 646

Java 2 Platform, Enterprise Edition (J2EE) 639, 644
Java Database Connectivity (JDBC™) 644
Java Message Service 644
Java Servlets 644
JavaServer Pages™ (JSP) 644, 646
portability 639-640
Supply chains 174-175, 186, 192, 211, 231, 234, 273, 301
definition 141
integration 141
managing with EDI 178
Supply webs 193, 211, 231-233
definition 175, 186
SVG (Scalable Vector Graphics) 5, 73-74
Synchronized Multimedia Integration Language
See SMIL (Synchronized Multimedia Integration Language)
SyncML 80
Syndication
requirements 303
Syntactic checks
definition 15

T

Tags 8, 441, 478, 569, 640
definition 95
element types vs. 688
elements vs. 95
names 95
rule-based 442-448
Template rules 556, 559, 835, 839
application 558-559
behaviors 560
patterns 557
renditions 559
templates 557
Templates 455, 587, 796, 799
TeX 21
Text
XPath text node vs. 810
Text processing
definition 7
development of 7
Thesauri 614-615
definition 614
and semantic networks 614
Three-tier models 107, 110-118, 121, 159, 649-650

Tokens 777, 782
Topic maps 432, 434, 479, 591, 600, 604, 607-623, 626-630, 673
definition 76, 608, 611
and workflow 627, 630-631, 633-635
applications of 616
applied to thesauri 614-615
association roles
definition 613
association types 614-615, 618-619
definition 613
associations 631
definition 626
control flow 626
distributed objects 627-628
facets 616
definition 616
indexes vs. 608, 611-612
occurrence roles 611, 618-619
definition 610
occurrences 611-613, 621, 631
definition 610
symmetrical 613
topic association
definition 612
topic types 612
transitive 614
Topic naming constraints 616
Topic types 619
as class-instance relationships 609
Top-level instructions
XSLT 846
tpaML (Trading Partner Agreement Markup Language) 85
Trading Partner Agreement Markup Language
See tpaML (Trading Partner Agreement Markup Language)
Transactional data
definition 423
Tree structure 644, 685
See also Hierarchy
Troff 7
Tweddle Litho Company 367-375
Parlance Document Manager 371, 373-374
Types
base 920
complex
definition 920

extension 921
vs. element types 919-920
Type-valid
definition 705

U

UI (User Interface) 122-123, 133, 580, 587, 649, 651
Unicode 36, 99, 233, 639, 678, 693, 805
definition 32, 764
(UTF-8) 32, 34
Uniform Resource Identifier
See URI (Uniform Resource Identifier)
Uniform Resource Locator
See URL (Uniform Resource Locator)
Unique identifiers
definition 95
Universal Resource Name (URN) 863
Universal Unique Identifier (UUID) 309
Unix™ 52
Unparsed entity declaration 740
URI (Uniform Resource Identifier) 706, 792, 795, 799, 801, 862-864
URI (Uniform Resource Identifier) reference
definition 802
URI (Uniform Resource Indentifier) reference
URI and XPath 862
URL (Uniform Resource Locator) 801
protocols 863
User Interface
See UI (User Interface)
userInterface.htm 121, 130, 132, 134-135

V

Validating parsers 19, 640, 642
Validating processors 703
Validity 43, 430, 448, 500, 525, 585-586, 640, 654-655
definition 42
and namespace compatibility 797
Value Added Network
See VAN (Value Added Network)
Value networks
definition 302
intermediaries 302
syndication 302
VAN (Value Added Network) 180, 188-189, 200
VBScript 124-125

Version info
definition 693
Verticals
definition 87
Vocabularies
definition 538
public 538-551

W

WAP (Wireless Application Protocol) 80, 83, 257, 259
WAP Binary XML
See WBXML (WAP Binary XML)
Wavo Corporation 277-298
MediaXpress 292-298
XMLNews 77
Wavo Internet News Delivery Service
See WINDS (Wavo Internet News Delivery Service)
WBXML (WAP Binary XML) 80
Web-based Distributed Authoring and Versioning
See WebDAV (Web-based Distributed Authoring and Versioning)
WebDAV (Web-based Distributed Authoring and Programming)
definition 50
Well-formed documents 43, 71, 640
definition 42
Wells Fargo & Company 151-156
Institutional Trust Group (ITG) 151, 154
What You See Is What You Get
See WYSIWYG (What You See Is What You Get)
Whitespace 850, 851
insignificant 773
xml:space attribute 770
WINDS (Wavo Internet News Delivery Service) 290, 293-294
Wireless Application Protocol
See WAP (Wireless Application Protocol)
WML (Wireless Markup Language) 259
WML/HDML 80
Workflow 358, 378, 475, 481, 627-628
definition 474
and content 627-628
and topic maps 627, 630, 631, 633-635
compound 632-635

loosely-coupled 627

management system 474, 476, 478-481

represented as XML documents 629

simple 630, 631, 633

tightly-coupled 627

XML-based 349

World Wide Web (WWW) 21, 50, 118, 187, 237, 320, 328, 331, 335,-336, 338, 345, 348, 350, 354-355, 368, 377, 379-380, 400, 414, 418, 440, 484, 536-537, 553, 560, 580, 587, 593, 598-599, 601, 603-604, 607, 616, 625, 639, 644-646, 667

browsers 593, 596, 602

development of 20

navigation 591

storefronts 171, 196-197, 199, 209-211

transactions 159

tutorial generator 563-576

World Wide Web Consortium (W3C) 5, 23, 39, 45, 47, 52, 73, 75, 77, 145, 250, 277, 330, 502, 509, 593, 602, 604, 787

adoption of stylesheets 22

WYSIWYG (What You See Is What You Get) 7, 12-13, 332-333, 437

X

XAS (XML Application Server) 255, 257-258, 262

XCare.net 607-635

XHTML (Extensible HTML) 43, 71, 81, 83

definition 42

XLink 43-44, 593, 598-599, 601-602, 604, 787, 795-796, 804

definition 875

actuate, for event-based linking 886

and HTML links 876-880

arcs 888, 890

definition 889

attributes 795

bidirectional 883

embed option 885-886

embed option vs. text entities 886

extended linking 598, 601

extended links 877, 887-890

extended links as annotations 880-883

for external links 44

HTML link vs. 878, 880

linkbases 882, 890

definition 882, 891

simple links 877-887

definition 888

traversal paths 889

traversals 876

XML 13, 29

definition 5-6

abstractions 429

and e-commerce 24, 485, 487, 528

and EDI (Electronic Data Interchange) 175-177, 179-198, 200, 203-204, 233

and enterprise applications 408-409

and HTML (Hypertext Markup Language) 67

and multimedia 73

and publishing 317

application server 253, 256

applications 472, 664

as a subset of SGML (Standard Generalized Markup Language) 6

content 563

content management 380, 386

content matching 671-672

conversion 471-473, 478, 481

data 348, 472

data extraction 273

data sharing 408

database publishing for 72-73

declaration 280

development of 23

digital representation of documents 30

document handler 656

document types 90, 410

documents 71, 73, 75, 79, 86, 93, 122, 142, 220-221, 223, 225, 250, 348-349, 413, 430, 526, 555, 575, 581, 597, 646

E-commerce 201

editing 430, 435, 437, 440

elements 31

email 221-226

enabling transforms 245

extended linking 429

extending existing data systems 412

extensibility 152, 247, 513

framework 671

guided editing 430-431

in distribution systems 669

infrastructure in 637

integration aids 234

ITEM element 126

markup 60, 294, 346, 433, 441, 472
messages 671
messaging 652
messaging between heterogeneous databases 416
metadata 98, 249, 359-360, 483, 486
metalanguage 99
middleware 644, 646-647
namespaces 296, 429
parsers 30, 34, 47, 71, 640
portability 639-640, 658
processing 656
processors 30, 34-35, 42, 585, 657, 679
schemas 521, 535-537, 787
serialization 653
specifications 90, 535-537
syntax 75, 451, 896
    definition 677
tags 477, 673
target language as 30
text 641
topic maps 429
tree structure 529
tree-structured data 346
uses of 10
vocabularies 536
workflow 634
XML Application Server
    See XAS (XML Application Server)
XML communication server 494
    definition 494
XML data
    mapping into relational schema 417-418
XML Data Source Object
    See XML DSO (XML Data Source Object)
XML declaration 692-694
XML document 99-100, 111, 156, 254, 262, 413, 432, 440, 572, 580, 582, 584-585, 587, 640, 644, 647, 651, 657
    definition 97
    as families 806
    as trees 806
    features in common with databases 18
    multimedia 30
    tutorial 566-569
    well-formed 188
XML documents
    self-identifying
        definition 693

XML DSO (XML Data Source Object) 133-134
XML E-commerce
    compared to traditional EDI (Electronic Data Interchange) 199-203
XML grammar 778-779
    production rules 777
XML messages 257
    message protocol
        definition 257
    message types
        definition 257
XML names 710
XML parser 60, 62, 187, 205, 416, 657-658
    definition 46
XML Path Language
    See XPath (XML Path Language)
XML Persistent Interchange Syntax for Assets
    See PISA (XML Persistent Interchange Syntax for Assets)
XML processor 48
    definition 46
XML Schema
    datatypes 897-898, 904-905
XML Schema Definition Language
    See XSDL (XML Schema Definition Language)
xml.org 536-537
XML-Data 509-510, 586
XML-DEV 48
XMLNews-Meta 277, 295-297
XMLNews-Story 277, 279-281, 283-284, 287, 295, 297, 400
XML-RPC 50-53, 83
XMLSolutions Corporation 199, 229-235, 483-495, 513-533
    Schema Central 234, 516-533
    Vocabulary Builder 521, 528-529, 531-532
    XEDI Translator 204
XMLXperts Ltd. 109-118
XPath (XML Path Language) 143, 258, 395, 400, 569, 570, 671, 787, 801, 830, 846
    definition 394
    and SQL 827
    expressions 395, 398
    functions 811, 816, 824
    ID function 826
    in XPointer 827
    in XSLT 827
    location paths 396-400, 811-826

definition 395
    examples 820
location steps
    parts of 815-820
node types 809-811
points 867
predicates 823-826
    definition 822
    examples 824
ranges 867-870
specification 394
tree addressing 806-808
XPointer 435, 437, 560, 596, 603-604, 610, 787, 804, 814
    definition 861
    bare names 866
    child sequences 866
    extension of XPath 861, 872
    here 870
    origin 871
    start-point 870
XQL (XML Query Language) 143
XSDL (XML Schema Definition Language) 509-510, 513, 530, 532, 895, 903-904, 906, 909-924
    content models 915-916
    syntax 912
XSDL (XML Schema Description Language) 703
XSL (Extensible Stylesheet Language) 155, 204, 250, 272, 354, 556, 563, 575, 579, 587, 787, 829
    definition 45
    and CSS 830
    and XSLT 830
    as a declarative language 836
    attribute sets 852
    filtering for 587
    formatting objects 832-833
    hypertext links 832, 856
    namespace alias 852-853
    numeric formats 852
    output descriptions 851
    processors 411

rendering XML for 588-589
stylesheets 156, 272, 349, 351, 585, 587-588, 647, 792, 834-835
to transform XML to EDI (Electronic Data Interchange) 205
to transform XML to HTML (Hypertext Markup Language) 204
XSL Formatting Objects
    See XSL-FO (XSL Formatting Objects)
XSL Parser 205
XSL Processor
    statements 416
XSL stylesheets 210
XSL Transformations
    See XSLT (XSL Transformations)
XSL Transformations (XSLT) 394
xsl:attribute-set 852
xsl:decimal-format 852
xsl:namespace-alias 852
xsl:output 851
XSL-FO (XSL Formatting Objects) 568, 571, 575
XSLT (XML Structured Language Translator) 79, 143, 262, 518, 568-569, 572, 802-803, 814
    example 804-805
XSLT (XSL Transformations) 829-830
    and ActiveX control 831
    and Java 831
    and Javascript 831
    and Perl 831
    and Python 831
    match patterns 837
    reordering output 841
    template rules 835-837
    transformations 830-831
    variables 853
XSLT Processor 416

Y

Y2K (Year 2000 bug) 483-486, 494-495
Yahoo™ 79

LICENSE AGREEMENT AND LIMITED WARRANTY

READ THE FOLLOWING TERMS AND CONDITIONS CAREFULLY BEFORE OPENING THIS SOFTWARE MEDIA PACKAGE. THIS LEGAL DOCUMENT IS AN AGREEMENT BETWEEN YOU AND PRENTICE-HALL, INC. (THE "COMPANY"). BY OPENING THIS SEALED SOFTWARE MEDIA PACKAGE, YOU ARE AGREEING TO BE BOUND BY THESE TERMS AND CONDITIONS. IF YOU DO NOT AGREE WITH THESE TERMS AND CONDITIONS, DO NOT OPEN THE SOFTWARE MEDIA PACKAGE. PROMPTLY RETURN THE UNOPENED PACKAGE AND ALL ACCOMPANYING ITEMS TO THE PLACE YOU OBTAINED THEM FOR A FULL REFUND OF ANY SUMS YOU HAVE PAID.

1. GRANT OF LICENSE: In consideration of your payment of the license fee, which is part of the price you paid for this product, and your agreement to abide by the terms and conditions of this Agreement, the Company grants to you a nonexclusive right to use and display the copy of the enclosed software program (hereinafter the "SOFTWARE") on a single computer (i.e., with a single CPU) at a single location so long as you comply with the terms of this Agreement. The Company reserves all rights not expressly granted to you under this Agreement.

2. OWNERSHIP OF SOFTWARE: You own only the magnetic or physical media (the enclosed CD-ROM) on which the SOFTWARE is recorded or fixed, but the Company retains all the rights, title, and ownership to the SOFTWARE recorded on the original CD-ROM copy(ies) and all subsequent copies of the SOFTWARE, regardless of the form or media on which the original or other copies may exist. This license is not a sale of the original SOFTWARE or any copy to you.

3. COPY RESTRICTIONS: This SOFTWARE and the accompanying printed materials and user manual (the "Documentation") are the subject of copyright. You may not copy the Documentation or the SOFTWARE, except that you may make a single copy of the SOFTWARE for backup or archival purposes only. You may be held legally responsible for any copying or copyright infringement which is caused or encouraged by your failure to abide by the terms of this restriction.

4. USE RESTRICTIONS: You may not network the SOFTWARE or otherwise use it on more than one computer or computer terminal at the same time. You may physically transfer the SOFTWARE from one computer to another provided that the SOFTWARE is used on only one computer at a time. You may not distribute copies of the SOFTWARE or Documentation to others. You may not reverse engineer, disassemble, decompile, modify, adapt, translate, or create derivative works based on the SOFTWARE or the Documentation without the prior written consent of the Company.

5. TRANSFER RESTRICTIONS: The enclosed SOFTWARE is licensed only to you and may not be transferred to any one else without the prior written consent of the Company. Any unauthorized transfer of the SOFTWARE shall result in the immediate termination of this Agreement.

6. TERMINATION: This license is effective until terminated. This license will terminate automatically without notice from the Company and become null and void if you fail to comply with any provisions or limitations of this license. Upon termination, you shall destroy the Documentation and all copies of the SOFTWARE. All provisions of this Agreement as to warranties, limitation of liability, remedies or damages, and our ownership rights shall survive termination.

7. MISCELLANEOUS: This Agreement shall be construed in accordance with the laws of the United States of America and the State of New York and shall benefit the Company, its affiliates, and assignees.

8. LIMITED WARRANTY AND DISCLAIMER OF WARRANTY: The Company warrants that the SOFTWARE, when properly used in accordance with the Documentation, will operate in substantial conformity with the description of the SOFTWARE set forth in the Documentation. The Company does not warrant that the SOFTWARE will meet your requirements or that the operation of the SOFTWARE will be uninterrupted or error-free. The Company warrants that the media on which the SOFTWARE is delivered shall be free from defects in materials and workmanship under normal use for a period of thirty (30) days from the date of your purchase. Your only remedy and the Company's only obligation under these limited warranties is, at the Company's option, return of the warranted item for a refund of any amounts paid by you or replacement of the item. Any replacement of SOFTWARE or media under the warranties shall not extend the original warranty period. The limited warranty set forth above shall not apply to any SOFTWARE which the Company determines in good faith has been subject to misuse, neglect, improper installation, repair, alteration, or damage by you. EXCEPT FOR THE EXPRESSED WARRANTIES SET FORTH ABOVE, THE COMPANY DISCLAIMS ALL WARRANTIES, EXPRESS OR IMPLIED, INCLUDING WITHOUT LIMITATION, THE IMPLIED WARRANTIES OF MERCHANTABILITY AND FITNESS FOR A PARTICULAR PURPOSE, EXCEPT FOR THE EXPRESS WARRANTY SET FORTH ABOVE, THE COMPANY DOES NOT WARRANT, GUARANTEE, OR MAKE ANY REPRESENTATION REGARDING THE USE OR THE RESULTS OF THE USE OF THE SOFTWARE IN TERMS OF ITS CORRECTNESS, ACCURACY, RELIABILITY, CURRENTNESS, OR OTHERWISE.

IN NO EVENT, SHALL THE COMPANY OR ITS EMPLOYEES, AGENTS, SUPPLIERS, OR CONTRACTORS BE LIABLE FOR ANY INCIDENTAL, INDIRECT, SPECIAL, OR CONSEQUENTIAL DAMAGES ARISING OUT OF OR IN

CONNECTION WITH THE LICENSE GRANTED UNDER THIS AGREEMENT, OR FOR LOSS OF USE, LOSS OF DATA, LOSS OF INCOME OR PROFIT, OR OTHER LOSSES, SUSTAINED AS A RESULT OF INJURY TO ANY PERSON, OR LOSS OF OR DAMAGE TO PROPERTY, OR CLAIMS OF THIRD PARTIES, EVEN IF THE COMPANY OR AN AUTHORIZED REPRESENTATIVE OF THE COMPANY HAS BEEN ADVISED OF THE POSSIBILITY OF SUCH DAMAGES. IN NO EVENT SHALL LIABILITY OF THE COMPANY FOR DAMAGES WITH RESPECT TO THE SOFTWARE EXCEED THE AMOUNTS ACTUALLY PAID BY YOU, IF ANY, FOR THE SOFTWARE.

SOME JURISDICTIONS DO NOT ALLOW THE LIMITATION OF IMPLIED WARRANTIES OR LIABILITY FOR INCIDENTAL, INDIRECT, SPECIAL, OR CONSEQUENTIAL DAMAGES, SO THE ABOVE LIMITATIONS MAY NOT ALWAYS APPLY. THE WARRANTIES IN THIS AGREEMENT GIVE YOU SPECIFIC LEGAL RIGHTS AND YOU MAY ALSO HAVE OTHER RIGHTS WHICH VARY IN ACCORDANCE WITH LOCAL LAW.

ACKNOWLEDGMENT

YOU ACKNOWLEDGE THAT YOU HAVE READ THIS AGREEMENT, UNDERSTAND IT, AND AGREE TO BE BOUND BY ITS TERMS AND CONDITIONS. YOU ALSO AGREE THAT THIS AGREEMENT IS THE COMPLETE AND EXCLUSIVE STATEMENT OF THE AGREEMENT BETWEEN YOU AND THE COMPANY AND SUPERSEDES ALL PROPOSALS OR PRIOR AGREEMENTS, ORAL, OR WRITTEN, AND ANY OTHER COMMUNICATIONS BETWEEN YOU AND THE COMPANY OR ANY REPRESENTATIVE OF THE COMPANY RELATING TO THE SUBJECT MATTER OF THIS AGREEMENT.

Should you have any questions concerning this Agreement or if you wish to contact the Company for any reason, please contact in writing at the address below.
Robin Short
Prentice Hall PTR
One Lake Street
Upper Saddle River, New Jersey 07458 USA

About the CD-ROM

Our two CD-ROMs are packed with useful XML tools and information. A full description can be found in "Resources" on pages 926-963.

There are three main areas, distributed over the two CD-ROMs:

- A hand-picked collection of genuine, productive, no-time-limit XML-centric free software. There are over 175 titles.
- A showcase for leading XML software and service providers. It features in-depth product and service information, white papers, XML samples, live demos, and trialware.
- The XML SPECtacular, a collection of the relevant specifications that you can browse, search, and print.

How to use the CD-ROMs

A CD-ROM is just another drive on your Windows 95/98/2000 or Windows NT computer. No special installation is necessary. Just do this:

1. Start your Web browser.
2. Select "Open File" from the File menu.
3. Type "d:\index.htm" as the file name, where "d" is your CD-ROM drive.

License Agreement

Use of the The XML Handbook CD-ROMs is subject to the terms of the License Agreement and Limited Warranty on the preceding pages.

FREE on the CD-ROMs:
The 175 best genuinely free XML software packages, including these from

Bean Markup Language: XML-based JavaBean component configuration
Dynamic XML for Java: Seamless embedding of Java in XML
Extensible Types (eTypes): Extensible datatype validator
LotusXSL: Conforming XSLT processor in Java
SVGView: Parse, process, and display SVG files on a Web browser
TaskGuide Viewer: Create wizards with XML
Visual XML Tools: Build documents and DTDs with IBM or SUN JDK 1.2.2
Voice XML: XML-based language for distributed vocal renditions
Xeena: Edit valid XML documents of any document type
XSL Editor: Tool for creating and testing XSL stylesheets
XMI Toolkit: Implements open information interchange model for objects
XML Generator: Generate random test cases from a DTD
XML Lightweight Extractor: DTD-driven data extractor
XML Enabler: Servlet that executes XSL stylesheets
XML Master (XMas): JavaBean designer for element editors
XML Parser for C++ (XML4C): Validating XML parser in portable C++
XML Parser for Java (XML4J): Configurable XML parser in Java
XML Security Suite: Add security to XML documents beyond SSL
XSL Trace: Realtime visual stylesheet tracing with breakpoints
XML Translator Generator: Inter-DTD translation from document instances
XML Viewer: View document markup, DTD, and hierarchical structure